M000309621

Principles of
Macroeconomics
for AP® Courses

Senior Contributing Authors
Steven A. Greenlaw, University Of Mary Washington
Timothy Taylor, Macalester College

Advanced Placement® and AP® are trademarks registered and/or owned by the College Board, which was not involved in the production of, and does not endorse, this product.

Download for free at https://openstax.org/details/books/principles-macroeconomics-ap-courses

Table of Contents

PREFACE

Welcome to *Principles of Macroeconomics for AP® Courses*, an OpenStax resource. This textbook has been created with several goals in mind: accessibility, customization, and student engagement—all while encouraging students toward high levels of academic scholarship. Instructors and students alike will find that this textbook offers a strong foundation in macroeconomics in an accessible format.

About OpenStax

OpenStax is a non-profit organization committed to improving student access to quality learning materials. Our free textbooks go through a rigorous editorial publishing process. Our texts are developed and peer-reviewed by educators to ensure they are readable, accurate, and meet the scope and sequence requirements of today's college courses. Unlike traditional textbooks, OpenStax resources live online and are owned by the community of educators using them. Through our partnerships with companies and foundations committed to reducing costs for students, OpenStax is working to improve access to higher education for all. OpenStax is an initiative of Rice University and is made possible through the generous support of several philanthropic foundations.

About OpenStax's Resources

OpenStax resources provide quality academic instruction. Three key features set our materials apart from others: they can be customized by instructors for each class, they are a "living" resource that grows online through contributions from science educators, and they are available free or for minimal cost.

Customization

OpenStax learning resources are designed to be customized for each course. Our textbooks provide a solid foundation on which instructors can build, and our resources are conceived and written with flexibility in mind. Instructors can select the sections most relevant to their curricula and create a textbook that speaks directly to the needs of their classes and student body. Teachers are encouraged to expand on existing examples by adding unique context via geographically localized applications and topical connections.

Principles of Macroeconomics for AP® Courses can be easily customized using our online platform (http://cnx.org/content/col11626/). Simply select the content most relevant to your current semester and create a textbook that speaks directly to the needs of your class. *Principles of Macroeconomics for AP® Courses* is organized as a collection of sections that can be rearranged, modified, and enhanced through localized examples or to incorporate a specific theme of your course. This customization feature will ensure that your textbook truly reflects the goals of your course.

Curation

To broaden access and encourage community curation, *Principles of Macroeconomics for AP® Courses* is "open source" licensed under a Creative Commons Attribution (CC-BY) license. The economics community is invited to submit examples, emerging research, and other feedback to enhance and strengthen the material and keep it current and relevant for today's students.

Cost

Our textbooks are available for free online, and in low-cost print and e-book editions.

About *Principles of Macroeconomics for AP® Courses*

Principles of Macroeconomics for AP® Courses has been developed to meet the scope and sequence of most introductory macroeconomics courses. At the same time, the book includes a number of innovative features designed to enhance student learning. Instructors can also customize the book, adapting it to the approach that works best in their classroom.

Coverage and Scope

To develop *Principles of Macroeconomics for AP® Courses*, we acquired the rights to Timothy Taylor's second edition of Principles of Economics and solicited ideas from economics instructors at all levels of higher education, from community colleges to Ph.D.-granting universities. They told us about their courses, students, challenges, resources, and how a textbook can best meet their and their students' needs.

The result is a book that covers the breadth of economics topics and also provides the necessary depth to ensure the course is manageable for instructors and students alike. And to make it more applied, we have incorporated many current topics. We hope students will be interested to know just how far-reaching the recent recession was (and still is). The housing bubble and housing crisis, Zimbabwe's hyperinflation, global unemployment, and the appointment of the United States' first female Federal Reserve chair, Janet Yellen, are just a few of the other important topics covered.

The pedagogical choices, chapter arrangements, and learning objective fulfillment were developed and vetted with feedback from educators dedicated to the project. They thoroughly read the material and offered critical and detailed commentary. The outcome is a balanced approach to macroeconomics, to both Keynesian and classical views, and to the theory and application of economics concepts. New 2015 data are incorporated for topics, such as the average U.S. household consumption in Chapter 2. Current events are treated in a politically-balanced way as well.

The book is organized into seven main parts:

What is Economics? The first two chapters introduce students to the study of economics with a focus on making choices in a world of scarce resources.

Supply and Demand, Chapters 3 and 4, introduces and explains the first analytical model in economics: supply, demand, and equilibrium, before showing applications in the markets for labor and finance.

Elasticity and Price, Chapter 5, introduces and explains elasticity and price, two key concepts in economics.

The Macroeconomic Perspective and Goals, Chapters 6 through 10, introduces a number of key concepts in macro: economic growth, unemployment and inflation, and international trade and capital flows.

A Framework for Macroeconomic Analysis, Chapters 11 through 13, introduces the principal analytic model in macro, namely the Aggregate Demand/Aggregate Supply Model. The model is then applied to the Keynesian and Neoclassical perspectives. The Expenditure/Output model is fully explained in a stand-alone appendix.

Monetary and Fiscal Policy, Chapters 14 through 18, explains the role of money and the banking system, as well as monetary policy and financial regulation. Then the discussion switches to government deficits and fiscal policy.

International Economics, Chapters 19 through 21, the final part of the text, introduces the international dimensions of economics, including international trade and protectionism.

Chapter 1 Welcome to Economics!
Chapter 2 Choice in a World of Scarcity
Chapter 3 Demand and Supply
Chapter 4 Labor and Financial Markets
Chapter 5 Elasticity
Chapter 6 The Macroeconomic Perspective
Chapter 7 Economic Growth
Chapter 8 Unemployment
Chapter 9 Inflation
Chapter 10 The International Trade and Capital Flows
Chapter 11 The Aggregate Demand/Aggregate Supply Model
Chapter 12 The Keynesian Perspective
Chapter 13 The Neoclassical Perspective
Chapter 14 Money and Banking
Chapter 15 Monetary Policy and Bank Regulation
Chapter 16 Exchange Rates and International Capital Flows
Chapter 17 Government Budgets and Fiscal Policy
Chapter 18 The Impacts of Government Borrowing
Chapter 19 Macroeconomic Policy Around the World
Chapter 20 International Trade
Chapter 21 Globalization and Protectionism

Appendix A The Use of Mathematics in Principles of Economics

Alternate Sequencing

Principles of Macroeconomics for AP® Courses was conceived and written to fit a particular topical sequence, but it can be used flexibly to accommodate other course structures. One such potential structure, which will fit reasonably well with the textbook content, is provided. Please consider, however, that the chapters were not written to be completely independent, and that the proposed alternate sequence should be carefully considered for student preparation and textual consistency.

Chapter 1 Welcome to Economics!
Chapter 2 Choice in a World of Scarcity
Chapter 3 Demand and Supply
Chapter 4 Labor and Financial Markets
Chapter 5 Elasticity
Chapter 20 International Trade
Chapter 6 The Macroeconomic Perspective
Chapter 7 Economic Growth
Chapter 8 Unemployment
Chapter 9 Inflation
Chapter 10 The International Trade and Capital Flows
Chapter 12 The Keynesian Perspective
Chapter 13 The Neoclassical Perspective
Chapter 14 Money and Banking
Chapter 15 Monetary Policy and Bank Regulation
Chapter 16 Exchange Rates and International Capital Flows
Chapter 17 Government Budgets and Fiscal Policy
Chapter 11 The Aggregate Demand/Aggregate Supply Model
Chapter 18 The Impacts of Government Borrowing
Chapter 19 Macroeconomic Policy Around the World
Chapter 21 Globalization and Protectionism

Appendix A The Use of Mathematics in Principles of Economics

Pedagogical Foundation

Throughout the OpenStax version of *Principles of Macroeconomics for AP® Courses*, you will find new features that engage the students in economic inquiry by taking selected topics a step further. Our features include:

Bring It Home: This added feature is a brief case study, specific to each chapter, which connects the chapter's main topic to the real word. It is broken up into two parts: the first at the beginning of the chapter (in the Intro module) and the second at chapter's end, when students have learned what's necessary to understand the case and "bring home" the chapter's core concepts.

Work It Out: This added feature asks students to work through a generally analytical or computational problem, and guides them step-by-step to find out how its solution is derived.

Clear It Up: This boxed feature, which includes pre-existing features from Taylor's text, addresses common student misconceptions about the content. Clear It Ups are usually deeper explanations of something in the main body of the text. Each CIU starts with a question. The rest of the feature explains the answer.

Link It Up: This added feature is a very brief introduction to a website that is pertinent to students' understanding and enjoyment of the topic at hand.

Questions for Each Level of Learning

The OpenStax version of *Principles of Macroeconomics for AP® Courses* further expands on Taylor's original end of chapter materials by offering four types of end-of-module questions for students.

Self-Checks: Are analytical self-assessment questions that appear at the end of each module. They "click–to-reveal" an answer in the web view so students can check their understanding before moving on to the next module. Self-Check questions are not simple look-up questions. They push the student to think a bit beyond what is said in the text. Self-Check questions are designed for formative (rather than summative) assessment. The questions and answers are explained so that students feel like they are being walked through the problem.

Review Questions: Have been retained from Taylor's version, and are simple recall questions from the chapter and are in open-response format (<u>not</u> multiple choice or true/false). The answers can be looked up in the text.

Critical Thinking Questions: Are new higher-level, conceptual questions that ask students to *demonstrate their understanding by applying* what they have learned in different contexts. They ask for outside-the-box thinking, for *reasoning* about the concepts. They push the student to places they wouldn't have thought of going themselves.

Problems: Are exercises that give students additional practice working with the analytic and computational concepts in the module.

Updated Art

Principles of Macroeconomics for AP® Courses includes an updated art program to better inform today's student, providing the latest data on covered topics.

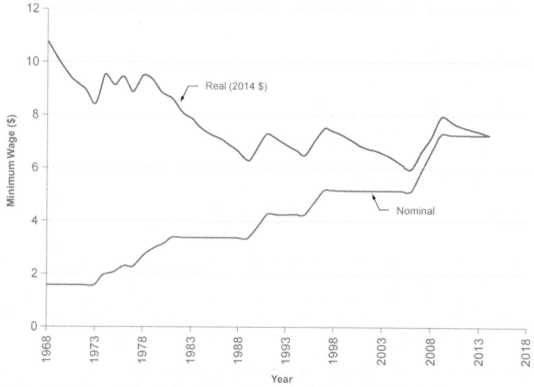

After adjusting for inflation, the federal minimum wage dropped more than 30 percent from 1967 to 2010, even though the nominal figure climbed from $1.40 to $7.25 per hour. Increases in the minimum wage in 2007, 2008, and 2009 kept the decline from being worse—as it would have been if the wage had remained the same as it did from 1997 through 2006. (Sources: http://www.dol.gov/whd/minwage/chart.htm; http://data.bls.gov/cgi-bin/surveymost?cu)

About Our Team
Senior Contributing Author

Timothy Taylor, Macalester College

Timothy Taylor has been writing and teaching about economics for 30 years, and is the Managing Editor of the *Journal of Economic Perspectives*, a post he's held since 1986. He has been a lecturer for The Teaching Company, the University of Minnesota, and the Hubert H. Humphrey Institute of Public Affairs, where students voted him Teacher of the Year in 1997. His writings include numerous pieces for journals such as the *Milken Institute*

Review and *The Public Interest*, and he has been an editor on many projects, most notably for the Brookings Institution and the World Bank, where he was Chief Outside Editor for the *World Development Report 1999/2000, Entering the 21st Century: The Changing Development Landscape*. He also blogs four to five times per week at http://conversableeconomist.blogspot.com. Timothy Taylor lives near Minneapolis with his wife Kimberley and their three children.

Senior Content Expert

Steven A. Greenlaw, University of Mary Washington
Steven Greenlaw has been teaching principles of economics for more than 30 years. In 1999, he received the Grellet C. Simpson Award for Excellence in Undergraduate Teaching at the University of Mary Washington. He is the author of *Doing Economics: A Guide to Doing and Understanding Economic Research*, as well as a variety of articles on economics pedagogy and instructional technology, published in the *Journal of Economic Education*, the *International Review of Economic Education*, and other outlets. He wrote the module on Quantitative Writing for *Starting Point: Teaching and Learning Economics*, the web portal on best practices in teaching economics. Steven Greenlaw lives in Alexandria, Virginia with his wife Kathy and their three children.

Senior Contributors

Eric Dodge	Hanover College
Cynthia Gamez	University of Texas at El Paso
Andres Jauregui	Columbus State University
Diane Keenan	Cerritos College
Dan MacDonald	California State University San Bernardino
Amyaz Moledina	The College of Wooster
Craig Richardson	Winston-Salem State University
David Shapiro	Pennsylvania State University
Ralph Sonenshine	American University

Reviewers

Bryan Aguiar	Northwest Arkansas Community College
Basil Al Hashimi	Mesa Community College
Emil Berendt	Mount St. Mary's University
Zena Buser	Adams State University
Douglas Campbell	The University of Memphis
Sanjukta Chaudhuri	University of Wisconsin - Eau Claire
Xueyu Cheng	Alabama State University
Robert Cunningham	Alma College
Rosa Lea Danielson	College of DuPage
Steven Deloach	Elon University
Michael Enz	Framingham State University
Debbie Evercloud	University of Colorado Denver

Reza Ghorashi	Richard Stockton College of New Jersey
Robert Gillette	University of Kentucky
Shaomin Huang	Lewis-Clark State College
George Jones	University of Wisconsin-Rock County
Charles Kroncke	College of Mount St. Joseph
Teresa Laughlin	Palomar Community College
Carlos Liard-Muriente	Central Connecticut State University
Heather Luea	Kansas State University
Steven Lugauer	University of Notre Dame
William Mosher	Nashua Community College
Michael Netta	Hudson County Community College
Nick Noble	Miami University
Joe Nowakowski	Muskingum University
Shawn Osell	University of Wisconsin, Superior
Mark Owens	Middle Tennessee State University
Sonia Pereira	Barnard College
Jennifer Platania	Elon University
Robert Rycroft	University of Mary Washington
Adrienne Sachse	Florida State College at Jacksonville
Hans Schumann	Texas AM
Gina Shamshak	Goucher College
Chris Warburton	John Jay College of Criminal Justice, CUNY
Mark Witte	Northwestern

Ancillaries

OpenStax projects offer an array of ancillaries for students and instructors. Please visit http://openstaxcollege.org and view the learning resources for this title.

1 | Welcome to Economics!

Figure 1.1 Do You Use Facebook? Economics is greatly impacted by how well information travels through society. Today, social media giants Twitter, Facebook, and Instagram are major forces on the information super highway. (Credit: Johan Larsson/Flickr)

Bring it Home

Decisions ... Decisions in the Social Media Age

To post or not to post? Every day we are faced with a myriad of decisions, from what to have for breakfast, to which route to take to class, to the more complex—"Should I double major and add possibly another semester of study to my education?" Our response to these choices depends on the information we have available at any given moment; information economists call "imperfect" because we rarely have all the data we need to make perfect decisions. Despite the lack of perfect information, we still make hundreds of decisions a day.

And now, we have another avenue in which to gather information—social media. Outlets like Facebook and Twitter are altering the process by which we make choices, how we spend our time, which movies we see, which products we buy, and more. How many of you chose a university without checking out its Facebook page or Twitter stream first for information and feedback?

As you will see in this course, what happens in economics is affected by how well and how fast information is disseminated through a society, such as how quickly information travels through Facebook. "Economists love nothing better than when deep and liquid markets operate under conditions of perfect information," says Jessica Irvine, National Economics Editor for News Corp Australia.

This leads us to the topic of this chapter, an introduction to the world of making decisions, processing information, and understanding behavior in markets —the world of economics. Each chapter in this book will start with a discussion about current (or sometimes past) events and revisit it at chapter's end—to "bring home" the concepts in play.

Introduction

In this chapter, you will learn about:

- What Is Economics, and Why Is It Important?

- Microeconomics and Macroeconomics

- How Economists Use Theories and Models to Understand Economic Issues

- How Economies Can Be Organized: An Overview of Economic Systems

What is economics and why should you spend your time learning it? After all, there are other disciplines you could be studying, and other ways you could be spending your time. As the Bring it Home feature just mentioned, making choices is at the heart of what economists study, and your decision to take this course is as much as economic decision as anything else.

Economics is probably not what you think. It is not primarily about money or finance. It is not primarily about business. It is not mathematics. What is it then? It is both a subject area and a way of viewing the world.

1.1 | What Is Economics, and Why Is It Important?

By the end of this section, you will be able to:
- Discuss the importance of studying economics
- Explain the relationship between production and division of labor
- Evaluate the significance of scarcity

Economics is the study of how humans make decisions in the face of scarcity. These can be individual decisions, family decisions, business decisions or societal decisions. If you look around carefully, you will see that scarcity is a fact of life. **Scarcity** means that human wants for goods, services and resources exceed what is available. Resources, such as labor, tools, land, and raw materials are necessary to produce the goods and services we want but they exist in limited supply. Of course, the ultimate scarce resource is time- everyone, rich or poor, has just 24 hours in the day to try to acquire the goods they want. At any point in time, there is only a finite amount of resources available.

Think about it this way: In 2015 the labor force in the United States contained over 158.6 million workers, according to the U.S. Bureau of Labor Statistics. Similarly, the total area of the United States is 3,794,101 square miles. These are large numbers for such crucial resources, however, they are limited. Because these resources are limited, so are the numbers of goods and services we produce with them. Combine this with the fact that human wants seem to be virtually infinite, and you can see why scarcity is a problem.

Figure 1.2 Scarcity of Resources Homeless people are a stark reminder that scarcity of resources is real. (Credit: "daveynin"/Flickr Creative Commons)

If you still do not believe that scarcity is a problem, consider the following: Does everyone need food to eat? Does everyone need a decent place to live? Does everyone have access to healthcare? In every country in the world, there are people who are hungry, homeless (for example, those who call park benches their beds, as shown in **Figure 1.2**), and in need of healthcare, just to focus on a few critical goods and services. Why is this the case? It is because of scarcity. Let's delve into the concept of scarcity a little deeper, because it is crucial to understanding economics.

The Problem of Scarcity

Think about all the things you consume: food, shelter, clothing, transportation, healthcare, and entertainment. How do you acquire those items? You do not produce them yourself. You buy them. How do you afford the things you buy? You work for pay. Or if you do not, someone else does on your behalf. Yet most of us never have enough to buy all the things we want. This is because of scarcity. So how do we solve it?

Link It Up ⚭

Visit this website (http://openstaxcollege.org/l/drought) to read about how the United States is dealing with scarcity in resources.

Every society, at every level, must make choices about how to use its resources. Families must decide whether to spend their money on a new car or a fancy vacation. Towns must choose whether to put more of the budget into police and fire protection or into the school system. Nations must decide whether to devote more funds to national defense or to protecting the environment. In most cases, there just isn't enough money in the budget to do everything. So why do we not each just produce all of the things we consume? The simple answer is most of us do not know how, but that is not the main reason. (When you study economics, you will discover that the obvious choice is not always the right answer—or at least the complete answer. Studying economics teaches you to think in a different of way.) Think back to pioneer days, when individuals knew how to do so much more than we do today, from building their homes, to growing their crops, to hunting for food, to repairing their equipment. Most of us do not know how to do all—or any—of those things. It is not because we could not learn. Rather, we do not have to. The reason why is something called *the division and specialization of labor*, a production innovation first put forth by Adam Smith, Figure 1.3, in his book, *The Wealth of Nations*.

Figure 1.3 Adam Smith Adam Smith introduced the idea of dividing labor into discrete tasks. (Credit: Wikimedia Commons)

The Division of and Specialization of Labor

The formal study of economics began when Adam Smith (1723–1790) published his famous book *The Wealth of Nations* in 1776. Many authors had written on economics in the centuries before Smith, but he was the first to address the subject in a comprehensive way. In the first chapter, Smith introduces the **division of labor**, which means that the way a good or service is produced is divided into a number of tasks that are performed by different workers, instead of all the tasks being done by the same person.

To illustrate the division of labor, Smith counted how many tasks went into making a pin: drawing out a piece of wire, cutting it to the right length, straightening it, putting a head on one end and a point on the other, and packaging pins for sale, to name just a few. Smith counted 18 distinct tasks that were often done by different people—all for a pin, believe it or not!

Modern businesses divide tasks as well. Even a relatively simple business like a restaurant divides up the task of serving meals into a range of jobs like top chef, sous chefs, less-skilled kitchen help, servers to wait on the tables, a greeter at the door, janitors to clean up, and a business manager to handle paychecks and bills—not to mention the economic connections a restaurant has with suppliers of food, furniture, kitchen equipment, and the building where it is located. A complex business like a large manufacturing factory, such as the shoe factory shown in Figure 1.4, or a hospital can have hundreds of job classifications.

Figure 1.4 Division of Labor Workers on an assembly line are an example of the divisions of labor. (Credit: Nina Hale/Flickr Creative Commons)

Why the Division of Labor Increases Production

When the tasks involved with producing a good or service are divided and subdivided, workers and businesses can produce a greater quantity of output. In his observations of pin factories, Smith observed that one worker alone might make 20 pins in a day, but that a small business of 10 workers (some of whom would need to do two or three of the 18 tasks involved with pin-making), could make 48,000 pins in a day. How can a group of workers, each specializing in certain tasks, produce so much more than the same number of workers who try to produce the entire good or service by themselves? Smith offered three reasons.

First, **specialization** in a particular small job allows workers to focus on the parts of the production process where they have an advantage. (In later chapters, we will develop this idea by discussing comparative advantage.) People have different skills, talents, and interests, so they will be better at some jobs than at others. The particular advantages may be based on educational choices, which are in turn shaped by interests and talents. Only those with medical degrees qualify to become doctors, for instance. For some goods, specialization will be affected by geography—it is easier to be a wheat farmer in North Dakota than in Florida, but easier to run a tourist hotel in Florida than in North Dakota. If you live in or near a big city, it is easier to attract enough customers to operate a successful dry cleaning business or movie theater than if you live in a sparsely populated rural area. Whatever the reason, if people specialize in the production of what they do best, they will be more productive than if they produce a combination of things, some of which they are good at and some of which they are not.

Second, workers who specialize in certain tasks often learn to produce more quickly and with higher quality. This pattern holds true for many workers, including assembly line laborers who build cars, stylists who cut hair, and doctors who perform heart surgery. In fact, specialized workers often know their jobs well enough to suggest innovative ways to do their work faster and better.

A similar pattern often operates within businesses. In many cases, a business that focuses on one or a few products (sometimes called its "core competency") is more successful than firms that try to make a wide range of products.

Third, specialization allows businesses to take advantage of **economies of scale**, which means that for many goods, as the level of production increases, the average cost of producing each individual unit declines. For example, if a factory produces only 100 cars per year, each car will be quite expensive to make on average. However, if a factory produces 50,000 cars each year, then it can set up an assembly line with huge machines and workers performing specialized tasks, and the average cost of production per car will be lower. The ultimate result of workers who can focus on their preferences and talents, learn to do their specialized jobs better, and work in larger organizations is that society as a whole can produce and consume far more than if each person tried to produce all of their own goods and services. The division and specialization of labor has been a force against the problem of scarcity.

Trade and Markets

Specialization only makes sense, though, if workers can use the pay they receive for doing their jobs to purchase the other goods and services that they need. In short, specialization requires trade.

You do not have to know anything about electronics or sound systems to play music—you just buy an iPod or MP3 player, download the music and listen. You do not have to know anything about artificial fibers or the construction of sewing machines if you need a jacket—you just buy the jacket and wear it. You do not need to know anything about internal combustion engines to operate a car—you just get in and drive. Instead of trying to acquire all the knowledge and skills involved in producing all of the goods and services that you wish to consume, the market allows you to learn a specialized set of skills and then use the pay you receive to buy the goods and services you need or want. This is how our modern society has evolved into a strong economy.

Why Study Economics?

Now that we have gotten an overview on what economics studies, let's quickly discuss why you are right to study it. Economics is not primarily a collection of facts to be memorized, though there are plenty of important concepts to be learned. Instead, economics is better thought of as a collection of questions to be answered or puzzles to be worked out. Most important, economics provides the tools to work out those puzzles. If you have yet to be been bitten by the economics "bug," there are other reasons why you should study economics.

- Virtually every major problem facing the world today, from global warming, to world poverty, to the conflicts in Syria, Afghanistan, and Somalia, has an economic dimension. If you are going to be part of solving those problems, you need to be able to understand them. Economics is crucial.

- It is hard to overstate the importance of economics to good citizenship. You need to be able to vote intelligently on budgets, regulations, and laws in general. When the U.S. government came close to a standstill at the end of 2012 due to the "fiscal cliff," what were the issues involved? Did you know?

- A basic understanding of economics makes you a well-rounded thinker. When you read articles about economic issues, you will understand and be able to evaluate the writer's argument. When you hear classmates, co-workers, or political candidates talking about economics, you will be able to distinguish between common sense and nonsense. You will find new ways of thinking about current events and about personal and business decisions, as well as current events and politics.

The study of economics does not dictate the answers, but it can illuminate the different choices.

1.2 | Microeconomics and Macroeconomics

By the end of this section, you will be able to:
- Describe microeconomics
- Describe macroeconomics
- Contrast monetary policy and fiscal policy

Economics is concerned with the well-being of *all* people, including those with jobs and those without jobs, as well as those with high incomes and those with low incomes. Economics acknowledges that production of useful goods and services can create problems of environmental pollution. It explores the question of how investing in education helps to develop workers' skills. It probes questions like how to tell when big businesses or big labor unions are operating in a way that benefits society as a whole and when they are operating in a way that benefits their owners or members at the expense of others. It looks at how government spending, taxes, and regulations affect decisions about production and consumption.

It should be clear by now that economics covers a lot of ground. That ground can be divided into two parts: **Microeconomics** focuses on the actions of individual agents within the economy, like households, workers, and businesses; **Macroeconomics** looks at the economy as a whole. It focuses on broad issues such as growth of production, the number of unemployed people, the inflationary increase in prices, government deficits, and levels of exports and imports. Microeconomics and macroeconomics are not separate subjects, but rather complementary perspectives on the overall subject of the economy.

To understand why both microeconomic and macroeconomic perspectives are useful, consider the problem of studying a biological ecosystem like a lake. One person who sets out to study the lake might focus on specific topics: certain kinds of algae or plant life; the characteristics of particular fish or snails; or the trees surrounding the lake. Another person might take an overall view and instead consider the entire ecosystem of the lake from top to bottom; what eats what, how the system stays in a rough balance, and what environmental stresses affect this balance. Both approaches are useful, and both examine the same lake, but the viewpoints are different. In a similar way, both microeconomics and macroeconomics study the same economy, but each has a different viewpoint.

Whether you are looking at lakes or economics, the micro and the macro insights should blend with each other. In studying a lake, the micro insights about particular plants and animals help to understand the overall food chain, while the macro insights about the overall food chain help to explain the environment in which individual plants and animals live.

In economics, the micro decisions of individual businesses are influenced by whether the macroeconomy is healthy; for example, firms will be more likely to hire workers if the overall economy is growing. In turn, the performance of the macroeconomy ultimately depends on the microeconomic decisions made by individual households and businesses.

Microeconomics

What determines how households and individuals spend their budgets? What combination of goods and services will best fit their needs and wants, given the budget they have to spend? How do people decide whether to work, and if so, whether to work full time or part time? How do people decide how much to save for the future, or whether they should borrow to spend beyond their current means?

What determines the products, and how many of each, a firm will produce and sell? What determines what prices a firm will charge? What determines how a firm will produce its products? What determines how many workers it will hire? How will a firm finance its business? When will a firm decide to expand, downsize, or even close? In the microeconomic part of this book, we will learn about the theory of consumer behavior and the theory of the firm.

Macroeconomics

What determines the level of economic activity in a society? In other words, what determines how many goods and services a nation actually produces? What determines how many jobs are available in an economy? What determines a nation's standard of living? What causes the economy to speed up or slow down? What causes firms to hire more workers or to lay workers off? Finally, what causes the economy to grow over the long term?

An economy's macroeconomic health can be defined by a number of goals: growth in the standard of living, low unemployment, and low inflation, to name the most important. How can macroeconomic policy be used to pursue these goals? **Monetary policy**, which involves policies that affect bank lending, interest rates, and financial capital markets, is conducted by a nation's central bank. For the United States, this is the Federal Reserve. **Fiscal policy**, which involves government spending and taxes, is determined by a nation's legislative body. For the United States, this is the Congress and the executive branch, which originates the federal budget. These are the main tools the government has to work with. Americans tend to expect that government can fix whatever economic problems we encounter, but to what extent is that expectation realistic? These are just some of the issues that will be explored in the macroeconomic chapters of this book.

1.3 | How Economists Use Theories and Models to Understand Economic Issues

By the end of this section, you will be able to:
- Interpret a circular flow diagram
- Explain the importance of economic theories and models
- Describe goods and services markets and labor markets

Figure 1.5 John Maynard Keynes One of the most influential economists in modern times was John Maynard Keynes. (Credit: Wikimedia Commons)

John Maynard Keynes (1883–1946), one of the greatest economists of the twentieth century, pointed out that economics is not just a subject area but also a way of thinking. Keynes, shown in Figure 1.5, famously wrote in the introduction to a fellow economist's book: "[Economics] is a method rather than a doctrine, an apparatus of the mind, a technique of thinking, which helps its possessor to draw correct conclusions." In other words, economics teaches you how to think, not what to think.

Link It Up

Watch this video (http://openstaxcollege.org/l/Keynes) about John Maynard Keynes and his influence on economics.

Economists see the world through a different lens than anthropologists, biologists, classicists, or practitioners of any other discipline. They analyze issues and problems with economic theories that are based on particular assumptions about human behavior, that are different than the assumptions an anthropologist or psychologist might use. A **theory** is a simplified representation of how two or more variables interact with each other. The purpose of a theory is to take a complex, real-world issue and simplify it down to its essentials. If done well, this enables the analyst to understand the issue and any problems around it. A good theory is simple enough to be understood, while complex enough to capture the key features of the object or situation being studied.

Sometimes economists use the term **model** instead of theory. Strictly speaking, a theory is a more abstract representation, while a model is more applied or empirical representation. Models are used to test theories, but for this course we will use the terms interchangeably.

For example, an architect who is planning a major office building will often build a physical model that sits on a tabletop to show how the entire city block will look after the new building is constructed. Companies often build models of their new products, which are more rough and unfinished than the final product will be, but can still demonstrate how the new product will work.

A good model to start with in economics is the **circular flow diagram**, which is shown in Figure 1.6. It pictures the economy as consisting of two groups—households and firms—that interact in two markets: the **goods and services market** in which firms sell and households buy and the **labor market** in which households sell labor to business firms or other employees.

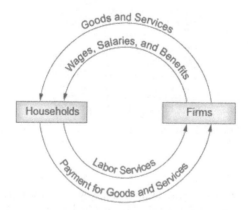

Figure 1.6 The Circular Flow Diagram The circular flow diagram shows how households and firms interact in the goods and services market, and in the labor market. The direction of the arrows shows that in the goods and services market, households receive goods and services and pay firms for them. In the labor market, households provide labor and receive payment from firms through wages, salaries, and benefits.

Of course, in the real world, there are many different markets for goods and services and markets for many different types of labor. The circular flow diagram simplifies this to make the picture easier to grasp. In the diagram, firms produce goods and services, which they sell to households in return for revenues. This is shown in the outer circle, and represents the two sides of the product market (for example, the market for goods and services) in which households demand and firms supply. Households sell their labor as workers to firms in return for wages, salaries and benefits. This is shown in the inner circle and represents the two sides of the labor market in which households supply and firms demand.

This version of the circular flow model is stripped down to the essentials, but it has enough features to explain how the product and labor markets work in the economy. We could easily add details to this basic model if we wanted to introduce more real-world elements, like financial markets, governments, and interactions with the rest of the globe (imports and exports).

Economists carry a set of theories in their heads like a carpenter carries around a toolkit. When they see an economic issue or problem, they go through the theories they know to see if they can find one that fits. Then they use the theory to derive insights about the issue or problem. In economics, theories are expressed as diagrams, graphs, or even as mathematical equations. (Do not worry. In this course, we will mostly use graphs.) Economists do not figure out the answer to the problem first and then draw the graph to illustrate. Rather, they use the graph of the theory to help them figure out the answer. Although at the introductory level, you can sometimes figure out the right answer without applying a model, if you keep studying economics, before too long you will run into issues and problems that you will need to graph to solve. Both micro and macroeconomics are explained in terms of theories and models. The most well-known theories are probably those of supply and demand, but you will learn a number of others.

1.4 | How Economies Can Be Organized: An Overview of Economic Systems

By the end of this section, you will be able to:
- Contrast traditional economies, command economies, and market economies
- Explain gross domestic product (GDP)
- Assess the importance and effects of globalization

Think about what a complex system a modern economy is. It includes all production of goods and services, all buying and selling, all employment. The economic life of every individual is interrelated, at least to a small extent, with the economic lives of thousands or even millions of other individuals. Who organizes and coordinates this system? Who insures that, for example, the number of televisions a society provides is the same as the amount it needs and wants? Who insures that the right number of employees work in the electronics industry? Who insures that televisions are produced in the best way possible? How does it all get done?

There are at least three ways societies have found to organize an economy. The first is the **traditional economy**, which is the oldest economic system and can be found in parts of Asia, Africa, and South America. Traditional economies organize their economic affairs the way they have always done (i.e., tradition). Occupations stay in the family. Most families are farmers who grow the crops they have always grown using traditional methods. What you produce is what you get to consume. Because things are driven by tradition, there is little economic progress or development.

Figure 1.7 A Command Economy Ancient Egypt was an example of a command economy. (Credit: Jay Bergesen/ Flickr Creative Commons)

Command economies are very different. In a **command economy**, economic effort is devoted to goals passed down from a ruler or ruling class. Ancient Egypt was a good example: a large part of economic life was devoted to building pyramids, like those shown in **Figure 1.7**, for the pharaohs. Medieval manor life is another example: the lord provided the land for growing crops and protection in the event of war. In return, vassals provided labor and soldiers to do the lord's bidding. In the last century, communism emphasized command economies.

In a command economy, the government decides what goods and services will be produced and what prices will be charged for them. The government decides what methods of production will be used and how much workers will be paid. Many necessities like healthcare and education are provided for free. Currently, Cuba and North Korea have command economies.

Figure 1.8 A Market Economy Nothing says "market" more than The New York Stock Exchange. (Credit: Erik Drost/ Flickr Creative Commons)

Although command economies have a very centralized structure for economic decisions, market economies have a very decentralized structure. A **market** is an institution that brings together buyers and sellers of goods or services, who may be either individuals or businesses. The New York Stock Exchange, shown in **Figure 1.8**, is a prime example of market in which buyers and sellers are brought together. In a **market economy**, decision-making is decentralized. Market economies are based on **private enterprise**: the means of production (resources and businesses) are owned and operated by private individuals or groups of private individuals. Businesses supply goods and services based on demand. (In a command economy, by contrast, resources and businesses are owned by the government.) What goods and services are supplied depends on what is demanded. A person's income is based on his or her ability to convert resources (especially labor) into something that society values. The more society values the person's output, the higher the income (think Lady Gaga or LeBron James). In this scenario, economic decisions are determined by market forces, not governments.

Most economies in the real world are mixed; they combine elements of command and market (and even traditional) systems. The U.S. economy is positioned toward the market-oriented end of the spectrum. Many countries in Europe and Latin America, while primarily market-oriented, have a greater degree of government involvement in economic decisions than does the U.S. economy. China and Russia, while they are closer to having a market-oriented system now than several decades ago, remain closer to the command economy end of the spectrum. A rich resource of information about countries and their economies can be found on the Heritage Foundation's website, as the following Clear It Up feature discusses.

What countries are considered economically free?

Who is in control of economic decisions? Are people free to do what they want and to work where they want? Are businesses free to produce when they want and what they choose, and to hire and fire as they wish? Are banks free to choose who will receive loans? Or does the government control these kinds of choices? Each year, researchers at the Heritage Foundation and the *Wall Street Journal* look at 50 different categories of economic freedom for countries around the world. They give each nation a score based on the extent of economic freedom in each category.

The 2015 Heritage Foundation's Index of Economic Freedom report ranked 178 countries around the world: some examples of the most free and the least free countries are listed in Table 1.1. Several countries were not ranked because of extreme instability that made judgments about economic freedom impossible. These countries include Afghanistan, Iraq, Syria, and Somalia.

The assigned rankings are inevitably based on estimates, yet even these rough measures can be useful for discerning trends. In 2015, 101 of the 178 included countries shifted toward greater economic freedom, although 77 of the countries shifted toward less economic freedom. In recent decades, the overall trend has been a *higher level of economic freedom around the world*.

Most Economic Freedom	Least Economic Freedom
1. Hong Kong	167. Timor-Leste
2. Singapore	168. Democratic Republic of Congo
3. New Zealand	169. Argentina
4. Australia	170. Republic of Congo
5. Switzerland	171. Iran
6. Canada	172. Turkmenistan
7. Chile	173. Equatorial Guinea
8. Estonia	174. Eritrea
9. Ireland	175. Zimbabwe
10. Mauritius	176. Venezuela
11. Denmark	177. Cuba
12. United States	178. North Korea

Table 1.1 Economic Freedoms, 2015   (Source: The Heritage Foundation, 2015 Index of Economic Freedom, Country Rankings, http://www.heritage.org/index/ranking)

Regulations: The Rules of the Game

Markets and government regulations are always entangled. There is no such thing as an absolutely free market. Regulations always define the "rules of the game" in the economy. Economies that are primarily market-oriented have fewer regulations—ideally just enough to maintain an even playing field for participants. At a minimum, these laws govern matters like safeguarding private property against theft, protecting people from violence, enforcing legal contracts, preventing fraud, and collecting taxes. Conversely, even the most command-oriented economies operate using markets. How else would buying and selling occur? But the decisions of what will be produced and what prices will be charged are heavily regulated. Heavily regulated economies often have **underground economies**, which are markets where the buyers and sellers make transactions without the government's approval.

The question of how to organize economic institutions is typically not a black-or-white choice between all market or all government, but instead involves a balancing act over the appropriate combination of market freedom and government rules.

Figure 1.9 Globalization Cargo ships are one mode of transportation for shipping goods in the global economy. (Credit: Raul Valdez/Flickr Creative Commons)

The Rise of Globalization

Recent decades have seen a trend toward **globalization**, which is the expanding cultural, political, and economic connections between people around the world. One measure of this is the increased buying and selling of goods, services, and assets across national borders—in other words, international trade and financial capital flows.

Globalization has occurred for a number of reasons. Improvements in shipping, as illustrated by the container ship shown in **Figure 1.9**, and air cargo have driven down transportation costs. Innovations in computing and telecommunications have made it easier and cheaper to manage long-distance economic connections of production and sales. Many valuable products and services in the modern economy can take the form of information—for example: computer software; financial advice; travel planning; music, books and movies; and blueprints for designing a building. These products and many others can be transported over telephones and computer networks at ever-lower costs. Finally, international agreements and treaties between countries have encouraged greater trade.

Table 1.2 presents one measure of globalization. It shows the percentage of domestic economic production that was exported for a selection of countries from 2010 to 2013, according to an entity known as The World Bank. **Exports** are the goods and services that are produced domestically and sold abroad. **Imports** are the goods and services that are produced abroad and then sold domestically. The size of total production in an economy is measured by the **gross domestic product (GDP)**. Thus, the ratio of exports divided by GDP measures what share of a country's total economic production is sold in other countries.

Country	2010	2011	2012	2013
Higher Income Countries				

Table 1.2 The Extent of Globalization (exports/GDP)   (Source: http://databank.worldbank.org/data/)

Country	2010	2011	2012	2013
United States	12.4	13.6	13.6	13.5
Belgium	76.2	81.4	82.2	82.8
Canada	29.1	30.7	30.0	30.1
France	26.0	27.8	28.1	28.3
Middle Income Countries				
Brazil	10.9	11.9	12.6	12.6
Mexico	29.9	31.2	32.6	31.7
South Korea	49.4	55.7	56.3	53.9
Lower Income Countries				
Chad	36.8	38.9	36.9	32.2
China	29.4	28.5	27.3	26.4
India	22.0	23.9	24.0	24.8
Nigeria	25.3	31.3	31.4	18.0

Table 1.2 The Extent of Globalization (exports/GDP)   (Source: http://databank.worldbank.org/data/)

In recent decades, the export/GDP ratio has generally risen, both worldwide and for the U.S. economy. Interestingly, the share of U.S. exports in proportion to the U.S. economy is well below the global average, in part because large economies like the United States can contain more of the division of labor inside their national borders. However, smaller economies like Belgium, Korea, and Canada need to trade across their borders with other countries to take full advantage of division of labor, specialization, and economies of scale. In this sense, the enormous U.S. economy is less affected by globalization than most other countries.

Table 1.2 also shows that many medium and low income countries around the world, like Mexico and China, have also experienced a surge of globalization in recent decades. If an astronaut in orbit could put on special glasses that make all economic transactions visible as brightly colored lines and look down at Earth, the astronaut would see the planet covered with connections.

So, hopefully, you now have an idea of what economics is about. Before you move to any other chapter of study, be sure to read the very important appendix to this chapter called The Use of Mathematics in Principles of Economics. It is essential that you learn more about how to read and use models in economics.

Bring it Home

Decisions ... Decisions in the Social Media Age

The world we live in today provides nearly instant access to a wealth of information. Consider that as recently as the late 1970s, the Farmer's Almanac, along with the Weather Bureau of the U.S. Department of Agriculture, were the primary sources American farmers used to determine when to plant and harvest their crops. Today, farmers are more likely to access, online, weather forecasts from the National Oceanic and Atmospheric Administration or watch the Weather Channel. After all, knowing the upcoming forecast could drive when to harvest crops. Consequently, knowing the upcoming weather could change the amount of crop harvested.

Some relatively new information forums, such as Facebook, are rapidly changing how information is distributed; hence, influencing decision making. In 2014, the Pew Research Center reported that 71% of online adults use Facebook. Facebook post topics range from the National Basketball Association, to celebrity singers and performers, to farmers.

Information helps us make decisions. Decisions as simple as what to wear today to how many reporters should be sent to cover a crash. Each of these decisions is an economic decision. After all, resources are scarce. If ten reporters are sent to cover an accident, they are not available to cover other stories or complete other tasks. Information provides the knowledge needed to make the best possible decisions on how to utilize scarce resources. Welcome to the world of economics!

KEY TERMS

circular flow diagram a diagram that views the economy as consisting of households and firms interacting in a goods and services market and a labor market

command economy an economy where economic decisions are passed down from government authority and where resources are owned by the government

division of labor the way in which the work required to produce a good or service is divided into tasks performed by different workers

economics the study of how humans make choices under conditions of scarcity

economies of scale when the average cost of producing each individual unit declines as total output increases

exports products (goods and services) made domestically and sold abroad

fiscal policy economic policies that involve government spending and taxes

globalization the trend in which buying and selling in markets have increasingly crossed national borders

goods and services market a market in which firms are sellers of what they produce and households are buyers

gross domestic product (GDP) measure of the size of total production in an economy

imports products (goods and services) made abroad and then sold domestically

labor market the market in which households sell their labor as workers to business firms or other employers

macroeconomics the branch of economics that focuses on broad issues such as growth, unemployment, inflation, and trade balance.

market interaction between potential buyers and sellers; a combination of demand and supply

market economy an economy where economic decisions are decentralized, resources are owned by private individuals, and businesses supply goods and services based on demand

microeconomics the branch of economics that focuses on actions of particular agents within the economy, like households, workers, and business firms

model see theory

monetary policy policy that involves altering the level of interest rates, the availability of credit in the economy, and the extent of borrowing

private enterprise system where the means of production (resources and businesses) are owned and operated by private individuals or groups of private individuals

scarcity when human wants for goods and services exceed the available supply

specialization when workers or firms focus on particular tasks for which they are well-suited within the overall production process

theory a representation of an object or situation that is simplified while including enough of the key features to help us understand the object or situation

traditional economy typically an agricultural economy where things are done the same as they have always been done

underground economy a market where the buyers and sellers make transactions in violation of one or more
government regulations

KEY CONCEPTS AND SUMMARY

1.1 What Is Economics, and Why Is It Important?
Economics seeks to solve the problem of scarcity, which is when human wants for goods and services exceed the available supply. A modern economy displays a division of labor, in which people earn income by specializing in what they produce and then use that income to purchase the products they need or want. The division of labor allows individuals and firms to specialize and to produce more for several reasons: a) It allows the agents to focus on areas of advantage due to natural factors and skill levels; b) It encourages the agents to learn and invent; c) It allows agents to take advantage of economies of scale. Division and specialization of labor only work when individuals can purchase what they do not produce in markets. Learning about economics helps you understand the major problems facing the world today, prepares you to be a good citizen, and helps you become a well-rounded thinker.

1.2 Microeconomics and Macroeconomics
Microeconomics and macroeconomics are two different perspectives on the economy. The microeconomic perspective focuses on parts of the economy: individuals, firms, and industries. The macroeconomic perspective looks at the economy as a whole, focusing on goals like growth in the standard of living, unemployment, and inflation. Macroeconomics has two types of policies for pursuing these goals: monetary policy and fiscal policy.

1.3 How Economists Use Theories and Models to Understand Economic Issues
Economists analyze problems differently than do other disciplinary experts. The main tools economists use are economic theories or models. A theory is not an illustration of the answer to a problem. Rather, a theory is a tool for determining the answer.

1.4 How Economies Can Be Organized: An Overview of Economic Systems
Societies can be organized as traditional, command, or market-oriented economies. Most societies are a mix. The last few decades have seen globalization evolve as a result of growth in commercial and financial networks that cross national borders, making businesses and workers from different economies increasingly interdependent.

SELF-CHECK QUESTIONS

1. What is scarcity? Can you think of two causes of scarcity?

2. Residents of the town of Smithfield like to consume hams, but each ham requires 10 people to produce it and takes a month. If the town has a total of 100 people, what is the maximum amount of ham the residents can consume in a month?

3. A consultant works for $200 per hour. She likes to eat vegetables, but is not very good at growing them. Why does it make more economic sense for her to spend her time at the consulting job and shop for her vegetables?

4. A computer systems engineer could paint his house, but it makes more sense for him to hire a painter to do it. Explain why.

5. What would be another example of a "system" in the real world that could serve as a metaphor for micro and macroeconomics?

6. Suppose we extend the circular flow model to add imports and exports. Copy the circular flow diagram onto a sheet of paper and then add a foreign country as a third agent. Draw a rough sketch of the flows of imports, exports, and the payments for each on your diagram.

7. What is an example of a problem in the world today, not mentioned in the chapter, that has an economic dimension?

8. The chapter defines *private enterprise* as a characteristic of market-oriented economies. What would *public enterprise* be? *Hint*: It is a characteristic of command economies.

9. Why might Belgium, France, Italy, and Sweden have a higher export to GDP ratio than the United States?

REVIEW QUESTIONS

10. Give the three reasons that explain why the division of labor increases an economy's level of production.

11. What are three reasons to study economics?

12. What is the difference between microeconomics and macroeconomics?

13. What are examples of individual economic agents?

14. What are the three main goals of macroeconomics?

15. How did John Maynard Keynes define economics?

16. Are households primarily buyers or sellers in the goods and services market? In the labor market?

17. Are firms primarily buyers or sellers in the goods and services market? In the labor market?

18. What are the three ways that societies can organize themselves economically?

19. What is globalization? How do you think it might have affected the economy over the past decade?

CRITICAL THINKING QUESTIONS

20. Suppose you have a team of two workers: one is a baker and one is a chef. Explain why the kitchen can produce more meals in a given period of time if each worker specializes in what they do best than if each worker tries to do everything from appetizer to dessert.

21. Why would division of labor without trade not work?

22. Can you think of any examples of *free* goods, that is, goods or services that are not scarce?

23. A balanced federal budget and a balance of trade are considered secondary goals of macroeconomics, while growth in the standard of living (for example) is considered a primary goal. Why do you think that is so?

24. Macroeconomics is an aggregate of what happens at the microeconomic level. Would it be possible for what happens at the macro level to differ from how economic agents would react to some stimulus at the micro level? *Hint:* Think about the behavior of crowds.

25. Why is it unfair or meaningless to criticize a theory as "unrealistic?"

26. Suppose, as an economist, you are asked to analyze an issue unlike anything you have ever done before. Also, suppose you do not have a specific model for analyzing that issue. What should you do? *Hint:* What would a carpenter do in a similar situation?

27. Why do you think that most modern countries' economies are a mix of command and market types?

28. Can you think of ways that globalization has helped you economically? Can you think of ways that it has not?

2 | Choice in a World of Scarcity

Figure 2.1 Choices and Tradeoffs In general, the higher the degree, the higher the salary. So why aren't more people pursuing higher degrees? The short answer: choices and tradeoffs. (Credit: modification of work by "Jim, the Photographer"/Flickr Creative Commons)

Bring it Home

Choices ... To What Degree?

In 2015, the median income for workers who hold master's degrees varies from males to females. The average of the two is $2,951 weekly. Multiply this average by 52 weeks, and you get an average salary of $153,452. Compare that to the median weekly earnings for a full-time worker over 25 with no higher than a bachelor's degree: $1,224 weekly and $63,648 a year. What about those with no higher than a high school diploma in 2015? They earn just $664 weekly and $34,528 over 12 months. In other words, says the Bureau of Labor Statistics (BLS), earning a bachelor's degree boosted salaries 54% over what you would have earned if you had stopped your education after high school. A master's degree yields a salary almost double that of a high school diploma.

Given these statistics, we might expect a lot of people to choose to go to college and at least earn a bachelor's degree. Assuming that people want to improve their material well-being, it seems like they would make those choices that give them the greatest opportunity to consume goods and services. As it turns out, the analysis is not nearly as simple as this. In fact, in 2014, the BLS reported that while almost 88% of the population in the United States had a high school diploma, only 33.6% of 25–65 year olds had bachelor's degrees, and only 7.4% of 25–65 year olds in 2014 had earned a master's.

This brings us to the subject of this chapter: why people make the choices they make and how economists go about explaining those choices.

Introduction to Choice in a World of Scarcity

In this chapter, you will learn about:

- How Individuals Make Choices Based on Their Budget Constraint
- The Production Possibilities Frontier and Social Choices
- Confronting Objections to the Economic Approach

You will learn quickly when you examine the relationship between economics and scarcity that choices involve tradeoffs. Every choice has a cost.

In 1968, the Rolling Stones recorded "You Can't Always Get What You Want." Economists chuckled, because they had been singing a similar tune for decades. English economist Lionel Robbins (1898–1984), in his *Essay on the Nature and Significance of Economic Science* in 1932, described not always getting what you want in this way:

> The time at our disposal is limited. There are only twenty-four hours in the day. We have to choose between the different uses to which they may be put. ... Everywhere we turn, if we choose one thing we must relinquish others which, in different circumstances, we would wish not to have relinquished. Scarcity of means to satisfy given ends is an almost ubiquitous condition of human nature.

Because people live in a world of scarcity, they cannot have all the time, money, possessions, and experiences they wish. Neither can society.

This chapter will continue our discussion of scarcity and the economic way of thinking by first introducing three critical concepts: opportunity cost, marginal decision making, and diminishing returns. Later, it will consider whether the economic way of thinking accurately describes either how choices *are* made or how they *should* be made.

2.1 | How Individuals Make Choices Based on Their Budget Constraint

By the end of this section, you will be able to:
- Calculate and graph budgets constraints
- Explain opportunity sets and opportunity costs
- Evaluate the law of diminishing marginal utility
- Explain how marginal analysis and utility influence choices

Consider the typical consumer's budget problem. Consumers have a limited amount of income to spend on the things they need and want. Suppose Alphonso has $10 in spending money each week that he can allocate between bus tickets for getting to work and the burgers that he eats for lunch. Burgers cost $2 each, and bus tickets are 50 cents each. **Figure 2.2** shows Alphonso's **budget constraint**, that is, the outer boundary of his **opportunity set**. The opportunity set identifies all the opportunities for spending within his budget. The budget constraint indicates all the combinations of burgers and bus tickets Alphonso can afford when he exhausts his budget, given the prices of the two goods. (There are actually many different kinds of budget constraints. You will learn more about them in the chapter on **Consumer Choices (http://cnx.org/content/m57229/latest/)** .)

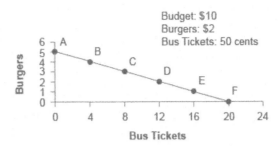

Figure 2.2 The Budget Constraint: Alphonso's Consumption Choice Opportunity Frontier   Each point on the budget constraint represents a combination of burgers and bus tickets whose total cost adds up to Alphonso's budget of $10. The slope of the budget constraint is determined by the relative price of burgers and bus tickets. All along the budget set, giving up one burger means gaining four bus tickets.

The vertical axis in the figure shows burger purchases and the horizontal axis shows bus ticket purchases. If Alphonso spends all his money on burgers, he can afford five per week. ($10 per week/$2 per burger = 5 burgers per week.) But if he does this, he will not be able to afford any bus tickets. This choice (zero bus tickets and five burgers) is shown by point A in the figure. Alternatively, if Alphonso spends all his money on bus tickets, he can afford 20 per week. ($10 per week/$0.50 per bus ticket = 20 bus tickets per week.) Then, however, he will not be able to afford any burgers. This alternative choice (20 bus tickets and zero burgers) is shown by point F.

If Alphonso is like most people, he will choose some combination that includes both bus tickets and burgers. That is, he will choose some combination on the budget constraint that connects points A and F. Every point on (or inside) the constraint shows a combination of burgers and bus tickets that Alphonso can afford. Any point outside the constraint is not affordable, because it would cost more money than Alphonso has in his budget.

The budget constraint clearly shows the tradeoff Alphonso faces in choosing between burgers and bus tickets. Suppose he is currently at point D, where he can afford 12 bus tickets and two burgers. What would it cost Alphonso for one more burger? It would be natural to answer $2, but that's not the way economists think. Instead they ask, how many bus tickets would Alphonso have to give up to get one more burger, while staying within his budget? The answer is four bus tickets. That is the true cost to Alphonso of one more burger.

The Concept of Opportunity Cost

Economists use the term **opportunity cost** to indicate what must be given up to obtain something that is desired. The idea behind opportunity cost is that the cost of one item is the lost opportunity to do or consume something else; in short, opportunity cost is the value of the next best alternative. For Alphonso, the opportunity cost of a burger is the four bus tickets he would have to give up. He would decide whether or not to choose the burger depending on whether the value of the burger exceeds the value of the forgone alternative—in this case, bus tickets. Since people must choose, they inevitably face tradeoffs in which they have to give up things they desire to get other things they desire more.

Link It Up

View this website (http://openstaxcollege.org/l/linestanding) for an example of opportunity cost—paying someone else to wait in line for you.

A fundamental principle of economics is that every choice has an opportunity cost. If you sleep through your economics class (not recommended, by the way), the opportunity cost is the learning you miss from not attending class. If you spend your income on video games, you cannot spend it on movies. If you choose to marry one person, you give up the opportunity to marry anyone else. In short, opportunity cost is all around us and part of human existence.

The following Work It Out feature shows a step-by-step analysis of a budget constraint calculation. Read through it to understand another important concept—slope—that is further explained in the appendix **The Use of Mathematics in Principles of Economics**.

Work It Out ─O─O─O

Understanding Budget Constraints

Budget constraints are easy to understand if you apply a little math. The appendix **The Use of Mathematics in Principles of Economics** explains all the math you are likely to need in this book. So if math is not your strength, you might want to take a look at the appendix.

Step 1: The equation for any budget constraint is:

$$Budget = P_1 \times Q_1 + P_2 \times Q_2$$

where P and Q are the price and quantity of items purchased and Budget is the amount of income one has to spend.

Step 2. Apply the budget constraint equation to the scenario. In Alphonso's case, this works out to be:

$$Budget = P_1 \times Q_1 + P_2 \times Q_2$$
$$\$10\ budget = \$2\ per\ burger \times quantity\ of\ burgers + \$0.50\ per\ bus\ ticket \times quantity\ of\ bus\ tickets$$
$$\$10 = \$2 \times Q_{burgers} + \$0.50 \times Q_{bus\ tickets}$$

Step 3. Using a little algebra, we can turn this into the familiar equation of a line:

$$y = b + mx$$

For Alphonso, this is:

$$\$10 = \$2 \times Q_{burgers} + \$0.50 \times Q_{bus\ tickets}$$

Step 4. Simplify the equation. Begin by multiplying both sides of the equation by 2:

$$2 \times 10 = 2 \times 2 \times Q_{burgers} + 2 \times 0.5 \times Q_{bus\ tickets}$$
$$20 = 4 \times Q_{burgers} + 1 \times Q_{bus\ tickets}$$

Step 5. Subtract one bus ticket from both sides:

$$20 - Q_{bus\ tickets} = 4 \times Q_{burgers}$$

Divide each side by 4 to yield the answer:

$$5 - 0.25 \times Q_{bus\ tickets} = Q_{burgers}$$
$$or$$
$$Q_{burgers} = 5 - 0.25 \times Q_{bus\ tickets}$$

Step 6. Notice that this equation fits the budget constraint in **Figure 2.2**. The vertical intercept is 5 and the slope is –0.25, just as the equation says. If you plug 20 bus tickets into the equation, you get 0 burgers. If you plug other numbers of bus tickets into the equation, you get the results shown in **Table 2.1**, which are the points on Alphonso's budget constraint.

Point	Quantity of Burgers (at $2)	Quantity of Bus Tickets (at 50 cents)
A	5	0
B	4	4
C	3	8
D	2	12
E	1	16
F	0	20

Table 2.1

Step 7. Notice that the slope of a budget constraint always shows the opportunity cost of the good which is on the horizontal axis. For Alphonso, the slope is −0.25, indicating that for every four bus tickets he buys, Alphonso must give up 1 burger.

There are two important observations here. First, the algebraic sign of the slope is negative, which means that the only way to get more of one good is to give up some of the other. Second, the slope is defined as the price of bus tickets (whatever is on the horizontal axis in the graph) divided by the price of burgers (whatever is on the vertical axis), in this case $0.50/$2 = 0.25. So if you want to determine the opportunity cost quickly, just divide the two prices.

Identifying Opportunity Cost

In many cases, it is reasonable to refer to the opportunity cost as the price. If your cousin buys a new bicycle for $300, then $300 measures the amount of "other consumption" that he has given up. For practical purposes, there may be no special need to identify the specific alternative product or products that could have been bought with that $300, but sometimes the price as measured in dollars may not accurately capture the true opportunity cost. This problem can loom especially large when costs of time are involved.

For example, consider a boss who decides that all employees will attend a two-day retreat to "build team spirit." The out-of-pocket monetary cost of the event may involve hiring an outside consulting firm to run the retreat, as well as room and board for all participants. But an opportunity cost exists as well: during the two days of the retreat, none of the employees are doing any other work.

Attending college is another case where the opportunity cost exceeds the monetary cost. The out-of-pocket costs of attending college include tuition, books, room and board, and other expenses. But in addition, during the hours that you are attending class and studying, it is impossible to work at a paying job. Thus, college imposes both an out-of-pocket cost and an opportunity cost of lost earnings.

What is the opportunity cost associated with increased airport security measures?

After the terrorist plane hijackings on September 11, 2001, many steps were proposed to improve air travel safety. For example, the federal government could provide armed "sky marshals" who would travel inconspicuously with the rest of the passengers. The cost of having a sky marshal on every flight would be roughly $3 billion per year. Retrofitting all U.S. planes with reinforced cockpit doors to make it harder for terrorists to take over the plane would have a price tag of $450 million. Buying more sophisticated security equipment for airports, like three-dimensional baggage scanners and cameras linked to face recognition software, could cost another $2 billion.

But the single biggest cost of greater airline security does not involve spending money. It is the opportunity cost of additional waiting time at the airport. According to the United States Department of Transportation (DOT), more than 800 million passengers took plane trips in the United States in 2012. Since the 9/11 hijackings, security screening has become more intensive, and consequently, the procedure takes longer than in the past. Say that, on average, each air passenger spends an extra 30 minutes in the airport per trip. Economists commonly place a value on time to convert an opportunity cost in time into a monetary figure. Because many air travelers are relatively high-paid business people, conservative estimates set the average price of time for air travelers at $20 per hour. By these back-of-the-envelope calculations, the opportunity cost of delays in airports could be as much as 800 million × 0.5 hours × $20/hour, or $8 billion per year. Clearly, the opportunity costs of waiting time can be just as important as costs that involve direct spending.

In some cases, realizing the opportunity cost can alter behavior. Imagine, for example, that you spend $8 on lunch every day at work. You may know perfectly well that bringing a lunch from home would cost only $3 a day, so the opportunity cost of buying lunch at the restaurant is $5 each day (that is, the $8 buying lunch costs minus the $3 your lunch from home would cost). $5 each day does not seem to be that much. However, if you project what that adds up to in a year—250 days a year × $5 per day equals $1,250, the cost, perhaps, of a decent vacation. If the opportunity cost is described as "a nice vacation" instead of "$5 a day," you might make different choices.

Marginal Decision-Making and Diminishing Marginal Utility

The budget constraint framework helps to emphasize that most choices in the real world are not about getting all of one thing or all of another; that is, they are not about choosing either the point at one end of the budget constraint or else the point all the way at the other end. Instead, most choices involve **marginal analysis**, which means comparing the benefits and costs of choosing a little more or a little less of a good.

People desire goods and services for the satisfaction or **utility** those goods and services provide. Utility, as we will see in the chapter on Consumer Choices (http://cnx.org/content/m57229/latest/) , is subjective but that does not make it less real. Economists typically assume that the more of some good one consumes (for example, slices of pizza), the more utility one obtains. At the same time, the utility a person receives from consuming the first unit of a good is typically more than the utility received from consuming the fifth or the tenth unit of that same good. When Alphonso chooses between burgers and bus tickets, for example, the first few bus rides that he chooses might provide him with a great deal of utility—perhaps they help him get to a job interview or a doctor's appointment. But later bus rides might provide much less utility—they may only serve to kill time on a rainy day. Similarly, the first burger that Alphonso chooses to buy may be on a day when he missed breakfast and is ravenously hungry. However, if Alphonso has a burger every single day, the last few burgers may taste pretty boring. The general pattern that consumption of the first few units of any good tends to bring a higher level of utility to a person than consumption of later units is a common pattern. Economists refer to this pattern as the **law of diminishing marginal utility**, which means that as a person receives more of a good, the additional (or marginal) utility from each additional unit of the good declines. In other words, the first slice of pizza brings more satisfaction than the sixth.

The law of diminishing marginal utility explains why people and societies rarely make all-or-nothing choices. You would not say, "My favorite food is ice cream, so I will eat nothing but ice cream from now on." Instead, even if you get a very high level of utility from your favorite food, if you ate it exclusively, the additional or marginal utility from those last few servings would not be very high. Similarly, most workers do not say: "I enjoy leisure, so I'll never work." Instead, workers recognize that even though some leisure is very nice, a combination of all leisure and no income is not so attractive. The budget constraint framework suggests that when people make choices in a world of scarcity, they will use marginal analysis and think about whether they would prefer a little more or a little less.

Sunk Costs

In the budget constraint framework, all decisions involve what will happen next: that is, what quantities of goods will you consume, how many hours will you work, or how much will you save. These decisions do not look back to past choices. Thus, the budget constraint framework assumes that **sunk costs**, which are costs that were incurred in the past and cannot be recovered, should not affect the current decision.

Consider the case of Selena, who pays $8 to see a movie, but after watching the film for 30 minutes, she knows that it is truly terrible. Should she stay and watch the rest of the movie because she paid for the ticket, or should she leave? The money she spent is a sunk cost, and unless the theater manager is feeling kindly, Selena will not get a refund. But staying in the movie still means paying an opportunity cost in time. Her choice is whether to spend the next 90 minutes suffering through a cinematic disaster or to do something—anything—else. The lesson of sunk costs is to forget about the money and time that is irretrievably gone and instead to focus on the marginal costs and benefits of current and future options.

For people and firms alike, dealing with sunk costs can be frustrating. It often means admitting an earlier error in judgment. Many firms, for example, find it hard to give up on a new product that is doing poorly because they spent so much money in creating and launching the product. But the lesson of sunk costs is to ignore them and make decisions based on what will happen in the future.

From a Model with Two Goods to One of Many Goods

The budget constraint diagram containing just two goods, like most models used in this book, is not realistic. After all, in a modern economy people choose from thousands of goods. However, thinking about a model with many goods is a straightforward extension of what we discussed here. Instead of drawing just one budget constraint, showing the tradeoff between two goods, you can draw multiple budget constraints, showing the possible tradeoffs between many different pairs of goods. Or in more advanced classes in economics, you would use mathematical equations that include many possible goods and services that can be purchased, together with their quantities and prices, and show how the total spending on all goods and services is limited to the overall budget available. The graph with two goods that was presented here clearly illustrates that every choice has an opportunity cost, which is the point that does carry over to the real world.

2.2 | The Production Possibilities Frontier and Social Choices

By the end of this section, you will be able to:
- Interpret production possibilities frontier graphs
- Contrast a budget constraint and a production possibilities frontier
- Explain the relationship between a production possibilities frontier and the law of diminishing returns
- Contrast productive efficiency and allocative efficiency
- Define comparative advantage

Just as individuals cannot have everything they want and must instead make choices, society as a whole cannot have everything it might want, either. This section of the chapter will explain the constraints faced by society, using a model called the **production possibilities frontier (PPF)**. There are more similarities than differences between individual choice and social choice. As you read this section, focus on the similarities.

Because society has limited resources (e.g., labor, land, capital, raw materials) at any point in time, there is a limit to the quantities of goods and services it can produce. Suppose a society desires two products, healthcare and education. This situation is illustrated by the production possibilities frontier in **Figure 2.3**.

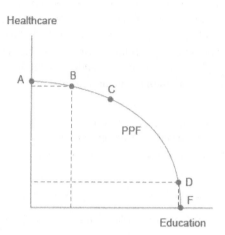

Figure 2.3 A Healthcare vs. Education Production Possibilities Frontier   This production possibilities frontier shows a tradeoff between devoting social resources to healthcare and devoting them to education. At A all resources go to healthcare and at B, most go to healthcare. At D most resources go to education, and at F, all go to education.

In **Figure 2.3**, healthcare is shown on the vertical axis and education is shown on the horizontal axis. If the society were to allocate all of its resources to healthcare, it could produce at point A. But it would not have any resources to produce education. If it were to allocate all of its resources to education, it could produce at point F. Alternatively, the society could choose to produce any combination of healthcare and education shown on the production possibilities frontier. In effect, the production possibilities frontier plays the same role for society as the budget constraint plays for Alphonso. Society can choose any combination of the two goods on or inside the PPF. But it does not have enough resources to produce outside the PPF.

Most important, the production possibilities frontier clearly shows the tradeoff between healthcare and education. Suppose society has chosen to operate at point B, and it is considering producing more education. Because the PPF is downward sloping from left to right, the only way society can obtain more education is by giving up some healthcare. That is the tradeoff society faces. Suppose it considers moving from point B to point C. What would the opportunity cost be for the additional education? The opportunity cost would be the healthcare society has to give up. Just as with Alphonso's budget constraint, the opportunity cost is shown by the slope of the production possibilities frontier. By now you might be saying, "Hey, this PPF is sounding like the budget constraint." If so, read the following Clear It Up feature.

Clear It Up $

What's the difference between a budget constraint and a PPF?

There are two major differences between a budget constraint and a production possibilities frontier. The first is the fact that the budget constraint is a straight line. This is because its slope is given by the relative prices of the two goods. In contrast, the PPF has a curved shape because of the law of the diminishing returns. The second is the absence of specific numbers on the axes of the PPF. There are no specific numbers because we do not know the exact amount of resources this imaginary economy has, nor do we know how many resources it takes to produce healthcare and how many resources it takes to produce education. If this were a real world example, that data would be available. An additional reason for the lack of numbers is that there is no single way to measure levels of education and healthcare. However, when you think of improvements in education, you can think of accomplishments like more years of school completed, fewer high-school dropouts, and higher scores on standardized tests. When you think of improvements in healthcare, you can think of longer life expectancies, lower levels of infant mortality, and fewer outbreaks of disease.

Whether or not we have specific numbers, conceptually we can measure the opportunity cost of additional education as society moves from point B to point C on the PPF. The additional education is measured by the horizontal distance between B and C. The foregone healthcare is given by the vertical distance between B and C. The slope of the PPF between B and C is (approximately) the vertical distance (the "rise") over the horizontal distance (the "run"). This is the opportunity cost of the additional education.

The Shape of the PPF and the Law of Diminishing Returns

The budget constraints presented earlier in this chapter, showing individual choices about what quantities of goods to consume, were all straight lines. The reason for these straight lines was that the slope of the budget constraint was determined by relative prices of the two goods in the consumption budget constraint. However, the production possibilities frontier for healthcare and education was drawn as a curved line. Why does the PPF have a different shape?

To understand why the PPF is curved, start by considering point A at the top left-hand side of the PPF. At point A, all available resources are devoted to healthcare and none are left for education. This situation would be extreme and even ridiculous. For example, children are seeing a doctor every day, whether they are sick or not, but not attending school. People are having cosmetic surgery on every part of their bodies, but no high school or college education exists. Now imagine that some of these resources are diverted from healthcare to education, so that the economy is at point B instead of point A. Diverting some resources away from A to B causes relatively little reduction in health because the last few marginal dollars going into healthcare services are not producing much additional gain in health. However, putting those marginal dollars into education, which is completely without resources at point A, can produce relatively large gains. For this reason, the shape of the PPF from A to B is relatively flat, representing a relatively small drop-off in health and a relatively large gain in education.

Now consider the other end, at the lower right, of the production possibilities frontier. Imagine that society starts at choice D, which is devoting nearly all resources to education and very few to healthcare, and moves to point F, which is devoting *all* spending to education and none to healthcare. For the sake of concreteness, you can imagine that in the movement from D to F, the last few doctors must become high school science teachers, the last few nurses must become school librarians rather than dispensers of vaccinations, and the last few emergency rooms are turned into kindergartens. The gains to education from adding these last few resources to education are very small. However, the opportunity cost lost to health will be fairly large, and thus the slope of the PPF between D and F is steep, showing a large drop in health for only a small gain in education.

The lesson is not that society is likely to make an extreme choice like devoting no resources to education at point A or no resources to health at point F. Instead, the lesson is that the gains from committing additional marginal resources to education depend on how much is already being spent. If on the one hand, very few resources are currently committed to education, then an increase in resources used can bring relatively large gains. On the other hand, if a large number of resources are already committed to education, then committing additional resources will bring relatively smaller gains.

This pattern is common enough that it has been given a name: the **law of diminishing returns**, which holds that as additional increments of resources are added to a certain purpose, the marginal benefit from those additional increments will decline. When government spends a certain amount more on reducing crime, for example, the original gains in reducing crime could be relatively large. But additional increases typically cause relatively smaller reductions in crime, and paying for enough police and security to reduce crime to nothing at all would be tremendously expensive.

The curvature of the production possibilities frontier shows that as additional resources are added to education, moving from left to right along the horizontal axis, the original gains are fairly large, but gradually diminish. Similarly, as additional resources are added to healthcare, moving from bottom to top on the vertical axis, the original gains are fairly large, but again gradually diminish. In this way, the law of diminishing returns produces the outward-bending shape of the production possibilities frontier.

Productive Efficiency and Allocative Efficiency

The study of economics does not presume to tell a society what choice it should make along its production possibilities frontier. In a market-oriented economy with a democratic government, the choice will involve a mixture of decisions by individuals, firms, and government. However, economics can point out that some choices are unambiguously better than others. This observation is based on the concept of efficiency. In everyday usage, efficiency refers to lack of waste. An inefficient machine operates at high cost, while an efficient machine operates at lower cost, because it is not wasting energy or materials. An inefficient organization operates with long delays and high costs, while an efficient organization meets schedules, is focused, and performs within budget.

The production possibilities frontier can illustrate two kinds of efficiency: productive efficiency and allocative efficiency. **Figure 2.4** illustrates these ideas using a production possibilities frontier between healthcare and education.

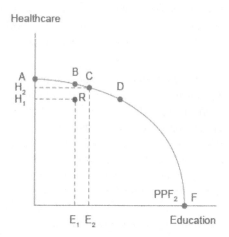

Figure 2.4 Productive and Allocative Efficiency   Productive efficiency means it is impossible to produce more of one good without decreasing the quantity that is produced of another good. Thus, all choices along a given PPF like B, C, and D display productive efficiency, but R does not. Allocative efficiency means that the particular mix of goods being produced—that is, the specific choice along the production possibilities frontier—represents the allocation that society most desires.

Productive efficiency means that, given the available inputs and technology, it is impossible to produce more of one good without decreasing the quantity that is produced of another good. All choices on the PPF in **Figure 2.4**, including A, B, C, D, and F, display productive efficiency. As a firm moves from any one of these choices to any other, either healthcare increases and education decreases or vice versa. However, any choice inside the production possibilities frontier is productively inefficient and wasteful because it is possible to produce more of one good, the other good, or some combination of both goods.

For example, point R is productively inefficient because it is possible at choice C to have more of both goods: education on the horizontal axis is higher at point C than point R (E_2 is greater than E_1), and healthcare on the vertical axis is also higher at point C than point R (H_2 is great than H_1).

The particular mix of goods and services being produced—that is, the specific combination of healthcare and education chosen along the production possibilities frontier—can be shown as a ray (line) from the origin to a specific point on the PPF. Output mixes that had more healthcare (and less education) would have a steeper ray, while those with more education (and less healthcare) would have a flatter ray.

Allocative efficiency means that the particular mix of goods a society produces represents the combination that society most desires. How to determine what a society desires can be a controversial question, and is usually discussed in political science, sociology, and philosophy classes as well as in economics. At its most basic, allocative efficiency means producers supply the quantity of each product that consumers demand. Only one of the productively efficient choices will be the allocatively efficient choice for society as a whole.

Why Society Must Choose

Every economy faces two situations in which it may be able to expand consumption of all goods. In the first case, a society may discover that it has been using its resources inefficiently, in which case by improving efficiency and producing on the production possibilities frontier, it can have more of all goods (or at least more of some and less of none). In the second case, as resources grow over a period of years (e.g., more labor and more capital), the economy grows. As it does, the production possibilities frontier for a society will tend to shift outward and society will be able to afford more of all goods.

But improvements in productive efficiency take time to discover and implement, and economic growth happens only gradually. So, a society must choose between tradeoffs in the present. For government, this process often involves trying to identify where additional spending could do the most good and where reductions in spending would do the least harm. At the individual and firm level, the market economy coordinates a process in which firms seek to produce goods and services in the quantity, quality, and price that people want. But for both the government and the market economy in the short term, increases in production of one good typically mean offsetting decreases somewhere else in the economy.

The PPF and Comparative Advantage

While every society must choose how much of each good it should produce, it does not need to produce every single good it consumes. Often how much of a good a country decides to produce depends on how expensive it is to produce it versus buying it from a different country. As we saw earlier, the curvature of a country's PPF gives us information about the tradeoff between devoting resources to producing one good versus another. In particular, its slope gives the opportunity cost of producing one more unit of the good in the x-axis in terms of the other good (in the y-axis). Countries tend to have different opportunity costs of producing a specific good, either because of different climates, geography, technology or skills.

Suppose two countries, the US and Brazil, need to decide how much they will produce of two crops: sugar cane and wheat. Due to its climatic conditions, Brazil can produce a lot of sugar cane per acre but not much wheat. Conversely, the U.S. can produce a lot of wheat per acre, but not much sugar cane. Clearly, Brazil has a lower opportunity cost of producing sugar cane (in terms of wheat) than the U.S. The reverse is also true; the U.S. has a lower opportunity cost of producing wheat than Brazil. This can be illustrated by the PPFs of the two countries in **Figure 2.5**

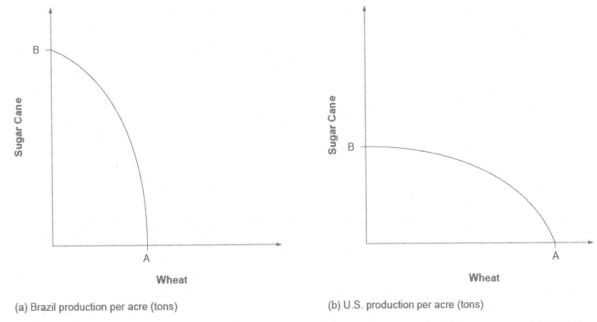

(a) Brazil production per acre (tons)   (b) U.S. production per acre (tons)

Figure 2.5 Production Possibility Frontier for the U.S. and Brazil The U.S. PPF is flatter than the Brazil PPF implying that the opportunity cost of wheat in term of sugar cane is lower in the U.S. than in Brazil. Conversely, the opportunity cost of sugar cane is lower in Brazil. The U.S. has comparative advantage in wheat and Brazil has comparative advantage in sugar cane.

When a country can produce a good at a lower opportunity cost than another country, we say that this country has a **comparative advantage** in that good. In our example, Brazil has a comparative advantage in sugar cane and the U.S. has a comparative advantage in wheat. One can easily see this with a simple observation of the extreme production points in the PPFs of the two countries. If Brazil devoted all of its resources to producing wheat, it would be producing at point A. If however it had devoted all of its resources to producing sugar cane instead, it would be producing a much larger amount, at point B. By moving from point A to point B Brazil would give up a relatively small quantity in wheat production to obtain a large production in sugar cane. The opposite is true for the U.S. If the U.S. moved from point A to B and produced only sugar cane, this would result in a large opportunity cost in terms of foregone wheat production.

The slope of the PPF gives the opportunity cost of producing an additional unit of wheat. While the slope is not constant throughout the PPFs, it is quite apparent that the PPF in Brazil is much steeper than in the U.S., and therefore the opportunity cost of wheat generally higher in Brazil. In the chapter on International Trade (http://cnx.org/content/m57383/latest/) you will learn that countries' differences in comparative advantage determine which goods they will choose to produce and trade. When countries engage in trade, they specialize in the production of the goods that they have comparative advantage in, and trade part of that production for goods they do not have comparative advantage in. With trade, goods are produced where the opportunity cost is lowest, so total production increases, benefiting both trading parties.

2.3 | Confronting Objections to the Economic Approach

By the end of this section, you will be able to:

- Analyze arguments against economic approaches to decision-making
- Interpret a tradeoff diagram
- Contrast normative statements and positive statements

It is one thing to understand the economic approach to decision-making and another thing to feel comfortable applying it. The sources of discomfort typically fall into two categories: that people do not act in the way that fits the economic way of thinking, and that even if people did act that way, they should try not to. Let's consider these arguments in turn.

First Objection: People, Firms, and Society Do Not Act Like This

The economic approach to decision-making seems to require more information than most individuals possess and more careful decision-making than most individuals actually display. After all, do you or any of your friends draw a budget constraint and mutter to yourself about maximizing utility before you head to the shopping mall? Do members of the U.S. Congress contemplate production possibilities frontiers before they vote on the annual budget? The messy ways in which people and societies operate somehow doesn't look much like neat budget constraints or smoothly curving production possibilities frontiers.

However, the economics approach can be a useful way to analyze and understand the tradeoffs of economic decisions even so. To appreciate this point, imagine for a moment that you are playing basketball, dribbling to the right, and throwing a bounce-pass to the left to a teammate who is running toward the basket. A physicist or engineer could work out the correct speed and trajectory for the pass, given the different movements involved and the weight and bounciness of the ball. But when you are playing basketball, you do not perform any of these calculations. You just pass the ball, and if you are a good player, you will do so with high accuracy.

Someone might argue: "The scientist's formula of the bounce-pass requires a far greater knowledge of physics and far more specific information about speeds of movement and weights than the basketball player actually has, so it must be an unrealistic description of how basketball passes are actually made." This reaction would be wrongheaded. The fact that a good player can throw the ball accurately because of practice and skill, without making a physics calculation, does not mean that the physics calculation is wrong.

Similarly, from an economic point of view, someone who goes shopping for groceries every week has a great deal of practice with how to purchase the combination of goods that will provide that person with utility, even if the shopper does not phrase decisions in terms of a budget constraint. Government institutions may work imperfectly and slowly, but in general, a democratic form of government feels pressure from voters and social institutions to make the choices that are most widely preferred by people in that society. So, when thinking about the economic actions of groups of people, firms, and society, it is reasonable, as a first approximation, to analyze them with the tools of economic analysis. For more on this, read about behavioral economics in the chapter on Consumer Choices (http://cnx.org/content/m57229/latest/) .

Second Objection: People, Firms, and Society Should Not Act This Way

The economics approach portrays people as self-interested. For some critics of this approach, even if self-interest is an accurate description of how people behave, these behaviors are not moral. Instead, the critics argue that people should be taught to care more deeply about others. Economists offer several answers to these concerns.

First, economics is not a form of moral instruction. Rather, it seeks to describe economic behavior as it actually exists. Philosophers draw a distinction between **positive statements**, which describe the world as it is, and **normative statements**, which describe how the world should be. For example, an economist could analyze a proposed subway system in a certain city. If the expected benefits exceed the costs, he concludes that the project is worth doing—an example of positive analysis. Another economist argues for extended unemployment compensation during the Great Depression because a rich country like the United States should take care of its less fortunate citizens—an example of normative analysis.

Even if the line between positive and normative statements is not always crystal clear, economic analysis does try to remain rooted in the study of the actual people who inhabit the actual economy. Fortunately however, the assumption that individuals are purely self-interested is a simplification about human nature. In fact, we need to look no further than to Adam Smith, the very father of modern economics to find evidence of this. The opening sentence of his book, *The Theory of Moral Sentiments*, puts it very clearly: "How selfish soever man may be supposed, there are evidently some principles in his nature, which interest him in the fortune of others, and render their happiness necessary to him, though he derives nothing from it except the pleasure of seeing it." Clearly, individuals are both self-interested and altruistic.

Second, self-interested behavior and profit-seeking can be labeled with other names, such as personal choice and freedom. The ability to make personal choices about buying, working, and saving is an important personal freedom. Some people may choose high-pressure, high-paying jobs so that they can earn and spend a lot of money on themselves. Others may earn a lot of money and give it to charity or spend it on their friends and family. Others may devote themselves to a career that can require a great deal of time, energy, and expertise but does not offer high financial rewards, like being an elementary school teacher or a social worker. Still others may choose a job that does not take lots of their time or provide a high level of income, but still leaves time for family, friends, and contemplation. Some people may prefer to work for a large company; others might want to start their own business. People's freedom to make their own economic choices has a moral value worth respecting.

Is a diagram by any other name the same?

When you study economics, you may feel buried under an avalanche of diagrams: diagrams in the text, diagrams in the lectures, diagrams in the problems, and diagrams on exams. Your goal should be to recognize the common underlying logic and pattern of the diagrams, not to memorize each of the individual diagrams.

This chapter uses only one basic diagram, although it is presented with different sets of labels. The consumption budget constraint and the production possibilities frontier for society, as a whole, are the same basic diagram. Figure 2.6 shows an individual budget constraint and a production possibilities frontier for two goods, Good 1 and Good 2. The tradeoff diagram always illustrates three basic themes: scarcity, tradeoffs, and economic efficiency.

The first theme is scarcity. It is not feasible to have unlimited amounts of both goods. But even if the budget constraint or a PPF shifts, scarcity remains—just at a different level. The second theme is tradeoffs. As depicted in the budget constraint or the production possibilities frontier, it is necessary to give up some of one good to gain more of the other good. The details of this tradeoff vary. In a budget constraint, the tradeoff is determined by the relative prices of the goods: that is, the relative price of two goods in the consumption choice budget constraint. These tradeoffs appear as a straight line. However, the tradeoffs in many production possibilities frontiers are represented by a curved line because the law of diminishing returns holds that as resources are added to an area, the marginal gains tend to diminish. Regardless of the specific shape, tradeoffs remain.

The third theme is economic efficiency, or getting the most benefit from scarce resources. All choices on the production possibilities frontier show productive efficiency because in such cases, there is no way to increase the quantity of one good without decreasing the quantity of the other. Similarly, when an individual makes a choice along a budget constraint, there is no way to increase the quantity of one good without decreasing the quantity of the other. The choice on a production possibilities set that is socially preferred, or the choice on an individual's budget constraint that is personally preferred, will display allocative efficiency.

The basic budget constraint/production possibilities frontier diagram will recur throughout this book. Some examples include using these tradeoff diagrams to analyze trade, labor supply versus leisure, saving versus consumption, environmental protection and economic output, equality of incomes and economic output, and the macroeconomic tradeoff between consumption and investment. Do not be confused by the different labels. The budget constraint/production possibilities frontier diagram is always just a tool for thinking carefully about scarcity, tradeoffs, and efficiency in a particular situation.

Figure 2.6 The Tradeoff Diagram Both the individual opportunity set (or budget constraint) and the social production possibilities frontier show the constraints under which individual consumers and society as a whole operate. Both diagrams show the tradeoff in choosing more of one good at the cost of less of the other.

Third, self-interested behavior can lead to positive social results. For example, when people work hard to make a living, they create economic output. Consumers who are looking for the best deals will encourage businesses to offer goods and services that meet their needs. Adam Smith, writing in *The Wealth of Nations*, christened this property the **invisible hand**. In describing how consumers and producers interact in a market economy, Smith wrote:

> Every individual…generally, indeed, neither intends to promote the public interest, nor knows how much he is promoting it. By preferring the support of domestic to that of foreign industry, he intends only his own security; and by directing that industry in such a manner as its produce may be of the greatest value, he intends only his own gain. And he is in this, as in many other cases, led by an invisible hand to promote an end which was no part of his intention…By pursuing his own interest he frequently promotes that of the society more effectually than when he really intends to promote it.

The metaphor of the invisible hand suggests the remarkable possibility that broader social good can emerge from selfish individual actions.

Fourth, even people who focus on their own self-interest in the economic part of their life often set aside their own narrow self-interest in other parts of life. For example, you might focus on your own self-interest when asking your employer for a raise or negotiating to buy a car. But then you might turn around and focus on other people when you volunteer to read stories at the local library, help a friend move to a new apartment, or donate money to a charity. Self-interest is a reasonable starting point for analyzing many economic decisions, without needing to imply that people never do anything that is not in their own immediate self-interest.

Bring it Home

Choices ... To What Degree?

What have we learned? We know that scarcity impacts all the choices we make. So, an economist might argue that people do not go on to get bachelor's degrees or master's degrees because they do not have the resources to make those choices or because their incomes are too low and/or the price of these degrees is too high. A bachelor's degree or a master's degree may not be available in their opportunity set.

The price of these degrees may be too high not only because the actual price, college tuition (and perhaps room and board), is too high. An economist might also say that for many people, the full opportunity cost of a bachelor's degree or a master's degree is too high. For these people, they are unwilling or unable to make the tradeoff of giving up years of working, and earning an income, to earn a degree.

Finally, the statistics introduced at the start of the chapter reveal information about intertemporal choices. An economist might say that people choose not to get a college degree because they may have to borrow money to go to college, and the interest they have to pay on that loan in the future will affect their decisions today. Also, it could be that some people have a preference for current consumption over future consumption, so they choose to work now at a lower salary and consume now, rather than putting that consumption off until after they graduate college.

KEY TERMS

allocative efficiency when the mix of goods being produced represents the mix that society most desires

budget constraint all possible consumption combinations of goods that someone can afford, given the prices of goods, when all income is spent; the boundary of the opportunity set

comparative advantage when a country can produce a good at a lower cost in terms of other goods; or, when a country has a lower opportunity cost of production

invisible hand idea that self-interested behavior by individuals can lead to positive social outcomes

law of diminishing marginal utility as we consume more of a good or service, the utility we get from additional units of the good or service tend to become smaller than what we received from earlier units

law of diminishing returns as additional increments of resources are added to producing a good or service, the marginal benefit from those additional increments will decline

marginal analysis examination of decisions on the margin, meaning a little more or a little less from the status quo

normative statement statement which describes how the world should be

opportunity cost measures cost by what is given up in exchange; opportunity cost measures the value of the forgone alternative

opportunity set all possible combinations of consumption that someone can afford given the prices of goods and the individual's income

positive statement statement which describes the world as it is

production possibilities frontier (PPF) a diagram that shows the productively efficient combinations of two products that an economy can produce given the resources it has available.

productive efficiency when it is impossible to produce more of one good (or service) without decreasing the quantity produced of another good (or service)

sunk costs costs that are made in the past and cannot be recovered

utility satisfaction, usefulness, or value one obtains from consuming goods and services

KEY CONCEPTS AND SUMMARY

2.1 How Individuals Make Choices Based on Their Budget Constraint

Economists see the real world as one of scarcity: that is, a world in which people's desires exceed what is possible. As a result, economic behavior involves tradeoffs in which individuals, firms, and society must give up something that they desire to obtain things that they desire more. Individuals face the tradeoff of what quantities of goods and services to consume. The budget constraint, which is the frontier of the opportunity set, illustrates the range of choices available. The slope of the budget constraint is determined by the relative price of the choices. Choices beyond the budget constraint are not affordable.

Opportunity cost measures cost by what is given up in exchange. Sometimes opportunity cost can be measured in money, but it is often useful to consider time as well, or to measure it in terms of the actual resources that must be given up.

Most economic decisions and tradeoffs are not all-or-nothing. Instead, they involve marginal analysis, which means they are about decisions on the margin, involving a little more or a little less. The law of diminishing marginal utility points out that as a person receives more of something—whether it is a specific good or another resource—the additional marginal gains tend to become smaller. Because sunk costs occurred in the past and cannot be recovered, they should be disregarded in making current decisions.

2.2 The Production Possibilities Frontier and Social Choices

A production possibilities frontier defines the set of choices society faces for the combinations of goods and services it can produce given the resources available. The shape of the PPF is typically curved outward, rather than straight. Choices outside the PPF are unattainable and choices inside the PPF are wasteful. Over time, a growing economy will tend to shift the PPF outwards.

The law of diminishing returns holds that as increments of additional resources are devoted to producing something, the marginal increase in output will become smaller and smaller. All choices along a production possibilities frontier display productive efficiency; that is, it is impossible to use society's resources to produce more of one good without decreasing production of the other good. The specific choice along a production possibilities frontier that reflects the mix of goods society prefers is the choice with allocative efficiency. The curvature of the PPF is likely to differ by country, which results in different countries having comparative advantage in different goods. Total production can increase if countries specialize in the goods they have comparative advantage in and trade some of their production for the remaining goods.

2.3 Confronting Objections to the Economic Approach

The economic way of thinking provides a useful approach to understanding human behavior. Economists make the careful distinction between positive statements, which describe the world as it is, and normative statements, which describe how the world should be. Even when economics analyzes the gains and losses from various events or policies, and thus draws normative conclusions about how the world should be, the analysis of economics is rooted in a positive analysis of how people, firms, and governments actually behave, not how they should behave.

SELF-CHECK QUESTIONS

1. Suppose Alphonso's town raised the price of bus tickets to $1 per trip (while the price of burgers stayed at $2 and his budget remained $10 per week.) Draw Alphonso's new budget constraint. What happens to the opportunity cost of bus tickets?

2. Return to the example in **Figure 2.4**. Suppose there is an improvement in medical technology that enables more healthcare to be provided with the same amount of resources. How would this affect the production possibilities curve and, in particular, how would it affect the opportunity cost of education?

3. Could a nation be producing in a way that is allocatively efficient, but productively inefficient?

4. What are the similarities between a consumer's budget constraint and society's production possibilities frontier, not just graphically but analytically?

5. Individuals may not act in the rational, calculating way described by the economic model of decision making, measuring utility and costs at the margin, but can you make a case that they behave approximately that way?

6. Would an op-ed piece in a newspaper urging the adoption of a particular economic policy be considered a positive or normative statement?

7. Would a research study on the effects of soft drink consumption on children's cognitive development be considered a positive or normative statement?

REVIEW QUESTIONS

8. Explain why scarcity leads to tradeoffs.

9. Explain why individuals make choices that are directly on the budget constraint, rather than inside the budget constraint or outside it.

10. What is comparative advantage?

11. What does a production possibilities frontier illustrate?

12. Why is a production possibilities frontier typically drawn as a curve, rather than a straight line?

13. Explain why societies cannot make a choice above their production possibilities frontier and should not make a choice below it.

14. What are diminishing marginal returns?

15. What is productive efficiency? Allocative efficiency?

16. What is the difference between a positive and a normative statement?

17. Is the economic model of decision-making intended as a literal description of how individuals, firms, and the governments actually make decisions?

18. What are four responses to the claim that people should not behave in the way described in this chapter?

CRITICAL THINKING QUESTIONS

19. Suppose Alphonso's town raises the price of bus tickets from $0.50 to $1 and the price of burgers rises from $2 to $4. Why is the opportunity cost of bus tickets unchanged? Suppose Alphonso's weekly spending money increases from $10 to $20. How is his budget constraint affected from all three changes? Explain.

20. During the Second World War, Germany's factories were decimated. It also suffered many human casualties, both soldiers and civilians. How did the war affect Germany's production possibilities curve?

21. It is clear that productive inefficiency is a waste since resources are being used in a way that produces

less goods and services than a nation is capable of. Why is allocative inefficiency also wasteful?

22. What assumptions about the economy must be true for the invisible hand to work? To what extent are those assumptions valid in the real world?

23. Do economists have any particular expertise at making normative arguments? In other words, they have expertise at making positive statements (i.e., what *will* happen) about some economic policy, for example, but do they have special expertise to judge whether or not the policy *should* be undertaken?

PROBLEMS

Use this information to answer the following 4 questions: Marie has a weekly budget of $24, which she likes to spend on magazines and pies.

24. If the price of a magazine is $4 each, what is the maximum number of magazines she could buy in a week?

25. If the price of a pie is $12, what is the maximum number of pies she could buy in a week?

26. Draw Marie's budget constraint with pies on the horizontal axis and magazines on the vertical axis. What is the slope of the budget constraint?

27. What is Marie's opportunity cost of purchasing a pie?

3 | Demand and Supply

Figure 3.1 Farmer's Market Organic vegetables and fruits that are grown and sold within a specific geographical region should, in theory, cost less than conventional produce because the transportation costs are less. That is not, however, usually the case. (Credit: modification of work by Natalie Maynor/Flickr Creative Commons)

Bring it Home

Why Can We Not Get Enough of Organic?

Organic food is increasingly popular, not just in the United States, but worldwide. At one time, consumers had to go to specialty stores or farmer's markets to find organic produce. Now it is available in most grocery stores. In short, organic is part of the mainstream.

Ever wonder why organic food costs more than conventional food? Why, say, does an organic Fuji apple cost $1.99 a pound, while its conventional counterpart costs $1.49 a pound? The same price relationship is true for just about every organic product on the market. If many organic foods are locally grown, would they not take less time to get to market and therefore be cheaper? What are the forces that keep those prices from coming down? Turns out those forces have a lot to do with this chapter's topic: demand and supply.

Introduction to Demand and Supply

In this chapter, you will learn about:

- Demand, Supply, and Equilibrium in Markets for Goods and Services
- Shifts in Demand and Supply for Goods and Services
- Changes in Equilibrium Price and Quantity: The Four-Step Process

- Price Ceilings and Price Floors

An auction bidder pays thousands of dollars for a dress Whitney Houston wore. A collector spends a small fortune for a few drawings by John Lennon. People usually react to purchases like these in two ways: their jaw drops because they think these are high prices to pay for such goods or they think these are rare, desirable items and the amount paid seems right.

Link It Up

Visit this website (http://openstaxcollege.org/l/celebauction) to read a list of bizarre items that have been purchased for their ties to celebrities. These examples represent an interesting facet of demand and supply.

When economists talk about prices, they are less interested in making judgments than in gaining a practical understanding of what determines prices and why prices change. Consider a price most of us contend with weekly: that of a gallon of gas. Why was the average price of gasoline in the United States $3.71 per gallon in June 2014? Why did the price for gasoline fall sharply to $2.07 per gallon by January 2015? To explain these price movements, economists focus on the determinants of what gasoline buyers are willing to pay and what gasoline sellers are willing to accept.

As it turns out, the price of gasoline in June of any given year is nearly always higher than the price in January of that same year; over recent decades, gasoline prices in midsummer have averaged about 10 cents per gallon more than their midwinter low. The likely reason is that people drive more in the summer, and are also willing to pay more for gas, but that does not explain how steeply gas prices fell. Other factors were at work during those six months, such as increases in supply and decreases in the demand for crude oil.

This chapter introduces the economic model of demand and supply—one of the most powerful models in all of economics. The discussion here begins by examining how demand and supply determine the price and the quantity sold in markets for goods and services, and how changes in demand and supply lead to changes in prices and quantities.

3.1 | Demand, Supply, and Equilibrium in Markets for Goods and Services

By the end of this section, you will be able to:
- Explain demand, quantity demanded, and the law of demand
- Identify a demand curve and a supply curve
- Explain supply, quantity supply, and the law of supply
- Explain equilibrium, equilibrium price, and equilibrium quantity

First let's first focus on what economists mean by demand, what they mean by supply, and then how demand and supply interact in a market.

Demand for Goods and Services

Economists use the term **demand** to refer to the amount of some good or service consumers are willing and able to purchase at each price. Demand is based on needs and wants—a consumer may be able to differentiate between a need and a want, but from an economist's perspective they are the same thing. Demand is also based on ability to pay. If you cannot pay for it, you have no effective demand.

What a buyer pays for a unit of the specific good or service is called **price**. The total number of units purchased at that price is called the **quantity demanded**. A rise in price of a good or service almost always decreases the quantity demanded of that good or service. Conversely, a fall in price will increase the quantity demanded. When the price of a gallon of gasoline goes up, for example, people look for ways to reduce their consumption by combining several errands, commuting by carpool or mass transit, or taking weekend or vacation trips closer to home. Economists call this inverse relationship between price and quantity demanded the **law of demand**. The law of demand assumes that all other variables that affect demand (to be explained in the next module) are held constant.

An example from the market for gasoline can be shown in the form of a table or a graph. A table that shows the quantity demanded at each price, such as **Table 3.1**, is called a **demand schedule**. Price in this case is measured in dollars per gallon of gasoline. The quantity demanded is measured in millions of gallons over some time period (for example, per day or per year) and over some geographic area (like a state or a country). A **demand curve** shows the relationship between price and quantity demanded on a graph like **Figure 3.2**, with quantity on the horizontal axis and the price per gallon on the vertical axis. (Note that this is an exception to the normal rule in mathematics that the independent variable (x) goes on the horizontal axis and the dependent variable (y) goes on the vertical. Economics is not math.)

The demand schedule shown by **Table 3.1** and the demand curve shown by the graph in **Figure 3.2** are two ways of describing the same relationship between price and quantity demanded.

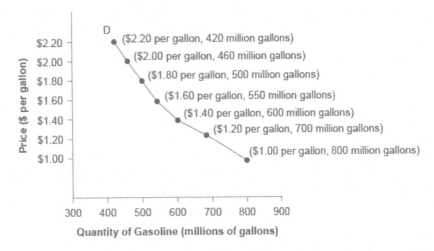

Figure 3.2 A Demand Curve for Gasoline The demand schedule shows that as price rises, quantity demanded decreases, and vice versa. These points are then graphed, and the line connecting them is the demand curve (D). The downward slope of the demand curve again illustrates the law of demand—the inverse relationship between prices and quantity demanded.

Price (per gallon)	Quantity Demanded (millions of gallons)
$1.00	800
$1.20	700
$1.40	600

Table 3.1 Price and Quantity Demanded of Gasoline

Price (per gallon)	Quantity Demanded (millions of gallons)
$1.60	550
$1.80	500
$2.00	460
$2.20	420

Table 3.1 Price and Quantity Demanded of Gasoline

Demand curves will appear somewhat different for each product. They may appear relatively steep or flat, or they may be straight or curved. Nearly all demand curves share the fundamental similarity that they slope down from left to right. So demand curves embody the law of demand: As the price increases, the quantity demanded decreases, and conversely, as the price decreases, the quantity demanded increases.

Confused about these different types of demand? Read the next Clear It Up feature.

Is demand the same as quantity demanded?

In economic terminology, demand is not the same as quantity demanded. When economists talk about demand, they mean the relationship between a range of prices and the quantities demanded at those prices, as illustrated by a demand curve or a demand schedule. When economists talk about quantity demanded, they mean only a certain point on the demand curve, or one quantity on the demand schedule. In short, demand refers to the curve and quantity demanded refers to the (specific) point on the curve.

Supply of Goods and Services

When economists talk about **supply**, they mean the amount of some good or service a producer is willing to supply at each price. Price is what the producer receives for selling one unit of a good or service. A rise in price almost always leads to an increase in the **quantity supplied** of that good or service, while a fall in price will decrease the quantity supplied. When the price of gasoline rises, for example, it encourages profit-seeking firms to take several actions: expand exploration for oil reserves; drill for more oil; invest in more pipelines and oil tankers to bring the oil to plants where it can be refined into gasoline; build new oil refineries; purchase additional pipelines and trucks to ship the gasoline to gas stations; and open more gas stations or keep existing gas stations open longer hours. Economists call this positive relationship between price and quantity supplied—that a higher price leads to a higher quantity supplied and a lower price leads to a lower quantity supplied—the **law of supply**. The law of supply assumes that all other variables that affect supply (to be explained in the next module) are held constant.

Still unsure about the different types of supply? See the following Clear It Up feature.

Is supply the same as quantity supplied?

In economic terminology, supply is not the same as quantity supplied. When economists refer to supply, they mean the relationship between a range of prices and the quantities supplied at those prices, a relationship that can be illustrated with a supply curve or a supply schedule. When economists refer to quantity supplied, they mean only a certain point on the supply curve, or one quantity on the supply schedule. In short, supply refers to the curve and quantity supplied refers to the (specific) point on the curve.

Figure 3.3 illustrates the law of supply, again using the market for gasoline as an example. Like demand, supply can be illustrated using a table or a graph. A **supply schedule** is a table, like Table 3.2, that shows the quantity supplied at a range of different prices. Again, price is measured in dollars per gallon of gasoline and quantity demanded is measured in millions of gallons. A **supply curve** is a graphic illustration of the relationship between price, shown on the vertical axis, and quantity, shown on the horizontal axis. The supply schedule and the supply curve are just two different ways of showing the same information. Notice that the horizontal and vertical axes on the graph for the supply curve are the same as for the demand curve.

Figure 3.3 A Supply Curve for Gasoline   The supply schedule is the table that shows quantity supplied of gasoline at each price. As price rises, quantity supplied also increases, and vice versa. The supply curve (S) is created by graphing the points from the supply schedule and then connecting them. The upward slope of the supply curve illustrates the law of supply—that a higher price leads to a higher quantity supplied, and vice versa.

Price (per gallon)	Quantity Supplied (millions of gallons)
$1.00	500
$1.20	550
$1.40	600
$1.60	640
$1.80	680
$2.00	700
$2.20	720

Table 3.2 Price and Supply of Gasoline

The shape of supply curves will vary somewhat according to the product: steeper, flatter, straighter, or curved. Nearly all supply curves, however, share a basic similarity: they slope up from left to right and illustrate the law of supply: as the price rises, say, from $1.00 per gallon to $2.20 per gallon, the quantity supplied increases from 500 gallons to 720 gallons. Conversely, as the price falls, the quantity supplied decreases.

Equilibrium—Where Demand and Supply Intersect

Because the graphs for demand and supply curves both have price on the vertical axis and quantity on the horizontal axis, the demand curve and supply curve for a particular good or service can appear on the same graph. Together, demand and supply determine the price and the quantity that will be bought and sold in a market.

Figure 3.4 illustrates the interaction of demand and supply in the market for gasoline. The demand curve (D) is identical to **Figure 3.2**. The supply curve (S) is identical to **Figure 3.3**. **Table 3.3** contains the same information in tabular form.

Figure 3.4 Demand and Supply for Gasoline   The demand curve (D) and the supply curve (S) intersect at the equilibrium point E, with a price of $1.40 and a quantity of 600. The equilibrium is the only price where quantity demanded is equal to quantity supplied. At a price above equilibrium like $1.80, quantity supplied exceeds the quantity demanded, so there is excess supply. At a price below equilibrium such as $1.20, quantity demanded exceeds quantity supplied, so there is excess demand.

Price (per gallon)	Quantity demanded (millions of gallons)	Quantity supplied (millions of gallons)
$1.00	800	500
$1.20	700	550
$1.40	**600**	**600**
$1.60	550	640
$1.80	500	680
$2.00	460	700
$2.20	420	720

Table 3.3 Price, Quantity Demanded, and Quantity Supplied

Remember this: When two lines on a diagram cross, this intersection usually means something. The point where the supply curve (S) and the demand curve (D) cross, designated by point E in **Figure 3.4**, is called the **equilibrium**. The **equilibrium price** is the only price where the plans of consumers and the plans of producers agree—that is, where the amount of the product consumers want to buy (quantity demanded) is equal to the amount producers want to sell (quantity supplied). This common quantity is called the **equilibrium quantity**. At any other price, the quantity demanded does not equal the quantity supplied, so the market is not in equilibrium at that price.

In **Figure 3.4**, the equilibrium price is $1.40 per gallon of gasoline and the equilibrium quantity is 600 million gallons. If you had only the demand and supply schedules, and not the graph, you could find the equilibrium by looking for the price level on the tables where the quantity demanded and the quantity supplied are equal.

The word "equilibrium" means "balance." If a market is at its equilibrium price and quantity, then it has no reason to move away from that point. However, if a market is not at equilibrium, then economic pressures arise to move the market toward the equilibrium price and the equilibrium quantity.

Imagine, for example, that the price of a gallon of gasoline was above the equilibrium price—that is, instead of $1.40 per gallon, the price is $1.80 per gallon. This above-equilibrium price is illustrated by the dashed horizontal line at the price of $1.80 in Figure 3.4. At this higher price, the quantity demanded drops from 600 to 500. This decline in quantity reflects how consumers react to the higher price by finding ways to use less gasoline.

Moreover, at this higher price of $1.80, the quantity of gasoline supplied rises from the 600 to 680, as the higher price makes it more profitable for gasoline producers to expand their output. Now, consider how quantity demanded and quantity supplied are related at this above-equilibrium price. Quantity demanded has fallen to 500 gallons, while quantity supplied has risen to 680 gallons. In fact, at any above-equilibrium price, the quantity supplied exceeds the quantity demanded. We call this an **excess supply** or a **surplus**.

With a surplus, gasoline accumulates at gas stations, in tanker trucks, in pipelines, and at oil refineries. This accumulation puts pressure on gasoline sellers. If a surplus remains unsold, those firms involved in making and selling gasoline are not receiving enough cash to pay their workers and to cover their expenses. In this situation, some producers and sellers will want to cut prices, because it is better to sell at a lower price than not to sell at all. Once some sellers start cutting prices, others will follow to avoid losing sales. These price reductions in turn will stimulate a higher quantity demanded. So, if the price is above the equilibrium level, incentives built into the structure of demand and supply will create pressures for the price to fall toward the equilibrium.

Now suppose that the price is below its equilibrium level at $1.20 per gallon, as the dashed horizontal line at this price in Figure 3.4 shows. At this lower price, the quantity demanded increases from 600 to 700 as drivers take longer trips, spend more minutes warming up the car in the driveway in wintertime, stop sharing rides to work, and buy larger cars that get fewer miles to the gallon. However, the below-equilibrium price reduces gasoline producers' incentives to produce and sell gasoline, and the quantity supplied falls from 600 to 550.

When the price is below equilibrium, there is **excess demand**, or a **shortage**—that is, at the given price the quantity demanded, which has been stimulated by the lower price, now exceeds the quantity supplied, which had been depressed by the lower price. In this situation, eager gasoline buyers mob the gas stations, only to find many stations running short of fuel. Oil companies and gas stations recognize that they have an opportunity to make higher profits by selling what gasoline they have at a higher price. As a result, the price rises toward the equilibrium level. Read Demand, Supply, and Efficiency for more discussion on the importance of the demand and supply model.

3.2 | Shifts in Demand and Supply for Goods and Services

By the end of this section, you will be able to:
- Identify factors that affect demand
- Graph demand curves and demand shifts
- Identify factors that affect supply
- Graph supply curves and supply shifts

The previous module explored how price affects the quantity demanded and the quantity supplied. The result was the demand curve and the supply curve. Price, however, is not the only thing that influences demand. Nor is it the only thing that influences supply. For example, how is demand for vegetarian food affected if, say, health concerns cause more consumers to avoid eating meat? Or how is the supply of diamonds affected if diamond producers discover several new diamond mines? What are the major factors, in addition to the price, that influence demand or supply?

Link It Up ⚯

Visit this website (http://openstaxcollege.org/l/toothfish) to read a brief note on how marketing strategies can influence supply and demand of products.

What Factors Affect Demand?

We defined demand as the amount of some product a consumer is willing and able to purchase at each price. That suggests at least two factors in addition to price that affect demand. Willingness to purchase suggests a desire, based on what economists call tastes and preferences. If you neither need nor want something, you will not buy it. Ability to purchase suggests that income is important. Professors are usually able to afford better housing and transportation than students, because they have more income. Prices of related goods can affect demand also. If you need a new car, the price of a Honda may affect your demand for a Ford. Finally, the size or composition of the population can affect demand. The more children a family has, the greater their demand for clothing. The more driving-age children a family has, the greater their demand for car insurance, and the less for diapers and baby formula.

These factors matter both for demand by an individual and demand by the market as a whole. Exactly how do these various factors affect demand, and how do we show the effects graphically? To answer those questions, we need the *ceteris paribus* assumption.

The *Ceteris Paribus* Assumption

A demand curve or a supply curve is a relationship between two, and only two, variables: quantity on the horizontal axis and price on the vertical axis. The assumption behind a demand curve or a supply curve is that no relevant economic factors, other than the product's price, are changing. Economists call this assumption **ceteris paribus**, a Latin phrase meaning "other things being equal." Any given demand or supply curve is based on the *ceteris paribus* assumption that all else is held equal. A demand curve or a supply curve is a relationship between two, and only two, variables when all other variables are kept constant. If all else is not held equal, then the laws of supply and demand will not necessarily hold, as the following Clear It Up feature shows.

Clear It Up

When does *ceteris paribus* apply?

Ceteris paribus is typically applied when we look at how changes in price affect demand or supply, but *ceteris paribus* can be applied more generally. In the real world, demand and supply depend on more factors than just price. For example, a consumer's demand depends on income and a producer's supply depends on the cost of producing the product. How can we analyze the effect on demand or supply if multiple factors are changing at the same time—say price rises and income falls? The answer is that we examine the changes one at a time, assuming the other factors are held constant.

For example, we can say that an increase in the price reduces the amount consumers will buy (assuming income, and anything else that affects demand, is unchanged). Additionally, a decrease in income reduces the amount consumers can afford to buy (assuming price, and anything else that affects demand, is unchanged). This is what the *ceteris paribus* assumption really means. In this particular case, after we analyze each factor separately, we can combine the results. The amount consumers buy falls for two reasons: first because of the higher price and second because of the lower income.

How Does Income Affect Demand?

Let's use income as an example of how factors other than price affect demand. Figure 3.5 shows the initial demand for automobiles as D_0. At point Q, for example, if the price is $20,000 per car, the quantity of cars demanded is 18 million. D_0 also shows how the quantity of cars demanded would change as a result of a higher or lower price. For example, if the price of a car rose to $22,000, the quantity demanded would decrease to 17 million, at point R.

The original demand curve D_0, like every demand curve, is based on the *ceteris paribus* assumption that no other economically relevant factors change. Now imagine that the economy expands in a way that raises the incomes of many people, making cars more affordable. How will this affect demand? How can we show this graphically?

Return to Figure 3.5. The price of cars is still $20,000, but with higher incomes, the quantity demanded has now increased to 20 million cars, shown at point S. As a result of the higher income levels, the demand curve shifts to the right to the new demand curve D_1, indicating an increase in demand. Table 3.4 shows clearly that this increased demand would occur at every price, not just the original one.

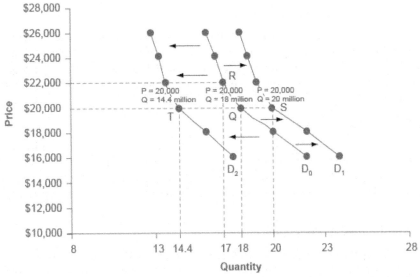

Figure 3.5 Shifts in Demand: A Car Example   Increased demand means that at every given price, the quantity demanded is higher, so that the demand curve shifts to the right from D_0 to D_1. Decreased demand means that at every given price, the quantity demanded is lower, so that the demand curve shifts to the left from D_0 to D_2.

Price	Decrease to D_2	Original Quantity Demanded D_0	Increase to D_1
$16,000	17.6 million	22.0 million	24.0 million
$18,000	16.0 million	20.0 million	22.0 million
$20,000	14.4 million	18.0 million	20.0 million
$22,000	13.6 million	17.0 million	19.0 million
$24,000	13.2 million	16.5 million	18.5 million
$26,000	12.8 million	16.0 million	18.0 million

Table 3.4 Price and Demand Shifts: A Car Example

Now, imagine that the economy slows down so that many people lose their jobs or work fewer hours, reducing their incomes. In this case, the decrease in income would lead to a lower quantity of cars demanded at every given price, and the original demand curve D_0 would shift left to D_2. The shift from D_0 to D_2 represents such a decrease in demand: At any given price level, the quantity demanded is now lower. In this example, a price of $20,000 means 18 million cars sold along the original demand curve, but only 14.4 million sold after demand fell.

When a demand curve shifts, it does not mean that the quantity demanded by every individual buyer changes by the same amount. In this example, not everyone would have higher or lower income and not everyone would buy or not buy an additional car. Instead, a shift in a demand curve captures an pattern for the market as a whole.

In the previous section, we argued that higher income causes greater demand at every price. This is true for most goods and services. For some—luxury cars, vacations in Europe, and fine jewelry—the effect of a rise in income can be especially pronounced. A product whose demand rises when income rises, and vice versa, is called a **normal good**. A few exceptions to this pattern do exist. As incomes rise, many people will buy fewer generic brand groceries and more name brand groceries. They are less likely to buy used cars and more likely to buy new cars. They will be less likely to rent an apartment and more likely to own a home, and so on. A product whose demand falls when income rises, and vice versa, is called an **inferior good**. In other words, when income increases, the demand curve shifts to the left.

Other Factors That Shift Demand Curves

Income is not the only factor that causes a shift in demand. Other things that change demand include tastes and preferences, the composition or size of the population, the prices of related goods, and even expectations. A change in any one of the underlying factors that determine what quantity people are willing to buy at a given price will cause a shift in demand. Graphically, the new demand curve lies either to the right (an increase) or to the left (a decrease) of the original demand curve. Let's look at these factors.

Changing Tastes or Preferences

From 1980 to 2014, the per-person consumption of chicken by Americans rose from 48 pounds per year to 85 pounds per year, and consumption of beef fell from 77 pounds per year to 54 pounds per year, according to the U.S. Department of Agriculture (USDA). Changes like these are largely due to movements in taste, which change the quantity of a good demanded at every price: that is, they shift the demand curve for that good, rightward for chicken and leftward for beef.

Changes in the Composition of the Population

The proportion of elderly citizens in the United States population is rising. It rose from 9.8% in 1970 to 12.6% in 2000, and will be a projected (by the U.S. Census Bureau) 20% of the population by 2030. A society with relatively more children, like the United States in the 1960s, will have greater demand for goods and services like tricycles and day care facilities. A society with relatively more elderly persons, as the United States is projected to have by 2030, has a higher demand for nursing homes and hearing aids. Similarly, changes in the size of the population can affect the demand for housing and many other goods. Each of these changes in demand will be shown as a shift in the demand curve.

The demand for a product can also be affected by changes in the prices of related goods such as substitutes or complements. A **substitute** is a good or service that can be used in place of another good or service. As electronic books, like this one, become more available, you would expect to see a decrease in demand for traditional printed books. A lower price for a substitute decreases demand for the other product. For example, in recent years as the price of tablet computers has fallen, the quantity demanded has increased (because of the law of demand). Since people are purchasing tablets, there has been a decrease in demand for laptops, which can be shown graphically as a leftward shift in the demand curve for laptops. A higher price for a substitute good has the reverse effect.

Other goods are **complements** for each other, meaning that the goods are often used together, because consumption of one good tends to enhance consumption of the other. Examples include breakfast cereal and milk; notebooks and pens or pencils, golf balls and golf clubs; gasoline and sport utility vehicles; and the five-way combination of bacon, lettuce, tomato, mayonnaise, and bread. If the price of golf clubs rises, since the quantity demanded of golf clubs falls (because of the law of demand), demand for a complement good like golf balls decreases, too. Similarly, a higher price for skis would shift the demand curve for a complement good like ski resort trips to the left, while a lower price for a complement has the reverse effect.

Changes in Expectations about Future Prices or Other Factors that Affect Demand

While it is clear that the price of a good affects the quantity demanded, it is also true that expectations about the future price (or expectations about tastes and preferences, income, and so on) can affect demand. For example, if people hear that a hurricane is coming, they may rush to the store to buy flashlight batteries and bottled water. If people learn that the price of a good like coffee is likely to rise in the future, they may head for the store to stock up on coffee now. These changes in demand are shown as shifts in the curve. Therefore, a **shift in demand** happens when a change in some economic factor (other than price) causes a different quantity to be demanded at every price. The following Work It Out feature shows how this happens.

Work It Out ⊸○─○─○

Shift in Demand

A shift in demand means that at any price (and at every price), the quantity demanded will be different than it was before. Following is an example of a shift in demand due to an income increase.

Step 1. Draw the graph of a demand curve for a normal good like pizza. Pick a price (like P_0). Identify the corresponding Q_0. An example is shown in Figure 3.6.

Figure 3.6 Demand Curve   The demand curve can be used to identify how much consumers would buy at any given price.

Step 2. Suppose income increases. As a result of the change, are consumers going to buy more or less pizza? The answer is more. Draw a dotted horizontal line from the chosen price, through the original quantity demanded, to the new point with the new Q_1. Draw a dotted vertical line down to the horizontal axis and label the new Q_1. An example is provided in Figure 3.7.

Figure 3.7 Demand Curve with Income Increase   With an increase in income, consumers will purchase larger quantities, pushing demand to the right.

Step 3. Now, shift the curve through the new point. You will see that an increase in income causes an upward (or rightward) shift in the demand curve, so that at any price the quantities demanded will be higher, as shown in Figure 3.8.

Figure 3.8 Demand Curve Shifted Right With an increase in income, consumers will purchase larger quantities, pushing demand to the right, and causing the demand curve to shift right.

Summing Up Factors That Change Demand

Six factors that can shift demand curves are summarized in **Figure 3.9**. The direction of the arrows indicates whether the demand curve shifts represent an increase in demand or a decrease in demand. Notice that a change in the price of the good or service itself is not listed among the factors that can shift a demand curve. A change in the price of a good or service causes a movement along a specific demand curve, and it typically leads to some change in the quantity demanded, but it does not shift the demand curve.

(a) Factors that increase demand

(b) Factors that decrease demand

Figure 3.9 Factors That Shift Demand Curves (a) A list of factors that can cause an increase in demand from D_0 to D_1. (b) The same factors, if their direction is reversed, can cause a decrease in demand from D_0 to D_1.

When a demand curve shifts, it will then intersect with a given supply curve at a different equilibrium price and quantity. We are, however, getting ahead of our story. Before discussing how changes in demand can affect equilibrium price and quantity, we first need to discuss shifts in supply curves.

How Production Costs Affect Supply

A supply curve shows how quantity supplied will change as the price rises and falls, assuming *ceteris paribus* so that no other economically relevant factors are changing. If other factors relevant to supply do change, then the entire supply curve will shift. Just as a shift in demand is represented by a change in the quantity demanded at every price, a **shift in supply** means a change in the quantity supplied at every price.

In thinking about the factors that affect supply, remember what motivates firms: profits, which are the difference between revenues and costs. Goods and services are produced using combinations of labor, materials, and machinery, or what we call **inputs** or **factors of production**. If a firm faces lower costs of production, while the prices for the good or service the firm produces remain unchanged, a firm's profits go up. When a firm's profits increase, it is more motivated to produce output, since the more it produces the more profit it will earn. So, when costs of production fall, a firm will tend to supply a larger quantity at any given price for its output. This can be shown by the supply curve shifting to the right.

Take, for example, a messenger company that delivers packages around a city. The company may find that buying gasoline is one of its main costs. If the price of gasoline falls, then the company will find it can deliver messages more cheaply than before. Since lower costs correspond to higher profits, the messenger company may now supply more of its services at any given price. For example, given the lower gasoline prices, the company can now serve a greater area, and increase its supply.

Conversely, if a firm faces higher costs of production, then it will earn lower profits at any given selling price for its products. As a result, a higher cost of production typically causes a firm to supply a smaller quantity at any given price. In this case, the supply curve shifts to the left.

Consider the supply for cars, shown by curve S_0 in **Figure 3.10**. Point J indicates that if the price is $20,000, the quantity supplied will be 18 million cars. If the price rises to $22,000 per car, *ceteris paribus*, the quantity supplied will rise to 20 million cars, as point K on the S_0 curve shows. The same information can be shown in table form, as in **Table 3.5**.

Figure 3.10 Shifts in Supply: A Car Example Decreased supply means that at every given price, the quantity supplied is lower, so that the supply curve shifts to the left, from S_0 to S_1. Increased supply means that at every given price, the quantity supplied is higher, so that the supply curve shifts to the right, from S_0 to S_2.

Price	Decrease to S_1	Original Quantity Supplied S_0	Increase to S_2
$16,000	10.5 million	12.0 million	13.2 million
$18,000	13.5 million	15.0 million	16.5 million
$20,000	16.5 million	18.0 million	19.8 million
$22,000	18.5 million	20.0 million	22.0 million
$24,000	19.5 million	21.0 million	23.1 million
$26,000	20.5 million	22.0 million	24.2 million

Table 3.5 Price and Shifts in Supply: A Car Example

Now, imagine that the price of steel, an important ingredient in manufacturing cars, rises, so that producing a car has become more expensive. At any given price for selling cars, car manufacturers will react by supplying a lower quantity. This can be shown graphically as a leftward shift of supply, from S_0 to S_1, which indicates that at any given price, the quantity supplied decreases. In this example, at a price of $20,000, the quantity supplied decreases from 18 million on the original supply curve (S_0) to 16.5 million on the supply curve S_1, which is labeled as point L.

Conversely, if the price of steel decreases, producing a car becomes less expensive. At any given price for selling cars, car manufacturers can now expect to earn higher profits, so they will supply a higher quantity. The shift of supply to the right, from S_0 to S_2, means that at all prices, the quantity supplied has increased. In this example, at a price of $20,000, the quantity supplied increases from 18 million on the original supply curve (S_0) to 19.8 million on the supply curve S_2, which is labeled M.

Other Factors That Affect Supply

In the example above, we saw that changes in the prices of inputs in the production process will affect the cost of production and thus the supply. Several other things affect the cost of production, too, such as changes in weather or other natural conditions, new technologies for production, and some government policies.

The cost of production for many agricultural products will be affected by changes in natural conditions. For example, in 2014 the Manchurian Plain in Northeastern China, which produces most of the country's wheat, corn, and soybeans, experienced its most severe drought in 50 years. A drought decreases the supply of agricultural products, which means that at any given price, a lower quantity will be supplied; conversely, especially good weather would shift the supply curve to the right.

When a firm discovers a new technology that allows the firm to produce at a lower cost, the supply curve will shift to the right, as well. For instance, in the 1960s a major scientific effort nicknamed the Green Revolution focused on breeding improved seeds for basic crops like wheat and rice. By the early 1990s, more than two-thirds of the wheat and rice in low-income countries around the world was grown with these Green Revolution seeds—and the harvest was twice as high per acre. A technological improvement that reduces costs of production will shift supply to the right, so that a greater quantity will be produced at any given price.

Government policies can affect the cost of production and the supply curve through taxes, regulations, and subsidies. For example, the U.S. government imposes a tax on alcoholic beverages that collects about $8 billion per year from producers. Taxes are treated as costs by businesses. Higher costs decrease supply for the reasons discussed above. Other examples of policy that can affect cost are the wide array of government regulations that require firms to spend money to provide a cleaner environment or a safer workplace; complying with regulations increases costs.

A government subsidy, on the other hand, is the opposite of a tax. A subsidy occurs when the government pays a firm directly or reduces the firm's taxes if the firm carries out certain actions. From the firm's perspective, taxes or regulations are an additional cost of production that shifts supply to the left, leading the firm to produce a lower quantity at every given price. Government subsidies reduce the cost of production and increase supply at every given price, shifting supply to the right. The following Work It Out feature shows how this shift happens.

Work It Out ─○─○─○

Shift in Supply

We know that a supply curve shows the minimum price a firm will accept to produce a given quantity of output. What happens to the supply curve when the cost of production goes up? Following is an example of a shift in supply due to a production cost increase.

Step 1. Draw a graph of a supply curve for pizza. Pick a quantity (like Q_0). If you draw a vertical line up from Q_0 to the supply curve, you will see the price the firm chooses. An example is shown in **Figure 3.11**.

Figure 3.11 Suppy Curve   The supply curve can be used to show the minimum price a firm will accept to produce a given quantity of output.

Step 2. Why did the firm choose that price and not some other? One way to think about this is that the price is composed of two parts. The first part is the average cost of production, in this case, the cost of the pizza ingredients (dough, sauce, cheese, pepperoni, and so on), the cost of the pizza oven, the rent on the shop, and the wages of the workers. The second part is the firm's desired profit, which is determined, among other factors, by the profit margins in that particular business. If you add these two parts together, you get the price the firm wishes to charge. The quantity Q0 and associated price P0 give you one point on the firm's supply curve, as shown in **Figure 3.12**.

Figure 3.12 Setting Prices   The cost of production and the desired profit equal the price a firm will set for a product.

Step 3. Now, suppose that the cost of production goes up. Perhaps cheese has become more expensive by $0.75 per pizza. If that is true, the firm will want to raise its price by the amount of the increase in cost ($0.75). Draw this point on the supply curve directly above the initial point on the curve, but $0.75 higher, as shown in **Figure 3.13**.

Figure 3.13 Increasing Costs Leads to Increasing Price   Because the cost of production and the desired profit equal the price a firm will set for a product, if the cost of production increases, the price for the product will also need to increase.

Step 4. Shift the supply curve through this point. You will see that an increase in cost causes an upward (or a leftward) shift of the supply curve so that at any price, the quantities supplied will be smaller, as shown in Figure 3.14.

Figure 3.14 Supply Curve Shifts   When the cost of production increases, the supply curve shifts upwardly to a new price level.

Summing Up Factors That Change Supply

Changes in the cost of inputs, natural disasters, new technologies, and the impact of government decisions all affect the cost of production. In turn, these factors affect how much firms are willing to supply at any given price.

Figure 3.15 summarizes factors that change the supply of goods and services. Notice that a change in the price of the product itself is not among the factors that shift the supply curve. Although a change in price of a good or service typically causes a change in quantity supplied or a movement along the supply curve for that specific good or service, it does not cause the supply curve itself to shift.

(a) Factors that increase supply (b) Factors that decrease supply

Figure 3.15 Factors That Shift Supply Curves (a) A list of factors that can cause an increase in supply from S_0 to S_1. (b) The same factors, if their direction is reversed, can cause a decrease in supply from S_0 to S_1.

Because demand and supply curves appear on a two-dimensional diagram with only price and quantity on the axes, an unwary visitor to the land of economics might be fooled into believing that economics is about only four topics: demand, supply, price, and quantity. However, demand and supply are really "umbrella" concepts: demand covers all the factors that affect demand, and supply covers all the factors that affect supply. Factors other than price that affect demand and supply are included by using shifts in the demand or the supply curve. In this way, the two-dimensional demand and supply model becomes a powerful tool for analyzing a wide range of economic circumstances.

3.3 | Changes in Equilibrium Price and Quantity: The Four-Step Process

By the end of this section, you will be able to:
- Identify equilibrium price and quantity through the four-step process
- Graph equilibrium price and quantity
- Contrast shifts of demand or supply and movements along a demand or supply curve
- Graph demand and supply curves, including equilibrium price and quantity, based on real-world examples

Let's begin this discussion with a single economic event. It might be an event that affects demand, like a change in income, population, tastes, prices of substitutes or complements, or expectations about future prices. It might be an event that affects supply, like a change in natural conditions, input prices, or technology, or government policies that affect production. How does this economic event affect equilibrium price and quantity? We will analyze this question using a four-step process.

Step 1. Draw a demand and supply model before the economic change took place. To establish the model requires four standard pieces of information: The law of demand, which tells us the slope of the demand curve; the law of supply, which gives us the slope of the supply curve; the shift variables for demand; and the shift variables for supply. From this model, find the initial equilibrium values for price and quantity.

Step 2. Decide whether the economic change being analyzed affects demand or supply. In other words, does the event refer to something in the list of demand factors or supply factors?

Step 3. Decide whether the effect on demand or supply causes the curve to shift to the right or to the left, and sketch the new demand or supply curve on the diagram. In other words, does the event increase or decrease the amount consumers want to buy or producers want to sell?

Step 4. Identify the new equilibrium and then compare the original equilibrium price and quantity to the new equilibrium price and quantity.

Let's consider one example that involves a shift in supply and one that involves a shift in demand. Then we will consider an example where both supply and demand shift.

Good Weather for Salmon Fishing

In the summer of 2000, weather conditions were excellent for commercial salmon fishing off the California coast. Heavy rains meant higher than normal levels of water in the rivers, which helps the salmon to breed. Slightly cooler ocean temperatures stimulated the growth of plankton, the microscopic organisms at the bottom of the ocean food chain, providing everything in the ocean with a hearty food supply. The ocean stayed calm during fishing season, so commercial fishing operations did not lose many days to bad weather. How did these climate conditions affect the quantity and price of salmon? Figure 3.16 illustrates the four-step approach, which is explained below, to work through this problem. Table 3.6 provides the information to work the problem as well.

Figure 3.16 Good Weather for Salmon Fishing: The Four-Step Process   Unusually good weather leads to changes in the price and quantity of salmon.

Price per Pound	Quantity Supplied in 1999	Quantity Supplied in 2000	Quantity Demanded
$2.00	80	400	840
$2.25	120	480	680
$2.50	160	550	550
$2.75	200	600	450
$3.00	230	640	350
$3.25	250	670	250
$3.50	270	700	200

Table 3.6 Salmon Fishing

Step 1. Draw a demand and supply model to illustrate the market for salmon in the year before the good weather conditions began. The demand curve D_0 and the supply curve S_0 show that the original equilibrium price is $3.25 per pound and the original equilibrium quantity is 250,000 fish. (This price per pound is what commercial buyers pay at the fishing docks; what consumers pay at the grocery is higher.)

Step 2. Did the economic event affect supply or demand? Good weather is an example of a natural condition that affects supply.

Step 3. Was the effect on supply an increase or a decrease? Good weather is a change in natural conditions that increases the quantity supplied at any given price. The supply curve shifts to the right, moving from the original supply curve S_0 to the new supply curve S_1, which is shown in both the table and the figure.

Step 4. Compare the new equilibrium price and quantity to the original equilibrium. At the new equilibrium E_1, the equilibrium price falls from \$3.25 to \$2.50, but the equilibrium quantity increases from 250,000 to 550,000 salmon. Notice that the equilibrium quantity demanded increased, even though the demand curve did not move.

In short, good weather conditions increased supply of the California commercial salmon. The result was a higher equilibrium quantity of salmon bought and sold in the market at a lower price.

Newspapers and the Internet

According to the Pew Research Center for People and the Press, more and more people, especially younger people, are getting their news from online and digital sources. The majority of U.S. adults now own smartphones or tablets, and most of those Americans say they use them in part to get the news. From 2004 to 2012, the share of Americans who reported getting their news from digital sources increased from 24% to 39%. How has this affected consumption of print news media, and radio and television news? **Figure 3.17** and the text below illustrates using the four-step analysis to answer this question.

Figure 3.17 The Print News Market: A Four-Step Analysis   A change in tastes from print news sources to digital sources results in a leftward shift in demand for the former. The result is a decrease in both equilibrium price and quantity.

Step 1. Develop a demand and supply model to think about what the market looked like before the event. The demand curve D_0 and the supply curve S_0 show the original relationships. In this case, the analysis is performed without specific numbers on the price and quantity axis.

Step 2. Did the change described affect supply or demand? A change in tastes, from traditional news sources (print, radio, and television) to digital sources, caused a change in demand for the former.

Step 3. Was the effect on demand positive or negative? A shift to digital news sources will tend to mean a lower quantity demanded of traditional news sources at every given price, causing the demand curve for print and other traditional news sources to shift to the left, from D_0 to D_1.

Step 4. Compare the new equilibrium price and quantity to the original equilibrium price. The new equilibrium (E_1) occurs at a lower quantity and a lower price than the original equilibrium (E_0).

The decline in print news reading predates 2004. Print newspaper circulation peaked in 1973 and has declined since then due to competition from television and radio news. In 1991, 55% of Americans indicated they got their news from print sources, while only 29% did so in 2012. Radio news has followed a similar path in recent decades, with the share of Americans getting their news from radio declining from 54% in 1991 to 33% in 2012. Television news has held its own over the last 15 years, with a market share staying in the mid to upper fifties. What does this suggest for the future, given that two-thirds of Americans under 30 years old say they do not get their news from television at all?

The Interconnections and Speed of Adjustment in Real Markets

In the real world, many factors that affect demand and supply can change all at once. For example, the demand for cars might increase because of rising incomes and population, and it might decrease because of rising gasoline prices (a complementary good). Likewise, the supply of cars might increase because of innovative new technologies that reduce the cost of car production, and it might decrease as a result of new government regulations requiring the installation of costly pollution-control technology.

Moreover, rising incomes and population or changes in gasoline prices will affect many markets, not just cars. How can an economist sort out all these interconnected events? The answer lies in the *ceteris paribus* assumption. Look at how each economic event affects each market, one event at a time, holding all else constant. Then combine the analyses to see the net effect.

A Combined Example

The U.S. Postal Service is facing difficult challenges. Compensation for postal workers tends to increase most years due to cost-of-living increases. At the same time, more and more people are using email, text, and other digital message forms such as Facebook and Twitter to communicate with friends and others. What does this suggest about the continued viability of the Postal Service? **Figure 3.18** and the text below illustrates using the four-step analysis to answer this question.

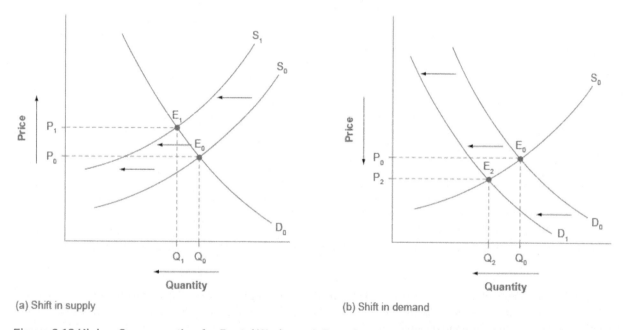

(a) Shift in supply

(b) Shift in demand

Figure 3.18 Higher Compensation for Postal Workers: A Four-Step Analysis   (a) Higher labor compensation causes a leftward shift in the supply curve, a decrease in the equilibrium quantity, and an increase in the equilibrium price. (b) A change in tastes away from Postal Services causes a leftward shift in the demand curve, a decrease in the equilibrium quantity, and a decrease in the equilibrium price.

Since this problem involves two disturbances, we need two four-step analyses, the first to analyze the effects of higher compensation for postal workers, the second to analyze the effects of many people switching from "snailmail" to email and other digital messages.

Figure 3.18 (a) shows the shift in supply discussed in the following steps.

Step 1. Draw a demand and supply model to illustrate what the market for the U.S. Postal Service looked like before this scenario starts. The demand curve D_0 and the supply curve S_0 show the original relationships.

Step 2. Did the change described affect supply or demand? Labor compensation is a cost of production. A change in production costs caused a change in supply for the Postal Service.

Step 3. Was the effect on supply positive or negative? Higher labor compensation leads to a lower quantity supplied of postal services at every given price, causing the supply curve for postal services to shift to the left, from S_0 to S_1.

Step 4. Compare the new equilibrium price and quantity to the original equilibrium price. The new equilibrium (E_1) occurs at a lower quantity and a higher price than the original equilibrium (E_0).

Figure 3.18 (b) shows the shift in demand discussed in the following steps.

Step 1. Draw a demand and supply model to illustrate what the market for U.S. Postal Services looked like before this scenario starts. The demand curve D_0 and the supply curve S_0 show the original relationships. Note that this diagram is independent from the diagram in panel (a).

Step 2. Did the change described affect supply or demand? A change in tastes away from snailmail toward digital messages will cause a change in demand for the Postal Service.

Step 3. Was the effect on supply positive or negative? Higher labor compensation leads to a lower quantity supplied of postal services at every given price, causing the supply curve for postal services to shift to the left, from D_0 to D_1.

Step 4. Compare the new equilibrium price and quantity to the original equilibrium price. The new equilibrium (E_2) occurs at a lower quantity and a lower price than the original equilibrium (E_0).

The final step in a scenario where both supply and demand shift is to combine the two individual analyses to determine what happens to the equilibrium quantity and price. Graphically, we superimpose the previous two diagrams one on top of the other, as in Figure 3.19.

Figure 3.19 Combined Effect of Decreased Demand and Decreased Supply   Supply and demand shifts cause changes in equilibrium price and quantity.

Following are the results:

Effect on Quantity: The effect of higher labor compensation on Postal Services because it raises the cost of production is to decrease the equilibrium quantity. The effect of a change in tastes away from snailmail is to decrease the equilibrium quantity. Since both shifts are to the left, the overall impact is a decrease in the equilibrium quantity of Postal Services (Q_3). This is easy to see graphically, since Q_3 is to the left of Q_0.

Effect on Price: The overall effect on price is more complicated. The effect of higher labor compensation on Postal Services, because it raises the cost of production, is to increase the equilibrium price. The effect of a change in tastes away from snailmail is to decrease the equilibrium price. Since the two effects are in opposite directions, unless we know the magnitudes of the two effects, the overall effect is unclear. This is not unusual. When both curves shift, typically we can determine the overall effect on price or on quantity, but not on both. In this case, we determined the overall effect on the equilibrium quantity, but not on the equilibrium price. In other cases, it might be the opposite.

The next Clear It Up feature focuses on the difference between shifts of supply or demand and movements along a curve.

What is the difference between shifts of demand or supply versus movements along a demand or supply curve?

One common mistake in applying the demand and supply framework is to confuse the shift of a demand or a supply curve with movement along a demand or supply curve. As an example, consider a problem that asks whether a drought will increase or decrease the equilibrium quantity and equilibrium price of wheat. Lee, a student in an introductory economics class, might reason:

"Well, it is clear that a drought reduces supply, so I will shift back the supply curve, as in the shift from the original supply curve S_0 to S_1 shown on the diagram (called Shift 1). So the equilibrium moves from E_0 to E_1, the equilibrium quantity is lower and the equilibrium price is higher. Then, a higher price makes farmers more likely to supply the good, so the supply curve shifts right, as shown by the shift from S_1 to S_2, on the diagram (shown as Shift 2), so that the equilibrium now moves from E_1 to E_2. The higher price, however, also reduces demand and so causes demand to shift back, like the shift from the original demand curve, D_0 to D_1 on the diagram (labeled Shift 3), and the equilibrium moves from E_2 to E_3."

Figure 3.20 Shifts of Demand or Supply versus Movements along a Demand or Supply Curve A shift in one curve never causes a shift in the other curve. Rather, a shift in one curve causes a movement along the second curve.

At about this point, Lee suspects that this answer is headed down the wrong path. Think about what might be wrong with Lee's logic, and then read the answer that follows.

Answer: Lee's first step is correct: that is, a drought shifts back the supply curve of wheat and leads to a prediction of a lower equilibrium quantity and a higher equilibrium price. This corresponds to a movement along the original demand curve (D_0), from E_0 to E_1. The rest of Lee's argument is wrong, because it mixes up shifts in supply with quantity supplied, and shifts in demand with quantity demanded. A higher or lower price never shifts the supply curve, as suggested by the shift in supply from S_1 to S_2. Instead, a price change leads to a movement along a given supply curve. Similarly, a higher or lower price never shifts a demand curve, as suggested in the shift from D_0 to D_1. Instead, a price change leads to a movement along a given demand curve. Remember, a change in the price of a good never causes the demand or supply curve for that good to shift.

Think carefully about the timeline of events: What happens first, what happens next? What is cause, what is effect? If you keep the order right, you are more likely to get the analysis correct.

In the four-step analysis of how economic events affect equilibrium price and quantity, the movement from the old to the new equilibrium seems immediate. As a practical matter, however, prices and quantities often do not zoom straight to equilibrium. More realistically, when an economic event causes demand or supply to shift, prices and quantities set off in the general direction of equilibrium. Indeed, even as they are moving toward one new equilibrium, prices are often then pushed by another change in demand or supply toward another equilibrium.

3.4 | Price Ceilings and Price Floors

By the end of this section, you will be able to:
- Explain price controls, price ceilings, and price floors
- Analyze demand and supply as a social adjustment mechanism

Controversy sometimes surrounds the prices and quantities established by demand and supply, especially for products that are considered necessities. In some cases, discontent over prices turns into public pressure on politicians, who may then pass legislation to prevent a certain price from climbing "too high" or falling "too low."

The demand and supply model shows how people and firms will react to the incentives provided by these laws to control prices, in ways that will often lead to undesirable consequences. Alternative policy tools can often achieve the desired goals of price control laws, while avoiding at least some of their costs and tradeoffs.

Price Ceilings

Laws that government enacts to regulate prices are called **Price controls**. Price controls come in two flavors. A **price ceiling** keeps a price from rising above a certain level (the "ceiling"), while a **price floor** keeps a price from falling below a certain level (the "floor"). This section uses the demand and supply framework to analyze price ceilings. The next section discusses price floors.

In many markets for goods and services, demanders outnumber suppliers. Consumers, who are also potential voters, sometimes unite behind a political proposal to hold down a certain price. In some cities, such as Albany, renters have pressed political leaders to pass rent control laws, a price ceiling that usually works by stating that rents can be raised by only a certain maximum percentage each year.

Rent control becomes a politically hot topic when rents begin to rise rapidly. Everyone needs an affordable place to live. Perhaps a change in tastes makes a certain suburb or town a more popular place to live. Perhaps locally-based businesses expand, bringing higher incomes and more people into the area. Changes of this sort can cause a change in the demand for rental housing, as **Figure 3.21** illustrates. The original equilibrium (E_0) lies at the intersection of supply curve S_0 and demand curve D_0, corresponding to an equilibrium price of \$500 and an equilibrium quantity of 15,000 units of rental housing. The effect of greater income or a change in tastes is to shift the demand curve for rental housing to the right, as shown by the data in **Table 3.7** and the shift from D_0 to D_1 on the graph. In this market, at the new equilibrium E_1, the price of a rental unit would rise to \$600 and the equilibrium quantity would increase to 17,000 units.

Figure 3.21 A Price Ceiling Example—Rent Control The original intersection of demand and supply occurs at E_0. If demand shifts from D_0 to D_1, the new equilibrium would be at E_1—unless a price ceiling prevents the price from rising. If the price is not permitted to rise, the quantity supplied remains at 15,000. However, after the change in demand, the quantity demanded rises to 19,000, resulting in a shortage.

Price	Original Quantity Supplied	Original Quantity Demanded	New Quantity Demanded
$400	12,000	18,000	23,000
$500	15,000	15,000	19,000
$600	17,000	13,000	17,000
$700	19,000	11,000	15,000
$800	20,000	10,000	14,000

Table 3.7 Rent Control

Suppose that a rent control law is passed to keep the price at the original equilibrium of $500 for a typical apartment. In **Figure 3.21**, the horizontal line at the price of $500 shows the legally fixed maximum price set by the rent control law. However, the underlying forces that shifted the demand curve to the right are still there. At that price ($500), the quantity supplied remains at the same 15,000 rental units, but the quantity demanded is 19,000 rental units. In other words, the quantity demanded exceeds the quantity supplied, so there is a shortage of rental housing. One of the ironies of price ceilings is that while the price ceiling was intended to help renters, there are actually fewer apartments rented out under the price ceiling (15,000 rental units) than would be the case at the market rent of $600 (17,000 rental units).

Price ceilings do not simply benefit renters at the expense of landlords. Rather, some renters (or potential renters) lose their housing as landlords convert apartments to co-ops and condos. Even when the housing remains in the rental market, landlords tend to spend less on maintenance and on essentials like heating, cooling, hot water, and lighting. The first rule of economics is you do not get something for nothing—everything has an opportunity cost. So if renters get "cheaper" housing than the market requires, they tend to also end up with lower quality housing.

Price ceilings have been proposed for other products. For example, price ceilings to limit what producers can charge have been proposed in recent years for prescription drugs, doctor and hospital fees, the charges made by some automatic teller bank machines, and auto insurance rates. Price ceilings are enacted in an attempt to keep prices low for those who demand the product. But when the market price is not allowed to rise to the equilibrium level, quantity demanded exceeds quantity supplied, and thus a shortage occurs. Those who manage to purchase the product at the lower price given by the price ceiling will benefit, but sellers of the product will suffer, along with those who are not able to purchase the product at all. Quality is also likely to deteriorate.

Price Floors

A price floor is the lowest legal price that can be paid in markets for goods and services, labor, or financial capital. Perhaps the best-known example of a price floor is the minimum wage, which is based on the normative view that someone working full time ought to be able to afford a basic standard of living. The federal minimum wage at the end of 2014 was $7.25 per hour, which yields an income for a single person slightly higher than the poverty line. As the cost of living rises over time, the Congress periodically raises the federal minimum wage.

Price floors are sometimes called "price supports," because they support a price by preventing it from falling below a certain level. Around the world, many countries have passed laws to create agricultural price supports. Farm prices and thus farm incomes fluctuate, sometimes widely. So even if, on average, farm incomes are adequate, some years they can be quite low. The purpose of price supports is to prevent these swings.

The most common way price supports work is that the government enters the market and buys up the product, adding to demand to keep prices higher than they otherwise would be. According to the Common Agricultural Policy reform passed in 2013, the European Union (EU) will spend about 60 billion euros per year, or 67 billion dollars per year, or roughly 38% of the EU budget, on price supports for Europe's farmers from 2014 to 2020.

Figure 3.22 illustrates the effects of a government program that assures a price above the equilibrium by focusing on the market for wheat in Europe. In the absence of government intervention, the price would adjust so that the quantity supplied would equal the quantity demanded at the equilibrium point E_0, with price P_0 and quantity Q_0. However, policies to keep prices high for farmers keeps the price above what would have been the market equilibrium level—the price Pf shown by the dashed horizontal line in the diagram. The result is a quantity supplied in excess of the quantity demanded (Qd). When quantity supplied exceeds quantity demanded, a surplus exists.

The high-income areas of the world, including the United States, Europe, and Japan, are estimated to spend roughly $1 billion per day in supporting their farmers. If the government is willing to purchase the excess supply (or to provide payments for others to purchase it), then farmers will benefit from the price floor, but taxpayers and consumers of food will pay the costs. Numerous proposals have been offered for reducing farm subsidies. In many countries, however, political support for subsidies for farmers remains strong. Either because this is viewed by the population as supporting the traditional rural way of life or because of the lobbying power of the agro-business industry.

For more detail on the effects price ceilings and floors have on demand and supply, see the following Clear It Up feature.

Figure 3.22 European Wheat Prices: A Price Floor Example The intersection of demand (D) and supply (S) would be at the equilibrium point E_0. However, a price floor set at Pf holds the price above E_0 and prevents it from falling. The result of the price floor is that the quantity supplied Qs exceeds the quantity demanded Qd. There is excess supply, also called a surplus.

Do price ceilings and floors change demand or supply?

Neither price ceilings nor price floors cause demand or supply to change. They simply set a price that limits what can be legally charged in the market. Remember, changes in price do not cause demand or supply to change. Price ceilings and price floors can cause a different choice of quantity demanded along a demand curve, but they do not move the demand curve. Price controls can cause a different choice of quantity supplied along a supply curve, but they do not shift the supply curve.

3.5 | Demand, Supply and Efficiency

The familiar demand and supply diagram holds within it the concept of economic efficiency. To economists, efficiency means it is impossible to improve the situation of one party without imposing a cost on another. Conversely, if a situation is inefficient, it becomes possible to benefit at least one party without imposing costs on others.

Efficiency in the demand and supply model has the same basic meaning: The economy is getting as much benefit as possible from its scarce resources and all the possible gains from trade have been achieved. In other words, the optimal amount of each good and service is being produced and consumed.

Consumer Surplus, Producer Surplus, Social Surplus

Consider a market for tablet computers, as shown in **Figure 3.23**. The equilibrium price is $80 and the equilibrium quantity is 28 million. To see the benefits to consumers, look at the segment of the demand curve above the equilibrium point and to the left. This portion of the demand curve shows that at least some demanders would have been willing to pay more than $80 for a tablet.

For example, point J shows that if the price was $90, 20 million tablets would be sold. Those consumers who would have been willing to pay $90 for a tablet based on the utility they expect to receive from it, but who were able to pay the equilibrium price of $80, clearly received a benefit beyond what they had to pay for. Remember, the demand curve traces consumers' willingness to pay for different quantities. The amount that individuals would have been willing to pay, minus the amount that they actually paid, is called consumer surplus. Consumer surplus is the area labeled F—that is, the area above the market price and below the demand curve.

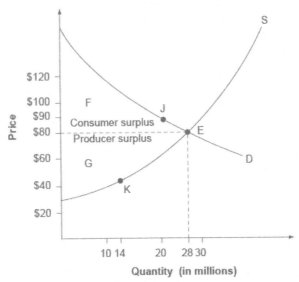

Figure 3.23 Consumer and Producer Surplus The somewhat triangular area labeled by F shows the area of consumer surplus, which shows that the equilibrium price in the market was less than what many of the consumers were willing to pay. Point J on the demand curve shows that, even at the price of $90, consumers would have been willing to purchase a quantity of 20 million. The somewhat triangular area labeled by G shows the area of producer surplus, which shows that the equilibrium price received in the market was more than what many of the producers were willing to accept for their products. For example, point K on the supply curve shows that at a price of $45, firms would have been willing to supply a quantity of 14 million.

The supply curve shows the quantity that firms are willing to supply at each price. For example, point K in **Figure 3.23** illustrates that, at $45, firms would still have been willing to supply a quantity of 14 million. Those producers who would have been willing to supply the tablets at $45, but who were instead able to charge the equilibrium price of $80, clearly received an extra benefit beyond what they required to supply the product. The amount that a seller is paid for a good minus the seller's actual cost is called producer surplus. In **Figure 3.23**, producer surplus is the area labeled G—that is, the area between the market price and the segment of the supply curve below the equilibrium.

The sum of consumer surplus and producer surplus is social surplus, also referred to as economic surplus. In **Figure 3.23**, social surplus would be shown as the area F + G. Social surplus is larger at equilibrium quantity and price than it would be at any other quantity. This demonstrates the economic efficiency of the market equilibrium. In addition, at the efficient level of output, it is impossible to produce greater consumer surplus without reducing producer surplus, and it is impossible to produce greater producer surplus without reducing consumer surplus.

Inefficiency of Price Floors and Price Ceilings

The imposition of a price floor or a price ceiling will prevent a market from adjusting to its equilibrium price and quantity, and thus will create an inefficient outcome. But there is an additional twist here. Along with creating inefficiency, price floors and ceilings will also transfer some consumer surplus to producers, or some producer surplus to consumers.

Imagine that several firms develop a promising but expensive new drug for treating back pain. If this therapy is left to the market, the equilibrium price will be $600 per month and 20,000 people will use the drug, as shown in **Figure 3.24** (a). The original level of consumer surplus is T + U and producer surplus is V + W + X. However, the government decides to impose a price ceiling of $400 to make the drug more affordable. At this price ceiling, firms in the market now produce only 15,000.

As a result, two changes occur. First, an inefficient outcome occurs and the total surplus of society is reduced. The loss in social surplus that occurs when the economy produces at an inefficient quantity is called deadweight loss. In a very real sense, it is like money thrown away that benefits no one. In **Figure 3.24** (a), the deadweight loss is the area U + W. When deadweight loss exists, it is possible for both consumer and producer surplus to be higher, in this case because the price control is blocking some suppliers and demanders from transactions they would both be willing to make.

A second change from the price ceiling is that some of the producer surplus is transferred to consumers. After the price ceiling is imposed, the new consumer surplus is T + V, while the new producer surplus is X. In other words, the price ceiling transfers the area of surplus (V) from producers to consumers. Note that the gain to consumers is less than the loss to producers, which is just another way of seeing the deadweight loss.

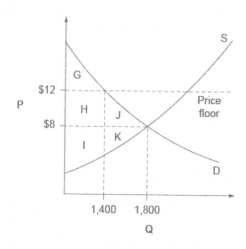

(a) Reduced social surplus from a price ceiling   (b) Reduced social surplus from a price floor

Figure 3.24 Efficiency and Price Floors and Ceilings (a) The original equilibrium price is $600 with a quantity of 20,000. Consumer surplus is T + U, and producer surplus is V + W + X. A price ceiling is imposed at $400, so firms in the market now produce only a quantity of 15,000. As a result, the new consumer surplus is T + V, while the new producer surplus is X. (b) The original equilibrium is $8 at a quantity of 1,800. Consumer surplus is G + H + J, and producer surplus is I + K. A price floor is imposed at $12, which means that quantity demanded falls to 1,400. As a result, the new consumer surplus is G, and the new producer surplus is H + I.

Figure 3.24 (b) shows a price floor example using a string of struggling movie theaters, all in the same city. The current equilibrium is $8 per movie ticket, with 1,800 people attending movies. The original consumer surplus is G + H + J, and producer surplus is I + K. The city government is worried that movie theaters will go out of business, reducing the entertainment options available to citizens, so it decides to impose a price floor of $12 per ticket. As a result, the quantity demanded of movie tickets falls to 1,400. The new consumer surplus is G, and the new producer surplus is H + I. In effect, the price floor causes the area H to be transferred from consumer to producer surplus, but also causes a deadweight loss of J + K.

This analysis shows that a price ceiling, like a law establishing rent controls, will transfer some producer surplus to consumers—which helps to explain why consumers often favor them. Conversely, a price floor like a guarantee that farmers will receive a certain price for their crops will transfer some consumer surplus to producers, which explains why producers often favor them. However, both price floors and price ceilings block some transactions that buyers and sellers would have been willing to make, and creates deadweight loss. Removing such barriers, so that prices and quantities can adjust to their equilibrium level, will increase the economy's social surplus.

KEY TERMS

ceteris paribus other things being equal

complements goods that are often used together so that consumption of one good tends to enhance consumption of the other

demand the relationship between price and the quantity demanded of a certain good or service

demand curve a graphic representation of the relationship between price and quantity demanded of a certain good or service, with quantity on the horizontal axis and the price on the vertical axis

demand schedule a table that shows a range of prices for a certain good or service and the quantity demanded at each price

equilibrium the situation where quantity demanded is equal to the quantity supplied; the combination of price and quantity where there is no economic pressure from surpluses or shortages that would cause price or quantity to change

equilibrium price the price where quantity demanded is equal to quantity supplied

equilibrium quantity the quantity at which quantity demanded and quantity supplied are equal for a certain price level

excess demand at the existing price, the quantity demanded exceeds the quantity supplied; also called a shortage

excess supply at the existing price, quantity supplied exceeds the quantity demanded; also called a surplus

factors of production the combination of labor, materials, and machinery that is used to produce goods and services; also called inputs

inferior good a good in which the quantity demanded falls as income rises, and in which quantity demanded rises and income falls

inputs the combination of labor, materials, and machinery that is used to produce goods and services; also called factors of production

law of demand the common relationship that a higher price leads to a lower quantity demanded of a certain good or service and a lower price leads to a higher quantity demanded, while all other variables are held constant

law of supply the common relationship that a higher price leads to a greater quantity supplied and a lower price leads to a lower quantity supplied, while all other variables are held constant

normal good a good in which the quantity demanded rises as income rises, and in which quantity demanded falls as income falls

price what a buyer pays for a unit of the specific good or service

price ceiling a legal maximum price

price control government laws to regulate prices instead of letting market forces determine prices

price floor a legal minimum price

quantity demanded the total number of units of a good or service consumers are willing to purchase at a given price

quantity supplied the total number of units of a good or service producers are willing to sell at a given price

shift in demand when a change in some economic factor (other than price) causes a different quantity to be demanded at every price

shift in supply when a change in some economic factor (other than price) causes a different quantity to be supplied at every price

shortage at the existing price, the quantity demanded exceeds the quantity supplied; also called excess demand

substitute a good that can replace another to some extent, so that greater consumption of one good can mean less of the other

supply the relationship between price and the quantity supplied of a certain good or service

supply curve a line that shows the relationship between price and quantity supplied on a graph, with quantity supplied on the horizontal axis and price on the vertical axis

supply schedule a table that shows a range of prices for a good or service and the quantity supplied at each price

surplus at the existing price, quantity supplied exceeds the quantity demanded; also called excess supply

total surplus see social surplus

KEY CONCEPTS AND SUMMARY

3.1 Demand, Supply, and Equilibrium in Markets for Goods and Services

A demand schedule is a table that shows the quantity demanded at different prices in the market. A demand curve shows the relationship between quantity demanded and price in a given market on a graph. The law of demand states that a higher price typically leads to a lower quantity demanded.

A supply schedule is a table that shows the quantity supplied at different prices in the market. A supply curve shows the relationship between quantity supplied and price on a graph. The law of supply says that a higher price typically leads to a higher quantity supplied.

The equilibrium price and equilibrium quantity occur where the supply and demand curves cross. The equilibrium occurs where the quantity demanded is equal to the quantity supplied. If the price is below the equilibrium level, then the quantity demanded will exceed the quantity supplied. Excess demand or a shortage will exist. If the price is above the equilibrium level, then the quantity supplied will exceed the quantity demanded. Excess supply or a surplus will exist. In either case, economic pressures will push the price toward the equilibrium level.

3.2 Shifts in Demand and Supply for Goods and Services

Economists often use the *ceteris paribus* or "other things being equal" assumption: while examining the economic impact of one event, all other factors remain unchanged for the purpose of the analysis. Factors that can shift the demand curve for goods and services, causing a different quantity to be demanded at any given price, include changes in tastes, population, income, prices of substitute or complement goods, and expectations about future conditions and prices. Factors that can shift the supply curve for goods and services, causing a different quantity to be supplied at any given price, include input prices, natural conditions, changes in technology, and government taxes, regulations, or subsidies.

3.3 Changes in Equilibrium Price and Quantity: The Four-Step Process

When using the supply and demand framework to think about how an event will affect the equilibrium price and quantity, proceed through four steps: (1) sketch a supply and demand diagram to think about what the market looked like before the event; (2) decide whether the event will affect supply or demand; (3) decide whether the effect on supply or demand is negative or positive, and draw the appropriate shifted supply or demand curve; (4) compare the new equilibrium price and quantity to the original ones.

3.4 Price Ceilings and Price Floors

Price ceilings prevent a price from rising above a certain level. When a price ceiling is set below the equilibrium price, quantity demanded will exceed quantity supplied, and excess demand or shortages will result. Price floors prevent a price from falling below a certain level. When a price floor is set above the equilibrium price, quantity supplied will exceed quantity demanded, and excess supply or surpluses will result. Price floors and price ceilings often lead to unintended consequences.

3.5 Demand, Supply and Efficiency

Consumer surplus is the gap between the price that consumers are willing to pay, based on their preferences, and the market equilibrium price. Producer surplus is the gap between the price for which producers are willing to sell a product, based on their costs, and the market equilibrium price. Social surplus is the sum of consumer surplus and producer surplus. Total surplus is larger at the equilibrium quantity and price than it will be at any other quantity and price. Deadweight loss is loss in total surplus that occurs when the economy produces at an inefficient quantity.

SELF-CHECK QUESTIONS

1. Review **Figure 3.4**. Suppose the price of gasoline is $1.60 per gallon. Is the quantity demanded higher or lower than at the equilibrium price of $1.40 per gallon? And what about the quantity supplied? Is there a shortage or a surplus in the market? If so, of how much?

2. Why do economists use the *ceteris paribus* assumption?

3. In an analysis of the market for paint, an economist discovers the facts listed below. State whether each of these changes will affect supply or demand, and in what direction.
   a. There have recently been some important cost-saving inventions in the technology for making paint.
   b. Paint is lasting longer, so that property owners need not repaint as often.
   c. Because of severe hailstorms, many people need to repaint now.
   d. The hailstorms damaged several factories that make paint, forcing them to close down for several months.

4. Many changes are affecting the market for oil. Predict how each of the following events will affect the equilibrium price and quantity in the market for oil. In each case, state how the event will affect the supply and demand diagram. Create a sketch of the diagram if necessary.
   a. Cars are becoming more fuel efficient, and therefore get more miles to the gallon.
   b. The winter is exceptionally cold.
   c. A major discovery of new oil is made off the coast of Norway.
   d. The economies of some major oil-using nations, like Japan, slow down.
   e. A war in the Middle East disrupts oil-pumping schedules.
   f. Landlords install additional insulation in buildings.
   g. The price of solar energy falls dramatically.
   h. Chemical companies invent a new, popular kind of plastic made from oil.

5. Let's think about the market for air travel. From August 2014 to January 2015, the price of jet fuel decreased roughly 47%. Using the four-step analysis, how do you think this fuel price decrease affected the equilibrium price and quantity of air travel?

6. A tariff is a tax on imported goods. Suppose the U.S. government cuts the tariff on imported flat screen televisions. Using the four-step analysis, how do you think the tariff reduction will affect the equilibrium price and quantity of flat screen TVs?

7. What is the effect of a price ceiling on the quantity demanded of the product? What is the effect of a price ceiling on the quantity supplied? Why exactly does a price ceiling cause a shortage?

8. Does a price ceiling change the equilibrium price?

9. What would be the impact of imposing a price floor below the equilibrium price?

10. Does a price ceiling increase or decrease the number of transactions in a market? Why? What about a price floor?

Assuming that people obey the price ceiling, the market price will be above equilibrium, which means that Qd will be less than Qs. Firms can only sell what is demanded, so the number of transactions will fall to Qd. This is easy to see graphically. By analogous reasoning, with a price floor the market price will be below the equilibrium price, so Qd will be greater than Qs. Since the limit on transactions here is demand, the number of transactions will fall to Qd. Note that because both price floors and price ceilings reduce the number of transactions, social surplus is less.

11. If a price floor benefits producers, why does a price floor reduce social surplus?

Because the losses to consumers are greater than the benefits to producers, so the net effect is negative. Since the lost consumer surplus is greater than the additional producer surplus, social surplus falls.

REVIEW QUESTIONS

12. What determines the level of prices in a market?

13. What does a downward-sloping demand curve mean about how buyers in a market will react to a higher price?

14. Will demand curves have the same exact shape in all markets? If not, how will they differ?

15. Will supply curves have the same shape in all markets? If not, how will they differ?

16. What is the relationship between quantity demanded and quantity supplied at equilibrium? What is the relationship when there is a shortage? What is the relationship when there is a surplus?

17. How can you locate the equilibrium point on a demand and supply graph?

18. If the price is above the equilibrium level, would you predict a surplus or a shortage? If the price is below the equilibrium level, would you predict a surplus or a shortage? Why?

19. When the price is above the equilibrium, explain how market forces move the market price to equilibrium. Do the same when the price is below the equilibrium.

20. What is the difference between the demand and the quantity demanded of a product, say milk? Explain in words and show the difference on a graph with a demand curve for milk.

21. What is the difference between the supply and the quantity supplied of a product, say milk? Explain in words and show the difference on a graph with the supply curve for milk.

22. When analyzing a market, how do economists deal with the problem that many factors that affect the market are changing at the same time?

23. Name some factors that can cause a shift in the demand curve in markets for goods and services.

24. Name some factors that can cause a shift in the supply curve in markets for goods and services.

25. How does one analyze a market where both demand and supply shift?

26. What causes a movement along the demand curve? What causes a movement along the supply curve?

27. Does a price ceiling attempt to make a price higher or lower?

28. How does a price ceiling set below the equilibrium level affect quantity demanded and quantity supplied?

29. Does a price floor attempt to make a price higher or lower?

30. How does a price floor set above the equilibrium level affect quantity demanded and quantity supplied?

31. What is consumer surplus? How is it illustrated on a demand and supply diagram?

32. What is producer surplus? How is it illustrated on a demand and supply diagram?

33. What is total surplus? How is it illustrated on a demand and supply diagram?

34. What is the relationship between total surplus and economic efficiency?

35. What is deadweight loss?

CRITICAL THINKING QUESTIONS

36. Review Figure 3.4. Suppose the government decided that, since gasoline is a necessity, its price should be legally capped at $1.30 per gallon. What do you anticipate would be the outcome in the gasoline market?

37. Explain why the following statement is false: "In the goods market, no buyer would be willing to pay more than the equilibrium price."

38. Explain why the following statement is false: "In the goods market, no seller would be willing to sell for less than the equilibrium price."

39. Consider the demand for hamburgers. If the price of a substitute good (for example, hot dogs) increases and the price of a complement good (for example, hamburger buns) increases, can you tell for sure what will happen to the demand for hamburgers? Why or why not? Illustrate your answer with a graph.

40. How do you suppose the demographics of an aging population of "Baby Boomers" in the United States will affect the demand for milk? Justify your answer.

41. We know that a change in the price of a product causes a movement along the demand curve. Suppose consumers believe that prices will be rising in the future. How will that affect demand for the product in the present? Can you show this graphically?

42. Suppose there is soda tax to curb obesity. What should a reduction in the soda tax do to the supply of sodas and to the equilibrium price and quantity? Can you show this graphically? *Hint*: assume that the soda tax is collected from the sellers

43. Use the four-step process to analyze the impact of the advent of the iPod (or other portable digital music players) on the equilibrium price and quantity of the

Sony Walkman (or other portable audio cassette players).

44. Use the four-step process to analyze the impact of a reduction in tariffs on imports of iPods on the equilibrium price and quantity of Sony Walkman-type products.

45. Suppose both of these events took place at the same time. Combine your analyses of the impacts of the iPod and the tariff reduction to determine the likely impact on the equilibrium price and quantity of Sony Walkman-type products. Show your answer graphically.

46. Most government policy decisions have winners and losers. What are the effects of raising the minimum wage? It is more complex than simply producers lose and workers gain. Who are the winners and who are the losers, and what exactly do they win and lose? To what extent does the policy change achieve its goals?

47. Agricultural price supports result in governments holding large inventories of agricultural products. Why do you think the government cannot simply give the products away to poor people?

48. Can you propose a policy that would induce the market to supply more rental housing units?

49. What term would an economist use to describe what happens when a shopper gets a "good deal" on a product?

50. Explain why voluntary transactions improve social welfare.

51. Why would a free market never operate at a quantity greater than the equilibrium quantity? (*Hint:* What would be required for a transaction to occur at that quantity?)

PROBLEMS

52. Review Figure 3.4 again. Suppose the price of gasoline is $1.00. Will the quantity demanded be lower or higher than at the equilibrium price of $1.40 per gallon? Will the quantity supplied be lower or higher? Is there a shortage or a surplus in the market? If so, of how much?

53. Table 3.8 shows information on the demand and supply for bicycles, where the quantities of bicycles are measured in thousands.

Price	Qd	Qs
$120	50	36
$150	40	40
$180	32	48

Table 3.8

Price	Qd	Qs
$210	28	56
$240	24	70

Table 3.8

a. What is the quantity demanded and the quantity supplied at a price of $210?
b. At what price is the quantity supplied equal to 48,000?
c. Graph the demand and supply curve for bicycles. How can you determine the equilibrium price and quantity from the graph? How can you determine the equilibrium price and quantity from the table? What are the equilibrium price and equilibrium quantity?
d. If the price was $120, what would the quantities demanded and supplied be? Would a shortage or surplus exist? If so, how large would the shortage or surplus be?

54. The computer market in recent years has seen many more computers sell at much lower prices. What shift in demand or supply is most likely to explain this outcome? Sketch a demand and supply diagram and explain your reasoning for each.

a. A rise in demand
b. A fall in demand
c. A rise in supply
d. A fall in supply

55. Demand and supply in the market for cheddar cheese is illustrated in Table 3.9. Graph the data and find the equilibrium. Next, create a table showing the change in quantity demanded or quantity supplied, and a graph of the new equilibrium, in each of the following situations:

a. The price of milk, a key input for cheese production, rises, so that the supply decreases by 80 pounds at every price.
b. A new study says that eating cheese is good for your health, so that demand increases by 20% at every price.

Price per Pound	Qd	Qs
$3.00	750	540

Table 3.9

Price per Pound	Qd	Qs
$3.20	700	600
$3.40	**650**	**650**
$3.60	620	700
$3.80	600	720
$4.00	590	730

Table 3.9

56. Supply and demand for movie tickets in a city are shown in Table 3.10. Graph demand and supply and identify the equilibrium. Then calculate in a table and graph the effect of the following two changes.

a. Three new nightclubs open. They offer decent bands and have no cover charge, but make their money by selling food and drink. As a result, demand for movie tickets falls by six units at every price.
b. The city eliminates a tax that it had been placing on all local entertainment businesses. The result is that the quantity supplied of movies at any given price increases by 10%.

Price per Pound	Qd	Qs
$5.00	26	16
$6.00	24	18
$7.00	22	20
$8.00	21	21
$9.00	20	22

Table 3.10

57. A low-income country decides to set a price ceiling on bread so it can make sure that bread is affordable to the poor. The conditions of demand and supply are given in Table 3.11. What are the equilibrium price and equilibrium quantity before the price ceiling? What will the excess demand or the shortage (that is, quantity demanded minus quantity supplied) be if the price ceiling is set at $2.40? At $2.00? At $3.60?

Price	Qd	Qs
$1.60	9,000	5,000
$2.00	8,500	5,500
$2.40	8,000	6,400
$2.80	**7,500**	**7,500**

Table 3.11

Price	Qd	Qs
$3.20	7,000	9,000
$3.60	6,500	11,000
$4.00	6,000	15,000

Table 3.11

Download for free at https://openstax.org/details/books/principles-macroeconomics-ap-courses

4 | Labor and Financial Markets

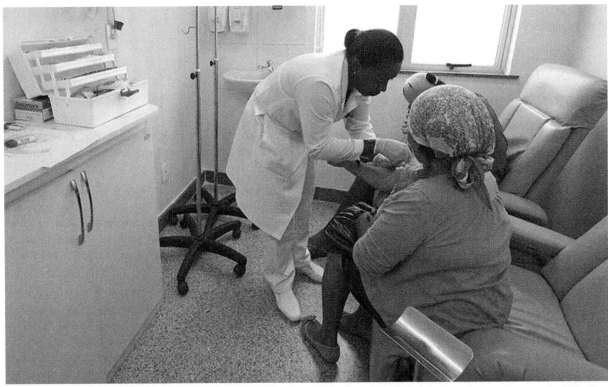

Figure 4.1 People often think of demand and supply in relation to goods, but labor markets, such as the nursing profession, can also apply to this analysis. (Credit: modification of work by "Fotos GOVBA"/Flickr Creative Commons)

Bring it Home

Baby Boomers Come of Age

The Census Bureau reports that as of 2013, 20% of the U.S. population was over 60 years old, which means that almost 63 million people are reaching an age when they will need increased medical care.

The baby boomer population, the group born between 1946 and 1964, is comprised of approximately 74 million people who have just reached retirement age. As this population grows older, they will be faced with common healthcare issues such as heart conditions, arthritis, and Alzheimer's that may require hospitalization, long-term, or at-home nursing care. Aging baby boomers and advances in life-saving and life-extending technologies will increase the demand for healthcare and nursing. Additionally, the Affordable Care Act, which expands access to healthcare for millions of Americans, will further increase the demand.

According to the Bureau of Labor Statistics, registered nursing jobs are expected to increase by 19% between 2012 and 2022. The median annual wage of $67,930 (in 2012) is also expected to increase. The BLS forecasts that 526,000 new nurses will be needed by 2022. One concern is the low rate of enrollment in nursing programs to help meet the growing demand. According to the American Association of Colleges of Nursing (AACN), enrollment in 2011 increased by only 5.1% due to a shortage of nursing educators and teaching facilities.

These data tell us, as economists, that the market for healthcare professionals, and nurses in particular, will face several challenges. Our study of supply and demand will help us to analyze in the second half of this case at chapter's end what might happen in the labor market for nursing and other healthcare professionals.

Introduction to Labor and Financial Markets

In this chapter, you will learn about:

- Demand and Supply at Work in Labor Markets

- Demand and Supply in Financial Markets

- The Market System as an Efficient Mechanism for Information

The theories of supply and demand do not apply just to markets for goods. They apply to any market, even markets for financial services like labor and financial investments. Labor markets are markets for employees or jobs. Financial services markets are markets for saving or borrowing.

When we think about demand and supply curves in goods and services markets, it is easy to picture who the demanders and suppliers are: businesses produce the products and households buy them. Who are the demanders and suppliers in labor and financial service markets? In labor markets job seekers (individuals) are the suppliers of labor, while firms and other employers who hire labor are the demanders for labor. In financial markets, any individual or firm who saves contributes to the supply of money, and any who borrows (person, firm, or government) contributes to the demand for money.

As a college student, you most likely participate in both labor and financial markets. Employment is a fact of life for most college students: In 2011, says the BLS, 52% of undergraduates worked part time and another 20% worked full time. Most college students are also heavily involved in financial markets, primarily as borrowers. Among full-time students, about half take out a loan to help finance their education each year, and those loans average about $6,000 per year. Many students also borrow for other expenses, like purchasing a car. As this chapter will illustrate, we can analyze labor markets and financial markets with the same tools we use to analyze demand and supply in the goods markets.

4.1 | Demand and Supply at Work in Labor Markets

By the end of this section, you will be able to:
- Predict shifts in the demand and supply curves of the labor market
- Explain the impact of new technology on the demand and supply curves of the labor market
- Explain price floors in the labor market such as minimum wage or a living wage

Markets for labor have demand and supply curves, just like markets for goods. The law of demand applies in labor markets this way: A higher **salary** or **wage**—that is, a higher price in the labor market—leads to a decrease in the quantity of labor demanded by employers, while a lower salary or wage leads to an increase in the quantity of labor demanded. The law of supply functions in labor markets, too: A higher price for labor leads to a higher quantity of labor supplied; a lower price leads to a lower quantity supplied.

Equilibrium in the Labor Market

In 2013, about 34,000 registered nurses worked in the Minneapolis-St. Paul-Bloomington, Minnesota-Wisconsin metropolitan area, according to the BLS. They worked for a variety of employers: hospitals, doctors' offices, schools, health clinics, and nursing homes. Figure 4.2 illustrates how demand and supply determine equilibrium in this labor market. The demand and supply schedules in Table 4.1 list the quantity supplied and quantity demanded of nurses at different salaries.

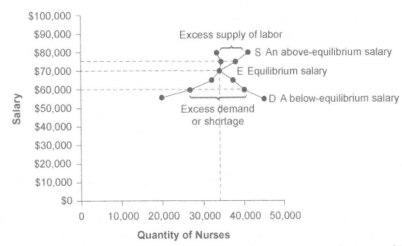

Figure 4.2 Labor Market Example: Demand and Supply for Nurses in Minneapolis-St. Paul-Bloomington The demand curve (D) of those employers who want to hire nurses intersects with the supply curve (S) of those who are qualified and willing to work as nurses at the equilibrium point (E). The equilibrium salary is $70,000 and the equilibrium quantity is 34,000 nurses. At an above-equilibrium salary of $75,000, quantity supplied increases to 38,000, but the quantity of nurses demanded at the higher pay declines to 33,000. At this above-equilibrium salary, an excess supply or surplus of nurses would exist. At a below-equilibrium salary of $60,000, quantity supplied declines to 27,000, while the quantity demanded at the lower wage increases to 40,000 nurses. At this below-equilibrium salary, excess demand or a surplus exists.

Annual Salary	Quantity Demanded	Quantity Supplied
$55,000	45,000	20,000
$60,000	40,000	27,000
$65,000	37,000	31,000
$70,000	34,000	34,000
$75,000	33,000	38,000
$80,000	32,000	41,000

Table 4.1 Demand and Supply of Nurses in Minneapolis-St. Paul-Bloomington

The horizontal axis shows the quantity of nurses hired. In this example, labor is measured by number of workers, but another common way to measure the quantity of labor is by the number of hours worked. The vertical axis shows the price for nurses' labor—that is, how much they are paid. In the real world, this "price" would be total labor compensation: salary plus benefits. It is not obvious, but benefits are a significant part (as high as 30 percent) of labor compensation. In this example, the price of labor is measured by salary on an annual basis, although in other cases the price of labor could be measured by monthly or weekly pay, or even the wage paid per hour. As the salary for nurses rises, the quantity demanded will fall. Some hospitals and nursing homes may cut back on the number of nurses they hire, or they may lay off some of their existing nurses, rather than pay them higher salaries. Employers who face higher nurses' salaries may also try to replace some nursing functions by investing in physical equipment, like computer monitoring and diagnostic systems to monitor patients, or by using lower-paid health care aides to reduce the number of nurses they need.

As the salary for nurses rises, the quantity supplied will rise. If nurses' salaries in Minneapolis-St. Paul-Bloomington are higher than in other cities, more nurses will move to Minneapolis-St. Paul-Bloomington to find jobs, more people will be willing to train as nurses, and those currently trained as nurses will be more likely to pursue nursing as a full-time job. In other words, there will be more nurses looking for jobs in the area.

At **equilibrium**, the quantity supplied and the quantity demanded are equal. Thus, every employer who wants to hire a nurse at this equilibrium wage can find a willing worker, and every nurse who wants to work at this equilibrium salary can find a job. In Figure 4.2, the supply curve (S) and demand curve (D) intersect at the equilibrium point (E). The equilibrium quantity of nurses in the Minneapolis-St. Paul-Bloomington area is 34,000, and the equilibrium salary is $70,000 per year. This example simplifies the nursing market by focusing on the "average" nurse. In reality, of course, the market for nurses is actually made up of many smaller markets, like markets for nurses with varying degrees of experience and credentials. Many markets contain closely related products that differ in quality; for instance, even a simple product like gasoline comes in regular, premium, and super-premium, each with a different price. Even in such cases, discussing the average price of gasoline, like the average salary for nurses, can still be useful because it reflects what is happening in most of the submarkets.

When the price of labor is not at the equilibrium, economic incentives tend to move salaries toward the equilibrium. For example, if salaries for nurses in Minneapolis-St. Paul-Bloomington were above the equilibrium at $75,000 per year, then 38,000 people want to work as nurses, but employers want to hire only 33,000 nurses. At that above-equilibrium salary, excess supply or a surplus results. In a situation of excess supply in the **labor market**, with many applicants for every job opening, employers will have an incentive to offer lower wages than they otherwise would have. Nurses' salary will move down toward equilibrium.

In contrast, if the salary is below the equilibrium at, say, $60,000 per year, then a situation of excess demand or a shortage arises. In this case, employers encouraged by the relatively lower wage want to hire 40,000 nurses, but only 27,000 individuals want to work as nurses at that salary in Minneapolis-St. Paul-Bloomington. In response to the shortage, some employers will offer higher pay to attract the nurses. Other employers will have to match the higher pay to keep their own employees. The higher salaries will encourage more nurses to train or work in Minneapolis-St. Paul-Bloomington. Again, price and quantity in the labor market will move toward equilibrium.

Shifts in Labor Demand

The demand curve for labor shows the quantity of labor employers wish to hire at any given salary or wage rate, under the *ceteris paribus* assumption. A change in the wage or salary will result in a change in the quantity demanded of labor. If the wage rate increases, employers will want to hire fewer employees. The quantity of labor demanded will decrease, and there will be a movement upward along the demand curve. If the wages and salaries decrease, employers are more likely to hire a greater number of workers. The quantity of labor demanded will increase, resulting in a downward movement along the demand curve.

Shifts in the demand curve for labor occur for many reasons. One key reason is that the demand for labor is based on the demand for the good or service that is being produced. For example, the more new automobiles consumers demand, the greater the number of workers automakers will need to hire. Therefore the demand for labor is called a "derived demand." Here are some examples of derived demand for labor:

- The demand for chefs is dependent on the demand for restaurant meals.

- The demand for pharmacists is dependent on the demand for prescription drugs.

- The demand for attorneys is dependent on the demand for legal services.

As the demand for the goods and services increases, the demand for labor will increase, or shift to the right, to meet employers' production requirements. As the demand for the goods and services decreases, the demand for labor will decrease, or shift to the left. Table 4.2 shows that in addition to the derived demand for labor, demand can also increase or decrease (shift) in response to several factors.

Factors	Results
Demand for Output	When the demand for the good produced (output) increases, both the output price and profitability increase. As a result, producers demand more labor to ramp up production.

Table 4.2 Factors That Can Shift Demand

Factors	Results
Education and Training	A well-trained and educated workforce causes an increase in the demand for that labor by employers. Increased levels of productivity within the workforce will cause the demand for labor to shift to the right. If the workforce is not well-trained or educated, employers will not hire from within that labor pool, since they will need to spend a significant amount of time and money training that workforce. Demand for such will shift to the left.
Technology	Technology changes can act as either substitutes for or complements to labor. When technology acts as a substitute, it replaces the need for the number of workers an employer needs to hire. For example, word processing decreased the number of typists needed in the workplace. This shifted the demand curve for typists left. An increase in the availability of certain technologies may increase the demand for labor. Technology that acts as a complement to labor will increase the demand for certain types of labor, resulting in a rightward shift of the demand curve. For example, the increased use of word processing and other software has increased the demand for information technology professionals who can resolve software and hardware issues related to a firm's network. More and better technology will increase demand for skilled workers who know how to use technology to enhance workplace productivity. Those workers who do not adapt to changes in technology will experience a decrease in demand.
Number of Companies	An increase in the number of companies producing a given product will increase the demand for labor resulting in a shift to the right. A decrease in the number of companies producing a given product will decrease the demand for labor resulting in a shift to the left.
Government Regulations	Complying with government regulations can increase or decrease the demand for labor at any given wage. In the healthcare industry, government rules may require that nurses be hired to carry out certain medical procedures. This will increase the demand for nurses. Less-trained healthcare workers would be prohibited from carrying out these procedures, and the demand for these workers will shift to the left.
Price and Availability of Other Inputs	Labor is not the only input into the production process. For example, a salesperson at a call center needs a telephone and a computer terminal to enter data and record sales. The demand for salespersons at the call center will increase if the number of telephones and computer terminals available increases. This will cause a rightward shift of the demand curve. As the amount of inputs increases, the demand for labor will increase. If the terminal or the telephones malfunction, then the demand for that labor force will decrease. As the quantity of other inputs decreases, the demand for labor will decrease. Similarly, if prices of other inputs fall, production will become more profitable and suppliers will demand more labor to increase production. The opposite is also true. Higher input prices lower demand for labor

Table 4.2 Factors That Can Shift Demand

Link It Up

Click here (http://openstaxcollege.org/l/Futurework) to read more about "Trends and Challenges for Work in the 21st Century."

Shifts in Labor Supply

The supply of labor is upward-sloping and adheres to the law of supply: The higher the price, the greater the quantity supplied and the lower the price, the less quantity supplied. The supply curve models the tradeoff between supplying labor into the market or using time in leisure activities at every given price level. The higher the wage, the more labor is willing to work and forego leisure activities. Table 4.3 lists some of the factors that will cause the supply to increase or decrease.

Factors	Results
Number of Workers	An increased number of workers will cause the supply curve to shift to the right. An increased number of workers can be due to several factors, such as immigration, increasing population, an aging population, and changing demographics. Policies that encourage immigration will increase the supply of labor, and vice versa. Population grows when birth rates exceed death rates; this eventually increases supply of labor when the former reach working age. An aging and therefore retiring population will decrease the supply of labor. Another example of changing demographics is more women working outside of the home, which increases the supply of labor.
Required Education	The more required education, the lower the supply. There is a lower supply of PhD mathematicians than of high school mathematics teachers; there is a lower supply of cardiologists than of primary care physicians; and there is a lower supply of physicians than of nurses.

Table 4.3 Factors that Can Shift Supply

Factors	Results
Government Policies	Government policies can also affect the supply of labor for jobs. On the one hand, the government may support rules that set high qualifications for certain jobs: academic training, certificates or licenses, or experience. When these qualifications are made tougher, the number of qualified workers will decrease at any given wage. On the other hand, the government may also subsidize training or even reduce the required level of qualifications. For example, government might offer subsidies for nursing schools or nursing students. Such provisions would shift the supply curve of nurses to the right. In addition, government policies that change the relative desirability of working versus not working also affect the labor supply. These include unemployment benefits, maternity leave, child care benefits and welfare policy. For example, child care benefits may increase the labor supply of working mothers. Long term unemployment benefits may discourage job searching for unemployed workers. All these policies must therefore be carefully designed to minimize any negative labor supply effects.

Table 4.3 Factors that Can Shift Supply

A change in salary will lead to a movement along labor demand or labor supply curves, but it will not shift those curves. However, other events like those outlined here will cause either the demand or the supply of labor to shift, and thus will move the labor market to a new equilibrium salary and quantity.

Technology and Wage Inequality: The Four-Step Process

Economic events can change the equilibrium salary (or wage) and quantity of labor. Consider how the wave of new information technologies, like computer and telecommunications networks, has affected low-skill and high-skill workers in the U.S. economy. From the perspective of employers who demand labor, these new technologies are often a substitute for low-skill laborers like file clerks who used to keep file cabinets full of paper records of transactions. However, the same new technologies are a complement to high-skill workers like managers, who benefit from the technological advances by being able to monitor more information, communicate more easily, and juggle a wider array of responsibilities. So, how will the new technologies affect the wages of high-skill and low-skill workers? For this question, the four-step process of analyzing how shifts in supply or demand affect a market (introduced in **Demand and Supply**) works in this way:

Step 1. What did the markets for low-skill labor and high-skill labor look like before the arrival of the new technologies? In **Figure 4.3** (a) and **Figure 4.3** (b), S_0 is the original supply curve for labor and D_0 is the original demand curve for labor in each market. In each graph, the original point of equilibrium, E_0, occurs at the price W_0 and the quantity Q_0.

(a) Technological change and low-skill labor

(b) Technological change and high-skill labor

Figure 4.3 Technology and Wages: Applying Demand and Supply (a) The demand for low-skill labor shifts to the left when technology can do the job previously done by these workers. (b) New technologies can also increase the demand for high-skill labor in fields such as information technology and network administration.

Step 2. Does the new technology affect the supply of labor from households or the demand for labor from firms? The technology change described here affects demand for labor by firms that hire workers.

Step 3. Will the new technology increase or decrease demand? Based on the description earlier, as the substitute for low-skill labor becomes available, demand for low-skill labor will shift to the left, from D_0 to D_1. As the technology complement for high-skill labor becomes cheaper, demand for high-skill labor will shift to the right, from D_0 to D_1.

Step 4. The new equilibrium for low-skill labor, shown as point E_1 with price W_1 and quantity Q_1, has a lower wage and quantity hired than the original equilibrium, E_0. The new equilibrium for high-skill labor, shown as point E_1 with price W_1 and quantity Q_1, has a higher wage and quantity hired than the original equilibrium (E_0).

So, the demand and supply model predicts that the new computer and communications technologies will raise the pay of high-skill workers but reduce the pay of low-skill workers. Indeed, from the 1970s to the mid-2000s, the wage gap widened between high-skill and low-skill labor. According to the National Center for Education Statistics, in 1980, for example, a college graduate earned about 30% more than a high school graduate with comparable job experience, but by 2012, a college graduate earned about 60% more than an otherwise comparable high school graduate. Many economists believe that the trend toward greater wage inequality across the U.S. economy was primarily caused by the new technologies.

Link It Up ⚭

Visit this website (http://openstaxcollege.org/l/oldtechjobs) to read about ten tech skills that have lost relevance in today's workforce.

Price Floors in the Labor Market: Living Wages and Minimum Wages

In contrast to goods and services markets, price ceilings are rare in labor markets, because rules that prevent people from earning income are not politically popular. There is one exception: sometimes limits are proposed on the high incomes of top business executives.

The labor market, however, presents some prominent examples of price floors, which are often used as an attempt to increase the wages of low-paid workers. The U.S. government sets a **minimum wage**, a price floor that makes it illegal for an employer to pay employees less than a certain hourly rate. In mid-2009, the U.S. minimum wage was raised to $7.25 per hour. Local political movements in a number of U.S. cities have pushed for a higher minimum wage, which they call a **living wage**. Promoters of living wage laws maintain that the minimum wage is too low to ensure a reasonable standard of living. They base this conclusion on the calculation that, if you work 40 hours a week at a minimum wage of $7.25 per hour for 50 weeks a year, your annual income is $14,500, which is less than the official U.S. government definition of what it means for a family to be in poverty. (A family with two adults earning minimum wage and two young children will find it more cost efficient for one parent to provide childcare while the other works for income. So the family income would be $14,500, which is significantly lower than the federal poverty line for a family of four, which was $23,850 in 2014.)

Supporters of the living wage argue that full-time workers should be assured a high enough wage so that they can afford the essentials of life: food, clothing, shelter, and healthcare. Since Baltimore passed the first living wage law in 1994, several dozen cities enacted similar laws in the late 1990s and the 2000s. The living wage ordinances do not apply to all employers, but they have specified that all employees of the city or employees of firms that are hired by the city be paid at least a certain wage that is usually a few dollars per hour above the U.S. minimum wage.

Figure 4.4 illustrates the situation of a city considering a living wage law. For simplicity, we assume that there is no federal minimum wage. The wage appears on the vertical axis, because the wage is the price in the labor market. Before the passage of the living wage law, the equilibrium wage is $10 per hour and the city hires 1,200 workers at this wage. However, a group of concerned citizens persuades the city council to enact a living wage law requiring employers to pay no less than $12 per hour. In response to the higher wage, 1,600 workers look for jobs with the city. At this higher wage, the city, as an employer, is willing to hire only 700 workers. At the price floor, the quantity supplied exceeds the quantity demanded, and a surplus of labor exists in this market. For workers who continue to have a job at a higher salary, life has improved. For those who were willing to work at the old wage rate but lost their jobs with the wage increase, life has not improved. Table 4.4 shows the differences in supply and demand at different wages.

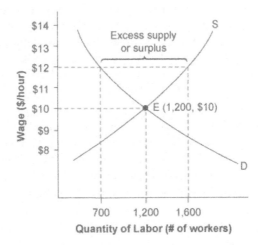

Figure 4.4 A Living Wage: Example of a Price Floor The original equilibrium in this labor market is a wage of $10/hour and a quantity of 1,200 workers, shown at point E. Imposing a wage floor at $12/hour leads to an excess supply of labor. At that wage, the quantity of labor supplied is 1,600 and the quantity of labor demanded is only 700.

Wage	Quantity Labor Demanded	Quantity Labor Supplied
$8/hr	1,900	500
$9/hr	1,500	900
$10/hr	1,200	1,200
$11/hr	900	1,400
$12/hr	700	1,600
$13/hr	500	1,800
$14/hr	400	1,900

Table 4.4 Living Wage: Example of a Price Floor

The Minimum Wage as an Example of a Price Floor

The U.S. minimum wage is a price floor that is set either very close to the equilibrium wage or even slightly below it. About 1% of American workers are actually paid the minimum wage. In other words, the vast majority of the U.S. labor force has its wages determined in the labor market, not as a result of the government price floor. But for workers with low skills and little experience, like those without a high school diploma or teenagers, the minimum wage is quite important. In many cities, the federal minimum wage is apparently below the market price for unskilled labor, because employers offer more than the minimum wage to checkout clerks and other low-skill workers without any government prodding.

Economists have attempted to estimate how much the minimum wage reduces the quantity demanded of low-skill labor. A typical result of such studies is that a 10% increase in the minimum wage would decrease the hiring of unskilled workers by 1 to 2%, which seems a relatively small reduction. In fact, some studies have even found no effect of a higher minimum wage on employment at certain times and places—although these studies are controversial.

Let's suppose that the minimum wage lies just slightly *below* the equilibrium wage level. Wages could fluctuate according to market forces above this price floor, but they would not be allowed to move beneath the floor. In this situation, the price floor minimum wage is said to be *nonbinding* —that is, the price floor is not determining the market outcome. Even if the minimum wage moves just a little higher, it will still have no effect on the quantity of employment in the economy, as long as it remains below the equilibrium wage. Even if the minimum wage is increased by enough so that it rises slightly above the equilibrium wage and becomes binding, there will be only a small excess supply gap between the quantity demanded and quantity supplied.

These insights help to explain why U.S. minimum wage laws have historically had only a small impact on employment. Since the minimum wage has typically been set close to the equilibrium wage for low-skill labor and sometimes even below it, it has not had a large effect in creating an excess supply of labor. However, if the minimum wage were increased dramatically—say, if it were doubled to match the living wages that some U.S. cities have considered—then its impact on reducing the quantity demanded of employment would be far greater. The following Clear It Up feature describes in greater detail some of the arguments for and against changes to minimum wage.

What's the harm in raising the minimum wage?

Because of the law of demand, a higher required wage will reduce the amount of low-skill employment either in terms of employees or in terms of work hours. Although there is controversy over the numbers, let's say for the sake of the argument that a 10% rise in the minimum wage will reduce the employment of low-skill workers by 2%. Does this outcome mean that raising the minimum wage by 10% is bad public policy? Not necessarily.

If 98% of those receiving the minimum wage have a pay increase of 10%, but 2% of those receiving the minimum wage lose their jobs, are the gains for society as a whole greater than the losses? The answer is not clear, because job losses, even for a small group, may cause more pain than modest income gains for others. For one thing, we need to consider which minimum wage workers are losing their jobs. If the 2% of minimum wage workers who lose their jobs are struggling to support families, that is one thing. If those who lose their job are high school students picking up spending money over summer vacation, that is something else.

Another complexity is that many minimum wage workers do not work full-time for an entire year. Imagine a minimum wage worker who holds different part-time jobs for a few months at a time, with bouts of unemployment in between. The worker in this situation receives the 10% raise in the minimum wage when working, but also ends up working 2% fewer hours during the year because the higher minimum wage reduces how much employers want people to work. Overall, this worker's income would rise because the 10% pay raise would more than offset the 2% fewer hours worked.

Of course, these arguments do not prove that raising the minimum wage is necessarily a good idea either. There may well be other, better public policy options for helping low-wage workers. (The Poverty and Economic Inequality (http://cnx.org/content/m57266/latest/) chapter discusses some possibilities.) The lesson from this maze of minimum wage arguments is that complex social problems rarely have simple answers. Even those who agree on how a proposed economic policy affects quantity demanded and quantity supplied may still disagree on whether the policy is a good idea.

4.2 | Demand and Supply in Financial Markets

By the end of this section, you will be able to:
- Identify the demanders and suppliers in a financial market.
- Explain how interest rates can affect supply and demand
- Analyze the economic effects of U.S. debt in terms of domestic financial markets
- Explain the role of price ceilings and usury laws in the U.S.

United States' households, institutions, and domestic businesses saved almost $1.9 trillion in 2013. Where did that savings go and what was it used for? Some of the savings ended up in banks, which in turn loaned the money to individuals or businesses that wanted to borrow money. Some was invested in private companies or loaned to government agencies that wanted to borrow money to raise funds for purposes like building roads or mass transit. Some firms reinvested their savings in their own businesses.

In this section, we will determine how the demand and supply model links those who wish to supply **financial capital** (i.e., savings) with those who demand financial capital (i.e., borrowing). Those who save money (or make financial investments, which is the same thing), whether individuals or businesses, are on the supply side of the financial market. Those who borrow money are on the demand side of the financial market. For a more detailed treatment of the different kinds of financial investments like bank accounts, stocks and bonds, see the Financial Markets (http://cnx.org/content/m57283/latest/) chapter.

Who Demands and Who Supplies in Financial Markets?

In any market, the price is what suppliers receive and what demanders pay. In financial markets, those who supply financial capital through saving expect to receive a rate of return, while those who demand financial capital by receiving funds expect to pay a rate of return. This rate of return can come in a variety of forms, depending on the type of investment.

The simplest example of a rate of return is the **interest rate**. For example, when you supply money into a savings account at a bank, you receive interest on your deposit. The interest paid to you as a percent of your deposits is the interest rate. Similarly, if you demand a loan to buy a car or a computer, you will need to pay interest on the money you borrow.

Let's consider the market for borrowing money with credit cards. In 2014, almost 200 million Americans were cardholders. Credit cards allow you to borrow money from the card's issuer, and pay back the borrowed amount plus interest, though most allow you a period of time in which you can repay the loan without paying interest. A typical credit card interest rate ranges from 12% to 18% per year. In 2014, Americans had about $793 billion outstanding in credit card debts. About half of U.S. families with credit cards report that they almost always pay the full balance on time, but one-quarter of U.S. families with credit cards say that they "hardly ever" pay off the card in full. In fact, in 2014, 56% of consumers carried an unpaid balance in the last 12 months. Let's say that, on average, the annual interest rate for credit card borrowing is 15% per year. So, Americans pay tens of billions of dollars every year in interest on their credit cards—plus basic fees for the credit card or fees for late payments.

Figure 4.5 illustrates demand and supply in the financial market for credit cards. The horizontal axis of the financial market shows the quantity of money that is loaned or borrowed in this market. The vertical or price axis shows the rate of return, which in the case of credit card borrowing can be measured with an interest rate. **Table 4.5** shows the quantity of financial capital that consumers demand at various interest rates and the quantity that credit card firms (often banks) are willing to supply.

Figure 4.5 Demand and Supply for Borrowing Money with Credit Cards   In this market for credit card borrowing, the demand curve (D) for borrowing financial capital intersects the supply curve (S) for lending financial capital at equilibrium €. At the equilibrium, the interest rate (the "price" in this market) is 15% and the quantity of financial capital being loaned and borrowed is $600 billion. The equilibrium price is where the quantity demanded and the quantity supplied are equal. At an above-equilibrium interest rate like 21%, the quantity of financial capital supplied would increase to $750 billion, but the quantity demanded would decrease to $480 billion. At a below-equilibrium interest rate like 13%, the quantity of financial capital demanded would increase to $700 billion, but the quantity of financial capital supplied would decrease to $510 billion.

Interest Rate (%)	Quantity of Financial Capital Demanded (Borrowing) ($ billions)	Quantity of Financial Capital Supplied (Lending) ($ billions)
11	$800	$420
13	$700	$510

Table 4.5 Demand and Supply for Borrowing Money with Credit Cards

Interest Rate (%)	Quantity of Financial Capital Demanded (Borrowing) ($ billions)	Quantity of Financial Capital Supplied (Lending) ($ billions)
15	$600	$600
17	$550	$660
19	$500	$720
21	$480	$750

Table 4.5 Demand and Supply for Borrowing Money with Credit Cards

The laws of demand and supply continue to apply in the financial markets. According to the **law of demand**, a higher rate of return (that is, a higher price) will decrease the quantity demanded. As the interest rate rises, consumers will reduce the quantity that they borrow. According to the law of supply, a higher price increases the quantity supplied. Consequently, as the interest rate paid on credit card borrowing rises, more firms will be eager to issue credit cards and to encourage customers to use them. Conversely, if the interest rate on credit cards falls, the quantity of financial capital supplied in the credit card market will decrease and the quantity demanded will fall.

Equilibrium in Financial Markets

In the financial market for credit cards shown in Figure 4.5, the supply curve (S) and the demand curve (D) cross at the equilibrium point (E). The equilibrium occurs at an interest rate of 15%, where the quantity of funds demanded and the quantity supplied are equal at an equilibrium quantity of $600 billion.

If the interest rate (remember, this measures the "price" in the financial market) is above the equilibrium level, then an excess supply, or a surplus, of financial capital will arise in this market. For example, at an interest rate of 21%, the quantity of funds supplied increases to $750 billion, while the quantity demanded decreases to $480 billion. At this above-equilibrium interest rate, firms are eager to supply loans to credit card borrowers, but relatively few people or businesses wish to borrow. As a result, some credit card firms will lower the interest rates (or other fees) they charge to attract more business. This strategy will push the interest rate down toward the equilibrium level.

If the interest rate is below the equilibrium, then excess demand or a shortage of funds occurs in this market. At an interest rate of 13%, the quantity of funds credit card borrowers demand increases to $700 billion; but the quantity credit card firms are willing to supply is only $510 billion. In this situation, credit card firms will perceive that they are overloaded with eager borrowers and conclude that they have an opportunity to raise interest rates or fees. The interest rate will face economic pressures to creep up toward the equilibrium level.

Shifts in Demand and Supply in Financial Markets

Those who supply financial capital face two broad decisions: how much to save, and how to divide up their savings among different forms of financial investments. We will discuss each of these in turn.

Participants in financial markets must decide when they prefer to consume goods: now or in the future. Economists call this **intertemporal decision making** because it involves decisions across time. Unlike a decision about what to buy from the grocery store, decisions about investment or saving are made across a period of time, sometimes a long period.

Most workers save for retirement because their income in the present is greater than their needs, while the opposite will be true once they retire. So they save today and supply financial markets. If their income increases, they save more. If their perceived situation in the future changes, they change the amount of their saving. For example, there is some evidence that Social Security, the program that workers pay into in order to qualify for government checks after retirement, has tended to reduce the quantity of financial capital that workers save. If this is true, Social Security has shifted the supply of financial capital at any interest rate to the left.

By contrast, many college students need money today when their income is low (or nonexistent) to pay their college expenses. As a result, they borrow today and demand from financial markets. Once they graduate and become employed, they will pay back the loans. Individuals borrow money to purchase homes or cars. A business seeks financial investment so that it has the funds to build a factory or invest in a research and development project that will not pay off for five years, ten years, or even more. So when consumers and businesses have greater confidence that they will be able to repay in the future, the quantity demanded of financial capital at any given interest rate will shift to the right.

For example, in the technology boom of the late 1990s, many businesses became extremely confident that investments in new technology would have a high rate of return, and their demand for financial capital shifted to the right. Conversely, during the Great Recession of 2008 and 2009, their demand for financial capital at any given interest rate shifted to the left.

To this point, we have been looking at saving in total. Now let us consider what affects saving in different types of financial investments. In deciding between different forms of financial investments, suppliers of financial capital will have to consider the rates of return and the risks involved. Rate of return is a positive attribute of investments, but risk is a negative. If Investment A becomes more risky, or the return diminishes, then savers will shift their funds to Investment B—and the supply curve of financial capital for Investment A will shift back to the left while the supply curve of capital for Investment B shifts to the right.

The United States as a Global Borrower

In the global economy, trillions of dollars of financial investment cross national borders every year. In the early 2000s, financial investors from foreign countries were investing several hundred billion dollars per year more in the U.S. economy than U.S. financial investors were investing abroad. The following Work It Out deals with one of the macroeconomic concerns for the U.S. economy in recent years.

Work It Out ⊶─○─○

The Effect of Growing U.S. Debt

Imagine that the U.S. economy became viewed as a less desirable place for foreign investors to put their money because of fears about the growth of the U.S. public debt. Using the four-step process for analyzing how changes in supply and demand affect equilibrium outcomes, how would increased U.S. public debt affect the equilibrium price and quantity for capital in U.S. financial markets?

Step 1. Draw a diagram showing demand and supply for financial capital that represents the original scenario in which foreign investors are pouring money into the U.S. economy. Figure 4.6 shows a demand curve, D, and a supply curve, S, where the supply of capital includes the funds arriving from foreign investors. The original equilibrium E_0 occurs at interest rate R_0 and quantity of financial investment Q_0.

Figure 4.6 The United States as a Global Borrower Before U.S. Debt Uncertainty   The graph shows the demand for financial capital from and supply of financial capital into the U.S. financial markets by the foreign sector before the increase in uncertainty regarding U.S. public debt. The original equilibrium (E_0) occurs at an equilibrium rate of return (R_0) and the equilibrium quantity is at Q_0.

Step 2. Will the diminished confidence in the U.S. economy as a place to invest affect demand or supply of financial capital? Yes, it will affect supply. Many foreign investors look to the U.S. financial markets to store their money in safe financial vehicles with low risk and stable returns. As the U.S. debt increases, debt servicing will increase—that is, more current income will be used to pay the interest rate on past debt. Increasing U.S. debt also means that businesses may have to pay higher interest rates to borrow money, because business is now competing with the government for financial resources.

Step 3. Will supply increase or decrease? When the enthusiasm of foreign investors' for investing their money in the U.S. economy diminishes, the supply of financial capital shifts to the left. Figure 4.7 shows the supply curve shift from S_0 to S_1.

Figure 4.7 The United States as a Global Borrower Before and After U.S. Debt Uncertainty The graph shows the demand for financial capital and supply of financial capital into the U.S. financial markets by the foreign sector before and after the increase in uncertainty regarding U.S. public debt. The original equilibrium (E_0) occurs at an equilibrium rate of return (R_0) and the equilibrium quantity is at Q_0.

Step 4. Thus, foreign investors' diminished enthusiasm leads to a new equilibrium, E_1, which occurs at the higher interest rate, R_1, and the lower quantity of financial investment, Q_1.

The economy has experienced an enormous inflow of foreign capital. According to the U.S. Bureau of Economic Analysis, by the third quarter of 2014, U.S. investors had accumulated $24.6 trillion of foreign assets, but foreign investors owned a total of $30.8 trillion of U.S. assets. If foreign investors were to pull their money out of the U.S. economy and invest elsewhere in the world, the result could be a significantly lower quantity of financial investment in the United States, available only at a higher interest rate. This reduced inflow of foreign financial investment could impose hardship on U.S. consumers and firms interested in borrowing.

In a modern, developed economy, financial capital often moves invisibly through electronic transfers between one bank account and another. Yet these flows of funds can be analyzed with the same tools of demand and supply as markets for goods or labor.

Price Ceilings in Financial Markets: Usury Laws

As we noted earlier, about 200 million Americans own credit cards, and their interest payments and fees total tens of billions of dollars each year. It is little wonder that political pressures sometimes arise for setting limits on the interest rates or fees that credit card companies charge. The firms that issue credit cards, including banks, oil companies, phone companies, and retail stores, respond that the higher interest rates are necessary to cover the losses created by those who borrow on their credit cards and who do not repay on time or at all. These companies also point out that cardholders can avoid paying interest if they pay their bills on time.

Consider the credit card market as illustrated in Figure 4.8. In this financial market, the vertical axis shows the interest rate (which is the price in the financial market). Demanders in the credit card market are households and businesses; suppliers are the companies that issue credit cards. This figure does not use specific numbers, which would be hypothetical in any case, but instead focuses on the underlying economic relationships. Imagine a law imposes a price ceiling that holds the interest rate charged on credit cards at the rate Rc, which lies below the interest rate R_0 that would otherwise have prevailed in the market. The price ceiling is shown by the horizontal dashed line in **Figure 4.8**. The demand and supply model predicts that at the lower price ceiling interest rate, the quantity demanded of credit card debt will increase from its original level of Q_0 to Qd; however, the quantity supplied of credit card debt will decrease from the original Q_0 to Qs. At the price ceiling (Rc), quantity demanded will exceed quantity supplied. Consequently, a number of people who want to have credit cards and are willing to pay the prevailing interest rate will find that companies are unwilling to issue cards to them. The result will be a credit shortage.

Figure 4.8 Credit Card Interest Rates: Another Price Ceiling Example The original intersection of demand D and supply S occurs at equilibrium E_0. However, a price ceiling is set at the interest rate Rc, below the equilibrium interest rate R_0, and so the interest rate cannot adjust upward to the equilibrium. At the price ceiling, the quantity demanded, Qd, exceeds the quantity supplied, Qs. There is excess demand, also called a shortage.

Many states do have **usury laws**, which impose an upper limit on the interest rate that lenders can charge. However, in many cases these upper limits are well above the market interest rate. For example, if the interest rate is not allowed to rise above 30% per year, it can still fluctuate below that level according to market forces. A price ceiling that is set at a relatively high level is nonbinding, and it will have no practical effect unless the equilibrium price soars high enough to exceed the price ceiling.

4.3 | The Market System as an Efficient Mechanism for Information

By the end of this section, you will be able to:
- Apply demand and supply models to analyze prices and quantities
- Explain the effects of price controls on the equilibrium of prices and quantities

Prices exist in markets for goods and services, for labor, and for financial capital. In all of these markets, prices serve as a remarkable social mechanism for collecting, combining, and transmitting information that is relevant to the market—namely, the relationship between demand and supply—and then serving as messengers to convey that information to buyers and sellers. In a market-oriented economy, no government agency or guiding intelligence oversees the set of responses and interconnections that result from a change in price. Instead, each consumer reacts according to that person's preferences and budget set, and each profit-seeking producer reacts to the impact on its expected profits. The following Clear It Up feature examines the **demand and supply models**.

Clear It Up

Why are demand and supply curves important?

The demand and supply model is the second fundamental diagram for this course. (The opportunity set model introduced in the Choice in a World of Scarcity chapter was the first.) Just as it would be foolish to try to learn the arithmetic of long division by memorizing every possible combination of numbers that can be divided by each other, it would be foolish to try to memorize every specific example of demand and supply in this chapter, this textbook, or this course. Demand and supply is not primarily a list of examples; it is a model to analyze prices and quantities. Even though demand and supply diagrams have many labels, they are fundamentally the same in their logic. Your goal should be to understand the underlying model so you can use it to analyze *any* market.

Figure 4.9 displays a generic demand and supply curve. The horizontal axis shows the different measures of quantity: a quantity of a good or service, or a quantity of labor for a given job, or a quantity of financial capital. The vertical axis shows a measure of price: the price of a good or service, the wage in the labor market, or the rate of return (like the interest rate) in the financial market.

The demand and supply model can explain the existing levels of prices, wages, and rates of return. To carry out such an analysis, think about the quantity that will be demanded at each price and the quantity that will be supplied at each price—that is, think about the shape of the demand and supply curves—and how these forces will combine to produce equilibrium.

Demand and supply can also be used to explain how economic events will cause changes in prices, wages, and rates of return. There are only four possibilities: the change in any single event may cause the demand curve to shift right or to shift left; or it may cause the supply curve to shift right or to shift left. The key to analyzing the effect of an economic event on equilibrium prices and quantities is to determine which of these four possibilities occurred. The way to do this correctly is to think back to the list of factors that shift the demand and supply curves. Note that if more than one variable is changing at the same time, the overall impact will depend on the degree of the shifts; when there are multiple variables, economists isolate each change and analyze it independently.

Figure 4.9 Demand and Supply Curves The figure displays a generic demand and supply curve. The horizontal axis shows the different measures of quantity: a quantity of a good or service, a quantity of labor for a given job, or a quantity of financial capital. The vertical axis shows a measure of price: the price of a good or service, the wage in the labor market, or the rate of return (like the interest rate) in the financial market. The demand and supply curves can be used to explain how economic events will cause changes in prices, wages, and rates of return.

An increase in the price of some product signals consumers that there is a shortage and the product should perhaps be economized on. For example, if you are thinking about taking a plane trip to Hawaii, but the ticket turns out to be expensive during the week you intend to go, you might consider other weeks when the ticket might be cheaper. The price could be high because you were planning to travel during a holiday when demand for traveling is high. Or, maybe the cost of an input like jet fuel increased or the airline has raised the price temporarily to see how many people are willing to pay it. Perhaps all of these factors are present at the same time. You do not need to analyze the market and break down the price change into its underlying factors. You just have to look at the price of a ticket and decide whether and when to fly.

In the same way, price changes provide useful information to producers. Imagine the situation of a farmer who grows oats and learns that the price of oats has risen. The higher price could be due to an increase in demand caused by a new scientific study proclaiming that eating oats is especially healthful. Or perhaps the price of a substitute grain, like corn, has risen, and people have responded by buying more oats. But the oat farmer does not need to know the details. The farmer only needs to know that the price of oats has risen and that it will be profitable to expand production as a result.

The actions of individual consumers and producers as they react to prices overlap and interlock in markets for goods, labor, and financial capital. A change in any single market is transmitted through these multiple interconnections to other markets. The vision of the role of flexible prices helping markets to reach equilibrium and linking different markets together helps to explain why price controls can be so counterproductive. Price controls are government laws that serve to regulate prices rather than allow the various markets to determine prices. There is an old proverb: "Don't kill the messenger." In ancient times, messengers carried information between distant cities and kingdoms. When they brought bad news, there was an emotional impulse to kill the messenger. But killing the messenger did not kill the bad news. Moreover, killing the messenger had an undesirable side effect: Other messengers would refuse to bring news to that city or kingdom, depriving its citizens of vital information.

Those who seek price controls are trying to kill the messenger—or at least to stifle an unwelcome message that prices are bringing about the equilibrium level of price and quantity. But price controls do nothing to affect the underlying forces of demand and supply, and this can have serious repercussions. During China's "Great Leap Forward" in the late 1950s, food prices were kept artificially low, with the result that 30 to 40 million people died of starvation because the low prices depressed farm production. Changes in demand and supply will continue to reveal themselves through consumers' and producers' behavior. Immobilizing the price messenger through price controls will deprive everyone in the economy of critical information. Without this information, it becomes difficult for everyone—buyers and sellers alike—to react in a flexible and appropriate manner as changes occur throughout the economy.

Bring it Home

Baby Boomers Come of Age

The theory of supply and demand can explain what happens in the labor markets and suggests that the demand for nurses will increase as healthcare needs of baby boomers increase, as Figure 4.10 shows. The impact of that increase will result in an average salary higher than the $67,930 earned in 2012 referenced in the first part of this case. The new equilibrium (E_1) will be at the new equilibrium price (Pe_1). Equilibrium quantity will also increase from Qe_0 to Qe_1.

Figure 4.10 Impact of Increasing Demand for Nurses 2012-2022 In 2012, the median salary for nurses was $67,930. As demand for services increases, the demand curve shifts to the right (from D_0 to D_1) and the equilibrium quantity of nurses increases from Qe_0 to Qe_1. The equilibrium salary increases from Pe_0 to Pe_1.

Suppose that as the demand for nurses increases, the supply shrinks due to an increasing number of nurses entering retirement and increases in the tuition of nursing degrees. The impact of a decreasing supply of nurses is captured by the leftward shift of the supply curve in Figure 4.11 The shifts in the two curves result in higher salaries for nurses, but the overall impact in the quantity of nurses is uncertain, as it depends on the relative shifts of supply and demand.

Figure 4.11 Impact of Decreasing Supply of Nurses between 2012 and 2022 Initially, salaries increase as demand for nursing increases to Pe_1. When demand increases, so too does the equilibrium quantity, from Qe_0 to Qe_1. The decrease in the supply of nurses due to nurses retiring from the workforce and fewer nursing graduates (*ceterus paribus*), causes a leftward shift of the supply curve resulting in even higher salaries for nurses, at Pe_2, but an uncertain outcome for the equilibrium quantity of nurses, which in this representation is less than Qe_1, but more than the initial Qe_0.

While we do not know if the number of nurses will increase or decrease relative to their initial employment, we know they will have higher salaries. The situation of the labor market for nurses described in the beginning of the chapter is different from this example, because instead of a shrinking supply, we had the supply growing at a lower rate than the growth in demand. Since both curves were shifting to the right, we would have an unequivocal increase in the quantity of nurses. And because the shift in the demand curve was larger than the one in the supply, we would expect higher wages as a result.

KEY TERMS

interest rate the "price" of borrowing in the financial market; a rate of return on an investment

minimum wage a price floor that makes it illegal for an employer to pay employees less than a certain hourly rate

usury laws laws that impose an upper limit on the interest rate that lenders can charge

KEY CONCEPTS AND SUMMARY

4.1 Demand and Supply at Work in Labor Markets

In the labor market, households are on the supply side of the market and firms are on the demand side. In the market for financial capital, households and firms can be on either side of the market: they are suppliers of financial capital when they save or make financial investments, and demanders of financial capital when they borrow or receive financial investments.

In the demand and supply analysis of labor markets, the price can be measured by the annual salary or hourly wage received. The quantity of labor can be measured in various ways, like number of workers or the number of hours worked.

Factors that can shift the demand curve for labor include: a change in the quantity demanded of the product that the labor produces; a change in the production process that uses more or less labor; and a change in government policy that affects the quantity of labor that firms wish to hire at a given wage. Demand can also increase or decrease (shift) in response to: workers' level of education and training, technology, the number of companies, and availability and price of other inputs.

The main factors that can shift the supply curve for labor are: how desirable a job appears to workers relative to the alternatives, government policy that either restricts or encourages the quantity of workers trained for the job, the number of workers in the economy, and required education.

4.2 Demand and Supply in Financial Markets

In the demand and supply analysis of financial markets, the "price" is the rate of return or the interest rate received. The quantity is measured by the money that flows from those who supply financial capital to those who demand it.

Two factors can shift the supply of financial capital to a certain investment: if people want to alter their existing levels of consumption, and if the riskiness or return on one investment changes relative to other investments. Factors that can shift demand for capital include business confidence and consumer confidence in the future—since financial investments received in the present are typically repaid in the future.

4.3 The Market System as an Efficient Mechanism for Information

The market price system provides a highly efficient mechanism for disseminating information about relative scarcities of goods, services, labor, and financial capital. Market participants do not need to know why prices have changed, only that the changes require them to revisit previous decisions they made about supply and demand. Price controls hide information about the true scarcity of products and thereby cause misallocation of resources.

SELF-CHECK QUESTIONS

1. In the labor market, what causes a movement along the demand curve? What causes a shift in the demand curve?

2. In the labor market, what causes a movement along the supply curve? What causes a shift in the supply curve?

3. Why is a living wage considered a price floor? Does imposing a living wage have the same outcome as a minimum wage?

4. In the financial market, what causes a movement along the demand curve? What causes a shift in the demand curve?

5. In the financial market, what causes a movement along the supply curve? What causes a shift in the supply curve?

6. If a usury law limits interest rates to no more than 35%, what would the likely impact be on the amount of loans made and interest rates paid?

7. Which of the following changes in the financial market will lead to a decline in interest rates:
    a. a rise in demand
    b. a fall in demand
    c. a rise in supply
    d. a fall in supply

8. Which of the following changes in the financial market will lead to an increase in the quantity of loans made and received:
    a. a rise in demand
    b. a fall in demand
    c. a rise in supply
    d. a fall in supply

9. Identify the most accurate statement. A price floor will have the largest effect if it is set:
    a. substantially above the equilibrium price
    b. slightly above the equilibrium price
    c. slightly below the equilibrium price
    d. substantially below the equilibrium price

Sketch all four of these possibilities on a demand and supply diagram to illustrate your answer.

10. A price ceiling will have the largest effect:
    a. substantially below the equilibrium price
    b. slightly below the equilibrium price
    c. substantially above the equilibrium price
    d. slightly above the equilibrium price

Sketch all four of these possibilities on a demand and supply diagram to illustrate your answer.

11. Select the correct answer. A price floor will usually shift:
    a. demand
    b. supply
    c. both
    d. neither

Illustrate your answer with a diagram.

12. Select the correct answer. A price ceiling will usually shift:
    a. demand
    b. supply
    c. both
    d. neither

REVIEW QUESTIONS

13. What is the "price" commonly called in the labor market?

14. Are households demanders or suppliers in the goods market? Are firms demanders or suppliers in the goods market? What about the labor market and the financial market?

15. Name some factors that can cause a shift in the demand curve in labor markets.

16. Name some factors that can cause a shift in the supply curve in labor markets.

17. How is equilibrium defined in financial markets?

18. What would be a sign of a shortage in financial markets?

19. Would usury laws help or hinder resolution of a shortage in financial markets?

CRITICAL THINKING QUESTIONS

21. Other than the demand for labor, what would be another example of a "derived demand?"

22. Suppose that a 5% increase in the minimum wage causes a 5% reduction in employment. How would this affect employers and how would it affect workers? In your opinion, would this be a good policy?

23. What assumption is made for a minimum wage to be a nonbinding price floor? What assumption is made for a living wage price floor to be binding?

24. Suppose the U.S. economy began to grow more rapidly than other countries in the world. What would be the likely impact on U.S. financial markets as part of the global economy?

25. If the government imposed a federal interest rate ceiling of 20% on all loans, who would gain and who would lose?

26. Why are the factors that shift the demand for a product different from the factors that shift the demand for labor? Why are the factors that shift the supply of

20. Whether the product market or the labor market, what happens to the equilibrium price and quantity for each of the four possibilities: increase in demand, decrease in demand, increase in supply, and decrease in supply.

a product different from those that shift the supply of labor?

27. During a discussion several years ago on building a pipeline to Alaska to carry natural gas, the U.S. Senate passed a bill stipulating that there should be a guaranteed minimum price for the natural gas that would be carried through the pipeline. The thinking behind the bill was that if private firms had a guaranteed price for their natural gas, they would be more willing to drill for gas and to pay to build the pipeline.
   a. Using the demand and supply framework, predict the effects of this price floor on the price, quantity demanded, and quantity supplied.
   b. With the enactment of this price floor for natural gas, what are some of the likely unintended consequences in the market?
   c. Suggest some policies other than the price floor that the government can pursue if it wishes to encourage drilling for natural gas and for a new pipeline in Alaska.

PROBLEMS

28. Identify each of the following as involving either demand or supply. Draw a circular flow diagram and label the flows A through F. (Some choices can be on both sides of the goods market.)
   a. Households in the labor market
   b. Firms in the goods market
   c. Firms in the financial market
   d. Households in the goods market
   e. Firms in the labor market
   f. Households in the financial market

29. Predict how each of the following events will raise or lower the equilibrium wage and quantity of coal miners in West Virginia. In each case, sketch a demand and supply diagram to illustrate your answer.
   a. The price of oil rises.
   b. New coal-mining equipment is invented that is cheap and requires few workers to run.

   c. Several major companies that do not mine coal open factories in West Virginia, offering a lot of well-paid jobs.
   d. Government imposes costly new regulations to make coal-mining a safer job.

30. Predict how each of the following economic changes will affect the equilibrium price and quantity in the financial market for home loans. Sketch a demand and supply diagram to support your answers.
   a. The number of people at the most common ages for home-buying increases.
   b. People gain confidence that the economy is growing and that their jobs are secure.
   c. Banks that have made home loans find that a larger number of people than they expected are not repaying those loans.
   d. Because of a threat of a war, people become uncertain about their economic future.

e. The overall level of saving in the economy diminishes.

f. The federal government changes its bank regulations in a way that makes it cheaper and easier for banks to make home loans.

31. Table 4.6 shows the amount of savings and borrowing in a market for loans to purchase homes, measured in millions of dollars, at various interest rates. What is the equilibrium interest rate and quantity in the capital financial market? How can you tell? Now, imagine that because of a shift in the perceptions of foreign investors, the supply curve shifts so that there will be $10 million less supplied at every interest rate. Calculate the new equilibrium interest rate and quantity, and explain why the direction of the interest rate shift makes intuitive sense.

Interest Rate	Qs	Qd
5%	130	170
6%	135	150
7%	140	140
8%	145	135

Table 4.6

Interest Rate	Qs	Qd
9%	150	125
10%	155	110

Table 4.6

32. Imagine that to preserve the traditional way of life in small fishing villages, a government decides to impose a price floor that will guarantee all fishermen a certain price for their catch.

a. Using the demand and supply framework, predict the effects on the price, quantity demanded, and quantity supplied.

b. With the enactment of this price floor for fish, what are some of the likely unintended consequences in the market?

c. Suggest some policies other than the price floor to make it possible for small fishing villages to continue.

33. What happens to the price and the quantity bought and sold in the cocoa market if countries producing cocoa experience a drought and a new study is released demonstrating the health benefits of cocoa? Illustrate your answer with a demand and supply graph.

5 | The Macroeconomic Perspective

Figure 5.1 The Great Depression At times, such as when many people are in need of government assistance, it is easy to tell how the economy is doing. This photograph shows people lined up during the Great Depression, waiting for relief checks. At other times, when some are doing well and others are not, it is more difficult to ascertain how the economy of a country is doing. (Credit: modification of work by the U.S. Library of Congress/Wikimedia Commons)

Bring it Home

How is the Economy Doing? How Does One Tell?

The 1990s were boom years for the U.S. economy. The late 2000s, from 2007 to 2014 were not. What causes the economy to expand or contract? Why do businesses fail when they are making all the right decisions? Why do workers lose their jobs when they are hardworking and productive? Are bad economic times a failure of the market system? Are they a failure of the government? These are all questions of macroeconomics, which we will begin to address in this chapter. We will not be able to answer all of these questions here, but we will start with the basics: How is the economy doing? How can we tell?

The macro economy includes all buying and selling, all production and consumption; everything that goes on in every market in the economy. How can we get a handle on that? The answer begins more than 80 years ago, during the Great Depression. President Franklin D. Roosevelt and his economic advisers knew things were bad—but how could they express and measure just how bad it was? An economist named Simon Kuznets, who later won the Nobel Prize for his work, came up with a way to track what the entire economy is producing. The result—gross domestic product (GDP)—remains our basic measure of macroeconomic activity. In this chapter, you will learn how GDP is constructed, how it is used, and why it is so important.

Introduction to the Macroeconomic Perspective

In this chapter, you will learn about:

- Measuring the Size of the Economy: Gross Domestic Product

- Adjusting Nominal Values to Real Values

- Tracking Real GDP over Time

- Comparing GDP among Countries

- How Well GDP Measures the Well-Being of Society

Macroeconomics focuses on the economy as a whole (or on whole economies as they interact). What causes recessions? What makes unemployment stay high when recessions are supposed to be over? Why do some countries grow faster than others? Why do some countries have higher standards of living than others? These are all questions that macroeconomics addresses. Macroeconomics involves adding up the economic activity of all households and all businesses in all markets to get the overall demand and supply in the economy. However, when we do that, something curious happens. It is not unusual that what results at the macro level is different from the sum of the microeconomic parts. Indeed, what seems sensible from a microeconomic point of view can have unexpected or counterproductive results at the macroeconomic level. Imagine that you are sitting at an event with a large audience, like a live concert or a basketball game. A few people decide that they want a better view, and so they stand up. However, when these people stand up, they block the view for other people, and the others need to stand up as well if they wish to see. Eventually, nearly everyone is standing up, and as a result, no one can see much better than before. The rational decision of some individuals at the micro level—to stand up for a better view—ended up being self-defeating at the macro level. This is not macroeconomics, but it is an apt analogy.

Macroeconomics is a rather massive subject. How are we going to tackle it? **Figure 5.2** illustrates the structure we will use. We will study macroeconomics from three different perspectives:

1. What are the macroeconomic goals? (Macroeconomics as a discipline does not have goals, but we do have goals for the macro economy.)

2. What are the frameworks economists can use to analyze the macroeconomy?

3. Finally, what are the policy tools governments can use to manage the macroeconomy?

Figure 5.2 Macroeconomic Goals, Framework, and Policies   This chart shows what macroeconomics is about. The box on the left indicates a consensus of what are the most important goals for the macro economy, the middle box lists the frameworks economists use to analyze macroeconomic changes (such as inflation or recession), and the box on the right indicates the two tools the federal government uses to influence the macro economy.

Goals

In thinking about the overall health of the macroeconomy, it is useful to consider three primary goals: economic growth, low unemployment, and low inflation.

- Economic growth ultimately determines the prevailing standard of living in a country. Economic growth is measured by the percentage change in real (inflation-adjusted) gross domestic product. A growth rate of more than 3% is considered good.

- Unemployment, as measured by the unemployment rate, is the percentage of people in the labor force who do not have a job. When people lack jobs, the economy is wasting a precious resource-labor, and the result is lower goods and services produced. Unemployment, however, is more than a statistic—it represents people's livelihoods. While measured unemployment is unlikely to ever be zero, a measured unemployment rate of 5% or less is considered low (good).

- Inflation is a sustained increase in the overall level of prices, and is measured by the consumer price index. If many people face a situation where the prices that they pay for food, shelter, and healthcare are rising much faster than the wages they receive for their labor, there will be widespread unhappiness as their standard of living declines. For that reason, low inflation—an inflation rate of 1–2%—is a major goal.

Frameworks

As you learn in the micro part of this book, principal tools used by economists are theories and models (see **Welcome to Economics!** for more on this). In microeconomics, we used the theories of supply and demand; in macroeconomics, we use the theories of aggregate demand (AD) and aggregate supply (AS). This book presents two perspectives on macroeconomics: the Neoclassical perspective and the Keynesian perspective, each of which has its own version of AD and AS. Between the two perspectives, you will obtain a good understanding of what drives the macroeconomy.

Policy Tools

National governments have two tools for influencing the macroeconomy. The first is monetary policy, which involves managing the money supply and interest rates. The second is fiscal policy, which involves changes in government spending/purchases and taxes.

Each of the items in **Figure 5.2** will be explained in detail in one or more other chapters. As you learn these things, you will discover that the goals and the policy tools are in the news almost every day.

5.1 | Measuring the Size of the Economy: Gross Domestic Product

By the end of this section, you will be able to:

- Identify the components of GDP on the demand side and on the supply side
- Evaluate how gross domestic product (GDP) is measured
- Contrast and calculate GDP, net exports, and net national product

Macroeconomics is an empirical subject, so the first step toward understanding it is to measure the economy.

How large is the U.S. economy? The size of a nation's overall economy is typically measured by its **gross domestic product (GDP)**, which is the value of all final goods and services produced within a country in a given year. The measurement of GDP involves counting up the production of millions of different goods and services—smart phones, cars, music downloads, computers, steel, bananas, college educations, and all other new goods and services produced in the current year—and summing them into a total dollar value. This task is straightforward: take the quantity of everything produced, multiply it by the price at which each product sold, and add up the total. In 2014, the U.S. GDP totaled $17.4 trillion, the largest GDP in the world.

Each of the market transactions that enter into GDP must involve both a buyer and a seller. The GDP of an economy can be measured either by the total dollar value of what is purchased in the economy, or by the total dollar value of what is produced. There is even a third way, as we will explain later.

GDP Measured by Components of Demand

Who buys all of this production? This demand can be divided into four main parts: consumer spending (consumption), business spending (investment), government spending on goods and services, and spending on net exports. (See the following Clear It Up feature to understand what is meant by investment.) **Table 5.1** shows how these four components added up to the GDP in 2014. **Figure 5.4** (a) shows the levels of consumption, investment, and government purchases over time, expressed as a percentage of GDP, while **Figure 5.4** (b) shows the levels of exports and imports as a percentage of GDP over time. A few patterns about each of these components are worth noticing. **Table 5.1** shows the components of GDP from the demand side. **Figure 5.3** provides a visual of the percentages.

	Components of GDP on the Demand Side (in trillions of dollars)	Percentage of Total
Consumption	$11.9	68.4%
Investment	$2.9	16.7%
Government	$3.2	18.4%
Exports	$2.3	13.2%
Imports	−$2.9	−16.7%
Total GDP	**$17.4**	**100%**

Table 5.1 Components of U.S. GDP in 2014: From the Demand Side   (Source: http://bea.gov/iTable/index_nipa.cfm)

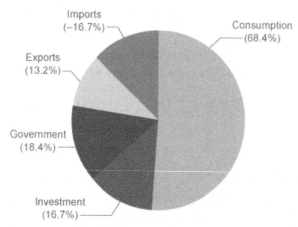

Figure 5.3 Percentage of Components of U.S. GDP on the Demand Side   Consumption makes up over half of the demand side components of the GDP. (Source: http://bea.gov/iTable/index_nipa.cfm)

What is meant by the word "investment"?

What do economists mean by investment, or business spending? In calculating GDP, investment does not refer to the purchase of stocks and bonds or the trading of financial assets. It refers to the purchase of new capital goods, that is, new commercial real estate (such as buildings, factories, and stores) and equipment, residential housing construction, and inventories. Inventories that are produced this year are included in this year's GDP—even if they have not yet sold. From the accountant's perspective, it is as if the firm invested in its own inventories. Business investment in 2014 was almost $3 trillion, according to the Bureau of Economic Analysis.

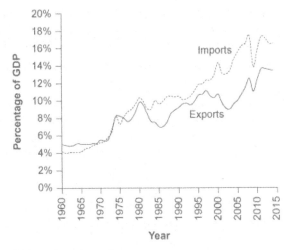

(a) Demand from consumption, investment, and government   (b) Imports and exports

Figure 5.4 Components of GDP on the Demand Side (a) Consumption is about two-thirds of GDP, but it moves relatively little over time. Business investment hovers around 15% of GDP, but it increases and declines more than consumption. Government spending on goods and services is around 20% of GDP. (b) Exports are added to total demand for goods and services, while imports are subtracted from total demand. If exports exceed imports, as in most of the 1960s and 1970s in the U.S. economy, a trade surplus exists. If imports exceed exports, as in recent years, then a trade deficit exists. (Source: http://bea.gov/iTable/index_nipa.cfm)

Consumption expenditure by households is the largest component of GDP, accounting for about two-thirds of the GDP in any year. This tells us that consumers' spending decisions are a major driver of the economy. However, consumer spending is a gentle elephant: when viewed over time, it does not jump around too much.

Investment expenditure refers to purchases of physical plant and equipment, primarily by businesses. If Starbucks builds a new store, or Amazon buys robots, these expenditures are counted under business investment. Investment demand is far smaller than consumption demand, typically accounting for only about 15–18% of GDP, but it is very important for the economy because this is where jobs are created. However, it fluctuates more noticeably than consumption. Business investment is volatile; new technology or a new product can spur business investment, but then confidence can drop and business investment can pull back sharply.

If you have noticed any of the infrastructure projects (new bridges, highways, airports) launched during the recession of 2009, you have seen how important government spending can be for the economy. Government expenditure in the United States is about 20% of GDP, and includes spending by all three levels of government: federal, state, and local. The only part of government spending counted in demand is government purchases of goods or services produced in the economy. Examples include the government buying a new fighter jet for the Air Force (federal government spending), building a new highway (state government spending), or a new school (local government spending). A significant portion of government budgets are transfer payments, like unemployment benefits, veteran's benefits, and Social Security payments to retirees. These payments are excluded from GDP because the government does not receive a new good or service in return or exchange. Instead they are transfers of income from taxpayers to others. If you are curious about the awesome undertaking of adding up GDP, read the following Clear It Up feature.

How do statisticians measure GDP?

Government economists at the Bureau of Economic Analysis (BEA), within the U.S. Department of Commerce, piece together estimates of GDP from a variety of sources.

Once every five years, in the second and seventh year of each decade, the Bureau of the Census carries out a detailed census of businesses throughout the United States. In between, the Census Bureau carries out a monthly survey of retail sales. These figures are adjusted with foreign trade data to account for exports that are produced in the United States and sold abroad and for imports that are produced abroad and sold here. Once every ten years, the Census Bureau conducts a comprehensive survey of housing and residential finance. Together, these sources provide the main basis for figuring out what is produced for consumers.

For investment, the Census Bureau carries out a monthly survey of construction and an annual survey of expenditures on physical capital equipment.

For what is purchased by the federal government, the statisticians rely on the U.S. Department of the Treasury. An annual Census of Governments gathers information on state and local governments. Because a lot of government spending at all levels involves hiring people to provide services, a large portion of government spending is also tracked through payroll records collected by state governments and by the Social Security Administration.

With regard to foreign trade, the Census Bureau compiles a monthly record of all import and export documents. Additional surveys cover transportation and travel, and adjustment is made for financial services that are produced in the United States for foreign customers.

Many other sources contribute to the estimates of GDP. Information on energy comes from the U.S. Department of Transportation and Department of Energy. Information on healthcare is collected by the Agency for Health Care Research and Quality. Surveys of landlords find out about rental income. The Department of Agriculture collects statistics on farming.

All of these bits and pieces of information arrive in different forms, at different time intervals. The BEA melds them together to produce estimates of GDP on a quarterly basis (every three months). These numbers are then "annualized" by multiplying by four. As more information comes in, these estimates are updated and revised. The "advance" estimate of GDP for a certain quarter is released one month after a quarter. The "preliminary" estimate comes out one month after that. The "final" estimate is published one month later, but it is not actually final. In July, roughly updated estimates for the previous calendar year are released. Then, once every five years, after the results of the latest detailed five-year business census have been processed, the BEA revises all of the past estimates of GDP according to the newest methods and data, going all the way back to 1929.

Link It Up ⌬

Visit this website (http://openstaxcollege.org/l/beafaq) to read FAQs on the BEA site. You can even email your own questions!

When thinking about the demand for domestically produced goods in a global economy, it is important to count spending on exports—domestically produced goods that are sold abroad. By the same token, we must also subtract spending on imports—goods produced in other countries that are purchased by residents of this country. The net export component of GDP is equal to the dollar value of exports (X) minus the dollar value of imports (M), (X – M). The gap between exports and imports is called the **trade balance**. If a country's exports are larger than its imports, then a country is said to have a **trade surplus**. In the United States, exports typically exceeded imports in the 1960s and 1970s, as shown in **Figure 5.4** (b).

Since the early 1980s, imports have typically exceeded exports, and so the United States has experienced a **trade deficit** in most years. Indeed, the trade deficit grew quite large in the late 1990s and in the mid-2000s. **Figure 5.4** (b) also shows that imports and exports have both risen substantially in recent decades, even after the declines during the

Great Recession between 2008 and 2009. As noted before, if exports and imports are equal, foreign trade has no effect on total GDP. However, even if exports and imports are balanced overall, foreign trade might still have powerful effects on particular industries and workers by causing nations to shift workers and physical capital investment toward one industry rather than another.

Based on these four components of demand, GDP can be measured as:

$$GDP = \text{Consumption} + \text{Investment} + \text{Government} + \text{Trade balance}$$
$$GDP = C + I + G + (X - M)$$

Understanding how to measure GDP is important for analyzing connections in the macro economy and for thinking about macroeconomic policy tools.

GDP Measured by What is Produced

Everything that is purchased must be produced first. Table 5.2 breaks down what is produced into five categories: **durable goods**, **nondurable goods**, **services**, **structures**, and the change in **inventories**. Before going into detail about these categories, notice that total GDP measured according to what is produced is exactly the same as the GDP measured by looking at the five components of demand. Figure 5.5 provides a visual representation of this information.

	Components of GDP on the Supply Side (in trillions of dollars)	Percentage of Total
Goods		
Durable goods	$2.9	16.7%
Nondurable goods	$2.3	13.2%
Services	$10.8	62.1%
Structures	$1.3	7.4%
Change in inventories	$0.1	0.6%
Total GDP	**$17.4**	**100%**

Table 5.2 Components of U.S. GDP on the Production Side, 2014   (Source: http://bea.gov/iTable/index_nipa.cfm)

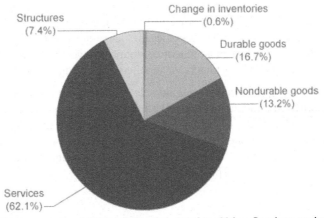

Figure 5.5 Percentage of Components of GDP on the Production Side   Services make up over half of the production side components of GDP in the United States.

Since every market transaction must have both a buyer and a seller, GDP must be the same whether measured by what is demanded or by what is produced. **Figure 5.6** shows these components of what is produced, expressed as a percentage of GDP, since 1960.

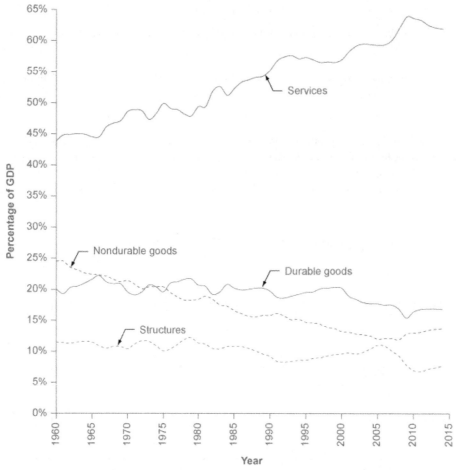

Figure 5.6 Types of Production   Services are the largest single component of total supply, representing over half of GDP. Nondurable goods used to be larger than durable goods, but in recent years, nondurable goods have been dropping closer to durable goods, which is about 20% of GDP. Structures hover around 10% of GDP. The change in inventories, the final component of aggregate supply, is not shown here; it is typically less than 1% of GDP.

In thinking about what is produced in the economy, many non-economists immediately focus on solid, long-lasting goods, like cars and computers. By far the largest part of GDP, however, is services. Moreover, services have been a growing share of GDP over time. A detailed breakdown of the leading service industries would include healthcare, education, and legal and financial services. It has been decades since most of the U.S. economy involved making solid objects. Instead, the most common jobs in a modern economy involve a worker looking at pieces of paper or a computer screen; meeting with co-workers, customers, or suppliers; or making phone calls.

Even within the overall category of goods, long-lasting durable goods like cars and refrigerators are about the same share of the economy as short-lived nondurable goods like food and clothing. The category of structures includes everything from homes, to office buildings, shopping malls, and factories. Inventories is a small category that refers to the goods that have been produced by one business but have not yet been sold to consumers, and are still sitting in warehouses and on shelves. The amount of inventories sitting on shelves tends to decline if business is better than expected, or to rise if business is worse than expected.

The Problem of Double Counting

GDP is defined as the current value of all final goods and services produced in a nation in a year. What are final goods? They are goods at the furthest stage of production at the end of a year. Statisticians who calculate GDP must avoid the mistake of **double counting**, in which output is counted more than once as it travels through the stages of production. For example, imagine what would happen if government statisticians first counted the value of tires produced by a tire manufacturer, and then counted the value of a new truck sold by an automaker that contains those tires. In this example, the value of the tires would have been counted twice-because the price of the truck includes the value of the tires.

To avoid this problem, which would overstate the size of the economy considerably, government statisticians count just the value of **final goods and services** in the chain of production that are sold for consumption, investment, government, and trade purposes. **Intermediate goods**, which are goods that go into the production of other goods, are excluded from GDP calculations. From the example above, only the value of the Ford truck will be counted. The value of what businesses provide to other businesses is captured in the final products at the end of the production chain.

The concept of GDP is fairly straightforward: it is just the dollar value of all final goods and services produced in the economy in a year. In our decentralized, market-oriented economy, actually calculating the more than $16 trillion-dollar U.S. GDP—along with how it is changing every few months—is a full-time job for a brigade of government statisticians.

What is Counted in GDP	What is not included in GDP
Consumption	Intermediate goods
Business investment	Transfer payments and non-market activities
Government spending on goods and services	Used goods
Net exports	Illegal goods

Table 5.3 Counting GDP

Notice the items that are not counted into GDP, as outlined in Table 5.3. The sales of used goods are not included because they were produced in a previous year and are part of that year's GDP. The entire underground economy of services paid "under the table" and illegal sales should be counted, but is not, because it is impossible to track these sales. In a recent study by Friedrich Schneider of shadow economies, the underground economy in the United States was estimated to be 6.6% of GDP, or close to $2 trillion dollars in 2013 alone. Transfer payments, such as payment by the government to individuals, are not included, because they do not represent production. Also, production of some goods—such as home production as when you make your breakfast—is not counted because these goods are not sold in the marketplace.

Link It Up

Visit this website (http://openstaxcollege.org/l/undergroundecon) to read about the "New Underground Economy."

Other Ways to Measure the Economy

Besides GDP, there are several different but closely related ways of measuring the size of the economy. We mentioned above that GDP can be thought of as total production and as total purchases. It can also be thought of as total income since anything produced and sold produces income.

One of the closest cousins of GDP is the **gross national product (GNP)**. GDP includes only what is produced within a country's borders. GNP adds what is produced by domestic businesses and labor abroad, and subtracts out any payments sent home to other countries by foreign labor and businesses located in the United States. In other words, GNP is based more on the production of citizens and firms of a country, wherever they are located, and GDP is based on what happens within the geographic boundaries of a certain country. For the United States, the gap between GDP and GNP is relatively small; in recent years, only about 0.2%. For small nations, which may have a substantial share of their population working abroad and sending money back home, the difference can be substantial.

Net national product (NNP) is calculated by taking GNP and then subtracting the value of how much physical capital is worn out, or reduced in value because of aging, over the course of a year. The process by which capital ages and loses value is called **depreciation**. The NNP can be further subdivided into **national income**, which includes all income to businesses and individuals, and personal income, which includes only income to people.

For practical purposes, it is not vital to memorize these definitions. However, it is important to be aware that these differences exist and to know what statistic you are looking at, so that you do not accidentally compare, say, GDP in one year or for one country with GNP or NNP in another year or another country. To get an idea of how these calculations work, follow the steps in the following Work It Out feature.

Work It Out —◯—◯—◯

Calculating GDP, Net Exports, and NNP

Based on the information in Table 5.4:

   a. What is the value of GDP?

   b. What is the value of net exports?

   c. What is the value of NNP?

Government purchases	$120 billion
Depreciation	$40 billion
Consumption	$400 billion
Business Investment	$60 billion
Exports	$100 billion
Imports	$120 billion
Income receipts from rest of the world	$10 billion
Income payments to rest of the world	$8 billion

Table 5.4

Step 1. To calculate GDP use the following formula:

$$
\begin{aligned}
\text{GDP} &= \text{Consumption} + \text{Investment} + \text{Government spending} + (\text{Exports} - \text{Imports}) \\
&= \text{C} + \text{I} + \text{G} + (\text{X} - \text{M}) \\
&= \$400 + \$60 + \$120 + (\$100 - \$120) \\
&= \$560 \text{ billion}
\end{aligned}
$$

Step 2. To calculate net exports, subtract imports from exports.

$$\text{Net exports} = X - M$$
$$= \$100 - \$120$$
$$= -\$20 \text{ billion}$$

Step 3. To calculate NNP, use the following formula:

$$\text{NNP} = \text{GDP} + \text{Income receipts from the rest of the world}$$
$$- \text{Income payments to the rest of the world} - \text{Depreciation}$$
$$= \$560 + \$10 - \$8 - \$40$$
$$= \$522 \text{ billion}$$

5.2 | Adjusting Nominal Values to Real Values

By the end of this section, you will be able to:
- Contrast nominal GDP and real GDP
- Explain GDP deflator
- Calculate real GDP based on nominal GDP values

When examining economic statistics, there is a crucial distinction worth emphasizing. The distinction is between nominal and real measurements, which refer to whether or not inflation has distorted a given statistic. Looking at economic statistics without considering inflation is like looking through a pair of binoculars and trying to guess how close something is: unless you know how strong the lenses are, you cannot guess the distance very accurately. Similarly, if you do not know the rate of inflation, it is difficult to figure out if a rise in GDP is due mainly to a rise in the overall level of prices or to a rise in quantities of goods produced. The **nominal value** of any economic statistic means the statistic is measured in terms of actual prices that exist at the time. The **real value** refers to the same statistic after it has been adjusted for inflation. Generally, it is the real value that is more important.

Converting Nominal to Real GDP

Table 5.5 shows U.S. GDP at five-year intervals since 1960 in nominal dollars; that is, GDP measured using the actual market prices prevailing in each stated year. This data is also reflected in the graph shown in Figure 5.7

Year	Nominal GDP (billions of dollars)	GDP Deflator (2005 = 100)
1960	543.3	19.0
1965	743.7	20.3
1970	1,075.9	24.8
1975	1,688.9	34.1
1980	2,862.5	48.3
1985	4,346.7	62.3
1990	5,979.6	72.7
1995	7,664.0	81.7
2000	10,289.7	89.0

Table 5.5 U.S. Nominal GDP and the GDP Deflator (Source: www.bea.gov)

Year	Nominal GDP (billions of dollars)	GDP Deflator (2005 = 100)
2005	13,095.4	100.0
2010	14,958.3	110.0

Table 5.5 U.S. Nominal GDP and the GDP Deflator   (Source: www.bea.gov)

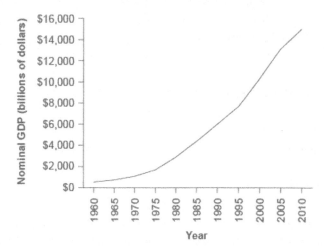

Figure 5.7 U.S. Nominal GDP, 1960–2010   Nominal GDP values have risen exponentially from 1960 through 2010, according to the BEA.

If an unwary analyst compared nominal GDP in 1960 to nominal GDP in 2010, it might appear that national output had risen by a factor of twenty-seven over this time (that is, GDP of $14,958 billion in 2010 divided by GDP of $543 billion in 1960). This conclusion would be highly misleading. Recall that nominal GDP is defined as the quantity of every good or service produced multiplied by the price at which it was sold, summed up for all goods and services. In order to see how much production has actually increased, we need to extract the effects of higher prices on nominal GDP. This can be easily done, using the GDP deflator.

GDP deflator is a price index measuring the average prices of all goods and services included in the economy. We explore price indices in detail and how they are computed in Inflation, but this definition will do in the context of this chapter. The data for the GDP deflator are given in Table 5.5 and shown graphically in Figure 5.8.

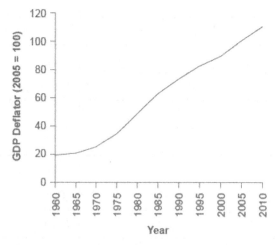

Figure 5.8 U.S. GDP Deflator, 1960–2010   Much like nominal GDP, the GDP deflator has risen exponentially from 1960 through 2010. (Source: BEA)

Figure 5.8 shows that the price level has risen dramatically since 1960. The price level in 2010 was almost six times higher than in 1960 (the deflator for 2010 was 110 versus a level of 19 in 1960). Clearly, much of the apparent growth in nominal GDP was due to inflation, not an actual change in the quantity of goods and services produced, in other words, not in real GDP. Recall that nominal GDP can rise for two reasons: an increase in output, and/or an increase in prices. What is needed is to extract the increase in prices from nominal GDP so as to measure only changes in output. After all, the dollars used to measure nominal GDP in 1960 are worth more than the inflated dollars of 1990—and the price index tells exactly how much more. This adjustment is easy to do if you understand that nominal measurements are in value terms, where

$$\text{Value} = \text{Price} \times \text{Quantity}$$
$$\text{or}$$
$$\text{Nominal GDP} = \text{GDP Deflator} \times \text{Real GDP}$$

Let's look at an example at the micro level. Suppose the t-shirt company, Coolshirts, sells 10 t-shirts at a price of $9 each.

$$
\begin{aligned}
\text{Coolshirt's nominal revenue from sales} &= \text{Price} \times \text{Quantity} \\
&= \$9 \times 10 \\
&= \$90
\end{aligned}
$$

Then,

$$
\begin{aligned}
\text{Coolshirt's real income} &= \frac{\text{Nominal revenue}}{\text{Price}} \\
&= \frac{\$90}{\$9} \\
&= 10
\end{aligned}
$$

In other words, when we compute "real" measurements we are trying to get at actual quantities, in this case, 10 t-shirts.

With GDP, it is just a tiny bit more complicated. We start with the same formula as above:

$$\text{Real GDP} = \frac{\text{Nominal GDP}}{\text{Price Index}}$$

For reasons that will be explained in more detail below, mathematically, a price index is a two-digit decimal number like 1.00 or 0.85 or 1.25. Because some people have trouble working with decimals, when the price index is published, it has traditionally been multiplied by 100 to get integer numbers like 100, 85, or 125. What this means is that when we "deflate" nominal figures to get real figures (by dividing the nominal by the price index). We also need to remember to divide the published price index by 100 to make the math work. So the formula becomes:

$$\text{Real GDP} = \frac{\text{Nominal GDP}}{\text{Price Index} / 100}$$

Now read the following Work It Out feature for more practice calculating real GDP.

Work It Out

Computing GDP

It is possible to use the data in Table 5.5 to compute real GDP.

Step 1. Look at Table 5.5, to see that, in 1960, nominal GDP was $543.3 billion and the price index (GDP deflator) was 19.0.

Step 2. To calculate the real GDP in 1960, use the formula:

$$\text{Real GDP} = \frac{\text{Nominal GDP}}{\text{Price Index} / 100}$$
$$= \frac{\$543.3 \text{ billion}}{19 / 100}$$
$$= \$2,859.5 \text{ billion}$$

We'll do this in two parts to make it clear. First adjust the price index: 19 divided by 100 = 0.19. Then divide into nominal GDP: $543.3 billion / 0.19 = $2,859.5 billion.

Step 3. Use the same formula to calculate the real GDP in 1965.

$$\text{Real GDP} = \frac{\text{Nominal GDP}}{\text{Price Index} / 100}$$
$$= \frac{\$743.7 \text{ billion}}{20.3 / 100}$$
$$= \$3,663.5 \text{ billion}$$

Step 4. Continue using this formula to calculate all of the real GDP values from 1960 through 2010. The calculations and the results are shown in Table 5.6.

Year	Nominal GDP (billions of dollars)	GDP Deflator (2005 = 100)	Calculations	Real GDP (billions of 2005 dollars)
1960	543.3	19.0	543.3 / (19.0/100)	2859.5
1965	743.7	20.3	743.7 / (20.3/100)	3663.5
1970	1075.9	24.8	1,075.9 / (24.8/100)	4338.3
1975	1688.9	34.1	1,688.9 / (34.1/100)	4952.8
1980	2862.5	48.3	2,862.5 / (48.3/100)	5926.5
1985	4346.7	62.3	4,346.7 / (62.3/100)	6977.0
1990	5979.6	72.7	5,979.6 / (72.7/100)	8225.0
1995	7664.0	82.0	7,664 / (82.0/100)	9346.3
2000	10289.7	89.0	10,289.7 / (89.0/100)	11561.5
2005	13095.4	100.0	13,095.4 / (100.0/100)	13095.4
2010	14958.3	110.0	14,958.3 / (110.0/100)	13598.5

There are a couple things to notice here. Whenever you compute a real statistic, one year (or period) plays a special role. It is called the base year (or base period). The base year is the year whose prices are used to compute the real statistic. When we calculate real GDP, for example, we take the quantities of goods and services produced in each year (for example, 1960 or 1973) and multiply them by their prices in the base year (in this case, 2005), so we get a measure of GDP that uses prices that do not change from year to year. That is why real GDP is labeled "Constant Dollars" or "2005 Dollars," which means that real GDP is constructed using prices that existed in 2005. The formula used is:

$$\text{GDP deflator} \ = \ \frac{\text{Nominal GDP}}{\text{Real GDP}} \times 100$$

Rearranging the formula and using the data from 2005:

$$
\begin{aligned}
\text{Real GDP} \ &= \ \frac{\text{Nominal GDP}}{\text{Price Index} / 100} \\
&= \ \frac{\$13{,}095.4 \text{ billion}}{100 / 100} \\
&= \ \$13{,}095.4 \text{ billion}
\end{aligned}
$$

Comparing real GDP and nominal GDP for 2005, you see they are the same. This is no accident. It is because 2005 has been chosen as the "base year" in this example. Since the price index in the base year always has a value of 100 (by definition), nominal and real GDP are always the same in the base year.

Look at the data for 2010.

$$
\begin{aligned}
\text{Real GDP} \ &= \ \frac{\text{Nominal GDP}}{\text{Price Index} / 100} \\
&= \ \frac{\$14{,}958.3 \text{ billion}}{110 / 100} \\
&= \ \$13{,}598.5 \text{ billion}
\end{aligned}
$$

Use this data to make another observation: As long as inflation is positive, meaning prices increase on average from year to year, real GDP should be less than nominal GDP in any year after the base year. The reason for this should be clear: The value of nominal GDP is "inflated" by inflation. Similarly, as long as inflation is positive, real GDP should be greater than nominal GDP in any year before the base year.

Figure 5.9 shows the U.S. nominal and real GDP since 1960. Because 2005 is the base year, the nominal and real values are exactly the same in that year. However, over time, the rise in nominal GDP looks much larger than the rise in real GDP (that is, the nominal GDP line rises more steeply than the real GDP line), because the rise in nominal GDP is exaggerated by the presence of inflation, especially in the 1970s.

Figure 5.9 U.S. Nominal and Real GDP, 1960–2012 The red line measures U.S. GDP in nominal dollars. The black line measures U.S. GDP in real dollars, where all dollar values have been converted to 2005 dollars. Since real GDP is expressed in 2005 dollars, the two lines cross in 2005. However, real GDP will appear higher than nominal GDP in the years before 2005, because dollars were worth less in 2005 than in previous years. Conversely, real GDP will appear lower in the years after 2005, because dollars were worth more in 2005 than in later years.

Let's return to the question posed originally: How much did GDP increase in real terms? What was the rate of growth of real GDP from 1960 to 2010? To find the real growth rate, we apply the formula for percentage change:

$$\frac{2010 \text{ real GDP} - 1960 \text{ real GDP}}{1960 \text{ real GDP}} \times 100 \;=\; \% \text{ change}$$

$$\frac{13{,}598.5 - 2{,}859.5}{2{,}859.5} \times 100 \;=\; 376\%$$

In other words, the U.S. economy has increased real production of goods and services by nearly a factor of four since 1960. Of course, that understates the material improvement since it fails to capture improvements in the quality of products and the invention of new products.

There is a quicker way to answer this question approximately, using another math trick. Because:

$$\begin{aligned} \text{Real GDP} \;&=\; \text{Price} \times \text{Quantity} \\ \% \text{ change in real GDP} \;&=\; \% \text{ change in price} + \% \text{ change in quantity} \\ &\quad \text{OR} \\ \% \text{ change in quantity} \;&=\; \% \text{ change in real GDP} - \% \text{ change in price} \end{aligned}$$

Therefore, the growth rate of real GDP (% change in quantity) equals the growth rate in nominal GDP (% change in value) minus the inflation rate (% change in price).

Note that using this equation provides an approximation for small changes in the levels. For more accurate measures, one should use the first formula shown.

5.3 | Tracking Real GDP over Time

By the end of this section, you will be able to:
- Explain recessions, depressions, peaks, and troughs
- Evaluate the importance of tracking real GDP over time
- Analyze the impact of economic fluctuations on a country's output and price level

When news reports indicate that "the economy grew 1.2% in the first quarter," the reports are referring to the percentage change in real GDP. By convention, GDP growth is reported at an annualized rate: Whatever the calculated growth in real GDP was for the quarter, it is multiplied by four when it is reported as if the economy were growing at that rate for a full year.

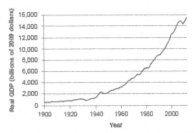

Figure 5.10 U.S. GDP, 1900–2014 Real GDP in the United States in 2014 was about $16 trillion. After adjusting to remove the effects of inflation, this represents a roughly 20-fold increase in the economy's production of goods and services since the start of the twentieth century. (Source: bea.gov)

Figure 5.10 shows the pattern of U.S. real GDP since 1900. The generally upward long-term path of GDP has been regularly interrupted by short-term declines. A significant decline in real GDP is called a **recession**. An especially lengthy and deep recession is called a **depression**. The severe drop in GDP that occurred during the Great Depression of the 1930s is clearly visible in the figure, as is the Great Recession of 2008–2009.

Real GDP is important because it is highly correlated with other measures of economic activity, like employment and unemployment. When real GDP rises, so does employment.

The most significant human problem associated with recessions (and their larger, uglier cousins, depressions) is that a slowdown in production means that firms need to lay off or fire some of the workers they have. Losing a job imposes painful financial and personal costs on workers, and often on their extended families as well. In addition, even those who keep their jobs are likely to find that wage raises are scanty at best—or they may even be asked to take pay cuts.

Table 5.7 lists the pattern of recessions and expansions in the U.S. economy since 1900. The highest point of the economy, before the recession begins, is called the **peak**; conversely, the lowest point of a recession, before a recovery begins, is called the **trough**. Thus, a recession lasts from peak to trough, and an economic upswing runs from trough to peak. The movement of the economy from peak to trough and trough to peak is called the **business cycle**. It is intriguing to notice that the three longest trough-to-peak expansions of the twentieth century have happened since 1960. The most recent recession started in December 2007 and ended formally in June 2009. This was the most severe recession since the Great Depression of the 1930's.

Trough	Peak	Months of Contraction	Months of Expansion
December 1900	September 1902	18	21
August 1904	May 1907	23	33
June 1908	January 1910	13	19
January 1912	January 1913	24	12
December 1914	August 1918	23	44
March 1919	January 1920	7	10
July 1921	May 1923	18	22
July 1924	October 1926	14	27
November 1927	August 1929	23	21

Table 5.7 U.S. Business Cycles since 1900   (Source: http://www.nber.org/cycles/main.html)

Trough	Peak	Months of Contraction	Months of Expansion
March 1933	May 1937	43	50
June 1938	February 1945	13	80
October 1945	November 1948	8	37
October 1949	July 1953	11	45
May 1954	August 1957	10	39
April 1958	April 1960	8	24
February 1961	December 1969	10	106
November 1970	November 1973	11	36
March 1975	January 1980	16	58
July 1980	July 1981	6	12
November 1982	July 1990	16	92
March 2001	November 2001	8	120
December 2007	June 2009	18	73

Table 5.7 U.S. Business Cycles since 1900   (Source: http://www.nber.org/cycles/main.html)

A private think tank, the National Bureau of Economic Research (NBER), is the official tracker of business cycles for the U.S. economy. However, the effects of a severe recession often linger on after the official ending date assigned by the NBER.

5.4 | Comparing GDP among Countries

By the end of this section, you will be able to:
- Explain how GDP can be used to compare the economic welfare of different nations
- Calculate the conversion of GDP to a common currency by using exchange rates
- Calculate GDP per capita using population data

It is common to use GDP as a measure of economic welfare or standard of living in a nation. When comparing the GDP of different nations for this purpose, two issues immediately arise. First, the GDP of a country is measured in its own currency: the United States uses the U.S. dollar; Canada, the Canadian dollar; most countries of Western Europe, the euro; Japan, the yen; Mexico, the peso; and so on. Thus, comparing GDP between two countries requires converting to a common currency. A second issue is that countries have very different numbers of people. For instance, the United States has a much larger economy than Mexico or Canada, but it also has roughly three times as many people as Mexico and nine times as many people as Canada. So, if we are trying to compare standards of living across countries, we need to divide GDP by population.

Converting Currencies with Exchange Rates

To compare the GDP of countries with different currencies, it is necessary to convert to a "common denominator" using an **exchange rate**, which is the value of one currency in terms of another currency. Exchange rates are expressed either as the units of country A's currency that need to be traded for a single unit of country B's currency (for example, Japanese yen per British pound), or as the inverse (for example, British pounds per Japanese yen). Two types of exchange rates can be used for this purpose, market exchange rates and purchasing power parity (PPP) equivalent exchange rates. Market exchange rates vary on a day-to-day basis depending on supply and demand in foreign exchange markets. PPP-equivalent exchange rates provide a longer run measure of the exchange rate. For this reason, PPP-equivalent exchange rates are typically used for cross country comparisons of GDP. Exchange rates will be discussed in more detail in Exchange Rates and International Capital Flows. The following Work It Out feature explains how to convert GDP to a common currency.

Converting GDP to a Common Currency

Using the exchange rate to convert GDP from one currency to another is straightforward. Say that the task is to compare Brazil's GDP in 2013 of 4.8 trillion reals with the U.S. GDP of $16.6 trillion for the same year.

Step 1. Determine the exchange rate for the specified year. In 2013, the exchange rate was 2.230 reals = $1. (These numbers are realistic, but rounded off to simplify the calculations.)

Step 2. Convert Brazil's GDP into U.S. dollars:

$$\text{Brazil's GDP in \$ U.S.} = \frac{\text{Brazil's GDP in reals}}{\text{Exchange rate (reals/\$ U.S.)}}$$

$$= \frac{\text{4.8 trillion reals}}{\text{2.230 reals per \$ U.S.}}$$

$$= \text{\$2.2 trillion}$$

Step 3. Compare this value to the GDP in the United States in the same year. The U.S. GDP was $16.6 trillion in 2013, which is nearly eight times that of GDP in Brazil in 2012.

Step 4. View Table 5.8 which shows the size of and variety of GDPs of different countries in 2013, all expressed in U.S. dollars. Each is calculated using the process explained above.

Country	GDP in Billions of Domestic Currency		Domestic Currency/U.S. Dollars (PPP Equivalent)	GDP (in billions of U.S. dollars)
Brazil	4,844.80	reals	2.157	2,246.00
Canada	1,881.20	dollars	1.030	1,826.80
China	58,667.30	yuan	6.196	9,469.10
Egypt	1,753.30	pounds	6.460	271.40
Germany	2,737.60	euros	0.753	3,636.00
India	113,550.70	rupees	60.502	1,876.80
Japan	478,075.30	yen	97.596	4,898.50
Mexico	16,104.40	pesos	12.772	1,260.90
South Korea	1,428,294.70	won	1,094.925	1,304.467
United Kingdom	1,612.80	pounds	0.639	2,523.20

Table 5.8 Comparing GDPs Across Countries, 2013   (Source: http://www.imf.org/external/pubs/ft/weo/2013/01/weodata/index.aspx)

Country	GDP in Billions of Domestic Currency		Domestic Currency/U.S. Dollars (PPP Equivalent)	GDP (in billions of U.S. dollars)
United States	16,768.10	dollars	1.000	16,768.10

Table 5.8 Comparing GDPs Across Countries, 2013   (Source: http://www.imf.org/external/pubs/ft/weo/2013/01/weodata/index.aspx)

GDP Per Capita

The U.S. economy has the largest GDP in the world, by a considerable amount. The United States is also a populous country; in fact, it is the third largest country by population in the world, although well behind China and India. So is the U.S. economy larger than other countries just because the United States has more people than most other countries, or because the U.S. economy is actually larger on a per-person basis? This question can be answered by calculating a country's **GDP per capita**; that is, the GDP divided by the population.

$$GDP \text{ per capita} = GDP/population$$

The second column of Table 5.9 lists the GDP of the same selection of countries that appeared in the previous Tracking Real GDP Over Time and Table 5.8, showing their GDP as converted into U.S. dollars (which is the same as the last column of the previous table). The third column gives the population for each country. The fourth column lists the GDP per capita. GDP per capita is obtained in two steps: First, by dividing column two (GDP, in billions of dollars) by 1000 so it has the same units as column three (Population, in millions). Then dividing the result (GDP in millions of dollars) by column three (Population, in millions).

Country	GDP (in billions of U.S. dollars)	Population (in millions)	Per Capita GDP (in U.S. dollars)
Brazil	2,246.00	199.20	11,172.50
Canada	1,826.80	35.10	52,037.10
China	9,469.10	1,360.80	6,958.70
Egypt	271.40	83.70	3,242.90
Germany	3,636.00	80.80	44,999.50
India	1,876.80	1,243.30	1,509.50
Japan	4,898.50	127.3	38,467.80
Mexico	1,260.90	118.40	10,649.90
South Korea	1,304.47	50.20	25,975.10
United Kingdom	2,523.20	64.10	39,371.70
United States	16,768.10	316.30	53,001.00

Table 5.9 GDP Per Capita, 2013   (Source: http://www.imf.org/external/pubs/ft/weo/2013/01/weodata/index.aspx)

Notice that the ranking by GDP is different from the ranking by GDP per capita. India has a somewhat larger GDP than Germany, but on a per capita basis, Germany has more than 10 times India's standard of living. Will China soon have a better standard of living than the U.S.? Read the following Clear It Up feature to find out.

Is China going to surpass the United States in terms of standard of living?

As shown in Table 5.9, China has the second largest GDP of the countries: $9.5 trillion compared to the United States' $16.8 trillion. Perhaps it will surpass the United States, but probably not any time soon. China has a much larger population so that in per capita terms, its GDP is less than one fifth that of the United States ($6,958.70 compared to $53,001). The Chinese people are still quite poor relative to the United States and other developed countries. One caveat: For reasons to be discussed shortly, GDP per capita can give us only a rough idea of the differences in living standards across countries.

The high-income nations of the world—including the United States, Canada, the Western European countries, and Japan—typically have GDP per capita in the range of $20,000 to $50,000. Middle-income countries, which include much of Latin America, Eastern Europe, and some countries in East Asia, have GDP per capita in the range of $6,000 to $12,000. The low-income countries in the world, many of them located in Africa and Asia, often have GDP per capita of less than $2,000 per year.

5.5 | How Well GDP Measures the Well-Being of Society

By the end of this section, you will be able to:
- Discuss how productivity influences the standard of living
- Explain the limitations of GDP as a measure of the standard of living
- Analyze the relationship between GDP data and fluctuations in the standard of living

The level of GDP per capita clearly captures some of what we mean by the phrase "standard of living." Most of the migration in the world, for example, involves people who are moving from countries with relatively low GDP per capita to countries with relatively high GDP per capita.

"Standard of living" is a broader term than GDP. While GDP focuses on production that is bought and sold in markets, **standard of living** includes all elements that affect people's well-being, whether they are bought and sold in the market or not. To illuminate the gap between GDP and standard of living, it is useful to spell out some things that GDP does not cover that are clearly relevant to standard of living.

Limitations of GDP as a Measure of the Standard of Living

While GDP includes spending on recreation and travel, it does not cover leisure time. Clearly, however, there is a substantial difference between an economy that is large because people work long hours, and an economy that is just as large because people are more productive with their time so they do not have to work as many hours. The GDP per capita of the U.S. economy is larger than the GDP per capita of Germany, as was shown in Table 5.9, but does that prove that the standard of living in the United States is higher? Not necessarily, since it is also true that the average U.S. worker works several hundred hours more per year more than the average German worker. The calculation of GDP does not take the German worker's extra weeks of vacation into account.

While GDP includes what is spent on environmental protection, healthcare, and education, it does not include actual levels of environmental cleanliness, health, and learning. GDP includes the cost of buying pollution-control equipment, but it does not address whether the air and water are actually cleaner or dirtier. GDP includes spending on medical care, but does not address whether life expectancy or infant mortality have risen or fallen. Similarly, it counts spending on education, but does not address directly how much of the population can read, write, or do basic mathematics.

GDP includes production that is exchanged in the market, but it does not cover production that is not exchanged in the market. For example, hiring someone to mow your lawn or clean your house is part of GDP, but doing these tasks yourself is not part of GDP. One remarkable change in the U.S. economy in recent decades is that, as of 1970, only about 42% of women participated in the paid labor force. By the second decade of the 2000s, nearly 60% of women participated in the paid labor force according to the Bureau of Labor Statistics. As women are now in the labor force, many of the services they used to produce in the non-market economy like food preparation and child care have shifted to some extent into the market economy, which makes the GDP appear larger even if more services are not actually being consumed.

GDP has nothing to say about the level of inequality in society. GDP per capita is only an average. When GDP per capita rises by 5%, it could mean that GDP for everyone in the society has risen by 5%, or that of some groups has risen by more while that of others has risen by less—or even declined. GDP also has nothing in particular to say about the amount of variety available. If a family buys 100 loaves of bread in a year, GDP does not care whether they are all white bread, or whether the family can choose from wheat, rye, pumpernickel, and many others—it just looks at whether the total amount spent on bread is the same.

Likewise, GDP has nothing much to say about what technology and products are available. The standard of living in, for example, 1950 or 1900 was not affected only by how much money people had—it was also affected by what they could buy. No matter how much money you had in 1950, you could not buy an iPhone or a personal computer.

In certain cases, it is not clear that a rise in GDP is even a good thing. If a city is wrecked by a hurricane, and then experiences a surge of rebuilding construction activity, it would be peculiar to claim that the hurricane was therefore economically beneficial. If people are led by a rising fear of crime, to pay for installation of bars and burglar alarms on all their windows, it is hard to believe that this increase in GDP has made them better off. In that same vein, some people would argue that sales of certain goods, like pornography or extremely violent movies, do not represent a gain to society's standard of living.

Does a Rise in GDP Overstate or Understate the Rise in the Standard of Living?

The fact that GDP per capita does not fully capture the broader idea of standard of living has led to a concern that the increases in GDP over time are illusory. It is theoretically possible that while GDP is rising, the standard of living could be falling if human health, environmental cleanliness, and other factors that are not included in GDP are worsening. Fortunately, this fear appears to be overstated.

In some ways, the rise in GDP understates the actual rise in the standard of living. For example, the typical workweek for a U.S. worker has fallen over the last century from about 60 hours per week to less than 40 hours per week. Life expectancy and health have risen dramatically, and so has the average level of education. Since 1970, the air and water in the United States have generally been getting cleaner. New technologies have been developed for entertainment, travel, information, and health. A much wider variety of basic products like food and clothing is available today than several decades ago. Because GDP does not capture leisure, health, a cleaner environment, the possibilities created by new technology, or an increase in variety, the actual rise in the standard of living for Americans in recent decades has exceeded the rise in GDP.

On the other side, rates of crime, levels of traffic congestion, and inequality of incomes are higher in the United States now than they were in the 1960s. Moreover, a substantial number of services that used to be provided, primarily by women, in the non-market economy are now part of the market economy that is counted by GDP. By ignoring these factors, GDP would tend to overstate the true rise in the standard of living.

Link It Up @⊘⊘

Visit this website (http://openstaxcollege.org/l/amdreamvalue) to read about the American Dream and standards of living.

GDP is Rough, but Useful

A high level of GDP should not be the only goal of macroeconomic policy, or government policy more broadly. Even though GDP does not measure the broader standard of living with any precision, it does measure production well and it does indicate when a country is materially better or worse off in terms of jobs and incomes. In most countries, a significantly higher GDP per capita occurs hand in hand with other improvements in everyday life along many dimensions, like education, health, and environmental protection.

No single number can capture all the elements of a term as broad as "standard of living." Nonetheless, GDP per capita is a reasonable, rough-and-ready measure of the standard of living.

Bring it Home

How is the Economy Doing? How Does One Tell?

To determine the state of the economy, one needs to examine economic indicators, such as GDP. To calculate GDP is quite an undertaking. It is the broadest measure of a nation's economic activity and we owe a debt to Simon Kuznets, the creator of the measurement, for that.

The sheer size of the U.S. economy as measured by GDP is huge—as of the third quarter of 2013, $16.6 trillion worth of goods and services were produced annually. Real GDP informed us that the recession of 2008–2009 was a severe one and that the recovery from that has been slow, but is improving. GDP per capita gives a rough estimate of a nation's standard of living. This chapter is the building block for other chapters that explore more economic indicators such as unemployment, inflation, or interest rates, and perhaps more importantly, will explain how they are related and what causes them to rise or fall.

KEY TERMS

business cycle the relatively short-term movement of the economy in and out of recession

depreciation the process by which capital ages over time and therefore loses its value

depression an especially lengthy and deep decline in output

double counting a potential mistake to be avoided in measuring GDP, in which output is counted more than once as it travels through the stages of production

durable good long-lasting good like a car or a refrigerator

exchange rate the price of one currency in terms of another currency

final good and service output used directly for consumption, investment, government, and trade purposes; contrast with "intermediate good"

GDP per capita GDP divided by the population

gross domestic product (GDP) the value of the output of all goods and services produced within a country in a year

gross national product (GNP) includes what is produced domestically and what is produced by domestic labor and business abroad in a year

intermediate good output provided to other businesses at an intermediate stage of production, not for final users; contrast with "final good and service"

inventory good that has been produced, but not yet been sold

national income includes all income earned: wages, profits, rent, and profit income

net national product (NNP) GDP minus depreciation

nominal value the economic statistic actually announced at that time, not adjusted for inflation; contrast with real value

nondurable good short-lived good like food and clothing

peak during the business cycle, the highest point of output before a recession begins

real value an economic statistic after it has been adjusted for inflation; contrast with nominal value

recession a significant decline in national output

service product which is intangible (in contrast to goods) such as entertainment, healthcare, or education

standard of living all elements that affect people's happiness, whether these elements are bought and sold in the market or not

structure building used as residence, factory, office building, retail store, or for other purposes

trade balance gap between exports and imports

trade deficit exists when a nation's imports exceed its exports and is calculated as imports –exports

trade surplus exists when a nation's exports exceed its imports and is calculated as exports – imports

trough during the business cycle, the lowest point of output in a recession, before a recovery begins

KEY CONCEPTS AND SUMMARY

5.1 Measuring the Size of the Economy: Gross Domestic Product

The size of a nation's economy is commonly expressed as its gross domestic product (GDP), which measures the value of the output of all goods and services produced within the country in a year. GDP is measured by taking the quantities of all goods and services produced, multiplying them by their prices, and summing the total. Since GDP measures what is bought and sold in the economy, it can be measured either by the sum of what is purchased in the economy or what is produced.

Demand can be divided into consumption, investment, government, exports, and imports. What is produced in the economy can be divided into durable goods, nondurable goods, services, structures, and inventories. To avoid double counting, GDP counts only final output of goods and services, not the production of intermediate goods or the value of labor in the chain of production.

5.2 Adjusting Nominal Values to Real Values

The nominal value of an economic statistic is the commonly announced value. The real value is the value after adjusting for changes in inflation. To convert nominal economic data from several different years into real, inflation-adjusted data, the starting point is to choose a base year arbitrarily and then use a price index to convert the measurements so that they are measured in the money prevailing in the base year.

5.3 Tracking Real GDP over Time

Over the long term, U.S. real GDP have increased dramatically. At the same time, GDP has not increased the same amount each year. The speeding up and slowing down of GDP growth represents the business cycle. When GDP declines significantly, a recession occurs. A longer and deeper decline is a depression. Recessions begin at the peak of the business cycle and end at the trough.

5.4 Comparing GDP among Countries

Since GDP is measured in a country's currency, in order to compare different countries' GDPs, we need to convert them to a common currency. One way to do that is with the exchange rate, which is the price of one country's currency in terms of another. Once GDPs are expressed in a common currency, we can compare each country's GDP per capita by dividing GDP by population. Countries with large populations often have large GDPs, but GDP alone can be a misleading indicator of the wealth of a nation. A better measure is GDP per capita.

5.5 How Well GDP Measures the Well-Being of Society

GDP is an indicator of a society's standard of living, but it is only a rough indicator. GDP does not directly take account of leisure, environmental quality, levels of health and education, activities conducted outside the market, changes in inequality of income, increases in variety, increases in technology, or the (positive or negative) value that society may place on certain types of output.

SELF-CHECK QUESTIONS

1. Country A has export sales of $20 billion, government purchases of $1,000 billion, business investment is $50 billion, imports are $40 billion, and consumption spending is $2,000 billion. What is the dollar value of GDP?

2. Which of the following are included in GDP, and which are not?
   a. The cost of hospital stays
   b. The rise in life expectancy over time
   c. Child care provided by a licensed day care center
   d. Child care provided by a grandmother
   e. The sale of a used car
   f. The sale of a new car
   g. The greater variety of cheese available in supermarkets
   h. The iron that goes into the steel that goes into a refrigerator bought by a consumer.

3. Using data from Table 5.5 how much of the nominal GDP growth from 1980 to 1990 was real GDP and how much was inflation?

4. Without looking at Table 5.7, return to Figure 5.10. If a recession is defined as a significant decline in national output, can you identify any post-1960 recessions in addition to the recession of 2008–2009? (This requires a judgment call.)

5. According to Table 5.7, how often have recessions occurred since the end of World War II (1945)?

6. According to Table 5.7, how long has the average recession lasted since the end of World War II?

7. According to Table 5.7, how long has the average expansion lasted since the end of World War II?

8. Is it possible for GDP to rise while at the same time per capita GDP is falling? Is it possible for GDP to fall while per capita GDP is rising?

9. The Central African Republic has a GDP of 1,107,689 million CFA francs and a population of 4.862 million. The exchange rate is 284.681CFA francs per dollar. Calculate the GDP per capita of Central African Republic.

10. Explain briefly whether each of the following would cause GDP to overstate or understate the degree of change in the broad standard of living.
   a. The environment becomes dirtier
   b. The crime rate declines
   c. A greater variety of goods become available to consumers
   d. Infant mortality declines

REVIEW QUESTIONS

11. What are the main components of measuring GDP with what is demanded?

12. What are the main components of measuring GDP with what is produced?

13. Would you usually expect GDP as measured by what is demanded to be greater than GDP measured by what is supplied, or the reverse?

14. Why must double counting be avoided when measuring GDP?

15. What is the difference between a series of economic data over time measured in nominal terms versus the same data series over time measured in real terms?

16. How do you convert a series of nominal economic data over time to real terms?

17. What are the typical patterns of GDP for a high-income economy like the United States in the long run and the short run?

18. What are the two main difficulties that arise in comparing the GDP of different countries?

19. List some of the reasons why GDP should not be considered an effective measure of the standard of living in a country.

CRITICAL THINKING QUESTIONS

20. U.S. macroeconomic data are thought to be among the best in the world. Given what you learned in the Clear It Up "How do statisticians measure GDP?", does this surprise you? Or does this simply reflect the complexity of a modern economy?

21. What does GDP not tell us about the economy?

22. Should people typically pay more attention to their real income or their nominal income? If you choose the latter, why would that make sense in today's world? Would your answer be the same for the 1970s?

23. Why do you suppose that U.S. GDP is so much higher today than 50 or 100 years ago?

24. Why do you think that GDP does not grow at a steady rate, but rather speeds up and slows down?

25. Cross country comparisons of GDP per capita typically use purchasing power parity equivalent exchange rates, which are a measure of the long run equilibrium value of an exchange rate. In fact, we used PPP equivalent exchange rates in this module. Why

could using market exchange rates, which sometimes change dramatically in a short period of time, be misleading?

26. Why might per capita GDP be only an imperfect measure of a country's standard of living?

27. How might a "green" GDP be measured?

PROBLEMS

28. Last year, a small nation with abundant forests cut down $200 worth of trees. $100 worth of trees were then turned into $150 worth of lumber. $100 worth of that lumber was used to produce $250 worth of bookshelves. Assuming the country produces no other outputs, and there are no other inputs used in the production of trees, lumber, and bookshelves, what is this nation's GDP? In other words, what is the value of the final goods produced including trees, lumber and bookshelves?

29. The "prime" interest rate is the rate that banks charge their best customers. Based on the nominal interest rates and inflation rates given in **Table 5.10**, in which of the years given would it have been best to be a lender? Based on the nominal interest rates and inflation rates given in **Table 5.10**, in which of the years given would it have been best to be a borrower?

Year	Prime Interest Rate	Inflation Rate
1970	7.9%	5.7%
1974	10.8%	11.0%
1978	9.1%	7.6%
1981	18.9%	10.3%

Table 5.10

30. A mortgage loan is a loan that a person makes to purchase a house. **Table 5.11** provides a list of the mortgage interest rate being charged for several different years and the rate of inflation for each of those years.

In which years would it have been better to be a person borrowing money from a bank to buy a home? In which years would it have been better to be a bank lending money?

Year	Mortgage Interest Rate	Inflation Rate
1984	12.4%	4.3%
1990	10%	5.4%
2001	7.0%	2.8%

Table 5.11

31. Ethiopia has a GDP of $8 billion (measured in U.S. dollars) and a population of 55 million. Costa Rica has a GDP of $9 billion (measured in U.S. dollars) and a population of 4 million. Calculate the per capita GDP for each country and identify which one is higher.

32. In 1980, Denmark had a GDP of $70 billion (measured in U.S. dollars) and a population of 5.1 million. In 2000, Denmark had a GDP of $160 billion (measured in U.S. dollars) and a population of 5.3 million. By what percentage did Denmark's GDP per capita rise between 1980 and 2000?

33. The Czech Republic has a GDP of 1,800 billion koruny. The exchange rate is 20 koruny/U.S. dollar. The Czech population is 20 million. What is the GDP per capita of the Czech Republic expressed in U.S. dollars?

6 | Economic Growth

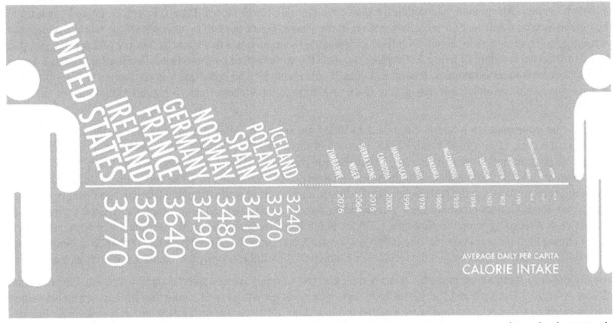

Figure 6.1 Average Daily Calorie Consumption Not only has the number of calories consumed per day increased, so has the amount of food calories that people are able to afford based on their working wages. (Credit: modification of work by Lauren Manning/Flickr Creative Commons)

Bring it Home

Calories and Economic Growth

On average, humans need about 2,500 calories a day to survive, depending on height, weight, and gender. The economist Brad DeLong estimates that the average worker in the early 1600s earned wages that could afford him 2,500 food calories. This worker lived in Western Europe. Two hundred years later, that same worker could afford 3,000 food calories. However, between 1800 and 1875, just a time span of just 75 years, economic growth was so rapid that western European workers could purchase 5,000 food calories a day. By 2012, a low skilled worker in an affluent Western European/North American country could afford to purchase 2.4 million food calories per day.

What caused such a rapid rise in living standards between 1800 and 1875 and thereafter? Why is it that many countries, especially those in Western Europe, North America, and parts of East Asia, can feed their populations more than adequately, while others cannot? We will look at these and other questions as we examine long-run economic growth.

Introduction to Economic Growth

In this chapter, you will learn about:

- The Relatively Recent Arrival of Economic Growth
- Labor Productivity and Economic Growth
- Components of Economic Growth

- Economic Convergence

Every country worries about economic growth. In the United States and other high-income countries, the question is whether economic growth continues to provide the same remarkable gains in our standard of living as it did during the twentieth century. Meanwhile, can middle-income countries like South Korea, Brazil, Egypt, or Poland catch up to the higher-income countries? Or must they remain in the second tier of per capita income? Of the world's population of roughly 6.7 billion people, about 2.6 billion are scraping by on incomes that average less than $2 per day, not that different from the standard of living 2,000 years ago. Can the world's poor be lifted from their fearful poverty? As the 1995 Nobel laureate in economics, Robert E. Lucas Jr., once noted: "The consequences for human welfare involved in questions like these are simply staggering: Once one starts to think about them, it is hard to think about anything else."

Dramatic improvements in a nation's standard of living are possible. After the Korean War in the late 1950s, the Republic of Korea, often called South Korea, was one of the poorest economies in the world. Most South Koreans worked in peasant agriculture. According to the British economist Angus Maddison, whose life's work was the measurement of GDP and population in the world economy, GDP per capita in 1990 international dollars was $854 per year. From the 1960s to the early twenty-first century, a time period well within the lifetime and memory of many adults, the South Korean economy grew rapidly. Over these four decades, GDP per capita increased by more than 6% per year. According to the World Bank, GDP for South Korea now exceeds $30,000 in nominal terms, placing it firmly among high-income countries like Italy, New Zealand, and Israel. Measured by total GDP in 2012, South Korea is the thirteenth-largest economy in the world. For a nation of 49 million people, this transformation is extraordinary.

South Korea is a standout example, but it is not the only case of rapid and sustained economic growth. Other nations of East Asia, like Thailand and Indonesia, have seen very rapid growth as well. China has grown enormously since market-oriented economic reforms were enacted around 1980. GDP per capita in high-income economies like the United States also has grown dramatically albeit over a longer time frame. Since the Civil War, the U.S. economy has been transformed from a primarily rural and agricultural economy to an economy based on services, manufacturing, and technology.

6.1 | The Relatively Recent Arrival of Economic Growth

By the end of this section, you will be able to:
- Explain the conditions that have allowed for modern economic growth in the last two centuries
- Analyze the influence of public policies on the long-run economic growth of an economy

Let's begin with a brief overview of the spectacular patterns of economic growth around the world in the last two centuries, commonly referred to as the period of **modern economic growth**. (Later in the chapter we will discuss lower rates of economic growth and some key ingredients for economic progress.) Rapid and sustained economic growth is a relatively recent experience for the human race. Before the last two centuries, although rulers, nobles, and conquerors could afford some extravagances and although economies rose above the subsistence level, the average person's standard of living had not changed much for centuries.

Progressive, powerful economic and institutional changes started to have a significant effect in the late eighteenth and early nineteenth centuries. According to the Dutch economic historian Jan Luiten van Zanden, slavery-based societies, favorable demographics, global trading routes, and standardized trading institutions that spread with different empires set the stage for the Industrial Revolution to succeed. The **Industrial Revolution** refers to the widespread use of power-driven machinery and the economic and social changes that resulted in the first half of the 1800s. Ingenious machines—the steam engine, the power loom, and the steam locomotive—performed tasks that otherwise would have taken vast numbers of workers to do. The Industrial Revolution began in Great Britain, and soon spread to the United States, Germany, and other countries.

The jobs for ordinary people working with these machines were often dirty and dangerous by modern standards, but the alternative jobs of that time in peasant agriculture and small-village industry were often dirty and dangerous, too. The new jobs of the Industrial Revolution typically offered higher pay and a chance for social mobility. A self-reinforcing cycle began: New inventions and investments generated profits, the profits provided funds for new investment and inventions, and the investments and inventions provided opportunities for further profits. Slowly, a group of national economies in Europe and North America emerged from centuries of sluggishness into a period of rapid modern growth. During the last two centuries, the average rate of growth of GDP per capita in the leading industrialized countries has averaged about 2% per year. What were times like before then? Read the following Clear It Up feature for the answer.

What were economic conditions like before 1870?

Angus Maddison, a quantitative economic historian, led the most systematic inquiry into national incomes before 1870. His methods recently have been refined and used to compile GDP per capita estimates from year 1 C.E. to 1348. Table 6.1 is an important counterpoint to most of the narrative in this chapter. It shows that nations can decline as well as rise. The declines in income are explained by a wide array of forces, such as epidemics, natural and weather-related disasters, the inability to govern large empires, and the remarkably slow pace of technological and institutional progress. Institutions are the traditions, laws, and so on by which people in a community agree to behave and govern themselves. Such institutions include marriage, religion, education, and laws of governance. Institutional progress is the development and codification of these institutions to reinforce social order, and thus, economic growth.

One example of such an institution is the Magna Carta (Great Charter), which the English nobles forced King John to sign in 1215. The Magna Carta codified the principles of due process, whereby a free man could not be penalized unless his peers had made a lawful judgment against him. This concept was later adopted by the United States in its own constitution. This social order may have contributed to England's GDP per capita in 1348, which was second to that of northern Italy.

In the study of economic growth, a country's institutional framework plays a critical role. Table 6.1 also shows relative global equality for almost 1,300 years. After this, we begin to see significant divergence in income (not shown in table).

Year	Northern Italy	Spain	England	Holland	Byzantium	Iraq	Egypt	Japan
1	$800	$600	$600	$600	$700	$700	$700	-
730	-	-	-	-	-	$920	$730	$402
1000	-	-	-	-	$600	$820	$600	-
1150	-	-	-	-	$580	$680	$660	$520
1280	-	-	-	-	-	-	$670	$527
1300	$1,588	$864	$892	-	-	-	$610	-
1348	$1,486	$907	$919	-	-	-	-	-

Table 6.1 GDP Per Capita Estimates in Current International Dollars from AD 1 to 1348 (Source: Bolt and van Zanden. "The First Update of the Maddison Project. Re-Estimating Growth Before 1820." 2013)

Another fascinating and underreported fact is the high levels of income, compared to others at that time, attained by the Islamic Empire Abbasid Caliphate—which was founded in present-day Iraq in 730 C.E. At its height, the empire spanned large regions of the Middle East, North Africa, and Spain until its gradual decline over 200 years.

The Industrial Revolution led to increasing inequality among nations. Some economies took off, whereas others, like many of those in Africa or Asia, remained close to a subsistence standard of living. General calculations show that the 17 countries of the world with the most-developed economies had, on average, 2.4 times the GDP per capita of the world's poorest economies in 1870. By 1960, the most developed economies had 4.2 times the GDP per capita of the poorest economies.

However, by the middle of the twentieth century, some countries had shown that catching up was possible. Japan's economic growth took off in the 1960s and 1970s, with a growth rate of real GDP per capita averaging 11% per year during those decades. Certain countries in Latin America experienced a boom in economic growth in the 1960s as well. In Brazil, for example, GDP per capita expanded by an average annual rate of 11.1% from 1968 to 1973. In the 1970s, some East Asian economies, including South Korea, Thailand, and Taiwan, saw rapid growth. In these countries, growth rates of 11% to 12% per year in GDP per capita were not uncommon. More recently, China, with its population of 1.3 billion people, grew at a per capita rate 9% per year from 1984 into the 2000s. India, with a population of 1.1 billion, has shown promising signs of economic growth, with growth in GDP per capita of about 4% per year during the 1990s and climbing toward 7% to 8% per year in the 2000s.

Link It Up

Visit this website (http://openstaxcollege.org/l/asiadevbank) to read about the Asian Development Bank.

These waves of catch-up economic growth have not reached all shores. In certain African countries like Niger, Tanzania, and Sudan, for example, GDP per capita at the start of the 2000s was still less than $300, not much higher than it was in the nineteenth century and for centuries before that. In the context of the overall situation of low-income people around the world, the good economic news from China (population: 1.3 billion) and India (population: 1.1 billion) is, nonetheless, astounding and heartening.

Economic growth in the last two centuries has made a striking change in the human condition. Richard Easterlin, an economist at the University of Southern California, wrote in 2000:

> By many measures, a revolution in the human condition is sweeping the world. Most people today are better fed, clothed, and housed than their predecessors two centuries ago. They are healthier, live longer, and are better educated. Women's lives are less centered on reproduction and political democracy has gained a foothold. Although Western Europe and its offshoots have been the leaders of this advance, most of the less developed nations have joined in during the 20th century, with the newly emerging nations of sub-Saharan Africa the latest to participate. Although the picture is not one of universal progress, it is the greatest advance in the human condition of the world's population ever achieved in such a brief span of time.

Rule of Law and Economic Growth

Economic growth depends on many factors. Key among those factors is adherence to the **rule of law** and protection of property rights and **contractual rights** by a country's government so that markets can work effectively and efficiently. Laws must be clear, public, fair, enforced, and equally applicable to all members of society. Property rights, as you might recall from **Environmental Protection and Negative Externalities (http://cnx.org/content/ m57254/latest/)** are the rights of individuals and firms to own property and use it as they see fit. If you have $100, you have the right to use that money, whether you spend it, lend it, or keep it in a jar. It is your property. The definition of property includes physical property as well as the right to your training and experience, especially since your training is what determines your livelihood. The use of this property includes the right to enter into contracts with other parties with your property. Individuals or firms must own the property to enter into a contract.

Contractual rights, then, are based on property rights and they allow individuals to enter into agreements with others regarding the use of their property providing recourse through the legal system in the event of noncompliance. One example is the employment agreement: a skilled surgeon operates on an ill person and expects to get paid. Failure to pay would constitute a theft of property by the patient; that property being the services provided by the surgeon. In a society with strong property rights and contractual rights, the terms of the patient–surgeon contract will be fulfilled, because the surgeon would have recourse through the court system to extract payment from that individual. Without a legal system that enforces contracts, people would not be likely to enter into contracts for current or future services because of the risk of non-payment. This would make it difficult to transact business and would slow economic growth.

The World Bank considers a country's legal system effective if it upholds property rights and contractual rights. The World Bank has developed a ranking system for countries' legal systems based on effective protection of property rights and rule-based governance using a scale from 1 to 6, with 1 being the lowest and 6 the highest rating. In 2013, the world average ranking was 2.9. The three countries with the lowest ranking of 1.5 were Afghanistan, the Central African Republic, and Zimbabwe; their GDP per capita was $679, $333, and $1,007 respectively. Afghanistan is cited by the World Bank as having a low standard of living, weak government structure, and lack of adherence to the rule of law, which has stymied its economic growth. The landlocked Central African Republic has poor economic resources as well as political instability and is a source of children used in human trafficking. Zimbabwe has had declining growth since 1998. Land redistribution and price controls have disrupted the economy, and corruption and violence have dominated the political process. Although global economic growth has increased, those countries lacking a clear system of property rights and an independent court system free from corruption have lagged far behind.

6.2 | Labor Productivity and Economic Growth

By the end of this section, you will be able to:

- Identify the role of labor productivity in promoting economic growth
- Analyze the sources of economic growth using the aggregate production function
- Measure an economy's rate of productivity growth
- Evaluate the power of sustained growth

Sustained long-term economic growth comes from increases in worker productivity, which essentially means how well we do things. In other words, how efficient is your nation with its time and workers? **Labor productivity** is the value that each employed person creates per unit of his or her input. The easiest way to comprehend labor productivity is to imagine a Canadian worker who can make 10 loaves of bread in an hour versus a U.S. worker who in the same hour can make only two loaves of bread. In this fictional example, the Canadians are more productive. Being more productive essentially means you can do more in the same amount of time. This in turn frees up resources to be used elsewhere.

What determines how productive workers are? The answer is pretty intuitive. The first determinant of labor productivity is human capital. **Human capital** is the accumulated knowledge (from education and experience), skills, and expertise that the average worker in an economy possesses. Typically the higher the average level of education in an economy, the higher the accumulated human capital and the higher the labor productivity.

The second factor that determines labor productivity is technological change. **Technological change** is a combination of **invention**—advances in knowledge—and **innovation**, which is putting that advance to use in a new product or service. For example, the transistor was invented in 1947. It allowed us to miniaturize the footprint of electronic devices and use less power than the tube technology that came before it. Innovations since then have produced smaller and better transistors that that are ubiquitous in products as varied as smart-phones, computers, and escalators. The development of the transistor has allowed workers to be anywhere with smaller devices. These devices can be used to communicate with other workers, measure product quality or do any other task in less time, improving worker productivity.

The third factor that determines labor productivity is economies of scale. Recall that economies of scale are the cost advantages that industries obtain due to size. (Read more about economies of scale in Cost and Industry

Structure (http://cnx.org/content/m57234/latest/) .) Consider again the case of the fictional Canadian worker who could produce 10 loaves of bread in an hour. If this difference in productivity was due only to economies of scale, it could be that Canadian workers had access to a large industrial-size oven while the U.S. worker was using a standard residential size oven.

Now that we have explored the determinants of worker productivity, let's turn to how economists measure economic growth and productivity.

Sources of Economic Growth: The Aggregate Production Function

To analyze the sources of economic growth, it is useful to think about a **production function**, which is the process of turning economic inputs like labor, machinery, and raw materials into outputs like goods and services used by consumers. A microeconomic production function describes the inputs and outputs of a firm, or perhaps an industry. In macroeconomics, the connection from inputs to outputs for the entire economy is called an **aggregate production function**.

Components of the Aggregate Production Function

Economists construct different production functions depending on the focus of their studies. Figure 6.2 presents two examples of aggregate production functions. In the first production function, shown in Figure 6.2 (a), the output is GDP. The inputs in this example are workforce, human capital, physical capital, and technology. We discuss these inputs further in the module, Components of Economic Growth.

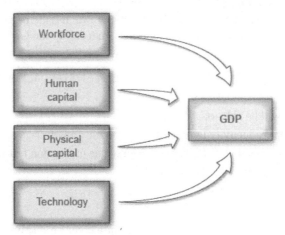

(a) Aggregate production function with GDP as its output

(b) Aggregate production function with GDP per capita as its output

Figure 6.2 Aggregate Production Functions   An aggregate production function shows what goes into producing the output for an overall economy. (a) This aggregate production function has GDP as its output. (b) This aggregate production function has GDP per capita as its output. Because it is calculated on a per-person basis, the labor input is already figured into the other factors and does not need to be listed separately.

Measuring Productivity

An economy's rate of productivity growth is closely linked to the growth rate of its GDP per capita, although the two are not identical. For example, if the percentage of the population who holds jobs in an economy increases, GDP per capita will increase but the productivity of individual workers may not be affected. Over the long term, the only way that GDP per capita can grow continually is if the productivity of the average worker rises or if there are complementary increases in capital.

A common measure of U.S. productivity per worker is dollar value per hour the worker contributes to the employer's output. This measure excludes government workers, because their output is not sold in the market and so their productivity is hard to measure. It also excludes farming, which accounts for only a relatively small share of the U.S. economy. Figure 6.3 shows an index of output per hour, with 2009 as the base year (when the index equals 100). The index equaled about 106 in 2014. In 1972, the index equaled 50, which shows that workers have more than doubled their productivity since then.

Figure 6.3 Output per Hour Worked in the U.S. Economy, 1947–2011 Output per hour worked is a measure of worker productivity. In the U.S. economy, worker productivity rose more quickly in the 1960s and the mid-1990s compared with the 1970s and 1980s. However, these growth-rate differences are only a few percentage points per year. Look carefully to see them in the changing slope of the line. The average U.S. worker produced over twice as much per hour in 2014 than he did in the early 1970s. (Source: U.S. Department of Labor, Bureau of Labor Statistics.)

According to the Department of Labor, U.S. productivity growth was fairly strong in the 1950s but then declined in the 1970s and 1980s before rising again in the second half of the 1990s and the first half of the 2000s. In fact, the rate of productivity measured by the change in output per hour worked averaged 3.2% per year from 1950 to 1970; dropped to 1.9% per year from 1970 to 1990; and then climbed back to over 2.3% from 1991 to the present, with another modest slowdown after 2001. Figure 6.4 shows average annual rates of productivity growth averaged over time since 1950.

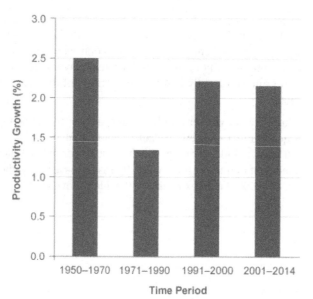

Figure 6.4 Productivity Growth Since 1950   U.S. growth in worker productivity was very high between 1950 and 1970. It then declined to lower levels in the 1970s and the 1980s. The late 1990s and early 2000s saw productivity rebound, but then productivity sagged a bit in the 2000s. Some think the productivity rebound of the late 1990s and early 2000s marks the start of a "new economy" built on higher productivity growth, but this cannot be determined until more time has passed. (Source: U.S. Department of Labor, Bureau of Labor Statistics.)

The "New Economy" Controversy

In recent years a controversy has been brewing among economists about the resurgence of U.S. productivity in the second half of the 1990s. One school of thought argues that the United States had developed a "new economy" based on the extraordinary advances in communications and information technology of the 1990s. The most optimistic proponents argue that it would generate higher average productivity growth for decades to come. The pessimists, on the other hand, argue that even five or ten years of stronger productivity growth does not prove that higher productivity will last for the long term. It is hard to infer anything about long-term productivity trends during the later part of the 2000s, because the steep recession of 2008–2009, with its sharp but not completely synchronized declines in output and employment, complicates any interpretation. While productivity growth was high in 2009 and 2010 (around 3%), it has slowed down since then.

Productivity growth is also closely linked to the average level of wages. Over time, the amount that firms are willing to pay workers will depend on the value of the output those workers produce. If a few employers tried to pay their workers less than what those workers produced, then those workers would receive offers of higher wages from other profit-seeking employers. If a few employers mistakenly paid their workers more than what those workers produced, those employers would soon end up with losses. In the long run, productivity per hour is the most important determinant of the average wage level in any economy. To learn how to compare economies in this regard, follow the steps in the following Work It Out feature.

Work It Out ─○─○─○

Comparing the Economies of Two Countries

The Organization for Economic Co-operation and Development (OECD) tracks data on the annual growth rate of real GDP per hour worked. You can find these data on the OECD data webpage "Labour productivity growth in the total economy" at this (http://stats.oecd.org/Index.aspx?DataSetCode=PDB_GR) website.

Step 1. Visit the OECD website given above and select two countries to compare.

Step 2. On the drop-down menu "Variable," select "Real GDP, Annual Growth, in percent" and record the data for the countries you have chosen for the five most recent years.

Step 3. Go back to the drop-down menu and select "Real GDP per Hour Worked, Annual Growth Rate, in percent" and select data for the same years for which you selected GDP data.

Step 4. Compare real GDP growth for both countries. Table 6.2 provides an example of a comparison between Australia and Belgium.

Australia	2009	2010	2011	2012	2013
Real GDP Growth (%)	0.1%	1.0%	2.2%	0.8	0.7%
Real GDP Growth/Hours Worked (%)	1.9%	−0.3%	2.4%	3.3%	1.4%
Belgium	2009	2010	2011	2012	2013
Real GDP Growth (%)	−3.4	1.6	0.8	−0.6	−0.2
Real GDP Growth/Hours Worked (%)	−1.3	−1.4	−0.5	−0.3	0.3

Table 6.2

Step 5. Consider the many factors can affect growth. For example, one factor that may have affected Australia is its isolation from Europe, which may have insulated the country from the effects of the global recession. In Belgium's case, the global recession seems to have had an impact on both GDP and real GDP per hours worked between 2009 and 2013, though productivity does seem to be recovering.

The Power of Sustained Economic Growth

Nothing is more important for people's standard of living than sustained economic growth. Even small changes in the rate of growth, when sustained and compounded over long periods of time, make an enormous difference in the standard of living. Consider Table 6.3, in which the rows of the table show several different rates of growth in GDP per capita and the columns show different periods of time. Assume for simplicity that an economy starts with a GDP per capita of 100. The table then applies the following formula to calculate what GDP will be at the given growth rate in the future:

$$\text{GDP at starting date} \times (1 + \text{growth rate of GDP})^{\text{years}} = \text{GDP at end date}$$

For example, an economy that starts with a GDP of 100 and grows at 3% per year will reach a GDP of 209 after 25 years; that is, $100 \, (1.03)^{25} = 209$.

The slowest rate of GDP per capita growth in the table, just 1% per year, is similar to what the United States experienced during its weakest years of productivity growth. The second highest rate, 3% per year, is close to what the U.S. economy experienced during the strong economy of the late 1990s and into the 2000s. Higher rates of per capita growth, such as 5% or 8% per year, represent the experience of rapid growth in economies like Japan, Korea, and China.

Table 6.3 shows that even a few percentage points of difference in economic growth rates will have a profound effect if sustained and compounded over time. For example, an economy growing at a 1% annual rate over 50 years will see its GDP per capita rise by a total of 64%, from 100 to 164 in this example. However, a country growing at a 5% annual rate will see (almost) the same amount of growth—from 100 to 163—over just 10 years. Rapid rates of economic growth can bring profound transformation. (See the following Clear It Up feature on the relationship between compound growth rates and compound interest rates.) If the rate of growth is 8%, young adults starting at age 20 will see the average standard of living in their country more than double by the time they reach age 30, and grow nearly sevenfold by the time they reach age 45.

Growth Rate	Value of an original 100 in 10 Years	Value of an original 100 in 25 Years	Value of an original 100 in 50 Years
1%	110	128	164
3%	134	209	438
5%	163	338	1,147
8%	216	685	4,690

Table 6.3 Growth of GDP over Different Time Horizons

How are compound growth rates and compound interest rates related?

The formula for growth rates of GDP over different periods of time, as shown in Figure 6.3, is exactly the same as the formula for how a given amount of financial savings grows at a certain interest rate over time, as presented in Choice in a World of Scarcity. Both formulas have the same ingredients:

- an original starting amount, in one case GDP and in the other case an amount of financial saving;
- a percentage increase over time, in one case the growth rate of GDP and in the other case an interest rate;
- and an amount of time over which this effect happens.

Recall that compound interest is interest that is earned on past interest. It causes the total amount of financial savings to grow dramatically over time. Similarly, compound rates of economic growth, or the **compound growth rate**, means that the rate of growth is being multiplied by a base that includes past GDP growth, with dramatic effects over time.

For example, in 2013, the World Fact Book, produced by the Central Intelligence Agency, reported that South Korea had a GDP of $1.67 trillion with a growth rate of 2.8%. We can estimate that at that growth rate, South Korea's GDP will be $1.92 trillion in five years. If we apply the growth rate to each year's ending GDP for the next five years, we will calculate that at the end of year one, GDP is $1.72 trillion. In year two, we start with the end-of-year one value of $1.67 and increase it by 2%. Year three starts with the end-of-year two GDP, and we increase it by 2% and so on, as depicted in the Table 6.4.

Year	Starting GDP	Growth Rate 2%	Year-End Amount
1	$1.67 Trillion ×	(1+0.028)	$1.72 Trillion
2	$1.72 Trillion ×	(1+0.028)	$1.76 Trillion
3	$1.76 Trillion ×	(1+0.028)	$1.81 Trillion
4	$1.81 Trillion ×	(1+0.028)	$1.87 Trillion
5	$1.87 Trillion ×	(1+0.028)	$1.92 Trillion

Table 6.4

Another way to calculate the growth rate is to apply the following formula:

$$\text{Future Value} = \text{Present Value} \times (1 + g)^n$$

Where "future value" is the value of GDP five years hence, "present value" is the starting GDP amount of $1.64 trillion, "g" is the growth rate of 2%, and "n" is the number of periods for which we are calculating growth.

$$\text{Future Value} = 1.67 \times (1+0.028)^5 = \$1.92 \text{ trillion}$$

6.3 | Components of Economic Growth

By the end of this section, you will be able to:
- Discuss the components of economic growth, including physical capital, human capital, and technology
- Explain capital deepening and its significance
- Analyze the methods employed in economic growth accounting studies
- Identify factors that contribute to a healthy climate for economic growth

Over decades and generations, seemingly small differences of a few percentage points in the annual rate of economic growth make an enormous difference in GDP per capita. In this module, we discuss some of the components of economic growth, including physical capital, human capital, and technology.

The category of **physical capital** includes the plant and equipment used by firms and also things like roads (also called **infrastructure**). Again, greater physical capital implies more output. Physical capital can affect productivity in two ways: (1) an increase in the *quantity* of physical capital (for example, more computers of the same quality); and (2) an increase in the *quality* of physical capital (same number of computers but the computers are faster, and so on). Human capital and physical capital accumulation are similar: In both cases, investment now pays off in longer-term productivity in the future.

The category of **technology** is the "joker in the deck." Earlier we described it as the combination of invention and innovation. When most people think of new technology, the invention of new products like the laser, the smartphone, or some new wonder drug come to mind. In food production, the development of more drought-resistant seeds is another example of technology. Technology, as economists use the term, however, includes still more. It includes new ways of organizing work, like the invention of the assembly line, new methods for ensuring better quality of output in factories, and innovative institutions that facilitate the process of converting inputs into output. In short, technology comprises all the advances that make the existing machines and other inputs produce more, and at higher quality, as well as altogether new products.

It may not make sense to compare the GDPs of China and say, Benin, simply because of the great difference in population size. To understand economic growth, which is really concerned with the growth in living standards of an average person, it is often useful to focus on GDP per capita. Using GDP per capita also makes it easier to compare countries with smaller numbers of people, like Belgium, Uruguay, or Zimbabwe, with countries that have larger populations, like the United States, the Russian Federation, or Nigeria.

To obtain a per capita production function, divide each input in Figure 6.2(a) by the population. This creates a second aggregate production function where the output is GDP per capita (that is, GDP divided by population). The inputs are the average level of human capital per person, the average level of physical capital per person, and the level of technology per person—see Figure 6.2(b). The result of having population in the denominator is mathematically appealing. Increases in population lower per capita income. However, increasing population is important for the average person only if the rate of income growth exceeds population growth. A more important reason for constructing a per capita production function is to understand the contribution of human and physical capital.

Capital Deepening

When society increases the level of capital per person, the result is called **capital deepening**. The idea of capital deepening can apply both to additional human capital per worker and to additional physical capital per worker.

Recall that one way to measure human capital is to look at the average levels of education in an economy. **Figure 6.5** illustrates the human capital deepening for U.S. workers by showing that the proportion of the U.S. population with a high school and a college degree is rising. As recently as 1970, for example, only about half of U.S. adults had at least a high school diploma; by the start of the twenty-first century, more than 80% of adults had graduated from high school. The idea of human capital deepening also applies to the years of experience that workers have, but the average experience level of U.S. workers has not changed much in recent decades. Thus, the key dimension for deepening human capital in the U.S. economy focuses more on additional education and training than on a higher average level of work experience.

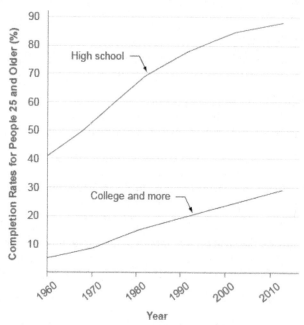

Figure 6.5 Human Capital Deepening in the U.S.   Rising levels of education for persons 25 and older show the deepening of human capital in the U.S. economy. Even today, relatively few U.S. adults have completed a four-year college degree. There is clearly room for additional deepening of human capital to occur. (Source: US Department of Education, National Center for Education Statistics)

Physical capital deepening in the U.S. economy is shown in **Figure 6.6**. The average U.S. worker in the late 2000s was working with physical capital worth almost three times as much as that of the average worker of the early 1950s.

Figure 6.6 Physical Capital per Worker in the United States The value of the physical capital, measured by plant and equipment, used by the average worker in the U.S. economy has risen over the decades. The increase may have leveled off a bit in the 1970s and 1980s, which were not, coincidentally, times of slower-than-usual growth in worker productivity. We see a renewed increase in physical capital per worker in the late 1990s, followed by a flattening in the early 2000s. (Source: Center for International Comparisons of Production, Income and Prices, University of Pennsylvania)

Not only does the current U.S. economy have better-educated workers with more and improved physical capital than it did several decades ago, but these workers have access to more advanced technologies. Growth in technology is impossible to measure with a simple line on a graph, but evidence that we live in an age of technological marvels is all around us—discoveries in genetics and in the structure of particles, the wireless Internet, and other inventions almost too numerous to count. The U.S. Patent and Trademark Office typically has issued more than 150,000 patents annually in recent years.

This recipe for economic growth—investing in labor productivity, with investments in human capital and technology, as well as increasing physical capital—also applies to other economies. In South Korea, for example, universal enrollment in primary school (the equivalent of kindergarten through sixth grade in the United States) had already been achieved by 1965, when Korea's GDP per capita was still near its rock bottom low. By the late 1980s, Korea had achieved almost universal secondary school education (the equivalent of a high school education in the United States). With regard to physical capital, Korea's rates of investment had been about 15% of GDP at the start of the 1960s, but doubled to 30–35% of GDP by the late 1960s and early 1970s. With regard to technology, South Korean students went to universities and colleges around the world to get scientific and technical training, and South Korean firms reached out to study and form partnerships with firms that could offer them technological insights. These factors combined to foster South Korea's high rate of economic growth.

Growth Accounting Studies

Since the late 1950s, economists have conducted growth accounting studies to determine the extent to which physical and human capital deepening and technology have contributed to growth. The usual approach uses an aggregate production function to estimate how much of per capita economic growth can be attributed to growth in physical capital and human capital. These two inputs can be measured, at least roughly. The part of growth that is unexplained by measured inputs, called the residual, is then attributed to growth in technology. The exact numerical estimates differ from study to study and from country to country, depending on how researchers measured these three main factors over what time horizons. For studies of the U.S. economy, three lessons commonly emerge from growth accounting studies.

First, technology is typically the most important contributor to U.S. economic growth. Growth in human capital and physical capital often explains only half or less than half of the economic growth that occurs. New ways of doing things are tremendously important.

Second, while investment in physical capital is essential to growth in labor productivity and GDP per capita, building human capital is at least as important. Economic growth is not just a matter of more machines and buildings. One vivid example of the power of human capital and technological knowledge occurred in Europe in the years after World War II (1939–1945). During the war, a large share of Europe's physical capital, such as factories, roads, and vehicles, was destroyed. Europe also lost an overwhelming amount of human capital in the form of millions of men, women, and children who died during the war. However, the powerful combination of skilled workers and technological knowledge, working within a market-oriented economic framework, rebuilt Europe's productive capacity to an even higher level within less than two decades.

A third lesson is that these three factors of human capital, physical capital, and technology work together. Workers with a higher level of education and skills are often better at coming up with new technological innovations. These technological innovations are often ideas that cannot increase production until they become a part of new investment in physical capital. New machines that embody technological innovations often require additional training, which builds worker skills further. If the recipe for economic growth is to succeed, an economy needs all the ingredients of the aggregate production function. See the following Clear It Up feature for an example of how human capital, physical capital, and technology can combine to significantly impact lives.

Clear It Up

How do girls' education and economic growth relate in low-income countries?

In the early 2000s, according to the World Bank, about 110 million children between the ages of 6 and 11 were not in school—and about two-thirds of them were girls. In Bangladesh, for example, the illiteracy rate for those aged 15 to 24 was 78% for females, compared to 75% for males. In Egypt, for this age group, illiteracy was 84% for females and 91% for males. Cambodia had 86% illiteracy for females and 88% for males. Nigeria had 66% illiteracy for females in the 15 to 24 age bracket and 78% for males.

Whenever any child does not receive a basic education, it is both a human and an economic loss. In low-income countries, wages typically increase by an average of 10 to 20% with each additional year of education. There is, however, some intriguing evidence that helping girls in low-income countries to close the education gap with boys may be especially important, because of the social role that many of the girls will play as mothers and homemakers.

Girls in low-income countries who receive more education tend to grow up to have fewer, healthier, better-educated children. Their children are more likely to be better nourished and to receive basic health care like immunizations. Economic research on women in low-income economies backs up these findings. When 20 women get one additional year of schooling, as a group they will, on average, have one less child. When 1,000 women get one additional year of schooling, on average one to two fewer women from that group will die in childbirth. When a woman stays in school an additional year, that factor alone means that, on average, each of her children will spend an additional half-year in school. Education for girls is a good investment because it is an investment in economic growth with benefits beyond the current generation.

A Healthy Climate for Economic Growth

While physical and human capital deepening and better technology are important, equally important to a nation's well-being is the climate or system within which these inputs are cultivated. Both the type of market economy and a legal system that governs and sustains property rights and contractual rights are important contributors to a healthy economic climate.

A healthy economic climate usually involves some sort of market orientation at the microeconomic, individual, or firm decision-making level. Markets that allow personal and business rewards and incentives for increasing human and physical capital encourage overall macroeconomic growth. For example, when workers participate in a competitive and well-functioning labor market, they have an incentive to acquire additional human capital, because additional education and skills will pay off in higher wages. Firms have an incentive to invest in physical capital and in training workers, because they expect to earn higher profits for their shareholders. Both individuals and firms look for new technologies, because even small inventions can make work easier or lead to product improvement. Collectively, such individual and business decisions made within a market structure add up to macroeconomic growth. Much of the rapid growth since the late nineteenth century has come from harnessing the power of competitive markets to allocate resources. This market orientation typically reaches beyond national borders and includes openness to international trade.

A general orientation toward markets does not rule out important roles for government. There are times when markets fail to allocate capital or technology in a manner that provides the greatest benefit for society as a whole. The role of the government is to correct these failures. In addition, government can guide or influence markets toward certain outcomes. The following examples highlight some important areas that governments around the world have chosen to invest in to facilitate capital deepening and technology:

- Education. The Danish government requires all children under 16 to attend school. They can choose to attend a public school (*Folkeskole*) or a private school. Students do not pay tuition to attend *Folkeskole*. Thirteen percent of primary/secondary (elementary/high) school is private, and the government supplies vouchers to citizens who choose private school.

- Savings and Investment. In the United States, as in other countries, private investment is taxed. Low capital gains taxes encourage investment and so also economic growth.

- Infrastructure. The Japanese government in the mid-1990s undertook significant infrastructure projects to improve roads and public works. This in turn increased the stock of physical capital and ultimately economic growth.

- Special Economic Zones. The island of Mauritius is one of the few African nations to encourage international trade in government-supported **special economic zones (SEZ)**. These are areas of the country, usually with access to a port where, among other benefits, the government does not tax trade. As a result of its SEZ, Mauritius has enjoyed above-average economic growth since the 1980s. Free trade does not have to occur in an SEZ however. Governments can encourage international trade across the board, or surrender to protectionism.

- Scientific Research. The European Union has strong programs to invest in scientific research. The researchers Abraham García and Pierre Mohnen demonstrate that firms which received support from the Austrian government actually increased their research intensity and had more sales. Governments can support scientific research and technical training that helps to create and spread new technologies. Governments can also provide a legal environment that protects the ability of inventors to profit from their inventions.

There are many more ways in which the government can play an active role in promoting economic growth; we explore them in other chapters and in particular in Macroeconomic Policy Around the World. A healthy climate for growth in GDP per capita and labor productivity includes human capital deepening, physical capital deepening, and technological gains, operating in a market-oriented economy with supportive government policies.

6.4 | Economic Convergence

By the end of this section, you will be able to:
- Explain economic convergence
- Analyze various arguments for and against economic convergence
- Evaluate the speed of economic convergence between high-income countries and the rest of the world

Some low-income and middle-income economies around the world have shown a pattern of **convergence**, in which their economies grow faster than those of high-income countries. GDP increased by an average rate of 2.7% per year in the 1990s and 2.3% per year from 2000 to 2008 in the high-income countries of the world, which include the United States, Canada, the countries of the European Union, Japan, Australia, and New Zealand.

Table 6.5 lists 10 countries of the world that belong to an informal "fast growth club." These countries averaged GDP growth (after adjusting for inflation) of at least 5% per year in both the time periods from 1990 to 2000 and from 2000 to 2008. Since economic growth in these countries has exceeded the average of the world's high-income economies, these countries may converge with the high-income countries. The second part of Table 6.5 lists the "slow growth club," which consists of countries that averaged GDP growth of 2% per year or less (after adjusting for inflation) during the same time periods. The final portion of Table 6.5 shows GDP growth rates for the countries of the world divided by income.

Country	Average Growth Rate of GDP 1990–2000	Average Growth Rate of GDP 2000–2008
Fast Growth Club (5% or more per year in both time periods)		
Cambodia	7.1%	9.1%
China	10.6%	9.9%
India	6.0%	7.1%
Ireland	7.5%	5.1%
Jordan	5.0%	6.3%
Laos	6.5%	6.8 %
Mozambique	6.4%	7.3%
Sudan	5.4%	7.3%
Uganda	7.1%	7.3%
Vietnam	7.9%	7.3%
Slow Growth Club (2% or less per year in both time periods)		
Central African Republic	2.0%	0.8%
France	2.0%	1.8%
Germany	1.8%	1.3%
Guinea-Bissau	1.2%	0.2%
Haiti	−1.5%	0.3%
Italy	1.6%	1.2%
Jamaica	0.9%	1.4%
Japan	1.3%	1.3%
Switzerland	1.0%	2.0%
United States	3.2%	2.2%

Table 6.5 Economic Growth around the World   (Source: http://databank.worldbank.org/data/views/variableSelection/selectvariables.aspx?source=world-development-indicators#c_u)

Country	Average Growth Rate of GDP 1990–2000	Average Growth Rate of GDP 2000–2008
World Overview		
High income	2.7%	2.3%
Low income	3.8%	5.6%
Middle income	4.7%	6.1%

Table 6.5 Economic Growth around the World (Source: http://databank.worldbank.org/data/views/variableSelection/selectvariables.aspx?source=world-development-indicators#c_u)

Each of the countries in **Table 6.5** has its own unique story of investments in human and physical capital, technological gains, market forces, government policies, and even lucky events, but an overall pattern of convergence is clear. The low-income countries have GDP growth that is faster than that of the middle-income countries, which in turn have GDP growth that is faster than that of the high-income countries. Two prominent members of the fast-growth club are China and India, which between them have nearly 40% of the world's population. Some prominent members of the slow-growth club are high-income countries like the United States, France, Germany, Italy, and Japan.

Will this pattern of economic convergence persist into the future? This is a controversial question among economists that we will consider by looking at some of the main arguments on both sides.

Arguments Favoring Convergence

Several arguments suggest that low-income countries might have an advantage in achieving greater worker productivity and economic growth in the future.

A first argument is based on diminishing marginal returns. Even though deepening human and physical capital will tend to increase GDP per capita, the law of diminishing returns suggests that as an economy continues to increase its human and physical capital, the marginal gains to economic growth will diminish. For example, raising the average education level of the population by two years from a tenth-grade level to a high school diploma (while holding all other inputs constant) would produce a certain increase in output. An additional two-year increase, so that the average person had a two-year college degree, would increase output further, but the marginal gain would be smaller. Yet another additional two-year increase in the level of education, so that the average person would have a four-year-college bachelor's degree, would increase output still further, but the marginal increase would again be smaller. A similar lesson holds for physical capital. If the quantity of physical capital available to the average worker increases, by, say, $5,000 to $10,000 (again, while holding all other inputs constant), it will increase the level of output. An additional increase from $10,000 to $15,000 will increase output further, but the marginal increase will be smaller.

Low-income countries like China and India tend to have lower levels of human capital and physical capital, so an investment in capital deepening should have a larger marginal effect in these countries than in high-income countries, where levels of human and physical capital are already relatively high. Diminishing returns implies that low-income economies could converge to the levels achieved by the high-income countries.

A second argument is that low-income countries may find it easier to improve their technologies than high-income countries. High-income countries must continually invent new technologies, whereas low-income countries can often find ways of applying technology that has already been invented and is well understood. The economist Alexander Gerschenkron (1904–1978) gave this phenomenon a memorable name: "the advantages of backwardness." Of course, he did not literally mean that it is an advantage to have a lower standard of living. He was pointing out that a country that is behind has some extra potential for catching up.

Finally, optimists argue that many countries have observed the experience of those that have grown more quickly and have learned from it. Moreover, once the people of a country begin to enjoy the benefits of a higher standard of living, they may be more likely to build and support the market-friendly institutions that will help provide this standard of living.

Link It Up

View this video (http://openstaxcollege.org/l/tedhansrosling) to learn about economic growth across the world.

Arguments That Convergence Is neither Inevitable nor Likely

If the growth of an economy depended only on the deepening of human capital and physical capital, then the growth rate of that economy would be expected to slow down over the long run because of diminishing marginal returns. However, there is another crucial factor in the aggregate production function: technology.

The development of new technology can provide a way for an economy to sidestep the diminishing marginal returns of capital deepening. Figure 6.7 shows how. The horizontal axis of the figure measures the amount of capital deepening, which on this figure is an overall measure that includes deepening of both physical and human capital. The amount of human and physical capital per worker increases as you move from left to right, from C_1 to C_2 to C_3. The vertical axis of the diagram measures per capita output. Start by considering the lowest line in this diagram, labeled Technology 1. Along this aggregate production function, the level of technology is being held constant, so the line shows only the relationship between capital deepening and output. As capital deepens from C_1 to C_2 to C_3 and the economy moves from R to U to W, per capita output does increase—but the way in which the line starts out steeper on the left but then flattens as it moves to the right shows the diminishing marginal returns, as additional marginal amounts of capital deepening increase output by ever-smaller amounts. The shape of the aggregate production line (Technology 1) shows that the ability of capital deepening, by itself, to generate sustained economic growth is limited, since diminishing returns will eventually set in.

Figure 6.7 Capital Deepening and New Technology   Imagine that the economy starts at point R, with the level of physical and human capital C_1 and the output per capita at G_1. If the economy relies only on capital deepening, while remaining at the technology level shown by the Technology 1 line, then it would face diminishing marginal returns as it moved from point R to point U to point W. However, now imagine that capital deepening is combined with improvements in technology. Then, as capital deepens from C_1 to C_2, technology improves from Technology 1 to Technology 2, and the economy moves from R to S. Similarly, as capital deepens from C_2 to C_3, technology increases from Technology 2 to Technology 3, and the economy moves from S to T. With improvements in technology, there is no longer any reason that economic growth must necessarily slow down.

Now, bring improvements in technology into the picture. Improved technology means that with a given set of inputs, more output is possible. The production function labeled Technology 1 in the figure is based on one level of technology, but Technology 2 is based on an improved level of technology, so for every level of capital deepening on the horizontal axis, it produces a higher level of output on the vertical axis. In turn, production function Technology 3 represents a still higher level of technology, so that for every level of inputs on the horizontal axis, it produces a higher level of output on the vertical axis than either of the other two aggregate production functions.

Most healthy, growing economies are deepening their human and physical capital and increasing technology at the same time. As a result, the economy can move from a choice like point R on the Technology 1 aggregate production line to a point like S on Technology 2 and a point like T on the still higher aggregate production line (Technology 3). With the combination of technology and capital deepening, the rise in GDP per capita in high-income countries does not need to fade away because of diminishing returns. The gains from technology can offset the diminishing returns involved with capital deepening.

Will technological improvements themselves run into diminishing returns over time? That is, will it become continually harder and more costly to discover new technological improvements? Perhaps someday, but, at least over the last two centuries since the Industrial Revolution, improvements in technology have not run into diminishing marginal returns. Modern inventions, like the Internet or discoveries in genetics or materials science, do not seem to provide smaller gains to output than earlier inventions like the steam engine or the railroad. One reason that technological ideas do not seem to run into diminishing returns is that the ideas of new technology can often be widely applied at a marginal cost that is very low or even zero. A specific additional machine, or an additional year of education, must be used by a specific worker or group of workers. A new technology or invention can be used by many workers across the economy at very low marginal cost.

The argument that it is easier for a low-income country to copy and adapt existing technology than it is for a high-income country to invent new technology is not necessarily true, either. When it comes to adapting and using new technology, a society's performance is not necessarily guaranteed, but is the result of whether the economic, educational, and public policy institutions of the country are supportive. In theory, perhaps, low-income countries have many opportunities to copy and adapt technology, but if they lack the appropriate supportive economic infrastructure and institutions, the theoretical possibility that backwardness might have certain advantages is of little practical relevance.

Link It Up

Visit this website (http://openstaxcollege.org/l/Indiapoverty) to read more about economic growth in India.

The Slowness of Convergence

Although economic convergence between the high-income countries and the rest of the world seems possible and even likely, it will proceed slowly. Consider, for example, a country that starts off with a GDP per capita of $40,000, which would roughly represent a typical high-income country today, and another country that starts out at $4,000, which is roughly the level in low-income but not impoverished countries like Indonesia, Guatemala, or Egypt. Say that the rich country chugs along at a 2% annual growth rate of GDP per capita, while the poorer country grows at the aggressive rate of 7% per year. After 30 years, GDP per capita in the rich country will be $72,450 (that is, $40,000 (1 + 0.02)^{30}$) while in the poor country it will be $30,450 (that is, $4,000 (1 + 0.07)^{30}$). Convergence has occurred; the rich country used to be 10 times as wealthy as the poor one, and now it is only about 2.4 times as wealthy. Even after 30 consecutive years of very rapid growth, however, people in the low-income country are still likely to feel quite poor compared to people in the rich country. Moreover, as the poor country catches up, its opportunities for catch-up growth are reduced, and its growth rate may slow down somewhat.

The slowness of convergence illustrates again that small differences in annual rates of economic growth become huge differences over time. The high-income countries have been building up their advantage in standard of living over decades—more than a century in some cases. Even in an optimistic scenario, it will take decades for the low-income countries of the world to catch up significantly.

Bring it Home

Calories and Economic Growth

The story of modern economic growth can be told by looking at calorie consumption over time. The dramatic rise in incomes allowed the average person to eat better and consume more calories. How did these incomes increase? The neoclassical growth consensus uses the aggregate production function to suggest that the period of modern economic growth came about because of increases in inputs such as technology and physical and human capital. Also important was the way in which technological progress combined with physical and human capital deepening to create growth and convergence. The issue of distribution of income notwithstanding, it is clear that the average worker can afford more calories in 2014 than in 1875.

Aside from increases in income, there is another reason why the average person can afford more food. Modern agriculture has allowed many countries to produce more food than they need. Despite having more than enough food, however, many governments and multilateral agencies have not solved the food distribution problem. In fact, food shortages, famine, or general food insecurity are caused more often by the failure of government macroeconomic policy, according to the Nobel Prize-winning economist Amartya Sen. Sen has conducted extensive research into issues of inequality, poverty, and the role of government in improving standards of living. Macroeconomic policies that strive toward stable inflation, full employment, education of women, and preservation of property rights are more likely to eliminate starvation and provide for a more even distribution of food.

Because we have more food per capita, global food prices have decreased since 1875. The prices of some foods, however, have decreased more than the prices of others. For example, researchers from the University of Washington have shown that in the United States, calories from zucchini and lettuce are 100 times more expensive than calories from oil, butter, and sugar. Research from countries like India, China, and the United States suggests that as incomes rise, individuals want more calories from fats and protein and fewer from carbohydrates. This has very interesting implications for global food production, obesity, and environmental consequences. Affluent urban India has an obesity problem much like many parts of the United States. The forces of convergence are at work.

KEY TERMS

aggregate production function the process whereby an economy as a whole turns economic inputs such as human capital, physical capital, and technology into output measured as GDP per capita

capital deepening an increase by society in the average level of physical and/or human capital per person

compound growth rate the rate of growth when multiplied by a base that includes past GDP growth

contractual rights the rights of individuals to enter into agreements with others regarding the use of their property providing recourse through the legal system in the event of noncompliance

convergence pattern in which economies with low per capita incomes grow faster than economies with high per capita incomes

human capital the accumulated skills and education of workers

Industrial Revolution the widespread use of power-driven machinery and the economic and social changes that occurred in the first half of the 1800s

infrastructure a component of physical capital such as roads, rail systems, and so on

innovation putting advances in knowledge to use in a new product or service

invention advances in knowledge

labor productivity the value of what is produced per worker, or per hour worked (sometimes called worker productivity)

modern economic growth the period of rapid economic growth from 1870 onward

physical capital the plant and equipment used by firms in production; this includes infrastructure

production function the process whereby a firm turns economic inputs like labor, machinery, and raw materials into outputs like goods and services used by consumers

rule of law the process of enacting laws that protect individual and entity rights to use their property as they see fit. Laws must be clear, public, fair, and enforced, and applicable to all members of society

special economic zone (SEZ) area of a country, usually with access to a port where, among other benefits, the government does not tax trade

technological change a combination of invention—advances in knowledge—and innovation

technology all the ways in which existing inputs produce more or higher quality, as well as different and altogether new products

KEY CONCEPTS AND SUMMARY

6.1 The Relatively Recent Arrival of Economic Growth

Since the early nineteenth century, there has been a spectacular process of long-run economic growth during which the world's leading economies—mostly those in Western Europe and North America—expanded GDP per capita at an average rate of about 2% per year. In the last half-century, countries like Japan, South Korea, and China have shown the potential to catch up. The extensive process of economic growth, often referred to as modern economic growth, was facilitated by the Industrial Revolution, which increased worker productivity and trade, as well as the development of governance and market institutions.

6.2 Labor Productivity and Economic Growth

Productivity, the value of what is produced per worker, or per hour worked, can be measured as the level of GDP per worker or GDP per hour. The United States experienced a productivity slowdown between 1973 and 1989. Since then, U.S. productivity has rebounded (the current global recession notwithstanding). It is not clear whether the current growth in productivity will be sustained. The rate of productivity growth is the primary determinant of an economy's rate of long-term economic growth and higher wages. Over decades and generations, seemingly small differences of a few percentage points in the annual rate of economic growth make an enormous difference in GDP per capita. An aggregate production function specifies how certain inputs in the economy, like human capital, physical capital, and technology, lead to the output measured as GDP per capita.

Compound interest and compound growth rates behave in the same way as productivity rates. Seemingly small changes in percentage points can have big impacts on income over time.

6.3 Components of Economic Growth

Over decades and generations, seemingly small differences of a few percentage points in the annual rate of economic growth make an enormous difference in GDP per capita. Capital deepening refers to an increase in the amount of capital per worker, either human capital per worker, in the form of higher education or skills, or physical capital per worker. Technology, in its economic meaning, refers broadly to all new methods of production, which includes major scientific inventions but also small inventions and even better forms of management or other types of institutions. A healthy climate for growth in GDP per capita consists of improvements in human capital, physical capital, and technology, in a market-oriented environment with supportive public policies and institutions.

6.4 Economic Convergence

When countries with lower levels of GDP per capita catch up to countries with higher levels of GDP per capita, the process is called convergence. Convergence can occur even when both high- and low-income countries increase investment in physical and human capital with the objective of growing GDP. This is because the impact of new investment in physical and human capital on a low-income country may result in huge gains as new skills or equipment are combined with the labor force. In higher-income countries, however, a level of investment equal to that of the low income country is not likely to have as big an impact, because the more developed country most likely has high levels of capital investment. Therefore, the marginal gain from this additional investment tends to be successively less and less. Higher income countries are more likely to have diminishing returns to their investments and must continually invent new technologies; this allows lower-income economies to have a chance for convergent growth. However, many high-income economies have developed economic and political institutions that provide a healthy economic climate for an ongoing stream of technological innovations. Continuous technological innovation can counterbalance diminishing returns to investments in human and physical capital.

SELF-CHECK QUESTIONS

1. Explain what the Industrial Revolution was and where it began.

2. Explain the difference between property rights and contractual rights. Why do they matter to economic growth?

3. Are there other ways in which we can measure productivity besides the amount produced per hour of work?

4. Assume there are two countries: South Korea and the United States. South Korea grows at 4% and the United States grows at 1%. For the sake of simplicity, assume they both start from the same fictional income level, $10,000. What will the incomes of the United States and South Korea be in 20 years? By how many multiples will each country's income grow in 20 years?

5. What do the growth accounting studies conclude are the determinants of growth? Which is more important, the determinants or how they are combined?

6. What policies can the government of a free-market economy implement to stimulate economic growth?

7. List the areas where government policy can help economic growth.

8. Use an example to explain why, after periods of rapid growth, a low-income country that has not caught up to a high-income country may feel poor.

9. Would the following events usually lead to capital deepening? Why or why not?
    a. A weak economy in which businesses become reluctant to make long-term investments in physical capital.
    b. A rise in international trade.
    c. A trend in which many more adults participate in continuing education courses through their employers and at colleges and universities.

10. What are the "advantages of backwardness" for economic growth?

11. Would you expect capital deepening to result in diminished returns? Why or why not? Would you expect improvements in technology to result in diminished returns? Why or why not?

12. Why does productivity growth in high-income economies not slow down as it runs into diminishing returns from additional investments in physical capital and human capital? Does this show one area where the theory of diminishing returns fails to apply? Why or why not?

REVIEW QUESTIONS

13. How did the Industrial Revolution increase the rate of economic growth and income levels in the United States?

14. How much should a nation be concerned if its rate of economic growth is just 2% slower than other nations?

15. How is GDP per capita calculated differently from labor productivity?

16. How do gains in labor productivity lead to gains in GDP per capita?

17. What is an aggregate production function?

18. What is capital deepening?

19. What do economists mean when they refer to improvements in technology?

20. For a high-income economy like the United States, what elements of the aggregate production function are most important in bringing about growth in GDP per capita? What about a middle-income country such as Brazil? A low-income country such as Niger?

21. List some arguments for and against the likelihood of convergence.

CRITICAL THINKING QUESTIONS

22. Over the past 50 years, many countries have experienced an annual growth rate in real GDP per capita greater than that of the United States. Some examples are China, Japan, South Korea, and Taiwan. Does that mean the United States is regressing relative to other countries? Does that mean these countries will eventually overtake the United States in terms of rate of growth of real GDP per capita? Explain.

23. Labor Productivity and Economic Growth outlined the logic of how increased productivity is associated with increased wages. Detail a situation where this is not the case and explain why it is not.

24. Change in labor productivity is one of the most watched international statistics of growth. Visit the St.

Louis Federal Reserve website and find the data section (http://research.stlouisfed.org). Find international comparisons of labor productivity, listed under the FRED Economic database (Growth Rate of Total Labor Productivity), and compare two countries in the recent past. State what you think the reasons for differences in labor productivity could be.

25. Refer back to the **Work It Out** about Comparing the Economies of Two Countries and examine the data for the two countries you chose. How are they similar? How are they different?

26. Education seems to be important for human capital deepening. As people become better educated and more knowledgeable, are there limits to how much additional benefit more education can provide? Why or why not?

27. Describe some of the political and social tradeoffs that might occur when a less developed country adopts a strategy to promote labor force participation and economic growth via investment in girls' education.

28. Why is investing in girls' education beneficial for growth?

29. How is the concept of technology, as defined with the aggregate production function, different from our everyday use of the word?

30. What sorts of policies can governments implement to encourage convergence?

31. As technological change makes us more sedentary and food costs increase, obesity is likely. What factors do you think may limit obesity?

PROBLEMS

32. An economy starts off with a GDP per capita of $5,000. How large will the GDP per capita be if it grows at an annual rate of 2% for 20 years? 2% for 40 years? 4% for 40 years? 6% for 40 years?

33. An economy starts off with a GDP per capita of 12,000 euros. How large will the GDP per capita be if it grows at an annual rate of 3% for 10 years? 3% for 30 years? 6% for 30 years?

34. Say that the average worker in Canada has a productivity level of $30 per hour while the average worker in the United Kingdom has a productivity level of $25 per hour (both measured in U.S. dollars). Over the next five years, say that worker productivity in Canada grows at 1% per year while worker productivity in the UK grows 3% per year. After five years, who will have the higher productivity level, and by how much?

35. Say that the average worker in the U.S. economy is eight times as productive as an average worker in Mexico. If the productivity of U.S. workers grows at 2% for 25 years and the productivity of Mexico's workers grows at 6% for 25 years, which country will have higher worker productivity at that point?

7 | Unemployment

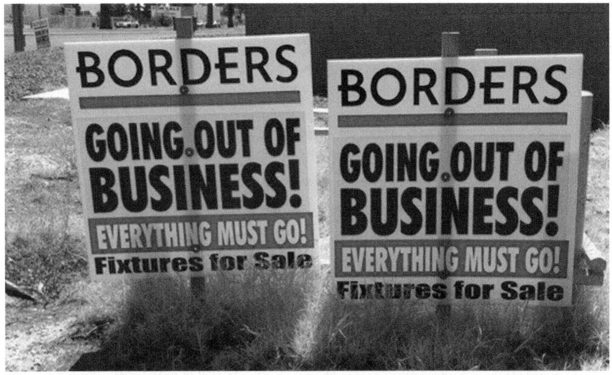

Figure 7.1 Out of Business   Borders was one of the many companies unable to recover from the economic recession of 2008-2009. (Credit: modification of work by Luis Villa del Campo/Flickr Creative Commons)

Bring it Home

The Mysterious Case of the Missing Candidates

Nearly eight million U.S. jobs were lost during the Great Recession of 2008-2009, with unemployment peaking at 10% in October 2009, according to the Bureau of Labor Statistics (BLS). That is a huge number of positions gone. During the tepid recovery, some positions were added, but as of summer 2013, unemployment had remained persistently higher than the pre-recession rate of less than 5%. Some economists and policymakers worried the recovery would be "jobless." With the economy growing, albeit slowly, why wasn't the unemployment number falling? Why were firms not hiring?

Peter Cappelli, noted Wharton management professor and Director of Wharton's Center for Human Resources, does not believe the job search process is akin to what he terms the "Home Depot" view of hiring. According to him, this view "basically says that filling a job is like replacing a part in a washing machine. You simply find someone who does the exact same job as that broken part, plug him or her into the washing machine and that is it." The job search, for both the prospective employee and the employer, is more complex than that.

In a hiring situation, employers hold all the cards. They write the job descriptions, determine the salaries, decide when and how to advertise positions, and set the controls on employment application screening software. Advertising for positions has increased as the economic recovery progresses, yet here's the kicker: Employers say there are no applicants out there who meet their needs. While the unemployment rate is now below 6% as of the beginning of 2015, many economists and policymakers (including the Chair of the Federal

Reserve, Janet Yellen) are still concerned about "slack" in the labor market. So the question arises: where are the job candidates?

That question leads us to the topic of this chapter—unemployment. What constitutes it? How is it measured? And if the economy is growing, why isn't the pool of job openings growing along with it? Sounds like the economy has a case of "missing" candidates.

Introduction to Unemployment

In this chapter, you will learn about:

- How the Unemployment Rate is Defined and Computed

- Patterns of Unemployment

- What Causes Changes in Unemployment over the Short Run

- What Causes Changes in Unemployment over the Long Run

Unemployment can be a terrible and wrenching life experience—like a serious automobile accident or a messy divorce—whose consequences can be fully understood only by someone who has gone through it. For unemployed individuals and their families, there is the day-to-day financial stress of not knowing where the next paycheck is coming from. There are painful adjustments, like watching your savings account dwindle, selling a car and buying a cheaper one, or moving to a less expensive place to live. Even when the unemployed person finds a new job, it may pay less than the previous one. For many people, their job is an important part of their self worth. When unemployment separates people from the workforce, it can affect family relationships as well as mental and physical health.

The human costs of unemployment alone would justify making a low level of unemployment an important public policy priority. But unemployment also includes economic costs to the broader society. When millions of unemployed but willing workers cannot find jobs, an economic resource is going unused. An economy with high unemployment is like a company operating with a functional but unused factory. The opportunity cost of unemployment is the output that could have been produced by the unemployed workers.

This chapter will discuss how the unemployment rate is defined and computed. It will examine the patterns of unemployment over time, for the U.S. economy as a whole, for different demographic groups in the U.S. economy, and for other countries. It will then consider an economic explanation for unemployment, and how it explains the patterns of unemployment and suggests public policies for reducing it.

7.1 | How the Unemployment Rate Is Defined and Computed

By the end of this section, you will be able to:
- Calculate the labor force percentage and the unemployment rate
- Explain hidden unemployment and what it means to be in or out of the labor force
- Evaluate the collection and interpretation of unemployment data

Unemployment is typically described in newspaper or television reports as a percentage or a rate. A recent report might have said, for example, *from August 2009 to November 2009, the U.S. unemployment rate rose from 9.7% to 10.0%, but by June 2010, it had fallen to 9.5%*. At a glance, the changes between the percentages may seem small. But remember that the U.S. economy has about 155 million adults who either have jobs or are looking for them. A rise or fall of just 0.1% in the unemployment rate of 155 million potential workers translates into 155,000 people, which is roughly the total population of a city like Syracuse, New York, Brownsville, Texas, or Pasadena, California. Large rises in the unemployment rate mean large numbers of job losses. In November 2009, at the peak of the recession, about 15 million people were out of work. Even with the unemployment rate now at 5.5% as of February 2015, about 8 million people total are out of work.

Link It Up

The Bureau of Labor Statistics (http://openstaxcollege.org/l/BLS1) tracks and reports all data related to unemployment.

Who's In or Out of the Labor Force?

Should everyone without a job be counted as unemployed? Of course not. Children, for example, should not be counted as unemployed. Surely, the retired should not be counted as unemployed. Many full-time college students have only a part-time job, or no job at all, but it seems inappropriate to count them as suffering the pains of unemployment. Some people are not working because they are rearing children, ill, on vacation, or on parental leave.

The point is that the adult population is not just divided into employed and unemployed. A third group exists: people who do not have a job, and for some reason—retirement, looking after children, taking a voluntary break before a new job—are not interested in having a job, either. It also includes those who do want a job but have quit looking, often due to being discouraged by their inability to find suitable employment. Economists refer to this third group of those who are not working and not looking for work as **out of the labor force** or not in the labor force.

The U.S. unemployment rate, which is based on a monthly survey carried out by the U.S. Bureau of the Census, asks a series of questions to divide up the adult population into employed, unemployed, or not in the labor force. To be classified as unemployed, a person must be without a job, currently available to work, and actively looking for work in the previous four weeks. Thus, a person who does not have a job but who is not currently available to work or has not actively looked for work in the last four weeks is counted as out of the labor force.

Employed: currently working for pay

Unemployed: Out of work and actively looking for a job

Out of the labor force: Out of paid work and not actively looking for a job

Labor force: the number of employed plus the unemployed

Calculating the Unemployment Rate

Figure 7.2 shows the three-way division of the over-16 adult population. In February 2015, about 62.8% of the adult population was "in the labor force"; that is, people are either employed or without a job but looking for work. Those in the labor force can be divided into the employed and the unemployed. These values are also shown in Table 7.1. The **unemployment rate** is not the percentage of the total adult population without jobs, but rather the percentage of adults who are in the labor force but who do not have jobs:

$$\text{Unemployment rate} \ = \ \frac{\text{Unemployed people}}{\text{Total labor force}} \times 100$$

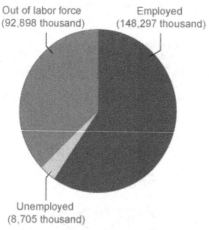

Out of labor force
(92,898 thousand)

Employed
(148,297 thousand)

Unemployed
(8,705 thousand)

Figure 7.2 Employed, Unemployed, and Out of the Labor Force Distribution of Adult Population (age 16 and older), February 2015 The total adult, working-age population in February 2015 was 249.9 million. Out of this total population, 148.3 were classified as employed, and 8.7 million were classified as unemployed. The remaining 92.9 were classified as out of the labor force. As you will learn, however, this seemingly simple chart does not tell the whole story.

Total adult population over the age of 16	249.9 million
In the labor force	157 million (62.8%)
Employed	148.3 million
Unemployed	8.7 million
Out of the labor force	92.9 million (37.2%)

Table 7.1 U.S. Employment and Unemployment, February 2015 (Source: http://www.bls.gov/news.release/empsit.t01.htm)

In this example, the unemployment rate can be calculated as 8.7 million unemployed people divided by 157 million people in the labor force, which works out to a 5.5% rate of unemployment. The following Work It Out feature will walk you through the steps of this calculation.

Work It Out ⎯◯⎯◯⎯◯

Calculating Labor Force Percentages

So how do economists arrive at the percentages in and out of the labor force and the unemployment rate? We will use the values in Table 7.1 to illustrate the steps.

To determine the percentage in the labor force:

Step 1. Divide the number of people in the labor force (157 million) by the total adult (working-age) population (249.9 million).

Step 2. Multiply by 100 to obtain the percentage.

$$
\begin{aligned}
\text{Percentage in the labor force} &= \frac{157}{249.9} \\
&= 0.6282 \\
&= 62.8\%
\end{aligned}
$$

To determine the percentage out of the labor force:

Step 1. Divide the number of people out the labor force (92.9 million) by the total adult (working-age) population (249.9 million).

Step 2. Multiply by 100 to obtain the percentage.

$$\text{Percentage in the labor force} = \frac{92.9}{249.9}$$
$$= 0.3717$$
$$= 37.2\%$$

To determine the unemployment rate:

Step 1. Divide the number of unemployed people (8.7 million) by the total labor force (157 million).

Step 2. Multiply by 100 to obtain the rate.

$$\text{Unemployment rate} = \frac{8.7}{157}$$
$$= 0.0554$$
$$= 5.5\%$$

Hidden Unemployment

Even with the "out of the labor force" category, there are still some people that are mislabeled in the categorization of employed, unemployed, or out of the labor force. There are some people who have only part time or temporary jobs and who are looking for full time and permanent employment that are counted as employed, though they are not employed in the way they would like or need to be. Additionally, there are individuals who are **underemployed**. This includes those that are trained or skilled for one type or level of work who are working in a lower paying job or one that does not utilize their skills. For example, an individual with a college degree in finance who is working as a sales clerk would be considered underemployed. They are, however, also counted in the employed group. All of these individuals fall under the umbrella of the term "hidden unemployment." **Discouraged workers**, those who have stopped looking for employment and, hence, are no longer counted in the unemployed also fall into this group

Labor Force Participation Rate

Another important statistic is the **labor force participation rate**. This is the percentage of adults in an economy who are either employed or who are unemployed and looking for a job. So, using the data in Figure 7.2 and Table 7.1, those included in this calculation would be the 157 million individuals in the labor force. The rate is calculated by taking the number of people in the labor force, that is, the number employed and the number unemployed, divided by the total adult population and multiplying by 100 to get the percentage. For the data from February 2015, the labor force participation rate is 62.8%. Historically, the civilian labor force participation rate in the United States climbed beginning in the 1960s as women increasingly entered the workforce, and it peaked at around 68% in late 1999 to early 2000. Since then, the labor force participation rate has steadily declined.

The Establishment Payroll Survey

When the unemployment report comes out each month, the Bureau of Labor Statistics (BLS) also reports on the number of jobs created—which comes from the establishment payroll survey. The payroll survey is based on a survey of about 140,000 businesses and government agencies throughout the United States. It generates payroll employment estimates by the following criteria: all employees, average weekly hours worked, and average hourly, weekly, and overtime earnings. One of the criticisms of this survey is that it does not count the self-employed. It also does not make a distinction between new, minimum wage, part time or temporary jobs and full time jobs with "decent" pay.

How Is the U.S. Unemployment Data Collected?

The unemployment rate announced by the U.S. Bureau of Labor Statistics each month is based on the Current Population Survey (CPS), which has been carried out every month since 1940. Great care is taken to make this survey representative of the country as a whole. The country is first divided into 3,137 areas. The U.S. Bureau of the Census then selects 729 of these areas to survey. The 729 areas are then divided into districts of about 300 households each, and each district is divided into clusters of about four dwelling units. Every month, Census Bureau employees call about 15,000 of the four-household clusters, for a total of 60,000 households. Households are interviewed for four consecutive months, then rotated out of the survey for eight months, and then interviewed again for the same four months the following year, before leaving the sample permanently.

Based on this survey, unemployment rates are calculated by state, industry, urban and rural areas, gender, age, race or ethnicity, and level of education. A wide variety of other information is available, too. For example, how long have people been unemployed? Did they become unemployed because they quit, or were laid off, or their employer went out of business? Is the unemployed person the only wage earner in the family? The Current Population Survey is a treasure trove of information about employment and unemployment. If you are wondering what the difference is between the CPS and EPS, read the following Clear it Up feature.

What is the difference between CPS and EPS?

The Current Population Survey (CPS) conducted by the United States Census Bureau measures the percentage of the labor force that is unemployed. The establishment payroll survey (EPS) by the Bureau of Labor Statistics is a payroll survey that measures the net change in jobs created for the month.

Criticisms of Measuring Unemployment

There are always complications in measuring the number of unemployed. For example, what about people who do not have jobs and would be available to work, but have gotten discouraged at the lack of available jobs in their area and stopped looking? Such people, and their families, may be suffering the pains of unemployment. But the survey counts them as out of the labor force because they are not actively looking for work. Other people may tell the Census Bureau that they are ready to work and looking for a job but, truly, they are not that eager to work and are not looking very hard at all. They are counted as unemployed, although they might more accurately be classified as out of the labor force. Still other people may have a job, perhaps doing something like yard work, child care, or cleaning houses, but are not reporting the income earned to the tax authorities. They may report being unemployed, when they actually are working.

Although the unemployment rate gets most of the public and media attention, economic researchers at the Bureau of Labor Statistics publish a wide array of surveys and reports that try to measure these kinds of issues and to develop a more nuanced and complete view of the labor market. It is not exactly a hot news flash that economic statistics are imperfect. Even imperfect measures like the unemployment rate, however, can still be quite informative, when interpreted knowledgeably and sensibly.

Link It Up

Click here (http://openstaxcollege.org/l/BLS_CPS) to learn more about the CPS to read frequently asked questions about employment and labor.

7.2 | Patterns of Unemployment

By the end of this section, you will be able to:
- Explain historical patterns of unemployment in the U.S.
- Identify trends of unemployment based on demographics
- Evaluate global unemployment rates

Let's look at how unemployment rates have changed over time and how various groups of people are affected by unemployment differently.

The Historical U.S. Unemployment Rate

Figure 7.3 shows the historical pattern of U.S. unemployment since 1955.

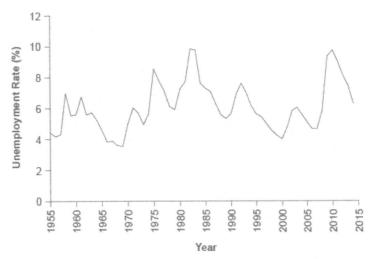

Figure 7.3 The U.S. Unemployment Rate, 1955–2015 The U.S. unemployment rate moves up and down as the economy moves in and out of recessions. But over time, the unemployment rate seems to return to a range of 4% to 6%. There does not seem to be a long-term trend toward the rate moving generally higher or generally lower. (Source: Federal Reserve Economic Data (FRED) https://research.stlouisfed.org/fred2/series/LRUN64TTUSA156S0)

As we look at this data, several patterns stand out:

1. Unemployment rates do fluctuate over time. During the deep recessions of the early 1980s and of 2007–2009, unemployment reached roughly 10%. For comparison, during the Great Depression of the 1930s, the unemployment rate reached almost 25% of the labor force.

2. Unemployment rates in the late 1990s and into the mid-2000s were rather low by historical standards. The unemployment rate was below 5% from 1997 to 2000 and near 5% during almost all of 2006–2007. The previous time unemployment had been less than 5% for three consecutive years was three decades earlier, from 1968 to 1970.

3. The unemployment rate never falls all the way to zero. Indeed, it never seems to get below 3%—and it stays that low only for very short periods. (Reasons why this is the case are discussed later in this chapter.)

4. The timing of rises and falls in unemployment matches fairly well with the timing of upswings and downswings in the overall economy. During periods of recession and depression, unemployment is high. During periods of economic growth, unemployment tends to be lower.

5. No significant upward or downward trend in unemployment rates is apparent. This point is especially worth noting because the U.S. population nearly quadrupled from 76 million in 1900 to over 314 million by 2012. Moreover, a higher proportion of U.S. adults are now in the paid workforce, because women have entered the paid labor force in significant numbers in recent decades. Women composed 18% of the paid workforce in 1900 and nearly half of the paid workforce in 2012. But despite the increased number of workers, as well as

other economic events like globalization and the continuous invention of new technologies, the economy has provided jobs without causing any long-term upward or downward trend in unemployment rates.

Unemployment Rates by Group

Unemployment is not distributed evenly across the U.S. population. **Figure 7.4** shows unemployment rates broken down in various ways: by gender, age, and race/ethnicity.

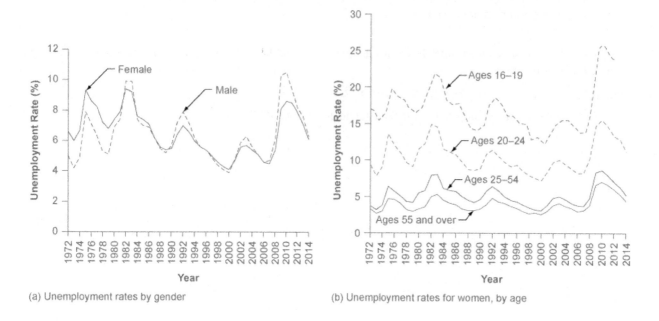

(a) Unemployment rates by gender

(b) Unemployment rates for women, by age

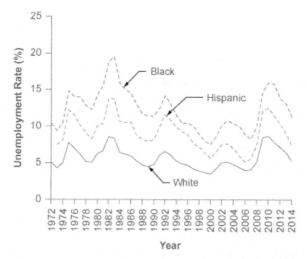

(c) Unemployment rates by race and ethnicity

Figure 7.4 Unemployment Rate by Demographic Group (a) By gender, 1972–2014. Unemployment rates for men used to be lower than unemployment rates for women, but in recent decades, the two rates have been very close, often with the unemployment rate for men somewhat higher. (b) By age, 1972–2014. Unemployment rates are highest for the very young and become lower with age. (c) By race and ethnicity, 1972–2014. Although unemployment rates for all groups tend to rise and fall together, the unemployment rate for whites has been lower than the unemployment rate for blacks and Hispanics in recent decades. (Source: www.bls.gov)

The unemployment rate for women had historically tended to be higher than the unemployment rate for men, perhaps reflecting the historical pattern that women were seen as "secondary" earners. By about 1980, however, the unemployment rate for women was essentially the same as that for men, as shown in **Figure 7.4** (a). During the recession of 2008-2009, the unemployment rate for men exceeded the unemployment rate for women. Through 2014, this pattern has remained, although the gap is narrowing.

Link It Up ⚭

Read this report (http://openstaxcollege.org/l/BLS_recession) for detailed information on the recession of 2008–2009. It also provides some very useful information on the statistics of unemployment.

Younger workers tend to have higher unemployment, while middle-aged workers tend to have lower unemployment, probably because the middle-aged workers feel the responsibility of needing to have a job more heavily. Younger workers move in and out of jobs (and in and out of the labor force) more easily. Elderly workers have extremely low rates of unemployment, because those who do not have jobs often exit the labor force by retiring, and thus are not counted in the unemployment statistics. **Figure 7.4** (b) shows unemployment rates for women divided by age; the pattern for men is similar.

The unemployment rate for African-Americans is substantially higher than the rate for other racial or ethnic groups, a fact that surely reflects, to some extent, a pattern of discrimination that has constrained blacks' labor market opportunities. However, the gaps between unemployment rates for whites and for blacks and Hispanics diminished in the 1990s, as shown in **Figure 7.4** (c). In fact, unemployment rates for blacks and Hispanics were at the lowest levels for several decades in the mid-2000s before rising during the recent Great Recession.

Finally, those with less education typically suffer higher unemployment. In February 2015, for example, the unemployment rate for those with a college degree was 2.7%; for those with some college but not a four year degree, the unemployment rate was 5.1%; for high school graduates with no additional degree, the unemployment rate was 5.4%; and for those without a high school diploma, the unemployment rate was 8.4%. This pattern may arise because additional education offers better connections to the labor market and higher demand, or it may occur because the labor market opportunities for low-skilled workers are less attractive than the opportunities for the more highly-skilled. Because of lower pay, low-skilled workers may be less motivated to find jobs.

Breaking Down Unemployment in Other Ways

The Bureau of Labor Statistics also gives information about the reasons for being unemployed as well as the length of time individuals have been unemployed. Table 7.2, for example, shows the four reasons for being unemployed and the percentages of the currently unemployed that fall into each category. Table 7.3 shows the length of unemployment. For both of these, the data is from February of 2015. (bls.gov)

Reason	Percentage
New Entrants	11.2%
Re-entrants	30.5%
Job Leavers	10.2%
Job Losers: Temporary	11.7%
Job Losers: Non Temporary	36.3%

Table 7.2 Reasons for Being Unemployed, February 2015

Length of Time	Percentage
Under 5 weeks	27.9%
5 to 14 weeks	25.6%
15 to 26 weeks	15.4%
Over 27 weeks	31.1%

Table 7.3 Length of Unemployment, February 2015

Link It Up

Watch this speech (http://openstaxcollege.org/l/droids) on the impact of droids on the labor market.

International Unemployment Comparisons

From an international perspective, the U.S. unemployment rate typically has looked a little better than average. **Table 7.4** compares unemployment rates for 1991, 1996, 2001, 2006 (just before the recession), and 2012 (somewhat after the recession) from several other high-income countries.

Country	1991	1996	2001	2006	2012
United States	6.8%	5.4%	4.8%	4.4%	8.1%
Canada	9.8%	8.8%	6.4%	6.2%	6.3%
Japan	2.1%	3.4%	5.1%	4.5%	3.9%
France	9.5%	12.5%	8.7%	10.1%	10.0%
Germany	5.6%	9.0%	8.9%	9.8%	5.5%
Italy	6.9%	11.7%	9.6%	7.8%	10.8%
Sweden	3.1%	9.9%	5.0%	5.2%	7.9%
United Kingdom	8.8%	8.1%	5.1%	5.5%	8.0%

Table 7.4 International Comparisons of Unemployment Rates

However, cross-country comparisons of unemployment rates need to be treated with care, because each country has slightly different survey tools for measuring unemployment and also different labor markets. For example, Japan's unemployment rates appear quite low, but Japan's economy has been mired in slow growth and recession since the late 1980s, and Japan's unemployment rate probably paints too rosy a picture of its labor market. In Japan, workers who lose their jobs are often quick to exit the labor force and not look for a new job, in which case they are not counted as unemployed. In addition, Japanese firms are often quite reluctant to fire workers, and so firms have substantial numbers of workers who are on reduced hours or officially employed, but doing very little. This Japanese pattern is perhaps best viewed as an unusual method for society to provide support for the unemployed, rather than a sign of a healthy economy.

Link It Up

We hear about the Chinese economy in the news all the time. The value of the Chinese yuan in comparison to the U.S. dollar is likely to be part of the nightly business report. So why is the Chinese economy not included in this discussion of international unemployment? The lack of reliable statistics is probably the reason. This article (http://openstaxcollege.org/l/ChinaEmployment) explains why.

Comparing unemployment rates in the United States and other high-income economies with unemployment rates in Latin America, Africa, Eastern Europe, and Asia is very difficult. One reason is that the statistical agencies in many poorer countries lack the resources and technical capabilities of the U.S. Bureau of the Census. But a more difficult problem with international comparisons is that in many low-income countries, most workers are not involved in the labor market through an employer who pays them regularly. Instead, workers in these countries are engaged in short-term work, subsistence activities, and barter. Moreover, the effect of unemployment is very different in high-income and low-income countries. Unemployed workers in the developed economies have access to various government programs like unemployment insurance, welfare, and food stamps; such programs may barely exist in poorer countries. Although unemployment is a serious problem in many low-income countries, it manifests itself in a different way than in high-income countries.

7.3 | What Causes Changes in Unemployment over the Short Run

By the end of this section, you will be able to:
- Analyze cyclical unemployment
- Explain the relationship between sticky wages and employment using various economic arguments
- Apply supply and demand models to unemployment and wages

We have seen that unemployment varies across times and places. What causes changes in unemployment? There are different answers in the short run and in the long run. Let's look at the short run first.

Cyclical Unemployment

Let's make the plausible assumption that in the short run, from a few months to a few years, the quantity of hours that the average person is willing to work for a given wage does not change much, so the labor supply curve does not shift much. In addition, make the standard *ceteris paribus* assumption that there is no substantial short-term change in the age structure of the labor force, institutions and laws affecting the labor market, or other possibly relevant factors.

One primary determinant of the demand for labor from firms is how they perceive the state of the macro economy. If firms believe that business is expanding, then at any given wage they will desire to hire a greater quantity of labor, and the labor demand curve shifts to the right. Conversely, if firms perceive that the economy is slowing down or entering a recession, then they will wish to hire a lower quantity of labor at any given wage, and the labor demand curve will shift to the left. The variation in unemployment caused by the economy moving from expansion to recession or from recession to expansion (i.e. the business cycle) is known as **cyclical unemployment**.

From the standpoint of the supply-and-demand model of competitive and flexible labor markets, unemployment represents something of a puzzle. In a supply-and-demand model of a labor market, as illustrated in **Figure 7.5**, the labor market should move toward an equilibrium wage and quantity. At the equilibrium wage (We), the equilibrium quantity (Qe) of labor supplied by workers should be equal to the quantity of labor demanded by employers.

Figure 7.5 The Unemployment and Equilibrium in the Labor Market In a labor market with flexible wages, the equilibrium will occur at wage We and quantity Qe, where the number of people looking for jobs (shown by S) equals the number of jobs available (shown by D).

One possibility for unemployment is that people who are unemployed are those who are not willing to work at the current equilibrium wage, say $10 an hour, but would be willing to work at a higher wage, like $20 per hour. The monthly Current Population Survey would count these people as unemployed, because they say they are ready and looking for work (at $20 per hour). But from an economist's point of view, these people are choosing to be unemployed.

Probably a few people are unemployed because of unrealistic expectations about wages, but they do not represent the majority of the unemployed. Instead, unemployed people often have friends or acquaintances of similar skill levels who are employed, and the unemployed would be willing to work at the jobs and wages similar to what is being received by those people. But the employers of their friends and acquaintances do not seem to be hiring. In other words, these people are involuntarily unemployed. What causes involuntary unemployment?

Why Wages Might Be Sticky Downward

If a labor market model with flexible wages does not describe unemployment very well—because it predicts that anyone willing to work at the going wage can always find a job—then it may prove useful to consider economic models in which wages are not flexible or adjust only very slowly. In particular, even though wage increases may occur with relative ease, wage decreases are few and far between.

One set of reasons why wages may be "sticky downward," as economists put it, involves economic laws and institutions. For low-skilled workers being paid the minimum wage, it is illegal to reduce their wages. For union workers operating under a multiyear contract with a company, wage cuts might violate the contract and create a labor dispute or a strike. However, minimum wages and union contracts are not a sufficient reason why wages would be sticky downward for the U.S. economy as a whole. After all, out of the 150 million or so workers in the U.S. economy, only about 1.4 million—less than 2% of the total—are paid the minimum wage. Similarly, only about 12% of American wage and salary workers are represented by a labor union. In other high-income countries, more workers may have their wages determined by unions or the minimum wage may be set at a level that applies to a larger share of workers. But for the United States, these two factors combined affect only about one-fifth or less of the labor force.

Economists looking for reasons why wages might be sticky downwards have focused on factors that may characterize most labor relationships in the economy, not just a few. A number of different theories have been proposed, but they share a common tone.

One argument is that even employees who are not union members often work under an **implicit contract**, which is that the employer will try to keep wages from falling when the economy is weak or the business is having trouble, and the employee will not expect huge salary increases when the economy or the business is strong. This wage-setting behavior acts like a form of insurance: the employee has some protection against wage declines in bad times, but pays for that protection with lower wages in good times. Clearly, this sort of implicit contract means that firms will be hesitant to cut wages, lest workers feel betrayed and work less hard or even leave the firm.

Efficiency wage theory argues that the productivity of workers depends on their pay, and so employers will often find it worthwhile to pay their employees somewhat more than market conditions might dictate. One reason is that employees who are paid better than others will be more productive because they recognize that if they were to lose their current jobs, they would suffer a decline in salary. As a result, they are motivated to work harder and to stay with the current employer. In addition, employers know that it is costly and time-consuming to hire and train new employees, so they would prefer to pay workers a little extra now rather than to lose them and have to hire and train new workers. Thus, by avoiding wage cuts, the employer minimizes costs of training and hiring new workers, and reaps the benefits of well-motivated employees.

The **adverse selection of wage cuts argument** points out that if an employer reacts to poor business conditions by reducing wages for all workers, then the best workers, those with the best employment alternatives at other firms, are the most likely to leave. The least attractive workers, with fewer employment alternatives, are more likely to stay. Consequently, firms are more likely to choose which workers should depart, through layoffs and firings, rather than trimming wages across the board. Sometimes companies that are going through tough times can persuade workers to take a pay cut for the short term, and still retain most of the firm's workers. But these stories are notable because they are so uncommon. It is far more typical for companies to lay off some workers, rather than to cut wages for everyone.

The **insider-outsider model** of the labor force, in simple terms, argues that those already working for firms are "insiders," while new employees, at least for a time, are "outsiders." A firm depends on its insiders to grease the wheels of the organization, to be familiar with routine procedures, to train new employees, and so on. However, cutting wages will alienate the insiders and damage the firm's productivity and prospects.

Finally, the **relative wage coordination argument** points out that even if most workers were hypothetically willing to see a decline in their own wages in bad economic times as long as everyone else also experiences such a decline, there is no obvious way for a decentralized economy to implement such a plan. Instead, workers confronted with the possibility of a wage cut will worry that other workers will not have such a wage cut, and so a wage cut means being worse off both in absolute terms and relative to others. As a result, workers fight hard against wage cuts.

These theories of why wages tend not to move downward differ in their logic and their implications, and figuring out the strengths and weaknesses of each theory is an ongoing subject of research and controversy among economists. All tend to imply that wages will decline only very slowly, if at all, even when the economy or a business is having tough times. When wages are inflexible and unlikely to fall, then either short-run or long-run unemployment can result. This can be seen in Figure 7.6.

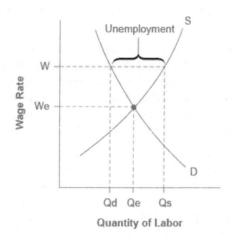

Figure 7.6 Sticky Wages in the Labor Market Because the wage rate is stuck at W, above the equilibrium, the number of job seekers (Qs) is greater than the number of job openings (Qd). The result is unemployment, shown by the bracket in the figure.

The interaction between shifts in labor demand and wages that are sticky downward are shown in **Figure 7.7**. **Figure 7.7** (a) illustrates the situation in which the demand for labor shifts to the right from D_0 to D_1. In this case, the equilibrium wage rises from W_0 to W_1 and the equilibrium quantity of labor hired increases from Q_0 to Q_1. It does not hurt employee morale at all for wages to rise.

Figure 7.7 (b) shows the situation in which the demand for labor shifts to the left, from D_0 to D_1, as it would tend to do in a recession. Because wages are sticky downward, they do not adjust toward what would have been the new equilibrium wage (Q_1), at least not in the short run. Instead, after the shift in the labor demand curve, the same quantity of workers is willing to work at that wage as before; however, the quantity of workers demanded at that wage has declined from the original equilibrium (Q_0) to Q_2. The gap between the original equilibrium quantity (Q_0) and the new quantity demanded of labor (Q_2) represents workers who would be willing to work at the going wage but cannot find jobs. The gap represents the economic meaning of unemployment.

(a) Rising demand for labor, wages rise

(b) Falling demand for labor, sticky wages, and unemployment

Figure 7.7 Rising Wage and Low Unemployment: Where Is the Unemployment in Supply and Demand? (a) In a labor market where wages are able to rise, an increase in the demand for labor from D_0 to D_1 leads to an increase in equilibrium quantity of labor hired from Q_0 to Q_1 and a rise in the equilibrium wage from W_0 to W_1. (b) In a labor market where wages do not decline, a fall in the demand for labor from D_0 to D_1 leads to a decline in the quantity of labor demanded at the original wage (W_0) from Q_0 to Q_2. These workers will want to work at the prevailing wage (W_0), but will not be able to find jobs.

This analysis helps to explain the connection noted earlier: that unemployment tends to rise in recessions and to decline during expansions. The overall state of the economy shifts the labor demand curve and, combined with wages that are sticky downwards, unemployment changes. The rise in unemployment that occurs because of a recession is cyclical unemployment.

Link It Up ᴑᴑᴑ

The St. Louis Federal Reserve Bank is the best resource for macroeconomic time series data, known as the Federal Reserve Economic Data (FRED). FRED (http://openstaxcollege.org/l/FRED_employment) provides complete data sets on various measures of the unemployment rate as well as the monthly Bureau of Labor Statistics report on the results of the household and employment surveys.

7.4 | What Causes Changes in Unemployment over the Long Run

By the end of this section, you will be able to:
- Explain frictional and structural unemployment
- Assess relationships between the natural rate of employment and potential real GDP, productivity, and public policy
- Identify recent patterns in the natural rate of employment
- Propose ways to combat unemployment

Cyclical unemployment explains why unemployment rises during a recession and falls during an economic expansion. But what explains the remaining level of unemployment even in good economic times? Why is the unemployment rate never zero? Even when the U.S. economy is growing strongly, the unemployment rate only rarely dips as low as 4%. Moreover, the discussion earlier in this chapter pointed out that unemployment rates in many European countries like Italy, France, and Germany have often been remarkably high at various times in the last few decades. Why does some level of unemployment persist even when economies are growing strongly? Why are unemployment rates continually higher in certain economies, through good economic years and bad? Economists have a term to describe the remaining level of unemployment that occurs even when the economy is healthy: it is called the **natural rate of unemployment**.

The Long Run: The Natural Rate of Unemployment

The natural rate of unemployment is not "natural" in the sense that water freezes at 32 degrees Fahrenheit or boils at 212 degrees Fahrenheit. It is not a physical and unchanging law of nature. Instead, it is only the "natural" rate because it is the unemployment rate that would result from the combination of economic, social, and political factors that exist at a time—assuming the economy was neither booming nor in recession. These forces include the usual pattern of companies expanding and contracting their workforces in a dynamic economy, social and economic forces that affect the labor market, or public policies that affect either the eagerness of people to work or the willingness of businesses to hire. Let's discuss these factors in more detail.

Frictional Unemployment

In a market economy, some companies are always going broke for a variety of reasons: old technology; poor management; good management that happened to make bad decisions; shifts in tastes of consumers so that less of the firm's product is desired; a large customer who went broke; or tough domestic or foreign competitors. Conversely, other companies will be doing very well for just the opposite reasons and looking to hire more employees. In a perfect world, all of those who lost jobs would immediately find new ones. But in the real world, even if the number of job seekers is equal to the number of job vacancies, it takes time to find out about new jobs, to interview and figure out if the new job is a good match, or perhaps to sell a house and buy another in proximity to a new job. The unemployment that occurs in the meantime, as workers move between jobs, is called **frictional unemployment**. Frictional unemployment is not inherently a bad thing. It takes time on part of both the employer and the individual to match those looking for employment with the correct job openings. For individuals and companies to be successful and productive, you want people to find the job for which they are best suited, not just the first job offered.

In the mid-2000s, before the recession of 2008–2009, it was true that about 7% of U.S. workers saw their jobs disappear in any three-month period. But in periods of economic growth, these destroyed jobs are counterbalanced for the economy as a whole by a larger number of jobs created. In 2005, for example, there were typically about 7.5 million unemployed people at any given time in the U.S. economy. Even though about two-thirds of those unemployed people found a job in 14 weeks or fewer, the unemployment rate did not change much during the year, because those who found new jobs were largely offset by others who lost jobs.

Of course, it would be preferable if people who were losing jobs could immediately and easily move into the new jobs being created, but in the real world, that is not possible. Someone who is laid off by a textile mill in South Carolina cannot turn around and immediately start working for a textile mill in California. Instead, the adjustment process happens in ripples. Some people find new jobs near their old ones, while others find that they must move to new locations. Some people can do a very similar job with a different company, while others must start new career paths. Some people may be near retirement and decide to look only for part-time work, while others want an employer that offers a long-term career path. The frictional unemployment that results from people moving between jobs in a dynamic economy may account for one to two percentage points of total unemployment.

The level of frictional unemployment will depend on how easy it is for workers to learn about alternative jobs, which may reflect the ease of communications about job prospects in the economy. The extent of frictional unemployment will also depend to some extent on how willing people are to move to new areas to find jobs—which in turn may depend on history and culture.

Frictional unemployment and the natural rate of unemployment also seem to depend on the age distribution of the population. Figure 7.4 (b) showed that unemployment rates are typically lower for people between 25–54 years of age than they are for those who are either younger or older. "Prime-age workers," as those in the 25–54 age bracket are sometimes called, are typically at a place in their lives when they want to have a job and income arriving at all times. But some proportion of those who are under 30 may still be trying out jobs and life options and some proportion of those over 55 are eyeing retirement. In both cases, the relatively young or old tend to worry less about unemployment than those in-between, and their periods of frictional unemployment may be longer as a result. Thus, a society with a relatively high proportion of relatively young or old workers will tend to have a higher unemployment rate than a society with a higher proportion of its workers in middle age.

Structural Unemployment

Another factor that influences the natural rate of unemployment is the amount of **structural unemployment**. The structurally unemployed are individuals who have no jobs because they lack skills valued by the labor market, either because demand has shifted away from the skills they do have, or because they never learned any skills. An example of the former would be the unemployment among aerospace engineers after the U.S. space program downsized in the 1970s. An example of the latter would be high school dropouts.

Some people worry that technology causes structural unemployment. In the past, new technologies have put lower skilled employees out of work, but at the same time they create demand for higher skilled workers to use the new technologies. Education seems to be the key in minimizing the amount of structural unemployment. Individuals who have degrees can be retrained if they become structurally unemployed. For people with no skills and little education, that option is more limited.

Natural Unemployment and Potential Real GDP

The natural unemployment rate is related to two other important concepts: full employment and potential real GDP. The economy is considered to be at full employment when the actual unemployment rate is equal to the natural unemployment. When the economy is at full employment, real GPD is equal to potential real GDP. By contrast, when the economy is below full employment, the unemployment rate is greater than the natural unemployment rate and real GDP is less than potential. Finally, when the economy above full employment, then the unemployment rate is less than the natural unemployment rate and real GDP is greater than potential. Operating above potential is only possible for a short while, since it is analogous to all workers working overtime.

Productivity Shifts and the Natural Rate of Unemployment

Unexpected shifts in productivity can have a powerful effect on the natural rate of unemployment. Over time, the level of wages in an economy will be determined by the productivity of workers. After all, if a business paid workers more than could be justified by their productivity, the business will ultimately lose money and go bankrupt. Conversely, if a business tries to pay workers less than their productivity then, in a competitive labor market, other businesses will find it worthwhile to hire away those workers and pay them more.

However, adjustments of wages to productivity levels will not happen quickly or smoothly. Wages are typically reviewed only once or twice a year. In many modern jobs, it is difficult to measure productivity at the individual level. For example, how precisely would one measure the quantity produced by an accountant who is one of many people working in the tax department of a large corporation? Because productivity is difficult to observe, wage increases are often determined based on recent experience with productivity; if productivity has been rising at, say, 2% per year, then wages rise at that level as well. However, when productivity changes unexpectedly, it can affect the natural rate of unemployment for a time.

The U.S. economy in the 1970s and 1990s provides two vivid examples of this process. In the 1970s, productivity growth slowed down unexpectedly (as discussed in Economic Growth). For example, output per hour of U.S. workers in the business sector increased at an annual rate of 3.3% per year from 1960 to 1973, but only 0.8% from 1973 to 1982. Figure 7.8 (a) illustrates the situation where the demand for labor—that is, the quantity of labor that business is willing to hire at any given wage—has been shifting out a little each year because of rising productivity, from D_0 to D_1 to D_2. As a result, equilibrium wages have been rising each year from W_0 to W_1 to W_2. But when productivity unexpectedly slows down, the pattern of wage increases does not adjust right away. Wages keep rising each year from W_2 to W_3 to W_4. But the demand for labor is no longer shifting up. A gap opens where the quantity of labor supplied at wage level W_4 is greater than the quantity demanded. The natural rate of unemployment rises; indeed, in the aftermath of this unexpectedly low productivity in the 1970s, the national unemployment rate did not fall below 7% from May, 1980 until 1986. Over time, the rise in wages will adjust to match the slower gains in productivity, and the unemployment rate will ease back down. But this process may take years.

(a) Productivity rises, and then stops rising

(b) Productivity doesn't change, and then rises

Figure 7.8 Unexpected Productivity Changes and Unemployment (a) Productivity is rising, increasing the demand for labor. Employers and workers become used to the pattern of wage increases. Then productivity suddenly stops increasing. However, the expectations of employers and workers for wage increases do not shift immediately, so wages keep rising as before. But the demand for labor has not increased, so at wage W_4, unemployment exists where the quantity supplied of labor exceeds the quantity demanded. (b) The rate of productivity increase has been zero for a time, so employers and workers have come to accept the equilibrium wage level (W). Then productivity increases unexpectedly, shifting demand for labor from D_0 to D_1. At the wage (W), this means that the quantity demanded of labor exceeds the quantity supplied, and with job offers plentiful, the unemployment rate will be low.

The late 1990s provide an opposite example: instead of the surprise decline in productivity in the 1970s, productivity unexpectedly rose in the mid-1990s. The annual growth rate of real output per hour of labor increased from 1.7% from 1980–1995, to an annual rate of 2.6% from 1995–2001. Let's simplify the situation a bit, so that the economic lesson of the story is easier to see graphically, and say that productivity had not been increasing at all in earlier years, so the intersection of the labor market was at point E in **Figure 7.8** (b), where the demand curve for labor (D_0) intersects the supply curve for labor. As a result, real wages were not increasing. Now, productivity jumps upward, which shifts the demand for labor out to the right, from D_0 to D_1. At least for a time, however, wages are still being set according to the earlier expectations of no productivity growth, so wages do not rise. The result is that at the prevailing wage level (W), the quantity of labor demanded (Qd) will for a time exceed the quantity of labor supplied (Qs), and unemployment will be very low—actually below the natural level of unemployment for a time. This pattern of unexpectedly high productivity helps to explain why the unemployment rate stayed below 4.5%—quite a low level by historical standards—from 1998 until after the U.S. economy had entered a recession in 2001.

Average levels of unemployment will tend to be somewhat higher on average when productivity is unexpectedly low, and conversely, will tend to be somewhat lower on average when productivity is unexpectedly high. But over time, wages do eventually adjust to reflect productivity levels.

Public Policy and the Natural Rate of Unemployment

Public policy can also have a powerful effect on the natural rate of unemployment. On the supply side of the labor market, public policies to assist the unemployed can affect how eager people are to find work. For example, if a worker who loses a job is guaranteed a generous package of unemployment insurance, welfare benefits, food stamps, and government medical benefits, then the opportunity cost of being unemployed is lower and that worker will be less eager to seek a new job.

What seems to matter most is not just the amount of these benefits, but how long they last. A society that provides generous help for the unemployed that cuts off after, say, six months, may provide less of an incentive for unemployment than a society that provides less generous help that lasts for several years. Conversely, government assistance for job search or retraining can in some cases encourage people back to work sooner. See the Clear it Up to learn how the U.S. handles unemployment insurance.

How does U.S. unemployment insurance work?

Unemployment insurance is a joint federal–state program, established by federal law in 1935. The federal government sets minimum standards for the program, but most of the administration is done by state governments.

The funding for the program is a federal tax collected from employers. The federal government requires that the tax be collected on the first $7,000 in wages paid to each worker; however, states can choose to collect the tax on a higher amount if they wish, and 41 states have set a higher limit. States can choose the length of time that benefits will be paid, although most states limit unemployment benefits to 26 weeks—with extensions possible in times of especially high unemployment. The fund is then used to pay benefits to those who become unemployed. Average unemployment benefits are equal to about one-third of the wage earned by the person in his or her previous job, but the level of unemployment benefits varies considerably across states.

Bottom 10 States That Pay the Lowest Benefit per Week		Top 10 States That Pay the Highest Benefit per Week	
Delaware	$330	Massachusetts	$674
Georgia	$330	Minnesota	$629
South Carolina	$326	New Jersey	$624
Missouri	$320	Washington	$624
Florida	$275	Connecticut	$590
Tennessee	$275	Pennsylvania	$573
Alabama	$265	Rhode Island	$566
Louisiana	$247	Ohio	$564
Arizona	$240	Hawaii	$560
Mississippi	$235	Oregon	$538

Table 7.5 Maximum Weekly Unemployment Benefits by State in 2014   (Source: http://jobsearch.about.com/od/unemployment/fl/unemployment-benefits-by-state-2014.htm)

One other interesting thing to note about the classifications of unemployment—an individual does not have to collect unemployment benefits to be classified as unemployed. While there are statistics kept and studied relating to how many people are collecting unemployment insurance, this is not the source of unemployment rate information.

Link It Up

View this article (http://openstaxcollege.org/l/NYT_Benefits) for an explanation of exactly who is eligible for unemployment benefits.

On the demand side of the labor market, government rules social institutions, and the presence of unions can affect the willingness of firms to hire. For example, if a government makes it hard for businesses to start up or to expand, by wrapping new businesses in bureaucratic red tape, then businesses will become more discouraged about hiring. Government regulations can make it harder to start a business by requiring that a new business obtain many permits and pay many fees, or by restricting the types and quality of products that can be sold. Other government regulations, like zoning laws, may limit where business can be done, or whether businesses are allowed to be open during evenings or on Sunday.

Whatever defenses may be offered for such laws in terms of social value—like the value some Christians place on not working on Sunday—these kinds of restrictions impose a barrier between some willing workers and other willing employers, and thus contribute to a higher natural rate of unemployment. Similarly, if government makes it difficult to fire or lay off workers, businesses may react by trying not to hire more workers than strictly necessary—since laying these workers off would be costly and difficult. High minimum wages may discourage businesses from hiring low-skill workers. Government rules may encourage and support powerful unions, which can then push up wages for union workers, but at a cost of discouraging businesses from hiring those workers.

The Natural Rate of Unemployment in Recent Years

The underlying economic, social, and political factors that determine the natural rate of unemployment can change over time, which means that the natural rate of unemployment can change over time, too.

Estimates by economists of the natural rate of unemployment in the U.S. economy in the early 2000s run at about 4.5 to 5.5%. This is a lower estimate than earlier. Three of the common reasons proposed by economists for this change are outlined below.

1. The Internet has provided a remarkable new tool through which job seekers can find out about jobs at different companies and can make contact with relative ease. An Internet search is far easier than trying to find a list of local employers and then hunting up phone numbers for all of their human resources departments, requesting a list of jobs and application forms, and so on. Social networking sites such as LinkedIn have changed how people find work as well.

2. The growth of the temporary worker industry has probably helped to reduce the natural rate of unemployment. In the early 1980s, only about 0.5% of all workers held jobs through temp agencies; by the early 2000s, the figure had risen above 2%. Temp agencies can provide jobs for workers while they are looking for permanent work. They can also serve as a clearinghouse, helping workers find out about jobs with certain employers and getting a tryout with the employer. For many workers, a temp job is a stepping-stone to a permanent job that they might not have heard about or gotten any other way, so the growth of temp jobs will also tend to reduce frictional unemployment.

3. The aging of the "baby boom generation"—the especially large generation of Americans born between 1946 and 1963—meant that the proportion of young workers in the economy was relatively high in the 1970s, as the boomers entered the labor market, but is relatively low today. As noted earlier, middle-aged workers are far more likely to keep steady jobs than younger workers, a factor that tends to reduce the natural rate of unemployment.

The combined result of these factors is that the natural rate of unemployment was on average lower in the 1990s and the early 2000s than in the 1980s. The Great Recession of 2008–2009 pushed monthly unemployment rates above 10% in late 2009. But even at that time, the Congressional Budget Office was forecasting that by 2015, unemployment rates would fall back to about 5%—lower than it currently is, though not by much. As of early 2015, policymakers still think that unemployment has not yet reached its natural rate.

The Natural Rate of Unemployment in Europe

By the standards of other high-income economies, the natural rate of unemployment in the U.S. economy appears relatively low. Through good economic years and bad, many European economies have had unemployment rates hovering near 10%, or even higher, since the 1970s. European rates of unemployment have been higher not because recessions in Europe have been deeper, but rather because the conditions underlying supply and demand for labor have been different in Europe, in a way that has created a much higher natural rate of unemployment.

Many European countries have a combination of generous welfare and unemployment benefits, together with nests of rules that impose additional costs on businesses when they hire. In addition, many countries have laws that require firms to give workers months of notice before laying them off and to provide substantial severance or retraining packages after laying them off. The legally required notice before laying off a worker can be more than three months in Spain, Germany, Denmark, and Belgium, and the legally required severance package can be as high as a year's salary or more in Austria, Spain, Portugal, Italy, and Greece. Such laws will surely discourage laying off or firing current workers. But when companies know that it will be difficult to fire or lay off workers, they also become hesitant about hiring in the first place.

The typically higher levels of unemployment in many European countries in recent years, which have prevailed even when economies are growing at a solid pace, are attributable to the fact that the sorts of laws and regulations that lead to a high natural rate of unemployment are much more prevalent in Europe than in the United States.

A Preview of Policies to Fight Unemployment

The Government Budgets and Fiscal Policy and Macroeconomic Policy Around the World chapters provide a detailed discussion of how to fight unemployment, when these policies can be discussed in the context of the full array of macroeconomic goals and frameworks for analysis. But even at this preliminary stage, it is useful to preview the main issues concerning policies to fight unemployment.

The remedy for unemployment will depend on the diagnosis. Cyclical unemployment is a short-term problem, caused because the economy is in a recession. Thus, the preferred solution will be to avoid or minimize recessions. As Government Budgets and Fiscal Policy discusses, this policy can be enacted by stimulating the overall buying power in the economy, so that firms perceive that sales and profits are possible, which makes them eager to hire.

Dealing with the natural rate of unemployment is trickier. There is not much to be done about the fact that in a market-oriented economy, firms will hire and fire workers. Nor is there much to be done about how the evolving age structure of the economy, or unexpected shifts in productivity, will affect the natural rate of unemployment for a time. However, as the example of high ongoing unemployment rates for many European countries illustrates, government policy clearly can affect the natural rate of unemployment that will persist even when GDP is growing.

When a government enacts policies that will affect workers or employers, it must examine how these policies will affect the information and incentives employees and employers have to seek each other out. For example, the government may have a role to play in helping some of the unemployed with job searches. The design of government programs that offer assistance to unemployed workers and protections to employed workers may need to be rethought so that they will not unduly discourage the supply of labor. Similarly, rules that make it difficult for businesses to begin or to expand may need to be redesigned so that they will not unduly discourage the demand for labor. The message is not that all laws affecting labor markets should be repealed, but only that when such laws are enacted, a society that cares about unemployment will need to consider the tradeoffs involved.

Bring it Home

The Mysterious Case of the Missing Candidates

After reading the chapter you might think the current unemployment conundrum may be due to structural unemployment. Indeed, there is a mismatch between the skills employers are seeking and the skills the unemployed possess. But Peter Cappelli has a slightly different view on this—it is called the purple squirrel. The what?

In human resource parlance, a purple squirrel is a job candidate who is a perfect fit for all of the many different responsibilities of a position. A purple squirrel candidate could step into a multi-faceted position with no training and permit the firm to higher fewer people because the worker is so versatile. During the Great Recession, Human Resources (HR) positions were reduced. This means today's hiring managers are drafting job descriptions and requirements without much, if any HR feedback. "It turns out it's typically the case that employers' requirements are crazy, they're not paying enough, or their applicant screening is so rigid that nobody gets through," Cappelli stated in a 2012 Knowledge@Wharton interview about the findings in his book, *Why Good People Can't Find Jobs: Chasing After the Purple Squirrel*. In short, managers are searching for "purple squirrels" when what they really need are just versatile workers. There really is not a shortage of "normal squirrels"—candidates who are versatile workers. The managers just cannot find them because their requirements, screening processes, and compensation will filter out all but the "purple" ones.

KEY TERMS

adverse selection of wage cuts argument if employers reduce wages for all workers, the best will leave

cyclical unemployment unemployment closely tied to the business cycle, like higher unemployment during a recession

discouraged workers those who have stopped looking for employment due to the lack of suitable positions available

efficiency wage theory the theory that the productivity of workers, either individually or as a group, will increase if they are paid more

frictional unemployment unemployment that occurs as workers move between jobs

implicit contract an unwritten agreement in the labor market that the employer will try to keep wages from falling when the economy is weak or the business is having trouble, and the employee will not expect huge salary increases when the economy or the business is strong

insider-outsider model those already working for the firm are "insiders" who know the procedures; the other workers are "outsiders" who are recent or prospective hires

labor force participation rate this is the percentage of adults in an economy who are either employed or who are unemployed and looking for a job

natural rate of unemployment the unemployment rate that would exist in a growing and healthy economy from the combination of economic, social, and political factors that exist at a given time

out of the labor force those who are not working and not looking for work—whether they want employment or not; also termed "not in the labor force"

relative wage coordination argument across-the-board wage cuts are hard for an economy to implement, and workers fight against them

structural unemployment unemployment that occurs because individuals lack skills valued by employers

underemployed individuals who are employed in a job that is below their skills

unemployment rate the percentage of adults who are in the labor force and thus seeking jobs, but who do not have jobs

KEY CONCEPTS AND SUMMARY

7.1 How the Unemployment Rate Is Defined and Computed

Unemployment imposes high costs. Unemployed individuals suffer from loss of income and from stress. An economy with high unemployment suffers an opportunity cost of unused resources. The adult population can be divided into those in the labor force and those out of the labor force. In turn, those in the labor force are divided into employed and unemployed. A person without a job must be willing and able to work and actively looking for work to be counted as unemployed; otherwise, a person without a job is counted as being out of the labor force. The unemployment rate is defined as the number of unemployed persons divided by the number of persons in the labor force (not the overall adult population). The Current Population Survey (CPS) conducted by the United States Census Bureau measures the percentage of the labor force that is unemployed. The establishment payroll survey by the Bureau of Labor Statistics measures the net change in jobs created for the month.

7.2 Patterns of Unemployment

The U.S. unemployment rate rises during periods of recession and depression, but falls back to the range of 4% to 6% when the economy is strong. The unemployment rate never falls to zero. Despite enormous growth in the size of the U.S. population and labor force in the twentieth century, along with other major trends like globalization and new technology, the unemployment rate shows no long-term rising trend.

Unemployment rates differ by group: higher for African-Americans and Hispanics than for whites; higher for less educated than more educated; higher for the young than the middle-aged. Women's unemployment rates used to be higher than men's, but in recent years men's and women's unemployment rates have been very similar. In recent years, unemployment rates in the United States have compared favorably with unemployment rates in most other high-income economies.

7.3 What Causes Changes in Unemployment over the Short Run

Cyclical unemployment rises and falls with the business cycle. In a labor market with flexible wages, wages will adjust in such a market so that quantity demanded of labor always equals the quantity supplied of labor at the equilibrium wage. Many theories have been proposed for why wages might not be flexible, but instead may adjust only in a "sticky" way, especially when it comes to downward adjustments: implicit contracts, efficiency wage theory, adverse selection of wage cuts, insider-outsider model, and relative wage coordination.

7.4 What Causes Changes in Unemployment over the Long Run

The natural rate of unemployment is the rate of unemployment that would be caused by the economic, social, and political forces in the economy even when the economy is not in a recession. These factors include the frictional unemployment that occurs when people are put out of work for a time by the shifts of a dynamic and changing economy and any laws concerning conditions of hiring and firing have the undesired side effect of discouraging job formation. They also include structural unemployment, which occurs when demand shifts permanently away from a certain type of job skill.

SELF-CHECK QUESTIONS

1. Suppose the adult population over the age of 16 is 237.8 million and the labor force is 153.9 million (of whom 139.1 million are employed). How many people are "not in the labor force?" What are the proportions of employed, unemployed and not in the labor force in the population? *Hint*: Proportions are percentages.

2. Using the above data, what is the unemployment rate? These data are U.S. statistics from 2010. How does it compare to the February 2015 unemployment rate computed earlier?

3. Over the long term, has the U.S. unemployment rate generally trended up, trended down, or remained at basically the same level?

4. Whose unemployment rates are commonly higher in the U.S. economy:
   a. Whites or nonwhites?
   b. The young or the middle-aged?
   c. College graduates or high school graduates?

5. Beginning in the 1970s and continuing for three decades, women entered the U.S. labor force in a big way. If we assume that wages are sticky in a downward direction, but that around 1970 the demand for labor equaled the supply of labor at the current wage rate, what do you imagine happened to the wage rate, employment, and unemployment as a result of increased labor force participation?

6. Is the increase in labor force participation rates among women better thought of as causing an increase in cyclical unemployment or an increase in the natural rate of unemployment? Why?

7. Many college students graduate from college before they have found a job. When graduates begin to look for a job, they are counted as what category of unemployed?

REVIEW QUESTIONS

8. What is the difference between being unemployed and being out of the labor force?

9. How is the unemployment rate calculated? How is the labor force participation rate calculated?

10. Are all adults who do not hold jobs counted as unemployed?

11. If you are out of school but working part time, are you considered employed or unemployed in U.S. labor statistics? If you are a full time student and working 12 hours a week at the college cafeteria are you considered employed or not in the labor force? If you are a senior citizen who is collecting social security and a pension and working as a greeter at Wal-Mart are you considered employed or not in the labor force?

12. What happens to the unemployment rate when unemployed workers are reclassified as discouraged workers?

13. What happens to the labor force participation rate when employed individuals are reclassified as unemployed? What happens when they are reclassified as discouraged workers?

14. What are some of the problems with using the unemployment rate as an accurate measure of overall joblessness?

15. What criteria are used by the BLS to count someone as employed? As unemployed?

16. Assess whether the following would be counted as "unemployed" in the Current Employment Statistics survey.
   a. A husband willingly stays home with children while his wife works.
   b. A manufacturing worker whose factory just closed down.
   c. A college student doing an unpaid summer internship.
   d. A retiree.
   e. Someone who has been out of work for two years but keeps looking for a job.
   f. Someone who has been out of work for two months but isn't looking for a job.
   g. Someone who hates her present job and is actively looking for another one.
   h. Someone who decides to take a part time job because she could not find a full time position.

17. Are U.S. unemployment rates typically higher, lower, or about the same as unemployment rates in other high-income countries?

18. Are U.S. unemployment rates distributed evenly across the population?

19. When would you expect cyclical unemployment to be rising? Falling?

20. Why is there unemployment in a labor market with flexible wages?

21. Name and explain some of the reasons why wages are likely to be sticky, especially in downward adjustments.

22. What term describes the remaining level of unemployment that occurs even when the economy is healthy?

23. What forces create the natural rate of unemployment for an economy?

24. Would you expect the natural rate of unemployment to be roughly the same in different countries?

25. Would you expect the natural rate of unemployment to remain the same within one country over the long run of several decades?

26. What is frictional unemployment? Give examples of frictional unemployment.

27. What is structural unemployment? Give examples of structural unemployment.

28. After several years of economic growth, would you expect the unemployment in an economy to be mainly cyclical or mainly due to the natural rate of unemployment? Why?

29. What type of unemployment (cyclical, frictional, or structural) applies to each of the following:
   a. landscapers laid off in response to drop in new housing construction during a recession.
   b. coal miners laid off due to EPA regulations that shut down coal fired power
   c. a financial analyst who quits his/her job in Chicago and is pursing similar work in Arizona
   d. printers laid off due to drop in demand for printed catalogues and flyers as firms go the internet to promote an advertise their products.

e.   factory workers in the U.S. laid off as the plants shut down and move to Mexico and Ireland.

CRITICAL THINKING QUESTIONS

30.   Using the definition of the unemployment rate, is an increase in the unemployment rate necessarily a bad thing for a nation?

31.   Is a decrease in the unemployment rate necessarily a good thing for a nation? Explain.

32.   If many workers become discouraged from looking for jobs, explain how the number of jobs could decline but the unemployment rate could fall at the same time.

33.   Would you expect hidden unemployment to be higher, lower, or about the same when the unemployment rate is high, say 10%, versus low, say 4%? Explain.

34.   Is the higher unemployment rates for minority workers necessarily an indication of discrimination? What could be some other reasons for the higher unemployment rate?

35.   While unemployment is highly negatively correlated with the level of economic activity, in the real world it responds with a lag. In other words, firms do not immediately lay off workers in response to a sales decline. They wait a while before responding. Similarly, firms do not immediately hire workers when sales pick up. What do you think accounts for the lag in response time?

36.   Why do you think that unemployment rates are lower for individuals with more education?

37.   Do you think it is rational for workers to prefer sticky wages to wage cuts, when the consequence of sticky wages is unemployment for some workers? Why

or why not? How do the reasons for sticky wages explained in this section apply to your argument?

38.   Under what condition would a decrease in unemployment be bad for the economy?

39.   Under what condition would an increase in the unemployment rate be a positive sign?

40.   As the baby boom generation retires, the ratio of retirees to workers will increase noticeably. How will this affect the Social Security program? How will this affect the standard of living of the average American?

41.   Unemployment rates have been higher in many European countries in recent decades than in the United States. Is the main reason for this long-term difference in unemployment rates more likely to be cyclical unemployment or the natural rate of unemployment? Explain briefly.

42.   Is it desirable to pursue a goal of zero unemployment? Why or why not?

43.   Is it desirable to eliminate natural unemployment? Why or why not? *Hint*: Think about what our economy would look like today and what assumptions would have to be met to have a zero rate of natural unemployment.

44.   The U.S. unemployment rate increased from 4.6% in July 2001 to 5.9% by June 2002. Without studying the subject in any detail, would you expect that a change of this kind is more likely to be due to cyclical unemployment or a change in the natural rate of unemployment? Why?

PROBLEMS

45.   A country with a population of eight million adults has five million employed, 500,000 unemployed, and the rest of the adult population is out of the labor force. What's the unemployment rate? What share of population is in the labor force? Sketch a pie chart that divides the adult population into these three groups.

46.   A government passes a family-friendly law that no companies can have evening, nighttime, or weekend

hours, so that everyone can be home with their families during these times. Analyze the effect of this law using a demand and supply diagram for the labor market: first assuming that wages are flexible, and then assuming that wages are sticky downward.

47.   As the baby boomer generation retires, what should happen to wages and employment? Can you show this graphically?

8 | Inflation

Figure 8.1 Big Bucks in Zimbabwe This bill was worth 100 billion Zimbabwean dollars when issued in 2008. There were even bills issued with a face value of 100 trillion Zimbabwean dollars. The bills had $100,000,000,000,000 written on them. Unfortunately, they were almost worthless. At one point, 621,984,228 Zimbabwean dollars were equal to one U.S. dollar. Eventually, the country abandoned its own currency and allowed foreign currency to be used for purchases. (Credit: modification of work by Samantha Marx/Flickr Creative Commons)

Bring it Home

A $550 Million Loaf of Bread?

If you were born within the last three decades in the United States, Canada, or many other countries in the developed world, you probably have no real experience with a high rate of inflation. Inflation is when most prices in an entire economy are rising. But there is an extreme form of inflation called hyperinflation. This occurred in Germany between 1921 and 1928, and more recently in Zimbabwe between 2008 and 2009. In November of 2008, Zimbabwe had an inflation rate of 79.6 billion percent. In contrast, in 2014, the United States had an average annual rate of inflation of 1.6%.

Zimbabwe's inflation rate was so high it is difficult to comprehend. So, let's put it into context. It is equivalent to price increases of 98% per day. This means that, from one day to the next, prices essentially double. What is life like in an economy afflicted with hyperinflation? Not like anything you are familiar with. Prices for commodities in Zimbabwean dollars were adjusted several times *each day*. There was no desire to hold on to currency since it lost value by the minute. The people there spent a great deal of time getting rid of any cash they acquired by purchasing whatever food or other commodities they could find. At one point, a loaf of bread cost 550 million Zimbabwean dollars. Teachers were paid in the trillions a month; however this was equivalent to only one U.S. dollar a day. At its height, it took 621,984,228 Zimbabwean dollars to purchase one U.S. dollar.

Government agencies had no money to pay their workers so they started printing money to pay their bills rather than raising taxes. Rising prices caused the government to enact price controls on private businesses, which led to shortages and the emergence of black markets. In 2009, the country abandoned its currency and allowed foreign currencies to be used for purchases.

How does this happen? How can both government and the economy fail to function at the most basic level? Before we consider these extreme cases of hyperinflation, let's first look at inflation itself.

Introduction to Inflation

In this chapter, you will learn about:

- Tracking Inflation

- How Changes in the Cost of Living are Measured

- How the U.S. and Other Countries Experience Inflation

- The Confusion Over Inflation

- Indexing and Its Limitations

Inflation is a general and ongoing rise in the level of prices in an entire economy. Inflation does not refer to a change in relative prices. A relative price change occurs when you see that the price of tuition has risen, but the price of laptops has fallen. Inflation, on the other hand, means that there is pressure for prices to rise in most markets in the economy. In addition, price increases in the supply-and-demand model were one-time events, representing a shift from a previous equilibrium to a new one. Inflation implies an ongoing rise in prices. If inflation happened for one year and then stopped—well, then it would not be inflation any more.

This chapter begins by showing how to combine prices of individual goods and services to create a measure of overall inflation. It discusses the historical and recent experience of inflation, both in the United States and in other countries around the world. Other chapters have sometimes included a note under an exhibit or a parenthetical reminder in the text saying that the numbers have been adjusted for inflation. In this chapter, it is time to show how to use inflation statistics to adjust other economic variables, so that you can tell how much of, say, the rise in GDP over different periods of time can be attributed to an actual increase in the production of goods and services and how much should be attributed to the fact that prices for most things have risen.

Inflation has consequences for people and firms throughout the economy, in their roles as lenders and borrowers, wage-earners, taxpayers, and consumers. The chapter concludes with a discussion of some imperfections and biases in the inflation statistics, and a preview of policies for fighting inflation that will be discussed in other chapters.

8.1 | Tracking Inflation

By the end of this section, you will be able to:
- Calculate the annual rate of inflation
- Explain and use index numbers and base years when simplifying the total quantity spent over a year for products
- Calculate inflation rates using index numbers

Dinner table conversations where you might have heard about inflation usually entail reminiscing about when "everything seemed to cost so much less. You used to be able to buy three gallons of gasoline for a dollar and then go see an afternoon movie for another dollar." Table 8.1 compares some prices of common goods in 1970 and 2014. Of course, the average prices shown in this table may not reflect the prices where you live. The cost of living in New York City is much higher than in Houston, Texas, for example. In addition, certain products have evolved over recent decades. A new car in 2014, loaded with antipollution equipment, safety gear, computerized engine controls, and many other technological advances, is a more advanced machine (and more fuel efficient) than your typical 1970s car. However, put details like these to one side for the moment, and look at the overall pattern. The primary reason behind the price rises in Table 8.1—and all the price increases for the other products in the economy—is not specific to the market for housing or cars or gasoline or movie tickets. Instead, it is part of a general rise in the level of all prices. In 2014, $1 had about the same purchasing power in overall terms of goods and services as 18 cents did in 1972, because of the amount of inflation that has occurred over that time period.

Items	1970	2014
Pound of ground beef	$0.66	$4.16
Pound of butter	$0.87	$2.93
Movie ticket	$1.55	$8.17
Sales price of new home (median)	$22,000	$280,000
New car	$3,000	$32,531
Gallon of gasoline	$0.36	$3.36
Average hourly wage for a manufacturing worker	$3.23	$19.55
Per capita GDP	$5,069	$53,041.98

Table 8.1 Price Comparisons, 1970 and 2014   (Sources: See chapter References at end of book.)

Moreover, the power of inflation does not affect just goods and services, but wages and income levels, too. The second-to-last row of Table 8.1 shows that the average hourly wage for a manufacturing worker increased nearly six-fold from 1970 to 2014. Sure, the average worker in 2014 is better educated and more productive than the average worker in 1970—but not six times more productive. Sure, per capita GDP increased substantially from 1970 to 2014, but is the average person in the U.S. economy really more than eight times better off in just 44 years? Not likely.

A modern economy has millions of goods and services whose prices are continually quivering in the breezes of supply and demand. How can all of these shifts in price be boiled down to a single inflation rate? As with many problems in economic measurement, the conceptual answer is reasonably straightforward: Prices of a variety of goods and services are combined into a single price level; the inflation rate is simply the percentage change in the price level. Applying the concept, however, involves some practical difficulties.

The Price of a Basket of Goods

To calculate the price level, economists begin with the concept of a **basket of goods and services**, consisting of the different items individuals, businesses, or organizations typically buy. The next step is to look at how the prices of those items change over time. In thinking about how to combine individual prices into an overall price level, many people find that their first impulse is to calculate the average of the prices. Such a calculation, however, could easily be misleading because some products matter more than others.

Changes in the prices of goods for which people spend a larger share of their incomes will matter more than changes in the prices of goods for which people spend a smaller share of their incomes. For example, an increase of 10% in the rental rate on housing matters more to most people than whether the price of carrots rises by 10%. To construct an overall measure of the price level, economists compute a weighted average of the prices of the items in the basket, where the weights are based on the actual quantities of goods and services people buy. The following Work It Out feature walks you through the steps of calculating the annual rate of inflation based on a few products.

Work It Out ―○―○―○

Calculating an Annual Rate of Inflation

Consider the simple basket of goods with only three items, represented in Table 8.2. Say that in any given month, a college student spends money on 20 hamburgers, one bottle of aspirin, and five movies. Prices for these items over four years are given in the table through each time period (Pd). Prices of some goods in the basket may rise while others fall. In this example, the price of aspirin does not change over the four years, while movies increase in price and hamburgers bounce up and down. Each year, the cost of buying the given basket of goods at the prices prevailing at that time is shown.

Items	Hamburger	Aspirin	Movies	Total	Inflation Rate
Qty	20	1 bottle	5	-	-
(Pd 1) Price	$3.00	$10.00	$6.00	-	-
(Pd 1) Amount Spent	$60.00	$10.00	$30.00	$100.00	-
(Pd 2) Price	$3.20	$10.00	$6.50	-	-
(Pd 2) Amount Spent	$64.00	$10.00	$32.50	$106.50	6.5%
(Pd 3) Price	$3.10	$10.00	$7.00	-	-
(Pd 3) Amount Spent	$62.00	$10.00	$35.00	$107.00	0.5%
(Pd 4) Price	$3.50	$10.00	$7.50	-	-
(Pd 4) Amount Spent	$70.00	$10.00	$37.50	$117.50	9.8%

Table 8.2 A College Student's Basket of Goods

To calculate the annual rate of inflation in this example:

Step 1. Find the percentage change in the cost of purchasing the overall basket of goods between the time periods. The general equation for percentage changes between two years, whether in the context of inflation or in any other calculation, is:

$$\frac{(\text{Level in new year} - \text{Level in previous year})}{\text{Level in previous year}} = \text{Percentage change}$$

Step 2. From period 1 to period 2, the total cost of purchasing the basket of goods in Table 8.2 rises from $100 to $106.50. Therefore, the percentage change over this time—the inflation rate—is:

$$\frac{(106.50 - 100)}{100.0} = 0.065 = 6.5\%$$

Step 3. From period 2 to period 3, the overall change in the cost of purchasing the basket rises from $106.50 to $107. Thus, the inflation rate over this time, again calculated by the percentage change, is approximately:

$$\frac{(107 - 106.50)}{106.50} = 0.0047 = 0.47\%$$

Step 4. From period 3 to period 4, the overall cost rises from $107 to $117.50. The inflation rate is thus:

$$\frac{(117.50 - 107)}{107} = 0.098 = 9.8\%$$

This calculation of the change in the total cost of purchasing a basket of goods takes into account how much is spent on each good. Hamburgers are the lowest-priced good in this example, and aspirin is the highest-priced. If an individual buys a greater quantity of a low-price good, then it makes sense that changes in the price of that good should have a larger impact on the buying power of that person's money. The larger impact of hamburgers shows up in the "amount spent" row, where, in all time periods, hamburgers are the largest item within the amount spent row.

Index Numbers

The numerical results of a calculation based on a basket of goods can get a little messy. The simplified example in Table 8.2 has only three goods and the prices are in even dollars, not numbers like 79 cents or $124.99. If the list of products was much longer, and more realistic prices were used, the total quantity spent over a year might be some messy-looking number like $17,147.51 or $27,654.92.

To simplify the task of interpreting the price levels for more realistic and complex baskets of goods, the price level in each period is typically reported as an **index number**, rather than as the dollar amount for buying the basket of goods. Price indices are created to calculate an overall average change in relative prices over time. To convert the money spent on the basket to an index number, economists arbitrarily choose one year to be the **base year**, or starting point from which we measure changes in prices. The base year, by definition, has an index number equal to 100. This sounds complicated, but it is really a simple math trick. In the example above, say that time period 3 is chosen as the base year. Since the total amount of spending in that year is $107, we divide that amount by itself ($107) and multiply by 100. Mathematically, that is equivalent to dividing $107 by 100, or $1.07. Doing either will give us an index in the base year of 100. Again, this is because the index number in the base year *always* has to have a value of 100. Then, to figure out the values of the index number for the other years, we divide the dollar amounts for the other years by 1.07 as well. Note also that the dollar signs cancel out so that index numbers have no units.

Calculations for the other values of the index number, based on the example presented in Table 8.2 are shown in Table 8.3. Because the index numbers are calculated so that they are in exactly the same proportion as the total dollar cost of purchasing the basket of goods, the inflation rate can be calculated based on the index numbers, using the percentage change formula. So, the inflation rate from period 1 to period 2 would be

$$\frac{(99.5 - 93.4)}{93.4} = 0.065 = 6.5\%$$

This is the same answer that was derived when measuring inflation based on the dollar cost of the basket of goods for the same time period.

	Total Spending	Index Number	Inflation Rate Since Previous Period
Period 1	$100	$\frac{100}{1.07} = 93.4$	
Period 2	$106.50	$\frac{106.50}{1.07} = 99.5$	$\frac{(99.5 - 93.4)}{93.4} = 0.065 = 6.5\%$
Period 3	$107	$\frac{107}{1.07} = 100.0$	$\frac{100 - 99.5}{99.5} = 0.005 = 0.5\%$
Period 4	$117.50	$\frac{117.50}{1.07} = 109.8$	$\frac{109.8 - 100}{100} = 0.098 = 9.8\%$

Table 8.3 Calculating Index Numbers When Period 3 is the Base Year

If the inflation rate is the same whether it is based on dollar values or index numbers, then why bother with the index numbers? The advantage is that indexing allows easier eyeballing of the inflation numbers. If you glance at two index numbers like 107 and 110, you know automatically that the rate of inflation between the two years is about, but not quite exactly equal to, 3%. By contrast, imagine that the price levels were expressed in absolute dollars of a large basket of goods, so that when you looked at the data, the numbers were $19,493.62 and $20,009.32. Most people find it difficult to eyeball those kinds of numbers and say that it is a change of about 3%. However, the two numbers expressed in absolute dollars are exactly in the same proportion of 107 to 110 as the previous example. If you're wondering why simple subtraction of the index numbers wouldn't work, read the following Clear It Up feature.

Clear It Up

Why do you not just subtract index numbers?

A word of warning: When a price index moves from, say, 107 to 110, the rate of inflation is not *exactly* 3%. Remember, the inflation rate is not derived by subtracting the index numbers, but rather through the percentage-change calculation. The precise inflation rate as the price index moves from 107 to 110 is calculated as (110 – 107) / 107 = 0.028 = 2.8%. When the base year is fairly close to 100, a quick subtraction is not a terrible shortcut to calculating the inflation rate—but when precision matters down to tenths of a percent, subtracting will not give the right answer.

Two final points about index numbers are worth remembering. First, index numbers have no dollar signs or other units attached to them. Although index numbers can be used to calculate a percentage inflation rate, the index numbers themselves do not have percentage signs. Index numbers just mirror the proportions found in other data. They transform the other data so that the data are easier to work with.

Second, the choice of a base year for the index number—that is, the year that is automatically set equal to 100—is arbitrary. It is chosen as a starting point from which changes in prices are tracked. In the official inflation statistics, it is common to use one base year for a few years, and then to update it, so that the base year of 100 is relatively close to the present. But any base year that is chosen for the index numbers will result in exactly the same inflation rate. To see this in the previous example, imagine that period 1, when total spending was $100, was also chosen as the base year, and given an index number of 100. At a glance, you can see that the index numbers would now exactly match the dollar figures, the inflation rate in the first period would be 6.5%, and so on.

Now that we see how indexes work to track inflation, the next module will show us how the cost of living is measured.

Link It Up

Watch this video (http://openstaxcollege.org/l/Duck_Tales) from the cartoon *Duck Tales* to view a mini-lesson on inflation.

8.2 | How Changes in the Cost of Living Are Measured

By the end of this section, you will be able to:
- Use the Consumer Price Index (CPI) to calculate U.S. inflation rates
- Identify several ways the Bureau of Labor Statistics avoids baises in the Consumer Price Index (CPI)
- Differentiate among the Consumer Price Index (CPI), the Producer Price Index (PPI), the International Price Index, the Employment Cost Index, and the GDP deflator.

The most commonly cited measure of inflation in the United States is the **Consumer Price Index (CPI)**. The CPI is calculated by government statisticians at the U.S. Bureau of Labor Statistics based on the prices in a fixed basket of goods and services that represents the purchases of the average family of four. In recent years, the statisticians have paid considerable attention to a subtle problem: that the change in the total cost of buying a fixed basket of goods and services over time is conceptually not quite the same as the change in the cost of living, because the cost of living represents how much it costs for a person to feel that his or her consumption provides an equal level of satisfaction or utility.

To understand the distinction, imagine that over the past 10 years, the cost of purchasing a fixed basket of goods increased by 25% and your salary also increased by 25%. Has your personal standard of living held constant? If you do not necessarily purchase an identical fixed basket of goods every year, then an inflation calculation based on the cost of a fixed basket of goods may be a misleading measure of how your cost of living has changed. Two problems arise here: substitution bias and quality/new goods bias.

When the price of a good rises, consumers tend to purchase less of it and to seek out substitutes instead. Conversely, as the price of a good falls, people will tend to purchase more of it. This pattern implies that goods with generally rising prices should tend over time to become less important in the overall basket of goods used to calculate inflation, while goods with falling prices should tend to become more important. Consider, as an example, a rise in the price of peaches by $100 per pound. If consumers were utterly inflexible in their demand for peaches, this would lead to a big rise in the price of food for consumers. Alternatively, imagine that people are utterly indifferent to whether they have peaches or other types of fruit. Now, if peach prices rise, people completely switch to other fruit choices and the average price of food does not change at all. A fixed and unchanging basket of goods assumes that consumers are locked into buying exactly the same goods, regardless of price changes—not a very likely assumption. Thus, **substitution bias**—the rise in the price of a fixed basket of goods over time—tends to overstate the rise in a consumer's true cost of living, because it does not take into account that the person can substitute away from goods whose relative prices have risen.

The other major problem in using a fixed basket of goods as the basis for calculating inflation is how to deal with the arrival of improved versions of older goods or altogether new goods. Consider the problem that arises if a cereal is improved by adding 12 essential vitamins and minerals—and also if a box of the cereal costs 5% more. It would clearly be misleading to count the entire resulting higher price as inflation, because the new price is being charged for a product of higher (or at least different) quality. Ideally, one would like to know how much of the higher price is due to the quality change, and how much of it is just a higher price. The Bureau of Labor Statistics, which is responsible for the computation of the Consumer Price Index, must deal with these difficulties in adjusting for quality changes.

Link It Up

Visit this website (http://openstaxcollege.org/l/Fords) to view a list of Ford car prices between 1909 and 1927. Consider how these prices compare to today's models. Is the product today of a different quality?

A new product can be thought of as an extreme improvement in quality—from something that did not exist to something that does. However, the basket of goods that was fixed in the past obviously does not include new goods created since then. The basket of goods and services used in the Consumer Price Index (CPI) is revised and updated over time, and so new products are gradually included. But the process takes some time. For example, room air conditioners were widely sold in the early 1950s, but were not introduced into the basket of goods behind the Consumer Price Index until 1964. The VCR and personal computer were available in the late 1970s and widely sold by the early 1980s, but did not enter the CPI basket of goods until 1987. By 1996, there were more than 40 million cellular phone subscribers in the United States—but cell phones were not yet part of the CPI basket of goods. The parade of inventions has continued, with the CPI inevitably lagging a few years behind.

The arrival of new goods creates problems with respect to the accuracy of measuring inflation. The reason people buy new goods, presumably, is that the new goods offer better value for money than existing goods. Thus, if the price index leaves out new goods, it overlooks one of the ways in which the cost of living is improving. In addition, the price of a new good is often higher when it is first introduced and then declines over time. If the new good is not included in the CPI for some years, until its price is already lower, the CPI may miss counting this price decline altogether. Taking these arguments together, the **quality/new goods bias** means that the rise in the price of a fixed basket of goods over time tends to overstate the rise in a consumer's true cost of living, because it does not take into account how improvements in the quality of existing goods or the invention of new goods improves the standard of living. The following Clear It Up feature is a must-read on how the CPI is comprised and calculated.

How do U.S. government statisticians measure the Consumer Price Index?

When the U.S. Bureau of Labor Statistics (BLS) calculates the Consumer Price Index, the first task is to decide on a basket of goods that is representative of the purchases of the average household. This is done by using the Consumer Expenditure Survey, a national survey of about 7,000 households, which provides detailed information on spending habits. Consumer expenditures are broken up into eight major groups, shown below, which in turn are broken up into more than 200 individual item categories. The BLS currently uses 1982–1984 as the base period.

For each of the 200 individual expenditure items, the BLS chooses several hundred very specific examples of that item and looks at the prices of those examples. So, in figuring out the "breakfast cereal" item under the overall category of "foods and beverages," the BLS picks several hundred examples of breakfast cereal. One example might be the price of a 24-oz. box of a particular brand of cereal sold at a particular store. The specific products and sizes and stores chosen are statistically selected to reflect what people buy and where they shop. The basket of goods in the Consumer Price Index thus consists of about 80,000 products; that is, several hundred specific products in over 200 broad-item categories. About one-quarter of these 80,000 specific products are rotated out of the sample each year, and replaced with a different set of products.

The next step is to collect data on prices. Data collectors visit or call about 23,000 stores in 87 urban areas all over the United States every month to collect prices on these 80,000 specific products. A survey of 50,000 landlords or tenants is also carried out to collect information about rents.

The Consumer Price Index is then calculated by taking the 80,000 prices of individual products and combining them, using weights (as shown in Figure 8.2) determined by the quantities of these products that people buy and allowing for factors like substitution between goods and quality improvements, into price indices for the 200 or so overall items. Then, the price indices for the 200 items are combined into an overall Consumer Price Index. According the Consumer Price Index website, there are eight categories used by data collectors:

The Eight Major Categories in the Consumer Price Index

1. Food and beverages (breakfast cereal, milk, coffee, chicken, wine, full-service meals, and snacks)

2. Housing (renter's cost of housing, homeowner's cost of housing, fuel oil, bedroom furniture)

3. Apparel (men's shirts and sweaters, women's dresses, jewelry)

4. Transportation (new vehicles, airline fares, gasoline, motor vehicle insurance)

5. Medical care (prescription drugs and medical supplies, physicians' services, eyeglasses and eye care, hospital services)

6. Recreation (televisions, cable television, pets and pet products, sports equipment, admissions)

7. Education and communication (college tuition, postage, telephone services, computer software and accessories)

8. Other goods and services (tobacco and smoking products, haircuts and other personal services, funeral expenses)

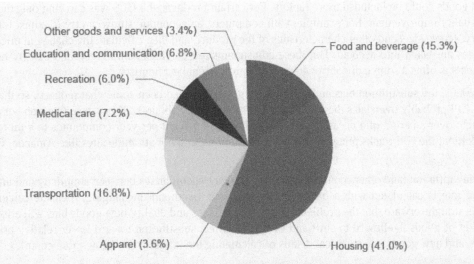

Figure 8.2 The Weighting of CPI Components Of the eight categories used to generate the Consumer Price Index, housing is the highest at 41%. The next highest category, transportation at 16.8%, is less than half the size of housing. Other goods and services, and apparel, are the lowest at 3.4% and 3.6%, respectively. (Source: www.bls.gov/cpi)

The CPI and Core Inflation Index

Imagine if you were driving a company truck across the country- you probably would care about things like the prices of available roadside food and motel rooms as well as the truck's operating condition. However, the manager of the firm might have different priorities. He would care mostly about the truck's on-time performance and much less so about the food you were eating and the places you were staying. In other words, the company manager would be paying attention to the production of the firm, while ignoring transitory elements that impacted you, but did not affect the company's bottom line.

In a sense, a similar situation occurs with regard to measures of inflation. As we've learned, CPI measures prices as they affect everyday household spending. Well, a **core inflation index** is typically calculated by taking the CPI and excluding volatile economic variables. In this way, economists have a better sense of the underlying trends in prices that affect the cost of living.

Examples of excluded variables include energy and food prices, which can jump around from month to month because of the weather. According to an article by Kent Bernhard, during Hurricane Katrina in 2005, a key supply point for the nation's gasoline was nearly knocked out. Gas prices quickly shot up across the nation, in some places up to 40 cents a gallon in one day. This was not the cause of an economic policy but rather a short-lived event until the pumps were restored in the region. In this case, the CPI that month would register the change as a cost of living event to households, but the core inflation index would remain unchanged. As a result, the Federal Reserve's decisions on interest rates would not be influenced. Similarly, droughts can cause world-wide spikes in food prices that, if temporary, do not affect the nation's economic capability.

As former Chairman of the Federal Reserve Ben Bernanke noted in 1999 about the core inflation index, "It provide(s) a better guide to monetary policy than the other indices, since it measures the more persistent underlying inflation rather than transitory influences on the price level." Bernanke also noted that it helps communicate that every inflationary shock need not be responded to by the Federal Reserve since some price changes are transitory and not part of a structural change in the economy.

In sum, both the CPI and the core inflation index are important, but serve different audiences. The CPI helps households understand their overall cost of living from month to month, while the core inflation index is a preferred gauge from which to make important government policy changes.

Practical Solutions for the Substitution and the Quality/New Goods Biases

By the early 2000s, the Bureau of Labor Statistics was using alternative mathematical methods for calculating the Consumer Price Index, more complicated than just adding up the cost of a fixed basket of goods, to allow for some substitution between goods. It was also updating the basket of goods behind the CPI more frequently, so that new and improved goods could be included more rapidly. For certain products, the BLS was carrying out studies to try to measure the quality improvement. For example, with computers, an economic study can try to adjust for changes in speed, memory, screen size, and other characteristics of the product, and then calculate the change in price after these product changes are taken into account. But these adjustments are inevitably imperfect, and exactly how to make these adjustments is often a source of controversy among professional economists.

By the early 2000s, the substitution bias and quality/new goods bias had been somewhat reduced, so that since then the rise in the CPI probably overstates the true rise in inflation by only about 0.5% per year. Over one or a few years, this is not much; over a period of a decade or two, even half of a percent per year compounds to a more significant amount. In addition, the CPI tracks prices from physical locations, and not at online sites like Amazon, where prices can be lower.

When measuring inflation (and other economic statistics, too), a tradeoff arises between simplicity and interpretation. If the inflation rate is calculated with a basket of goods that is fixed and unchanging, then the calculation of an inflation rate is straightforward, but the problems of substitution bias and quality/new goods bias will arise. However, when the basket of goods is allowed to shift and evolve to reflect substitution toward lower relative prices, quality improvements, and new goods, the technical details of calculating the inflation rate grow more complex.

Additional Price Indices: PPI, GDP Deflator, and More

The basket of goods behind the Consumer Price Index represents an average hypothetical U.S. household, which is to say that it does not exactly capture anyone's personal experience. When the task is to calculate an average level of inflation, this approach works fine. What if, however, you are concerned about inflation experienced by a certain group, like the elderly, or the poor, or single-parent families with children, or Hispanic-Americans? In specific situations, a price index based on the buying power of the average consumer may not feel quite right.

This problem has a straightforward solution. If the Consumer Price Index does not serve the desired purpose, then invent another index, based on a basket of goods appropriate for the group of interest. Indeed, the Bureau of Labor Statistics publishes a number of experimental price indices: some for particular groups like the elderly or the poor, some for different geographic areas, and some for certain broad categories of goods like food or housing.

The BLS also calculates several price indices that are not based on baskets of consumer goods. For example, the **Producer Price Index (PPI)** is based on prices paid for supplies and inputs by producers of goods and services. It can be broken down into price indices for different industries, commodities, and stages of processing (like finished goods, intermediate goods, crude materials for further processing, and so on). There is an **International Price Index** based on the prices of merchandise that is exported or imported. An **Employment Cost Index** measures wage inflation in the labor market. The **GDP deflator**, measured by the Bureau of Economic Analysis, is a price index that includes all the components of GDP (that is, consumption plus investment plus government plus exports minus imports). Unlike the CPI, its baskets are not fixed but re-calculate what that year's GDP would have been worth using the base-year's prices. MIT's Billion Prices Project is a more recent alternative attempt to measure prices: data are collected online from retailers and then composed into an index that is compared to the CPI (Source: http://bpp.mit.edu/usa/).

What's the best measure of inflation? If concerned with the most accurate measure of inflation, use the GDP deflator as it picks up the prices of goods and services produced. However, it is not a good measure of cost of living as it includes prices of many products not purchased by households (for example, aircraft, fire engines, factory buildings, office complexes, and bulldozers). If one wants the most accurate measure of inflation as it impacts households, use the CPI, as it only picks up prices of products purchased by households. That is why the CPI is sometimes referred to as the cost-of-living index. As the Bureau of Labor Statistics states on its website: "The 'best' measure of inflation for a given application depends on the intended use of the data."

8.3 | How the U.S. and Other Countries Experience Inflation

By the end of this section, you will be able to:
- Identify patterns of inflation for the United States using data from the Consumer Price Index
- Identify patterns of inflation on an international level

In the last three decades, inflation has been relatively low in the U.S. economy, with the Consumer Price Index typically rising 2% to 4% per year. Looking back over the twentieth century, there have been several periods where inflation caused the price level to rise at double-digit rates, but nothing has come close to hyperinflation.

Historical Inflation in the U.S. Economy

Figure 8.3 (a) shows the level of prices in the Consumer Price Index stretching back to 1916. In this case, the base years (when the CPI is defined as 100) are set for the average level of prices that existed from 1982 to 1984. Figure 8.3 (b) shows the annual percentage changes in the CPI over time, which is the inflation rate.

(a) U.S. price level 1913-2014

(b) U.S. inflation rate 1913-2014

Figure 8.3 U.S. Price Level and Inflation Rates since 1913 Graph a shows the trends in the U.S. price level from the year 1916 to 2014. In 1916, the graph starts out close to $10, rises to around $20 in 1920, stays around $16 or $17 until 1931, when it jumps to around $15. It gradually increases, with periodic dips, until 2014, when it is around $236. Graph b shows the trends in U.S. inflation rates from the year 1916 to 2014. In 1916, the graph starts out at 7.7%, jumps to close to 18% in 1917, drops drastically to close to –11% in 1921, goes up and down periodically, until settling to around 1.5% in 2014.

The first two waves of inflation are easy to characterize in historical terms: they are right after World War I and World War II. However, there are also two periods of severe negative inflation—called **deflation**—in the early decades of the twentieth century: one following the deep recession of 1920–21 and the other during the Great Depression of the 1930s. (Since inflation is a time when the buying power of money in terms of goods and services is reduced, deflation will be a time when the buying power of money in terms of goods and services increases.) For the period from 1900 to about 1960, the major inflations and deflations nearly balanced each other out, so the average annual rate of inflation over these years was only about 1% per year. A third wave of more severe inflation arrived in the 1970s and departed in the early 1980s.

Link It Up

Visit this website (http://openstaxcollege.org/l/CPI_calculator) to use an inflation calculator and discover how prices have changed in the last 100 years.

Times of recession or depression often seem to be times when the inflation rate is lower, as in the recession of 1920–1921, the Great Depression, the recession of 1980–1982, and the Great Recession in 2008–2009. There were a few months in 2009 that were deflationary, but not at an annual rate. Recessions are typically accompanied by higher levels of unemployment, and the total demand for goods falls, pulling the price level down. Conversely, the rate of inflation often, but not always, seems to start moving up when the economy is growing very strongly, like right after wartime or during the 1960s. The frameworks for macroeconomic analysis, developed in other chapters, will explain why recession often accompanies higher unemployment and lower inflation, while rapid economic growth often brings lower unemployment but higher inflation.

Inflation around the World

Around the rest of the world, the pattern of inflation has been very mixed, as can be seen in **Figure 8.4** which shows inflation rates over the last several decades. Many industrialized countries, not just the United States, had relatively high inflation rates in the 1970s. For example, in 1975, Japan's inflation rate was over 8% and the inflation rate for the United Kingdom was almost 25%. In the 1980s, inflation rates came down in the United States and in Europe and have largely stayed down.

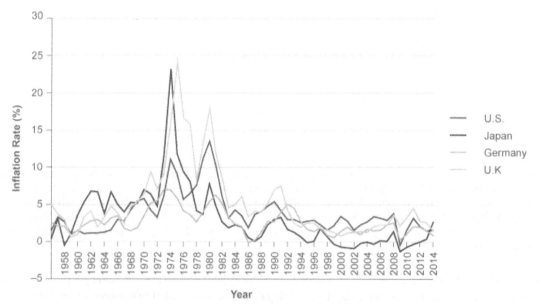

Figure 8.4 Countries with Relatively Low Inflation Rates, 1960–2014 This chart shows the annual percentage change in consumer prices compared with the previous year's consumer prices in the United States, the United Kingdom, Japan, and Germany.

Countries with controlled economies in the 1970s, like the Soviet Union and China, historically had very low rates of measured inflation—because prices were forbidden to rise by law, except for the cases where the government deemed a price increase to be due to quality improvements. However, these countries also had perpetual shortages of goods, since forbidding prices to rise acts like a price ceiling and creates a situation where quantity demanded often exceeds quantity supplied. As Russia and China made a transition toward more market-oriented economies, they also experienced outbursts of inflation, although the statistics for these economies should be regarded as somewhat shakier. Inflation in China averaged about 10% per year for much of the 1980s and early 1990s, although it has dropped off since then. Russia experienced **hyperinflation**—an outburst of high inflation—of 2,500% per year in the early 1990s, although by 2006 Russia's consumer price inflation had dipped below 10% per year, as shown in **Figure 8.5**. The closest the United States has ever gotten to hyperinflation was during the Civil War, 1860–1865, in the Confederate states.

(a) Inflation rates 1980-1995

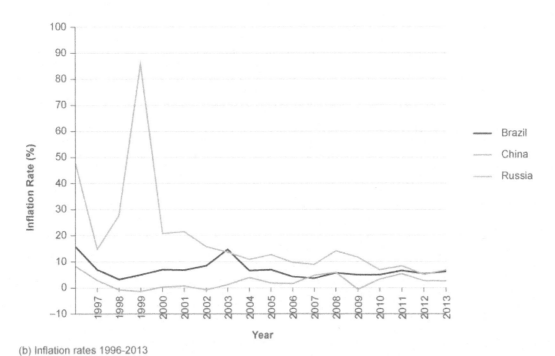

(b) Inflation rates 1996-2013

Figure 8.5 Countries with Relatively High Inflation Rates, 1980–2013 These charts show the percentage change in consumer prices compared with the previous year's consumer prices in Brazil, China, and Russia. (a) Of these, Brazil and Russia experienced hyperinflation at some point between the mid-1980s and mid-1990s. (b) Though not as high, China and Nigeria also had high inflation rates in the mid-1990s. Even though their inflation rates have come down over the last two decades, several of these countries continue to see significant inflation rates. (Sources: http://research.stlouisfed.org/fred2/series/FPCPITOTLZGBRA; http://research.stlouisfed.org/fred2/series/CHNCPIALLMINMEI; http://research.stlouisfed.org/fred2/series/FPCPITOTLZGRUS)

Many countries in Latin America experienced raging hyperinflation during the 1980s and early 1990s, with inflation rates often well above 100% per year. In 1990, for example, both Brazil and Argentina saw inflation climb above 2000%. Certain countries in Africa experienced extremely high rates of inflation, sometimes bordering on hyperinflation, in the 1990s. Nigeria, the most populous country in Africa, had an inflation rate of 75% in 1995.

In the early 2000s, the problem of inflation appears to have diminished for most countries, at least in comparison to the worst times of recent decades. As we noted in this earlier Bring it Home feature, in recent years, the world's worst example of hyperinflation was in Zimbabwe, where at one point the government was issuing bills with a face value of $100 trillion (in Zimbabwean dollars)—that is, the bills had $100,000,000,000,000 written on the front, but were almost worthless. In many countries, the memory of double-digit, triple-digit, and even quadruple-digit inflation is not very far in the past.

8.4 | The Confusion Over Inflation

By the end of this section, you will be able to:
- Explain how inflation can cause redistributions of purchasing power
- Identify ways inflation can blur the perception of supply and demand
- Explain the economic benefits and challenges of inflation

Economists usually oppose high inflation, but they oppose it in a milder way than many non-economists. Robert Shiller, one of 2013's Nobel Prize winners in economics, carried out several surveys during the 1990s about attitudes toward inflation. One of his questions asked, "Do you agree that preventing high inflation is an important national priority, as important as preventing drug abuse or preventing deterioration in the quality of our schools?" Answers were on a scale of 1–5, where 1 meant "Fully agree" and 5 meant "Completely disagree." For the U.S. population as a whole, 52% answered "Fully agree" that preventing high inflation was a highly important national priority and just 4% said "Completely disagree." However, among professional economists, only 18% answered "Fully agree," while the same percentage of 18% answered "Completely disagree."

The Land of Funny Money

What are the economic problems caused by inflation, and why do economists often regard them with less concern than the general public? Consider a very short story: "The Land of Funny Money."

One morning, everyone in the Land of Funny Money awakened to find that everything denominated in money had increased by 20%. The change was completely unexpected. Every price in every store was 20% higher. Paychecks were 20% higher. Interest rates were 20 % higher. The amount of money, everywhere from wallets to savings accounts, was 20% larger. This overnight inflation of prices made newspaper headlines everywhere in the Land of Funny Money. But the headlines quickly disappeared, as people realized that in terms of what they could actually buy with their incomes, this inflation had no economic impact. Everyone's pay could still buy exactly the same set of goods as it did before. Everyone's savings were still sufficient to buy exactly the same car, vacation, or retirement that they could have bought before. Equal levels of inflation in all wages and prices ended up not mattering much at all.

When the people in Robert Shiller's surveys explained their concern about inflation, one typical reason was that they feared that as prices rose, they would not be able to afford to buy as much. In other words, people were worried because they did not live in a place like the Land of Funny Money, where all prices and wages rose simultaneously. Instead, people live here on Planet Earth, where prices might rise while wages do not rise at all, or where wages rise more slowly than prices.

Economists note that over most periods, the inflation level in prices is roughly similar to the inflation level in wages, and so they reason that, on average, over time, people's economic status is not greatly changed by inflation. If all prices, wages, and interest rates adjusted automatically and immediately with inflation, as in the Land of Funny Money, then no one's purchasing power, profits, or real loan payments would change. However, if other economic variables do not move exactly in sync with inflation, or if they adjust for inflation only after a time lag, then inflation can cause three types of problems: unintended redistributions of purchasing power, blurred price signals, and difficulties in long-term planning.

Unintended Redistributions of Purchasing Power

Inflation can cause redistributions of purchasing power that hurt some and help others. People who are hurt by inflation include those who are holding a lot of cash, whether it is in a safe deposit box or in a cardboard box under the bed. When inflation happens, the buying power of cash is diminished. But cash is only an example of a more general problem: anyone who has financial assets invested in a way that the nominal return does not keep up with inflation will tend to suffer from inflation. For example, if a person has money in a bank account that pays 4% interest, but inflation rises to 5%, then the real rate of return for the money invested in that bank account is negative 1%.

The problem of a good-looking nominal interest rate being transformed into an ugly-looking real interest rate can be worsened by taxes. The U.S. income tax is charged on the nominal interest received in dollar terms, without an adjustment for inflation. So, a person who invests $10,000 and receives a 5% nominal rate of interest is taxed on the $500 received—no matter whether the inflation rate is 0%, 5%, or 10%. If inflation is 0%, then the real interest rate is 5% and all $500 is a gain in buying power. But if inflation is 5%, then the real interest rate is zero and the person had no real gain—but owes income tax on the nominal gain anyway. If inflation is 10%, then the real interest rate is *negative* 5% and the person is actually falling behind in buying power, but would still owe taxes on the $500 in nominal gains.

Inflation can cause unintended redistributions for wage earners, too. Wages do typically creep up with inflation over time eventually. The last row of Table 8.1 at the start of this chapter showed that average hourly wage in the U.S. economy increased from $3.23 in 1970 to $19.55 in 2014, which is an increase by a factor of almost six. Over that time period, the Consumer Price Index increased by an almost identical amount. However, increases in wages may lag behind inflation for a year or two, since wage adjustments are often somewhat sticky and occur only once or twice a year. Moreover, the extent to which wages keep up with inflation creates insecurity for workers and may involve painful, prolonged conflicts between employers and employees. If the minimum wage is adjusted for inflation only infrequently, minimum wage workers are losing purchasing power from their nominal wages, as shown in Figure 8.6.

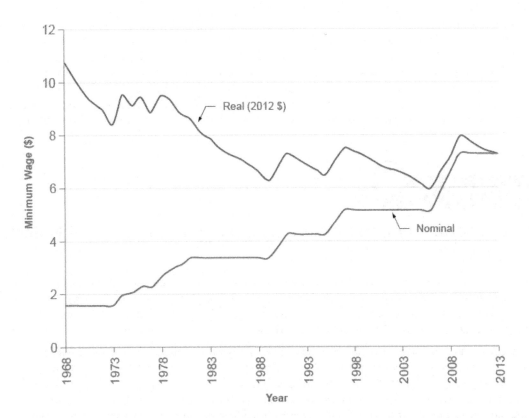

Figure 8.6 U.S. Minimum Wage and Inflation After adjusting for inflation, the federal minimum wage dropped more than 30 percent from 1967 to 2010, even though the nominal figure climbed from $1.40 to $7.25 per hour. Increases in the minimum wage in between 2008 and 2010 kept the decline from being worse—as it would have been if the wage had remained the same as it did from 1997 through 2007. (Sources: http://www.dol.gov/whd/minwage/chart.htm; http://data.bls.gov/cgi-bin/surveymost?cu)

One sizable group of people has often received a large share of their income in a form that does not increase over time: retirees who receive a private company pension. Most pensions have traditionally been set as a fixed nominal dollar amount per year at retirement. For this reason, pensions are called "defined benefits" plans. Even if inflation is low, the combination of inflation and a fixed income can create a substantial problem over time. A person who retires on a fixed income at age 65 will find that losing just 1% to 2% of buying power per year to inflation compounds to a considerable loss of buying power after a decade or two.

Fortunately, pensions and other defined benefits retirement plans are increasingly rare, replaced instead by "defined contribution" plans, such as 401(k)s and 403(b)s. In these plans, the employer contributes a fixed amount to the worker's retirement account on a regular basis (usually every pay check). The employee often contributes as well. The worker invests these funds in a wide range of investment vehicles. These plans are tax deferred, and they are portable so that if the individual takes a job with a different employer, their 401(k) comes with them. To the extent that the investments made generate real rates of return, retirees do not suffer from the inflation costs of traditional pensioners.

However, ordinary people can sometimes benefit from the unintended redistributions of inflation. Consider someone who borrows $10,000 to buy a car at a fixed interest rate of 9%. If inflation is 3% at the time the loan is made, then the loan must be repaid at a real interest rate of 6%. But if inflation rises to 9%, then the real interest rate on the loan is zero. In this case, the borrower's benefit from inflation is the lender's loss. A borrower paying a fixed interest rate, who benefits from inflation, is just the flip side of an investor receiving a fixed interest rate, who suffers from inflation. The lesson is that when interest rates are fixed, rises in the rate of inflation tend to penalize suppliers of financial capital, who end up being repaid in dollars that are worth less because of inflation, while demanders of financial capital end up better off, because they can repay their loans in dollars that are worth less than originally expected.

The unintended redistributions of buying power caused by inflation may have a broader effect on society. America's widespread acceptance of market forces rests on a perception that people's actions have a reasonable connection to market outcomes. When inflation causes a retiree who built up a pension or invested at a fixed interest rate to suffer, however, while someone who borrowed at a fixed interest rate benefits from inflation, it is hard to believe that this outcome was deserved in any way. Similarly, when homeowners benefit from inflation because the price of their homes rises, while renters suffer because they are paying higher rent, it is hard to see any useful incentive effects. One of the reasons that inflation is so disliked by the general public is a sense that it makes economic rewards and penalties more arbitrary—and therefore likely to be perceived as unfair – even dangerous, as the next Clear It Up feature shows.

Is there a connection between German hyperinflation and Hitler's rise to power?

Germany suffered an intense hyperinflation of its currency, the Mark, in the years after World War I, when the Weimar Republic in Germany resorted to printing money to pay its bills and the onset of the Great Depression created the social turmoil that Adolf Hitler could take advantage of in his rise to power. Shiller described the connection this way in a National Bureau of Economic Research 1996 Working Paper:

> A fact that is probably little known to young people today, even in Germany, is that the final collapse of the Mark in 1923, the time when the Mark's inflation reached astronomical levels (inflation of 35,974.9% in November 1923 alone, for an annual rate that month of 4.69×10^{28}%), came in the same month as did Hitler's Beer Hall Putsch, his Nazi Party's armed attempt to overthrow the German government. This failed putsch resulted in Hitler's imprisonment, at which time he wrote his book *Mein Kampf*, setting forth an inspirational plan for Germany's future, suggesting plans for world domination. . .

> . . . Most people in Germany today probably do not clearly remember these events; this lack of attention to it may be because its memory is blurred by the more dramatic events that succeeded it (the Nazi seizure of power and World War II). However, to someone living through these historical events in sequence . . . [the putsch] may have been remembered as vivid evidence of the potential effects of inflation.

Blurred Price Signals

Prices are the messengers in a market economy, conveying information about conditions of demand and supply. Inflation blurs those price messages. Inflation means that price signals are perceived more vaguely, like a radio program received with a lot of static. If the static becomes severe, it is hard to tell what is happening.

In Israel, when inflation accelerated to an annual rate of 500% in 1985, some stores stopped posting prices directly on items, since they would have had to put new labels on the items or shelves every few days to reflect inflation. Instead, a shopper just took items from a shelf and went up to the checkout register to find out the price for that day. Obviously, this situation makes comparing prices and shopping for the best deal rather difficult. When the levels and changes of prices become uncertain, businesses and individuals find it harder to react to economic signals. In a world where inflation is at a high rate, but bouncing up and down to some extent, does a higher price of a good mean that inflation has risen, or that supply of that good has decreased, or that demand for that good has increased? Should a buyer of the good take the higher prices as an economic hint to start substituting other products—or have the prices of the substitutes risen by an equal amount? Should a seller of the good take a higher price as a reason to increase production—or is the higher price only a sign of a general inflation in which the prices of all inputs to production are rising as well? The true story will presumably become clear over time, but at a given moment, who can say?

High and variable inflation means that the incentives in the economy to adjust in response to changes in prices are weaker. Markets will adjust toward their equilibrium prices and quantities more erratically and slowly, and many individual markets will experience a greater chance of surpluses and shortages.

Problems of Long-Term Planning

Inflation can make long-term planning difficult. In discussing unintended redistributions, we considered the case of someone trying to plan for retirement with a pension that is fixed in nominal terms and a high rate of inflation. Similar problems arise for all people trying to save for retirement, because they must consider what their money will really buy several decades in the future when the rate of future inflation cannot be known with certainty.

Inflation, especially at moderate or high levels, will pose substantial planning problems for businesses, too. A firm can make money from inflation—for example, by paying bills and wages as late as possible so that it can pay in inflated dollars, while collecting revenues as soon as possible. A firm can also suffer losses from inflation, as in the case of a retail business that gets stuck holding too much cash, only to see the value of that cash eroded by inflation. But when a business spends its time focusing on how to profit by inflation, or at least how to avoid suffering from it, an inevitable tradeoff strikes: less time is spent on improving products and services or on figuring out how to make existing products and services more cheaply. An economy with high inflation rewards businesses that have found clever ways of profiting from inflation, which are not necessarily the businesses that excel at productivity, innovation, or quality of service.

In the short term, low or moderate levels of inflation may not pose an overwhelming difficulty for business planning, because costs of doing business and sales revenues may rise at similar rates. If, however, inflation varies substantially over the short or medium term, then it may make sense for businesses to stick to shorter-term strategies. The evidence as to whether relatively low rates of inflation reduce productivity is controversial among economists. There is some evidence that if inflation can be held to moderate levels of less than 3% per year, it need not prevent a nation's real economy from growing at a healthy pace. For some countries that have experienced hyperinflation of several thousand percent per year, an annual inflation rate of 20–30% may feel basically the same as zero. However, several economists have pointed to the suggestive fact that when U.S. inflation heated up in the early 1970s—to 10%—U.S. growth in productivity slowed down, and when inflation slowed down in the 1980s, productivity edged up again not long thereafter, as shown in **Figure 8.7**.

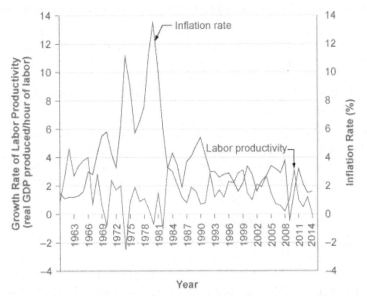

Figure 8.7 U.S. Inflation Rate and U.S. Labor Productivity, 1961–2014 Over the last several decades in the United States, there have been times when rising inflation rates have been closely followed by lower productivity rates and lower inflation rates have corresponded to increasing productivity rates. As the graph shows, however, this correlation does not always exist.

Any Benefits of Inflation?

Although the economic effects of inflation are primarily negative, two countervailing points are worth noting. First, the impact of inflation will differ considerably according to whether it is creeping up slowly at 0% to 2% per year, galloping along at 10% to 20% per year, or racing to the point of hyperinflation at, say, 40% per month. Hyperinflation can rip an economy and a society apart. An annual inflation rate of 2%, 3%, or 4%, however, is a long way from a national crisis. Low inflation is also better than deflation which occurs with severe recessions.

Second, an argument is sometimes made that moderate inflation may help the economy by making wages in labor markets more flexible. The discussion in Unemployment pointed out that wages tend to be sticky in their downward movements and that unemployment can result. A little inflation could nibble away at real wages, and thus help real wages to decline if necessary. In this way, even if a moderate or high rate of inflation may act as sand in the gears of the economy, perhaps a low rate of inflation serves as oil for the gears of the labor market. This argument is controversial. A full analysis would have to take all the effects of inflation into account. It does, however, offer another reason to believe that, all things considered, very low rates of inflation may not be especially harmful.

8.5 | Indexing and Its Limitations

By the end of this section, you will be able to:
- Explain the relationship between indexing and inflation
- Identify three ways the government can control inflation through macroeconomic policy

When a price, wage, or interest rate is adjusted automatically with inflation, it is said to be **indexed**. An indexed payment increases according to the index number that measures inflation. A wide array of indexing arrangements is observed in private markets and government programs. Since the negative effects of inflation depend in large part on having inflation unexpectedly affect one part of the economy but not another—say, increasing the prices that people pay but not the wages that workers receive—indexing will take some of the sting out of inflation.

Indexing in Private Markets

In the 1970s and 1980s, labor unions commonly negotiated wage contracts that had **cost-of-living adjustments (COLAs)** which guaranteed that their wages would keep up with inflation. These contracts were sometimes written as, for example, COLA plus 3%. Thus, if inflation was 5%, the wage increase would automatically be 8%, but if inflation rose to 9%, the wage increase would automatically be 12%. COLAs are a form of indexing applied to wages.

Loans often have built-in inflation adjustments, too, so that if the inflation rate rises by two percentage points, then the interest rate charged on the loan rises by two percentage points as well. An **adjustable-rate mortgage (ARM)** is a kind of loan used to purchase a home in which the interest rate varies with the rate of inflation. Often, a borrower will be able receive a lower interest rate if borrowing with an ARM, compared to a fixed-rate loan. The reason is that with an ARM, the lender is protected against the risk that higher inflation will reduce the real loan payments, and so the risk premium part of the interest rate can be correspondingly lower.

A number of ongoing or long-term business contracts also have provisions that prices will be adjusted automatically according to inflation. Sellers like such contracts because they are not locked into a low nominal selling price if inflation turns out higher than expected; buyers like such contracts because they are not locked into a high buying price if inflation turns out to be lower than expected. A contract with automatic adjustments for inflation in effect agrees on a real price to be paid, rather than a nominal price.

Indexing in Government Programs

Many government programs are indexed to inflation. The U.S. income tax code is designed so that as a person's income rises above certain levels, the tax rate on the marginal income earned rises as well; this is what is meant by the expression "move into a higher tax bracket." For example, according to the basic tax tables from the Internal Revenue Service, in 2014 a single person owed 10% of all taxable income from $0 to $9,075; 15% of all income from $9,076 to $36,900; 25% of all taxable income from $36,901 to $89,350; 28% of all taxable income from $89,351 to $186,350; 33% of all taxable income from $186,351 to $405,100; 35% of all taxable income from $405,101 to $406,750; and 39.6% of all income from $406,751 and above.

Because of the many complex provisions in the rest of the tax code, the taxes owed by any individual cannot be exactly determined based on these numbers, but the numbers illustrate the basic theme that tax rates rise as the marginal dollar of income rises. Until the late 1970s, if nominal wages increased along with inflation, people were moved into higher tax brackets and owed a higher proportion of their income in taxes, even though their real income had not risen. This "bracket creep," as it was called, was eliminated by law in 1981. Now, the income levels where higher tax rates kick in are indexed to rise automatically with inflation.

The Social Security program offers two examples of indexing. Since the passage of the Social Security Indexing Act of 1972, the level of Social Security benefits increases each year along with the Consumer Price Index. Also, Social

Security is funded by payroll taxes, which are imposed on the income earned up to a certain amount—$117,000 in 2014. This level of income is adjusted upward each year according to the rate of inflation, so that the indexed rise in the benefit level is accompanied by an indexed increase in the Social Security tax base.

As yet another example of a government program affected by indexing, in 1996 the U.S., government began offering indexed bonds. Bonds are means by which the U.S. government (and many private-sector companies as well) borrows money; that is, investors buy the bonds, and then the government repays the money with interest. Traditionally, government bonds have paid a fixed rate of interest. This policy gave a government that had borrowed an incentive to encourage inflation, because it could then repay its past borrowing in inflated dollars at a lower real interest rate. But indexed bonds promise to pay a certain real rate of interest above whatever inflation rate occurs. In the case of a retiree trying to plan for the long term and worried about the risk of inflation, for example, indexed bonds that guarantee a rate of return higher than inflation—no matter the level of inflation—can be a very comforting investment.

Might Indexing Reduce Concern over Inflation?

Indexing may seem like an obviously useful step. After all, when individuals, firms, and government programs are indexed against inflation, then people can worry less about arbitrary redistributions and other effects of inflation.

However, some of the fiercest opponents of inflation express grave concern about indexing. They point out that indexing is always partial. Not every employer will provide COLAs for workers. Not all companies can assume that costs and revenues will rise in lockstep with the general rates of inflation. Not all interest rates for borrowers and savers will change to match inflation exactly. But as partial inflation indexing spreads, the political opposition to inflation may diminish. After all, older people whose Social Security benefits are protected against inflation, or banks that have loaned their money with adjustable-rate loans, no longer have as much reason to care whether inflation heats up. In a world where some people are indexed against inflation and some are not, financially savvy businesses and investors may seek out ways to be protected against inflation, while the financially unsophisticated and small businesses may suffer from it most.

A Preview of Policy Discussions of Inflation

This chapter has focused on how inflation is measured, historical experience with inflation, how to adjust nominal variables into real ones, how inflation affects the economy, and how indexing works. The causes of inflation have barely been hinted at, and government policies to deal with inflation have not been addressed at all. These issues will be taken up in depth in other chapters. However, it is useful to offer a preview here.

The cause of inflation can be summed up in one sentence: Too many dollars chasing too few goods. The great surges of inflation early in the twentieth century came after wars, which are a time when government spending is very high, but consumers have little to buy, because production is going to the war effort. Governments also commonly impose price controls during wartime. After the war, the price controls end and pent-up buying power surges forth, driving up inflation. On the other hand, if too few dollars are chasing too many goods, then inflation will decline or even turn into deflation. Therefore, slowdowns in economic activity, as in major recessions and the Great Depression, are typically associated with a reduction in inflation or even outright deflation.

The policy implications are clear. If inflation is to be avoided, the amount of purchasing power in the economy must grow at roughly the same rate as the production of goods. Macroeconomic policies that the government can use to affect the amount of purchasing power—through taxes, spending, and regulation of interest rates and credit—can thus cause inflation to rise or reduce inflation to lower levels.

Bring it Home

A $550 Million Loaf of Bread?

As we will learn in Money and Banking, the existence of money provides enormous benefits to an economy. In a real sense, money is the lubrication that enhances the workings of markets. Money makes transactions easier. It allows people to find employment producing one product, then use the money earned to purchase the other products they need to live on. However, too much money in circulation can lead to inflation. Extreme cases of governments recklessly printing money lead to hyperinflation. Inflation reduces the value of money. Hyperinflation, because money loses value so quickly, ultimately results in people no longer using money.

The economy reverts to barter, or it adopts another country's more stable currency, like U.S. dollars. In the meantime, the economy literally falls apart as people leave jobs and fend for themselves because it is not worth the time to work for money that will be worthless in a few days.

Only national governments have the power to cause hyperinflation. Hyperinflation typically happens when government faces extraordinary demands for spending, which it cannot finance by taxes or borrowing. The only option is to print money—more and more of it. With more money in circulation chasing the same amount (or even less) goods and services, the only result is higher and higher prices until the economy and/or the government collapses. This is why economists are generally wary of letting inflation get out of control.

KEY TERMS

adjustable-rate mortgage (ARM) a loan used to purchase a home in which the interest rate varies with market interest rates

base year arbitrary year whose value as an index number is defined as 100; inflation from the base year to other years can easily be seen by comparing the index number in the other year to the index number in the base year—for example, 100; so, if the index number for a year is 105, then there has been exactly 5% inflation between that year and the base year

basket of goods and services a hypothetical group of different items, with specified quantities of each one meant to represent a "typical" set of consumer purchases, used as a basis for calculating how the price level changes over time

Consumer Price Index (CPI) a measure of inflation calculated by U.S. government statisticians based on the price level from a fixed basket of goods and services that represents the purchases of the average consumer

core inflation index a measure of inflation typically calculated by taking the CPI and excluding volatile economic variables such as food and energy prices to better measure the underlying and persistent trend in long-term prices

cost-of-living adjustments (COLAs) a contractual provision that wage increases will keep up with inflation

deflation negative inflation; most prices in the economy are falling

Employment Cost Index a measure of inflation based on wages paid in the labor market

GDP deflator a measure of inflation based on the prices of all the components of GDP

hyperinflation an outburst of high inflation that is often seen (although not exclusively) when economies shift from a controlled economy to a market-oriented economy

index number a unit-free number derived from the price level over a number of years, which makes computing inflation rates easier, since the index number has values around 100

indexed a price, wage, or interest rate is adjusted automatically for inflation

inflation a general and ongoing rise in the level of prices in an economy

International Price Index a measure of inflation based on the prices of merchandise that is exported or imported

Producer Price Index (PPI) a measure of inflation based on prices paid for supplies and inputs by producers of goods and services

quality/new goods bias inflation calculated using a fixed basket of goods over time tends to overstate the true rise in cost of living, because it does not take into account improvements in the quality of existing goods or the invention of new goods

substitution bias an inflation rate calculated using a fixed basket of goods over time tends to overstate the true rise in the cost of living, because it does not take into account that the person can substitute away from goods whose prices rise by a lot

KEY CONCEPTS AND SUMMARY

8.1 Tracking Inflation

The price level is measured by using a basket of goods and services and calculating how the total cost of buying that basket of goods will increase over time. The price level is often expressed in terms of index numbers, which transform the cost of buying the basket of goods and services into a series of numbers in the same proportion to each other, but with an arbitrary base year of 100. The rate of inflation is measured as the percentage change between price levels or index numbers over time.

8.2 How Changes in the Cost of Living Are Measured

Measuring price levels with a fixed basket of goods will always have two problems: the substitution bias, by which a fixed basket of goods does not allow for buying more of what is relatively less expensive and less of what is relatively more expensive; and the quality/new goods bias, by which a fixed basket cannot take into account improvements in quality and the advent of new goods. These problems can be reduced in degree—for example, by allowing the basket of goods to evolve over time—but they cannot be totally eliminated. The most commonly cited measure of inflation is the Consumer Price Index (CPI), which is based on a basket of goods representing what the typical consumer buys. The Core Inflation Index further breaks down the CPI by excluding volatile economic variables. Several price indices are not based on baskets of consumer goods. The GDP deflator is based on all the components of GDP. The Producer Price Index is based on prices of supplies and inputs bought by producers of goods and services. An Employment Cost Index measures wage inflation in the labor market. An International Price Index is based on the prices of merchandise that is exported or imported.

8.3 How the U.S. and Other Countries Experience Inflation

In the U.S. economy, the annual inflation rate in the last two decades has typically been around 2% to 4%. The periods of highest inflation in the United States in the twentieth century occurred during the years after World Wars I and II, and in the 1970s. The period of lowest inflation—actually, with deflation—was the Great Depression of the 1930s.

8.4 The Confusion Over Inflation

Unexpected inflation will tend to hurt those whose money received, in terms of wages and interest payments, does not rise with inflation. In contrast, inflation can help those who owe money that can be paid in less valuable, inflated dollars. Low rates of inflation have relatively little economic impact over the short term. Over the medium and the long term, even low rates of inflation can complicate future planning. High rates of inflation can muddle price signals in the short term and prevent market forces from operating efficiently, and can vastly complicate long-term savings and investment decisions.

8.5 Indexing and Its Limitations

A payment is said to be indexed if it is automatically adjusted for inflation. Examples of indexing in the private sector include wage contracts with cost-of-living adjustments (COLAs) and loan agreements like adjustable-rate mortgages (ARMs). Examples of indexing in the public sector include tax brackets and Social Security payments.

SELF-CHECK QUESTIONS

1. Table 8.4 shows the prices of fruit purchased by the typical college student from 2001 to 2004. What is the amount spent each year on the "basket" of fruit with the quantities shown in column 2?

Items	Qty	(2001) Price	(2001) Amount Spent	(2002) Price	(2002) Amount Spent	(2003) Price	(2003) Amount Spent	(2004) Price	(2004) Amount Spent
Apples	10	$0.50		$0.75		$0.85		$0.88	
Bananas	12	$0.20		$0.25		$0.25		$0.29	

Table 8.4

Items	Qty	(2001) Price	(2001) Amount Spent	(2002) Price	(2002) Amount Spent	(2003) Price	(2003) Amount Spent	(2004) Price	(2004) Amount Spent
Grapes	2	$0.65		$0.70		$0.90		$0.95	
Raspberries	1	$2.00		$1.90		$2.05		$2.13	$2.13
Total									

Table 8.4

2. Construct the price index for a "fruit basket" in each year using 2003 as the base year.

3. Compute the inflation rate for fruit prices from 2001 to 2004.

4. Edna is living in a retirement home where most of her needs are taken care of, but she has some discretionary spending. Based on the basket of goods in Table 8.5, by what percentage does Edna's cost of living increase between time 1 and time 2?

Items	Quantity	(Time 1) Price	(Time 2) Price
Gifts for grandchildren	12	$50	$60
Pizza delivery	24	$15	$16
Blouses	6	$60	$50
Vacation trips	2	$400	$420

Table 8.5

5. How Changes in the Cost of Living are Measured introduced a number of different price indices. Which price index would be best to use to adjust your paycheck for inflation?

6. The Consumer Price Index is subject to the substitution bias and the quality/new goods bias. Are the Producer Price Index and the GDP Deflator also subject to these biases? Why or why not?

7. Go to this website (http://www.measuringworth.com/ppowerus/) for the Purchasing Power Calculator at MeasuringWorth.com. How much money would it take today to purchase what one dollar would have bought in the year of your birth?

8. If inflation rises unexpectedly by 5%, would a state government that had recently borrowed money to pay for a new highway benefit or lose?

9. How should an increase in inflation affect the interest rate on an adjustable-rate mortgage?

10. A fixed-rate mortgage has the same interest rate over the life of the loan, whether the mortgage is for 15 or 30 years. By contrast, an adjustable-rate mortgage changes with market interest rates over the life of the mortgage. If inflation falls unexpectedly by 3%, what would likely happen to a homeowner with an adjustable-rate mortgage?

REVIEW QUESTIONS

11. How is a basket of goods and services used to measure the price level?

12. Why are index numbers used to measure the price level rather than dollar value of goods?

13. What is the difference between the price level and the rate of inflation?

14. Why does "substitution bias" arise if the inflation rate is calculated based on a fixed basket of goods?

15. Why does the "quality/new goods bias" arise if the inflation rate is calculated based on a fixed basket of goods?

16. What has been a typical range of inflation in the U.S. economy in the last decade or so?

17. Over the last century, during what periods was the U.S. inflation rate highest and lowest?

18. What is deflation?

19. Identify several parties likely to be helped and hurt by inflation.

20. What is indexing?

21. Name several forms of indexing in the private and public sector.

CRITICAL THINKING QUESTIONS

22. Inflation rates, like most statistics, are imperfect measures. Can you identify some ways that the inflation rate for fruit does not perfectly capture the rising price of fruit?

23. Given the federal budget deficit in recent years, some economists have argued that by adjusting Social Security payments for inflation using the CPI, Social Security is overpaying recipients. What is the argument being made, and do you agree or disagree with it?

24. Why is the GDP deflator not an accurate measure of inflation as it impacts a household?

25. Imagine that the government statisticians who calculate the inflation rate have been updating the basic basket of goods once every 10 years, but now they decide to update it every five years. How will this change affect the amount of substitution bias and quality/new goods bias?

26. Describe a situation, either a government policy situation, an economic problem, or a private sector situation, where using the CPI to convert from nominal to real would be more appropriate than using the GDP deflator.

27. Describe a situation, either a government policy situation, an economic problem, or a private sector situation, where using the GDP deflator to convert from nominal to real would be more appropriate than using the CPI.

28. Why do you think the U.S. experience with inflation over the last 50 years has been so much milder than in many other countries?

29. If, over time, wages and salaries on average rise at least as fast as inflation, why do people worry about how inflation affects incomes?

30. Who in an economy is the big winner from inflation?

31. If a government gains from unexpected inflation when it borrows, why would it choose to offer indexed bonds?

32. Do you think perfect indexing is possible? Why or why not?

PROBLEMS

33. The index number representing the price level changes from 110 to 115 in one year, and then from 115 to 120 the next year. Since the index number increases by five each year, is five the inflation rate each year? Is the inflation rate the same each year? Explain your answer.

34. The total price of purchasing a basket of goods in the United Kingdom over four years is: year 1=£940, year 2=£970, year 3=£1000, and year 4=£1070. Calculate two price indices, one using year 1 as the base

year (set equal to 100) and the other using year 4 as the base year (set equal to 100). Then, calculate the inflation rate based on the first price index. If you had used the other price index, would you get a different inflation rate? If you are unsure, do the calculation and find out.

35. Within 1 or 2 percentage points, what has the U.S. inflation rate been during the last 20 years? Draw a graph to show the data.

36. If inflation rises unexpectedly by 5%, indicate for each of the following whether the economic actor is helped, hurt, or unaffected:
   a. A union member with a COLA wage contract
   b. Someone with a large stash of cash in a safe deposit box
   c. A bank lending money at a fixed rate of interest
   d. A person who is not due to receive a pay raise for another 11 months

37. Rosalie the Retiree knows that when she retires in 16 years, her company will give her a one-time payment of $20,000. However, if the inflation rate is 6% per year, how much buying power will that $20,000 have when measured in today's dollars? *Hint*: Start by calculating the rise in the price level over the 16 years.

9 | The International Trade and Capital Flows

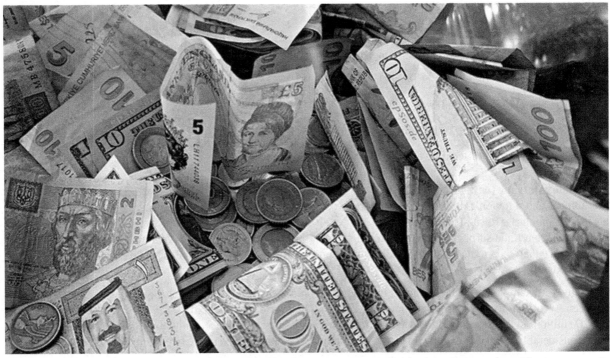

Figure 9.1 A World of Money We are all part of the global financial system, which includes many different currencies. (Credit: modification of work by epSos.de/Flickr Creative Commons)

Bring it Home

More than Meets the Eye in the Congo

How much do you interact with the global financial system? Do you think not much? Think again. Suppose you take out a student loan, or you deposit money into your bank account. You just affected domestic savings and borrowing. Now say you are at the mall and buy two T-shirts "made in China," and later contribute to a charity that helps refugees. What is the impact? You affected how much money flows into and out of the United States. If you open an IRA savings account and put money in an international mutual fund, you are involved in the flow of money overseas. While your involvement may not seem as influential as someone like the president, who can increase or decrease foreign aid and, thereby, have a huge impact on money flows in and out of the country, you do interact with the global financial system on a daily basis.

The balance of payments—a term you will meet soon—seems like a huge topic, but once you learn the specific components of trade and money, it all makes sense. Along the way, you may have to give up some common misunderstandings about trade and answer some questions: If a country is running a trade deficit, is that bad? Is a trade surplus good? For example, look at the Democratic Republic of Congo (often referred to as "Congo"), a large country in Central Africa. In 2013, it ran a trade surplus of $1 billion, so it must be doing well, right? In contrast, the trade deficit in the United States was $508 billion in 2013. Do these figures suggest that the economy in the United States is doing worse than the Congolese economy? Not necessarily. The U.S. trade deficit tends to worsen as the economy strengthens. In contrast, high poverty rates in the Congo persist, and these rates are not going down even with the positive trade balance. Clearly, it is more complicated than simply asserting that running a trade deficit is bad for the economy. You will learn more about these issues and others in this chapter.

Introduction to International Trade and Capital Flows

In this chapter, you will learn about:

- Measuring Trade Balances
- Trade Balances in Historical and International Context
- Trade Balances and Flows of Financial Capital
- The National Saving and Investment Identity
- The Pros and Cons of Trade Deficits and Surpluses
- The Difference between Level of Trade and the Trade Balance

The **balance of trade** (or trade balance) is any gap between a nation's dollar value of its exports, or what its producers sell abroad, and a nation's dollar worth of imports, or the foreign-made products and services that households and businesses purchase. Recall from **The Macroeconomic Perspective** that if exports exceed imports, the economy is said to have a trade surplus. If imports exceed exports, the economy is said to have a trade deficit. If exports and imports are equal, then trade is balanced. But what happens when trade is out of balance and large trade surpluses or deficits exist?

Germany, for example, has had substantial trade surpluses in recent decades, in which exports have greatly exceeded imports. According to the Central Intelligence Agency's The World Factbook, in 2013, Germany ran a trade surplus of $260 billion. In contrast, the U.S. economy in recent decades has experienced large trade deficits, in which imports have considerably exceeded exports. In 2014, for example, U.S. imports exceeded exports by $539 billion.

A series of financial crises triggered by unbalanced trade can lead economies into deep recessions. These crises begin with large trade deficits. At some point, foreign investors become pessimistic about the economy and move their money to other countries. The economy then drops into deep recession, with real GDP often falling up to 10% or more in a single year. This happened to Mexico in 1995 when their GDP fell 8.1%. A number of countries in East Asia—Thailand, South Korea, Malaysia, and Indonesia—came down with the same economic illness in 1997–1998 (called the Asian Financial Crisis). In the late 1990s and into the early 2000s, Russia and Argentina had the identical experience. What are the connections between imbalances of trade in goods and services and the flows of international financial capital that set off these economic avalanches?

We will start by examining the balance of trade in more detail, by looking at some patterns of trade balances in the United States and around the world. Then we will examine the intimate connection between international flows of goods and services and international flows of financial capital, which to economists are really just two sides of the same coin. It is often assumed that trade surpluses like those in Germany must be a positive sign for an economy, while trade deficits like those in the United States must be harmful. As it turns out, both trade surpluses and deficits can be either good or bad. We will see why in this chapter.

9.1 | Measuring Trade Balances

By the end of this section, you will be able to:

- Explain merchandise trade balance, current account balance, and unilateral transfers
- Identify components of the U.S. current account balance
- Calculate the merchandise trade balance and current account balance using import and export data for a country

A few decades ago, it was common to track the solid or physical items that were transported by planes, trains, and trucks between countries as a way of measuring the balance of trade. This measurement is called the **merchandise trade balance**. In most high-income economies, including the United States, goods make up less than half of a country's total production, while services compose more than half. The last two decades have seen a surge in international trade in services, powered by technological advances in telecommunications and computers that have made it possible to export or import customer services, finance, law, advertising, management consulting, software, construction engineering, and product design. Most global trade still takes the form of goods rather than services, and the merchandise trade balance is still announced by the government and reported prominently in the newspapers. Old habits are hard to break. Economists, however, typically rely on broader measures such as the balance of trade or the **current account balance** which includes other international flows of income and foreign aid.

Components of the U.S. Current Account Balance

Table 9.1 breaks down the four main components of the U.S. current account balance for the last quarter of 2014 (seasonally adjusted). The first line shows the merchandise trade balance; that is, exports and imports of goods. Because imports exceed exports, the trade balance in the final column is negative, showing a merchandise trade deficit. How this trade information is collected is explained in the following Clear It Up feature.

	Value of Exports (money flowing into the United States)	Value of Imports (money flowing out of the United States)	Balance
Goods	$410.0	$595.5	–$185.3
Services	$180.4	$122.3	$58.1
Income receipts and payments	$203.0	$152.4	$50.6
Unilateral transfers	$27.3	$64.4	–$37.1
Current account balance	$820.7	$934.4	–$113.7

Table 9.1 Components of the U.S. Current Account Balance for 2014 (in billions)

How does the U.S. government collect trade statistics?

Do not confuse the balance of trade (which tracks imports and exports), with the current account balance, which includes not just exports and imports, but also income from investment and transfers.

Statistics on the balance of trade are compiled by the Bureau of Economic Analysis (BEA) within the U.S. Department of Commerce, using a variety of different sources. Importers and exporters of merchandise must file monthly documents with the Census Bureau, which provides the basic data for tracking trade. To measure international trade in services—which can happen over a telephone line or computer network without any physical goods being shipped—the BEA carries out a set of surveys. Another set of BEA surveys track investment flows, and there are even specific surveys to collect travel information from U.S. residents visiting Canada and Mexico. For measuring unilateral transfers, the BEA has access to official U.S. government spending on aid, and then also carries out a survey of charitable organizations that make foreign donations.

This information on international flows of goods and capital is then cross-checked against other available data. For example, the Census Bureau also collects data from the shipping industry, which can be used to check the data on trade in goods. All companies involved in international flows of capital—including banks and companies making financial investments like stocks—must file reports, which are ultimately compiled by the U.S. Department of the Treasury. Information on foreign trade can also be cross-checked by looking at data collected by other countries on their foreign trade with the United States, and also at the data collected by various international organizations. Take these data sources, stir carefully, and you have the U.S. balance of trade statistics. Much of the statistics cited in this chapter come from these sources.

The second row of Table 9.1 provides data on trade in services. Here, the U.S. economy is running a surplus. Although the level of trade in services is still relatively small compared to trade in goods, the importance of services has expanded substantially over the last few decades. For example, U.S. exports of services were equal to about one-half of U.S. exports of goods in 2014, compared to one-fifth in 1980.

The third component of the current account balance, labeled "income payments," refers to money received by U.S. financial investors on their foreign investments (money flowing into the United States) and payments to foreign investors who had invested their funds here (money flowing out of the United States). The reason for including this money on foreign investment in the overall measure of trade, along with goods and services, is that, from an economic perspective, income is just as much an economic transaction as shipments of cars or wheat or oil: it is just trade that is happening in the financial capital market.

The final category of the current account balance is **unilateral transfers**, which are payments made by government, private charities, or individuals in which money is sent abroad without any direct good or service being received. Economic or military assistance from the U.S. government to other countries fits into this category, as does spending abroad by charities to address poverty or social inequalities. When an individual in the United States sends money overseas, it is also counted in this category. The current account balance treats these unilateral payments like imports, because they also involve a stream of payments leaving the country. For the U.S. economy, unilateral transfers are almost always negative. This pattern, however, does not always hold. In 1991, for example, when the United States led an international coalition against Saddam Hussein's Iraq in the Gulf War, many other nations agreed that they would make payments to the United States to offset the U.S. war expenses. These payments were large enough that, in 1991, the overall U.S. balance on unilateral transfers was a positive $10 billion.

The following Work It Out feature steps you through the process of using the values for goods, services, and income payments to calculate the merchandise balance and the current account balance.

Work It Out ─○─○─○

Calculating the Merchandise Balance and the Current Account Balance

	Exports (in $ billions)	Imports (in $ billions)	Balance
Goods			
Services			
Income payments			
Unilateral transfers			
Current account balance			

Table 9.2 Calculating Merchandise Balance and Current Account Balance

Use the information given below to fill in Table 9.2, and then calculate:

- The merchandise balance
- The current account balance

Known information:

- Unilateral transfers: $130
- Exports in goods: $1,046
- Exports in services: $509
- Imports in goods: $1,562
- Imports in services: $371
- Income received by U.S. investors on foreign stocks and bonds: $561
- Income received by foreign investors on U.S. assets: $472

Step 1. Focus on goods and services first. Enter the dollar amount of exports of both goods and services under the Export column.

Step 2. Enter imports of goods and services under the Import column.

Step 3. Under the Export column and in the row for Income payments, enter the financial flows of money coming back to the United States. U.S. investors are earning this income from abroad.

Step 4. Under the Import column and in the row for Income payments, enter the financial flows of money going out of the United States to foreign investors. Foreign investors are earning this money on U.S. assets, like stocks.

Step 5. Unilateral transfers are money flowing out of the United States in the form of military aid, foreign aid, global charities, and so on. Because the money leaves the country, it is entered under Imports and in the final column as well, as a negative.

Step 6. Calculate the trade balance by subtracting imports from exports in both goods and services. Enter this in the final Balance column. This can be positive or negative.

Step 7. Subtract the income payments flowing out of the country (under Imports) from the money coming back to the United States (under Exports) and enter this amount under the Balance column.

Step 8. Enter unilateral transfers as a negative amount under the Balance column.

Step 9. The merchandise trade balance is the difference between exports of goods and imports of goods—the first number under Balance.

Step 10. Now sum up your columns for Exports, Imports, and Balance. The final balance number is the current account balance.

The merchandise balance of trade is the difference between exports and imports. In this case, it is the difference between $1,046 – $1,562, a trade deficit of –$516 billion. The current account balance is –$419 billion. See the completed Table 9.3.

	Exports	Imports	Balance
Goods	$1,046	$1,562	–$516
Services	$509	$371	$138
Income payments	$561	$472	$89
Unilateral transfers	-	$130	–$130

Table 9.3 Completed Merchandise Balance and Current Account Balance

	Exports	Imports	Balance
Current account balance	$2,116	$2,535	–$419

Table 9.3 Completed Merchandise Balance and Current Account Balance

9.2 | Trade Balances in Historical and International Context

By the end of this section, you will be able to:
- Analyze graphs of the current account balance and the merchandise trade balance
- Identify patterns in U.S. trade surpluses and deficits
- Compare the U.S. trade surpluses and deficits to other countries' trade surpluses and deficits

The history of the U.S. current account balance in recent decades is presented in several different ways. **Figure 9.2** (a) shows the current account balance and the merchandise trade balance in dollar terms. **Figure 9.2** (b) shows the current account balance and merchandise account balance yet again, this time presented as a share of the GDP for that year. By dividing the trade deficit in each year by GDP in that year, **Figure 9.2** (b) factors out both inflation and growth in the real economy.

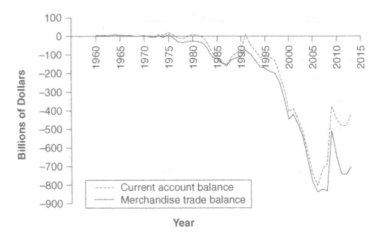

(a) The current account and merchandise trade balance in nominal dollars

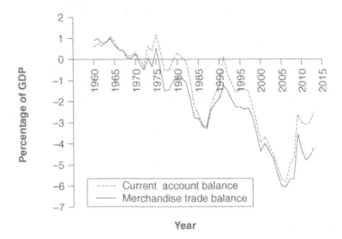

(b) The current account and merchandise trade balance as a percentage of GDP

Figure 9.2 Current Account Balance and Merchandise Trade Balance, 1960–2013 (a) The current account balance and the merchandise trade balance in billions of dollars from 1960 to 2013. If the lines are above zero dollars, the United States was running a positive trade balance and current account balance. If the lines fall below zero dollars, the United States is running a trade deficit and a deficit in its current account balance. (b) These same items—trade balance and current account balance—are shown in relationship to the size of the U.S. economy, or GDP, from 1960 to 2012.

By either measure, the general pattern of the U.S. balance of trade is clear. From the 1960s into the 1970s, the U.S. economy had mostly small trade surpluses—that is, the graphs of **Figure 9.2** show positive numbers. However, starting in the 1980s, the trade deficit increased rapidly, and after a tiny surplus in 1991, the current account trade deficit got even larger in the late 1990s and into the mid-2000s. However, the trade deficit declined in 2009 after the recession had taken hold.

Table 9.4 shows the U.S. trade picture in 2013 compared with some other economies from around the world. While the U.S. economy has consistently run trade deficits in recent years, Japan and many European nations, among them France and Germany, have consistently run trade surpluses. Some of the other countries listed include Brazil, the largest economy in Latin America; Nigeria, the largest economy in Africa; and China, India, and Korea. The first column offers one measure of the globalization of an economy: **exports of goods and services as a percentage of GDP**. The second column shows the trade balance. Most of the time, most countries have trade surpluses or deficits that are less than 5% of GDP. As you can see, the U.S. current account balance is –2.3% of GDP, while Germany's is 7.4% of GDP.

	Exports of Goods and Services	Current Account Balance
United States	13.5%	−2.3%
Japan	16.2%	0.7%
Germany	45.6%	7.4%
United Kingdom	29.8%	−4.2%
Canada	30.1%	−3.2%
Sweden	43.8%	6.7%
Korea	53.9%	5.4%
Mexico	31.7%	−2.3%
Brazil	12.6%	−3.6%
China	26.4%	2.0%
India	24.8%	−2.6%
Nigeria	18.0%	4.1%
World	-	0.0%

Table 9.4 Level and Balance of Trade in 2013 (figures as a percentage of GDP, Source: http://data.worldbank.org/indicator/BN.CAB.XOKA.GD.ZS)

9.3 | Trade Balances and Flows of Financial Capital

By the end of this section, you will be able to:
- Explain the connection between trade balances and flows of financial capital
- Calculate comparative advantage
- Explain balanced trade in terms of investment and capital flows

As economists see it, trade surpluses can be either good or bad, depending on circumstances, and trade deficits can be good or bad, too. The challenge is to understand how the international flows of goods and services are connected with international flows of **financial capital**. In this module we will illustrate the intimate connection between trade balances and flows of financial capital in two ways: a parable of trade between Robinson Crusoe and Friday, and a circular flow diagram representing flows of trade and payments.

A Two-Person Economy: Robinson Crusoe and Friday

To understand how economists view trade deficits and surpluses, consider a parable based on the story of Robinson Crusoe. Crusoe, as you may remember from the classic novel by Daniel Defoe first published in 1719, was shipwrecked on a desert island. After living alone for some time, he is joined by a second person, whom he names Friday. Think about the balance of trade in a two-person economy like that of Robinson and Friday.

Robinson and Friday trade goods and services. Perhaps Robinson catches fish and trades them to Friday for coconuts. Or Friday weaves a hat out of tree fronds and trades it to Robinson for help in carrying water. For a period of time, each individual trade is self-contained and complete. Because each trade is voluntary, both Robinson and Friday must feel that they are receiving fair value for what they are giving. As a result, each person's exports are always equal to his imports, and trade is always in balance between the two. Neither person experiences either a trade deficit or a trade surplus.

However, one day Robinson approaches Friday with a proposition. Robinson wants to dig ditches for an irrigation system for his garden, but he knows that if he starts this project, he will not have much time left to fish and gather coconuts to feed himself each day. He proposes that Friday supply him with a certain number of fish and coconuts for several months, and after that time, he promises to repay Friday out of the extra produce that he will be able to grow in his irrigated garden. If Friday accepts this offer, then a trade imbalance comes into being. For several months, Friday will have a trade surplus: that is, he is exporting to Robinson more than he is importing. More precisely, he is giving Robinson fish and coconuts, and at least for the moment, he is receiving nothing in return. Conversely, Robinson will have a trade deficit, because he is importing more from Friday than he is exporting.

This parable raises several useful issues in thinking about what a trade deficit and a trade surplus really mean in economic terms. The first issue raised by this story of Robinson and Friday is this: Is it better to have a trade surplus or a trade deficit? The answer, as in any voluntary market interaction, is that if both parties agree to the transaction, then they may both be better off. Over time, if Robinson's irrigated garden is a success, it is certainly possible that both Robinson and Friday can benefit from this agreement.

A second issue raised by the parable: What can go wrong? Robinson's proposal to Friday introduces an element of uncertainty. Friday is, in effect, making a loan of fish and coconuts to Robinson, and Friday's happiness with this arrangement will depend on whether that loan is repaid as planned, in full and on time. Perhaps Robinson spends several months loafing and never builds the irrigation system. Or perhaps Robinson has been too optimistic about how much he will be able to grow with the new irrigation system, which turns out not to be very productive. Perhaps, after building the irrigation system, Robinson decides that he does not want to repay Friday as much as previously agreed. Any of these developments will prompt a new round of negotiations between Friday and Robinson. Friday's attitude toward these renegotiations is likely to be shaped by why the repayment failed. If Robinson worked very hard and the irrigation system just did not increase production as intended, Friday may have some sympathy. If Robinson loafed or if he just refuses to pay, Friday may become irritated.

A third issue raised by the parable of Robinson and Friday is that an intimate relationship exists between a trade deficit and international borrowing, and between a trade surplus and international lending. The size of Friday's trade surplus is exactly how much he is lending to Robinson. The size of Robinson's trade deficit is exactly how much he is borrowing from Friday. Indeed, to economists, a trade surplus literally means the same thing as an outflow of financial capital, and a trade deficit literally means the same thing as an inflow of financial capital. This last insight is worth exploring in greater detail, which we will do in the following section.

The story of Robinson and Friday also provides a good opportunity to consider the law of comparative advantage, which you learn more about in the International Trade (http://cnx.org/content/m57383/latest/) chapter. The following Work It Out feature steps you through calculating comparative advantage for the wheat and cloth traded between the United States and Great Britain in the 1800s.

Calculating Comparative Advantage

In the 1800s, the United States and Britain traded wheat and cloth. Table 9.5 shows the varying hours of labor per unit of output.

	Wheat (in bushels)	Cloth (in yards)	Relative labor cost of wheat (Pw/Pc)	Relative labor cost of cloth (Pc/Pw)
United States	8	9	8/9	9/8
Britain	4	3	4/3	3/4

Table 9.5

Step 1. Observe from Table 9.5 that, in the United States, it takes eight hours to supply a bushel of wheat and nine hours to supply a yard of cloth. In contrast, it takes four hours to supply a bushel of wheat and three hours to supply a yard of cloth in Britain.

Step 2. Recognize the difference between absolute advantage and comparative advantage. Britain has an absolute advantage (lowest cost) in each good, since it takes a lower amount of labor to make each good in Britain. Britain also has a comparative advantage in the production of cloth (lower opportunity cost in cloth (3/4 versus 9/8)). The United States has a comparative advantage in wheat production (lower opportunity cost of 8/9 versus 4/3).

Step 3. Determine the relative price of one good in terms of the other good. The price of wheat, in this example, is the amount of cloth you have to give up. To find this price, convert the hours per unit of wheat and cloth into units per hour. To do so, observe that in the United States it takes eight hours to make a bushel of wheat, so 1/8 of a bushel of wheat can be made in an hour. It takes nine hours to make a yard of cloth in the United States, so 1/9 of a yard of cloth can be made in an hour. If you divide the amount of cloth (1/9 of a yard) by the amount of wheat you give up (1/8 of a bushel) in an hour, you find the price (8/9) of one good (wheat) in terms of the other (cloth).

The Balance of Trade as the Balance of Payments

The connection between trade balances and international flows of financial capital is so close that the balance of trade is sometimes described as the balance of payments. Each category of the current account balance involves a corresponding flow of payments between a given country and the rest of the world economy.

Figure 9.3 shows the flow of goods and services and payments between one country—the United States in this example—and the rest of the world. The top line shows U.S. exports of goods and services, while the second line shows financial payments from purchasers in other countries back to the U.S. economy. The third line then shows U.S. imports of goods, services, and investment, and the fourth line shows payments from the home economy to the rest of the world. Flow of goods and services (lines one and three) show up in the current account, while flow of funds (lines two and four) are found in the financial account.

The bottom four lines of the Figure 9.3 show the flow of investment income. In the first of the bottom lines, we see investments made abroad with funds flowing from the home country to rest of the world. Investment income stemming from an investment abroad then runs in the other direction from the rest of the world to the home country. Similarly, we see on the bottom third line, an investment from rest of the world into the home country and investment income (bottom fourth line) flowing from the home country to the rest of the world. The investment income (bottom lines two and four) are found in the current account, while investment to the rest of the world or into the home country (lines one and three) are found in the financial account. Unilateral transfers, the fourth item in the current account, are not shown in this figure.

Figure 9.3 Flow of Investment Goods and Capital Each element of the current account balance involves a flow of financial payments between countries. The top line shows exports of goods and services leaving the home country; the second line shows the money received by the home country for those exports. The third line shows imports received by the home country; the fourth line shows the payments sent abroad by the home country in exchange for these imports.

A current account deficit means that, the country is a net borrower from abroad. Conversely, a positive current account balance means a country is a net lender to the rest of the world. Just like the parable of Robinson and Friday, the lesson is that a trade surplus means an overall outflow of financial investment capital, as domestic investors put their funds abroad, while the deficit in the current account balance is exactly equal to the overall or net inflow of foreign investment capital from abroad.

It is important to recognize that an inflow and outflow of foreign capital does not necessarily refer to a debt that governments owe to other governments, although government debt may be part of the picture. Instead, these international flows of financial capital refer to all of the ways in which private investors in one country may invest in another country—by buying real estate, companies, and financial investments like stocks and bonds.

9.4 | The National Saving and Investment Identity

By the end of this section, you will be able to:
- Explain the determinants of trade and current account balance
- Identify and calculate supply and demand for financial capital
- Explain how a nation's balance of trade is determined by that nation's own level of domestic saving and investment
- Predict the rising and falling of trade deficits based on a nation's saving and investment identity

The close connection between trade balances and international flows of savings and investments leads to a macroeconomic analysis. This approach views trade balances—and their associated flows of financial capital—in the context of the overall levels of savings and financial investment in the economy.

Understanding the Determinants of the Trade and Current Account Balance

The **national saving and investment identity** provides a useful way to understand the determinants of the trade and current account balance. In a nation's financial capital market, the quantity of financial capital supplied at any given time must equal the quantity of financial capital demanded for purposes of making investments. What is on the supply and demand sides of financial capital? See the following Clear It Up feature for the answer to this question.

What comprises the supply and demand of financial capital?

A country's national savings is the total of its domestic savings by household and companies (private savings) as well as the government (public savings). If a country is running a trade deficit, it means money from abroad is entering the country and is considered part of the supply of financial capital.

The demand for financial capital (money) represents groups that are borrowing the money. Businesses need to borrow to finance their investments in factories, materials, and personnel. When the federal government runs a budget deficit, it is also borrowing money from investors by selling Treasury bonds. So both business investment and the federal government can demand (or borrow) the supply of savings.

There are two main sources for the supply of financial capital in the U.S. economy: saving by individuals and firms, called S, and the inflow of financial capital from foreign investors, which is equal to the trade deficit $(M - X)$, or imports minus exports. There are also two main sources of demand for financial capital in the U.S. economy: private sector investment, I, and government borrowing, where the government needs to borrow when government spending, G, is higher than the taxes collected, T. This national savings and investment identity can be expressed in algebraic terms:

$$\text{Supply of financial capital} = \text{Demand for financial capital}$$
$$S + (M - X) = I + (G - T)$$

Again, in this equation, S is private savings, T is taxes, G is government spending, M is imports, X is exports, and I is investment. This relationship is true as a matter of definition because, for the macro economy, the quantity supplied of financial capital must be equal to the quantity demanded.

However, certain components of the national savings and investment identity can switch between the supply side and the demand side. Some countries, like the United States in most years since the 1970s, have budget deficits, which mean the government is spending more than it collects in taxes, and so the government needs to borrow funds. In this case, the government term would be $G - T > 0$, showing that spending is larger than taxes, and the government would be a demander of financial capital on the right-hand side of the equation (that is, a borrower), not a supplier of financial capital on the right-hand side. However, if the government runs a budget surplus so that the taxes exceed spending, as the U.S. government did from 1998 to 2001, then the government in that year was contributing to the supply of financial capital $(T - G > 0)$, and would appear on the left (saving) side of the national savings and investment identity.

Similarly, if a national economy runs a trade surplus, the trade sector will involve an outflow of financial capital to other countries. A trade surplus means that the domestic financial capital is in surplus within a country and can be invested in other countries.

The fundamental notion that total quantity of financial capital demanded equals total quantity of financial capital supplied must always remain true. Domestic savings will always appear as part of the supply of financial capital and domestic investment will always appear as part of the demand for financial capital. However, the government and trade balance elements of the equation can move back and forth as either suppliers or demanders of financial capital, depending on whether government budgets and the trade balance are in surplus or deficit.

Domestic Saving and Investment Determine the Trade Balance

One insight from the national saving and investment identity is that a nation's balance of trade is determined by that nation's own levels of domestic saving and domestic investment. To understand this point, rearrange the identity to put the balance of trade all by itself on one side of the equation. Consider first the situation with a trade deficit, and then the situation with a trade surplus.

In the case of a trade deficit, the national saving and investment identity can be rewritten as:

$$\text{Trade deficit} = \text{Domestic investment} - \text{Private domestic saving} - \text{Government (or public) savings}$$
$$(M - X) = I - S - (T - G)$$

In this case, domestic investment is higher than domestic saving, including both private and government saving. The only way that domestic investment can exceed domestic saving is if capital is flowing into a country from abroad. After all, that extra financial capital for investment has to come from someplace.

Now consider a trade *surplus* from the standpoint of the national saving and investment identity:

$$\text{Trade surplus} \ = \ \text{Private domestic saving} + \text{Public saving} - \text{Domestic investment}$$
$$(X - M) \ = \ S + (T - G) - I$$

In this case, domestic savings (both private and public) is higher than domestic investment. That extra financial capital will be invested abroad.

This connection of domestic saving and investment to the trade balance explains why economists view the balance of trade as a fundamentally macroeconomic phenomenon. As the national saving and investment identity shows, the trade balance is not determined by the performance of certain sectors of an economy, like cars or steel. Nor is the trade balance determined by whether the nation's trade laws and regulations encourage free trade or protectionism (see **Globalization and Protectionism (http://cnx.org/content/m57388/latest/)**).

Exploring Trade Balances One Factor at a Time

The national saving and investment identity also provides a framework for thinking about what will cause trade deficits to rise or fall. Begin with the version of the identity that has domestic savings and investment on the left and the trade deficit on the right:

$$\text{Domestic investment} - \text{Private domestic savings} - \text{Public domestic savings} \ = \ \text{Trade deficit}$$
$$I - S - (T - G) \ = \ (M - X)$$

Now, consider the factors on the left-hand side of the equation one at a time, while holding the other factors constant.

As a first example, assume that the level of domestic investment in a country rises, while the level of private and public saving remains unchanged. The result is shown in the first row of **Table 9.6** under the equation. Since the equality of the national savings and investment identity must continue to hold—it is, after all, an identity that must be true by definition—the rise in domestic investment will mean a higher trade deficit. This situation occurred in the U.S. economy in the late 1990s. Because of the surge of new information and communications technologies that became available, business investment increased substantially. A fall in private saving during this time and a rise in government saving more or less offset each other. As a result, the financial capital to fund that business investment came from abroad, which is one reason for the very high U.S. trade deficits of the late 1990s and early 2000s.

Domestic Investment	−	Private Domestic Savings	−	Public Domestic Savings	=	Trade Deficit
I	−	S	−	(T − G)	=	(M − X)
Up		No change		No change		Then M − X must rise
No change		Up		No change		Then M − X must fall
No change		No change		Down		Then M − X must rise

Table 9.6 Causes of a Changing Trade Balance

As a second scenario, assume that the level of domestic savings rises, while the level of domestic investment and public savings remain unchanged. In this case, the trade deficit would decline. As domestic savings rises, there would be less need for foreign financial capital to meet investment needs. For this reason, a policy proposal often made for reducing the U.S. trade deficit is to increase private saving—although exactly how to increase the overall rate of saving has proven controversial.

As a third scenario, imagine that the government budget deficit increased dramatically, while domestic investment and private savings remained unchanged. This scenario occurred in the U.S. economy in the mid-1980s. The federal budget deficit increased from $79 billion in 1981 to $221 billion in 1986—an increase in the demand for financial capital of $142 billion. The current account balance collapsed from a surplus of $5 billion in 1981 to a deficit of $147 million in 1986—an increase in the supply of financial capital from abroad of $152 billion. The two numbers do not match exactly, since in the real world, private savings and investment did not remain fixed. The connection at that time is clear: a sharp increase in government borrowing increased the U.S. economy's demand for financial capital, and that increase was primarily supplied by foreign investors through the trade deficit. The following Work It Out feature walks you through a scenario in which private domestic savings has to rise by a certain amount to reduce a trade deficit.

Work It Out ─O─O─O

Solving Problems with the Saving and Investment Identity

Use the saving and investment identity to answer the following question: Country A has a trade deficit of $200 billion, private domestic savings of $500 billion, a government deficit of $200 billion, and private domestic investment of $500 billion. To reduce the $200 billion trade deficit by $100 billion, by how much does private domestic savings have to increase?

Step 1. Write out the savings investment formula solving for the trade deficit or surplus on the left:

$$(X - M) = S + (T - G) - I$$

Step 2. In the formula, put the amount for the trade deficit in as a negative number $(X - M)$. The left side of your formula is now:

$$-200 = S + (T - G) - I$$

Step 3. Enter the private domestic savings (S) of $500 in the formula:

$$-200 = 500 + (T - G) - I$$

Step 4. Enter domestic investment (I) of $500 into the formula:

$$-200 = 500 + (T - G) - 500$$

Step 5. The government budget surplus or balance is represented by $(T - G)$. Enter a budget deficit amount for $(T - G)$ of −200:

$$-200 = 500 + (-200) - 500$$

Step 6. Your formula now is:

$$(X - M) = S + (T - G) - I$$
$$-200 = 500 + (-200) - 500$$

The question is: To reduce your trade deficit $(X - M)$ of −200 to −100 (in billions of dollars), by how much will savings have to rise?

$$(X - M) = S + (T - G) - I$$
$$-100 = S + (-200) - 500$$
$$600 = S$$

Step 7. Summarize the answer: Private domestic savings needs to rise by $100 billion, to a total of $600 billion, for the two sides of the equation to remain equal (−100 = −100).

Short-Term Movements in the Business Cycle and the Trade Balance

In the short run, trade imbalances can be affected by whether an economy is in a recession or on the upswing. A recession tends to make a trade deficit smaller, or a trade surplus larger, while a period of strong economic growth tends to make a trade deficit larger, or a trade surplus smaller.

As an example, note in **Figure 9.2** that the U.S. trade deficit declined by almost half from 2006 to 2009. One primary reason for this change is that during the recession, as the U.S. economy slowed down, it purchased fewer of all goods, including fewer imports from abroad. However, buying power abroad fell less, and so U.S. exports did not fall by as much.

Conversely, in the mid-2000s, when the U.S. trade deficit became very large, a contributing short-term reason is that the U.S. economy was growing. As a result, there was lots of aggressive buying in the U.S. economy, including the buying of imports. Thus, a rapidly growing domestic economy is often accompanied by a trade deficit (or a much lower trade surplus), while a slowing or recessionary domestic economy is accompanied by a trade surplus (or a much lower trade deficit).

When the trade deficit rises, it necessarily means a greater net inflow of foreign financial capital. The national saving and investment identity teaches that the rest of the economy can absorb this inflow of foreign financial capital in several different ways. For example, the additional inflow of financial capital from abroad could be offset by reduced private savings, leaving domestic investment and public saving unchanged. Alternatively, the inflow of foreign financial capital could result in higher domestic investment, leaving private and public saving unchanged. Yet another possibility is that the inflow of foreign financial capital could be absorbed by greater government borrowing, leaving domestic saving and investment unchanged. The national saving and investment identity does not specify which of these scenarios, alone or in combination, will occur—only that one of them must occur.

9.5 | The Pros and Cons of Trade Deficits and Surpluses

By the end of this section, you will be able to:
- Identify three ways in which borrowing money or running a trade deficit can result in a healthy economy
- Identify three ways in which borrowing money or running a trade deficit can result in a weaker economy

Because flows of trade always involve flows of financial payments, flows of international trade are actually the same as flows of international financial capital. The question of whether trade deficits or surpluses are good or bad for an economy is, in economic terms, exactly the same question as whether it is a good idea for an economy to rely on net inflows of financial capital from abroad or to make net investments of financial capital abroad. Conventional wisdom often holds that borrowing money is foolhardy, and that a prudent country, like a prudent person, should always rely on its own resources. While it is certainly possible to borrow too much—as anyone with an overloaded credit card can testify—borrowing at certain times can also make sound economic sense. For both individuals and countries, there is no economic merit in a policy of abstaining from participation in financial capital markets.

It makes economic sense to borrow when you are buying something with a long-run payoff; that is, when you are making an investment. For this reason, it can make economic sense to borrow for a college education, because the education will typically allow you to earn higher wages, and so to repay the loan and still come out ahead. It can also make sense for a business to borrow in order to purchase a machine that will last 10 years, as long as the machine will increase output and profits by more than enough to repay the loan. Similarly, it can make economic sense for a national economy to borrow from abroad, as long as the money is wisely invested in ways that will tend to raise the nation's economic growth over time. Then, it will be possible for the national economy to repay the borrowed money over time and still end up better off than before.

One vivid example of a country that borrowed heavily from abroad, invested wisely, and did perfectly well is the United States during the nineteenth century. The United States ran a trade deficit in 40 of the 45 years from 1831 to 1875, which meant that it was importing capital from abroad over that time. However, that financial capital was, by and large, invested in projects like railroads that brought a substantial economic payoff. (See the following Clear It Up feature for more on this.)

A more recent example along these lines is the experience of South Korea, which had trade deficits during much of the 1970s—and so was an importer of capital over that time. However, South Korea also had high rates of investment in physical plant and equipment, and its economy grew rapidly. From the mid-1980s into the mid-1990s, South Korea often had trade surpluses—that is, it was repaying its past borrowing by sending capital abroad.

In contrast, some countries have run large trade deficits, borrowed heavily in global capital markets, and ended up in all kinds of trouble. Two specific sorts of trouble are worth examining. First, a borrower nation can find itself in a bind if the incoming funds from abroad are not invested in a way that leads to increased productivity. Several of the large economies of Latin America, including Mexico and Brazil, ran large trade deficits and borrowed heavily from abroad in the 1970s, but the inflow of financial capital did not boost productivity sufficiently, which meant that these countries faced enormous troubles repaying the money borrowed when economic conditions shifted during the 1980s. Similarly, it appears that a number of African nations that borrowed foreign funds in the 1970s and 1980s did not invest in productive economic assets. As a result, several of those countries later faced large interest payments, with no economic growth to show for the borrowed funds.

Are trade deficits always harmful?

For most years of the nineteenth century, U.S. imports exceeded exports and the U.S. economy had a trade deficit. Yet the string of trade deficits did not hold back the economy at all; instead, the trade deficits contributed to the strong economic growth that gave the U.S. economy the highest per capita GDP in the world by around 1900.

The U.S. trade deficits meant that the U.S. economy was receiving a net inflow of foreign capital from abroad. Much of that foreign capital flowed into two areas of investment—railroads and public infrastructure like roads, water systems, and schools—which were important to helping the growth of the U.S. economy.

The effect of foreign investment capital on U.S. economic growth should not be overstated. In most years the foreign financial capital represented no more than 6–10% of the funds used for overall physical investment in the economy. Nonetheless, the trade deficit and the accompanying investment funds from abroad were clearly a help, not a hindrance, to the U.S. economy in the nineteenth century.

A second "trouble" is: What happens if the foreign money flows in, and then suddenly flows out again? This scenario was raised at the start of the chapter. In the mid-1990s, a number of countries in East Asia—Thailand, Indonesia, Malaysia, and South Korea—ran large trade deficits and imported capital from abroad. However, in 1997 and 1998 many foreign investors became concerned about the health of these economies, and quickly pulled their money out of stock and bond markets, real estate, and banks. The extremely rapid departure of that foreign capital staggered the banking systems and economies of these countries, plunging them into deep recession. We investigate and discuss the links between international capital flows, banks, and recession in **The Impacts of Government Borrowing**.

While a trade deficit is not always harmful, there is no guarantee that running a trade surplus will bring robust economic health. For example, Germany and Japan ran substantial trade surpluses for most of the last three decades. Regardless of their persistent trade surpluses, both countries have experienced occasional recessions and neither country has had especially robust annual growth in recent years. Read more about Japan's trade surplus in the next Clear It Up feature.

Link It Up

Watch this video (http://openstaxcollege.org/l/tradedeficit) on whether or not trade deficit is good for the economy.

The sheer size and persistence of the U.S. trade deficits and inflows of foreign capital since the 1980s are a legitimate cause for concern. The huge U.S. economy will not be destabilized by an outflow of international capital as easily as, say, the comparatively tiny economies of Thailand and Indonesia were in 1997–1998. Even an economy that is not knocked down, however, can still be shaken. American policymakers should certainly be paying attention to those cases where a pattern of extensive and sustained current account deficits and foreign borrowing has gone badly—if only as a cautionary tale.

Clear It Up

Are trade surpluses always beneficial? Considering Japan since the 1990s.

Perhaps no economy around the world is better known for its trade surpluses than Japan. Since 1990, the size of these surpluses has often been near $100 billion per year. When Japan's economy was growing vigorously in the 1960s and 1970s, its large trade surpluses were often described, especially by non-economists, as either a cause or a result of its robust economic health. But from a standpoint of economic growth, Japan's economy has been teetering in and out of recession since 1990, with real GDP growth averaging only about 1% per year, and an unemployment rate that has been creeping higher. Clearly, a whopping trade surplus is no guarantee of economic good health.

Instead, Japan's trade surplus reflects that Japan has a very high rate of domestic savings, more than the Japanese economy can invest domestically, and so the extra funds are invested abroad. In Japan's slow economy, the growth of consumption is relatively low, which also means that consumption of imports is relatively low. Thus, Japan's exports continually exceed its imports, leaving the trade surplus continually high. Recently, Japan's trade surpluses began to deteriorate. In 2013, Japan ran a trade deficit due to the high cost of imported oil.

9.6 | The Difference between Level of Trade and the Trade Balance

By the end of this section, you will be able to:
- Identify three factors that influence a country's level of trade
- Differentiate between balance of trade and level of trade

A nation's *level* of trade may at first sound like much the same issue as the *balance* of trade, but these two are actually quite separate. It is perfectly possible for a country to have a very high level of trade—measured by its exports of goods and services as a share of its GDP—while it also has a near-balance between exports and imports. A high level of trade indicates that a good portion of the nation's production is exported. It is also possible for a country's trade to be a relatively low share of GDP, relative to global averages, but for the imbalance between its exports and its imports to be quite large. This general theme was emphasized earlier in **Measuring Trade Balances**, which offered some illustrative figures on trade levels and balances.

A country's level of trade tells how much of its production it exports. This is measured by the percent of exports out of GDP. It indicates how globalized an economy is. Some countries, such as Germany, have a high level of trade—they export almost 50% of their total production. The balance of trade tells us if the country is running a trade surplus or trade deficit. A country can have a low level of trade but a high trade deficit. (For example, the United States only exports 14% of GDP, but it has a trade deficit of $540 billion.)

Three factors strongly influence a nation's level of trade: the size of its economy, its geographic location, and its history of trade. Large economies like the United States can do much of their trading internally, while small economies like Sweden have less ability to provide what they want internally and tend to have higher ratios of exports and imports to GDP. Nations that are neighbors tend to trade more, since costs of transportation and communication are lower. Moreover, some nations have long and established patterns of international trade, while others do not.

Consequently, a relatively small economy like Sweden, with many nearby trading partners across Europe and a long history of foreign trade, has a high level of trade. Brazil and India, which are fairly large economies that have often sought to inhibit trade in recent decades, have lower levels of trade. Whereas, the United States and Japan are extremely large economies that have comparatively few nearby trading partners. Both countries actually have quite low levels of trade by world standards. The ratio of exports to GDP in either the United States or in Japan is about half of the world average.

The balance of trade is a separate issue from the level of trade. The United States has a low level of trade, but had enormous trade deficits for most years from the mid-1980s into the 2000s. Japan has a low level of trade by world standards, but has typically shown large trade surpluses in recent decades. Nations like Germany and the United Kingdom have medium to high levels of trade by world standards, but Germany had a moderate trade surplus in 2008, while the United Kingdom had a moderate trade deficit. Their trade picture was roughly in balance in the late 1990s. Sweden had a high level of trade and a large trade surplus in 2007, while Mexico had a high level of trade and a moderate trade deficit that same year.

In short, it is quite possible for nations with a relatively low level of trade, expressed as a percentage of GDP, to have relatively large trade deficits. It is also quite possible for nations with a near balance between exports and imports to worry about the consequences of high levels of trade for the economy. It is not inconsistent to believe that a high level of trade is potentially beneficial to an economy, because of the way it allows nations to play to their comparative advantages, and to also be concerned about any macroeconomic instability caused by a long-term pattern of large trade deficits. The following Clear It Up feature discusses how this sort of dynamic played out in Colonial India.

Clear It Up

Are trade surpluses always beneficial? Considering Colonial India.

India was formally under British rule from 1858 to 1947. During that time, India consistently had trade surpluses with Great Britain. Anyone who believes that trade surpluses are a sign of economic strength and dominance while trade deficits are a sign of economic weakness must find this pattern odd, since it would mean that colonial India was successfully dominating and exploiting Great Britain for almost a century—which was not true.

Instead, India's trade surpluses with Great Britain meant that each year there was an overall flow of financial capital from India to Great Britain. In India, this flow of financial capital was heavily criticized as the "drain," and eliminating the drain of financial capital was viewed as one of the many reasons why India would benefit from achieving independence.

Final Thoughts about Trade Balances

Trade deficits can be a good or a bad sign for an economy, and trade surpluses can be a good or a bad sign. Even a trade balance of zero—which just means that a nation is neither a net borrower nor lender in the international economy—can be either a good or bad sign. The fundamental economic question is not whether a nation's economy is borrowing or lending at all, but whether the particular borrowing or lending in the particular economic conditions of that country makes sense.

It is interesting to reflect on how public attitudes toward trade deficits and surpluses might change if we could somehow change the labels that people and the news media affix to them. If a trade deficit was called "attracting foreign financial capital"—which accurately describes what a trade deficit means—then trade deficits might look more attractive. Conversely, if a trade surplus were called "shipping financial capital abroad"—which accurately captures what a trade surplus does—then trade surpluses might look less attractive. Either way, the key to understanding trade balances is to understand the relationships between flows of trade and flows of international payments, and what these relationships imply about the causes, benefits, and risks of different kinds of trade balances. The first step along this journey of understanding is to move beyond knee-jerk reactions to terms like "trade surplus," "trade balance," and "trade deficit."

Bring it Home

More than Meets the Eye in the Congo

Now that you see the big picture, you undoubtedly realize that all of the economic choices you make, such as depositing savings or investing in an international mutual fund, do influence the flow of goods and services as well as the flows of money around the world.

You now know that a trade surplus does not necessarily tell us whether an economy is doing well or not. The Democratic Republic of Congo ran a trade surplus in 2013, as we learned in the beginning of the chapter. Yet its current account balance was –$2.8 billion. However, the return of political stability and the rebuilding in the aftermath of the civil war there has meant a flow of investment and financial capital into the country. In this case, a negative current account balance means the country is being rebuilt—and that is a good thing.

KEY TERMS

balance of trade (trade balance) the gap, if any, between a nation's exports and imports

current account balance a broad measure of the balance of trade that includes trade in goods and services, as well as international flows of income and foreign aid

exports of goods and services as a percentage of GDP the dollar value of exports divided by the dollar value of a country's GDP

financial capital the international flows of money that facilitates trade and investment

merchandise trade balance the balance of trade looking only at goods

national savings and investment identity the total of private savings and public savings (a government budget surplus)

unilateral transfers "one-way payments" made by governments, private entities, or individuals that are sent abroad with nothing received in return

KEY CONCEPTS AND SUMMARY

9.1 Measuring Trade Balances
The trade balance measures the gap between a country's exports and its imports. In most high-income economies, goods make up less than half of a country's total production, while services compose more than half. The last two decades have seen a surge in international trade in services; however, most global trade still takes the form of goods rather than services. The current account balance includes the trade in goods, services, and money flowing into and out of a country from investments and unilateral transfers.

9.2 Trade Balances in Historical and International Context
The United States developed large trade surpluses in the early 1980s, swung back to a tiny trade surplus in 1991, and then had even larger trade deficits in the late 1990s and early 2000s. As we will see below, a trade deficit necessarily means a net inflow of financial capital from abroad, while a trade surplus necessarily means a net outflow of financial capital from an economy to other countries.

9.3 Trade Balances and Flows of Financial Capital
International flows of goods and services are closely connected to the international flows of financial capital. A current account deficit means that, after taking all the flows of payments from goods, services, and income together, the country is a net borrower from the rest of the world. A current account surplus is the opposite and means the country is a net lender to the rest of the world.

9.4 The National Saving and Investment Identity
The national saving and investment identity is based on the relationship that the total quantity of financial capital supplied from all sources must equal the total quantity of financial capital demanded from all sources. If S is private saving, T is taxes, G is government spending, M is imports, X is exports, and I is investment, then for an economy with a current account deficit and a budget deficit:

$$\text{Supply of financial capital} \quad = \quad \text{Demand for financial capital}$$
$$S + (M - X) \quad = \quad I + (G - T)$$

A recession tends to increase the trade balance (meaning a higher trade surplus or lower trade deficit), while economic boom will tend to decrease the trade balance (meaning a lower trade surplus or a larger trade deficit).

9.5 The Pros and Cons of Trade Deficits and Surpluses

Trade surpluses are no guarantee of economic health, and trade deficits are no guarantee of economic weakness. Either trade deficits or trade surpluses can work out well or poorly, depending on whether the corresponding flows of financial capital are wisely invested.

9.6 The Difference between Level of Trade and the Trade Balance

There is a difference between the level of a country's trade and the balance of trade. The level of trade is measured by the percentage of exports out of GDP, or the size of the economy. Small economies that have nearby trading partners and a history of international trade will tend to have higher levels of trade. Larger economies with few nearby trading partners and a limited history of international trade will tend to have lower levels of trade. The level of trade is different from the trade balance. The level of trade depends on a country's history of trade, its geography, and the size of its economy. A country's balance of trade is the dollar difference between its exports and imports.

Trade deficits and trade surpluses are not necessarily good or bad—it depends on the circumstances. Even if a country is borrowing, if that money is invested in productivity-boosting investments it can lead to an improvement in long-term economic growth.

SELF-CHECK QUESTIONS

1. If foreign investors buy more U.S. stocks and bonds, how would that show up in the current account balance?

2. If the trade deficit of the United States increases, how is the current account balance affected?

3. State whether each of the following events involves a financial flow to the Mexican economy or a financial flow out of the Mexican economy:
    a. Mexico imports services from Japan
    b. Mexico exports goods to Canada
    c. U.S. investors receive a return from past financial investments in Mexico

4. In what way does comparing a country's exports to GDP reflect how globalized it is?

5. Canada's GDP is $1,800 billion and its exports are $542 billion. What is Canada's export ratio?

6. The GDP for the United States is $16,800 billion and its current account balance is –$400 billion. What percent of GDP is the current account balance?

7. Why does the trade balance and the current account balance track so closely together over time?

8. State whether each of the following events involves a financial flow to the U.S. economy or away from the U.S. economy:
    a. Export sales to Germany
    b. Returns being paid on past U.S. financial investments in Brazil
    c. Foreign aid from the U.S. government to Egypt
    d. Imported oil from the Russian Federation
    e. Japanese investors buying U.S. real estate

9. How does the bottom portion of **Figure 9.3**, showing the international flow of investments and capital, differ from the upper portion?

10. Explain the relationship between a current account deficit or surplus and the flow of funds.

11. Using the national savings and investment identity, explain how each of the following changes (*ceteris paribus*) will increase or decrease the trade balance:
    a. A lower domestic savings rate
    b. The government changes from running a budget surplus to running a budget deficit
    c. The rate of domestic investment surges

12. If a country is running a government budget surplus, why is (T − G) on the left side of the saving-investment identity?

13. What determines the size of a country's trade deficit?

14. If domestic investment increases, and there is no change in the amount of private and public saving, what must happen to the size of the trade deficit?

15. Why does a recession cause a trade deficit to increase?

16. Both the United States and global economies are booming. Will U.S. imports and/or exports increase?

17. For each of the following, indicate which type of government spending would justify a budget deficit and which would not.
   a. Increased federal spending on Medicare
   b. Increased spending on education
   c. Increased spending on the space program
   d. Increased spending on airports and air traffic control

18. How did large trade deficits hurt the East Asian countries in the mid 1980's? (Recall that trade deficits are equivalent to inflows of financial capital from abroad.)

19. Describe a scenario in which a trade surplus benefits an economy and one in which a trade surplus is occurring in an economy that performs poorly. What key factor or factors are making the difference in the outcome that results from a trade surplus?

20. The United States exports 14% of GDP while Germany exports about 50% of its GDP. Explain what that means.

21. Explain briefly whether each of the following would be more likely to lead to a higher level of trade for an economy, or a greater imbalance of trade for an economy.
   a. Living in an especially large country
   b. Having a domestic investment rate much higher than the domestic savings rate
   c. Having many other large economies geographically nearby
   d. Having an especially large budget deficit
   e. Having countries with a tradition of strong protectionist legislation shutting out imports

REVIEW QUESTIONS

22. If imports exceed exports, is it a trade deficit or a trade surplus? What about if exports exceed imports?

23. What is included in the current account balance?

24. In recent decades, has the U.S. trade balance usually been in deficit, surplus, or balanced?

25. Does a trade surplus mean an overall inflow of financial capital to an economy, or an overall outflow of financial capital? What about a trade deficit?

26. What are the two main sides of the national savings and investment identity?

27. What are the main components of the national savings and investment identity?

28. When is a trade deficit likely to work out well for an economy? When is it likely to work out poorly?

29. Does a trade surplus help to guarantee strong economic growth?

30. What three factors will determine whether a nation has a higher or lower share of trade relative to its GDP?

31. What is the difference between trade deficits and balance of trade?

CRITICAL THINKING QUESTIONS

32. From time to time, a government official will argue that a country should strive for both a trade surplus and a healthy inflow of capital from abroad. Explain why such a statement is economically impossible.

33. A government official announces a new policy. The country wishes to eliminate its trade deficit, but will strongly encourage financial investment from foreign firms. Explain why such a statement is contradictory.

34. If a country is a big exporter, is it more exposed to global financial crises?

35. If countries reduced trade barriers, would the international flows of money increase?

36. Is it better for your country to be an international lender or borrower?

37. Many think that the size of a trade deficit is due to a lack of competitiveness of domestic sectors, such as autos. Explain why this is not true.

38. If you observed a country with a rapidly growing trade surplus over a period of a year or so, would you be more likely to believe that the economy of that country was in a period of recession or of rapid growth? Explain.

39. From time to time, a government official will argue that a country should strive for both a trade surplus and a healthy inflow of capital from abroad. Is this possible?

40. What is more important, a country's current account balance or the growth of GDP? Why?

41. Will nations that are more involved in foreign trade tend to have higher trade imbalances, lower trade imbalances, or is the pattern unpredictable?

42. Some economists warn that the persistent trade deficits and a negative current account balance that the United States has run will be a problem in the long run. Do you agree or not? Explain your answer.

PROBLEMS

43. In 2001, the economy of the United Kingdom exported goods worth £192 billion and services worth another £77 billion. It imported goods worth £225 billion and services worth £66 billion. Receipts of income from abroad were £140 billion while income payments going abroad were £131 billion. Government transfers from the United Kingdom to the rest of the world were £23 billion, while various U.K government agencies received payments of £16 billion from the rest of the world.
   a. Calculate the U.K. merchandise trade deficit for 2001.
   b. Calculate the current account balance for 2001.
   c. Explain how you decided whether payments on foreign investment and government transfers counted on the positive or the negative side of the current account balance for the United Kingdom in 2001.

44. Imagine that the U.S. economy finds itself in the following situation: a government budget deficit of $100 billion, total domestic savings of $1,500 billion, and total domestic physical capital investment of $1,600 billion. According to the national saving and investment identity, what will be the current account balance? What will be the current account balance if investment rises by $50 billion, while the budget deficit and national savings remain the same?

45. Table 9.7 provides some hypothetical data on macroeconomic accounts for three countries represented by A, B, and C and measured in billions of currency units. In Table 9.7, private household saving is SH, tax revenue is T, government spending is G, and investment spending is I.

	A	B	C
SH	700	500	600
T	00	500	500
G	600	350	650
I	800	400	450

Table 9.7 Macroeconomic Accounts

   a. Calculate the trade balance and the net inflow of foreign saving for each country.
   b. State whether each one has a trade surplus or deficit (or balanced trade).
   c. State whether each is a net lender or borrower internationally and explain.

46. Imagine that the economy of Germany finds itself in the following situation: the government budget has a surplus of 1% of Germany's GDP; private savings is 20% of GDP; and physical investment is 18% of GDP.

a. Based on the national saving and investment identity, what is the current account balance?

b. If the government budget surplus falls to zero, how will this affect the current account balance?

10 | The Aggregate Demand/ Aggregate Supply Model

Figure 10.1 New Home Construction At the peak of the housing bubble, many people across the country were able to secure the loans necessary to build new houses. (Credit: modification of work by Tim Pierce/Flickr Creative Commons)

Bring it Home

From Housing Bubble to Housing Bust

The United States experienced rising home ownership rates for most of the last two decades. Between 1990 and 2006, the U.S. housing market grew. Homeownership rates grew from 64% to a high of over 69% between 2004 and 2005. For many people, this was a period in which they could either buy first homes or buy a larger and more expensive home. During this time mortgage values tripled. Housing became more accessible to Americans and was considered to be a safe financial investment. Figure 10.2 shows how new single family home sales peaked in 2005 at 107,000 units.

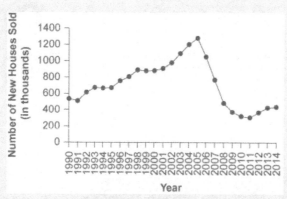

Figure 10.2 New Single Family Houses Sold From the early 1990s up through 2005, the number of new single family houses sold rose steadily. In 2006, the number dropped dramatically and this dramatic decline continued through 2011. By 2014, the number of new houses sold had begun to climb back up, but the levels are still lower than those of 1990. (Source: U.S. Census Bureau)

The housing bubble began to show signs of bursting in 2005, as delinquency and late payments began to grow and an oversupply of new homes on the market became apparent. Dropping home values contributed to a decrease in the overall wealth of the household sector and caused homeowners to pull back on spending. Several mortgage lenders were forced to file for bankruptcy because homeowners were not making their payments, and by 2008 the problem had spread throughout the financial markets. Lenders clamped down on credit and the housing bubble burst. Financial markets were now in crisis and unable or unwilling to even extend credit to credit-worthy customers.

The housing bubble and the crisis in the financial markets were major contributors to the Great Recession that led to unemployment rates over 10% and falling GDP. While the United States is still recovering from the impact of the Great Recession, it has made substantial progress in restoring financial market stability through the implementation of aggressive fiscal and monetary policy.

The economic history of the United States is cyclical in nature with recessions and expansions. Some of these fluctuations are severe, such as the economic downturn experienced during Great Depression of the 1930's which lasted several years. Why does the economy grow at different rates in different years? What are the causes of the cyclical behavior of the economy? This chapter will introduce an important model, the aggregate demand–aggregate supply model, to begin our understanding of why economies expand and contract over time.

Introduction to the Aggregate Supply–Aggregate Demand Model

In this chapter, you will learn about:

- Macroeconomic Perspectives on Demand and Supply

- Building a Model of Aggregate Supply and Aggregate Demand

- Shifts in Aggregate Supply

- Shifts in Aggregate Demand

- How the AS–AD Model Incorporates Growth, Unemployment, and Inflation

- Keynes' Law and Say's Law in the AS–AD Model

A key part of macroeconomics is the use of models to analyze macro issues and problems. How is the rate of economic growth connected to changes in the unemployment rate? Is there a reason why unemployment and inflation seem to move in opposite directions: lower unemployment and higher inflation from 1997 to 2000, higher unemployment and lower inflation in the early 2000s, lower unemployment and higher inflation in the mid-2000s, and then higher unemployment and lower inflation in 2009? Why did the current account deficit rise so high, but then decline in 2009?

To analyze questions like these, we must move beyond discussing macroeconomic issues one at a time, and begin building economic models that will capture the relationships and interconnections between them. The next three chapters take up this task. This chapter introduces the macroeconomic model of aggregate supply and aggregate demand, how the two interact to reach a macroeconomic equilibrium, and how shifts in aggregate demand or aggregate supply will affect that equilibrium. This chapter also relates the model of aggregate supply and aggregate demand to the three goals of economic policy (growth, unemployment, and inflation), and provides a framework for thinking about many of the connections and tradeoffs between these goals. The chapter on The Keynesian Perspective focuses on the macroeconomy in the short run, where aggregate demand plays a crucial role. The chapter on The Neoclassical Perspective explores the macroeconomy in the long run, where aggregate supply plays a crucial role.

10.1 | Macroeconomic Perspectives on Demand and Supply

By the end of this section, you will be able to:

- Explain Say's Law and determine whether it applies in the short run or the long run
- Explain Keynes' Law and determine whether it applies in the short run or the long run

Macroeconomists over the last two centuries have often divided into two groups: those who argue that supply is the most important determinant of the size of the macroeconomy while demand just tags along, and those who argue that demand is the most important factor in the size of the macroeconomy while supply just tags along.

Say's Law and the Macroeconomics of Supply

Those economists who emphasize the role of supply in the macroeconomy often refer to the work of a famous French economist of the early nineteenth century named Jean-Baptiste Say (1767–1832). **Say's law** is: "Supply creates its own demand." As a matter of historical accuracy, it seems clear that Say never actually wrote down this law and that it oversimplifies his beliefs, but the law lives on as useful shorthand for summarizing a point of view.

The intuition behind Say's law is that each time a good or service is produced and sold, it generates income that is earned for someone: a worker, a manager, an owner, or those who are workers, managers, and owners at firms that supply inputs along the chain of production. The forces of supply and demand in individual markets will cause prices to rise and fall. The bottom line remains, however, that every sale represents income to someone, and so, Say's law argues, a given value of supply must create an equivalent value of demand somewhere else in the economy. Because Jean-Baptiste Say, Adam Smith, and other economists writing around the turn of the nineteenth century who discussed this view were known as "classical" economists, modern economists who generally subscribe to the Say's law view on the importance of supply for determining the size of the macroeconomy are called **neoclassical economists**.

If supply always creates exactly enough demand at the macroeconomic level, then (as Say himself recognized) it is hard to understand why periods of recession and high unemployment should ever occur. To be sure, even if total supply always creates an equal amount of total demand, the economy could still experience a situation of some firms earning profits while other firms suffer losses. Nevertheless, a recession is not a situation where all business failures are exactly counterbalanced by an offsetting number of successes. A recession is a situation in which the economy as a whole is shrinking in size, business failures outnumber the remaining success stories, and many firms end up suffering losses and laying off workers.

Say's law that supply creates its own demand does seem a good approximation for the long run. Over periods of some years or decades, as the productive power of an economy to supply goods and services increases, total demand in the economy grows at roughly the same pace. However, over shorter time horizons of a few months or even years, recessions or even depressions occur in which firms, as a group, seem to face a lack of demand for their products.

Keynes' Law and the Macroeconomics of Demand

The alternative to Say's law, with its emphasis on supply, can be named **Keynes' law**: "Demand creates its own supply." As a matter of historical accuracy, just as Jean-Baptiste Say never wrote down anything as simpleminded as

Say's law, John Maynard Keynes never wrote down Keynes' law, but the law is a useful simplification that conveys a certain point of view.

When Keynes wrote his great work *The General Theory of Employment, Interest, and Money* during the Great Depression of the 1930s, he pointed out that during the Depression, the capacity of the economy to supply goods and services had not changed much. U.S. unemployment rates soared higher than 20% from 1933 to 1935, but the number of possible workers had not increased or decreased much. Factories were closed and shuttered, but machinery and equipment had not disappeared. Technologies that had been invented in the 1920s were not un-invented and forgotten in the 1930s. Thus, Keynes argued that the Great Depression—and many ordinary recessions as well—were not caused by a drop in the ability of the economy to supply goods as measured by labor, physical capital, or technology. He argued the economy often produced less than its full potential, not because it was technically impossible to produce more with the existing workers and machines, but because a lack of demand in the economy as a whole led to inadequate incentives for firms to produce. In such cases, he argued, the level of GDP in the economy was not primarily determined by the potential of what the economy could supply, but rather by the amount of total demand.

Keynes' law seems to apply fairly well in the short run of a few months to a few years, when many firms experience either a drop in demand for their output during a recession or so much demand that they have trouble producing enough during an economic boom. However, demand cannot tell the whole macroeconomic story, either. After all, if demand was all that mattered at the macroeconomic level, then the government could make the economy as large as it wanted just by pumping up total demand through a large increase in the government spending component or by legislating large tax cuts to push up the consumption component. Economies do, however, face genuine limits to how much they can produce, limits determined by the quantity of labor, physical capital, technology, and the institutional and market structures that bring these factors of production together. These constraints on what an economy can supply at the macroeconomic level do not disappear just because of an increase in demand.

Combining Supply and Demand in Macroeconomics

Two insights emerge from this overview of Say's law with its emphasis on macroeconomic supply and Keynes' law with its emphasis on macroeconomic demand. The first conclusion, which is not exactly a hot news flash, is that an economic approach focused only on the supply side or only on the demand side can be only a partial success. Both supply and demand need to be taken into account. The second conclusion is that since Keynes' law applies more accurately in the short run and Say's law applies more accurately in the long run, the tradeoffs and connections between the three goals of macroeconomics may be different in the short run and the long run.

10.2 | Building a Model of Aggregate Demand and Aggregate Supply

By the end of this section, you will be able to:
- Explain the aggregate supply curve and how it relates to real GDP and potential GDP
- Explain the aggregate demand curve and how it is influenced by price levels
- Interpret the aggregate demand/aggregate supply model
- Identify the point of equilibrium in the aggregate demand/aggregate supply model
- Define short run aggregate supply and long run aggregate supply

To build a useful macroeconomic model, we need a model that shows what determines total supply or total demand for the economy, and how total demand and total supply interact at the macroeconomic level. This model is called the **aggregate demand/aggregate supply model**. This module will explain aggregate supply, aggregate demand, and the equilibrium between them. The following modules will discuss the causes of shifts in aggregate supply and aggregate demand.

The Aggregate Supply Curve and Potential GDP

Firms make decisions about what quantity to supply based on the profits they expect to earn. Profits, in turn, are also determined by the price of the outputs the firm sells and by the price of the inputs, like labor or raw materials, the firm needs to buy. **Aggregate supply (AS)** refers to the total quantity of output (i.e. real GDP) firms will produce and sell. The **aggregate supply (AS) curve** shows the total quantity of output (i.e. real GDP) that firms will produce and sell at each price level.

Figure 10.3 shows an aggregate supply curve. In the following paragraphs, we will walk through the elements of the diagram one at a time: the horizontal and vertical axes, the aggregate supply curve itself, and the meaning of the potential GDP vertical line.

Figure 10.3 The Aggregate Supply Curve Aggregate supply (AS) slopes up, because as the price level for outputs rises, with the price of inputs remaining fixed, firms have an incentive to produce more and to earn higher profits. The potential GDP line shows the maximum that the economy can produce with full employment of workers and physical capital.

The horizontal axis of the diagram shows real GDP—that is, the level of GDP adjusted for inflation. The vertical axis shows the price level. Remember that the price level is different from the inflation rate. Visualize the price level as an index number, like the GDP deflator, while the inflation rate is the percentage change between price levels over time.

As the price level (the average price of all goods and services produced in the economy) rises, the aggregate quantity of goods and services supplied rises as well. Why? The price level shown on the vertical axis represents prices for final goods or outputs bought in the economy—like the GDP deflator—not the price level for intermediate goods and services that are inputs to production. Thus, the AS curve describes how suppliers will react to a higher price level for final outputs of goods and services, while holding the prices of inputs like labor and energy constant. If firms across the economy face a situation where the price level of what they produce and sell is rising, but their costs of production are not rising, then the lure of higher profits will induce them to expand production.

The slope of an AS curve changes from nearly flat at its far left to nearly vertical at its far right. At the far left of the aggregate supply curve, the level of output in the economy is far below **potential GDP**, which is defined as the quantity that an economy can produce by fully employing its existing levels of labor, physical capital, and technology, in the context of its existing market and legal institutions. At these relatively low levels of output, levels of unemployment are high, and many factories are running only part-time, or have closed their doors. In this situation, a relatively small increase in the prices of the outputs that businesses sell—while making the assumption of no rise in input prices—can encourage a considerable surge in the quantity of aggregate supply because so many workers and factories are ready to swing into production.

As the quantity produced increases, however, certain firms and industries will start running into limits: perhaps nearly all of the expert workers in a certain industry will have jobs or factories in certain geographic areas or industries will be running at full speed. In the intermediate area of the AS curve, a higher price level for outputs continues to encourage a greater quantity of output—but as the increasingly steep upward slope of the aggregate supply curve shows, the increase in quantity in response to a given rise in the price level will not be quite as large. (Read the following Clear It Up feature to learn why the AS curve crosses potential GDP.)

Why does AS cross potential GDP?

The aggregate supply curve is typically drawn to cross the potential GDP line. This shape may seem puzzling: How can an economy produce at an output level which is higher than its "potential" or "full employment" GDP? The economic intuition here is that if prices for outputs were high enough, producers would make fanatical efforts to produce: all workers would be on double-overtime, all machines would run 24 hours a day, seven days a week. Such hyper-intense production would go beyond using potential labor and physical capital resources fully, to using them in a way that is not sustainable in the long term. Thus, it is indeed possible for production to sprint above potential GDP, but only in the short run.

At the far right, the aggregate supply curve becomes nearly vertical. At this quantity, higher prices for outputs cannot encourage additional output, because even if firms want to expand output, the inputs of labor and machinery in the economy are fully employed. In this example, the vertical line in the exhibit shows that potential GDP occurs at a total output of 9,500. When an economy is operating at its potential GDP, machines and factories are running at capacity, and the unemployment rate is relatively low—at the natural rate of unemployment. For this reason, potential GDP is sometimes also called **full-employment GDP**.

The Aggregate Demand Curve

Aggregate demand (AD) refers to the amount of total spending on domestic goods and services in an economy. (Strictly speaking, AD is what economists call total planned expenditure. This distinction will be further explained in the appendix **The Expenditure-Output Model**. For now, just think of aggregate demand as total spending.) It includes all four components of demand: consumption, investment, government spending, and net exports (exports minus imports). This demand is determined by a number of factors, but one of them is the price level—recall though, that the price level is an index number such as the GDP deflator that measures the average price of the things we buy. The **aggregate demand (AD) curve** shows the total spending on domestic goods and services at each price level.

Figure 10.4 presents an aggregate demand (AD) curve. Just like the aggregate supply curve, the horizontal axis shows real GDP and the vertical axis shows the price level. The AD curve slopes down, which means that increases in the price level of outputs lead to a lower quantity of total spending. The reasons behind this shape are related to how changes in the price level affect the different components of aggregate demand. The following components make up aggregate demand: consumption spending (C), investment spending (I), government spending (G), and spending on exports (X) minus imports (M): C + I + G + X – M.

Figure 10.4 The Aggregate Demand Curve Aggregate demand (AD) slopes down, showing that, as the price level rises, the amount of total spending on domestic goods and services declines.

The wealth effect holds that as the price level increases, the buying power of savings that people have stored up in bank accounts and other assets will diminish, eaten away to some extent by inflation. Because a rise in the price level reduces people's wealth, consumption spending will fall as the price level rises.

The interest rate effect is that as prices for outputs rise, the same purchases will take more money or credit to accomplish. This additional demand for money and credit will push interest rates higher. In turn, higher interest rates will reduce borrowing by businesses for investment purposes and reduce borrowing by households for homes and cars—thus reducing consumption and investment spending.

The foreign price effect points out that if prices rise in the United States while remaining fixed in other countries, then goods in the United States will be relatively more expensive compared to goods in the rest of the world. U.S. exports will be relatively more expensive, and the quantity of exports sold will fall. U.S. imports from abroad will be relatively cheaper, so the quantity of imports will rise. Thus, a higher domestic price level, relative to price levels in other countries, will reduce net export expenditures.

Truth be told, among economists all three of these effects are controversial, in part because they do not seem to be very large. For this reason, the aggregate demand curve in Figure 10.4 slopes downward fairly steeply; the steep slope indicates that a higher price level for final outputs reduces aggregate demand for all three of these reasons, but that the change in the quantity of aggregate demand as a result of changes in price level is not very large.

Read the following Work It Out feature to learn how to interpret the AD/AS model. In this example, aggregate supply, aggregate demand, and the price level are given for the imaginary country of Xurbia.

Work It Out

Interpreting the AD/AS Model

Table 10.1 shows information on aggregate supply, aggregate demand, and the price level for the imaginary country of Xurbia. What information does Table 10.1 tell you about the state of the Xurbia's economy? Where is the equilibrium price level and output level (this is the SR macroequilibrium)? Is Xurbia risking inflationary pressures or facing high unemployment? How can you tell?

Price Level	Aggregate Demand	Aggregate Supply
110	$700	$600
120	$690	$640
130	$680	$680
140	$670	$720
150	$660	$740
160	$650	$760
170	$640	$770

Table 10.1 Price Level: Aggregate Demand/Aggregate Supply

To begin to use the AD/AS model, it is important to plot the AS and AD curves from the data provided. What is the equilibrium?

Step 1. Draw your x- and y-axis. Label the x-axis Real GDP and the y-axis Price Level.

Step 2. Plot AD on your graph.

Step 3. Plot AS on your graph.

Step 4. Look at Figure 10.5 which provides a visual to aid in your analysis.

Figure 10.5 The AD/AS Curves AD and AS curves created from the data in Table 10.1.

Step 5. Determine where AD and AS intersect. This is the equilibrium with price level at 130 and real GDP at $680.

Step 6. Look at the graph to determine where equilibrium is located. We can see that this equilibrium is fairly far from where the AS curve becomes near-vertical (or at least quite steep) which seems to start at about $750 of real output. This implies that the economy is not close to potential GDP. Thus, unemployment will be high. In the relatively flat part of the AS curve, where the equilibrium occurs, changes in the price level will not be a major concern, since such changes are likely to be small.

Step 7. Determine what the steep portion of the AS curve indicates. Where the AS curve is steep, the economy is at or close to potential GDP.

Step 8. Draw conclusions from the given information:

- If equilibrium occurs in the flat range of AS, then economy is not close to potential GDP and will be experiencing unemployment, but stable price level.

- If equilibrium occurs in the steep range of AS, then the economy is close or at potential GDP and will be experiencing rising price levels or inflationary pressures, but will have a low unemployment rate.

Equilibrium in the Aggregate Demand/Aggregate Supply Model

The intersection of the aggregate supply and aggregate demand curves shows the equilibrium level of real GDP and the equilibrium price level in the economy. At a relatively low price level for output, firms have little incentive to produce, although consumers would be willing to purchase a high quantity. As the price level for outputs rises, aggregate supply rises and aggregate demand falls until the equilibrium point is reached.

Figure 10.6 combines the AS curve from Figure 10.3 and the AD curve from Figure 10.4 and places them both on a single diagram. In this example, the equilibrium point occurs at point E, at a price level of 90 and an output level of 8,800.

Figure 10.6 Aggregate Supply and Aggregate Demand The equilibrium, where aggregate supply (AS) equals aggregate demand (AD), occurs at a price level of 90 and an output level of 8,800.

Confusion sometimes arises between the aggregate supply and aggregate demand model and the microeconomic analysis of demand and supply in particular markets for goods, services, labor, and capital. Read the following Clear It Up feature to gain an understanding of whether AS and AD are macro or micro.

Are AS and AD macro or micro?

These aggregate supply and aggregate demand model and the microeconomic analysis of demand and supply in particular markets for goods, services, labor, and capital have a superficial resemblance, but they also have many underlying differences.

For example, the vertical and horizontal axes have distinctly different meanings in macroeconomic and microeconomic diagrams. The vertical axis of a microeconomic demand and supply diagram expresses a price (or wage or rate of return) for an individual good or service. This price is implicitly relative: it is intended to be compared with the prices of other products (for example, the price of pizza relative to the price of fried chicken). In contrast, the vertical axis of an aggregate supply and aggregate demand diagram expresses the level of a price index like the Consumer Price Index or the GDP deflator—combining a wide array of prices from across the economy. The price level is absolute: it is not intended to be compared to any other prices since it is essentially the average price of all products in an economy. The horizontal axis of a microeconomic supply and demand curve measures the quantity of a particular good or service. In contrast, the horizontal axis of the aggregate demand and aggregate supply diagram measures GDP, which is the sum of all the final goods and services produced in the economy, not the quantity in a specific market.

In addition, the economic reasons for the shapes of the curves in the macroeconomic model are different from the reasons behind the shapes of the curves in microeconomic models. Demand curves for individual goods or services slope down primarily because of the existence of substitute goods, not the wealth effects, interest rate, and foreign price effects associated with aggregate demand curves. The slopes of individual supply and demand curves can have a variety of different slopes, depending on the extent to which quantity demanded and quantity supplied react to price in that specific market, but the slopes of the AS and AD curves are much the same in every diagram (although as we shall see in later chapters, short-run and long-run perspectives will emphasize different parts of the AS curve).

In short, just because the AD/AS diagram has two lines that cross, do not assume that it is the same as every other diagram where two lines cross. The intuitions and meanings of the macro and micro diagrams are only distant cousins from different branches of the economics family tree.

Defining SRAS and LRAS

In the Clear It Up feature titled "Why does AS cross potential GDP?" we differentiated between short run changes in aggregate supply which are shown by the AS curve and long run changes in aggregate supply which are defined by the vertical line at potential GDP. In the short run, if demand is too low (or too high), it is possible for producers to supply less GDP (or more GDP) than potential. In the long run, however, producers are limited to producing at potential GDP. For this reason, what we have been calling the AS curve, will from this point on may also be referred to as the **short run aggregate supply (SRAS) curve**. The vertical line at potential GDP may also be referred to as the **long run aggregate supply (LRAS) curve**.

10.3 | Shifts in Aggregate Supply

By the end of this section, you will be able to:
- Explain how productivity growth changes the aggregate supply curve
- Explain how changes in input prices changes the aggregate supply curve

The original equilibrium in the AD/AS diagram will shift to a new equilibrium if the AS or AD curve shifts. When the aggregate supply curve shifts to the right, then at every price level, a greater quantity of real GDP is produced. When the SRAS curve shifts to the left, then at every price level, a lower quantity of real GDP is produced. This module discusses two of the most important factors that can lead to shifts in the AS curve: productivity growth and input prices.

How Productivity Growth Shifts the AS Curve

In the long run, the most important factor shifting the AS curve is productivity growth. Productivity means how much output can be produced with a given quantity of labor. One measure of this is output per worker or GDP per capita. Over time, productivity grows so that the same quantity of labor can produce more output. Historically, the real growth in GDP per capita in an advanced economy like the United States has averaged about 2% to 3% per year, but productivity growth has been faster during certain extended periods like the 1960s and the late 1990s through the early 2000s, or slower during periods like the 1970s. A higher level of productivity shifts the AS curve to the right, because with improved productivity, firms can produce a greater quantity of output at every price level. **Figure 10.7** (a) shows an outward shift in productivity over two time periods. The AS curve shifts out from $SRAS_0$ to $SRAS_1$ to $SRAS_2$, reflecting the rise in potential GDP in this economy, and the equilibrium shifts from E_0 to E_1 to E_2.

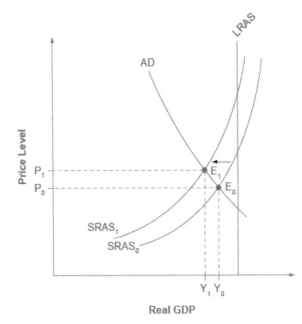

(a) Productivity growth shifts AS to the right   (b) Higher prices for key inputs shifts AS to the left

Figure 10.7 Shifts in Aggregate Supply (a) The rise in productivity causes the SRAS curve to shift to the right. The original equilibrium E_0 is at the intersection of AD and $SRAS_0$. When SRAS shifts right, then the new equilibrium E_1 is at the intersection of AD and $SRAS_1$, and then yet another equilibrium, E_2, is at the intersection of AD and $SRAS_2$. Shifts in SRAS to the right, lead to a greater level of output and to downward pressure on the price level. (b) A higher price for inputs means that at any given price level for outputs, a lower quantity will be produced so aggregate supply will shift to the left from $SRAS_0$ to AS_1. The new equilibrium, E_1, has a reduced quantity of output and a higher price level than the original equilibrium (E_0).

A shift in the SRAS curve to the right will result in a greater real GDP and downward pressure on the price level, if aggregate demand remains unchanged. However, if this shift in SRAS results from gains in productivity growth, which are typically measured in terms of a few percentage points per year, the effect will be relatively small over a few months or even a couple of years.

How Changes in Input Prices Shift the AS Curve

Higher prices for inputs that are widely used across the entire economy can have a macroeconomic impact on aggregate supply. Examples of such widely used inputs include wages and energy products. Increases in the price of such inputs will cause the SRAS curve to shift to the left, which means that at each given price level for outputs, a higher price for inputs will discourage production because it will reduce the possibilities for earning profits. **Figure 10.7** (b) shows the aggregate supply curve shifting to the left, from $SRAS_0$ to $SRAS_1$, causing the equilibrium to move from E_0 to E_1. The movement from the original equilibrium of E_0 to the new equilibrium of E_1 will bring a nasty set of effects: reduced GDP or recession, higher unemployment because the economy is now further away from potential GDP, and an inflationary higher price level as well. For example, the U.S. economy experienced recessions in 1974–1975, 1980–1982, 1990–91, 2001, and 2007–2009 that were each preceded or accompanied by a rise in the key input of oil prices. In the 1970s, this pattern of a shift to the left in SRAS leading to a stagnant economy with high unemployment and inflation was nicknamed **stagflation**.

Conversely, a decline in the price of a key input like oil will shift the SRAS curve to the right, providing an incentive for more to be produced at every given price level for outputs. From 1985 to 1986, for example, the average price of crude oil fell by almost half, from $24 a barrel to $12 a barrel. Similarly, from 1997 to 1998, the price of a barrel of crude oil dropped from $17 per barrel to $11 per barrel. In both cases, the plummeting price of oil led to a situation like that presented earlier in **Figure 10.7** (a), where the outward shift of SRAS to the right allowed the economy to expand, unemployment to fall, and inflation to decline.

Along with energy prices, two other key inputs that may shift the SRAS curve are the cost of labor, or wages, and the cost of imported goods that are used as inputs for other products. In these cases as well, the lesson is that lower prices for inputs cause SRAS to shift to the right, while higher prices cause it to shift back to the left.

Other Supply Shocks

The aggregate supply curve can also shift due to shocks to input goods or labor. For example, an unexpected early freeze could destroy a large number of agricultural crops, a shock that would shift the AS curve to the left since there would be fewer agricultural products available at any given price.

Similarly, shocks to the labor market can affect aggregate supply. An extreme example might be an overseas war that required a large number of workers to cease their ordinary production in order to go fight for their country. In this case, aggregate supply would shift to the left because there would be fewer workers available to produce goods at any given price.

10.4 | Shifts in Aggregate Demand

By the end of this section, you will be able to:
- Explain how imports influence aggregate demand
- Identify ways in which business confidence and consumer confidence can affect aggregate demand
- Explain how government policy can change aggregate demand
- Evaluate why economists disagree on the topic of tax cuts

As mentioned previously, the components of aggregate demand are consumption spending (C), investment spending (I), government spending (G), and spending on exports (X) minus imports (M). (Read the following Clear It Up feature for explanation of why imports are subtracted from exports and what this means for aggregate demand.) A shift of the AD curve to the right means that at least one of these components increased so that a greater amount of total spending would occur at every price level. A shift of the AD curve to the left means that at least one of these components decreased so that a lesser amount of total spending would occur at every price level. **The Keynesian Perspective** will discuss the components of aggregate demand and the factors that affect them. Here, the discussion will sketch two broad categories that could cause AD curves to shift: changes in the behavior of consumers or firms and changes in government tax or spending policy.

Do imports diminish aggregate demand?

We have seen that the formula for aggregate demand is AD = C + I + G + X - M, where M is the total value of imported goods. Why is there a minus sign in front of imports? Does this mean that more imports will result in a lower level of aggregate demand?

When an American buys a foreign product, for example, it gets counted along with all the other consumption. So the income generated does not go to American producers, but rather to producers in another country; it would be wrong to count this as part of domestic demand. Therefore, imports added in consumption are subtracted back out in the M term of the equation.

Because of the way in which the demand equation is written, it is easy to make the mistake of thinking that imports are bad for the economy. Just keep in mind that every negative number in the M term has a corresponding positive number in the C or I or G term, and they always cancel out.

How Changes by Consumers and Firms Can Affect AD

When consumers feel more confident about the future of the economy, they tend to consume more. If business confidence is high, then firms tend to spend more on investment, believing that the future payoff from that investment will be substantial. Conversely, if consumer or business confidence drops, then consumption and investment spending decline.

The University of Michigan publishes a survey of consumer confidence and constructs an index of consumer confidence each month. The survey results are then reported at **http://www.sca.isr.umich.edu (http://www.sca.isr.umich.edu/)** , which break down the change in consumer confidence among different income levels. According to that index, consumer confidence averaged around 90 prior to the Great Recession, and then it fell to below 60 in late 2008, which was the lowest it had been since 1980. Since then, confidence has climbed from a 2011 low of 55.8 back to a level in the low 80s, which is considered close to being considered a healthy state.

One measure of business confidence is published by the OECD: the "business tendency surveys". Business opinion survey data are collected for 21 countries on future selling prices and employment, among other elements of the business climate. After sharply declining during the Great Recession, the measure has risen above zero again and is back to long-term averages (the indicator dips below zero when business outlook is weaker than usual). Of course, either of these survey measures is not very precise. They can however, suggest when confidence is rising or falling, as well as when it is relatively high or low compared to the past.

Because a rise in confidence is associated with higher consumption and investment demand, it will lead to an outward shift in the AD curve, and a move of the equilibrium, from E_0 to E_1, to a higher quantity of output and a higher price level, as shown in **Figure 10.8** (a).

Consumer and business confidence often reflect macroeconomic realities; for example, confidence is usually high when the economy is growing briskly and low during a recession. However, economic confidence can sometimes rise or fall for reasons that do not have a close connection to the immediate economy, like a risk of war, election results, foreign policy events, or a pessimistic prediction about the future by a prominent public figure. U.S. presidents, for example, must be careful in their public pronouncements about the economy. If they offer economic pessimism, they risk provoking a decline in confidence that reduces consumption and investment and shifts AD to the left, and in a self-fulfilling prophecy, contributes to causing the recession that the president warned against in the first place. A shift of AD to the left, and the corresponding movement of the equilibrium, from E_0 to E_1, to a lower quantity of output and a lower price level, is shown in **Figure 10.8** (b).

(a) Aggregate demand shifts right   (b) Aggregate demand shifts left

Figure 10.8 Shifts in Aggregate Demand (a) An increase in consumer confidence or business confidence can shift AD to the right, from AD_0 to AD_1. When AD shifts to the right, the new equilibrium (E_1) will have a higher quantity of output and also a higher price level compared with the original equilibrium (E_0). In this example, the new equilibrium (E_1) is also closer to potential GDP. An increase in government spending or a cut in taxes that leads to a rise in consumer spending can also shift AD to the right. (b) A decrease in consumer confidence or business confidence can shift AD to the left, from AD_0 to AD_1. When AD shifts to the left, the new equilibrium (E_1) will have a lower quantity of output and also a lower price level compared with the original equilibrium (E_0). In this example, the new equilibrium (E_1) is also farther below potential GDP. A decrease in government spending or higher taxes that leads to a fall in consumer spending can also shift AD to the left.

How Government Macroeconomic Policy Choices Can Shift AD

Government spending is one component of AD. Thus, higher government spending will cause AD to shift to the right, as in **Figure 10.8** (a), while lower government spending will cause AD to shift to the left, as in **Figure 10.8** (b). For example, in the United States, government spending declined by 3.2% of GDP during the 1990s, from 21% of GDP in 1991, and to 17.8% of GDP in 1998. However, from 2005 to 2009, the peak of the Great Recession, government spending increased from 19% of GDP to 21.4% of GDP. If changes of a few percentage points of GDP seem small to you, remember that since GDP was about $14.4 trillion in 2009, a seemingly small change of 2% of GDP is equal to close to $300 billion.

Tax policy can affect consumption and investment spending, too. Tax cuts for individuals will tend to increase consumption demand, while tax increases will tend to diminish it. Tax policy can also pump up investment demand by offering lower tax rates for corporations or tax reductions that benefit specific kinds of investment. Shifting C or I will shift the AD curve as a whole.

During a recession, when unemployment is high and many businesses are suffering low profits or even losses, the U.S. Congress often passes tax cuts. During the recession of 2001, for example, a tax cut was enacted into law. At such times, the political rhetoric often focuses on how people going through hard times need relief from taxes. The aggregate supply and aggregate demand framework, however, offers a complementary rationale, as illustrated in **Figure 10.9**. The original equilibrium during a recession is at point E_0, relatively far from the full employment level of output. The tax cut, by increasing consumption, shifts the AD curve to the right. At the new equilibrium (E_1), real GDP rises and unemployment falls and, because in this diagram the economy has not yet reached its potential or full employment level of GDP, any rise in the price level remains muted. Read the following Clear It Up feature to consider the question of whether economists favor tax cuts or oppose them.

Figure 10.9 Recession and Full Employment in the AD/AS Model Whether the economy is in a recession is illustrated in the AD/AS model by how close the equilibrium is to the potential GDP line as indicated by the vertical LRAS line. In this example, the level of output Y_0 at the equilibrium E_0 is relatively far from the potential GDP line, so it can represent an economy in recession, well below the full employment level of GDP. In contrast, the level of output Y_1 at the equilibrium E_1 is relatively close to potential GDP, and so it would represent an economy with a lower unemployment rate.

Do economists favor tax cuts or oppose them?

One of the most fundamental divisions in American politics over the last few decades has been between those who believe that the government should cut taxes substantially and those who disagree. Ronald Reagan rode into the presidency in 1980 partly because of his promise, soon carried out, to enact a substantial tax cut. George Bush lost his bid for reelection against Bill Clinton in 1992 partly because he had broken his 1988 promise: "Read my lips! No new taxes!" In the 2000 presidential election, both George W. Bush and Al Gore advocated substantial tax cuts and Bush succeeded in pushing a package of tax cuts through Congress early in 2001. Disputes over tax cuts often ignite at the state and local level as well.

What side are economists on? Do they support broad tax cuts or oppose them? The answer, unsatisfying to zealots on both sides, is that it depends. One issue is whether the tax cuts are accompanied by equally large government spending cuts. Economists differ, as does any broad cross-section of the public, on how large government spending should be and what programs might be cut back. A second issue, more relevant to the discussion in this chapter, concerns how close the economy is to the full employment level of output. In a recession, when the intersection of the AD and AS curves is far below the full employment level, tax cuts can make sense as a way of shifting AD to the right. However, when the economy is already doing extremely well, tax cuts may shift AD so far to the right as to generate inflationary pressures, with little gain to GDP.

With the AD/AS framework in mind, many economists might readily believe that the Reagan tax cuts of 1981, which took effect just after two serious recessions, were beneficial economic policy. Similarly, the Bush tax cuts of 2001 and the Obama tax cuts of 2009 were enacted during recessions. However, some of the same economists who favor tax cuts in time of recession would be much more dubious about identical tax cuts at a time the economy is performing well and cyclical unemployment is low.

The use of government spending and tax cuts can be a useful tool to affect aggregate demand and it will be discussed in greater detail in the Government Budgets and Fiscal Policy chapter and The Impacts of Government Borrowing. Other policy tools can shift the aggregate demand curve as well. For example, as discussed in the Monetary policy and Bank Regulation chapter, the Federal Reserve can affect interest rates and the availability of credit. Higher interest rates tend to discourage borrowing and thus reduce both household spending on big-ticket items like houses and cars and investment spending by business. Conversely, lower interest rates will stimulate consumption and investment demand. Interest rates can also affect exchange rates, which in turn will have effects on the export and import components of aggregate demand.

Spelling out the details of these alternative policies and how they affect the components of aggregate demand can wait for The Keynesian Perspective chapter. Here, the key lesson is that a shift of the aggregate demand curve to the right leads to a greater real GDP and to upward pressure on the price level. Conversely, a shift of aggregate demand to the left leads to a lower real GDP and a lower price level. Whether these changes in output and price level are relatively large or relatively small, and how the change in equilibrium relates to potential GDP, depends on whether the shift in the AD curve is happening in the relatively flat or relatively steep portion of the AS curve.

10.5 | How the AD/AS Model Incorporates Growth, Unemployment, and Inflation

By the end of this section, you will be able to:
- Identify periods of economic growth and recession using the aggregate demand/aggregate supply model
- Explain how unemployment and inflation impact the aggregate demand/aggregate supply model
- Evaluate the importance of the aggregate demand/aggregate supply model

The AD/AS model can convey a number of interlocking relationships between the four macroeconomic goals of growth, unemployment, inflation, and a sustainable balance of trade. Moreover, the AD/AS framework is flexible enough to accommodate both the Keynes' law approach that focuses on aggregate demand and the short run, while also including the Say's law approach that focuses on aggregate supply and the long run. These advantages are considerable. Every model is a simplified version of the deeper reality and, in the context of the AD/AS model, the three macroeconomic goals arise in ways that are sometimes indirect or incomplete. In this module, we consider how the AD/AS model illustrates the three macroeconomic goals of economic growth, low unemployment, and low inflation.

Growth and Recession in the AD/AS Diagram

In the AD/AS diagram, long-run economic growth due to productivity increases over time will be represented by a gradual shift to the right of aggregate supply. The vertical line representing potential GDP (or the "full employment level of GDP") will gradually shift to the right over time as well. A pattern of economic growth over three years, with the AS curve shifting slightly out to the right each year, was shown earlier in Figure 10.7 (a). However, the factors that determine the speed of this long-term economic growth rate—like investment in physical and human capital, technology, and whether an economy can take advantage of catch-up growth—do not appear directly in the AD/AS diagram.

In the short run, GDP falls and rises in every economy, as the economy dips into recession or expands out of recession. Recessions are illustrated in the AD/AS diagram when the equilibrium level of real GDP is substantially below potential GDP, as occurred at the equilibrium point E_0 in Figure 10.9. On the other hand, in years of resurgent economic growth the equilibrium will typically be close to potential GDP, as shown at equilibrium point E_1 in that earlier figure.

Unemployment in the AD/AS Diagram

Two types of unemployment were described in the Unemployment chapter. Cyclical unemployment bounces up and down according to the short-run movements of GDP. Over the long run, in the United States, the unemployment rate typically hovers around 5% (give or take one percentage point or so), when the economy is healthy. In many of the national economies across Europe, the rate of unemployment in recent decades has only dropped to about 10%

or a bit lower, even in good economic years. This baseline level of unemployment that occurs year-in and year-out is called the natural rate of unemployment and is determined by how well the structures of market and government institutions in the economy lead to a matching of workers and employers in the labor market. Potential GDP can imply different unemployment rates in different economies, depending on the natural rate of unemployment for that economy.

Link It Up

Visit this website (http://openstaxcollege.org/l/consumerconfid) for data on consumer confidence.

In the AD/AS diagram, cyclical unemployment is shown by how close the economy is to the potential or full employment level of GDP. Returning to **Figure 10.9**, relatively low cyclical unemployment for an economy occurs when the level of output is close to potential GDP, as in the equilibrium point E_1. Conversely, high cyclical unemployment arises when the output is substantially to the left of potential GDP on the AD/AS diagram, as at the equilibrium point E_0. The factors that determine the natural rate of unemployment are not shown separately in the AD/AS model, although they are implicitly part of what determines potential GDP or full employment GDP in a given economy.

Inflationary Pressures in the AD/AS Diagram

Inflation fluctuates in the short run. Higher inflation rates have typically occurred either during or just after economic booms: for example, the biggest spurts of inflation in the U.S. economy during the twentieth century followed the wartime booms of World War I and World War II. Conversely, rates of inflation generally decline during recessions. As an extreme example, inflation actually became negative—a situation called "deflation"—during the Great Depression. Even during the relatively short recession of 1991–1992, the rate of inflation declined from 5.4% in 1990 to 3.0% in 1992. During the relatively short recession of 2001, the rate of inflation declined from 3.4% in 2000 to 1.6% in 2002. During the deep recession of 2007–2009, the rate of inflation declined from 3.8% in 2008 to –0.4% in 2009. Some countries have experienced bouts of high inflation that lasted for years. In the U.S. economy since the mid–1980s, inflation does not seem to have had any long-term trend to be substantially higher or lower; instead, it has stayed in the range of 1–5% annually.

Link It Up

Visit this website (http://openstaxcollege.org/l/businessconfid) for data on business confidence.

The AD/AS framework implies two ways that inflationary pressures may arise. One possible trigger is if aggregate demand continues to shift to the right when the economy is already at or near potential GDP and full employment, thus pushing the macroeconomic equilibrium into the steep portion of the AS curve. In **Figure 10.10** (a), there is a shift of aggregate demand to the right; the new equilibrium E_1 is clearly at a higher price level than the original equilibrium E_0. In this situation, the aggregate demand in the economy has soared so high that firms in the economy are not capable of producing additional goods, because labor and physical capital are fully employed, and so additional increases in aggregate demand can only result in a rise in the price level.

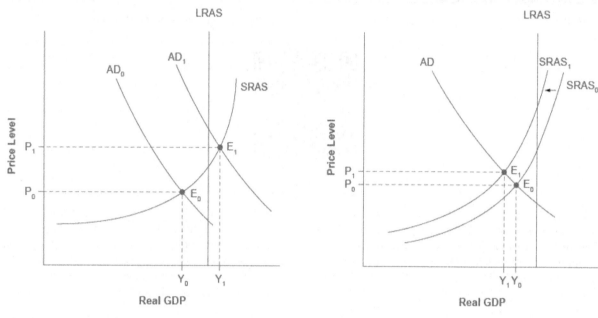

(a) Inflationary pressure from a shift in AD

(b) Inflationary pressure from a shift in AS

Figure 10.10 Sources of Inflationary Pressure in the AD/AS Model (a) A shift in aggregate demand, from AD_0 to AD_1, when it happens in the area of the SRAS curve that is near potential GDP, will lead to a higher price level and to pressure for a higher price level and inflation. The new equilibrium (E1) is at a higher price level (P1) than the original equilibrium. (b) A shift in aggregate supply, from $SRAS_0$ to $SRAS_1$, will lead to a lower real GDP and to pressure for a higher price level and inflation. The new equilibrium (E_1) is at a higher price level (P_1), while the original equilibrium (E_0) is at the lower price level (P_0).

An alternative source of inflationary pressures can occur due to a rise in input prices that affects many or most firms across the economy—perhaps an important input to production like oil or labor—and causes the aggregate supply curve to shift back to the left. In **Figure 10.10** (b), the shift of the SRAS curve to the left also increases the price level from P_0 at the original equilibrium (E_0) to a higher price level of P_1 at the new equilibrium (E_1). In effect, the rise in input prices ends up, after the final output is produced and sold, being passed along in the form of a higher price level for outputs.

The AD/AS diagram shows only a one-time shift in the price level. It does not address the question of what would cause inflation either to vanish after a year, or to sustain itself for several years. There are two explanations for why inflation may persist over time. One way that continual inflationary price increases can occur is if the government continually attempts to stimulate aggregate demand in a way that keeps pushing the AD curve when it is already in the steep portion of the SRAS curve. A second possibility is that, if inflation has been occurring for several years, a certain level of inflation may come to be expected. For example, if consumers, workers, and businesses all expect prices and wages to rise by a certain amount, then these expected rises in the price level can become built into the annual increases of prices, wages, and interest rates of the economy. These two reasons are interrelated, because if a government fosters a macroeconomic environment with inflationary pressures, then people will grow to expect inflation. However, the AD/AS diagram does not show these patterns of ongoing or expected inflation in a direct way.

Importance of the Aggregate Demand/Aggregate Supply Model

Macroeconomics takes an overall view of the economy, which means that it needs to juggle many different concepts. For example, start with the three macroeconomic goals of growth, low inflation, and low unemployment. Aggregate demand has four elements: consumption, investment, government spending, and exports less imports. Aggregate supply reveals how businesses throughout the economy will react to a higher price level for outputs. Finally, a wide array of economic events and policy decisions can affect aggregate demand and aggregate supply, including government tax and spending decisions; consumer and business confidence; changes in prices of key inputs like oil; and technology that brings higher levels of productivity.

The aggregate demand/aggregate supply model is one of the fundamental diagrams in this course (like the budget constraint diagram introduced in the Choice in a World of Scarcity chapter and the supply and demand diagram introduced in the Demand and Supply chapter) because it provides an overall framework for bringing these factors together in one diagram. Indeed, some version of the AD/AS model will appear in every chapter in the rest of this book.

10.6 | Keynes' Law and Say's Law in the AD/AS Model

By the end of this section, you will be able to:
- Identify the neoclassical zone, the intermediate zone, and the Keynesian zone in the aggregate demand/aggregate supply model
- Use an aggregate demand/aggregate supply model as a diagnostic test to understand the current state of the economy

The AD/AS model can be used to illustrate both Say's law that supply creates its own demand and Keynes' law that demand creates its own supply. Consider the three zones of the SRAS curve as identified in Figure 10.11: the Keynesian zone, the neoclassical zone, and the intermediate zone.

Figure 10.11 Keynes, Neoclassical, and Intermediate Zones in the Aggregate Supply Curve Near the equilibrium Ek, in the Keynesian zone at the far left of the SRAS curve, small shifts in AD, either to the right or the left, will affect the output level Yk, but will not much affect the price level. In the Keynesian zone, AD largely determines the quantity of output. Near the equilibrium En, in the neoclassical zone at the far right of the SRAS curve, small shifts in AD, either to the right or the left, will have relatively little effect on the output level Yn, but instead will have a greater effect on the price level. In the neoclassical zone, the near-vertical SRAS curve close to the level of potential GDP largely determines the quantity of output. In the intermediate zone around equilibrium Ei, movement in AD to the right will increase both the output level and the price level, while a movement in AD to the left would decrease both the output level and the price level.

Focus first on the **Keynesian zone**, that portion of the SRAS curve on the far left which is relatively flat. If the AD curve crosses this portion of the SRAS curve at an equilibrium point like Ek, then certain statements about the economic situation will follow. In the Keynesian zone, the equilibrium level of real GDP is far below potential GDP, the economy is in recession, and cyclical unemployment is high. If aggregate demand shifted to the right or left in the Keynesian zone, it will determine the resulting level of output (and thus unemployment). However, inflationary price pressure is not much of a worry in the Keynesian zone, since the price level does not vary much in this zone.

Now, focus your attention on the **neoclassical zone** of the SRAS curve, which is the near-vertical portion on the right-hand side. If the AD curve crosses this portion of the SRAS curve at an equilibrium point like En where output is at or near potential GDP, then the size of potential GDP pretty much determines the level of output in the economy. Since the equilibrium is near potential GDP, cyclical unemployment is low in this economy, although structural unemployment may remain an issue. In the neoclassical zone, shifts of aggregate demand to the right or the left have little effect on the level of output or employment. The only way to increase the size of the real GDP in the neoclassical zone is for AS to shift to the right. However, shifts in AD in the neoclassical zone will create pressures to change the price level.

Finally, consider the **intermediate zone** of the SRAS curve in Figure 10.11. If the AD curve crosses this portion of the SRAS curve at an equilibrium point like Ei, then we might expect unemployment and inflation to move in opposing directions. For instance, a shift of AD to the right will move output closer to potential GDP and thus reduce unemployment, but will also lead to a higher price level and upward pressure on inflation. Conversely, a shift of AD to the left will move output further from potential GDP and raise unemployment, but will also lead to a lower price level and downward pressure on inflation.

This approach of dividing the SRAS curve into different zones works as a diagnostic test that can be applied to an economy, like a doctor checking a patient for symptoms. First, figure out what zone the economy is in and then the economic issues, tradeoffs, and policy choices will be clarified. Some economists believe that the economy is strongly predisposed to be in one zone or another. Thus, hard-line Keynesian economists believe that the economies are in the Keynesian zone most of the time, and so they view the neoclassical zone as a theoretical abstraction. Conversely, hard-line neoclassical economists argue that economies are in the neoclassical zone most of the time and that the Keynesian zone is a distraction. **The Keynesian Perspective** and **The Neoclassical Perspective** should help to clarify the underpinnings and consequences of these contrasting views of the macroeconomy.

Bring it Home

From Housing Bubble to Housing Bust

Economic fluctuations, whether those experienced during the Great Depression of the 1930s, the stagflation of the 1970s, or the Great Recession of 2008–2009, can be explained using the AD/AS diagram. Short-run fluctuations in output occur due to shifts of the SRAS curve, the AD curve, or both. In the case of the housing bubble, rising home values caused the AD curve to shift to the right as more people felt that rising home values increased their overall wealth. Many homeowners took on mortgages that exceeded their ability to pay because, as home values continued to go up, the increased value would pay off any debt outstanding. Increased wealth due to rising home values lead to increased home equity loans and increased spending. All these activities pushed AD to the right, contributing to low unemployment rates and economic growth in the United States. When the housing bubble burst, overall wealth dropped dramatically, wiping out the recent gains. This drop in the value of homes was a demand shock to the U.S. economy because of its impact directly on the wealth of the household sector, and its contagion into the financial that essentially locked up new credit. The AD curve shifted to the left as evidenced by the rising unemployment of the Great Recession.

Understanding the source of these macroeconomic fluctuations provided monetary and fiscal policy makers with insight about what policy actions to take to mitigate the impact of the housing crisis. From a monetary policy perspective, the Federal Reserve lowered short-term interest rates to between 0% and 0.25 %, to loosen up credit throughout the financial system. Discretionary fiscal policy measures included the passage of the Emergency Economic Stabilization Act of 2008 that allowed for the purchase of troubled assets, such as mortgages, from financial institutions and the American Recovery and Reinvestment Act of 2009 that increased government spending on infrastructure, provided for tax cuts, and increased transfer payments. In combination, both monetary and fiscal policy measures were designed to help stimulate aggregate demand in the U.S. economy, pushing the AD curve to the right.

While most economists agree on the usefulness of the AD/AS diagram in analyzing the sources of these fluctuations, there is still some disagreement about the effectiveness of policy decisions that are useful in stabilizing these fluctuations. We discuss the possible policy actions and the differences among economists about their effectiveness in more detail in **The Keynesian Perspective, Monetary Policy and Bank Regulation**, and **Government Budgets and Fiscal Policy**.

KEY TERMS

aggregate demand (AD) the amount of total spending on domestic goods and services in an economy

aggregate demand (AD) curve the total spending on domestic goods and services at each price level

aggregate demand/aggregate supply model a model that shows what determines total supply or total demand for the economy, and how total demand and total supply interact at the macroeconomic level

aggregate supply (AS) the total quantity of output (i.e. real GDP) firms will produce and sell

aggregate supply (AS) curve the total quantity of output (i.e. real GDP) that firms will produce and sell at each price level

full-employment GDP another name for potential GDP, when the economy is producing at its potential and unemployment is at the natural rate of unemployment

intermediate zone portion of the SRAS curve where GDP is below potential but not so far below as in the Keynesian zone; the SRAS curve is upward-sloping, but not vertical in the intermediate zone

Keynesian zone portion of the SRAS curve where GDP is far below potential and the SRAS curve is flat

Keynes' law "demand creates its own supply"

long run aggregate supply (LRAS) curve vertical line at potential GDP showing no relationship between the price level for output and real GDP in the long run

neoclassical economists economists who generally emphasize the importance of aggregate supply in determining the size of the macroeconomy over the long run

neoclassical zone portion of the SRAS curve where GDP is at or near potential output where the SRAS curve is steep

potential GDP the maximum quantity that an economy can produce given full employment of its existing levels of labor, physical capital, technology, and institutions

Say's law "supply creates its own demand"

short run aggregate supply (SRAS) curve positive short run relationship between the price level for output and real GDP, holding the prices of inputs fixed

stagflation an economy experiences stagnant growth and high inflation at the same time

KEY CONCEPTS AND SUMMARY

10.1 Macroeconomic Perspectives on Demand and Supply

Neoclassical economists emphasize Say's law, which holds that supply creates its own demand. Keynesian economists emphasize Keynes' law, which holds that demand creates its own supply. Many mainstream economists take a Keynesian perspective, emphasizing the importance of aggregate demand, for the short run, and a neoclassical perspective, emphasizing the importance of aggregate supply, for the long run.

10.2 Building a Model of Aggregate Demand and Aggregate Supply

The upward-sloping short run aggregate supply (SRAS) curve shows the positive relationship between the price level and the level of real GDP in the short run. Aggregate supply slopes up because when the price level for outputs increases, while the price level of inputs remains fixed, the opportunity for additional profits encourages more production. The aggregate supply curve is near-horizontal on the left and near-vertical on the right. In the long run, aggregate supply is shown by a vertical line at the level of potential output, which is the maximum level of output the economy can produce with its existing levels of workers, physical capital, technology, and economic institutions.

The downward-sloping aggregate demand (AD) curve shows the relationship between the price level for outputs and the quantity of total spending in the economy. It slopes down because of: (a) the wealth effect, which means that a higher price level leads to lower real wealth, which reduces the level of consumption; (b) the interest rate effect, which holds that a higher price level will mean a greater demand for money, which will tend to drive up interest rates and reduce investment spending; and (c) the foreign price effect, which holds that a rise in the price level will make domestic goods relatively more expensive, discouraging exports and encouraging imports.

10.3 Shifts in Aggregate Supply

The aggregate demand/aggregate supply (AD/AS) diagram shows how AD and AS interact. The intersection of the AD and AS curves shows the equilibrium output and price level in the economy. Movements of either AS or AD will result in a different equilibrium output and price level. The aggregate supply curve will shift out to the right as productivity increases. It will shift back to the left as the price of key inputs rises, and will shift out to the right if the price of key inputs falls. If the AS curve shifts back to the left, the combination of lower output, higher unemployment, and higher inflation, called stagflation, occurs. If AS shifts out to the right, a combination of lower inflation, higher output, and lower unemployment is possible.

10.4 Shifts in Aggregate Demand

The AD curve will shift out as the components of aggregate demand—C, I, G, and X–M—rise. It will shift back to the left as these components fall. These factors can change because of different personal choices, like those resulting from consumer or business confidence, or from policy choices like changes in government spending and taxes. If the AD curve shifts to the right, then the equilibrium quantity of output and the price level will rise. If the AD curve shifts to the left, then the equilibrium quantity of output and the price level will fall. Whether equilibrium output changes relatively more than the price level or whether the price level changes relatively more than output is determined by where the AD curve intersects with the AS curve.

The AD/AS diagram superficially resembles the microeconomic supply and demand diagram on the surface, but in reality, what is on the horizontal and vertical axes and the underlying economic reasons for the shapes of the curves are very different. Long-term economic growth is illustrated in the AD/AS framework by a gradual shift of the aggregate supply curve to the right. A recession is illustrated when the intersection of AD and AS is substantially below potential GDP, while an expanding economy is illustrated when the intersection of AS and AD is near potential GDP.

10.5 How the AD/AS Model Incorporates Growth, Unemployment, and Inflation

Cyclical unemployment is relatively large in the AD/AS framework when the equilibrium is substantially below potential GDP. Cyclical unemployment is small in the AD/AS framework when the equilibrium is near potential GDP. The natural rate of unemployment, as determined by the labor market institutions of the economy, is built into what is meant by potential GDP, but does not otherwise appear in an AD/AS diagram. Pressures for inflation to rise or fall are shown in the AD/AS framework when the movement from one equilibrium to another causes the price level to rise or to fall. The balance of trade does not appear directly in the AD/AS diagram, but it appears indirectly in several ways. Increases in exports or declines in imports can cause shifts in AD. Changes in the price of key imported inputs to production, like oil, can cause shifts in AS. The AD/AS model is the key model used in this book to understand macroeconomic issues.

10.6 Keynes' Law and Say's Law in the AD/AS Model

The SRAS curve can be divided into three zones. Keynes' law says demand creates its own supply, so that changes in aggregate demand cause changes in real GDP and employment. Keynes' law can be shown on the horizontal Keynesian zone of the aggregate supply curve. The Keynesian zone occurs at the left of the SRAS curve where it is fairly flat, so movements in AD will affect output, but have little effect on the price level. Say's law says supply creates its own demand. Changes in aggregate demand have no effect on real GDP and employment, only on the price level. Say's law can be shown on the vertical neoclassical zone of the aggregate supply curve. The neoclassical zone occurs at the right of the SRAS curve where it is fairly vertical, and so movements in AD will affect the price level, but have little impact on output. The intermediate zone in the middle of the SRAS curve is upward-sloping, so a rise in AD will cause higher output and price level, while a fall in AD will lead to a lower output and price level.

SELF-CHECK QUESTIONS

1. Describe the mechanism by which supply creates its own demand.

2. Describe the mechanism by which demand creates its own supply.

3. The short run aggregate supply curve was constructed assuming that as the price of outputs increases, the price of inputs stays the same. How would an increase in the prices of important inputs, like energy, affect aggregate supply?

4. In the AD/AS model, what prevents the economy from achieving equilibrium at potential output?

5. Suppose the U.S. Congress passes significant immigration reform that makes it easier for foreigners to come to the United States to work. Use the AD/AS model to explain how this would affect the equilibrium level of GDP and the price level.

6. Suppose concerns about the size of the federal budget deficit lead the U.S. Congress to cut all funding for research and development for ten years. Assuming this has an impact on technology growth, what does the AD/AS model predict would be the likely effect on equilibrium GDP and the price level?

7. How would a dramatic increase in the value of the stock market shift the AD curve? What effect would the shift have on the equilibrium level of GDP and the price level?

8. Suppose Mexico, one of our largest trading partners and purchaser of a large quantity of our exports, goes into a recession. Use the AD/AS model to determine the likely impact on our equilibrium GDP and price level.

9. A policymaker claims that tax cuts led the economy out of a recession. Can we use the AD/AS diagram to show this?

10. Many financial analysts and economists eagerly await the press releases for the reports on the home price index and consumer confidence index. What would be the effects of a negative report on both of these? What about a positive report?

11. What impact would a decrease in the size of the labor force have on GDP and the price level according to the AD/AS model?

12. Suppose, after five years of sluggish growth, the economy of the European Union picks up speed. What would be the likely impact on the U.S. trade balance, GDP, and employment?

13. Suppose the Federal Reserve begins to increase the supply of money at an increasing rate. What impact would that have on GDP, unemployment, and inflation?

14. If the economy is operating in the neoclassical zone of the SRAS curve and aggregate demand falls, what is likely to happen to real GDP?

15. If the economy is operating in the Keynesian zone of the SRAS curve and aggregate demand falls, what is likely to happen to real GDP?

REVIEW QUESTIONS

16. What is Say's law?

17. What is Keynes' law?

18. Do neoclassical economists believe in Keynes' law or Say's law?

19. Does Say's law apply more accurately in the long run or the short run? What about Keynes' law?

20. What is on the horizontal axis of the AD/AS diagram? What is on the vertical axis?

21. What is the economic reason why the SRAS curve slopes up?

22. What are the components of the aggregate demand (AD) curve?

23. What are the economic reasons why the AD curve slopes down?

24. Briefly explain the reason for the near-horizontal shape of the SRAS curve on its far left.

25. Briefly explain the reason for the near-vertical shape of the SRAS curve on its far right.

26. What is potential GDP?

27. Name some factors that could cause the SRAS curve to shift, and say whether they would shift SRAS to the right or to the left.

28. Will the shift of SRAS to the right tend to make the equilibrium quantity and price level higher or lower? What about a shift of SRAS to the left?

29. What is stagflation?

30. Name some factors that could cause AD to shift, and say whether they would shift AD to the right or to the left.

31. Would a shift of AD to the right tend to make the equilibrium quantity and price level higher or lower? What about a shift of AD to the left?

32. How is long-term growth illustrated in an AD/AS model?

33. How is recession illustrated in an AD/AS model?

34. How is cyclical unemployment illustrated in an AD/AS model?

35. How is the natural rate of unemployment illustrated in an AD/AS model?

36. How is pressure for inflationary price increases shown in an AD/AS model?

37. What are some of the ways in which exports and imports can affect the AD/AS model?

38. What is the Keynesian zone of the SRAS curve? How much is the price level likely to change in the Keynesian zone?

39. What is the neoclassical zone of the SRAS curve? How much is the output level likely to change in the neoclassical zone?

40. What is the intermediate zone of the SRAS curve? Will a rise in output be accompanied by a rise or a fall in the price level in this zone?

CRITICAL THINKING QUESTIONS

41. Why would an economist choose either the neoclassical perspective or the Keynesian perspective, but not both?

42. On a microeconomic demand curve, a decrease in price causes an increase in quantity demanded because the product in question is now relatively less expensive than substitute products. Explain why aggregate demand does not increase for the same reason in response to a decrease in the aggregate price level. In other words, what causes total spending to increase if it is not because goods are now cheaper?

43. Economists expect that as the labor market continues to tighten going into the latter part of 2015 that workers should begin to expect wage increases in 2015 and 2016. Assuming this occurs and it was the only development in the labor market that year, how would this affect the AS curve? What if it was also accompanied by an increase in worker productivity?

44. If new government regulations require firms to use a cleaner technology that is also less efficient than what was previously used, what would the effect be on

output, the price level, and employment using the AD/AS diagram?

45. During the spring of 2016 the Midwestern United States, which has a large agricultural base, experiences above-average rainfall. Using the AD/AS diagram, what is the effect on output, the price level, and employment?

46. Hydraulic fracturing (fracking) has the potential to significantly increase the amount of natural gas produced in the United States. If a large percentage of factories and utility companies use natural gas, what will happen to output, the price level, and employment as fracking becomes more widely used?

47. Some politicians have suggested tying the minimum wage to the consumer price index (CPI). Using the AD/AS diagram, what effects would this policy most likely have on output, the price level, and employment?

48. If households decide to save a larger portion of their income, what effect would this have on the output, employment, and price level in the short run? What about the long run?

49. If firms become more optimistic about the future of the economy and, at the same time, innovation in 3-D printing makes most workers more productive, what is the combined effect on output, employment, and the price-level?

50. If Congress cuts taxes at the same time that businesses become more pessimistic about the economy, what is the combined effect on output, the price level, and employment using the AD/AS diagram?

51. Suppose the level of structural unemployment increases. How would the increase in structural unemployment be illustrated in the AD/AS model? *Hint*: How does structural unemployment affect potential GDP?

52. If foreign wealth-holders decide that the United States is the safest place to invest their savings, what would the effect be on the economy here? Show graphically using the AD/AS model.

53. The AD/AS model is static. It shows a snapshot of the economy at a given point in time. Both economic growth and inflation are dynamic phenomena. Suppose economic growth is 3% per year and aggregate demand is growing at the same rate. What does the AD/AS model say the inflation rate should be?

54. Explain why the short-run aggregate supply curve might be fairly flat in the Keynesian zone of the SRAS curve. How might we tell if we are in the Keynesian zone of the AS?

55. Explain why the short-run aggregate supply curve might be vertical in the neoclassical zone of the SRAS curve. How might we tell if we are in the neoclassical zone of the AS?

56. Why might it be important for policymakers to know which zone of the SRAS curve the economy is in?

57. In your view, is the economy currently operating in the Keynesian, intermediate or neoclassical portion of the economy's aggregate supply curve?

58. Are Say's law and Keynes' law necessarily mutually exclusive?

PROBLEMS

59. Review the problem shown in the Work It Out titled "Interpreting the AD/AS Model." Like the information provided in that feature, Table 10.2 shows information on aggregate supply, aggregate demand, and the price level for the imaginary country of Xurbia.

Price Level	AD	AS
110	700	600
120	690	640
130	680	680
140	670	720
150	660	740
160	650	760
170	640	770

Table 10.2 Price Level: AD/AS

a. Plot the AD/AS diagram from the data shown. Identify the equilibrium.
b. Imagine that, as a result of a government tax cut, aggregate demand becomes higher by 50 at every price level. Identify the new equilibrium.

c. How will the new equilibrium alter output? How will it alter the price level? What do you think will happen to employment?

60. The imaginary country of Harris Island has the aggregate supply and aggregate demand curves as shown in Table 10.3.

Price Level	AD	AS
100	700	200
120	600	325
140	500	500
160	400	570
180	300	620

Table 10.3 Price Level: AD/AS

a. Plot the AD/AS diagram. Identify the equilibrium.
b. Would you expect unemployment in this economy to be relatively high or low?
c. Would you expect concern about inflation in this economy to be relatively high or low?

d. Imagine that consumers begin to lose confidence about the state of the economy, and so AD becomes lower by 275 at every price level. Identify the new aggregate equilibrium.

e. How will the shift in AD affect the original output, price level, and employment?

61. Santher is an economy described by Table 10.4.

Price Level	AD	AS
50	1,000	250
60	950	580
70	900	750
80	850	850

Table 10.4 Price Level: AD/AS

Price Level	AD	AS
90	800	900

Table 10.4 Price Level: AD/AS

a. Plot the AD/AS curves and identify the equilibrium.

b. Would you expect unemployment in this economy to be relatively high or low?

c. Would you expect prices to be a relatively large or small concern for this economy?

d. Imagine that input prices fall and so AS shifts to the right by 150 units. Identify the new equilibrium.

e. How will the shift in AS affect the original output, price level, and employment?

11 | The Keynesian Perspective

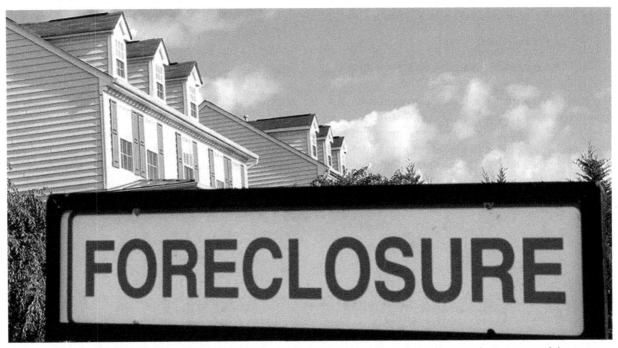

Figure 11.1 Signs of a Recession Home foreclosures were just one of the many signs and symptoms of the recent Great Recession. During that time, many businesses closed and many people lost their jobs. (Credit: modification of work by Taber Andrew Bain/Flickr Creative Commons)

Bring it Home

The Great Recession

The Great Recession of 2008–2009 hit the U.S. economy hard. According to the Bureau of Labor Statistics (BLS), the number of unemployed Americans rose from 6.8 million in May 2007 to 15.4 million in October 2009. During that time, the U.S. Census Bureau estimated that approximately 170,000 small businesses closed. Mass layoffs peaked in February 2009 when 326,392 workers were given notice. U.S. productivity and output fell as well. Job losses, declining home values, declining incomes, and uncertainty about the future caused consumption expenditures to decrease. According to the BLS, household spending dropped by 7.8%.

Home foreclosures and the meltdown in U.S. financial markets called for immediate action by Congress, the President, and the Federal Reserve Bank. For example, programs such as the American Restoration and Recovery Act were implemented to help millions of people by providing tax credits for homebuyers, paying "cash for clunkers," and extending unemployment benefits. From cutting back on spending, filing for unemployment, and losing homes, millions of people were affected by the recession. And while the United States is now on the path to recovery, the impact will be felt for many years to come.

What caused this recession and what prevented the economy from spiraling further into another depression? Policymakers looked to the lessons learned from the Great Depression of the 1930s and to the models developed by John Maynard Keynes to analyze the causes and find solutions to the country's economic woes. The Keynesian perspective is the subject of this chapter.

Introduction to the Keynesian Perspective

In this chapter, you will learn about:

- Aggregate Demand in Keynesian Analysis
- The Building Blocks of Keynesian Analysis
- The Expenditure-Output (or Keynesian Cross) Model
- The Phillips Curve
- The Keynesian Perspective on Market Forces

We have learned that the level of economic activity, for example output, employment, and spending, tends to grow over time. In **The Keynesian Perspective** we learned the reasons for this trend. **The Macroeconomic Perspective** pointed out that the economy tends to cycle around the long-run trend. In other words, the economy does not always grow at its average growth rate. Sometimes economic activity grows at the trend rate, sometimes it grows more than the trend, sometimes it grows less than the trend, and sometimes it actually declines. You can see this cyclical behavior in **Figure 11.2**.

Figure 11.2 U.S. Gross Domestic Product, Percent Changes 1930–2014 The chart tracks the percent change in GDP since 1930. The magnitude of both recessions and peaks was quite large between 1930 and 1945. (Source: Bureau of Economic Analysis, "National Economic Accounts")

This empirical reality raises two important questions: How can we explain the cycles, and to what extent can they be moderated? This chapter (on the Keynesian perspective) and **The Neoclassical Perspective** explore those questions from two different points of view, building on what we learned in **The Aggregate Demand/Aggregate Supply Model**.

11.1 | Aggregate Demand in Keynesian Analysis

By the end of this section, you will be able to:
- Explain real GDP, recessionary gaps, and inflationary gaps
- Recognize the Keynesian AD/AS model
- Identify the determining factors of both consumption expenditure and investment expenditure
- Analyze the factors that determine government spending and net exports

The Keynesian perspective focuses on aggregate demand. The idea is simple: firms produce output only if they expect it to sell. Thus, while the availability of the factors of production determines a nation's potential GDP, the amount of goods and services actually being sold, known as **real GDP**, depends on how much demand exists across the economy. This point is illustrated in Figure 11.3.

Figure 11.3 The Keynesian AD/AS Model The Keynesian View of the AD/AS Model uses an SRAS curve, which is horizontal at levels of output below potential and vertical at potential output. Thus, when beginning from potential output, any decrease in AD affects only output, but not prices; any increase in AD affects only prices, not output.

Keynes argued that, for reasons we explain shortly, aggregate demand is not stable—that it can change unexpectedly. Suppose the economy starts where AD intersects SRAS at P_0 and Yp. Because Yp is potential output, the economy is at full employment. Because AD is volatile, it can easily fall. Thus, even if we start at Yp, if AD falls, then we find ourselves in what Keynes termed a **recessionary gap**. The economy is in equilibrium but with less than full employment, as shown at Y_1 in the Figure 11.3. Keynes believed that the economy would tend to stay in a recessionary gap, with its attendant unemployment, for a significant period of time.

In the same way (though not shown in the figure), if AD increases, the economy could experience an **inflationary gap**, where demand is attempting to push the economy past potential output. As a consequence, the economy experiences inflation. The key policy implication for either situation is that government needs to step in and close the gap, increasing spending during recessions and decreasing spending during booms to return aggregate demand to match potential output.

Recall from The Aggregate Supply-Aggregate Demand Model that aggregate demand is total spending, economy-wide, on domestic goods and services. (Aggregate demand (AD) is actually what economists call total planned expenditure. Read the appendix on The Expenditure-Output Model for more on this.) You may also remember that aggregate demand is the sum of four components: consumption expenditure, investment expenditure, government spending, and spending on net exports (exports minus imports). In the following sections, we will examine each component through the Keynesian perspective.

What Determines Consumption Expenditure?

Consumption expenditure is spending by households and individuals on durable goods, nondurable goods, and services. Durable goods are things that last and provide value over time, such as automobiles. Nondurable goods are things like groceries—once you consume them, they are gone. Recall from The Macroeconomic Perspective that services are intangible things consumers buy, like healthcare or entertainment.

Keynes identified three factors that affect consumption:

- Disposable income: For most people, the single most powerful determinant of how much they consume is how much income they have in their take-home pay, also known as **disposable income**, which is income after taxes.

- Expected future income: Consumer expectations about future income also are important in determining consumption. If consumers feel optimistic about the future, they are more likely to spend and increase overall aggregate demand. News of recession and troubles in the economy will make them pull back on consumption.

- Wealth or credit: When households experience a rise in wealth, they may be willing to consume a higher share of their income and to save less. When the U.S. stock market rose dramatically in the late 1990s, for example, U.S. rates of saving declined, probably in part because people felt that their wealth had increased and there was less need to save. How do people spend beyond their income, when they perceive their wealth increasing? The answer is borrowing. On the other side, when the U.S. stock market declined about 40% from March 2008 to March 2009, people felt far greater uncertainty about their economic future, so rates of saving increased while consumption declined.

Finally, Keynes noted that a variety of other factors combine to determine how much people save and spend. If household preferences about saving shift in a way that encourages consumption rather than saving, then AD will shift out to the right.

Link It Up

Visit this website (http://openstaxcollege.org/l/Diane_Rehm) for more information about how the recession affected various groups of people.

What Determines Investment Expenditure?

Spending on new capital goods is called investment expenditure. Investment falls into four categories: producer's durable equipment and software, new nonresidential structures (such as factories, offices, and retail locations), changes in inventories, and residential structures (such as single-family homes, townhouses, and apartment buildings). The first three types of investment are conducted by businesses, while the last is conducted by households.

Keynes's treatment of investment focuses on the key role of expectations about the future in influencing business decisions. When a business decides to make an investment in physical assets, like plants or equipment, or in intangible assets, like skills or a research and development project, that firm considers both the expected benefits of the investment (expectations of future profits) and the costs of the investment (interest rates).

- Expectations of future profits: The clearest driver of the benefits of an investment is expectations for future profits. When an economy is expected to grow, businesses perceive a growing market for their products. Their higher degree of business confidence will encourage new investment. For example, in the second half of the 1990s, U.S. investment levels surged from 18% of GDP in 1994 to 21% in 2000. However, when a recession started in 2001, U.S. investment levels quickly sank back to 18% of GDP by 2002.

- Interest rates also play a significant role in determining how much investment a firm will make. Just as individuals need to borrow money to purchase homes, so businesses need financing when they purchase big ticket items. The cost of investment thus includes the interest rate. Even if the firm has the funds, the interest rate measures the opportunity cost of purchasing business capital. Lower interest rates stimulate investment spending and higher interest rates reduce it.

Many factors can affect the expected profitability on investment. For example, if the price of energy declines, then investments that use energy as an input will yield higher profits. If government offers special incentives for investment (for example, through the tax code), then investment will look more attractive; conversely, if government removes special investment incentives from the tax code, or increases other business taxes, then investment will look less attractive. As Keynes noted, business investment is the most variable of all the components of aggregate demand.

What Determines Government Spending?

The third component of aggregate demand is spending by federal, state, and local governments. Although the United States is usually thought of as a market economy, government still plays a significant role in the economy. As we discuss in **Environmental Protection and Negative Externalities (http://cnx.org/content/m57254/**

latest/) and **Positive Externalities and Public Goods** (http://cnx.org/content/m57262/latest/) , government provides important public services such as national defense, transportation infrastructure, and education.

Keynes recognized that the government budget offered a powerful tool for influencing aggregate demand. Not only could AD be stimulated by more government spending (or reduced by less government spending), but consumption and investment spending could be influenced by lowering or raising tax rates. Indeed, Keynes concluded that during extreme times like deep recessions, only the government had the power and resources to move aggregate demand.

What Determines Net Exports?

Recall that exports are products produced domestically and sold abroad while imports are products produced abroad but purchased domestically. Since aggregate demand is defined as spending on domestic goods and services, export expenditures add to AD, while import expenditures subtract from AD.

Two sets of factors can cause shifts in export and import demand: changes in relative growth rates between countries and changes in relative prices between countries. The level of demand for a nation's exports tends to be most heavily affected by what is happening in the economies of the countries that would be purchasing those exports. For example, if major importers of American-made products like Canada, Japan, and Germany have recessions, exports of U.S. products to those countries are likely to decline. Conversely, the quantity of a nation's imports is directly affected by the amount of income in the domestic economy: more income will bring a higher level of imports.

Exports and imports can also be affected by relative prices of goods in domestic and international markets. If U.S. goods are relatively cheaper compared with goods made in other places, perhaps because a group of U.S. producers has mastered certain productivity breakthroughs, then U.S. exports are likely to rise. If U.S. goods become relatively more expensive, perhaps because a change in the exchange rate between the U.S. dollar and other currencies has pushed up the price of inputs to production in the United States, then exports from U.S. producers are likely to decline.

Table 11.1 summarizes the reasons given here for changes in aggregate demand.

Reasons for a Decrease in Aggregate Demand	Reasons for an Increase in Aggregate Demand
Consumption • Rise in taxes • Fall in income • Rise in interest • Desire to save more • Decrease in wealth • Fall in future expected income	**Consumption** • Decrease in taxes • Increase in income • Fall in interest rates • Desire to save less • Rise in wealth • Rise in future expected income
Investment • Fall in expected rate of return • Rise in interest rates • Drop in business confidence	**Investment** • Rise in expected rate of return • Drop in interest rates • Rise in business confidence
Government • Reduction in government spending • Increase in taxes	**Government** • Increase in government spending • Decrease in taxes

Table 11.1 Determinants of Aggregate Demand

Reasons for a Decrease in Aggregate Demand	Reasons for an Increase in Aggregate Demand
Net Exports • Decrease in foreign demand • Relative price increase of U.S. goods	*Net Exports* • Increase in foreign demand • Relative price drop of U.S. goods

Table 11.1 Determinants of Aggregate Demand

11.2 | The Building Blocks of Keynesian Analysis

By the end of this section, you will be able to:
- Evaluate the Keynesian view of recessions through an understanding of sticky wages and prices and the importance of aggregate demand
- Explain the coordination argument, menu costs, and macroeconomic externality
- Analyze the impact of the expenditure multiplier

Now that we have a clear understanding of what constitutes aggregate demand, we return to the Keynesian argument using the model of aggregate demand/aggregate supply (AD/AS). (For a similar treatment using Keynes' income-expenditure model, see the appendix on **The Expenditure-Output Model.**)

Keynesian economics focuses on explaining why recessions and depressions occur and offering a policy prescription for minimizing their effects. The Keynesian view of recession is based on two key building blocks. First, aggregate demand is not always automatically high enough to provide firms with an incentive to hire enough workers to reach full employment. Second, the macroeconomy may adjust only slowly to shifts in aggregate demand because of **sticky wages and prices**, which are wages and prices that do not respond to decreases or increases in demand. We will consider these two claims in turn, and then see how they are represented in the AD/AS model.

The first building block of the Keynesian diagnosis is that recessions occur when the level of household and business sector demand for goods and services is less than what is produced when labor is fully employed. In other words, the intersection of aggregate supply and aggregate demand occurs at a level of output less than the level of GDP consistent with full employment. Suppose the stock market crashes, as occurred in 1929. Or, suppose the housing market collapses, as occurred in 2008. In either case, household wealth will decline, and consumption expenditure will follow. Suppose businesses see that consumer spending is falling. That will reduce expectations of the profitability of investment, so businesses will decrease investment expenditure.

This seemed to be the case during the Great Depression, since the physical capacity of the economy to supply goods did not alter much. No flood or earthquake or other natural disaster ruined factories in 1929 or 1930. No outbreak of disease decimated the ranks of workers. No key input price, like the price of oil, soared on world markets. The U.S. economy in 1933 had just about the same factories, workers, and state of technology as it had had four years earlier in 1929—and yet the economy had shrunk dramatically. This also seems to be what happened in 2008.

As Keynes recognized, the events of the Depression contradicted Say's law that "supply creates its own demand." Although production capacity existed, the markets were not able to sell their products. As a result, real GDP was less than potential GDP.

Visit this website (http://openstaxcollege.org/l/expenditures) for raw data used to calculate GDP.

Wage and Price Stickiness

Keynes also pointed out that although AD fluctuated, prices and wages did not immediately respond as economists often expected. Instead, prices and wages are "sticky," making it difficult to restore the economy to full employment and potential GDP. Keynes emphasized one particular reason why wages were sticky: the **coordination argument**. This argument points out that, even if most people would be willing—at least hypothetically—to see a decline in their own wages in bad economic times as long as everyone else also experienced such a decline, a market-oriented economy has no obvious way to implement a plan of coordinated wage reductions. Unemployment proposed a number of reasons why wages might be sticky downward, most of which center on the argument that businesses avoid wage cuts because they may in one way or another depress morale and hurt the productivity of the existing workers.

Some modern economists have argued in a Keynesian spirit that, along with wages, other prices may be sticky, too. Many firms do not change their prices every day or even every month. When a firm considers changing prices, it must consider two sets of costs. First, changing prices uses company resources: managers must analyze the competition and market demand and decide what the new prices will be, sales materials must be updated, billing records will change, and product labels and price labels must be redone. Second, frequent price changes may leave customers confused or angry—especially if they find out that a product now costs more than expected. These costs of changing prices are called **menu costs**—like the costs of printing up a new set of menus with different prices in a restaurant. Prices do respond to forces of supply and demand, but from a macroeconomic perspective, the process of changing all prices throughout the economy takes time.

To understand the effect of sticky wages and prices in the economy, consider Figure 11.4 (a) illustrating the overall labor market, while Figure 11.4 (b) illustrates a market for a specific good or service. The original equilibrium (E_0) in each market occurs at the intersection of the demand curve (D_0) and supply curve (S_0). When aggregate demand declines, the demand for labor shifts to the left (to D_1) in Figure 11.4 (a) and the demand for goods shifts to the left (to D_1) in Figure 11.4 (b). However, because of sticky wages and prices, the wage remains at its original level (W_0) for a period of time and the price remains at its original level (P_0).

As a result, a situation of excess supply—where the quantity supplied exceeds the quantity demanded at the existing wage or price—exists in markets for both labor and goods, and Q_1 is less than Q_0 in both Figure 11.4 (a) and Figure 11.4 (b). When many labor markets and many goods markets all across the economy find themselves in this position, the economy is in a recession; that is, firms cannot sell what they wish to produce at the existing market price and do not wish to hire all who are willing to work at the existing market wage. The Clear It Up feature discusses this problem in more detail.

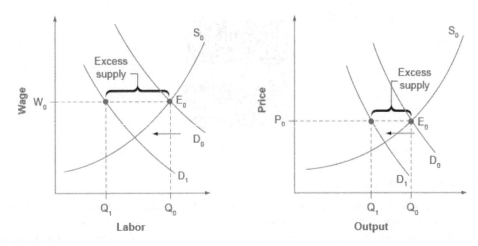

(a) Sticky wages in the labor market   (b) Sticky prices in the goods market

Figure 11.4 Sticky Prices and Falling Demand in the Labor and Goods Market In both (a) and (b), demand shifts left from D_0 to D_1. However, the wage in (a) and the price in (b) do not immediately decline. In (a), the quantity demanded of labor at the original wage (W_0) is Q_0, but with the new demand curve for labor (D_1), it will be Q_1. Similarly, in (b), the quantity demanded of goods at the original price (P_0) is Q_0, but at the new demand curve (D_1) it will be Q_1. An excess supply of labor will exist, which is called unemployment. An excess supply of goods will also exist, where the quantity demanded is substantially less than the quantity supplied. Thus, sticky wages and sticky prices, combined with a drop in demand, bring about unemployment and recession.

Why Is the Pace of Wage Adjustments Slow?

The recovery after the Great Recession in the United States has been slow, with wages stagnant, if not declining. In fact, many low-wage workers at McDonalds, Dominos, and Walmart have threatened to strike for higher wages. Their plight is part of a larger trend in job growth and pay in the post–recession recovery.

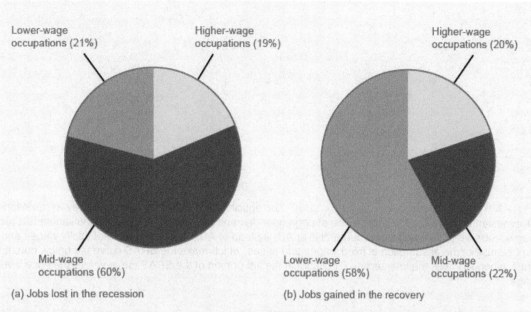

Figure 11.5 Jobs Lost/Gained in the Recession/Recovery Data in the aftermath of the Great Recession suggests that jobs lost were in mid-wage occupations, while jobs gained were in low-wage occupations.

The National Employment Law Project compiled data from the Bureau of Labor Statistics and found that, during the Great Recession, 60% of job losses were in medium-wage occupations. Most of them were replaced during the recovery period with lower-wage jobs in the service, retail, and food industries. This data is illustrated in Figure 11.5.

Wages in the service, retail, and food industries are at or near minimum wage and tend to be both downwardly and upwardly "sticky." Wages are downwardly sticky due to minimum wage laws; they may be upwardly sticky if insufficient competition in low-skilled labor markets enables employers to avoid raising wages that would reduce their profits. At the same time, however, the Consumer Price Index increased 11% between 2007 and 2012, pushing real wages down.

The Two Keynesian Assumptions in the AD/AS Model

These two Keynesian assumptions—the importance of aggregate demand in causing recession and the stickiness of wages and prices—are illustrated by the AD/AS diagram in Figure 11.6. Note that because of the stickiness of wages and prices, the aggregate supply curve is flatter than either supply curve (labor or specific good). In fact, if wages and prices were so sticky that they did not fall at all, the aggregate supply curve would be completely flat below potential GDP, as shown in Figure 11.6. This outcome is an important example of a **macroeconomic externality**, where what happens at the macro level is different from and inferior to what happens at the micro level. For example, a firm should respond to a decrease in demand for its product by cutting its price to increase sales. But if all firms experience a decrease in demand for their products, sticky prices in the aggregate prevent aggregate demand from rebounding (which would be shown as a movement along the AD curve in response to a lower price level).

The original equilibrium of this economy occurs where the aggregate demand function (AD_0) intersects with AS. Since this intersection occurs at potential GDP (Yp), the economy is operating at full employment. When aggregate demand shifts to the left, all the adjustment occurs through decreased real GDP. There is no decrease in the price level. Since the equilibrium occurs at Y_1, the economy experiences substantial unemployment.

Figure 11.6 A Keynesian Perspective of Recession The equilibrium (E_0) illustrates the two key assumptions behind Keynesian economics. The importance of aggregate demand is shown because this equilibrium is a recession which has occurred because aggregate demand is at AD_1 instead of AD_0. The importance of sticky wages and prices is shown because of the assumption of fixed wages and prices, which make the SRAS curve flat below potential GDP. Thus, when AD falls, the intersection E_1 occurs in the flat portion of the SRAS curve where the price level does not change.

The Expenditure Multiplier

A key concept in Keynesian economics is the **expenditure multiplier**. The expenditure multiplier is the idea that not only does spending affect the equilibrium level of GDP, but that spending is powerful. More precisely, it means that a change in spending causes a more than proportionate change in GDP.

$$\frac{\Delta Y}{\Delta \text{Spending}} > 1$$

The reason for the expenditure multiplier is that one person's spending becomes another person's income, which leads to additional spending and additional income, and so forth, so that the cumulative impact on GDP is larger than the initial increase in spending. While the multiplier is important for understanding the effectiveness of fiscal policy, it occurs whenever any autonomous increase in spending occurs. Additionally, the multiplier operates in a negative as well as a positive direction. Thus, when investment spending collapsed during the Great Depression, it caused a much larger decrease in real GDP. The size of the multiplier is critical and was a key element in recent discussions of the effectiveness of the Obama administration's fiscal stimulus package, officially titled the American Recovery and Reinvestment Act of 2009.

11.3 | The Expenditure-Output (or Keynesian Cross) Model

The fundamental ideas of Keynesian economics were developed before the AD/AS model was popularized. From the 1930s until the 1970s, Keynesian economics was usually explained with a different model, known as the expenditure-output approach. This approach is strongly rooted in the fundamental assumptions of Keynesian economics: it focuses on the total amount of spending in the economy, with no explicit mention of aggregate supply or of the price level (although as you will see, it is possible to draw some inferences about aggregate supply and price levels based on the diagram).

The Axes of the Expenditure-Output Diagram

The expenditure-output model, sometimes also called the Keynesian cross diagram, determines the equilibrium level of real GDP by the point where the total or aggregate expenditures in the economy are equal to the amount of output produced. The axes of the Keynesian cross diagram presented in **Figure 11.7** show real GDP on the horizontal axis as a measure of output and aggregate expenditures on the vertical axis as a measure of spending.

Figure 11.7 The Expenditure-Output Diagram The aggregate expenditure-output model shows aggregate expenditures on the vertical axis and real GDP on the horizontal axis. A vertical line shows potential GDP where full employment occurs. The 45-degree line shows all points where aggregate expenditures and output are equal. The aggregate expenditure schedule shows how total spending or aggregate expenditure increases as output or real GDP rises. The intersection of the aggregate expenditure schedule and the 45-degree line will be the equilibrium. Equilibrium occurs at E_0, where aggregate expenditure AE_0 is equal to the output level Y_0.

Remember that GDP can be thought of in several equivalent ways: it measures both the value of spending on final goods and also the value of the production of final goods. All sales of the final goods and services that make up GDP will eventually end up as income for workers, for managers, and for investors and owners of firms. The sum of all the income received for contributing resources to GDP is called national income (Y). At some points in the discussion that follows, it will be useful to refer to real GDP as "national income." Both axes are measured in real (inflation-adjusted) terms.

The Potential GDP Line and the 45-degree Line

The Keynesian cross diagram contains two lines that serve as conceptual guideposts to orient the discussion. The first is a vertical line showing the level of potential GDP. Potential GDP means the same thing here that it means in the AD/AS diagrams: it refers to the quantity of output that the economy can produce with full employment of its labor and physical capital.

The second conceptual line on the Keynesian cross diagram is the 45-degree line, which starts at the origin and reaches up and to the right. A line that stretches up at a 45-degree angle represents the set of points (1, 1), (2, 2), (3, 3) and so on, where the measurement on the vertical axis is equal to the measurement on the horizontal axis. In this diagram, the 45-degree line shows the set of points where the level of aggregate expenditure in the economy, measured on the vertical axis, is equal to the level of output or national income in the economy, measured by GDP on the horizontal axis.

When the macroeconomy is in equilibrium, it must be true that the aggregate expenditures in the economy are equal to the real GDP—because by definition, GDP is the measure of what is spent on final sales of goods and services in the economy. Thus, the equilibrium calculated with a Keynesian cross diagram will always end up where aggregate expenditure and output are equal—which will only occur along the 45-degree line.

The Aggregate Expenditure Schedule

The final ingredient of the Keynesian cross or expenditure-output diagram is the aggregate expenditure schedule, which will show the total expenditures in the economy for each level of real GDP. The intersection of the aggregate expenditure line with the 45-degree line—at point E_0 in **Figure 11.7**—will show the equilibrium for the economy, because it is the point where aggregate expenditure is equal to output or real GDP. After developing an understanding of what the aggregate expenditures schedule means, we will return to this equilibrium and how to interpret it.

Building the Aggregate Expenditure Schedule

Aggregate expenditure is the key to the expenditure-income model. The aggregate expenditure schedule shows, either in the form of a table or a graph, how aggregate expenditures in the economy rise as real GDP or national income rises.

Thus, in thinking about the components of the aggregate expenditure line—consumption, investment, government spending, exports and imports—the key question is how expenditures in each category will adjust as national income rises.

Consumption as a Function of National Income

How do consumption expenditures increase as national income rises? People can do two things with their income: consume it or save it (for the moment, let's ignore the need to pay taxes with some of it). Each person who receives an additional dollar faces this choice. The marginal propensity to consume (MPC), is the share of the additional dollar of income a person decides to devote to consumption expenditures. The marginal propensity to save (MPS) is the share of the additional dollar a person decides to save. It must always hold true that:

$$MPC + MPS = 1$$

For example, if the marginal propensity to consume out of the marginal amount of income earned is 0.9, then the marginal propensity to save is 0.1.

With this relationship in mind, consider the relationship among income, consumption, and savings shown in **Figure 11.8**. (Note that we use "Aggregate Expenditure" on the vertical axis in this and the following figures, because all consumption expenditures are parts of aggregate expenditures.)

An assumption commonly made in this model is that even if income were zero, people would have to consume something. In this example, consumption would be $600 even if income were zero. Then, the MPC is 0.8 and the MPS is 0.2. Thus, when income increases by $1,000, consumption rises by $800 and savings rises by $200. At an income of $4,000, total consumption will be the $600 that would be consumed even without any income, plus $4,000 multiplied by the marginal propensity to consume of 0.8, or $ 3,200, for a total of $ 3,800. The total amount of consumption and saving must always add up to the total amount of income. (Exactly how a situation of zero income and negative savings would work in practice is not important, because even low-income societies are not literally at zero income, so the point is hypothetical.) This relationship between income and consumption, illustrated in **Figure 11.8** and **Table 11.2**, is called the consumption function.

Figure 11.8 The Consumption Function In the expenditure-output model, how does consumption increase with the level of national income? Output on the horizontal axis is conceptually the same as national income, since the value of all final output that is produced and sold must be income to someone, somewhere in the economy. At a national income level of zero, $600 is consumed. Then, each time income rises by $1,000, consumption rises by $800, because in this example, the marginal propensity to consume is 0.8.

The pattern of consumption shown in Table 11.2 is plotted in Figure 11.8. To calculate consumption, multiply the income level by 0.8, for the marginal propensity to consume, and add $600, for the amount that would be consumed even if income was zero. Consumption plus savings must be equal to income.

Income	Consumption	Savings
$0	$600	−$600
$1,000	$1,400	−$400
$2,000	$2,200	−$200
$3,000	$3,000	$0
$4,000	$3,800	$200
$5,000	$4,600	$400
$6,000	$5,400	$600
$7,000	$6,200	$800
$8,000	$7,000	$1,000
$9,000	$7,800	$1,200

Table 11.2 The Consumption Function

However, a number of factors other than income can also cause the entire consumption function to shift. These factors were summarized in the earlier discussion of consumption, and listed in Table 11.2. When the consumption function moves, it can shift in two ways: either the entire consumption function can move up or down in a parallel manner, or the slope of the consumption function can shift so that it becomes steeper or flatter. For example, if a tax cut leads consumers to spend more, but does not affect their marginal propensity to consume, it would cause an upward shift to a new consumption function that is parallel to the original one. However, a change in household preferences for saving that reduced the marginal propensity to save would cause the slope of the consumption function to become steeper: that is, if the savings rate is lower, then every increase in income leads to a larger rise in consumption.

Investment as a Function of National Income

Investment decisions are forward-looking, based on expected rates of return. Precisely because investment decisions depend primarily on perceptions about future economic conditions, they do *not* depend primarily on the level of GDP in the current year. Thus, on a Keynesian cross diagram, the investment function can be drawn as a horizontal line, at a fixed level of expenditure. Figure 11.9 shows an investment function where the level of investment is, for the sake of concreteness, set at the specific level of 500. Just as a consumption function shows the relationship between consumption levels and real GDP (or national income), the investment function shows the relationship between investment levels and real GDP.

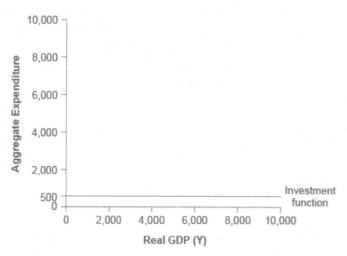

Figure 11.9 The Investment Function The investment function is drawn as a flat line because investment is based on interest rates and expectations about the future, and so it does not change with the level of current national income. In this example, investment expenditures are at a level of 500. However, changes in factors like technological opportunities, expectations about near-term economic growth, and interest rates would all cause the investment function to shift up or down.

The appearance of the investment function as a horizontal line does not mean that the level of investment never moves. It means only that in the context of this two-dimensional diagram, the level of investment on the vertical aggregate expenditure axis does not vary according to the current level of real GDP on the horizontal axis. However, all the other factors that vary investment—new technological opportunities, expectations about near-term economic growth, interest rates, the price of key inputs, and tax incentives for investment—can cause the horizontal investment function to shift up or down.

Government Spending and Taxes as a Function of National Income

In the Keynesian cross diagram, government spending appears as a horizontal line, as in **Figure 11.10**, where government spending is set at a level of 1,300. As in the case of investment spending, this horizontal line does not mean that government spending is unchanging. It means only that government spending changes when Congress decides on a change in the budget, rather than shifting in a predictable way with the current size of the real GDP shown on the horizontal axis.

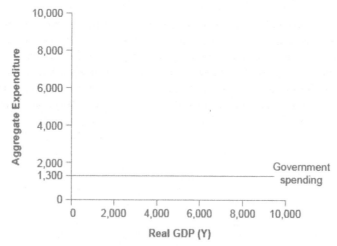

Figure 11.10 The Government Spending Function The level of government spending is determined by political factors, not by the level of real GDP in a given year. Thus, government spending is drawn as a horizontal line. In this example, government spending is at a level of 1,300. Congressional decisions to increase government spending will cause this horizontal line to shift up, while decisions to reduce spending would cause it to shift down.

The situation of taxes is different because taxes often rise or fall with the volume of economic activity. For example, income taxes are based on the level of income earned and sales taxes are based on the amount of sales made, and both income and sales tend to be higher when the economy is growing and lower when the economy is in a recession. For the purposes of constructing the basic Keynesian cross diagram, it is helpful to view taxes as a proportionate share of GDP. In the United States, for example, taking federal, state, and local taxes together, government typically collects about 30–35 % of income as taxes.

Table 11.3 revises the earlier table on the consumption function so that it takes taxes into account. The first column shows national income. The second column calculates taxes, which in this example are set at a rate of 30%, or 0.3. The third column shows after-tax income; that is, total income minus taxes. The fourth column then calculates consumption in the same manner as before: multiply after-tax income by 0.8, representing the marginal propensity to consume, and then add $600, for the amount that would be consumed even if income was zero. When taxes are included, the marginal propensity to consume is reduced by the amount of the tax rate, so each additional dollar of income results in a smaller increase in consumption than before taxes. For this reason, the consumption function, with taxes included, is flatter than the consumption function without taxes, as Figure 11.11 shows.

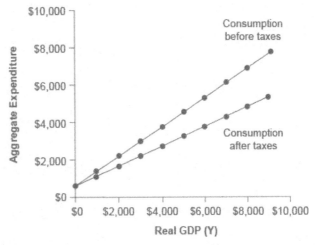

Figure 11.11 The Consumption Function Before and After Taxes The upper line repeats the consumption function from Figure 11.8. The lower line shows the consumption function if taxes must first be paid on income, and then consumption is based on after-tax income.

Income	Taxes	After-Tax Income	Consumption	Savings
$0	$0	$0	$600	–$600
$1,000	$300	$700	$1,160	–$460
$2,000	$600	$1,400	$1,720	–$320
$3,000	$900	$2,100	$2,280	–$180
$4,000	$1,200	$2,800	$2,840	–$40
$5,000	$1,500	$3,500	$3,400	$100
$6,000	$1,800	$4,200	$3,960	$240
$7,000	$2,100	$4,900	$4,520	$380
$8,000	$2,400	$5,600	$5,080	$520

Table 11.3 The Consumption Function Before and After Taxes

Income	Taxes	After-Tax Income	Consumption	Savings
$9,000	$2,700	$6,300	$5,640	$660

Table 11.3 The Consumption Function Before and After Taxes

Exports and Imports as a Function of National Income

The export function, which shows how exports change with the level of a country's own real GDP, is drawn as a horizontal line, as in the example in Figure 11.12 (a) where exports are drawn at a level of $840. Again, as in the case of investment spending and government spending, drawing the export function as horizontal does not imply that exports never change. It just means that they do not change because of what is on the horizontal axis—that is, a country's own level of domestic production—and instead are shaped by the level of aggregate demand in other countries. More demand for exports from other countries would cause the export function to shift up; less demand for exports from other countries would cause it to shift down.

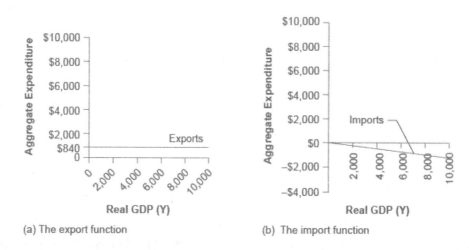

(a) The export function

(b) The import function

Figure 11.12 The Export and Import Functions (a) The export function is drawn as a horizontal line because exports are determined by the buying power of other countries and thus do not change with the size of the domestic economy. In this example, exports are set at 840. However, exports can shift up or down, depending on buying patterns in other countries. (b) The import function is drawn in negative territory because expenditures on imported products are a subtraction from expenditures in the domestic economy. In this example, the marginal propensity to import is 0.1, so imports are calculated by multiplying the level of income by –0.1.

Imports are drawn in the Keynesian cross diagram as a downward-sloping line, with the downward slope determined by the marginal propensity to import (MPI), out of national income. In Figure 11.12 (b), the marginal propensity to import is 0.1. Thus, if real GDP is $5,000, imports are $500; if national income is $6,000, imports are $600, and so on. The import function is drawn as downward sloping and negative, because it represents a subtraction from the aggregate expenditures in the domestic economy. A change in the marginal propensity to import, perhaps as a result of changes in preferences, would alter the slope of the import function.

Work It Out ─○─○─○

Using an Algebraic Approach to the Expenditure-Output Model

In the expenditure-output or Keynesian cross model, the equilibrium occurs where the aggregate expenditure line (AE line) crosses the 45-degree line. Given algebraic equations for two lines, the point where they cross can be readily calculated. Imagine an economy with the following characteristics.

Y = Real GDP or national income

T = Taxes = 0.3Y

C = Consumption = 140 + 0.9(Y – T)

I = Investment = 400

G = Government spending = 800

X = Exports = 600

M = Imports = 0.15Y

Step 1. Determine the aggregate expenditure function. In this case, it is:

$$\begin{aligned} AE &= C + I + G + X - M \\ AE &= 140 + 0.9(Y - T) + 400 + 800 + 600 - 0.15Y \end{aligned}$$

Step 2. The equation for the 45-degree line is the set of points where GDP or national income on the horizontal axis is equal to aggregate expenditure on the vertical axis. Thus, the equation for the 45-degree line is: AE = Y.

Step 3. The next step is to solve these two equations for Y (or AE, since they will be equal to each other). Substitute Y for AE:

$$Y = 140 + 0.9(Y - T) + 400 + 800 + 600 - 0.15Y$$

Step 4. Insert the term 0.3Y for the tax rate T. This produces an equation with only one variable, Y.

Step 5. Work through the algebra and solve for Y.

$$\begin{aligned} Y &= 140 + 0.9(Y - 0.3Y) + 400 + 800 + 600 - 0.15Y \\ Y &= 140 + 0.9Y - 0.27Y + 1800 - 0.15Y \\ Y &= 1940 + 0.48Y \\ Y - 0.48Y &= 1940 \\ 0.52Y &= 1940 \\ \frac{0.52Y}{0.52} &= \frac{1940}{0.52} \\ Y &= 3730 \end{aligned}$$

This algebraic framework is flexible and useful in predicting how economic events and policy actions will affect real GDP.

Step 6. Say, for example, that because of changes in the relative prices of domestic and foreign goods, the marginal propensity to import falls to 0.1. Calculate the equilibrium output when the marginal propensity to import is changed to 0.1.

$$\begin{aligned} Y &= 140 + 0.9(Y - 0.3Y) + 400 + 800 + 600 - 0.1Y \\ Y &= 1940 - 0.53Y \\ 0.47Y &= 1940 \\ Y &= 4127 \end{aligned}$$

Step 7. Because of a surge of business confidence, investment rises to 500. Calculate the equilibrium output.

$$\begin{aligned} Y &= 140 + 0.9(Y - 0.3Y) + 500 + 800 + 600 - 0.15Y \\ Y &= 2040 + 0.48Y \\ Y - 0.48Y &= 2040 \\ 0.52Y &= 2040 \\ Y &= 3923 \end{aligned}$$

For issues of policy, the key questions would be how to adjust government spending levels or tax rates so that the equilibrium level of output is the full employment level. In this case, let the economic parameters be:

Y = National income

T = Taxes = 0.3Y

C = Consumption = 200 + 0.9(Y – T)

I = Investment = 600

G = Government spending = 1,000

X = Exports = 600

Y = Imports = 0.1(Y – T)

Step 8. Calculate the equilibrium for this economy (remember Y = AE).

$$Y = 200 + 0.9(Y - 0.3Y) + 600 + 1000 + 600 - 0.1(Y - 0.3Y)$$
$$Y - 0.63Y + 0.07Y = 2400$$
$$0.44Y = 2400$$
$$Y = 5454$$

Step 9. Assume that the full employment level of output is 6,000. What level of government spending would be necessary to reach that level? To answer this question, plug in 6,000 as equal to Y, but leave G as a variable, and solve for G. Thus:

$$6000 = 200 + 0.9(6000 - 0.3(6000)) + 600 + G + 600 - 0.1(6000 - 0.3(6000))$$

Step 10. Solve this problem arithmetically. The answer is: G = 1,240. In other words, increasing government spending by 240, from its original level of 1,000, to 1,240, would raise output to the full employment level of GDP.

Indeed, the question of how much to increase government spending so that equilibrium output will rise from 5,454 to 6,000 can be answered without working through the algebra, just by using the multiplier formula. The multiplier equation in this case is:

$$\frac{1}{1 - 0.56} = 2.27$$

Thus, to raise output by 546 would require an increase in government spending of 546/2.27=240, which is the same as the answer derived from the algebraic calculation.

This algebraic framework is highly flexible. For example, taxes can be treated as a total set by political considerations (like government spending) and not dependent on national income. Imports might be based on before-tax income, not after-tax income. For certain purposes, it may be helpful to analyze the economy without exports and imports. A more complicated approach could divide up consumption, investment, government, exports and imports into smaller categories, or to build in some variability in the rates of taxes, savings, and imports. A wise economist will shape the model to fit the specific question under investigation.

Building the Combined Aggregate Expenditure Function

All the components of aggregate demand—consumption, investment, government spending, and the trade balance—are now in place to build the Keynesian cross diagram. Figure 11.13 builds up an aggregate expenditure function, based on the numerical illustrations of C, I, G, X, and M that have been used throughout this text. The first three columns in Table 11.4 are lifted from the earlier Table 11.3, which showed how to bring taxes into the consumption function. The first column is real GDP or national income, which is what appears on the horizontal axis of the income-expenditure diagram. The second column calculates after-tax income, based on the assumption, in this case, that 30% of real GDP is collected in taxes. The third column is based on an MPC of 0.8, so that as after-tax income rises by $700 from one row to the next, consumption rises by $560 (700 × 0.8) from one row to the next. Investment, government spending, and exports do not change with the level of current national income. In the previous discussion, investment was $500, government spending was $1,300, and exports were $840, for a total of $2,640. This total is shown in the fourth column. Imports are 0.1 of real GDP in this example, and the level of imports is calculated in the fifth column. The final column, aggregate expenditures, sums up C + I + G + X – M. This aggregate expenditure line is illustrated in Figure 11.13.

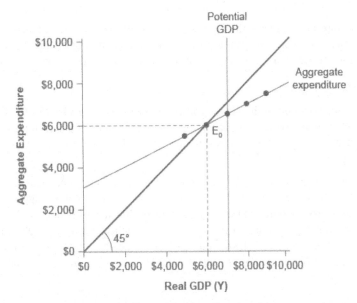

Figure 11.13 A Keynesian Cross Diagram Each combination of national income and aggregate expenditure (after-tax consumption, government spending, investment, exports, and imports) is graphed. The equilibrium occurs where aggregate expenditure is equal to national income; this occurs where the aggregate expenditure schedule crosses the 45-degree line, at a real GDP of $6,000. Potential GDP in this example is $7,000, so the equilibrium is occurring at a level of output or real GDP below the potential GDP level.

National Income	After-Tax Income	Consumption	Government Spending + Investment + Exports	Imports	Aggregate Expenditure
$3,000	$2,100	$2,280	$2,640	$300	$4,620
$4,000	$2,800	$2,840	$2,640	$400	$5,080
$5,000	$3,500	$3,400	$2,640	$500	$5,540
$6,000	$4,200	$3,960	$2,640	$600	$6,000
$7,000	$4,900	$4,520	$2,640	$700	$6,460
$8,000	$5,600	$5,080	$2,640	$800	$6,920
$9,000	$6,300	$5,640	$2,640	$900	$7,380

Table 11.4 National Income-Aggregate Expenditure Equilibrium

The aggregate expenditure function is formed by stacking on top of each other the consumption function (after taxes), the investment function, the government spending function, the export function, and the import function. The point at which the aggregate expenditure function intersects the vertical axis will be determined by the levels of investment, government, and export expenditures—which do not vary with national income. The upward slope of the aggregate expenditure function will be determined by the marginal propensity to save, the tax rate, and the marginal propensity to import. A higher marginal propensity to save, a higher tax rate, and a higher marginal propensity to import will all make the slope of the aggregate expenditure function flatter—because out of any extra income, more is going to savings or taxes or imports and less to spending on domestic goods and services.

The equilibrium occurs where national income is equal to aggregate expenditure, which is shown on the graph as the point where the aggregate expenditure schedule crosses the 45-degree line. In this example, the equilibrium occurs at 6,000. This equilibrium can also be read off the table under the figure; it is the level of national income where aggregate expenditure is equal to national income.

Equilibrium in the Keynesian Cross Model

With the aggregate expenditure line in place, the next step is to relate it to the two other elements of the Keynesian cross diagram. Thus, the first subsection interprets the intersection of the aggregate expenditure function and the 45-degree line, while the next subsection relates this point of intersection to the potential GDP line.

Where Equilibrium Occurs

The point where the aggregate expenditure line that is constructed from C + I + G + X – M crosses the 45-degree line will be the equilibrium for the economy. It is the only point on the aggregate expenditure line where the total amount being spent on aggregate demand equals the total level of production. In **Figure 11.13**, this point of equilibrium (E_0) happens at 6,000, which can also be read off **Table 11.4**.

The meaning of "equilibrium" remains the same; that is, equilibrium is a point of balance where no incentive exists to shift away from that outcome. To understand why the point of intersection between the aggregate expenditure function and the 45-degree line is a macroeconomic equilibrium, consider what would happen if an economy found itself to the right of the equilibrium point E, say point H in **Figure 11.14**, where output is higher than the equilibrium. At point H, the level of aggregate expenditure is below the 45-degree line, so that the level of aggregate expenditure in the economy is less than the level of output. As a result, at point H, output is piling up unsold—not a sustainable state of affairs.

Figure 11.14 Equilibrium in the Keynesian Cross Diagram If output was above the equilibrium level, at H, then the real output is greater than the aggregate expenditure in the economy. This pattern cannot hold, because it would mean that goods are produced but piling up unsold. If output was below the equilibrium level at L, then aggregate expenditure would be greater than output. This pattern cannot hold either, because it would mean that spending exceeds the number of goods being produced. Only point E can be at equilibrium, where output, or national income and aggregate expenditure, are equal. The equilibrium (E) must lie on the 45-degree line, which is the set of points where national income and aggregate expenditure are equal.

Conversely, consider the situation where the level of output is at point L—where real output is lower than the equilibrium. In that case, the level of aggregate demand in the economy is above the 45-degree line, indicating that the level of aggregate expenditure in the economy is greater than the level of output. When the level of aggregate demand has emptied the store shelves, it cannot be sustained, either. Firms will respond by increasing their level of production. Thus, the equilibrium must be the point where the amount produced and the amount spent are in balance, at the intersection of the aggregate expenditure function and the 45-degree line.

Work It Out ⚬—⚬—⚬

Finding Equilibrium

Table 11.5 gives some information on an economy. The Keynesian model assumes that there is some level of consumption even without income. That amount is $236 − $216 = $20. $20 will be consumed when national income equals zero. Assume that taxes are 0.2 of real GDP. Let the marginal propensity to save of after-tax income be 0.1. The level of investment is $70, the level of government spending is $80, and the level of exports is $50. Imports are 0.2 of after-tax income.

Given these values, you need to complete Table 11.5 and then answer these questions:

- What is the consumption function?
- What is the equilibrium?
- Why is a national income of $300 not at equilibrium?
- How do expenditures and output compare at this point?

National Income	Taxes	After-Tax income	Consumption	I + G + X	Imports	Aggregate Expenditures
$300			$236			
$400						
$500						
$600						
$700						

Table 11.5

Step 1. Calculate the amount of taxes for each level of national income(reminder: GDP = national income) for each level of national income using the following as an example:

$$\begin{array}{ll} \text{National Income (Y)} & \$300 \\ \text{Taxes} = 0.2 \text{ or } 20\% & \times 0.2 \\ \text{Tax amount (T)} & \$60 \end{array}$$

Step 2. Calculate after-tax income by subtracting the tax amount from national income for each level of national income using the following as an example:

$$\begin{array}{ll} \text{National income minus taxes} & \$300 \\ & -\$60 \\ \text{After-tax income} & \$240 \end{array}$$

Step 3. Calculate consumption. The marginal propensity to save is given as 0.1. This means that the marginal propensity to consume is 0.9, since MPS + MPC = 1. Therefore, multiply 0.9 by the after-tax income amount using the following as an example:

$$\begin{array}{ll} \text{After-tax Income} & \$240 \\ \text{MPC} & \times 0.9 \\ \text{Consumption} & \$216 \end{array}$$

Step 4. Consider why the table shows consumption of $236 in the first row. As mentioned earlier, the Keynesian model assumes that there is some level of consumption even without income. That amount is $236 − $216 = $20.

Step 5. There is now enough information to write the consumption function. The consumption function is found by figuring out the level of consumption that will happen when income is zero.

Remember that:

$$C = \text{Consumption when national income is zero} + \text{MPC (after-tax income)}$$

Let C represent the consumption function, Y represent national income, and T represent taxes.

$$
\begin{aligned}
C &= \$20 + 0.9(Y - T) \\
&= \$20 + 0.9(\$300 - \$60) \\
&= \$236
\end{aligned}
$$

Step 6. Use the consumption function to find consumption at each level of national income.

Step 7. Add investment (I), government spending (G), and exports (X). Remember that these do not change as national income changes:

Step 8. Find imports, which are 0.2 of after-tax income at each level of national income. For example:

After-tax income	$240
Imports of 0.2 or 20% of Y – T	× 0.2
Imports	$48

Step 9. Find aggregate expenditure by adding C + I + G + X – I for each level of national income. Your completed table should look like Table 11.6.

National Income (Y)	Tax = 0.2 × Y (T)	After-Tax income (Y – T)	Consumption C = $20 + 0.9(Y – T)	I + G + X	Minus Imports (M)	Aggregate Expenditures AE = C + I + G + X – M
$300	$60	$240	$236	$200	$48	$388
$400	$80	$320	$308	$200	$64	$444
$500	$100	$400	$380	$200	$80	$500
$600	$120	$480	$452	$200	$96	$556
$700	$140	$560	$524	$200	$112	$612

Table 11.6

Step 10. Answer the question: What is equilibrium? Equilibrium occurs where AE = Y. Table 11.6 shows that equilibrium occurs where national income equals aggregate expenditure at $500.

Step 11. Find equilibrium mathematically, knowing that national income is equal to aggregate expenditure.

$$
\begin{aligned}
Y &= AE \\
&= C + I + G + X - M \\
&= \$20 + 0.9(Y - T) + \$70 + \$80 + \$50 - 0.2(Y - T) \\
&= \$220 + 0.9(Y - T) - 0.2(Y - T)
\end{aligned}
$$

Since T is 0.2 of national income, substitute T with 0.2 Y so that:

$$
\begin{aligned}
Y &= \$220 + 0.9(Y - 0.2Y) - 0.2(Y - 0.2Y) \\
&= \$220 + 0.9Y - 0.18Y - 0.2Y + 0.04Y \\
&= \$220 + 0.56Y
\end{aligned}
$$

Solve for Y.

$$\begin{aligned}
Y &= \$220 + 0.56Y \\
Y - 0.56Y &= \$220 \\
0.44Y &= \$220 \\
\frac{0.44Y}{0.44} &= \frac{\$220}{0.44} \\
Y &= \$500
\end{aligned}$$

Step 12. Answer this question: Why is a national income of $300 not an equilibrium? At national income of $300, aggregate expenditures are $388.

Step 13. Answer this question: How do expenditures and output compare at this point? Aggregate expenditures cannot exceed output (GDP) in the long run, since there would not be enough goods to be bought.

Recessionary and Inflationary Gaps

In the Keynesian cross diagram, if the aggregate expenditure line intersects the 45-degree line at the level of potential GDP, then the economy is in sound shape. There is no recession, and unemployment is low. But there is no guarantee that the equilibrium will occur at the potential GDP level of output. The equilibrium might be higher or lower.

For example, Figure 11.15 (a) illustrates a situation where the aggregate expenditure line intersects the 45-degree line at point E_0, which is a real GDP of $6,000, and which is below the potential GDP of $7,000. In this situation, the level of aggregate expenditure is too low for GDP to reach its full employment level, and unemployment will occur.

The distance between an output level like E_0 that is below potential GDP and the level of potential GDP is called a recessionary gap. Because the equilibrium level of real GDP is so low, firms will not wish to hire the full employment number of workers, and unemployment will be high.

(a) Policy to address a recessionary gap.   (b) Policy to address an inflationary gap.

Figure 11.15 Addressing Recessionary and Inflationary Gaps (a) If the equilibrium occurs at an output below potential GDP, then a recessionary gap exists. The policy solution to a recessionary gap is to shift the aggregate expenditure schedule up from AE_0 to AE_1, using policies like tax cuts or government spending increases. Then the new equilibrium E_1 occurs at potential GDP. (b) If the equilibrium occurs at an output above potential GDP, then an inflationary gap exists. The policy solution to an inflationary gap is to shift the aggregate expenditure schedule down from AE_0 to AE_1, using policies like tax increases or spending cuts. Then, the new equilibrium E_1 occurs at potential GDP.

What might cause a recessionary gap? Anything that shifts the aggregate expenditure line down is a potential cause of recession, including a decline in consumption, a rise in savings, a fall in investment, a drop in government spending or a rise in taxes, or a fall in exports or a rise in imports. Moreover, an economy that is at equilibrium with a recessionary gap may just stay there and suffer high unemployment for a long time; remember, the meaning of equilibrium is that there is no particular adjustment of prices or quantities in the economy to chase the recession away.

The appropriate response to a recessionary gap is for the government to reduce taxes or increase spending so that the aggregate expenditure function shifts up from AE_0 to AE_1. When this shift occurs, the new equilibrium E_1 now occurs at potential GDP as shown in **Figure 11.15** (a).

Conversely, **Figure 11.15** (b) shows a situation where the aggregate expenditure schedule (AE_0) intersects the 45-degree line above potential GDP. The gap between the level of real GDP at the equilibrium E_0 and potential GDP is called an inflationary gap. The inflationary gap also requires a bit of interpreting. After all, a naïve reading of the Keynesian cross diagram might suggest that if the aggregate expenditure function is just pushed up high enough, real GDP can be as large as desired—even doubling or tripling the potential GDP level of the economy. This implication is clearly wrong. An economy faces some supply-side limits on how much it can produce at a given time with its existing quantities of workers, physical and human capital, technology, and market institutions.

The inflationary gap should be interpreted, not as a literal prediction of how large real GDP will be, but as a statement of how much extra aggregate expenditure is in the economy beyond what is needed to reach potential GDP. An inflationary gap suggests that because the economy cannot produce enough goods and services to absorb this level of aggregate expenditures, the spending will instead cause an inflationary increase in the price level. In this way, even though changes in the price level do not appear explicitly in the Keynesian cross equation, the notion of inflation is implicit in the concept of the inflationary gap.

The appropriate Keynesian response to an inflationary gap is shown in **Figure 11.15** (b). The original intersection of aggregate expenditure line AE_0 and the 45-degree line occurs at $8,000, which is above the level of potential GDP at $7,000. If AE_0 shifts down to AE_1, so that the new equilibrium is at E_1, then the economy will be at potential GDP without pressures for inflationary price increases. The government can achieve a downward shift in aggregate expenditure by increasing taxes on consumers or firms, or by reducing government expenditures.

The Multiplier Effect

The Keynesian policy prescription has one final twist. Assume that for a certain economy, the intersection of the aggregate expenditure function and the 45-degree line is at a GDP of 700, while the level of potential GDP for this economy is $800. By how much does government spending need to be increased so that the economy reaches the full employment GDP? The obvious answer might seem to be $800 – $700 = $100; so raise government spending by $100. But that answer is incorrect. A change of, for example, $100 in government expenditures will have an effect of more than $100 on the equilibrium level of real GDP. The reason is that a change in aggregate expenditures circles through the economy: households buy from firms, firms pay workers and suppliers, workers and suppliers buy goods from other firms, those firms pay their workers and suppliers, and so on. In this way, the original change in aggregate expenditures is actually spent more than once. This is called the multiplier effect: An initial increase in spending, cycles repeatedly through the economy and has a larger impact than the initial dollar amount spent.

How Does the Multiplier Work?

To understand how the multiplier effect works, return to the example in which the current equilibrium in the Keynesian cross diagram is a real GDP of $700, or $100 short of the $800 needed to be at full employment, potential GDP. If the government spends $100 to close this gap, someone in the economy receives that spending and can treat it as income. Assume that those who receive this income pay 30% in taxes, save 10% of after-tax income, spend 10% of total income on imports, and then spend the rest on domestically produced goods and services.

As shown in the calculations in **Figure 11.16** and **Table 11.7**, out of the original $100 in government spending, $53 is left to spend on domestically produced goods and services. That $53 which was spent, becomes income to someone, somewhere in the economy. Those who receive that income also pay 30% in taxes, save 10% of after-tax income, and spend 10% of total income on imports, as shown in **Figure 11.16**, so that an additional $28.09 (that is, $0.53 \times 53) is spent in the third round. The people who receive that income then pay taxes, save, and buy imports, and the amount spent in the fourth round is $14.89 (that is, $0.53 \times 28.09).

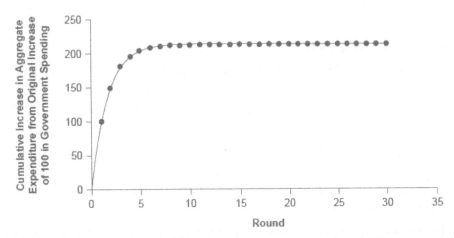

Figure 11.16 The Multiplier Effect An original increase of government spending of $100 causes a rise in aggregate expenditure of $100. But that $100 is income to others in the economy, and after they save, pay taxes, and buy imports, they spend $53 of that $100 in a second round. In turn, that $53 is income to others. Thus, the original government spending of $100 is multiplied by these cycles of spending, but the impact of each successive cycle gets smaller and smaller. Given the numbers in this example, the original government spending increase of $100 raises aggregate expenditure by $213; therefore, the multiplier in this example is $213/$100 = 2.13.

Original increase in aggregate expenditure from government spending	100
Which is income to people throughout the economy: Pay 30% in taxes. Save 10% of after-tax income. Spend 10% of income on imports. Second-round increase of…	70 – 7 – 10 = 53
Which is $53 of income to people through the economy: Pay 30% in taxes. Save 10% of after-tax income. Spend 10% of income on imports. Third-round increase of…	37.1 – 3.71 – 5.3 = 28.09
Which is $28.09 of income to people through the economy: Pay 30% in taxes. Save 10% of after-tax income. Spend 10% of income on imports. Fourth-round increase of…	19.663 – 1.96633 – 2.809 = 14.89

Table 11.7 Calculating the Multiplier Effect

Thus, over the first four rounds of aggregate expenditures, the impact of the original increase in government spending of $100 creates a rise in aggregate expenditures of $100 + $53 + $28.09 + $14.89 = $195.98. **Figure 11.16** shows these total aggregate expenditures after these first four rounds, and then the figure shows the total aggregate expenditures after 30 rounds. The additional boost to aggregate expenditures is shrinking in each round of consumption. After about 10 rounds, the additional increments are very small indeed—nearly invisible to the naked eye. After 30 rounds, the additional increments in each round are so small that they have no practical consequence. After 30 rounds, the cumulative value of the initial boost in aggregate expenditure is approximately $213. Thus, the government spending increase of $100 eventually, after many cycles, produced an increase of $213 in aggregate expenditure and real GDP. In this example, the multiplier is $213/$100 = 2.13.

Calculating the Multiplier

Fortunately for everyone who is not carrying around a computer with a spreadsheet program to project the impact of an original increase in expenditures over 20, 50, or 100 rounds of spending, there is a formula for calculating the multiplier.

$$\text{Spending Multiplier} = 1/(1 – \text{MPC} * (1 – \text{tax rate}) + \text{MPI})$$

The data from **Figure 11.16** and **Table 11.7** is:

- Marginal Propensity to Save (MPS) = 30%

- Tax rate = 10%

- Marginal Propensity to Import (MPI) = 10%

The MPC is equal to 1 − MPS, or 0.7. Therefore, the spending multiplier is:

$$\text{Spending Multiplier} = \frac{1}{1 - (0.7 - (0.10)(0.7) - 0.10)}$$
$$= \frac{1}{0.47}$$
$$= 2.13$$

A change in spending of $100 multiplied by the spending multiplier of 2.13 is equal to a change in GDP of $213. Not coincidentally, this result is exactly what was calculated in **Figure 11.16** after many rounds of expenditures cycling through the economy.

The size of the multiplier is determined by what proportion of the marginal dollar of income goes into taxes, saving, and imports. These three factors are known as "leakages," because they determine how much demand "leaks out" in each round of the multiplier effect. If the leakages are relatively small, then each successive round of the multiplier effect will have larger amounts of demand, and the multiplier will be high. Conversely, if the leakages are relatively large, then any initial change in demand will diminish more quickly in the second, third, and later rounds, and the multiplier will be small. Changes in the size of the leakages—a change in the marginal propensity to save, the tax rate, or the marginal propensity to import—will change the size of the multiplier.

Calculating Keynesian Policy Interventions

Returning to the original question: How much should government spending be increased to produce a total increase in real GDP of $100? If the goal is to increase aggregate demand by $100, and the multiplier is 2.13, then the increase in government spending to achieve that goal would be $100/2.13 = $47. Government spending of approximately $47, when combined with a multiplier of 2.13 (which is, remember, based on the specific assumptions about tax, saving, and import rates), produces an overall increase in real GDP of $100, restoring the economy to potential GDP of $800, as **Figure 11.17** shows.

Figure 11.17 The Multiplier Effect in an Expenditure-Output Model The power of the multiplier effect is that an increase in expenditure has a larger increase on the equilibrium output. The increase in expenditure is the vertical increase from AE_0 to AE_1. However, the increase in equilibrium output, shown on the horizontal axis, is clearly larger.

The multiplier effect is also visible on the Keynesian cross diagram. **Figure 11.17** shows the example we have been discussing: a recessionary gap with an equilibrium of $700, potential GDP of $800, the slope of the aggregate expenditure function (AE_0) determined by the assumptions that taxes are 30% of income, savings are 0.1 of after-tax income, and imports are 0.1 of before-tax income. At AE_1, the aggregate expenditure function is moved up to reach potential GDP.

Now, compare the vertical shift upward in the aggregate expenditure function, which is $47, with the horizontal shift outward in real GDP, which is $100 (as these numbers were calculated earlier). The rise in real GDP is more than double the rise in the aggregate expenditure function. (Similarly, if you look back at Figure 11.15, you will see that the vertical movements in the aggregate expenditure functions are smaller than the change in equilibrium output that is produced on the horizontal axis. Again, this is the multiplier effect at work.) In this way, the power of the multiplier is apparent in the income–expenditure graph, as well as in the arithmetic calculation.

The multiplier does not just affect government spending, but applies to any change in the economy. Say that business confidence declines and investment falls off, or that the economy of a leading trading partner slows down so that export sales decline. These changes will reduce aggregate expenditures, and then will have an even larger effect on real GDP because of the multiplier effect. Read the following Clear It Up feature to learn how the multiplier effect can be applied to analyze the economic impact of professional sports.

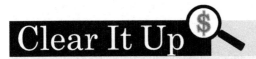

How can the multiplier be used to analyze the economic impact of professional sports?

Attracting professional sports teams and building sports stadiums to create jobs and stimulate business growth is an economic development strategy adopted by many communities throughout the United States. In his recent article, "Public Financing of Private Sports Stadiums," James Joyner of *Outside the Beltway* looked at public financing for NFL teams. Joyner's findings confirm the earlier work of John Siegfried of Vanderbilt University and Andrew Zimbalist of Smith College.

Siegfried and Zimbalist used the multiplier to analyze this issue. They considered the amount of taxes paid and dollars spent locally to see if there was a positive multiplier effect. Since most professional athletes and owners of sports teams are rich enough to owe a lot of taxes, let's say that 40% of any marginal income they earn is paid in taxes. Because athletes are often high earners with short careers, let's assume that they save one-third of their after-tax income.

However, many professional athletes do not live year-round in the city in which they play, so let's say that one-half of the money that they do spend is spent outside the local area. One can think of spending outside a local economy, in this example, as the equivalent of imported goods for the national economy.

Now, consider the impact of money spent at local entertainment venues other than professional sports. While the owners of these other businesses may be comfortably middle-income, few of them are in the economic stratosphere of professional athletes. Because their incomes are lower, so are their taxes; say that they pay only 35% of their marginal income in taxes. They do not have the same ability, or need, to save as much as professional athletes, so let's assume their MPC is just 0.8. Finally, because more of them live locally, they will spend a higher proportion of their income on local goods—say, 65%.

If these general assumptions hold true, then money spent on professional sports will have less local economic impact than money spent on other forms of entertainment. For professional athletes, out of a dollar earned, 40 cents goes to taxes, leaving 60 cents. Of that 60 cents, one-third is saved, leaving 40 cents, and half is spent outside the area, leaving 20 cents. Only 20 cents of each dollar is cycled into the local economy in the first round. For locally-owned entertainment, out of a dollar earned, 35 cents goes to taxes, leaving 65 cents. Of the rest, 20% is saved, leaving 52 cents, and of that amount, 65% is spent in the local area, so that 33.8 cents of each dollar of income is recycled into the local economy.

Siegfried and Zimbalist make the plausible argument that, within their household budgets, people have a fixed amount to spend on entertainment. If this assumption holds true, then money spent attending professional sports events is money that was not spent on other entertainment options in a given metropolitan area. Since the multiplier is lower for professional sports than for other local entertainment options, the arrival of professional sports to a city would reallocate entertainment spending in a way that causes the local economy to shrink, rather than to grow. Thus, their findings seem to confirm what Joyner reports and what newspapers across the country are reporting. A quick Internet search for "economic impact of sports" will yield numerous reports questioning this economic development strategy.

Multiplier Tradeoffs: Stability versus the Power of Macroeconomic Policy

Is an economy healthier with a high multiplier or a low one? With a high multiplier, any change in aggregate demand will tend to be substantially magnified, and so the economy will be more unstable. With a low multiplier, by contrast, changes in aggregate demand will not be multiplied much, so the economy will tend to be more stable.

However, with a low multiplier, government policy changes in taxes or spending will tend to have less impact on the equilibrium level of real output. With a higher multiplier, government policies to raise or reduce aggregate expenditures will have a larger effect. Thus, a low multiplier means a more stable economy, but also weaker government macroeconomic policy, while a high multiplier means a more volatile economy, but also an economy in which government macroeconomic policy is more powerful.

11.4 | The Phillips Curve

By the end of this section, you will be able to:
- Explain the Phillips curve, noting its impact on the theories of Keynesian economics
- Graph a Phillips curve
- Identify factors that cause the instability of the Phillips curve
- Analyze the Keynesian policy for reducing unemployment and inflation

The simplified AD/AS model that we have used so far is fully consistent with Keynes's original model. More recent research, though, has indicated that in the real world, an aggregate supply curve is more curved than the right angle used in this chapter. Rather, the real-world AS curve is very flat at levels of output far below potential ("the Keynesian zone"), very steep at levels of output above potential ("the neoclassical zone") and curved in between ("the intermediate zone"). This is illustrated in **Figure 11.18**. The typical aggregate supply curve leads to the concept of the Phillips curve.

Figure 11.18 Keynes, Neoclassical, and Intermediate Zones in the Aggregate Supply Curve Near the equilibrium Ek, in the Keynesian zone at the far left of the SRAS curve, small shifts in AD, either to the right or the left, will affect the output level Yk, but will not much affect the price level. In the Keynesian zone, AD largely determines the quantity of output. Near the equilibrium En, in the neoclassical zone, at the far right of the SRAS curve, small shifts in AD, either to the right or the left, will have relatively little effect on the output level Yn, but instead will have a greater effect on the price level. In the neoclassical zone, the near-vertical SRAS curve close to the level of potential GDP (as represented by the LRAS line) largely determines the quantity of output. In the intermediate zone around equilibrium Ei, movement in AD to the right will increase both the output level and the price level, while a movement in AD to the left would decrease both the output level and the price level.

The Discovery of the Phillips Curve

In the 1950s, A.W. Phillips, an economist at the London School of Economics, was studying the Keynesian analytical framework. The Keynesian theory implied that during a recession inflationary pressures are low, but when the level of output is at or even pushing beyond potential GDP, the economy is at greater risk for inflation. Phillips analyzed 60 years of British data and did find that tradeoff between unemployment and inflation, which became known as a **Phillips curve**. Figure 11.19 shows a theoretical Phillips curve, and the following Work It Out feature shows how the pattern appears for the United States.

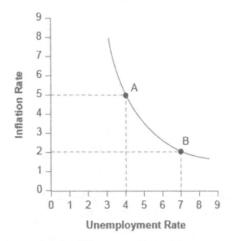

Figure 11.19 A Keynesian Phillips Curve Tradeoff between Unemployment and Inflation A Phillips curve illustrates a tradeoff between the unemployment rate and the inflation rate; if one is higher, the other must be lower. For example, point A illustrates an inflation rate of 5% and an unemployment rate of 4%. If the government attempts to reduce inflation to 2%, then it will experience a rise in unemployment to 7%, as shown at point B.

The Phillips Curve for the United States

Step 1. Go to this website (http://1.usa.gov/1c3psdL) to see the 2005 *Economic Report of the President.*

Step 2. Scroll down and locate Table B-63 in the Appendices. This table is titled "Changes in special consumer price indexes, 1960–2004."

Step 3. Download the table in Excel by selecting the XLS option and then selecting the location in which to save the file.

Step 4. Open the downloaded Excel file.

Step 5. View the third column (labeled "Year to year"). This is the inflation rate, measured by the percentage change in the Consumer Price Index.

Step 6. Return to the website and scroll to locate the Appendix Table B-42 "Civilian unemployment rate, 1959–2004.

Step 7. Download the table in Excel.

Step 8. Open the downloaded Excel file and view the second column. This is the overall unemployment rate.

Step 9. Using the data available from these two tables, plot the Phillips curve for 1960–69, with unemployment rate on the x-axis and the inflation rate on the y-axis. Your graph should look like Figure 11.20.

Figure 11.20 The Phillips Curve from 1960–1969 This chart shows the negative relationship between unemployment and inflation.

Step 10. Plot the Phillips curve for 1960–1979. What does the graph look like? Do you still see the tradeoff between inflation and unemployment? Your graph should look like **Figure 11.21**.

Figure 11.21 U.S. Phillips Curve, 1960–1979 The tradeoff between unemployment and inflation appeared to break down during the 1970s as the Phillips Curve shifted out to the right.

Over this longer period of time, the Phillips curve appears to have shifted out. There is no tradeoff any more.

The Instability of the Phillips Curve

During the 1960s, the Phillips curve was seen as a policy menu. A nation could choose low inflation and high unemployment, or high inflation and low unemployment, or anywhere in between. Fiscal and monetary policy could be used to move up or down the Phillips curve as desired. Then a curious thing happened. When policymakers tried to exploit the tradeoff between inflation and unemployment, the result was an increase in both inflation and unemployment. What had happened? The Phillips curve shifted.

The U.S. economy experienced this pattern in the deep recession from 1973 to 1975, and again in back-to-back recessions from 1980 to 1982. Many nations around the world saw similar increases in unemployment and inflation. This pattern became known as stagflation. (Recall from **The Aggregate Demand/Aggregate Supply Model** that stagflation is an unhealthy combination of high unemployment and high inflation.) Perhaps most important, stagflation was a phenomenon that could not be explained by traditional Keynesian economics.

Economists have concluded that two factors cause the Phillips curve to shift. The first is supply shocks, like the Oil Crisis of the mid-1970s, which first brought stagflation into our vocabulary. The second is changes in people's expectations about inflation. In other words, there may be a tradeoff between inflation and unemployment when people expect no inflation, but when they realize inflation is occurring, the tradeoff disappears. Both factors (supply shocks and changes in inflationary expectations) cause the aggregate supply curve, and thus the Phillips curve, to shift.

In short, a downward-sloping Phillips curve should be interpreted as valid for short-run periods of several years, but over longer periods, when aggregate supply shifts, the downward-sloping Phillips curve can shift so that unemployment and inflation are both higher (as in the 1970s and early 1980s) or both lower (as in the early 1990s or first decade of the 2000s).

Keynesian Policy for Fighting Unemployment and Inflation

Keynesian macroeconomics argues that the solution to a recession is **expansionary fiscal policy**, such as tax cuts to stimulate consumption and investment, or direct increases in government spending that would shift the aggregate demand curve to the right. For example, if aggregate demand was originally at ADr in **Figure 11.22**, so that the economy was in recession, the appropriate policy would be for government to shift aggregate demand to the right from ADr to ADf, where the economy would be at potential GDP and full employment.

Keynes noted that while it would be nice if the government could spend additional money on housing, roads, and other amenities, he also argued that if the government could not agree on how to spend money in practical ways, then it could spend in impractical ways. For example, Keynes suggested building monuments, like a modern equivalent of the Egyptian pyramids. He proposed that the government could bury money underground, and let mining companies get started to dig the money up again. These suggestions were slightly tongue-in-cheek, but their purpose was to emphasize that a Great Depression is no time to quibble over the specifics of government spending programs and tax cuts when the goal should be to pump up aggregate demand by enough to lift the economy to potential GDP.

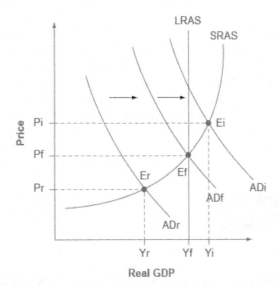

Figure 11.22 Fighting Recession and Inflation with Keynesian Policy If an economy is in recession, with an equilibrium at Er, then the Keynesian response would be to enact a policy to shift aggregate demand to the right from ADr toward ADf. If an economy is experiencing inflationary pressures with an equilibrium at Ei, then the Keynesian response would be to enact a policy response to shift aggregate demand to the left, from ADi toward ADf.

The other side of Keynesian policy occurs when the economy is operating above potential GDP. In this situation, unemployment is low, but inflationary rises in the price level are a concern. The Keynesian response would be **contractionary fiscal policy**, using tax increases or government spending cuts to shift AD to the left. The result would be downward pressure on the price level, but very little reduction in output or very little rise in unemployment. If aggregate demand was originally at ADi in **Figure 11.22**, so that the economy was experiencing inflationary rises in the price level, the appropriate policy would be for government to shift aggregate demand to the left, from ADi toward ADf, which reduces the pressure for a higher price level while the economy remains at full employment.

In the Keynesian economic model, too little aggregate demand brings unemployment and too much brings inflation. Thus, you can think of Keynesian economics as pursuing a "Goldilocks" level of aggregate demand: not too much, not too little, but looking for what is just right.

11.5 | The Keynesian Perspective on Market Forces

By the end of this section, you will be able to:
- Explain the Keynesian perspective on market forces
- Analyze the role of government policy in economic management

Ever since the birth of Keynesian economics in the 1930s, controversy has simmered over the extent to which government should play an active role in managing the economy. In the aftermath of the human devastation and misery of the Great Depression, many people—including many economists—became more aware of vulnerabilities within the market-oriented economic system. Some supporters of Keynesian economics advocated a high degree of government planning in all parts of the economy.

However, Keynes himself was careful to separate the issue of aggregate demand from the issue of how well individual markets worked. He argued that individual markets for goods and services were appropriate and useful, but that sometimes that level of aggregate demand was just too low. When 10 million people are willing and able to work, but one million of them are unemployed, he argued, individual markets may be doing a perfectly good job of allocating the efforts of the nine million workers—the problem is that insufficient aggregate demand exists to support jobs for all 10 million. Thus, he believed that, while government should ensure that overall level of aggregate demand is sufficient for an economy to reach full employment, this task did not imply that the government should attempt to set prices and wages throughout the economy, nor to take over and manage large corporations or entire industries directly.

Even if one accepts the Keynesian economic theory, a number of practical questions remain. In the real world, can government economists identify potential GDP accurately? Is a desired increase in aggregate demand better accomplished by a tax cut or by an increase in government spending? Given the inevitable delays and uncertainties as policies are enacted into law, is it reasonable to expect that the government can implement Keynesian economics? Can fixing a recession really be just as simple as pumping up aggregate demand? Government Budgets and Fiscal Policy will probe these issues. The Keynesian approach, with its focus on aggregate demand and sticky prices, has proved useful in understanding how the economy fluctuates in the short run and why recessions and cyclical unemployment occur. In The Neoclassical Perspective, we will consider some of the shortcomings of the Keynesian approach and why it is not especially well-suited for long-run macroeconomic analysis.

Bring it Home

The Great Recession

The lessons learned during the Great Depression of the 1930s and the aggregate expenditure model proposed by John Maynard Keynes gave the modern economists and policymakers of today the tools to effectively navigate the treacherous economy in the latter half of the 2000s. In "How the Great Recession Was Brought to an End," Alan S. Blinder and Mark Zandi wrote that the actions taken by today's policymakers stand in sharp contrast to those of the early years of the Great Depression. Today's economists and policymakers were not content to let the markets recover from recession without taking proactive measures to support consumption and investment. The Federal Reserve actively lowered short-term interest rates and developed innovative ways to pump money into the economy so that credit and investment would not dry up. Both Presidents Bush and Obama and Congress implemented a variety of programs ranging from tax rebates to "Cash for Clunkers" to the Troubled Asset Relief Program to stimulate and stabilize household consumption and encourage investment. Although these policies came under harsh criticism from the public and many politicians, they lessened the impact of the economic downturn and may have saved the country from a second Great Depression.

KEY TERMS

contractionary fiscal policy tax increases or cuts in government spending designed to decrease aggregate demand and reduce inflationary pressures

coordination argument downward wage and price flexibility requires perfect information about the level of lower compensation acceptable to other laborers and market participants

disposable income income after taxes

expansionary fiscal policy tax cuts or increases in government spending designed to stimulate aggregate demand and move the economy out of recession

expenditure multiplier Keynesian concept that asserts that a change in autonomous spending causes a more than proportionate change in real GDP

inflationary gap equilibrium at a level of output above potential GDP

macroeconomic externality occurs when what happens at the macro level is different from and inferior to what happens at the micro level; an example would be where upward sloping supply curves for firms become a flat aggregate supply curve, illustrating that the price level cannot fall to stimulate aggregate demand

menu costs costs firms face in changing prices

Phillips curve the tradeoff between unemployment and inflation

real GDP the amount of goods and services actually being sold in a nation

recessionary gap equilibrium at a level of output below potential GDP

sticky wages and prices a situation where wages and prices do not fall in response to a decrease in demand, or do not rise in response to an increase in demand

KEY CONCEPTS AND SUMMARY

11.1 Aggregate Demand in Keynesian Analysis

Aggregate demand is the sum of four components: consumption, investment, government spending, and net exports. Consumption will change for a number of reasons, including movements in income, taxes, expectations about future income, and changes in wealth levels. Investment will change in response to its expected profitability, which in turn is shaped by expectations about future economic growth, the creation of new technologies, the price of key inputs, and tax incentives for investment. Investment will also change when interest rates rise or fall. Government spending and taxes are determined by political considerations. Exports and imports change according to relative growth rates and prices between two economies.

11.2 The Building Blocks of Keynesian Analysis

Keynesian economics is based on two main ideas: (1) aggregate demand is more likely than aggregate supply to be the primary cause of a short-run economic event like a recession; (2) wages and prices can be sticky, and so, in an economic downturn, unemployment can result. The latter is an example of a macroeconomic externality. While surpluses cause prices to fall at the micro level, they do not necessarily at the macro level; instead the adjustment to a decrease in demand occurs only through decreased quantities. One reason why prices may be sticky is menu costs, the costs of changing prices. These include internal costs a business faces in changing prices in terms of labeling, recordkeeping, and accounting, and also the costs of communicating the price change to (possibly unhappy) customers. Keynesians also believe in the existence of the expenditure multiplier—the notion that a change in autonomous expenditure causes a more than proportionate change in GDP.

11.3 The Expenditure-Output (or Keynesian Cross) Model

The expenditure-output model or Keynesian cross diagram shows how the level of aggregate expenditure (on the vertical axis) varies with the level of economic output (shown on the horizontal axis). Since the value of all macroeconomic output also represents income to someone somewhere else in the economy, the horizontal axis can also be interpreted as national income. The equilibrium in the diagram will occur where the aggregate expenditure line crosses the 45-degree line, which represents the set of points where aggregate expenditure in the economy is equal to output (or national income). Equilibrium in a Keynesian cross diagram can happen at potential GDP, or below or above that level.

The consumption function shows the upward-sloping relationship between national income and consumption. The marginal propensity to consume (MPC) is the amount consumed out of an additional dollar of income. A higher marginal propensity to consume means a steeper consumption function; a lower marginal propensity to consume means a flatter consumption function. The marginal propensity to save (MPS) is the amount saved out of an additional dollar of income. It is necessarily true that MPC + MPS = 1. The investment function is drawn as a flat line, showing that investment in the current year does not change with regard to the current level of national income. However, the investment function will move up and down based on the expected rate of return in the future. Government spending is drawn as a horizontal line in the Keynesian cross diagram, because its level is determined by political considerations, not by the current level of income in the economy. Taxes in the basic Keynesian cross diagram are taken into account by adjusting the consumption function. The export function is drawn as a horizontal line in the Keynesian cross diagram, because exports do not change as a result of changes in domestic income, but they move as a result of changes in foreign income, as well as changes in exchange rates. The import function is drawn as a downward-sloping line, because imports rise with national income, but imports are a subtraction from aggregate demand. Thus, a higher level of imports means a lower level of expenditure on domestic goods.

In a Keynesian cross diagram, the equilibrium may be at a level below potential GDP, which is called a recessionary gap, or at a level above potential GDP, which is called an inflationary gap.

The multiplier effect describes how an initial change in aggregate demand generated several times as much as cumulative GDP. The size of the spending multiplier is determined by three leakages: spending on savings, taxes, and imports. The formula for the multiplier is:

$$\text{Multiplier} = \frac{1}{1 - (\text{MPC} \times (1 - \text{tax rate}) + \text{MPI})}$$

An economy with a lower multiplier is more stable—it is less affected either by economic events or by government policy than an economy with a higher multiplier.

11.4 The Phillips Curve

A Phillips curve shows the tradeoff between unemployment and inflation in an economy. From a Keynesian viewpoint, the Phillips curve should slope down so that higher unemployment means lower inflation, and vice versa. However, a downward-sloping Phillips curve is a short-term relationship that may shift after a few years.

Keynesian macroeconomics argues that the solution to a recession is expansionary fiscal policy, such as tax cuts to stimulate consumption and investment, or direct increases in government spending that would shift the aggregate demand curve to the right. The other side of Keynesian policy occurs when the economy is operating above potential GDP. In this situation, unemployment is low, but inflationary rises in the price level are a concern. The Keynesian response would be contractionary fiscal policy, using tax increases or government spending cuts to shift AD to the left.

11.5 The Keynesian Perspective on Market Forces

The Keynesian prescription for stabilizing the economy implies government intervention at the macroeconomic level—increasing aggregate demand when private demand falls and decreasing aggregate demand when private demand rises. This does not imply that the government should be passing laws or regulations that set prices and quantities in microeconomic markets.

SELF-CHECK QUESTIONS

1.   In the Keynesian framework, which of the following events might cause a recession? Which might cause inflation? Sketch AD/AS diagrams to illustrate your answers.
   a.   A large increase in the price of the homes people own.
   b.   Rapid growth in the economy of a major trading partner.
   c.   The development of a major new technology offers profitable opportunities for business.
   d.   The interest rate rises.
   e.   The good imported from a major trading partner become much less expensive.

2.   In a Keynesian framework, using an AD/AS diagram, which of the following government policy choices offer a possible solution to recession? Which offer a possible solution to inflation?
   a.   A tax increase on consumer income.
   b.   A surge in military spending.
   c.   A reduction in taxes for businesses that increase investment.
   d.   A major increase in what the U.S. government spends on healthcare.

3.   Use the AD/AS model to explain how an inflationary gap occurs, beginning from the initial equilibrium in Figure 11.6.

4.   Suppose the U.S. Congress cuts federal government spending in order to balance the Federal budget. Use the AD/AS model to analyze the likely impact on output and employment. *Hint*: revisit Figure 11.6.

5.   Sketch the aggregate expenditure-output diagram with the recessionary gap.

6.   Sketch the aggregate expenditure-output diagram with an inflationary gap.

7.   An economy has the following characteristics:

Y = National income

Taxes = T = 0.25Y

C = Consumption = 400 + 0.85(Y − T)

I = 300

G = 200

X = 500

M = 0.1(Y − T)

Find the equilibrium for this economy. If potential GDP is 3,500, then what change in government spending is needed to achieve this level? Do this problem two ways. First, plug 3,500 into the equations and solve for G. Second, calculate the multiplier and figure it out that way.

8.   Table 11.8 represents the data behind a Keynesian cross diagram. Assume that the tax rate is 0.4 of national income; the MPC out of the after-tax income is 0.8; investment is $2,000; government spending is $1,000; exports are $2,000 and imports are 0.05 of after-tax income. What is the equilibrium level of output for this economy?

National Income	After-Tax Income	Consumption	I + G + X	Minus Imports	Aggregate Expenditures
$8,000		$4,340			
$9,000					
$10,000					
$11,000					

Table 11.8

National Income	After-Tax Income	Consumption	I + G + X	Minus Imports	Aggregate Expenditures
$12,000					
$13,000					

Table 11.8

9. Explain how the multiplier works. Use an MPC of 80% in an example.

10. How would a decrease in energy prices affect the Phillips curve?

11. Does Keynesian economics require government to set controls on prices, wages, or interest rates?

12. List three practical problems with the Keynesian perspective.

REVIEW QUESTIONS

13. Name some economic events not related to government policy that could cause aggregate demand to shift.

14. Name some government policies that could cause aggregate demand to shift.

15. From a Keynesian point of view, which is more likely to cause a recession: aggregate demand or aggregate supply, and why?

16. Why do sticky wages and prices increase the impact of an economic downturn on unemployment and recession?

17. Explain what economists mean by "menu costs."

18. What is on the axes of an expenditure-output diagram?

19. What does the 45-degree line show?

20. What determines the slope of a consumption function?

21. What is the marginal propensity to consume, and how is it related to the marginal propensity to import?

22. Why are the investment function, the government spending function, and the export function all drawn as flat lines?

23. Why does the import function slope down? What is the marginal propensity to import?

24. What are the components on which the aggregate expenditure function is based?

25. Is the equilibrium in a Keynesian cross diagram usually expected to be at or near potential GDP?

26. What is an inflationary gap? A recessionary gap?

27. What is the multiplier effect?

28. Why are savings, taxes, and imports referred to as "leakages" in calculating the multiplier effect?

29. Will an economy with a high multiplier be more stable or less stable than an economy with a low multiplier in response to changes in the economy or in government policy?

30. How do economists use the multiplier?

31. What tradeoff is shown by a Phillips curve?

32. Would you expect to see long-run data trace out a stable downward-sloping Phillips curve?

33. What is the Keynesian prescription for recession? For inflation?

34. How did the Keynesian perspective address the economic market failure of the Great Depression?

CRITICAL THINKING QUESTIONS

35. In its recent report, The Conference Board's *Global Economic Outlook 2015*, updated November 2014 (http://www.conference-board.org/data/globaloutlook.cfm), projects China's growth between

2015 and 2019 to be about 5.5%. *International Business Times* (http://www.ibtimes.com/us-exports-china-have-grown-294-over-past-decade-1338693) reports that China is the United States' third largest export market, with exports to China growing 294% over the last ten years. Explain what impact China has on the U.S. economy.

36. What may happen if growth in China continues or contracts?

37. Does it make sense that wages would be sticky downwards but not upwards? Why or why not?

38. Suppose the economy is operating at potential GDP when it experiences an increase in export demand. How might the economy increase production of exports to meet this demand, given that the economy is already at full employment?

39. What does it mean when the aggregate expenditure line crosses the 45-degree line? In other words, how would you explain the intersection in words?

40. Which model, the AD/AS or the AE model better explains the relationship between rising price levels and GDP? Why?

41. What are some reasons that the economy might be in a recession, and what is the appropriate government action to alleviate the recession?

42. What should the government do to relieve inflationary pressures if the aggregate expenditure is greater than potential GDP?

43. Two countries are in a recession. Country A has an MPC of 0.8 and Country B has an MPC of 0.6. In which country will government spending have the greatest impact?

44. Compare two policies: a tax cut on income or an increase in government spending on roads and bridges. What are both the short-term and long-term impacts of such policies on the economy?

45. What role does government play in stabilizing the economy and what are the tradeoffs that must be considered?

46. If there is a recessionary gap of $100 billion, should the government increase spending by $100 billion to close the gap? Why? Why not?

47. What other changes in the economy can be evaluated by using the multiplier?

48. Do you think the Phillips curve is a useful tool for analyzing the economy today? Why or why not?

49. Return to the table from the *Economic Report of the President* in the earlier **The Phillips Curve for the United States** feature titled "The Phillips Curve for the United States." How would you expect government spending to have changed over the last six years?

50. Explain what types of policies the federal government may have implemented to restore aggregate demand and the potential obstacles policymakers may have encountered.

12 | The Neoclassical Perspective

Figure 12.1 Impact of the Great Recession The impact of the Great Recession can be seen in many areas of the economy that impact our daily lives. One of the most visible signs can be seen in the housing market where many homes and other buildings are abandoned, including ones that midway through construction. (Credit: modification of work by A McLin/Flickr Creative Commons)

Bring it Home

Navigating Unchartered Waters

The Great Recession ended in June 2009 after 18 months, according to the National Bureau of Economic Research (NBER). The NBER examines a variety of measures of economic activity to gauge the overall health of the economy. These measures include real income, wholesale and retail sales, employment, and industrial production. In the years since the official end of this historic economic downturn, it has become clear that the Great Recession was two-pronged, hitting the U.S. economy with the collapse of the housing market and the failure of the financial system's credit institutions, further contaminating global economies. While the stock market rapidly lost trillions of dollars of value, consumer spending dried up, and companies began cutting jobs, economic policymakers were struggling with how to best combat and prevent a national, and even global economic collapse. In the end, policymakers used a number of controversial monetary and fiscal policies to support the housing market and domestic industries as well as to stabilize the financial sector. Some of these initiatives included:

- Federal Reserve Bank purchase of both traditional and nontraditional assets off banks' balance sheets. By doing this, the Fed injected money into the banking system and increased the amounts of funds available to lend to the business sector and consumers. This also dropped short-term interest rates to as low as zero percent and had the effect of devaluing U.S. dollars in the global market and boosting exports.

- The Congress and the President also passed several pieces of legislation that would stabilize the financial market. The Troubled Asset Relief Program (TARP), passed in late 2008, allowed the government to inject cash into troubled banks and other financial institutions and help support General Motors and Chrysler as they faced bankruptcy and threatened job losses throughout their supply chain. The American Recovery and Reinvestment Act in early 2009 provided tax rebates to low- and middle-income households to encourage consumer spending.

Four years after the end of the Great Recession, the economy has yet to return to its pre-recession levels of productivity and growth. Annual productivity increased only 1.9% between 2009 and 2012 compared to its 2.7% annual growth rate between 2000 and 2007, unemployment remains above the natural rate, and real GDP continues to lag behind potential growth. The actions taken to stabilize the economy are still under scrutiny and debate about their effectiveness continues. In this chapter, we will discuss the neoclassical perspective on economics and compare it to the Keynesian perspective. At the end of the chapter, we will use the neoclassical perspective to analyze the actions taken in the Great Recession.

Introduction to the Neoclassical Perspective

In this chapter, you will learn about:

- The Building Blocks of Neoclassical Analysis
- The Policy Implications of the Neoclassical Perspective
- Balancing Keynesian and Neoclassical Models

In Chicago, Illinois, the highest recorded temperature was 105° in July 1995, while the lowest recorded temperature was 27° below zero in January 1958. Understanding why these extreme weather patterns occurred would be interesting. However, if you wanted to understand the typical weather pattern in Chicago, instead of focusing on one-time extremes, you would need to look at the entire pattern of data over time.

A similar lesson applies to the study of macroeconomics. It is interesting to study extreme situations, like the Great Depression of the 1930s or what many have called the Great Recession of 2008–2009. If you want to understand the whole picture, however, you need to look at the long term. Consider the unemployment rate. The unemployment rate has fluctuated from as low as 3.5% in 1969 to as high as 9.7% in 1982 and 9.6% in 2009. Even as the U.S. unemployment rate rose during recessions and declined during expansions, it kept returning to the general neighborhood of 5.0–5.5%. When the nonpartisan Congressional Budget Office carried out its long-range economic forecasts in 2010, it assumed that from 2015 to 2020, after the recession has passed, the unemployment rate would be 5.0%. From a long-run perspective, the economy seems to keep adjusting back to this rate of unemployment.

As the name "neoclassical" implies, this perspective of how the macroeconomy works is a "new" view of the "old" classical model of the economy. The classical view, the predominant economic philosophy until the Great Depression, was that short-term fluctuations in economic activity would rather quickly, with flexible prices, adjust back to full employment. This view of the economy implied a vertical aggregate supply curve at full employment GDP, and prescribed a "hands off" policy approach. For example, if the economy were to slip into recession (a leftward shift of the aggregate demand curve), it would temporarily exhibit a surplus of goods. This surplus would be eliminated with falling prices, and the economy would return to full employment level of GDP; no active fiscal or monetary policy was needed. In fact, the classical view was that expansionary fiscal or monetary policy would only cause inflation, rather than increase GDP. The deep and lasting impact of the Great Depression changed this thinking and Keynesian economics, which prescribed active fiscal policy to alleviate weak aggregate demand, became the more mainstream perspective.

12.1 | The Building Blocks of Neoclassical Analysis

By the end of this section, you will be able to:

- Explain the importance of potential GDP in the long run
- Analyze the role of flexible prices
- Interpret a neoclassical model of aggregate demand and aggregate supply
- Evaluate different ways for measuring the speed of macroeconomic adjustment

The **neoclassical perspective** on macroeconomics holds that, in the long run, the economy will fluctuate around its potential GDP and its natural rate of unemployment. This chapter begins with two building blocks of neoclassical economics: (1) the size of the economy is determined by potential GDP, and (2) wages and prices will adjust in a flexible manner so that the economy will adjust back to its potential GDP level of output. The key policy implication is this: Should the government focus more on long-term growth and on controlling inflation than on worrying about recession or cyclical unemployment? This focus on long-run growth rather than the short-run fluctuations in the business cycle means that neoclassical economics is more useful for long-run macroeconomic analysis and Keynesian economics is more useful for analyzing the macroeconomic short run. Let's consider the two neoclassical building blocks in turn, and how they can be embodied in the aggregate demand/aggregate supply model.

The Importance of Potential GDP in the Long Run

Over the long run, the level of potential GDP determines the size of real GDP. When economists refer to "potential GDP" they are referring to that level of output that can be achieved when all resources (land, labor, capital, and entrepreneurial ability) are fully employed. While the unemployment rate in labor markets will never be zero, full employment in the labor market refers to zero cyclical unemployment. There will still be some level of unemployment due to frictional or structural unemployment, but when the economy is operating with zero cyclical unemployment, the economy is said to be at the natural rate of unemployment or at full employment.

Actual or real GDP is benchmarked against the potential GDP to determine how well the economy is performing. Growth in GDP can be explained by increases and investment in physical capital and human capital per person as well as advances in technology. **Physical capital per person** refers to the amount and kind of machinery and equipment available to help people get work done. Compare, for example, your productivity in typing a term paper on a typewriter to working on your laptop with word processing software. Clearly, you will be able to be more productive using word processing software. The technology and level of capital of your laptop and software has increased your productivity. More broadly, the development of GPS technology and Universal Product Codes (those barcodes on every product we buy) has made it much easier for firms to track shipments, tabulate inventories, and sell and distribute products. These two technological innovations, and many others, have increased a nation's ability to produce goods and services for a given population. Likewise, increasing human capital involves increasing levels of knowledge, education, and skill sets per person through vocational or higher education. Physical and human capital improvements with technological advances will increase overall productivity and, thus, GDP.

To see how these improvements have increased productivity and output at the national level, we should examine evidence from the United States. The United States experienced significant growth in the twentieth century due to phenomenal changes in infrastructure, equipment, and technological improvements in physical capital and human capital. The population more than tripled in the twentieth century, from 76 million in 1900 to over 300 million in 2012. The human capital of modern workers is far higher today because the education and skills of workers have risen dramatically. In 1900, only about one-eighth of the U.S. population had completed high school and just one person in 40 had completed a four-year college degree. By 2010, more than 87% of Americans had a high school degree and over 29% had a four-year college degree as well. In 2014, 40% of working-age Americans had a four-year college degree. The average amount of physical capital per worker has grown dramatically. The technology available to modern workers is extraordinarily better than a century ago: cars, airplanes, electrical machinery, smartphones, computers, chemical and biological advances, materials science, health care—the list of technological advances could run on and on. More workers, higher skill levels, larger amounts of physical capital per worker, and amazingly better technology, and potential GDP for the U.S. economy has clearly increased a great deal since 1900.

This growth has fallen below its potential GDP and, at times, has exceeded its potential. For example from 2008 to 2009, the U.S. economy tumbled into recession and remains below its potential. At other times, like in the late

1990s, the economy ran at potential GDP—or even slightly ahead. **Figure 12.2** shows the actual data for the increase in nominal GDP since 1960. The slightly smoother line shows the potential GDP since 1960 as estimated by the nonpartisan Congressional Budget Office. Most economic recessions and upswings are times when the economy is 1–3% below or above potential GDP in a given year. Clearly, short-run fluctuations around potential GDP do exist, but over the long run, the upward trend of potential GDP determines the size of the economy.

Figure 12.2 Potential and Actual GDP (in Nominal Dollars) Actual GDP falls below potential GDP during and after recessions, like the recessions of 1980 and 1981–82, 1990–91, 2001, and 2008–2009 and continues below potential GDP through 2014. In other cases, actual GDP can be above potential GDP for a time, as in the late 1990s.

In the aggregate demand/aggregate supply model, potential GDP is shown as a vertical line. Neoclassical economists who focus on potential GDP as the primary determinant of real GDP argue that the long-run aggregate supply curve is located at potential GDP—that is, the long-run aggregate supply curve is a vertical line drawn at the level of potential GDP, as shown in **Figure 12.3**. A vertical LRAS curve means that the level of aggregate supply (or potential GDP) will determine the real GDP of the economy, regardless of the level of aggregate demand. Over time, increases in the quantity and quality of physical capital, increases in human capital, and technological advancements shift potential GDP and the vertical LRAS curve gradually to the right. This gradual increase in an economy's potential GDP is often described as a nation's long-term economic growth.

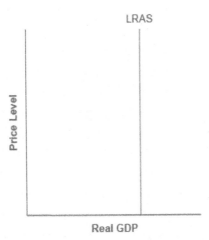

Figure 12.3 A Vertical AS Curve In the neoclassical model, the aggregate supply curve is drawn as a vertical line at the level of potential GDP. If AS is vertical, then it determines the level of real output, no matter where the aggregate demand curve is drawn. Over time, the LRAS curve shifts to the right as productivity increases and potential GDP expands.

The Role of Flexible Prices

How does the macroeconomy adjust back to its level of potential GDP in the long run? What if aggregate demand increases or decreases? The neoclassical view of how the macroeconomy adjusts is based on the insight that even if wages and prices are "sticky", or slow to change, in the short run, they are flexible over time. To understand this better, let's follow the connections from the short-run to the long-run macroeconomic equilibrium.

The aggregate demand and aggregate supply diagram shown in Figure 12.4 shows two aggregate supply curves. The original upward sloping aggregate supply curve (SRAS$_0$) is a short-run or Keynesian AS curve. The vertical aggregate supply curve (LRASn) is the long-run or neoclassical AS curve, which is located at potential GDP. The original aggregate demand curve, labeled AD$_0$, is drawn so that the original equilibrium occurs at point E$_0$, at which point the economy is producing at its potential GDP.

Figure 12.4 The Rebound to Potential GDP after AD Increases The original equilibrium (E_0), at an output level of 500 and a price level of 120, happens at the intersection of the aggregate demand curve (AD_0) and the short-run aggregate supply curve ($SRAS_0$). The output at E_0 is equal to potential GDP. Aggregate demand shifts right from AD_0 to AD_1. The new equilibrium is E_1, with a higher output level of 550 and an increase in the price level to 125. With unemployment rates unsustainably low, wages are bid up by eager employers, which shifts short-run aggregate supply to the left, from $SRAS_0$ to $SRAS_1$. The new equilibrium (E_2) is at the same original level of output, 500, but at a higher price level of 130. Thus, the long-run aggregate supply curve (LRASn), which is vertical at the level of potential GDP, determines the level of real GDP in this economy in the long run.

Now, imagine that some economic event boosts aggregate demand: perhaps a surge of export sales or a rise in business confidence that leads to more investment, perhaps a policy decision like higher government spending, or perhaps a tax cut that leads to additional aggregate demand. The short-run Keynesian analysis is that the rise in aggregate demand will shift the aggregate demand curve out to the right, from AD_0 to AD_1, leading to a new equilibrium at point E_1 with higher output, lower unemployment, and pressure for an inflationary rise in the price level.

In the long-run neoclassical analysis, however, the chain of economic events is just beginning. As economic output rises above potential GDP, the level of unemployment falls. The economy is now above full employment and there is a shortage of labor. Eager employers are trying to bid workers away from other companies and to encourage their current workers to exert more effort and to put in longer hours. This high demand for labor will drive up wages. Most workers have their salaries reviewed only once or twice a year, and so it will take time before the higher wages filter through the economy. As wages do rise, it will mean a leftward shift in the short-run Keynesian aggregate supply curve back to $SRAS_1$, because the price of a major input to production has increased. The economy moves to a new equilibrium (E_2). The new equilibrium has the same level of real GDP as did the original equilibrium (E_0), but there has been an inflationary increase in the price level.

This description of the short-run shift from E_0 to E_1 and the long-run shift from E_1 to E_2 is a step-by-step way of making a simple point: the economy cannot sustain production above its potential GDP in the long run. An economy may produce above its level of potential GDP in the short run, under pressure from a surge in aggregate demand. Over the long run, however, that surge in aggregate demand ends up as an increase in the price level, not as a rise in output.

The rebound of the economy back to potential GDP also works in response to a shift to the left in aggregate demand. **Figure 12.5** again starts with two aggregate supply curves, with $SRAS_0$ showing the original upward sloping short-run Keynesian AS curve and LRASn showing the vertical long-run neoclassical aggregate supply curve. A decrease in aggregate demand—for example, because of a decline in consumer confidence that leads to less consumption and more saving—causes the original aggregate demand curve AD_0 to shift back to AD_1. The shift from the original equilibrium (E_0) to the new equilibrium (E_1) results in a decline in output. The economy is now below full employment and there is a surplus of labor. As output falls below potential GDP, unemployment rises. While a lower price level (i.e., deflation) is rare in the United States, it does happen from time to time during very weak periods of economic activity. For practical purposes, we might consider a lower price level in the AD–AS model as indicative of disinflation, which is a decline in the rate of inflation. Thus, the long-run aggregate supply curve LRASn, which is vertical at the level of potential GDP, ultimately determines the real GDP of this economy.

Figure 12.5 A Rebound Back to Potential GDP from a Shift to the Left in Aggregate Demand The original equilibrium (E_0), at an output level of 500 and a price level of 120, happens at the intersection of the aggregate demand curve (AD_0) and the short-run aggregate supply curve ($SRAS_0$). The output at E_0 is equal to potential GDP. Aggregate demand shifts left, from AD_0 to AD_1. The new equilibrium is at E_1, with a lower output level of 450 and downward pressure on the price level of 115. With high unemployment rates, wages are held down. Lower wages are an economy-wide decrease in the price of a key input, which shifts short-run aggregate supply to the right, from $SRAS_0$ to $SRAS_1$. The new equilibrium (E_2) is at the same original level of output, 500, but at a lower price level of 110.

Again, from the neoclassical perspective, this short-run scenario is only the beginning of the chain of events. The higher level of unemployment means more workers looking for jobs. As a result, employers can hold down on pay increases—or perhaps even replace some of their higher-paid workers with unemployed people willing to accept a lower wage. As wages stagnate or fall, this decline in the price of a key input means that the short-run Keynesian aggregate supply curve shifts to the right from its original ($SRAS_0$ to $SRAS_1$). The overall impact in the long run, as the macroeconomic equilibrium shifts from E_0 to E_1 to E_2, is that the level of output returns to potential GDP, where it started. There is, however, downward pressure on the price level. Thus, in the neoclassical view, changes in aggregate demand can have a short-run impact on output and on unemployment—but only a short-run impact. In the long run, when wages and prices are flexible, potential GDP and aggregate supply determine the size of real GDP.

How Fast Is the Speed of Macroeconomic Adjustment?

How long does it take for wages and prices to adjust, and for the economy to rebound back to its potential GDP? This subject is highly contentious. Keynesian economists argue that if the adjustment from recession to potential GDP takes a very long time, then neoclassical theory may be more hypothetical than practical. In response to those immortal words of John Maynard Keynes, "In the long run we are all dead," neoclassical economists respond that even if the adjustment takes as long as, say, ten years the neoclassical perspective remains of central importance in understanding the economy.

One subset of neoclassical economists holds that the adjustment of wages and prices in the macroeconomy might be quite rapid indeed. The theory of **rational expectations** holds that people form the most accurate possible expectations about the future that they can, using all information available to them. In an economy where most people have rational expectations, economic adjustments may happen very quickly.

To understand how rational expectations may affect the speed of price adjustments, think about a situation in the real estate market. Imagine that several events seem likely to push up the value of homes in the neighborhood. Perhaps a local employer announces that it is going to hire many more people or the city announces that it is going to build a local park or a library in that neighborhood. The theory of rational expectations points out that even though none of the changes will happen immediately, home prices in the neighborhood will rise immediately, because the expectation that homes will be worth more in the future will lead buyers to be willing to pay more in the present. The amount of the immediate increase in home prices will depend on how likely it seems that the announcements about the future will actually happen and on how distant the local jobs and neighborhood improvements are in the future. The key point is that, because of rational expectations, prices do not wait on events, but adjust immediately.

At a macroeconomic level, the theory of rational expectations points out that if the aggregate supply curve is vertical over time, then people should rationally expect this pattern. When a shift in aggregate demand occurs, people and businesses with rational expectations will know that its impact on output and employment will be temporary, while its impact on the price level will be permanent. If firms and workers perceive the outcome of the process in advance, and if all firms and workers know that everyone else is perceiving the process in the same way, then they have no incentive to go through an extended series of short-run scenarios, like a firm first hiring more people when aggregate demand shifts out and then firing those same people when aggregate supply shifts back. Instead, everyone will recognize where this process is heading—toward a change in the price level—and then will act on that expectation. In this scenario, the expected long-run change in the price level may happen very quickly, without a drawn-out zigzag of output and employment first moving one way and then the other.

The theory that people and firms have rational expectations can be a useful simplification, but as a statement about how people and businesses actually behave, the assumption seems too strong. After all, many people and firms are not especially well informed, either about what is happening in the economy or about how the economy works. An alternate assumption is that people and firms act with **adaptive expectations**: they look at past experience and gradually adapt their beliefs and behavior as circumstances change, but are not perfect synthesizers of information and accurate predictors of the future in the sense of rational expectations theory. If most people and businesses have some form of adaptive expectations, then the adjustment from the short run and long run will be traced out in incremental steps that occur over time.

The empirical evidence on the speed of macroeconomic adjustment of prices and wages is not clear-cut. Indeed, the speed of macroeconomic adjustment probably varies among different countries and time periods. A reasonable guess is that the initial short-run effect of a shift in aggregate demand might last two to five years, before the adjustments in wages and prices cause the economy to adjust back to potential GDP. Thus, one might think of the short run for applying Keynesian analysis as time periods less than two to five years, and the long run for applying neoclassical analysis as longer than five years. For practical purposes, this guideline is frustratingly imprecise, but when analyzing a complex social mechanism like an economy as it evolves over time, some imprecision seems unavoidable.

12.2 | The Policy Implications of the Neoclassical Perspective

By the end of this section, you will be able to:
- Discuss why and how inflation expectations are measured
- Analyze the impacts of fiscal policy and monetary policy on aggregate supply and aggregate demand
- Explain the neoclassical Phillips curve, noting its tradeoff between inflation and unemployment
- Identify clear distinctions between neoclassical economics and Keynesian economics

To understand the policy recommendations of the neoclassical economists, it helps to start with the Keynesian perspective. Suppose a decrease in aggregate demand causes the economy to go into recession with high unemployment. The Keynesian response would be to use government policy to stimulate aggregate demand and eliminate the recessionary gap. The neoclassical economists believe that the Keynesian response, while perhaps well intentioned, will not have a good outcome for reasons we will discuss shortly. Since the neoclassical economists believe that the economy will correct itself over time, the only advantage of a Keynesian stabilization policy would be to speed up the process and minimize the time that the unemployed are out of work. Is that the likely outcome?

Keynesian macroeconomic policy requires some optimism about the ability of the government to recognize a situation of too little or too much aggregate demand, and to adjust aggregate demand accordingly with the right level of changes in taxes or spending, all enacted in a timely fashion. After all, neoclassical economists argue, it takes government statisticians months to produce even preliminary estimates of GDP so that politicians know whether a recession is occurring—and those preliminary estimates may be revised substantially later. Moreover, there is the question of timely action. The political process can take more months to enact a tax cut or a spending increase; the amount of those tax or spending changes may be determined as much by political considerations as economic ones; and then the economy will take still more months to put changes in aggregate demand into effect through spending and production. When all of these time lags and political realities are considered, active fiscal policy may fail to address the current problem, and could even make the future economy worse. The average U.S. post-World War II recession has lasted only about a year. By the time government policy kicks in, the recession will likely be over. As a consequence, the only result of government fine-tuning will be to stimulate the economy when it is already recovering (or to contract the economy when it is already falling). In other words, an active macroeconomic policy is likely to exacerbate the cycles rather than dampen them. Indeed, some neoclassical economists believe a large part of the business cycles we observe are due to flawed government policy. To learn about this issue further, read the following Clear It Up feature.

Clear It Up 🔍

Why and how are inflation expectations measured?

People take expectations about inflation into consideration every time they make a major purchase, such as a house or a car. As inflation fluctuates, so too does the nominal interest rate on loans to buy these goods. The nominal interest rate is comprised of the real rate, plus an **expected inflation** factor. Expected inflation also tells economists about how the public views the direction of the economy. Suppose the public expects inflation to increase. This could be the result of positive demand shock due to an expanding economy and increasing aggregate demand. It could also be the result of a negative supply shock, perhaps from rising energy prices, and decreasing aggregate supply. In either case, the public may expect the central bank to engage in contractionary monetary policy to reduce inflation, and this policy results in higher interest rates. If, on the other hand, inflation is expected to decrease, the public may anticipate a recession. In turn, the public may expect expansionary monetary policy, and the lowering of interest rates, in the short run. By monitoring expected inflation, economists garner information about the effectiveness of macroeconomic policies. Additionally, monitoring expected inflation allows for projecting the direction of real interest rates that isolate for the effect of inflation. This information is necessary for making decisions about financing investments.

Expectations about inflation may seem like a highly theoretical concept, but, in fact, inflation expectations are measured by the Federal Reserve Bank based upon early research conducted by Joseph Livingston, a financial journalist for the *Philadelphia Inquirer*. In 1946, he started a twice-a-year survey of economists about their expectations of inflation. After Livingston's death in 1969, the survey was continued by the Federal Reserve Bank and other economic research agencies such as the Survey Research Center at the University of Michigan, the American Statistical Association, and the National Bureau of Economic Research.

Current research by the Federal Reserve compares these expectations to actual inflation that has occurred, and the results, so far, are mixed. Economists' forecasts, however, have become notably more accurate in the last few decades. Economists are actively researching how expectations of inflation and other economic variables are formed and changed.

Link It Up 🔗

Visit this website (http://openstaxcollege.org/l/Haubrich) to read "The Federal Reserve Bank of Cleveland's Economic Commentary: A New Approach to Gauging Inflation Expectations" by Joseph G. Haubrich for more information about how expected inflation is forecast.

The Neoclassical Phillips Curve Tradeoff

The Keynesian Perspective introduced the Phillips curve and explained how it is derived from the aggregate supply curve. The short run upward sloping aggregate supply curve implies a downward sloping Phillips curve; thus, there is a tradeoff between inflation and unemployment in the short run. By contrast, a neoclassical long-run aggregate supply curve will imply a vertical shape for the Phillips curve, indicating no long run tradeoff between inflation and unemployment. **Figure 12.6** (a) shows the vertical AS curve, with three different levels of aggregate demand, resulting in three different equilibria, at three different price levels. At every point along that vertical AS curve, potential GDP and the rate of unemployment remains the same. Assume that for this economy, the natural rate of unemployment is 5%. As a result, the long-run Phillips curve relationship, shown in **Figure 12.6** (b), is a vertical line, rising up from 5% unemployment, at any level of inflation. Read the following Work It Out feature for additional information on how to interpret inflation and unemployment rates.

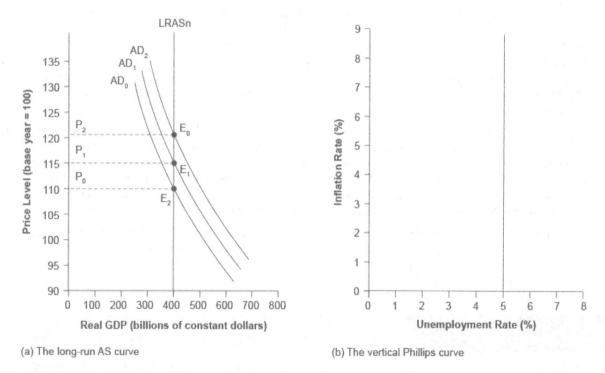

(a) The long-run AS curve   (b) The vertical Phillips curve

Figure 12.6 From a Long-Run AS Curve to a Long-Run Phillips Curve (a) With a vertical LRAS curve, shifts in aggregate demand do not alter the level of output but do lead to changes in the price level. Because output is unchanged between the equilibria E_0, E_1, and E_2, all unemployment in this economy will be due to the natural rate of unemployment. (b) If the natural rate of unemployment is 5%, then the Phillips curve will be vertical. That is, regardless of changes in the price level, the unemployment rate remains at 5%.

Work It Out ─○─○─○

Tracking Inflation and Unemployment Rates

Suppose that you have collected data for years on the rates of inflation and unemployment and recorded them in a table, such as Table 12.1. How do you interpret that information?

Year	Inflation Rate	Unemployment Rate
1970	2%	4%
1975	3%	3%
1980	2%	4%
1985	1%	6%
1990	1%	4%
1995	4%	2%
2000	5%	4%

Table 12.1

Step 1. Plot the data points in a graph with inflation rate on the vertical axis and unemployment rate on the horizontal axis. Your graph will appear similar to Figure 12.7.

Figure 12.7 Inflation Rates

Step 2. What patterns do you see in the data? You should notice that there are years when unemployment falls but inflation rises, and other years where unemployment rises and inflation falls.

Step 3. Can you determine the natural rate of unemployment from the data or from the graph? As you analyze the graph, it appears that the natural rate of unemployment lies at 4%; this is the rate that the economy appears to adjust back to after an apparent change in the economy. For example, in 1975 the economy appeared to have an increase in aggregate demand; the unemployment rate fell to 3% but inflation increased from 2% to 3%. By 1980, the economy had adjusted back to 4% unemployment and the inflation rate had returned to 2%. In 1985, the economy looks to have suffered a recession as unemployment rose to 6% and inflation fell to 1%. This would be consistent with a decrease in aggregate demand. By 1990, the economy recovered back to 4% unemployment, but at a lower inflation rate of 1%. In 1995 the economy again rebounded and unemployment fell to 2%, but inflation increased to 4%, which is consistent with a large increase in aggregate demand. The economy adjusted back to 4% unemployment but at a higher rate of inflation of 5%. Then in 2000, both unemployment and inflation increased to 5% and 4%, respectively.

Step 4. Do you see the Phillips curve(s) in the data? If we trace the downward sloping trend of data points, we could see a short-run Phillips curve that exhibits the inverse tradeoff between higher unemployment and lower inflation rates. If we trace the vertical line of data points, we could see a long-run Phillips curve at the 4% natural rate of unemployment.

The unemployment rate on the long-run Phillips curve will be the natural rate of unemployment. A small inflationary increase in the price level from AD_0 to AD_1 will have the same natural rate of unemployment as a larger inflationary increase in the price level from AD_0 to AD_2. The macroeconomic equilibrium along the vertical aggregate supply curve can occur at a variety of different price levels, and the natural rate of unemployment can be consistent with all different rates of inflation. The great economist Milton Friedman (1912–2006) summed up the neoclassical view of the long-term Phillips curve tradeoff in a 1967 speech: "[T]here is always a temporary trade-off between inflation and unemployment; there is no permanent trade-off."

In the Keynesian perspective, the primary focus is on getting the level of aggregate demand right in relationship to an upward-sloping aggregate supply curve. That is, AD should be adjusted so that the economy produces at its potential GDP, not so low that cyclical unemployment results and not so high that inflation results. In the neoclassical perspective, aggregate supply will determine output at potential GDP, unemployment is determined by the natural rate of unemployment churned out by the forces of supply and demand in the labor market, and shifts in aggregate demand are the primary determinant of changes in the price level.

Link It Up @@

Visit this website (http://openstaxcollege.org/l/modeledbehavior) to read about the effects of economic intervention.

Fighting Unemployment or Inflation?

As explained in **Unemployment**, unemployment can be divided into two categories: cyclical unemployment and the natural rate of unemployment, which is the sum of frictional and structural unemployment. Cyclical unemployment results from fluctuations in the business cycle and is created when the economy is producing below potential GDP—giving potential employers less incentive to hire. When the economy is producing at potential GDP, cyclical unemployment will be zero. Because of the dynamics of the labor market, in which people are always entering or exiting the labor force, the unemployment rate never falls to 0%, not even when the economy is producing at or even slightly above potential GDP. Probably the best we can hope for is for the number of job vacancies to equal the number of job seekers. We know that it takes time for job seekers and employers to find each other, and this time is the cause of frictional unemployment. Most economists do not consider frictional unemployment to be a "bad" thing. After all, there will always be workers who are unemployed while looking for a job that is a better match for their skills. There will always be employers that have an open position, while looking for a worker that is a better match for the job. Ideally, these matches happen quickly, but even when the economy is very strong there will be some natural unemployment and this is what is measured by the natural rate of unemployment.

The neoclassical view of unemployment tends to focus attention away from the problem of cyclical unemployment—that is, unemployment caused by recession—while putting more attention on the issue of the rates of unemployment that prevail even when the economy is operating at potential GDP. To put it another way, the neoclassical view of unemployment tends to focus on how public policy can be adjusted to reduce the natural rate of unemployment. Such policy changes might involve redesigning unemployment and welfare programs so that they support those in need, but also offer greater encouragement for job-hunting. It might involve redesigning business rules with an eye to whether they are unintentionally discouraging businesses from taking on new employees. It might involve building institutions to improve the flow of information about jobs and the mobility of workers, to help bring workers and employers together more quickly. For those workers who find that their skills are permanently no longer in demand (for example, the structurally unemployed), policy can be designed to provide opportunities for retraining so that these workers can reenter the labor force and seek employment.

Neoclassical economists will not tend to see aggregate demand as a useful tool for reducing unemployment; after all, if economic output is determined by a vertical aggregate supply curve, then aggregate demand has no long-run effect on unemployment. Instead, neoclassical economists believe that aggregate demand should be allowed to expand only to match the gradual shifts of aggregate supply to the right—keeping the price level much the same and inflationary pressures low.

If aggregate demand rises rapidly in the neoclassical model, in the long run it leads only to inflationary pressures. **Figure 12.8** shows a vertical LRAS curve and three different levels of aggregate demand, rising from AD_0 to AD_1 to AD_2. As the macroeconomic equilibrium rises from E_0 to E_1 to E_2, the price level rises, but real GDP does not budge; nor does the rate of unemployment, which adjusts to its natural rate. Conversely, reducing inflation has no long-term costs, either. Think about **Figure 12.8** in reverse, as the aggregate demand curve shifts from AD_2 to AD_1 to AD_0, and the equilibrium moves from E_2 to E_1 to E_0. During this process, the price level falls, but, in the long run, neither real GDP nor the natural rate of unemployment is changed.

Figure 12.8 How Aggregate Demand Determines the Price Level in the Long Run As aggregate demand shifts to the right, from AD_0 to AD_1 to AD_2, real GDP in this economy and the level of unemployment do not change. However, there is inflationary pressure for a higher price level as the equilibrium changes from E_0 to E_1 to E_2.

Link It Up 🔗

Visit this website (http://openstaxcollege.org/l/inflatemploy) to read about how inflation and unemployment are related.

Fighting Recession or Encouraging Long-Term Growth?

Neoclassical economists believe that the economy will rebound out of a recession or eventually contract during an expansion because prices and wage rates are flexible and will adjust either upward or downward to restore the economy to its potential GDP. Thus, the key policy question for neoclassicals is how to promote growth of potential GDP. We know that economic growth ultimately depends on the growth rate of long-term productivity. Productivity measures how effective inputs are at producing outputs. We know that U.S. productivity has grown on average about 2% per year. That means that the same amount of inputs produce 2% more output than the year before. We also know that productivity growth varies a great deal in the short term due to cyclical factors. It also varies somewhat in the long term. From 1953–1972, U.S. labor productivity (as measured by output per hour in the business sector) grew at 3.2% per year. From 1973–1992, productivity growth declined significantly to 1.8% per year. Then, from 1993–2014, productivity growth increased slightly to 2% per year. The neoclassical economists believe the underpinnings of long-run productivity growth to be an economy's investments in human capital, physical capital, and technology, operating together in a market-oriented environment that rewards innovation. Promotion of these factors is what government policy should focus on.

Summary of Neoclassical Macroeconomic Policy Recommendations

Let's summarize what neoclassical economists recommend for macroeconomic policy. Neoclassical economists do not believe in "fine-tuning" the economy. They believe that economic growth is fostered by a stable economic environment with a low rate of inflation. Similarly, tax rates should be low and unchanging. In this environment, private economic agents can make the best possible investment decisions, which will lead to optimal investment in physical and human capital as well as research and development to promote improvements in technology.

Summary of Neoclassical Economics versus Keynesian Economics

Table 12.2 summarizes the key differences between the two schools of thought.

Summary	Neoclassical Economics	Keynesian Economics
Focus: long-term or short term	Long-term	Short-term
Prices and wages: sticky or flexible?	Flexible	Sticky
Economic output: Primarily determined by aggregate demand or aggregate supply?	Aggregate supply	Aggregate demand
Aggregate supply: vertical or upward-sloping?	Vertical	Upward-sloping
Phillips curve vertical or downward-sloping	Vertical	Downward sloping

Table 12.2 Neoclassical versus Keynesian Economics

Summary	Neoclassical Economics	Keynesian Economics
Is aggregate demand a useful tool for controlling inflation?	Yes	Yes
What should be the primary area of policy emphasis for reducing unemployment?	Reform labor market institutions to reduce natural rate of unemployment	Increase aggregate demand to eliminate cyclical unemployment
Is aggregate demand a useful tool for ending recession?	At best, only in the short-run temporary sense, but may just increase inflation instead	Yes

Table 12.2 Neoclassical versus Keynesian Economics

12.3 | Balancing Keynesian and Neoclassical Models

By the end of this section, you will be able to:
- Evaluate how neoclassical economists and Keynesian economists react to recessions
- Analyze the interrelationship between the neoclassical and Keynesian economic models

Finding the balance between Keynesian and Neoclassical models can be compared to the challenge of riding two horses simultaneously. When a circus performer stands on two horses, with a foot on each one, much of the excitement for the viewer lies in contemplating the gap between the two. As modern macroeconomists ride into the future on two horses—with one foot on the short-term Keynesian perspective and one foot on the long-term neoclassical perspective—the balancing act may look uncomfortable, but there does not seem to be any way to avoid it. Each approach, Keynesian and neoclassical, has its strengths and weaknesses.

The short-term Keynesian model, built on the importance of aggregate demand as a cause of business cycles and a degree of wage and price rigidity, does a sound job of explaining many recessions and why cyclical unemployment rises and falls. By focusing on the short-run adjustments of aggregate demand, Keynesian economics risks overlooking the long-term causes of economic growth or the natural rate of unemployment that exists even when the economy is producing at potential GDP.

The neoclassical model, with its emphasis on aggregate supply, focuses on the underlying determinants of output and employment in markets, and thus tends to put more emphasis on economic growth and how labor markets work. However, the neoclassical view is not especially helpful in explaining why unemployment moves up and down over short time horizons of a few years. Nor is the neoclassical model especially helpful when the economy is mired in an especially deep and long-lasting recession, like the Great Depression of the 1930s. Keynesian economics tends to view inflation as a price that might sometimes be paid for lower unemployment; neoclassical economics tends to view inflation as a cost that offers no offsetting gains in terms of lower unemployment.

Macroeconomics cannot, however, be summed up as an argument between one group of economists who are pure Keynesians and another group who are pure neoclassicists. Instead, many mainstream economists believe both the Keynesian and neoclassical perspectives. Robert Solow, the Nobel laureate in economics in 1987, described the dual approach in this way:

> At short time scales, I think, something sort of 'Keynesian' is a good approximation, and surely better than anything straight 'neoclassical.' At very long time scales, the interesting questions are best studied in a neoclassical framework, and attention to the Keynesian side of things would be a minor distraction. At the five-to-ten-year time scale, we have to piece things together as best we can, and look for a hybrid model that will do the job.

Many modern macroeconomists spend considerable time and energy trying to construct models that blend the most attractive aspects of the Keynesian and neoclassical approaches. It is possible to construct a somewhat complex mathematical model where aggregate demand and sticky wages and prices matter in the short run, but wages, prices, and aggregate supply adjust in the long run. However, creating an overall model that encompasses both short-term Keynesian and long-term neoclassical models is not easy.

Bring it Home

Navigating Unchartered Waters

Were the policies implemented to stabilize the economy and financial markets during the Great Recession effective? Many economists from both the Keynesian and neoclassical schools have found that they were, although to varying degrees. Alan Blinder of Princeton University and Mark Zandi for Moody's Analytics found that, without fiscal policy, GDP decline would have been significantly more than its 3.3% in 2008 followed by its 0.1% decline in 2009. They also estimated that there would have been 8.5 million more job losses had the government not intervened in the market with the TARP to support the financial industry and key automakers General Motors and Chrysler. Federal Reserve Bank economists Carlos Carvalho, Stefano Eusip, and Christian Grisse found in their study, *Policy Initiatives in the Global Recession: What Did Forecasters Expect?* that once policies were implemented, forecasters adapted their expectations to these policies. They were more likely to anticipate increases in investment due to lower interest rates brought on by monetary policy and increased economic growth resulting from fiscal policy.

The difficulty with evaluating the effectiveness of the stabilization policies that were taken in response to the Great Recession is that we will never know what would have happened had those policies not have been implemented. Surely some of the programs were more effective at creating and saving jobs, while other programs were less so. The final conclusion on the effectiveness of macroeconomic policies is still up for debate, and further study will no doubt consider the impact of these policies on the U.S. budget and deficit, as well as the value of the U.S. dollar in the financial market.

KEY TERMS

adaptive expectations the theory that people look at past experience and gradually adapt their beliefs and behavior as circumstances change

expected inflation a future rate of inflation that consumers and firms build into current decision making

neoclassical perspective the philosophy that, in the long run, the business cycle will fluctuate around the potential, or full-employment, level of output

physical capital per person the amount and kind of machinery and equipment available to help a person produce a good or service

rational expectations the theory that people form the most accurate possible expectations about the future that they can, using all information available to them

KEY CONCEPTS AND SUMMARY

12.1 The Building Blocks of Neoclassical Analysis
Neoclassical perspective argues that, in the long run, the economy will adjust back to its potential GDP level of output through flexible price levels. Thus, the neoclassical perspective views the long-run AS curve as vertical. A rational expectations perspective argues that people have excellent information about economic events and how the economy works and that, as a result, price and other economic adjustments will happen very quickly. In adaptive expectations theory, people have limited information about economic information and how the economy works, and so price and other economic adjustments can be slow.

12.2 The Policy Implications of the Neoclassical Perspective
Neoclassical economists tend to put relatively more emphasis on long-term growth than on fighting recession, because they believe that recessions will fade in a few years and long-term growth will ultimately determine the standard of living. They tend to focus more on reducing the natural rate of unemployment caused by economic institutions and government policies than the cyclical unemployment caused by recession.

Neoclassical economists also see no social benefit to inflation. With an upward-sloping Keynesian AS curve, inflation can arise because an economy is approaching full employment. With a vertical long-run neoclassical AS curve, inflation does not accompany any rise in output. If aggregate supply is vertical, then aggregate demand does not affect the quantity of output. Instead, aggregate demand can only cause inflationary changes in the price level. A vertical aggregate supply curve, where the quantity of output is consistent with many different price levels, also implies a vertical Phillips curve.

12.3 Balancing Keynesian and Neoclassical Models
The Keynesian perspective considers changes to aggregate demand to be the cause of business cycle fluctuations. Keynesians are likely to advocate that policy makers actively attempt to reverse recessionary and inflationary periods because they are not convinced that the self-correcting economy can easily return to full employment.

The neoclassical perspective places more emphasis on aggregate supply. The level of potential GDP is determined by long term productivity growth and that the economy typically will return to full employment after a change in aggregate demand. Skeptical of the effectiveness and timeliness of Keynesian policy, neoclassical economists are more likely to advocate a hands-off, or fairly limited, role for active stabilization policy.

While Keynesians would tend to advocate an acceptable tradeoff between inflation and unemployment when counteracting a recession, neoclassical economists argue that no such tradeoff exists; any short-term gains in lower unemployment will eventually vanish and the result of active policy will only be inflation.

SELF-CHECK QUESTIONS

1. Do rational expectations tend to look back at past experience while adaptive expectations look ahead to the future? Explain your answer.

2. Legislation proposes that the government should use macroeconomic policy to achieve an unemployment rate of zero percent, by increasing aggregate demand for as much and as long as necessary to accomplish this goal. From a neoclassical perspective, how will this policy affect output and the price level in the short run and in the long run? Sketch an aggregate demand/aggregate supply diagram to illustrate your answer. *Hint*: revisit Figure 12.4.

3. Would it make sense to argue that rational expectations economics is an extreme version of neoclassical economics? Explain.

4. Summarize the Keynesian and Neoclassical models.

REVIEW QUESTIONS

5. Does neoclassical economics focus on the long term or the short term? Explain your answer.

6. Does neoclassical economics view prices and wages as sticky or flexible? Why?

7. What shape is the long-run aggregate supply curve? Why does it have this shape?

8. What is the difference between rational expectations and adaptive expectations?

9. A neoclassical economist and a Keynesian economist are studying the economy of Vineland. It appears that Vineland is beginning to experience a mild recession with a decrease in aggregate demand. Which of these two economists would likely advocate that the government of Vineland take active measures to reverse this decline in aggregate demand? Why?

10. Do neoclassical economists tend to focus more on long term economic growth or on recessions? Explain briefly.

11. Do neoclassical economists tend to focus more on cyclical unemployment or on inflation? Explain briefly.

12. Do neoclassical economists see a value in tolerating a little more inflation if it brings additional economic output? Explain your answer.

13. If aggregate supply is vertical, what role does aggregate demand play in determining output? In determining the price level?

14. What is the shape of the neoclassical long-run Phillips curve? What assumptions are made that lead to this shape?

15. When the economy is experiencing a recession, why would a neoclassical economist be unlikely to argue for aggressive policy to stimulate aggregate demand and return the economy to full employment? Explain your answer.

16. If the economy is suffering through a rampant inflationary period, would a Keynesian economist advocate for stabilization policy that involves higher taxes and higher interest rates? Explain your answer.

CRITICAL THINKING QUESTIONS

17. If most people have rational expectations, how long will recessions last?

18. Explain why the neoclassical economists believe that nothing much needs to be done about unemployment. Do you agree or disagree? Explain.

19. The American Recovery and Reinvestment Act was criticized by economists from all theoretical persuasions. The "Stimulus Package" was arguably a Keynesian measure so why would a Keynesian economist be critical of it? Why would neoclassical economists be critical?

20. Is it a logical contradiction to be a neoclassical Keynesian? Explain.

PROBLEMS

21. Use Table 12.3 to answer the following questions.

Price Level	Aggregate Supply	Aggregate Demand
90	3,000	3,500
95	3,000	3,000
100	3,000	2,500
105	3,000	2,200
110	3,000	2,100

Table 12.3

a. Sketch an aggregate supply and aggregate demand diagram.
b. What is the equilibrium output and price level?
c. If aggregate demand shifts right, what is equilibrium output?
d. If aggregate demand shifts left, what is equilibrium output?
e. In this scenario, would you suggest using aggregate demand to alter the level of output or to control any inflationary increases in the price level?

13 | Money and Banking

Figure 13.1 Cowrie Shell or Money? Is this an image of a cowrie shell or money? The answer is: Both. For centuries, the extremely durable cowrie shell was used as a medium of exchange in various parts of the world. (Credit: modification of work by "prilfish"/Flickr Creative Commons)

Bring it Home

The Many Disguises of Money: From Cowries to Bitcoins

Here is a trivia question: In the history of the world, what item was used for money over the broadest geographic area and for the longest period of time? The answer is not gold, silver, or any precious metal. It is the cowrie, a mollusk shell found mainly off the Maldives Islands in the Indian Ocean. Cowries served as money as early as 700 B.C. in China. By the 1500s, they were in widespread use across India and Africa. For several centuries after that, cowries were used in markets including southern Europe, western Africa, India, and China for a wide range of purchases: everything from buying lunch or a ferry ride to paying for a shipload of silk or rice. Cowries were still acceptable as a way of paying taxes in certain African nations in the early twentieth century.

What made cowries work so well as money? First, they are extremely durable—lasting a century or more. As the late economic historian Karl Polyani put it, they can be "poured, sacked, shoveled, hoarded in heaps" while remaining "clean, dainty, stainless, polished, and milk-white." Second, parties could use cowries either by counting shells of a certain size, or—for large purchases—by measuring the weight or volume of the total shells to be exchanged. Third, it was impossible to counterfeit a cowrie shell, but gold or silver coins could be counterfeited by making copies with cheaper metals. Finally, in the heyday of cowrie money, from the 1500s into the 1800s, the collection of cowries was tightly controlled, first by the Portuguese and later by the Dutch and the English. As a result, the supply of cowries was allowed to grow quickly enough to serve the needs of commerce, but not so quickly that they were no longer scarce. Money throughout the ages has taken many different forms and continues to evolve even today. What do you think money is?

Introduction to Money and Banking

In this chapter, you will learn about:

- Defining Money by Its Functions
- Measuring Money: Currency, M1, and M2
- The Role of Banks
- How Banks Create Money

The discussion of money and banking is a central component in the study of macroeconomics. At this point, you should have firmly in mind the main goals of macroeconomics from **Welcome to Economics!**: economic growth, low unemployment, and low inflation. We have yet to discuss money and its role in helping to achieve our macroeconomic goals.

You should also understand Keynesian and neoclassical frameworks for macroeconomic analysis and how these frameworks can be embodied in the aggregate demand/aggregate supply (AD/AS) model. With the goals and frameworks for macroeconomic analysis in mind, the final step is to discuss the two main categories of macroeconomic policy: monetary policy, which focuses on money, banking and interest rates; and fiscal policy, which focuses on government spending, taxes, and borrowing. This chapter discusses what economists mean by money, and how money is closely interrelated with the banking system. **Monetary Policy and Bank Regulation** furthers this discussion.

13.1 | Defining Money by Its Functions

By the end of this section, you will be able to:
- Explain the various functions of money
- Contrast commodity money and fiat money

Money for the sake of money is not an end in itself. You cannot eat dollar bills or wear your bank account. Ultimately, the usefulness of money rests in exchanging it for goods or services. As the American writer and humorist Ambrose Bierce (1842–1914) wrote in 1911, money is a "blessing that is of no advantage to us excepting when we part with it." Money is what people regularly use when purchasing or selling goods and services, and thus money must be widely accepted by both buyers and sellers. This concept of money is intentionally flexible, because money has taken a wide variety of forms in different cultures.

Barter and the Double Coincidence of Wants

To understand the usefulness of money, we must consider what the world would be like without money. How would people exchange goods and services? Economies without money typically engage in the barter system. **Barter**—literally trading one good or service for another—is highly inefficient for trying to coordinate the trades in a modern advanced economy. In an economy without money, an exchange between two people would involve a **double coincidence of wants**, a situation in which two people each want some good or service that the other person can provide. For example, if an accountant wants a pair of shoes, this accountant must find someone who has a pair of shoes in the correct size and who is willing to exchange the shoes for some hours of accounting services. Such a trade is likely to be difficult to arrange. Think about the complexity of such trades in a modern economy, with its extensive division of labor that involves thousands upon thousands of different jobs and goods.

Another problem with the barter system is that it does not allow us to easily enter into future contracts for the purchase of many goods and services. For example, if the goods are perishable it may be difficult to exchange them for other goods in the future. Imagine a farmer wanting to buy a tractor in six months using a fresh crop of strawberries.

Additionally, while the barter system might work adequately in small economies, it will keep these economies from growing. The time that individuals would otherwise spend producing goods and services and enjoying leisure time is spent bartering.

Functions for Money

Money solves the problems created by the barter system. (We will get to its definition soon.) First, money serves as a **medium of exchange**, which means that money acts as an intermediary between the buyer and the seller. Instead of exchanging accounting services for shoes, the accountant now exchanges accounting services for money. This money is then used to buy shoes. To serve as a medium of exchange, money must be very widely accepted as a method of payment in the markets for goods, labor, and financial capital.

Second, money must serve as a **store of value**. In a barter system, we saw the example of the shoemaker trading shoes for accounting services. But she risks having her shoes go out of style, especially if she keeps them in a warehouse for future use—their value will decrease with each season. Shoes are not a good store of value. Holding money is a much easier way of storing value. You know that you do not need to spend it immediately because it will still hold its value the next day, or the next year. This function of money does not require that money is a *perfect* store of value. In an economy with inflation, money loses some buying power each year, but it remains money.

Third, money serves as a **unit of account**, which means that it is the ruler by which other values are measured. For example, an accountant may charge $100 to file your tax return. That $100 can purchase two pair of shoes at $50 a pair. Money acts as a common denominator, an accounting method that simplifies thinking about trade-offs.

Finally, another function of money is that money must serve as a **standard of deferred payment**. This means that if money is usable today to make purchases, it must also be acceptable to make purchases today that will be paid in the *future*. Loans and future agreements are stated in monetary terms and the standard of deferred payment is what allows us to buy goods and services today and pay in the future. So **money** serves all of these functions— it is a medium of exchange, store of value, unit of account, and standard of deferred payment.

Commodity versus Fiat Money

Money has taken a wide variety of forms in different cultures. Gold, silver, cowrie shells, cigarettes, and even cocoa beans have been used as money. Although these items are used as **commodity money**, they also have a value from use as something other than money. Gold, for example, has been used throughout the ages as money although today it is not used as money but rather is valued for its other attributes. Gold is a good conductor of electricity and is used in the electronics and aerospace industry. Gold is also used in the manufacturing of energy efficient reflective glass for skyscrapers and is used in the medical industry as well. Of course, gold also has value because of its beauty and malleability in the creation of jewelry.

As commodity money, gold has historically served its purpose as a medium of exchange, a store of value, and as a unit of account. **Commodity-backed currencies** are dollar bills or other currencies with values backed up by gold or other commodity held at a bank. During much of its history, the money supply in the United States was backed by gold and silver. Interestingly, antique dollars dated as late as 1957, have "Silver Certificate" printed over the portrait of George Washington, as shown in Figure 13.2. This meant that the holder could take the bill to the appropriate bank and exchange it for a dollar's worth of silver.

Figure 13.2 A Silver Certificate and a Modern U.S. Bill Until 1958, silver certificates were commodity-backed money—backed by silver, as indicated by the words "Silver Certificate" printed on the bill. Today, U.S. bills are backed by the Federal Reserve, but as fiat money. (Credit: "The.Comedian"/Flickr Creative Commons)

As economies grew and became more global in nature, the use of commodity monies became more cumbersome. Countries moved towards the use of **fiat money**. Fiat money has no intrinsic value, but is declared by a government to be the legal tender of a country. The United States' paper money, for example, carries the statement: "THIS NOTE IS LEGAL TENDER FOR ALL DEBTS, PUBLIC AND PRIVATE." In other words, by government decree, if you owe a debt, then legally speaking, you can pay that debt with the U.S. currency, even though it is not backed by a commodity. The only backing of our money is universal faith and trust that the currency has value, and nothing more.

Link It Up ⚭

Watch this video (http://openstaxcollege.org/l/moneyhistory) on the "History of Money."

13.2 | Measuring Money: Currency, M1, and M2

By the end of this section, you will be able to:
- Contrast M1 money supply and M2 money supply
- Classify monies as M1 money supply or M2 money supply

Cash in your pocket certainly serves as money. But what about checks or credit cards? Are they money, too? Rather than trying to state a single way of measuring money, economists offer broader definitions of money based on liquidity. Liquidity refers to how quickly a financial asset can be used to buy a good or service. For example, cash is very liquid. Your $10 bill can be easily used to buy a hamburger at lunchtime. However, $10 that you have in your savings account is not so easy to use. You must go to the bank or ATM machine and withdraw that cash to buy your lunch. Thus, $10 in your savings account is *less* liquid.

The Federal Reserve Bank, which is the central bank of the United States, is a bank regulator and is responsible for monetary policy and defines money according to its liquidity. There are two definitions of money: M1 and M2 money supply. **M1 money supply** includes those monies that are very liquid such as cash, checkable (demand) deposits, and traveler's checks **M2 money supply** is less liquid in nature and includes M1 plus savings and time deposits, certificates of deposits, and money market funds.

M1 money supply includes **coins and currency in circulation**—the coins and bills that circulate in an economy that are not held by the U.S. Treasury, at the Federal Reserve Bank, or in bank vaults. Closely related to currency are checkable deposits, also known as **demand deposits**. These are the amounts held in checking accounts. They are called demand deposits or checkable deposits because the banking institution must give the deposit holder his money "on demand" when a check is written or a debit card is used. These items together—currency, and checking accounts in banks—make up the definition of money known as M1, which is measured daily by the Federal Reserve System. Traveler's checks are a also included in M1, but have decreased in use over the recent past.

A broader definition of money, M2 includes everything in M1 but also adds other types of deposits. For example, M2 includes **savings deposits** in banks, which are bank accounts on which you cannot write a check directly, but from which you can easily withdraw the money at an automatic teller machine or bank. Many banks and other financial institutions also offer a chance to invest in **money market funds**, where the deposits of many individual investors are pooled together and invested in a safe way, such as short-term government bonds. Another ingredient of M2 are the relatively small (that is, less than about $100,000) certificates of deposit (CDs) or **time deposits**, which are accounts that the depositor has committed to leaving in the bank for a certain period of time, ranging from a few months to a few years, in exchange for a higher interest rate. In short, all these types of M2 are money that you can withdraw and spend, but which require a greater effort to do so than the items in M1 **Figure 13.3** should help in visualizing the relationship between M1 and M2. Note that M1 is included in the M2 calculation.

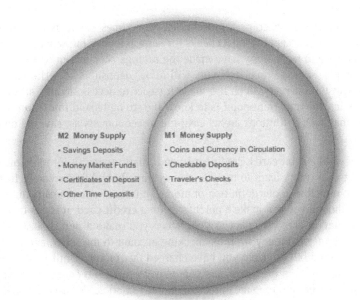

Figure 13.3 The Relationship between M1 and M2 Money M1 and M2 money have several definitions, ranging from narrow to broad. M1 = coins and currency in circulation + checkable (demand) deposit + traveler's checks. M2 = M1 + savings deposits + money market funds + certificates of deposit + other time deposits.

The Federal Reserve System is responsible for tracking the amounts of M1 and M2 and prepares a weekly release of information about the money supply. To provide an idea of what these amounts sound like, according to the Federal Reserve Bank's measure of the U.S. money stock, at the end of February 2015, M1 in the United States was $3 trillion, while M2 was $11.8 trillion. A breakdown of the portion of each type of money that comprised M1 and M2 in February 2015, as provided by the Federal Reserve Bank, is provided in **Table 13.1**.

Components of M1 in the U.S. (February 2015, Seasonally Adjusted)	$ billions
Currency	$1,271.8
Traveler's checks	$2.9
Demand deposits and other checking accounts	$1,713.5
Total M1	*$2,988.2 (or $3 trillion)*
Components of M2 in the U.S. (February 2015, Seasonally Adjusted)	**$ billions**
M1 money supply	$2,988.2
Savings accounts	$7,712.1
Time deposits	$509.2
Individual money market mutual fund balances	$610.8
Total M2	*$11,820.3 (or $11.8 trillion)*

Table 13.1 M1 and M2 Federal Reserve Statistical Release, Money Stock Measures   (Source: Federal Reserve Statistical Release, http://www.federalreserve.gov/RELEASES/h6/current/default.htm#t2tg1link)

The lines separating M1 and M2 can become a little blurry. Sometimes elements of M1 are not treated alike; for example, some businesses will not accept personal checks for large amounts, but will accept traveler's checks or cash. Changes in banking practices and technology have made the savings accounts in M2 more similar to the checking accounts in M1. For example, some savings accounts will allow depositors to write checks, use automatic teller machines, and pay bills over the Internet, which has made it easier to access savings accounts. As with many other economic terms and statistics, the important point is to know the strengths and limitations of the various definitions of money, not to believe that such definitions are as clear-cut to economists as, say, the definition of nitrogen is to chemists.

Where does "plastic money" like debit cards, credit cards, and smart money fit into this picture? A **debit card**, like a check, is an instruction to the user's bank to transfer money directly and immediately from your bank account to the seller. It is important to note that in our definition of money, it is *checkable deposits* that are money, not the paper check or the debit card. Although you can make a purchase with a **credit card**, it is not considered money but rather a short term loan from the credit card company to you. When you make a purchase with a credit card, the credit card company immediately transfers money from its checking account to the seller, and at the end of the month, the credit card company sends you a bill for what you have charged that month. Until you pay the credit card bill, you have effectively borrowed money from the credit card company. With a **smart card**, you can store a certain value of money on the card and then use the card to make purchases. Some "smart cards" used for specific purposes, like long-distance phone calls or making purchases at a campus bookstore and cafeteria, are not really all that smart, because they can only be used for certain purchases or in certain places.

In short, credit cards, debit cards, and smart cards are different ways to move money when a purchase is made. But having more credit cards or debit cards does not change the quantity of money in the economy, any more than having more checks printed increases the amount of money in your checking account.

One key message underlying this discussion of M1 and M2 is that money in a modern economy is not just paper bills and coins; instead, money is closely linked to bank accounts. Indeed, the macroeconomic policies concerning money are largely conducted through the banking system. The next section explains how banks function and how a nation's banking system has the power to create money.

Link It Up

Read a brief article (http://openstaxcollege.org/l/Sweden) on the current monetary challenges in Sweden.

13.3 | The Role of Banks

By the end of this section, you will be able to:

- Explain how banks act as intermediaries between savers and borrowers
- Evaluate the relationship between banks, savings and loans, and credit unions
- Analyze the causes of bankruptcy and recessions

The late bank robber named Willie Sutton was once asked why he robbed banks. He answered: "That's where the money is." While this may have been true at one time, from the perspective of modern economists, Sutton is both right and wrong. He is wrong because the overwhelming majority of money in the economy is not in the form of currency sitting in vaults or drawers at banks, waiting for a robber to appear. Most money is in the form of bank accounts, which exist only as electronic records on computers. From a broader perspective, however, the bank robber was more right than he may have known. Banking is intimately interconnected with money and consequently, with the broader economy.

Banks make it far easier for a complex economy to carry out the extraordinary range of transactions that occur in goods, labor, and financial capital markets. Imagine for a moment what the economy would be like if all payments had to be made in cash. When shopping for a large purchase or going on vacation you might need to carry hundreds of dollars in a pocket or purse. Even small businesses would need stockpiles of cash to pay workers and to purchase supplies. A bank allows people and businesses to store this money in either a checking account or savings account, for example, and then withdraw this money as needed through the use of a direct withdrawal, writing a check, or using a debit card.

Banks are a critical intermediary in what is called the **payment system**, which helps an economy exchange goods and services for money or other financial assets. Also, those with extra money that they would like to save can store their money in a bank rather than look for an individual that is willing to borrow it from them and then repay them at a later date. Those who want to borrow money can go directly to a bank rather than trying to find someone to lend them cash **Transaction costs** are the costs associated with finding a lender or a borrower for this money. Thus, banks lower transactions costs and act as financial intermediaries—they bring savers and borrowers together. Along with making transactions much safer and easier, banks also play a key role in the creation of money.

Banks as Financial Intermediaries

An "intermediary" is one who stands between two other parties. Banks are a **financial intermediary**—that is, an institution that operates between a saver who deposits money in a bank and a borrower who receives a loan from that bank. Financial intermediaries include other institutions in the financial market such as insurance companies and pension funds, but they will not be included in this discussion because they are not considered to be **depository institutions**, which are institutions that accept money *deposits* and then use these to make loans. All the funds deposited are mingled in one big pool, which is then loaned out. **Figure 13.4** illustrates the position of banks as financial intermediaries, with deposits flowing into a bank and loans flowing out. Of course, when banks make loans to firms, the banks will try to funnel financial capital to healthy businesses that have good prospects for repaying the loans, not to firms that are suffering losses and may be unable to repay.

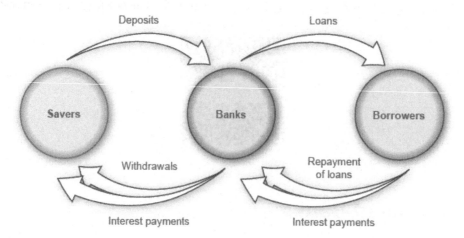

Figure 13.4 Banks as Financial Intermediaries Banks act as financial intermediaries because they stand between savers and borrowers. Savers place deposits with banks, and then receive interest payments and withdraw money. Borrowers receive loans from banks and repay the loans with interest. In turn, banks return money to savers in the form of withdrawals, which also include interest payments from banks to savers.

How are banks, savings and loans, and credit unions related?

Banks have a couple of close cousins: savings institutions and credit unions. Banks, as explained, receive deposits from individuals and businesses and make loans with the money. Savings institutions are also sometimes called "savings and loans" or "thrifts." They also take loans and make deposits. However, from the 1930s until the 1980s, federal law limited how much interest savings institutions were allowed to pay to depositors. They were also required to make most of their loans in the form of housing-related loans, either to homebuyers or to real-estate developers and builders.

A credit union is a nonprofit financial institution that its members own and run. Members of each credit union decide who is eligible to be a member. Usually, potential members would be everyone in a certain community, or groups of employees, or members of a certain organization. The credit union accepts deposits from members and focuses on making loans back to its members. While there are more credit unions than banks and more banks than savings and loans, the total assets of credit unions are growing.

In 2008, there were 7,085 banks. Due to the bank failures of 2007–2009 and bank mergers, there were 5,571 banks in the United States at the end of the fourth quarter in 2014. According to the Credit Union National Association, as of December 2014 there were 6,535 credit unions with assets totaling $1.1 billion. A day of "Transfer Your Money" took place in 2009 out of general public disgust with big bank bailouts. People were encouraged to transfer their deposits to credit unions. This has grown into the ongoing Move Your Money Project. Consequently, some now hold deposits as large as $50 million. However, as of 2013, the 12 largest banks (0.2%) controlled 69 percent of all banking assets, according to the Dallas Federal Reserve.

A Bank's Balance Sheet

A **balance sheet** is an accounting tool that lists assets and liabilities. An **asset** is something of value that is owned and can be used to produce something. For example, the cash you own can be used to pay your tuition. If you own a home, this is also considered an asset. A **liability** is a debt or something you owe. Many people borrow money to buy homes. In this case, a home is the asset, but the mortgage is the liability. The **net worth** is the asset value minus how much is owed (the liability). A bank's balance sheet operates in much the same way. A bank's net worth is also referred to as **bank capital**. A bank has assets such as cash held in its vaults, monies that the bank holds at the Federal Reserve bank (called "reserves"), loans that are made to customers, and bonds.

Figure 13.5 illustrates a hypothetical and simplified balance sheet for the Safe and Secure Bank. Because of the two-column format of the balance sheet, with the T-shape formed by the vertical line down the middle and the horizontal line under "Assets" and "Liabilities," it is sometimes called a **T-account**.

Assets		Liabilities + Net Worth	
Loans	$5 million	Deposits	$10 million
U.S. Government Securities (USGS)	$4 million		
Reserves	$2 million	Net Worth	$1 million

Figure 13.5 A Balance Sheet for the Safe and Secure Bank

The "T" in a T-account separates the assets of a firm, on the left, from its liabilities, on the right. All firms use T-accounts, though most are much more complex. For a bank, the assets are the financial instruments that either the bank is holding (its reserves) or those instruments where other parties owe money to the bank—like loans made by the bank and U.S. Government Securities, such as U.S. treasury bonds purchased by the bank. Liabilities are what the bank owes to others. Specifically, the bank owes any deposits made in the bank to those who have made them. The net worth of the bank is the total assets minus total liabilities. Net worth is included on the liabilities side to have the T account balance to zero. For a healthy business, net worth will be positive. For a bankrupt firm, net worth will be negative. In either case, on a bank's T-account, assets will always equal liabilities plus net worth.

When bank customers deposit money into a checking account, savings account, or a certificate of deposit, the bank views these deposits as liabilities. After all, the bank owes these deposits to its customers, when the customers wish to withdraw their money. In the example shown in **Figure 13.5**, the Safe and Secure Bank holds $10 million in deposits.

Loans are the first category of bank assets shown in **Figure 13.5**. Say that a family takes out a 30-year mortgage loan to purchase a house, which means that the borrower will repay the loan over the next 30 years. This loan is clearly an asset from the bank's perspective, because the borrower has a legal obligation to make payments to the bank over time. But in practical terms, how can the value of the mortgage loan that is being paid over 30 years be measured in the present? One way of measuring the value of something—whether a loan or anything else—is by estimating what another party in the market is willing to pay for it. Many banks issue home loans, and charge various handling and processing fees for doing so, but then sell the loans to other banks or financial institutions who collect the loan payments. The market where loans are made to borrowers is called the primary loan market, while the market in which these loans are bought and sold by financial institutions is the secondary loan market.

One key factor that affects what financial institutions are willing to pay for a loan, when they buy it in the secondary loan market, is the perceived riskiness of the loan: that is, given the characteristics of the borrower, such as income level and whether the local economy is performing strongly, what proportion of loans of this type will be repaid? The greater the risk that a loan will not be repaid, the less that any financial institution will pay to acquire the loan. Another key factor is to compare the interest rate charged on the original loan with the current interest rate in the economy. If the original loan made at some point in the past requires the borrower to pay a low interest rate, but current interest rates are relatively high, then a financial institution will pay less to acquire the loan. In contrast, if the original loan requires the borrower to pay a high interest rate, while current interest rates are relatively low, then a financial institution will pay more to acquire the loan. For the Safe and Secure Bank in this example, the total value of its loans if they were sold to other financial institutions in the secondary market is $5 million.

The second category of bank asset is bonds, which are a common mechanism for borrowing, used by the federal and local government, and also private companies, and nonprofit organizations. A bank takes some of the money it has received in deposits and uses the money to buy bonds—typically bonds issued by the U.S. government. Government bonds are low-risk because the government is virtually certain to pay off the bond, albeit at a low rate of interest. These bonds are an asset for banks in the same way that loans are an asset: The bank will receive a stream of payments in the future. In our example, the Safe and Secure Bank holds bonds worth a total value of $4 million.

The final entry under assets is **reserves**, which is money that the bank keeps on hand, and that is not loaned out or invested in bonds—and thus does not lead to interest payments. The Federal Reserve requires that banks keep a certain percentage of depositors' money on "reserve," which means either in their vaults or kept at the Federal Reserve Bank. This is called a reserve requirement. (**Monetary Policy and Bank Regulation** will explain how the level of these required reserves are one policy tool that governments have to influence bank behavior.) Additionally, banks may also want to keep a certain amount of reserves on hand in excess of what is required. The Safe and Secure Bank is holding $2 million in reserves.

The net worth of a bank is defined as its total assets minus its total liabilities. For the Safe and Secure Bank shown in Figure 13.5, net worth is equal to $1 million; that is, $11 million in assets minus $10 million in liabilities. For a financially healthy bank, the net worth will be positive. If a bank has negative net worth and depositors tried to withdraw their money, the bank would not be able to give all depositors their money.

Link It Up

For some concrete examples of what banks do, watch this video (http://openstaxcollege.org/l/makingsense) from Paul Solman's "Making Sense of Financial News."

How Banks Go Bankrupt

A bank that is bankrupt will have a negative net worth, meaning its assets will be worth less than its liabilities. How can this happen? Again, looking at the balance sheet helps to explain.

A well-run bank will assume that a small percentage of borrowers will not repay their loans on time, or at all, and factor these missing payments into its planning. Remember, the calculations of the expenses of banks every year includes a factor for loans that are not repaid, and the value of a bank's loans on its balance sheet assumes a certain level of riskiness because some loans will not be repaid. Even if a bank expects a certain number of loan defaults, it will suffer if the number of loan defaults is much greater than expected, as can happen during a recession. For example, if the Safe and Secure Bank in Figure 13.5 experienced a wave of unexpected defaults, so that its loans declined in value from $5 million to $3 million, then the assets of the Safe and Secure Bank would decline so that the bank had negative net worth.

Clear It Up

What led to the financial crisis of 2008–2009?

Many banks make mortgage loans so that people can buy a home, but then do not keep the loans on their books as an asset. Instead, the bank sells the loan. These loans are "securitized," which means that they are bundled together into a financial security that is sold to investors. Investors in these mortgage-backed securities receive a rate of return based on the level of payments that people make on all the mortgages that stand behind the security.

Securitization offers certain advantages. If a bank makes most of its loans in a local area, then the bank may be financially vulnerable if the local economy declines, so that many people are unable to make their payments. But if a bank sells its local loans, and then buys a mortgage-backed security based on home loans in many parts of the country, it can avoid being exposed to local financial risks. (In the simple example in the text, banks just own "bonds." In reality, banks can own a number of financial instruments, as long as these financial investments are safe enough to satisfy the government bank regulators.) From the standpoint of a local homebuyer, securitization offers the benefit that a local bank does not need to have lots of extra funds to make a loan, because the bank is only planning to hold that loan for a short time, before selling the loan so that it can be pooled into a financial security.

But securitization also offers one potentially large disadvantage. If a bank is going to hold a mortgage loan as an asset, the bank has an incentive to scrutinize the borrower carefully to ensure that the loan is likely to be repaid. However, a bank that is going to sell the loan may be less careful in making the loan in the first place. The bank will be more willing to make what are called "subprime loans," which are loans that have characteristics like low or zero down-payment, little scrutiny of whether the borrower has a reliable income, and sometimes low payments for the first year or two that will be followed by much higher payments after that. Some subprime loans made in the mid-2000s were later dubbed NINJA loans: loans made even though the borrower had demonstrated No Income, No Job, or Assets.

These subprime loans were typically sold and turned into financial securities—but with a twist. The idea was that if losses occurred on these mortgage-backed securities, certain investors would agree to take the first, say, 5% of such losses. Other investors would agree to take, say, the next 5% of losses. By this approach, still other investors would not need to take any losses unless these mortgage-backed financial securities lost 25% or 30% or more of their total value. These complex securities, along with other economic factors, encouraged a large expansion of subprime loans in the mid-2000s.

The economic stage was now set for a banking crisis. Banks thought they were buying only ultra-safe securities, because even though the securities were ultimately backed by risky subprime mortgages, the banks only invested in the part of those securities where they were protected from small or moderate levels of losses. But as housing prices fell after 2007, and the deepening recession made it harder for many people to make their mortgage payments, many banks found that their mortgage-backed financial assets could end up being worth much less than they had expected—and so the banks were staring bankruptcy in the face. In the 2008–2011 period, 318 banks failed in the United States.

The risk of an unexpectedly high level of loan defaults can be especially difficult for banks because a bank's liabilities, namely the deposits of its customers, can be withdrawn quickly, but many of the bank's assets like loans and bonds will only be repaid over years or even decades. This **asset-liability time mismatch**—a bank's liabilities can be withdrawn in the short term while its assets are repaid in the long term—can cause severe problems for a bank. For example, imagine a bank that has loaned a substantial amount of money at a certain interest rate, but then sees interest rates rise substantially. The bank can find itself in a precarious situation. If it does not raise the interest rate it pays to depositors, then deposits will flow to other institutions that offer the higher interest rates that are now prevailing. However, if the bank raises the interest rates that it pays to depositors, it may end up in a situation where it is paying a higher interest rate to depositors than it is collecting from those past loans that were made at lower interest rates. Clearly, the bank cannot survive in the long term if it is paying out more in interest to depositors than it is receiving from borrowers.

How can banks protect themselves against an unexpectedly high rate of loan defaults and against the risk of an asset-liability time mismatch? One strategy is for a bank to **diversify** its loans, which means lending to a variety of customers. For example, suppose a bank specialized in lending to a niche market—say, making a high proportion of its loans to construction companies that build offices in one downtown area. If that one area suffers an unexpected economic downturn, the bank will suffer large losses. However, if a bank loans both to consumers who are buying homes and cars and also to a wide range of firms in many industries and geographic areas, the bank is less exposed to risk. When a bank diversifies its loans, those categories of borrowers who have an unexpectedly large number of defaults will tend to be balanced out, according to random chance, by other borrowers who have an unexpectedly low number of defaults. Thus, diversification of loans can help banks to keep a positive net worth. However, if a widespread recession occurs that touches many industries and geographic areas, diversification will not help.

Along with diversifying their loans, banks have several other strategies to reduce the risk of an unexpectedly large number of loan defaults. For example, banks can sell some of the loans they make in the secondary loan market, as described earlier, and instead hold a greater share of assets in the form of government bonds or reserves. Nevertheless, in a lengthy recession, most banks will see their net worth decline because a higher share of loans will not be repaid in tough economic times.

13.4 | How Banks Create Money

By the end of this section, you will be able to:
- Utilize the money multiplier formulate to determine how banks create money
- Analyze and create T-account balance sheets
- Evaluate the risks and benefits of money and banks

Banks and money are intertwined. It is not just that most money is in the form of bank accounts. The banking system can literally create money through the process of making loans. Let's see how.

Money Creation by a Single Bank

Start with a hypothetical bank called Singleton Bank. The bank has $10 million in deposits. The T-account balance sheet for Singleton Bank, when it holds all of the deposits in its vaults, is shown in Figure 13.6. At this stage, Singleton Bank is simply storing money for depositors and is using these deposits to make loans. In this simplified example, Singleton Bank cannot earn any interest income from these loans and cannot pay its depositors an interest rate either.

Assets		Liabilities + Net Worth	
Reserves	$10 million	Deposits	$10 million

Figure 13.6 Singleton Bank's Balance Sheet: Receives $10 million in Deposits

Singleton Bank is required by the Federal Reserve to keep $1 million on reserve (10% of total deposits). It will loan out the remaining $9 million. By loaning out the $9 million and charging interest, it will be able to make interest payments to depositors and earn interest income for Singleton Bank (for now, we will keep it simple and not put interest income on the balance sheet). Instead of becoming just a storage place for deposits, Singleton Bank can become a financial intermediary between savers and borrowers.

This change in business plan alters Singleton Bank's balance sheet, as shown in Figure 13.7. Singleton's assets have changed; it now has $1 million in reserves and a loan to Hank's Auto Supply of $9 million. The bank still has $10 million in deposits.

Assets		Liabilities + Net Worth	
Reserves	$1 million	Deposits	$10 million
Loan to Hank's Auto Supply	$9 million		

Figure 13.7 Singleton Bank's Balance Sheet: 10% Reserves, One Round of Loans

Singleton Bank lends $9 million to Hank's Auto Supply. The bank records this loan by making an entry on the balance sheet to indicate that a loan has been made. This loan is an asset, because it will generate interest income for the bank. Of course, the loan officer is not going to let Hank walk out of the bank with $9 million in cash. The bank issues Hank's Auto Supply a cashier's check for the $9 million. Hank deposits the loan in his regular checking account with First National. The deposits at First National rise by $9 million and its reserves also rise by $9 million, as Figure 13.8 shows. First National must hold 10% of additional deposits as required reserves but is free to loan out the rest

Assets		Liabilities + Net Worth	
Reserves	+ $9 million	Deposits	+ $9 million

Figure 13.8 First National Balance Sheet

Making loans that are deposited into a demand deposit account increases the M1 money supply. Remember the definition of M1 includes checkable (demand) deposits, which can be easily used as a medium of exchange to buy goods and services. Notice that the money supply is now $19 million: $10 million in deposits in Singleton bank and $9 million in deposits at First National. Obviously these deposits will be drawn down as Hank's Auto Supply writes checks to pay its bills. But the bigger picture is that a bank must hold enough money in reserves to meet its liabilities; the rest the bank loans out. In this example so far, bank lending has expanded the money supply by $9 million.

Now, First National must hold only 10% as required reserves ($900,000) but can lend out the other 90% ($8.1 million) in a loan to Jack's Chevy Dealership as shown in **Figure 13.9**.

Assets		Liabilities + Net Worth	
Reserves	$900,000	Deposits	+ $9 million
Loans	$8.1 million		

Figure 13.9 First National Balance Sheet

If Jack's deposits the loan in its checking account at Second National, the money supply just increased by an additional $8.1 million, as **Figure 13.10** shows.

Assets		Liabilities + Net Worth	
Reserves	+ $8.1 million	Deposits	+ $8.1 million

Figure 13.10 Second National Bank's Balance Sheet

How is this money creation possible? It is possible because there are multiple banks in the financial system, they are required to hold only a fraction of their deposits, and loans end up deposited in other banks, which increases deposits and, in essence, the money supply.

Link It Up

Watch this video (http://openstaxcollege.org/l/createmoney) to learn more about how banks create money.

The Money Multiplier and a Multi-Bank System

In a system with multiple banks, the initial excess reserve amount that Singleton Bank decided to lend to Hank's Auto Supply was deposited into Frist National Bank, which is free to loan out $8.1 million. If all banks loan out their excess reserves, the money supply will expand. In a multi-bank system, the amount of money that the system can create is found by using the money multiplier. The money multiplier tells us by how many times a loan will be "multiplied" as it is spent in the economy and then re-deposited in other banks.

Fortunately, a formula exists for calculating the total of these many rounds of lending in a banking system. The **money multiplier formula** is:

$$\frac{1}{\text{Reserve Requirement}}$$

The money multiplier is then multiplied by the change in excess reserves to determine the total amount of M1 money supply created in the banking system. See the Work it Out feature to walk through the multiplier calculation.

Work It Out

Using the Money Multiplier Formula

Using the money multiplier for the example in this text:

Step 1. In the case of Singleton Bank, for whom the reserve requirement is 10% (or 0.10), the money multiplier is 1 divided by .10, which is equal to 10.

Step 2. We have identified that the excess reserves are $9 million, so, using the formula we can determine the total change in the M1 money supply:

$$
\begin{aligned}
\text{Total Change in the M1 Money Supply} \ &= \ \frac{1}{\text{Reserve Requirement}} \times \text{Excess Requirement} \\
&= \ \frac{1}{0.10} \times \$9 \text{ million} \\
&= \ 10 \times \$9 \text{ million} \\
&= \ \$90 \text{ million}
\end{aligned}
$$

Step 3. Thus, we can say that, in this example, the total quantity of money generated in this economy after all rounds of lending are completed will be $90 million.

Cautions about the Money Multiplier

The money multiplier will depend on the proportion of reserves that banks are required to hold by the Federal Reserve Bank. Additionally, a bank can also choose to hold extra reserves. Banks may decide to vary how much they hold in reserves for two reasons: macroeconomic conditions and government rules. When an economy is in recession, banks are likely to hold a higher proportion of reserves because they fear that loans are less likely to be repaid when the economy is slow. The Federal Reserve may also raise or lower the required reserves held by banks as a policy move to affect the quantity of money in an economy, as **Monetary Policy and Bank Regulation** will discuss.

The process of how banks create money shows how the quantity of money in an economy is closely linked to the quantity of lending or credit in the economy. Indeed, all of the money in the economy, except for the original reserves, is a result of bank loans that are re-deposited and loaned out, again, and again.

Finally, the money multiplier depends on people re-depositing the money that they receive in the banking system. If people instead store their cash in safe-deposit boxes or in shoeboxes hidden in their closets, then banks cannot recirculate the money in the form of loans. Indeed, central banks have an incentive to assure that bank deposits are safe because if people worry that they may lose their bank deposits, they may start holding more money in cash, instead of depositing it in banks, and the quantity of loans in an economy will decline. Low-income countries have what economists sometimes refer to as "mattress savings," or money that people are hiding in their homes because they do not trust banks. When mattress savings in an economy are substantial, banks cannot lend out those funds and the money multiplier cannot operate as effectively. The overall quantity of money and loans in such an economy will decline.

Link It Up

Watch a video (http://openstaxcollege.org/l/moneymyth) of Jem Bendell discussing "The Money Myth."

Money and Banks—Benefits and Dangers

Money and banks are marvelous social inventions that help a modern economy to function. Compared with the alternative of barter, money makes market exchanges vastly easier in goods, labor, and financial markets. Banking makes money still more effective in facilitating exchanges in goods and labor markets. Moreover, the process of banks making loans in financial capital markets is intimately tied to the creation of money.

But the extraordinary economic gains that are possible through money and banking also suggest some possible corresponding dangers. If banks are not working well, it sets off a decline in convenience and safety of transactions throughout the economy. If the banks are under financial stress, because of a widespread decline in the value of their assets, loans may become far less available, which can deal a crushing blow to sectors of the economy that depend on borrowed money like business investment, home construction, and car manufacturing. The Great Recession of 2008–2009 illustrated this pattern.

Bring it Home

The Many Disguises of Money: From Cowries to Bit Coins

The global economy has come a long way since it started using cowrie shells as currency. We have moved away from commodity and commodity-backed paper money to fiat currency. As technology and global integration increases, the need for paper currency is diminishing, too. Every day, we witness the increased use of debit and credit cards.

The latest creation and perhaps one of the purest forms of fiat money is the Bitcoin. Bitcoins are a digital currency that allows users to buy goods and services online. Products and services such as videos and books may be purchased using Bitcoins. It is not backed by any commodity nor has it been decreed by any government as legal tender, yet it used as a medium of exchange and its value (online at least) can be stored. It is also unregulated by any central bank, but is created online through people solving very complicated mathematics problems and getting paid afterward. Bitcoin.org is an information source if you are curious. Bitcoins are a relatively new type of money. At present, because it is not sanctioned as a legal currency by any country nor regulated by any central bank, it lends itself for use in illegal trading activities as well as legal ones. As technology increases and the need to reduce transactions costs associated with using traditional forms of money increases, Bitcoins or some sort of digital currency may replace our dollar bill, just as the cowrie shell was replaced.

KEY TERMS

asset item of value owned by a firm or an individual

asset–liability time mismatch a bank's liabilities can be withdrawn in the short term while its assets are repaid in the long term

balance sheet an accounting tool that lists assets and liabilities

bank capital a bank's net worth

barter literally, trading one good or service for another, without using money

coins and currency in circulation the coins and bills that circulate in an economy that are not held by the U.S Treasury, at the Federal Reserve Bank, or in bank vaults

commodity money an item that is used as money, but which also has value from its use as something other than money

commodity-backed currencies are dollar bills or other currencies with values backed up by gold or another commodity

credit card immediately transfers money from the credit card company's checking account to the seller, and at the end of the month the user owes the money to the credit card company; a credit card is a short-term loan

debit card like a check, is an instruction to the user's bank to transfer money directly and immediately from your bank account to the seller

demand deposit checkable deposit in banks that is available by making a cash withdrawal or writing a check

depository institution institution that accepts money deposits and then uses these to make loans

diversify making loans or investments with a variety of firms, to reduce the risk of being adversely affected by events at one or a few firms

double coincidence of wants a situation in which two people each want some good or service that the other person can provide

fiat money has no intrinsic value, but is declared by a government to be the legal tender of a country

financial intermediary an institution that operates between a saver with financial assets to invest and an entity who will borrow those assets and pay a rate of return

liability any amount or debt owed by a firm or an individual

M1 money supply a narrow definition of the money supply that includes currency and checking accounts in banks, and to a lesser degree, traveler's checks.

M2 money supply a definition of the money supply that includes everything in M1, but also adds savings deposits, money market funds, and certificates of deposit

medium of exchange whatever is widely accepted as a method of payment

money whatever serves society in four functions: as a medium of exchange, a store of value, a unit of account, and a standard of deferred payment.

money market fund the deposits of many investors are pooled together and invested in a safe way like short-term government bonds

money multiplier formula total money in the economy divided by the original quantity of money, or change in the total money in the economy divided by a change in the original quantity of money

net worth the excess of the asset value over and above the amount of the liability; total assets minus total liabilities

payment system helps an economy exchange goods and services for money or other financial assets

reserves funds that a bank keeps on hand and that are not loaned out or invested in bonds

savings deposit bank account where you cannot withdraw money by writing a check, but can withdraw the money at a bank—or can transfer it easily to a checking account

smart card stores a certain value of money on a card and then the card can be used to make purchases

standard of deferred payment money must also be acceptable to make purchases today that will be paid in the future

store of value something that serves as a way of preserving economic value that can be spent or consumed in the future

T-account a balance sheet with a two-column format, with the T-shape formed by the vertical line down the middle and the horizontal line under the column headings for "Assets" and "Liabilities"

time deposit account that the depositor has committed to leaving in the bank for a certain period of time, in exchange for a higher rate of interest; also called certificate of deposit

transaction costs the costs associated with finding a lender or a borrower for money

unit of account the common way in which market values are measured in an economy

KEY CONCEPTS AND SUMMARY

13.1 Defining Money by Its Functions
Money is what people in a society regularly use when purchasing or selling goods and services. If money were not available, people would need to barter with each other, meaning that each person would need to identify others with whom they have a double coincidence of wants—that is, each party has a specific good or service that the other desires. Money serves several functions: a medium of exchange, a unit of account, a store of value, and a standard of deferred payment. There are two types of money: commodity money, which is an item used as money, but which also has value from its use as something other than money; and fiat money, which has no intrinsic value, but is declared by a government to be the legal tender of a country.

13.2 Measuring Money: Currency, M1, and M2
Money is measured with several definitions: M1 includes currency and money in checking accounts (demand deposits). Traveler's checks are also a component of M1, but are declining in use. M2 includes all of M1, plus savings deposits, time deposits like certificates of deposit, and money market funds.

13.3 The Role of Banks
Banks facilitate the use of money for transactions in the economy because people and firms can use bank accounts when selling or buying goods and services, when paying a worker or being paid, and when saving money or receiving a loan. In the financial capital market, banks are financial intermediaries; that is, they operate between savers who supply financial capital and borrowers who demand loans. A balance sheet (sometimes called a T-account) is an accounting tool which lists assets in one column and liabilities in another column. The liabilities of a bank are its deposits. The assets of a bank include its loans, its ownership of bonds, and its reserves (which are not loaned out). The net worth of a bank is calculated by subtracting the bank's liabilities from its assets. Banks run a risk of negative net worth if the value of their assets declines. The value of assets can decline because of an unexpectedly high number of defaults on loans, or if interest rates rise and the bank suffers an asset-liability time mismatch in which the bank is receiving a low rate of interest on its long-term loans but must pay the currently higher market rate of interest to

attract depositors. Banks can protect themselves against these risks by choosing to diversify their loans or to hold a greater proportion of their assets in bonds and reserves. If banks hold only a fraction of their deposits as reserves, then the process of banks' lending money, those loans being re-deposited in banks, and the banks making additional loans will create money in the economy.

13.4 How Banks Create Money

The money multiplier is defined as the quantity of money that the banking system can generate from each $1 of bank reserves. The formula for calculating the multiplier is 1/reserve ratio, where the reserve ratio is the fraction of deposits that the bank wishes to hold as reserves. The quantity of money in an economy and the quantity of credit for loans are inextricably intertwined. Much of the money in an economy is created by the network of banks making loans, people making deposits, and banks making more loans.

Given the macroeconomic dangers of a malfunctioning banking system, Monetary Policy and Bank Regulation will discuss government policies for controlling the money supply and for keeping the banking system safe.

SELF-CHECK QUESTIONS

1. In many casinos, a person buys chips to use for gambling. Within the walls of the casino, these chips can often be used to buy food and drink or even a hotel room. Do chips in a gambling casino serve all three functions of money?

2. Can you name some item that is a store of value, but does not serve the other functions of money?

3. If you are out shopping for clothes and books, what is easiest and most convenient for you to spend: M1 or M2? Explain your answer.

4. For the following list of items, indicate if they are in M1, M2, or neither:
   a. Your $5,000 line of credit on your Bank of America card
   b. $50 dollars' worth of traveler's checks you have not used yet
   c. $1 in quarters in your pocket
   d. $1200 in your checking account
   e. $2000 you have in a money market account

5. Explain why the money listed under assets on a bank balance sheet may not actually be in the bank?

6. Imagine that you are in the position of buying loans in the secondary market (that is, buying the right to collect the payments on loans made by banks) for a bank or other financial services company. Explain why you would be willing to pay more or less for a given loan if:
   a. The borrower has been late on a number of loan payments
   b. Interest rates in the economy as a whole have risen since the loan was made
   c. The borrower is a firm that has just declared a high level of profits
   d. Interest rates in the economy as a whole have fallen since the loan was made

REVIEW QUESTIONS

7. What are the four functions served by money?

8. How does the existence of money simplify the process of buying and selling?

9. What is the double-coincidence of wants?

10. What components of money are counted as part of M1?

11. What components of money are counted in M2?

12. Why is a bank called a financial intermediary?

13. What does a balance sheet show?

14. What are the assets of a bank? What are its liabilities?

15. How do you calculate the net worth of a bank?

16. How can a bank end up with negative net worth?

17. What is the asset-liability time mismatch that all banks face?

18. What is the risk if a bank does not diversify its loans?

19. How do banks create money?

20. What is the formula for the money multiplier?

CRITICAL THINKING QUESTIONS

21. The Bring it Home Feature discusses the use of cowrie shells as money. Although cowrie shells are no longer used as money, do you think other forms of commodity monies are possible? What role might technology play in our definition of money?

22. Imagine that you are a barber in a world without money. Explain why it would be tricky to obtain groceries, clothing, and a place to live.

23. Explain why you think the Federal Reserve Bank tracks M1 and M2.

24. The total amount of U.S. currency in circulation divided by the U.S. population comes out to about $3,500 per person. That is more than most of us carry. Where is all the cash?

25. Explain the difference between how you would characterize bank deposits and loans as assets and liabilities on your own personal balance sheet and how a bank would characterize deposits and loans as assets and liabilities on its balance sheet.

26. Should banks have to hold 100% of their deposits? Why or why not?

27. Explain what will happen to the money multiplier process if there is an increase in the reserve requirement?

28. What do you think the Federal Reserve Bank did to the reserve requirement during the Great Recession of 2008–2009?

PROBLEMS

29. If you take $100 out of your piggy bank and deposit it in your checking account, how did M1 change? Did M2 change?

30. A bank has deposits of $400. It holds reserves of $50. It has purchased government bonds worth $70. It has made loans of $500. Set up a T-account balance sheet for the bank, with assets and liabilities, and calculate the bank's net worth.

31. Humongous Bank is the only bank in the economy. The people in this economy have $20 million in money, and they deposit all their money in Humongous Bank.

a. Humongous Bank decides on a policy of holding 100% reserves. Draw a T-account for the bank.
b. Humongous Bank is required to hold 5% of its existing $20 million as reserves, and to loan out the rest. Draw a T-account for the bank after this first round of loans has been made.
c. Assume that Humongous bank is part of a multibank system. How much will money supply increase with that original loan of $19 million?

14 | Monetary Policy and Bank Regulation

Figure 14.1 Marriner S. Eccles Federal Reserve Headquarters, Washington D.C. Some of the most influential decisions regarding monetary policy in the United States are made behind these doors. (Credit: modification of work by "squirrel83"/Flickr Creative Commons)

Bring it Home

The Problem of the Zero Percent Interest Rate Lower Bound

Most economists believe that monetary policy (the manipulation of interest rates and credit conditions by a nation's central bank) has a powerful influence on a nation's economy. Monetary policy works when the central bank reduces interest rates and makes credit more available. As a result, business investment and other types of spending increase, causing GDP and employment to grow.

But what if the interest rates banks pay are close to zero already? They cannot be made negative, can they? That would mean that lenders pay borrowers for the privilege of taking their money. Yet, this was the situation the U.S. Federal Reserve found itself in at the end of the 2008–2009 recession. The federal funds rate, which is the interest rate for banks that the Federal Reserve targets with its monetary policy, was slightly above 5% in 2007. By 2009, it had fallen to 0.16%.

The Federal Reserve's situation was further complicated because fiscal policy, the other major tool for managing the economy, was constrained by fears that the federal budget deficit and the public debt were already too high. What were the Federal Reserve's options? How could monetary policy be used to stimulate the economy? The answer, as we will see in this chapter, was to change the rules of the game.

Introduction to Monetary Policy and Bank Regulation

In this chapter, you will learn about:

- The Federal Reserve Banking System and Central Banks

- Bank Regulation

- How a Central Bank Executes Monetary Policy

- Monetary Policy and Economic Outcomes

- Pitfalls for Monetary Policy

Money, loans, and banks are all tied together. Money is deposited in bank accounts, which is then loaned to businesses, individuals, and other banks. When the interlocking system of money, loans, and banks works well, economic transactions are made smoothly in goods and labor markets and savers are connected with borrowers. If the money and banking system does not operate smoothly, the economy can either fall into recession or suffer prolonged inflation.

The government of every country has public policies that support the system of money, loans, and banking. But these policies do not always work perfectly. This chapter discusses how monetary policy works and what may prevent it from working perfectly.

14.1 | The Federal Reserve Banking System and Central Banks

By the end of this section, you will be able to:
- Explain the structure and organization of the U.S. Federal Reserve
- Discuss how central banks impact monetary policy, promote financial stability, and provide banking services

In making decisions about the money supply, a central bank decides whether to raise or lower interest rates and, in this way, to influence macroeconomic policy, whose goal is low unemployment and low inflation. The central bank is also responsible for regulating all or part of the nation's banking system to protect bank depositors and insure the health of the bank's balance sheet.

The organization responsible for conducting monetary policy and ensuring that a nation's financial system operates smoothly is called the **central bank**. Most nations have central banks or currency boards. Some prominent central banks around the world include the European Central Bank, the Bank of Japan, and the Bank of England. In the United States, the central bank is called the Federal Reserve—often abbreviated as just "the Fed." This section explains the organization of the U.S. Federal Reserve and identifies the major responsibilities of a central bank.

Structure/Organization of the Federal Reserve

Unlike most central banks, the Federal Reserve is semi-decentralized, mixing government appointees with representation from private-sector banks. At the national level, it is run by a Board of Governors, consisting of seven members appointed by the President of the United States and confirmed by the Senate. Appointments are for 14-year terms and they are arranged so that one term expires January 31 of every even-numbered year. The purpose of the long and staggered terms is to insulate the Board of Governors as much as possible from political pressure so that policy decisions can be made based only on their economic merits. Additionally, except when filling an unfinished term, each member only serves one term, further insulating decision-making from politics. Policy decisions of the Fed do not require congressional approval, and the President cannot ask for the resignation of a Federal Reserve Governor as the President can with cabinet positions.

One member of the Board of Governors is designated as the Chair. For example, from 1987 until early 2006, the Chair was Alan Greenspan. From 2006 until 2014, Ben Bernanke held the post. The current Chair, Janet Yellen, has made many headlines already. Why? See the following Clear It Up feature to find out.

Who has the most immediate economic power in the world?

Figure 14.2 Chair of the Federal Reserve Board   Janet L. Yellen is the first woman to hold the position of Chair of the Federal Reserve Board of Governors. (Credit: Board of Governors of the Federal Reserve System)

What individual can make financial market crash or soar just by making a public statement? It is not Bill Gates or Warren Buffett. It is not even the President of the United States. The answer is the Chair of the Federal Reserve Board of Governors. In early 2014, Janet L. Yellen, shown in Figure 14.2 became the first woman to hold this post. Yellen has been described in the media as "perhaps the most qualified Fed chair in history." With a Ph.D. in economics from Yale University, Yellen has taught macroeconomics at Harvard, the London School of Economics, and most recently at the University of California at Berkeley. From 2004–2010, Yellen was President of the Federal Reserve Bank of San Francisco. Not an ivory tower economist, Yellen became one of the few economists who warned about a possible bubble in the housing market, more than two years before the financial crisis occurred. Yellen served on the Board of Governors of the Federal Reserve twice, most recently as Vice Chair. She also spent two years as Chair of the President's Council of Economic Advisors. If experience and credentials mean anything, Yellen is likely to be an effective Fed chair.

The Fed Chair is first among equals on the Board of Governors. While he or she has only one vote, the Chair controls the agenda, and is the public voice of the Fed, so he or she has more power and influence than one might expect.

Link It Up

Visit this website (http://openstaxcollege.org/l/Governors) to see who the current members of the Federal Reserve Board of Governors are. You can follow the links provided for each board member to learn more about their backgrounds, experiences, and when their terms on the board will end.

The Federal Reserve is more than the Board of Governors. The Fed also includes 12 regional Federal Reserve banks, each of which is responsible for supporting the commercial banks and economy generally in its district. The Federal Reserve districts and the cities where their regional headquarters are located are shown in **Figure 14.3**. The commercial banks in each district elect a Board of Directors for each regional Federal Reserve bank, and that board chooses a president for each regional Federal Reserve district. Thus, the Federal Reserve System includes both federally and private-sector appointed leaders.

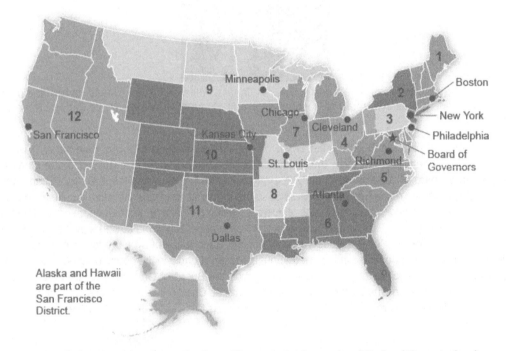

Figure 14.3 The Twelve Federal Reserve Districts There are twelve regional Federal Reserve banks, each with its district.

What Does a Central Bank Do?

The Federal Reserve, like most central banks, is designed to perform three important functions:

1. To conduct monetary policy
2. To promote stability of the financial system
3. To provide banking services to commercial banks and other depository institutions, and to provide banking services to the federal government.

The first two functions are sufficiently important that we will discuss them in their own modules; the third function we will discuss here.

The Federal Reserve provides many of the same services to banks as banks provide to their customers. For example, all commercial banks have an account at the Fed where they deposit reserves. Similarly, banks can obtain loans from the Fed through the "discount window" facility, which will be discussed in more detail later. The Fed is also responsible for check processing. When you write a check, for example, to buy groceries, the grocery store deposits the check in its bank account. Then, the physical check (or an image of that actual check) is returned to your bank, after which funds are transferred from your bank account to the account of the grocery store. The Fed is responsible for each of these actions.

On a more mundane level, the Federal Reserve ensures that enough currency and coins are circulating through the financial system to meet public demands. For example, each year the Fed increases the amount of currency available in banks around the Christmas shopping season and reduces it again in January.

Finally, the Fed is responsible for assuring that banks are in compliance with a wide variety of consumer protection laws. For example, banks are forbidden from discriminating on the basis of age, race, sex, or marital status. Banks are also required to disclose publicly information about the loans they make for buying houses and how those loans are distributed geographically, as well as by sex and race of the loan applicants.

14.2 | Bank Regulation

By the end of this section, you will be able to:
- Discuss the relationship between bank regulation and monetary policy
- Explain bank supervision
- Explain how deposit insurance and lender of last resort are two strategies to protect against bank runs

A safe and stable national financial system is a critical concern of the Federal Reserve. The goal is not only to protect individuals' savings, but to protect the integrity of the financial system itself. This esoteric task is usually behind the scenes, but came into view during the 2008–2009 financial crisis, when for a brief period of time, critical parts of the financial system failed and firms became unable to obtain financing for ordinary parts of their business. Imagine if suddenly you were unable to access the money in your bank accounts because your checks were not accepted for payment and your debit cards were declined. This gives an idea of what a failure of the payments/financial system is like.

Bank regulation is intended to maintain the solvency of banks by avoiding excessive risk. Regulation falls into a number of categories, including reserve requirements, capital requirements, and restrictions on the types of investments banks may make. In **Money and Banking**, we learned that banks are required to hold a minimum percentage of their deposits on hand as reserves. "On hand" is a bit of a misnomer because, while a portion of bank reserves are held as cash in the bank, the majority are held in the bank's account at the Federal Reserve, and their purpose is to cover desired withdrawals by depositors. Another part of bank regulation is restrictions on the types of investments banks are allowed to make. Banks are allowed to make loans to businesses, individuals, and other banks. They are allowed to purchase U.S. Treasury securities but, to protect depositors, they are not permitted to invest in the stock market or other assets that are perceived as too risky.

Bank capital is the difference between a bank's assets and its liabilities. In other words, it is a bank's net worth. A bank must have positive net worth; otherwise it is insolvent or bankrupt, meaning it would not have enough assets to pay back its liabilities. Regulation requires that banks maintain a minimum net worth, usually expressed as a percent of their assets, to protect their depositors and other creditors.

Link It Up

Visit this website (http://openstaxcollege.org/l/bankregulation) to read the brief article, "Stop Confusing Monetary Policy and Bank Regulation."

Bank Supervision

Several government agencies monitor the balance sheets of banks to make sure they have positive net worth and are not taking too high a level of risk. Within the U.S. Department of the Treasury, the Office of the Comptroller of the Currency has a national staff of bank examiners who conduct on-site reviews of the 1,500 or so of the largest national banks. The bank examiners also review any foreign banks that have branches in the United States. The Office of the Comptroller of the Currency also monitors and regulates about 800 savings and loan institutions.

The National Credit Union Administration (NCUA) supervises credit unions, which are nonprofit banks owned and run by their members. There are over 6,000 credit unions in the U.S. economy, though the typical credit union is small compared to most banks.

The Federal Reserve also has some responsibility for supervising financial institutions. For example, conglomerate firms that own banks and other businesses are called "bank holding companies." While other regulators like the Office of the Comptroller of the Currency supervises the banks, the Federal Reserve supervises the holding companies.

When the supervision of banks (and bank-like institutions such as savings and loans and credit unions) works well, most banks will remain financially healthy most of the time. If the bank supervisors find that a bank has low or negative net worth, or is making too high a proportion of risky loans, they can require that the bank change its behavior—or, in extreme cases, even force the bank to be closed or sold to a financially healthy bank.

Bank supervision can run into both practical and political questions. The practical question is that measuring the value of a bank's assets is not always straightforward. As discussed in **Money and Banking**, a bank's assets are its loans, and the value of these assets depends on estimates about the risk that these loans will not be repaid. These issues can become even more complex when a bank makes loans to banks or firms in other countries, or arranges financial deals that are much more complex than a basic loan.

The political question arises because the decision by a bank supervisor to require a bank to close or to change its financial investments is often controversial, and the bank supervisor often comes under political pressure from the owners of the bank and the local politicians to keep quiet and back off.

For example, many observers have pointed out that Japan's banks were in deep financial trouble through most of the 1990s; however, nothing substantial had been done about it by the early 2000s. A similar unwillingness to confront problems with struggling banks is visible across the rest of the world, in East Asia, Latin America, Eastern Europe, Russia, and elsewhere.

In the United States, laws were passed in the 1990s requiring that bank supervisors make their findings open and public, and that they act as soon as a problem is identified. However, as many U.S. banks were staggered by the recession of 2008–2009, critics of the bank regulators asked pointed questions about why the regulators had not foreseen the financial shakiness of the banks earlier, before such large losses had a chance to accumulate.

Bank Runs

Back in the nineteenth century and during the first few decades of the twentieth century (around and during the Great Depression), putting your money in a bank could be nerve-wracking. Imagine that the net worth of your bank became negative, so that the bank's assets were not enough to cover its liabilities. In this situation, whoever withdrew their deposits first received all of their money, and those who did not rush to the bank quickly enough, lost their money. Depositors racing to the bank to withdraw their deposits, as shown in **Figure 14.4** is called a **bank run**. In the movie *It's a Wonderful Life*, the bank manager, played by Jimmy Stewart, faces a mob of worried bank depositors who want to withdraw their money, but manages to allay their fears by allowing some of them to withdraw a portion of their deposits—using the money from his own pocket that was supposed to pay for his honeymoon.

Figure 14.4 A Run on the Bank   Bank runs during the Great Depression only served to worsen the economic situation. (Credit: National Archives and Records Administration)

The risk of bank runs created instability in the banking system. Even a rumor that a bank might experience negative net worth could trigger a bank run and, in a bank run, even healthy banks could be destroyed. Because a bank loans out most of the money it receives, and because it keeps only limited reserves on hand, a bank run of any size would quickly drain any of the bank's available cash. When the bank had no cash remaining, it only intensified the fears of remaining depositors that they could lose their money. Moreover, a bank run at one bank often triggered a chain reaction of runs on other banks. In the late nineteenth and early twentieth century, bank runs were typically not the original cause of a recession—but they could make a recession much worse.

Deposit Insurance

To protect against bank runs, Congress has put two strategies into place: **deposit insurance** and the lender of last resort. Deposit insurance is an insurance system that makes sure depositors in a bank do not lose their money, even if the bank goes bankrupt. About 70 countries around the world, including all of the major economies, have deposit insurance programs. In the United States, the Federal Deposit Insurance Corporation (FDIC) is responsible for deposit insurance. Banks pay an insurance premium to the FDIC. The insurance premium is based on the bank's level of deposits, and then adjusted according to the riskiness of a bank's financial situation. In 2009, for example, a fairly safe bank with a high net worth might have paid 10–20 cents in insurance premiums for every $100 in bank deposits, while a risky bank with very low net worth might have paid 50–60 cents for every $100 in bank deposits.

Bank examiners from the FDIC evaluate the balance sheets of banks, looking at the value of assets and liabilities, to determine the level of riskiness. The FDIC provides deposit insurance for about 6,509 banks (as of the end of 2014). Even if a bank fails, the government guarantees that depositors will receive up to $250,000 of their money in each account, which is enough for almost all individuals, although not sufficient for many businesses. Since the United States enacted deposit insurance in the 1930s, no one has lost any of their insured deposits. Bank runs no longer happen at insured banks.

Lender of Last Resort

The problem with bank runs is not that insolvent banks will fail; they are, after all, bankrupt and need to be shut down. The problem is that bank runs can cause solvent banks to fail and spread to the rest of the financial system. To prevent this, the Fed stands ready to lend to banks and other financial institutions when they cannot obtain funds from anywhere else. This is known as the **lender of last resort** role. For banks, the central bank acting as a lender of last resort helps to reinforce the effect of deposit insurance and to reassure bank customers that they will not lose their money.

The lender of last resort task can come up in other financial crises, as well. During the panic of the stock market crash in 1987, when the value of U.S. stocks fell by 25% in a single day, the Federal Reserve made a number of short-term emergency loans so that the financial system could keep functioning. During the recession of 2008–2009, the "quantitative easing" policies (discussed below) of the Federal Reserve can be interpreted as a willingness to make short-term credit available as needed in a time when the banking and financial system was under stress.

14.3 | How a Central Bank Executes Monetary Policy

By the end of this section, you will be able to:
- Explain the reason for open market operations
- Evaluate reserve requirements and discount rates
- Interpret and show bank activity through balance sheets

The most important function of the Federal Reserve is to conduct the nation's monetary policy. Article I, Section 8 of the U.S. Constitution gives Congress the power "to coin money" and "to regulate the value thereof." As part of the 1913 legislation that created the Federal Reserve, Congress delegated these powers to the Fed. Monetary policy involves managing interest rates and credit conditions, which influences the level of economic activity, as described in more detail below.

A central bank has three traditional tools to implement monetary policy in the economy:

- Open market operations
- Changing reserve requirements
- Changing the discount rate

In discussing how these three tools work, it is useful to think of the central bank as a "bank for banks"—that is, each private-sector bank has its own account at the central bank. We will discuss each of these monetary policy tools in the sections below.

Open Market Operations

The most commonly used tool of monetary policy in the U.S. is **open market operations**. Open market operations take place when the central bank sells or buys U.S. Treasury bonds in order to influence the quantity of bank reserves and the level of interest rates. The specific interest rate targeted in open market operations is the federal funds rate. The name is a bit of a misnomer since the federal funds rate is the interest rate charged by commercial banks making overnight loans to other banks. As such, it is a very short term interest rate, but one that reflects credit conditions in financial markets very well.

The **Federal Open Market Committee (FOMC)** makes the decisions regarding these open market operations. The FOMC is made up of the seven members of the Federal Reserve's Board of Governors. It also includes five voting members who are drawn, on a rotating basis, from the regional Federal Reserve Banks. The New York district president is a permanent voting member of the FOMC and the other four spots are filled on a rotating, annual basis, from the other 11 districts. The FOMC typically meets every six weeks, but it can meet more frequently if necessary. The FOMC tries to act by consensus; however, the chairman of the Federal Reserve has traditionally played a very powerful role in defining and shaping that consensus. For the Federal Reserve, and for most central banks, open market operations have, over the last few decades, been the most commonly used tool of monetary policy.

Visit this website (http://openstaxcollege.org/l/monetarypolicy) for the Federal Reserve to learn more about current monetary policy.

To understand how open market operations affect the money supply, consider the balance sheet of Happy Bank, displayed in **Figure 14.5**. **Figure 14.5** (a) shows that Happy Bank starts with $460 million in assets, divided among reserves, bonds and loans, and $400 million in liabilities in the form of deposits, with a net worth of $60 million. When the central bank purchases $20 million in bonds from Happy Bank, the bond holdings of Happy Bank fall by $20 million and the bank's reserves rise by $20 million, as shown in **Figure 14.5** (b). However, Happy Bank only wants to hold $40 million in reserves (the quantity of reserves that it started with in **Figure 14.5**) (a), so the bank decides to loan out the extra $20 million in reserves and its loans rise by $20 million, as shown in **Figure 14.5** (c). The open market operation by the central bank causes Happy Bank to make loans instead of holding its assets in the form of government bonds, which expands the money supply. As the new loans are deposited in banks throughout the economy, these banks will, in turn, loan out some of the deposits they receive, triggering the money multiplier discussed in **Money and Banking**.

Assets		Liabilities + Net Worth	
Reserves	40	Deposits	400
Bonds	120		
Loans	300	Net Worth	60

(a) The original balance sheet

Assets		Liabilities + Net Worth	
Reserves	40 + 20 = 60	Deposits	400
Bonds	120 – 20 = 100		
Loans	300	Net Worth	60

(b) The central bank buys bonds

Assets		Liabilities + Net Worth	
Reserves	60 – 20 = 40	Deposits	400
Bonds	100		
Loans	300 + 20 = 320	Net Worth	60

(c) The bank makes additional loans

Figure 14.5

Where did the Federal Reserve get the $20 million that it used to purchase the bonds? A central bank has the power to create money. In practical terms, the Federal Reserve would write a check to Happy Bank, so that Happy Bank can have that money credited to its bank account at the Federal Reserve. In truth, the Federal Reserve created the money to purchase the bonds out of thin air—or with a few clicks on some computer keys.

Open market operations can also reduce the quantity of money and loans in an economy. **Figure 14.6** (a) shows the balance sheet of Happy Bank before the central bank sells bonds in the open market. When Happy Bank purchases $30 million in bonds, Happy Bank sends $30 million of its reserves to the central bank, but now holds an additional $30 million in bonds, as shown in **Figure 14.6** (b). However, Happy Bank wants to hold $40 million in reserves, as in **Figure 14.6** (a), so it will adjust down the quantity of its loans by $30 million, to bring its reserves back to the desired level, as shown in **Figure 14.6** (c). In practical terms, a bank can easily reduce its quantity of loans. At any given time, a bank is receiving payments on loans that it made previously and also making new loans. If the bank just slows down or briefly halts making new loans, and instead adds those funds to its reserves, then its overall quantity of loans will decrease. A decrease in the quantity of loans also means fewer deposits in other banks, and other banks reducing their lending as well, as the money multiplier discussed in **Money and Banking** takes effect. And what about all those bonds? How do they affect the money supply? Read the following Clear It Up feature for the answer.

Assets		Liabilities + Net Worth	
Reserves	40	Deposits	400
Bonds	120		
Loans	300	Net Worth	60

(a) The original balance sheet

Assets		Liabilities + Net Worth	
Reserves	40 - 30 = 10	Deposits	400
Bonds	120 + 30 = 150		
Loans	300	Net Worth	60

(b) The central bank sells bonds to the bank

Assets		Liabilities + Net Worth	
Reserves	10 + 30 = 40	Deposits	400
Bonds	150		
Loans	300 – 30 = 270	Net Worth	60

(c) The bank makes fewer loans

Figure 14.6

Clear It Up

Does selling or buying bonds increase the money supply?

Is it a sale of bonds by the central bank which increases bank reserves and lowers interest rates or is it a purchase of bonds by the central bank? The easy way to keep track of this is to treat the central bank as being *outside* the banking system. When a central bank buys bonds, money is flowing from the central bank to individual banks in the economy, increasing the supply of money in circulation. When a central bank sells bonds, then money from individual banks in the economy is flowing into the central bank—reducing the quantity of money in the economy.

Changing Reserve Requirements

A second method of conducting monetary policy is for the central bank to raise or lower the **reserve requirement**, which, as we noted earlier, is the percentage of each bank's deposits that it is legally required to hold either as cash in their vault or on deposit with the central bank. If banks are required to hold a greater amount in reserves, they have less money available to lend out. If banks are allowed to hold a smaller amount in reserves, they will have a greater amount of money available to lend out.

In early 2015, the Federal Reserve required banks to hold reserves equal to 0% of the first $14.5 million in deposits, then to hold reserves equal to 3% of the deposits up to $103.6 million, and 10% of any amount above $103.6 million. Small changes in the reserve requirements are made almost every year. For example, the $103.6 million dividing line is sometimes bumped up or down by a few million dollars. In practice, large changes in reserve requirements are rarely used to execute monetary policy. A sudden demand that all banks increase their reserves would be extremely disruptive and difficult to comply with, while loosening requirements too much would create a danger of banks being unable to meet the demand for withdrawals.

Changing the Discount Rate

The Federal Reserve was founded in the aftermath of the Financial Panic of 1907 when many banks failed as a result of bank runs. As mentioned earlier, since banks make profits by lending out their deposits, no bank, even those that are not bankrupt, can withstand a bank run. As a result of the Panic, the Federal Reserve was founded to be the "lender of last resort." In the event of a bank run, sound banks, (banks that were not bankrupt) could borrow as much cash as they needed from the Fed's discount "window" to quell the bank run. The interest rate banks pay for such loans is called the **discount rate**. (They are so named because loans are made against the bank's outstanding loans "at a discount" of their face value.) Once depositors became convinced that the bank would be able to honor their withdrawals, they no longer had a reason to make a run on the bank. In short, the Federal Reserve was originally intended to provide credit passively, but in the years since its founding, the Fed has taken on a more active role with monetary policy.

So, the third traditional method for conducting monetary policy is to raise or lower the discount rate. If the central bank raises the discount rate, then commercial banks will reduce their borrowing of reserves from the Fed, and instead call in loans to replace those reserves. Since fewer loans are available, the money supply falls and market interest rates rise. If the central bank lowers the discount rate it charges to banks, the process works in reverse.

In recent decades, the Federal Reserve has made relatively few discount loans. Before a bank borrows from the Federal Reserve to fill out its required reserves, the bank is expected to first borrow from other available sources, like other banks. This is encouraged by Fed's charging a higher discount rate, than the federal funds rate. Given that most banks borrow little at the discount rate, changing the discount rate up or down has little impact on their behavior. More importantly, the Fed has found from experience that open market operations are a more precise and powerful means of executing any desired monetary policy.

In the Federal Reserve Act, the phrase "...to afford means of rediscounting commercial paper" is contained in its long title. This tool was seen as the main tool for monetary policy when the Fed was initially created. This illustrates how monetary policy has evolved and how it continues to do so.

14.4 | Monetary Policy and Economic Outcomes

By the end of this section, you will be able to:
- Contrast expansionary monetary policy and contractionary monetary policy
- Explain how monetary policy impacts interest rates and aggregate demand
- Evaluate Federal Reserve decisions over the last forty years
- Explain the significance of quantitative easing (QE)

A monetary policy that lowers interest rates and stimulates borrowing is known as an **expansionary monetary policy** or **loose monetary policy**. Conversely, a monetary policy that raises interest rates and reduces borrowing in the economy is a **contractionary monetary policy** or **tight monetary policy**. This module will discuss how expansionary and contractionary monetary policies affect interest rates and aggregate demand, and how such policies will affect macroeconomic goals like unemployment and inflation. We will conclude with a look at the Fed's monetary policy practice in recent decades.

The Effect of Monetary Policy on Interest Rates

Consider the market for loanable bank funds, shown in Figure 14.7. The original equilibrium (E_0) occurs at an interest rate of 8% and a quantity of funds loaned and borrowed of $10 billion. An expansionary monetary policy will shift the supply of loanable funds to the right from the original supply curve (S_0) to S_1, leading to an equilibrium (E_1) with a lower interest rate of 6% and a quantity of funds loaned of $14 billion. Conversely, a contractionary monetary policy will shift the supply of loanable funds to the left from the original supply curve (S_0) to S_2, leading to an equilibrium (E_2) with a higher interest rate of 10% and a quantity of funds loaned of $8 billion.

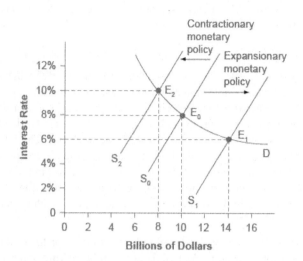

Figure 14.7 Monetary Policy and Interest Rates The original equilibrium occurs at E_0. An expansionary monetary policy will shift the supply of loanable funds to the right from the original supply curve (S_0) to the new supply curve (S_1) and to a new equilibrium of E_1, reducing the interest rate from 8% to 6%. A contractionary monetary policy will shift the supply of loanable funds to the left from the original supply curve (S_0) to the new supply (S_2), and raise the interest rate from 8% to 10%.

So how does a central bank "raise" interest rates? When describing the monetary policy actions taken by a central bank, it is common to hear that the central bank "raised interest rates" or "lowered interest rates." We need to be clear about this: more precisely, through open market operations the central bank changes bank reserves in a way which affects the supply curve of loanable funds. As a result, interest rates change, as shown in **Figure 14.7**. If they do not meet the Fed's target, the Fed can supply more or less reserves until interest rates do.

Recall that the specific interest rate the Fed targets is the **federal funds rate**. The Federal Reserve has, since 1995, established its target federal funds rate in advance of any open market operations.

Of course, financial markets display a wide range of interest rates, representing borrowers with different risk premiums and loans that are to be repaid over different periods of time. In general, when the federal funds rate drops substantially, other interest rates drop, too, and when the federal funds rate rises, other interest rates rise. However, a fall or rise of one percentage point in the federal funds rate—which remember is for borrowing overnight—will typically have an effect of less than one percentage point on a 30-year loan to purchase a house or a three-year loan to purchase a car. Monetary policy can push the entire spectrum of interest rates higher or lower, but the specific interest rates are set by the forces of supply and demand in those specific markets for lending and borrowing.

The Effect of Monetary Policy on Aggregate Demand

Monetary policy affects interest rates and the available quantity of loanable funds, which in turn affects several components of aggregate demand. Tight or contractionary monetary policy that leads to higher interest rates and a reduced quantity of loanable funds will reduce two components of aggregate demand. Business investment will decline because it is less attractive for firms to borrow money, and even firms that have money will notice that, with higher interest rates, it is relatively more attractive to put those funds in a financial investment than to make an investment in physical capital. In addition, higher interest rates will discourage consumer borrowing for big-ticket items like houses and cars. Conversely, loose or expansionary monetary policy that leads to lower interest rates and a higher quantity of loanable funds will tend to increase business investment and consumer borrowing for big-ticket items.

If the economy is suffering a recession and high unemployment, with output below potential GDP, expansionary monetary policy can help the economy return to potential GDP. **Figure 14.8** (a) illustrates this situation. This example uses a short-run upward-sloping Keynesian aggregate supply curve (SRAS). The original equilibrium during a recession of E_0 occurs at an output level of 600. An expansionary monetary policy will reduce interest rates and stimulate investment and consumption spending, causing the original aggregate demand curve (AD_0) to shift right to AD_1, so that the new equilibrium (E_1) occurs at the potential GDP level of 700.

(a) Expansionary monetary policy

(b) Contractionary monetary policy

Figure 14.8 Expansionary or Contractionary Monetary Policy (a) The economy is originally in a recession with the equilibrium output and price level shown at E_0. Expansionary monetary policy will reduce interest rates and shift aggregate demand to the right from AD_0 to AD_1, leading to the new equilibrium (E_1) at the potential GDP level of output with a relatively small rise in the price level. (b) The economy is originally producing above the potential GDP level of output at the equilibrium E_0 and is experiencing pressures for an inflationary rise in the price level. Contractionary monetary policy will shift aggregate demand to the left from AD_0 to AD_1, thus leading to a new equilibrium (E_1) at the potential GDP level of output.

Conversely, if an economy is producing at a quantity of output above its potential GDP, a contractionary monetary policy can reduce the inflationary pressures for a rising price level. In **Figure 14.8** (b), the original equilibrium (E_0) occurs at an output of 750, which is above potential GDP. A contractionary monetary policy will raise interest rates, discourage borrowing for investment and consumption spending, and cause the original demand curve (AD_0) to shift left to AD_1, so that the new equilibrium (E_1) occurs at the potential GDP level of 700.

These examples suggest that monetary policy should be **countercyclical**; that is, it should act to counterbalance the business cycles of economic downturns and upswings. Monetary policy should be loosened when a recession has caused unemployment to increase and tightened when inflation threatens. Of course, countercyclical policy does pose a danger of overreaction. If loose monetary policy seeking to end a recession goes too far, it may push aggregate demand so far to the right that it triggers inflation. If tight monetary policy seeking to reduce inflation goes too far, it may push aggregate demand so far to the left that a recession begins. **Figure 14.9** (a) summarizes the chain of effects that connect loose and tight monetary policy to changes in output and the price level.

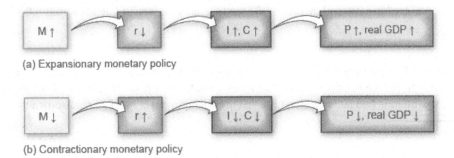

(a) Expansionary monetary policy

(b) Contractionary monetary policy

Figure 14.9 The Pathways of Monetary Policy (a) In expansionary monetary policy the central bank causes the supply of money and loanable funds to increase, which lowers the interest rate, stimulating additional borrowing for investment and consumption, and shifting aggregate demand right. The result is a higher price level and, at least in the short run, higher real GDP. (b) In contractionary monetary policy, the central bank causes the supply of money and credit in the economy to decrease, which raises the interest rate, discouraging borrowing for investment and consumption, and shifting aggregate demand left. The result is a lower price level and, at least in the short run, lower real GDP.

Federal Reserve Actions Over Last Four Decades

For the period from the mid-1970s up through the end of 2007, Federal Reserve monetary policy can largely be summed up by looking at how it targeted the federal funds interest rate using open market operations.

Of course, telling the story of the U.S. economy since 1975 in terms of Federal Reserve actions leaves out many other macroeconomic factors that were influencing unemployment, recession, economic growth, and inflation over this time. The nine episodes of Federal Reserve action outlined in the sections below also demonstrate that the central bank should be considered one of the leading actors influencing the macro economy. As noted earlier, the single person with the greatest power to influence the U.S. economy is probably the chairperson of the Federal Reserve.

Figure 14.10 shows how the Federal Reserve has carried out monetary policy by targeting the federal funds interest rate in the last few decades. The graph shows the federal funds interest rate (remember, this interest rate is set through open market operations), the unemployment rate, and the inflation rate since 1975. Different episodes of monetary policy during this period are indicated in the figure.

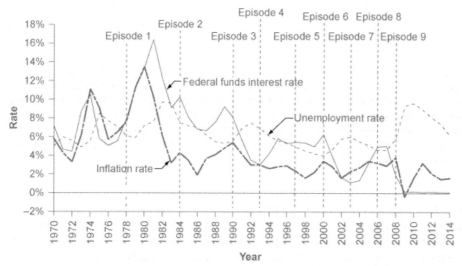

Figure 14.10 Monetary Policy, Unemployment, and Inflation   Through the episodes shown here, the Federal Reserve typically reacted to higher inflation with a contractionary monetary policy and a higher interest rate, and reacted to higher unemployment with an expansionary monetary policy and a lower interest rate.

Episode 1

Consider Episode 1 in the late 1970s. The rate of inflation was very high, exceeding 10% in 1979 and 1980, so the Federal Reserve used tight monetary policy to raise interest rates, with the federal funds rate rising from 5.5% in 1977 to 16.4% in 1981. By 1983, inflation was down to 3.2%, but aggregate demand contracted sharply enough that back-to-back recessions occurred in 1980 and in 1981–1982, and the unemployment rate rose from 5.8% in 1979 to 9.7% in 1982.

Episode 2

In Episode 2, when the Federal Reserve was persuaded in the early 1980s that inflation was declining, the Fed began slashing interest rates to reduce unemployment. The federal funds interest rate fell from 16.4% in 1981 to 6.8% in 1986. By 1986 or so, inflation had fallen to about 2% and the unemployment rate had come down to 7%, and was still falling.

Episode 3

However, in Episode 3 in the late 1980s, inflation appeared to be creeping up again, rising from 2% in 1986 up toward 5% by 1989. In response, the Federal Reserve used contractionary monetary policy to raise the federal funds rates from 6.6% in 1987 to 9.2% in 1989. The tighter monetary policy stopped inflation, which fell from above 5% in 1990 to under 3% in 1992, but it also helped to cause the recession of 1990–1991, and the unemployment rate rose from 5.3% in 1989 to 7.5% by 1992.

Episode 4

In Episode 4, in the early 1990s, when the Federal Reserve was confident that inflation was back under control, it reduced interest rates, with the federal funds interest rate falling from 8.1% in 1990 to 3.5% in 1992. As the economy expanded, the unemployment rate declined from 7.5% in 1992 to less than 5% by 1997.

Episodes 5 and 6

In Episodes 5 and 6, the Federal Reserve perceived a risk of inflation and raised the federal funds rate from 3% to 5.8% from 1993 to 1995. Inflation did not rise, and the period of economic growth during the 1990s continued. Then in 1999 and 2000, the Fed was concerned that inflation seemed to be creeping up so it raised the federal funds interest rate from 4.6% in December 1998 to 6.5% in June 2000. By early 2001, inflation was declining again, but a recession occurred in 2001. Between 2000 and 2002, the unemployment rate rose from 4.0% to 5.8%.

Episodes 7 and 8

In Episodes 7 and 8, the Federal Reserve conducted a loose monetary policy and slashed the federal funds rate from 6.2% in 2000 to just 1.7% in 2002, and then again to 1% in 2003. They actually did this because of fear of Japan-style deflation; this persuaded them to lower the Fed funds further than they otherwise would have. The recession ended, but, unemployment rates were slow to decline in the early 2000s. Finally, in 2004, the unemployment rate declined and the Federal Reserve began to raise the federal funds rate until it reached 5% by 2007.

Episode 9

In Episode 9, as the Great Recession took hold in 2008, the Federal Reserve was quick to slash interest rates, taking them down to 2% in 2008 and to nearly 0% in 2009. When the Fed had taken interest rates down to near-zero by December 2008, the economy was still deep in recession. Open market operations could not make the interest rate turn negative. The Federal Reserve had to think "outside the box."

Quantitative Easing

The most powerful and commonly used of the three traditional tools of monetary policy—open market operations—works by expanding or contracting the money supply in a way that influences the interest rate. In late 2008, as the U.S. economy struggled with recession, the Federal Reserve had already reduced the interest rate to near-zero. With the recession still ongoing, the Fed decided to adopt an innovative and nontraditional policy known as **quantitative easing (QE)**. This is the purchase of long-term government and private mortgage-backed securities by central banks to make credit available so as to stimulate aggregate demand.

Quantitative easing differed from traditional monetary policy in several key ways. First, it involved the Fed purchasing long term Treasury bonds, rather than short term Treasury bills. In 2008, however, it was impossible to stimulate the economy any further by lowering short term rates because they were already as low as they could get. (Read the closing Bring it Home feature for more on this.) Therefore, Bernanke sought to lower long-term rates utilizing quantitative easing.

This leads to a second way QE is different from traditional monetary policy. Instead of purchasing Treasury securities, the Fed also began purchasing private mortgage-backed securities, something it had never done before. During the financial crisis, which precipitated the recession, mortgage-backed securities were termed "toxic assets," because when the housing market collapsed, no one knew what these securities were worth, which put the financial institutions which were holding those securities on very shaky ground. By offering to purchase mortgage-backed securities, the Fed was both pushing long term interest rates down and also removing possibly "toxic assets" from the balance sheets of private financial firms, which would strengthen the financial system.

Quantitative easing (QE) occurred in three episodes:

1. During QE_1, which began in November 2008, the Fed purchased $600 billion in mortgage-backed securities from government enterprises Fannie Mae and Freddie Mac.

2. In November 2010, the Fed began QE_2, in which it purchased $600 billion in U.S. Treasury bonds.

3. QE_3, began in September 2012 when the Fed commenced purchasing $40 billion of additional mortgage-backed securities per month. This amount was increased in December 2012 to $85 billion per month. The Fed stated that, when economic conditions permit, it will begin tapering (or reducing the monthly purchases). By October 2014, the Fed had announced the final $15 billion purchase of bonds, ending Quantitative Easing.

The quantitative easing policies adopted by the Federal Reserve (and by other central banks around the world) are usually thought of as temporary emergency measures. If these steps are, indeed, to be temporary, then the Federal

Reserve will need to stop making these additional loans and sell off the financial securities it has accumulated. The concern is that the process of quantitative easing may prove more difficult to reverse than it was to enact. The evidence suggests that QE_1 was somewhat successful, but that QE_2 and QE_3 have been less so.

14.5 | Pitfalls for Monetary Policy

By the end of this section, you will be able to:
- Analyze whether monetary policy decisions should be made more democratically
- Calculate the velocity of money
- Evaluate the central bank's influence on inflation, unemployment, asset bubbles, and leverage cycles
- Calculate the effects of monetary stimulus

In the real world, effective monetary policy faces a number of significant hurdles. Monetary policy affects the economy only after a time lag that is typically long and of variable length. Remember, monetary policy involves a chain of events: the central bank must perceive a situation in the economy, hold a meeting, and make a decision to react by tightening or loosening monetary policy. The change in monetary policy must percolate through the banking system, changing the quantity of loans and affecting interest rates. When interest rates change, businesses must change their investment levels and consumers must change their borrowing patterns when purchasing homes or cars. Then it takes time for these changes to filter through the rest of the economy.

As a result of this chain of events, monetary policy has little effect in the immediate future; instead, its primary effects are felt perhaps one to three years in the future. The reality of long and variable time lags does not mean that a central bank should refuse to make decisions. It does mean that central banks should be humble about taking action, because of the risk that their actions can create as much or more economic instability as they resolve.

Excess Reserves

Banks are legally required to hold a minimum level of reserves, but no rule prohibits them from holding additional **excess reserves** above the legally mandated limit. For example, during a recession banks may be hesitant to lend, because they fear that when the economy is contracting, a high proportion of loan applicants become less likely to repay their loans.

When many banks are choosing to hold excess reserves, expansionary monetary policy may not work well. This may occur because the banks are concerned about a deteriorating economy, while the central bank is trying to expand the money supply. If the banks prefer to hold excess reserves above the legally required level, the central bank cannot force individual banks to make loans. Similarly, sensible businesses and consumers may be reluctant to borrow substantial amounts of money in a recession, because they recognize that firms' sales and employees' jobs are more insecure in a recession, and they do not want to face the need to make interest payments. The result is that during an especially deep recession, an expansionary monetary policy may have little effect on either the price level or the real GDP.

Japan experienced this situation in the 1990s and early 2000s. Japan's economy entered a period of very slow growth, dipping in and out of recession, in the early 1990s. By February 1999, the Bank of Japan had lowered the equivalent of its federal funds rate to 0%. It kept it there most of the time through 2003. Moreover, in the two years from March 2001 to March 2003, the Bank of Japan also expanded the money supply of the country by about 50%—an enormous increase. Even this highly expansionary monetary policy, however, had no substantial effect on stimulating aggregate demand. Japan's economy continued to experience extremely slow growth into the mid-2000s.

Should monetary policy decisions be made more democratically?

Should monetary policy be conducted by a nation's Congress or legislature comprised of elected representatives? Or should it be conducted by a politically appointed central bank that is more independent of voters? Here are some of the arguments made by each side.

The Case for Greater Democratic Control of Monetary Policy

Elected representatives conduct fiscal policy by passing tax and spending bills. They could handle monetary policy in the same way. Sure, they will sometimes make mistakes, but in a democracy, it is better to have mistakes made by elected officials accountable to voters than by political appointees. After all, the people appointed to the top governing positions at the Federal Reserve—and to most central banks around the world—are typically bankers and economists. They are not representatives of borrowers like small businesses or farmers nor are they representatives of labor unions. Central banks might not be so quick to raise interest rates if they had to pay more attention to firms and people in the real economy.

The Case for an Independent Central Bank

Because the central bank has some insulation from day-to-day politics, its members can take a nonpartisan look at specific economic situations and make tough, immediate decisions when necessary. The idea of giving a legislature the ability to create money and hand out loans is likely to end up badly, sooner or later. It is simply too tempting for lawmakers to expand the money supply to fund their projects. The long term result will be rampant inflation. Also, a central bank, acting according to the laws passed by elected officials, can respond far more quickly than a legislature. For example, the U.S. budget takes months to debate, pass, and be signed into law, but monetary policy decisions can be made much more rapidly. Day-to-day democratic control of monetary policy is impractical and seems likely to lead to an overly expansionary monetary policy and higher inflation.

The problem of excess reserves does not affect contractionary policy. Central bankers have an old saying that monetary policy can be like pulling and pushing on a string: when the central bank pulls on the string and uses contractionary monetary policy, it can definitely raise interest rates and reduce aggregate demand. However, when the central bank tries to push on the string of expansionary monetary policy, the string may sometimes just fold up limp and have little effect, because banks decide not to loan out their excess reserves. This analogy should not be taken too literally—expansionary monetary policy usually does have real effects, after that inconveniently long and variable lag. There are also times, like Japan's economy in the late 1990s and early 2000s, when expansionary monetary policy has been insufficient to lift a recession-prone economy.

Unpredictable Movements of Velocity

Velocity is a term that economists use to describe how quickly money circulates through the economy. The **velocity** of money in a year is defined as:

$$\text{Velocity} = \frac{\text{nominal GDP}}{\text{money supply}}$$

Specific measurements of velocity depend on the definition of the money supply being used. Consider the velocity of M1, the total amount of currency in circulation and checking account balances. In 2009, for example, M1 was $1.7 trillion and nominal GDP was $14.3 trillion, so the velocity of M1 was 8.4 ($14.3 trillion/$1.7 trillion). A higher velocity of money means that the average dollar circulates more times in a year; a lower velocity means that the average dollar circulates fewer times in a year.

Perhaps you heard the "d" word mentioned during our recent economic downturn. See the following Clear It Up feature for a discussion of how deflation could affect monetary policy.

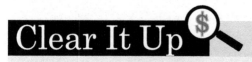

What happens during episodes of deflation?

Deflation occurs when the rate of inflation is negative; that is, instead of money having less purchasing power over time, as occurs with inflation, money is worth more. Deflation can make it very difficult for monetary policy to address a recession.

Remember that the real interest rate is the nominal interest rate minus the rate of inflation. If the nominal interest rate is 7% and the rate of inflation is 3%, then the borrower is effectively paying a 4% real interest rate. If the nominal interest rate is 7% and there is *deflation* of 2%, then the real interest rate is actually 9%. In this way, an unexpected deflation raises the real interest payments for borrowers. It can lead to a situation where an unexpectedly high number of loans are not repaid, and banks find that their net worth is decreasing or negative. When banks are suffering losses, they become less able and eager to make new loans. Aggregate demand declines, which can lead to recession.

Then the double-whammy: After causing a recession, deflation can make it difficult for monetary policy to work. Say that the central bank uses expansionary monetary policy to reduce the nominal interest rate all the way to zero—but the economy has 5% deflation. As a result, the real interest rate is 5%, and because a central bank cannot make the nominal interest rate negative, expansionary policy cannot reduce the real interest rate further.

In the U.S. economy during the early 1930s, deflation was 6.7% per year from 1930–1933, which caused many borrowers to default on their loans and many banks to end up bankrupt, which in turn contributed substantially to the Great Depression. Not all episodes of deflation, however, end in economic depression. Japan, for example, experienced deflation of slightly less than 1% per year from 1999–2002, which hurt the Japanese economy, but it still grew by about 0.9% per year over this period. Indeed, there is at least one historical example of deflation coexisting with rapid growth. The U.S. economy experienced deflation of about 1.1% per year over the quarter-century from 1876–1900, but real GDP also expanded at a rapid clip of 4% per year over this time, despite some occasional severe recessions.

The central bank should be on guard against deflation and, if necessary, use expansionary monetary policy to prevent any long-lasting or extreme deflation from occurring. Except in severe cases like the Great Depression, deflation does not guarantee economic disaster.

Changes in velocity can cause problems for monetary policy. To understand why, rewrite the definition of velocity so that the money supply is on the left-hand side of the equation. That is:

$$\text{Money supply} \times \text{velocity} = \text{Nominal GDP}$$

Recall from **The Macroeconomic Perspective** that

$$\text{Nominal GDP} = \text{Price Level (or GDP Deflator)} \times \text{Real GDP}.$$

Therefore,

$$\text{Money Supply} \times \text{velocity} = \text{Nominal GDP} = \text{Price Level} \times \text{Real GDP}.$$

This equation is sometimes called the **basic quantity equation of money** but, as you can see, it is just the definition of velocity written in a different form. This equation must hold true, by definition.

If velocity is constant over time, then a certain percentage rise in the money supply on the left-hand side of the basic quantity equation of money will inevitably lead to the same percentage rise in nominal GDP—although this change could happen through an increase in inflation, or an increase in real GDP, or some combination of the two. If velocity is changing over time but in a constant and predictable way, then changes in the money supply will continue to have a predictable effect on nominal GDP. If velocity changes unpredictably over time, however, then the effect of changes in the money supply on nominal GDP becomes unpredictable.

The actual velocity of money in the U.S. economy as measured by using M1, the most common definition of the money supply, is illustrated in **Figure 14.11**. From 1960 up to about 1980, velocity appears fairly predictable; that is, it is increasing at a fairly constant rate. In the early 1980s, however, velocity as calculated with M1 becomes more variable. The reasons for these sharp changes in velocity remain a puzzle. Economists suspect that the changes in velocity are related to innovations in banking and finance which have changed how money is used in making economic transactions: for example, the growth of electronic payments; a rise in personal borrowing and credit card usage; and accounts that make it easier for people to hold money in savings accounts, where it is counted as M2, right up to the moment that they want to write a check on the money and transfer it to M1. So far at least, it has proven difficult to draw clear links between these kinds of factors and the specific up-and-down fluctuations in M1. Given many changes in banking and the prevalence of electronic banking, M2 is now favored as a measure of money rather than the narrower M1.

Figure 14.11 Velocity Calculated Using M1 Velocity is the nominal GDP divided by the money supply for a given year. Different measures of velocity can be calculated by using different measures of the money supply. Velocity, as calculated by using M1, has lacked a steady trend since the 1980s, instead bouncing up and down. (credit: Federal Reserve Bank of St. Louis)

In the 1970s, when velocity as measured by M1 seemed predictable, a number of economists, led by Nobel laureate Milton Friedman (1912–2006), argued that the best monetary policy was for the central bank to increase the money supply at a constant growth rate. These economists argued that with the long and variable lags of monetary policy, and the political pressures on central bankers, central bank monetary policies were as likely to have undesirable as to have desirable effects. Thus, these economists believed that the monetary policy should seek steady growth in the money supply of 3% per year. They argued that a steady rate of monetary growth would be correct over longer time periods, since it would roughly match the growth of the real economy. In addition, they argued that giving the central bank less discretion to conduct monetary policy would prevent an overly activist central bank from becoming a source of economic instability and uncertainty. In this spirit, Friedman wrote in 1967: "The first and most important lesson that history teaches about what monetary policy can do—and it is a lesson of the most profound importance—is that monetary policy can prevent money itself from being a major source of economic disturbance."

As the velocity of M1 began to fluctuate in the 1980s, having the money supply grow at a predetermined and unchanging rate seemed less desirable, because as the quantity theory of money shows, the combination of constant growth in the money supply and fluctuating velocity would cause nominal GDP to rise and fall in unpredictable ways. The jumpiness of velocity in the 1980s caused many central banks to focus less on the rate at which the quantity of money in the economy was increasing, and instead to set monetary policy by reacting to whether the economy was experiencing or in danger of higher inflation or unemployment.

Unemployment and Inflation

If you were to survey central bankers around the world and ask them what they believe should be the primary task of monetary policy, the most popular answer by far would be fighting inflation. Most central bankers believe that the neoclassical model of economics accurately represents the economy over the medium to long term. Remember that in the neoclassical model of the economy, the aggregate supply curve is drawn as a vertical line at the level of potential GDP, as shown in **Figure 14.12**. In the neoclassical model, the level of potential GDP (and the natural rate of unemployment that exists when the economy is producing at potential GDP) is determined by real economic factors. If the original level of aggregate demand is AD_0, then an expansionary monetary policy that shifts aggregate demand to AD$_1$ only creates an inflationary increase in the price level, but it does not alter GDP or unemployment. From this perspective, all that monetary policy can do is to lead to low inflation or high inflation—and low inflation provides a better climate for a healthy and growing economy. After all, low inflation means that businesses making investments can focus on real economic issues, not on figuring out ways to protect themselves from the costs and risks of inflation. In this way, a consistent pattern of low inflation can contribute to long-term growth.

Figure 14.12 Monetary Policy in a Neoclassical Model   In a neoclassical view, monetary policy affects only the price level, not the level of output in the economy. For example, an expansionary monetary policy causes aggregate demand to shift from the original AD$_0$ to AD$_1$. However, the adjustment of the economy from the original equilibrium (E$_0$) to the new equilibrium (E$_1$) represents an inflationary increase in the price level from P$_0$ to P$_1$, but has no effect in the long run on output or the unemployment rate. In fact, no shift in AD will affect the equilibrium quantity of output in this model.

This vision of focusing monetary policy on a low rate of inflation is so attractive that many countries have rewritten their central banking laws since in the 1990s to have their bank practice **inflation targeting**, which means that the central bank is legally required to focus primarily on keeping inflation low. By 2014, central banks in 28 countries, including Austria, Brazil, Canada, Israel, Korea, Mexico, New Zealand, Spain, Sweden, Thailand, and the United Kingdom faced a legal requirement to target the inflation rate. A notable exception is the Federal Reserve in the United States, which does not practice inflation-targeting. Instead, the law governing the Federal Reserve requires it to take both unemployment and inflation into account.

Economists have no final consensus on whether a central bank should be required to focus only on inflation or should have greater discretion. For those who subscribe to the inflation targeting philosophy, the fear is that politicians who are worried about slow economic growth and unemployment will constantly pressure the central bank to conduct a loose monetary policy—even if the economy is already producing at potential GDP. In some countries, the central bank may lack the political power to resist such pressures, with the result of higher inflation, but no long-term reduction in unemployment. The U.S. Federal Reserve has a tradition of independence, but central banks in other countries may be under greater political pressure. For all of these reasons—long and variable lags, excess reserves, unstable velocity, and controversy over economic goals—monetary policy in the real world is often difficult. The basic message remains, however, that central banks can affect aggregate demand through the conduct of monetary policy and in that way influence macroeconomic outcomes.

Asset Bubbles and Leverage Cycles

One long-standing concern about having the central bank focus on inflation and unemployment is that it may be overlooking certain other economic problems that are coming in the future. For example, from 1994 to 2000 during what was known as the "dot-com" boom, the U.S. stock market, which is measured by the Dow Jones Industrial Index (which includes 30 very large companies from across the U.S. economy), nearly tripled in value. The Nasdaq index, which includes many smaller technology companies, increased in value by a multiple of five from 1994 to 2000. These rates of increase were clearly not sustainable. Indeed, stock values as measured by the Dow Jones were almost 20% lower in 2009 than they had been in 2000. Stock values in the Nasdaq index were 50% lower in 2009 than they had been in 2000. The drop-off in stock market values contributed to the recession of 2001 and the higher unemployment that followed.

A similar story can be told about housing prices in the mid-2000s. During the 1970s, 1980s, and 1990s, housing prices increased at about 6% per year on average. During what came to be known as the "housing bubble" from 2003 to 2005, housing prices increased at almost double this annual rate. These rates of increase were clearly not sustainable. When the price of housing fell in 2007 and 2008, many banks and households found that their assets were worth less than they expected, which contributed to the recession that started in 2007.

At a broader level, some economists worry about a leverage cycle, where "leverage" is a term used by financial economists to mean "borrowing." When economic times are good, banks and the financial sector are eager to lend, and people and firms are eager to borrow. Remember that the amount of money and credit in an economy is determined by a money multiplier—a process of loans being made, money being deposited, and more loans being made. In good economic times, this surge of lending exaggerates the episode of economic growth. It can even be part of what lead prices of certain assets—like stock prices or housing prices—to rise at unsustainably high annual rates. At some point, when economic times turn bad, banks and the financial sector become much less willing to lend, and credit becomes expensive or unavailable to many potential borrowers. The sharp reduction in credit, perhaps combined with the deflating prices of a dot-com stock price bubble or a housing bubble, makes the economic downturn worse than it would otherwise be.

Thus, some economists have suggested that the central bank should not just look at economic growth, inflation, and unemployment rates, but should also keep an eye on asset prices and leverage cycles. Such proposals are quite controversial. If a central bank had announced in 1997 that stock prices were rising "too fast" or in 2004 that housing prices were rising "too fast," and then taken action to hold down price increases, many people and their elected political representatives would have been outraged. Neither the Federal Reserve nor any other central banks want to take the responsibility of deciding when stock prices and housing prices are too high, too low, or just right. As further research explores how asset price bubbles and leverage cycles can affect an economy, central banks may need to think about whether they should conduct monetary policy in a way that would seek to moderate these effects.

Let's end this chapter with a Work it Out exercise in how the Fed—or any central bank—would stir up the economy by increasing the money supply.

Work It Out ─○─○─○

Calculating the Effects of Monetary Stimulus

Suppose that the central bank wants to stimulate the economy by increasing the money supply. The bankers estimate that the velocity of money is 3, and that the price level will increase from 100 to 110 due to the stimulus. Using the quantity equation of money, what will be the impact of an $800 billion dollar increase in the money supply on the quantity of goods and services in the economy given an initial money supply of $4 trillion?

Step 1. We begin by writing the quantity equation of money: MV = PQ. We know that initially V = 3, M = 4,000 (billion) and P = 100. Substituting these numbers in, we can solve for Q:

$$
\begin{aligned}
MV &= PQ \\
4,000 \times 3 &= 100 \times Q \\
Q &= 120
\end{aligned}
$$

Step 2. Now we want to find the effect of the addition $800 billion in the money supply, together with the increase in the price level. The new equation is:

$$
\begin{aligned}
MV &= PQ \\
4,800 \times 3 &= 110 \times Q \\
Q &= 130.9
\end{aligned}
$$

Step 3. If we take the difference between the two quantities, we find that the monetary stimulus increased the quantity of goods and services in the economy by 10.9 billion.

The discussion in this chapter has focused on domestic monetary policy; that is, the view of monetary policy within an economy. **Exchange Rates and International Capital Flows** explores the international dimension of monetary policy, and how monetary policy becomes involved with exchange rates and international flows of financial capital.

Bring it Home

The Problem of the Zero Percent Interest Rate Lower Bound

In 2008, the U.S. Federal Reserve found itself in a difficult position. The federal funds rate was on its way to near zero, which meant that traditional open market operations, by which the Fed purchases U.S. Treasury Bills to lower short term interest rates, was no longer viable. This so called "zero bound problem," prompted the Fed, under then Chair Ben Bernanke, to attempt some unconventional policies, collectively called quantitative easing. By early 2014, quantitative easing nearly quintupled the amount of bank reserves. This likely contributed to the U.S. economy's recovery, but the impact was muted, probably due to some of the hurdles mentioned in the last section of this module. The unprecedented increase in bank reserves also led to fears of inflation. As of early 2015, however, there have been no serious signs of a boom, with core inflation around a stable 1.7%.

KEY TERMS

bank run when depositors race to the bank to withdraw their deposits for fear that otherwise they would be lost

basic quantity equation of money money supply × velocity = nominal GDP

central bank institution which conducts a nation's monetary policy and regulates its banking system

contractionary monetary policy a monetary policy that reduces the supply of money and loans

countercyclical moving in the opposite direction of the business cycle of economic downturns and upswings

deposit insurance an insurance system that makes sure depositors in a bank do not lose their money, even if the bank goes bankrupt

discount rate the interest rate charged by the central bank on the loans that it gives to other commercial banks

excess reserves reserves banks hold that exceed the legally mandated limit

expansionary monetary policy a monetary policy that increases the supply of money and the quantity of loans

federal funds rate the interest rate at which one bank lends funds to another bank overnight

inflation targeting a rule that the central bank is required to focus only on keeping inflation low

lender of last resort an institution that provides short-term emergency loans in conditions of financial crisis

loose monetary policy see expansionary monetary policy

open market operations the central bank selling or buying Treasury bonds to influence the quantity of money and the level of interest rates

quantitative easing (QE) the purchase of long term government and private mortgage-backed securities by central banks to make credit available in hopes of stimulating aggregate demand

reserve requirement the percentage amount of its total deposits that a bank is legally obligated to to either hold as cash in their vault or deposit with the central bank

tight monetary policy see contractionary monetary policy

velocity the speed with which money circulates through the economy; calculated as the nominal GDP divided by the money supply

KEY CONCEPTS AND SUMMARY

14.1 The Federal Reserve Banking System and Central Banks

The most prominent task of a central bank is to conduct monetary policy, which involves changes to interest rates and credit conditions, affecting the amount of borrowing and spending in an economy. Some prominent central banks around the world include the U.S. Federal Reserve, the European Central Bank, the Bank of Japan, and the Bank of England.

14.2 Bank Regulation

A bank run occurs when there are rumors (possibly true, possibly false) that a bank is at financial risk of having negative net worth. As a result, depositors rush to the bank to withdraw their money and put it someplace safer. Even false rumors, if they cause a bank run, can force a healthy bank to lose its deposits and be forced to close. Deposit insurance guarantees bank depositors that, even if the bank has negative net worth, their deposits will be protected. In the United States, the Federal Deposit Insurance Corporation (FDIC) collects deposit insurance premiums from banks and guarantees bank deposits up to $250,000. Bank supervision involves inspecting the balance sheets of banks to make sure that they have positive net worth and that their assets are not too risky. In the United States, the Office of the Comptroller of the Currency (OCC) is responsible for supervising banks and inspecting savings and loans and the National Credit Union Administration (NCUA) is responsible for inspecting credit unions. The FDIC and the Federal Reserve also play a role in bank supervision.

When a central bank acts as a lender of last resort, it makes short-term loans available in situations of severe financial panic or stress. The failure of a single bank can be treated like any other business failure. Yet if many banks fail, it can reduce aggregate demand in a way that can bring on or deepen a recession. The combination of deposit insurance, bank supervision, and lender of last resort policies help to prevent weaknesses in the banking system from causing recessions.

14.3 How a Central Bank Executes Monetary Policy

A central bank has three traditional tools to conduct monetary policy: open market operations, which involves buying and selling government bonds with banks; reserve requirements, which determine what level of reserves a bank is legally required to hold; and discount rates, which is the interest rate charged by the central bank on the loans that it gives to other commercial banks. The most commonly used tool is open market operations.

14.4 Monetary Policy and Economic Outcomes

An expansionary (or loose) monetary policy raises the quantity of money and credit above what it otherwise would have been and reduces interest rates, boosting aggregate demand, and thus countering recession. A contractionary monetary policy, also called a tight monetary policy, reduces the quantity of money and credit below what it otherwise would have been and raises interest rates, seeking to hold down inflation. During the 2008–2009 recession, central banks around the world also used quantitative easing to expand the supply of credit.

14.5 Pitfalls for Monetary Policy

Monetary policy is inevitably imprecise, for a number of reasons: (a) the effects occur only after long and variable lags; (b) if banks decide to hold excess reserves, monetary policy cannot force them to lend; and (c) velocity may shift in unpredictable ways. The basic quantity equation of money is $MV = PQ$, where M is the money supply, V is the velocity of money, P is the price level, and Q is the real output of the economy. Some central banks, like the European Central Bank, practice inflation targeting, which means that the only goal of the central bank is to keep inflation within a low target range. Other central banks, such as the U.S. Federal Reserve, are free to focus on either reducing inflation or stimulating an economy that is in recession, whichever goal seems most important at the time.

SELF-CHECK QUESTIONS

1. Why is it important for the members of the Board of Governors of the Federal Reserve to have longer terms in office than elected officials, like the President?

2. Given the danger of bank runs, why do banks not keep the majority of deposits on hand to meet the demands of depositors?

3. Bank runs are often described as "self-fulfilling prophecies." Why is this phrase appropriate to bank runs?

4. If the central bank sells $500 in bonds to a bank that has issued $10,000 in loans and is exactly meeting the reserve requirement of 10%, what will happen to the amount of loans and to the money supply in general?

5. What would be the effect of increasing the reserve requirements of banks on the money supply?

6. Why does contractionary monetary policy cause interest rates to rise?

7. Why does expansionary monetary policy causes interest rates to drop?

8. Why might banks want to hold excess reserves in time of recession?

9. Why might the velocity of money change unexpectedly?

REVIEW QUESTIONS

10. How is a central bank different from a typical commercial bank?

11. List the three traditional tools that a central bank has for controlling the money supply.

12. How is bank regulation linked to the conduct of monetary policy?

13. What is a bank run?

14. In a program of deposit insurance as it is operated in the United States, what is being insured and who pays the insurance premiums?

15. In government programs of bank supervision, what is being supervised?

16. What is the lender of last resort?

17. Name and briefly describe the responsibilities of each of the following agencies: FDIC, NCUA, and OCC.

18. Explain how to use an open market operation to expand the money supply.

19. Explain how to use the reserve requirement to expand the money supply.

20. Explain how to use the discount rate to expand the money supply.

21. How do the expansionary and contractionary monetary policy affect the quantity of money?

22. How do tight and loose monetary policy affect interest rates?

23. How do expansionary, tight, contractionary, and loose monetary policy affect aggregate demand?

24. Which kind of monetary policy would you expect in response to high inflation: expansionary or contractionary? Why?

25. Explain how to use quantitative easing to stimulate aggregate demand.

26. Which kind of monetary policy would you expect in response to recession: expansionary or contractionary? Why?

27. How might each of the following factors complicate the implementation of monetary policy: long and variable lags, excess reserves, and movements in velocity?

28. Define the velocity of the money supply.

29. What is the basic quantity equation of money?

30. How does a monetary policy of inflation targeting work?

CRITICAL THINKING QUESTIONS

31. Why do presidents typically reappoint Chairs of the Federal Reserve Board even when they were originally appointed by a president of a different political party?

32. In what ways might monetary policy be superior to fiscal policy? In what ways might it be inferior?

33. The term "moral hazard" describes increases in risky behavior resulting from efforts to make that behavior safer. How does the concept of moral hazard apply to deposit insurance and other bank regulations?

34. Explain what would happen if banks were notified they had to increase their required reserves by one percentage point from, say, 9% to10% of deposits. What would their options be to come up with the cash?

35. A well-known economic model called the Phillips Curve (discussed in **The Keynesian Perspective** chapter) describes the short run tradeoff typically observed between inflation and unemployment. Based on the discussion of expansionary and contractionary monetary policy, explain why one of these variables usually falls when the other rises.

36. How does rule-based monetary policy differ from discretionary monetary policy (that is, monetary policy not based on a rule)? What are some of the arguments for each?

37. Is it preferable for central banks to primarily target inflation or unemployment? Why?

PROBLEMS

38. Suppose the Fed conducts an open market purchase by buying $10 million in Treasury bonds from Acme Bank. Sketch out the balance sheet changes that will occur as Acme converts the bond sale proceeds to new loans. The initial Acme bank balance sheet contains the following information: Assets – reserves 30, bonds 50, and loans 50; Liabilities – deposits 300 and equity 30.

39. Suppose the Fed conducts an open market sale by selling $10 million in Treasury bonds to Acme Bank. Sketch out the balance sheet changes that will occur as Acme restores its required reserves (10% of deposits) by reducing its loans. The initial balance sheet for Acme Bank contains the following information: Assets – reserves 30, bonds 50, and loans 250; Liabilities – deposits 300 and equity 30.

40. All other things being equal, by how much will nominal GDP expand if the central bank increases the money supply by $100 billion, and the velocity of money is 3? (Use this information as necessary to answer the following 4 questions.)

41. Suppose now that economists expect the velocity of money to increase by 50% as a result of the monetary stimulus. What will be the total increase in nominal GDP?

42. If GDP is 1,500 and the money supply is 400, what is velocity?

43. If GDP now rises to 1,600, but the money supply does not change, how has velocity changed?

44. If GDP now falls back to 1,500 and the money supply falls to 350, what is velocity?

15 | Exchange Rates and International Capital Flows

Figure 15.1 Trade Around the World Is a trade deficit between the United States and the European Union good or bad for the U.S. economy? (Credit: modification of work by Milad Mosapoor/Wikimedia Commons)

Bring it Home

Is a Stronger Dollar Good for the U.S. Economy?

From 2002 to 2008, the U.S. dollar lost more than a quarter of its value in foreign currency markets. On January 1, 2002, one dollar was worth 1.11 euros. On April 24, 2008 it hit its lowest point with a dollar being worth 0.64 euros. During this period, the trade deficit between the United States and the European Union grew from a yearly total of approximately –85.7 billion dollars in 2002 to 95.8 billion dollars in 2008. Was this a good thing or a bad thing for the U.S. economy?

We live in a global world. U.S. consumers buy trillions of dollars worth of imported goods and services each year, not just from the European Union, but from all over the world. U.S. businesses sell trillions of dollars' worth of exports. U.S. citizens, businesses, and governments invest trillions of dollars abroad every year. Foreign investors, businesses, and governments invest trillions of dollars in the United States each year. Indeed, foreigners are a major buyer of U.S. federal debt.

Many people feel that a weaker dollar is bad for America, that it's an indication of a weak economy. But is it? This chapter will help answer that question.

Introduction to Exchange Rates and International Capital Flows

In this chapter, you will learn about:

- How the Foreign Exchange Market Works

- Demand and Supply Shifts in Foreign Exchange Markets

- Macroeconomic Effects of Exchange Rates

- Exchange Rate Policies

The world has over 150 different currencies, from the Afghanistan afghani and the Albanian lek all the way through the alphabet to the Zambian kwacha and the Zimbabwean dollar. For international economic transactions, households or firms will wish to exchange one currency for another. Perhaps the need for exchanging currencies will come from a German firm that exports products to Russia, but then wishes to exchange the Russian rubles it has earned for euros, so that the firm can pay its workers and suppliers in Germany. Perhaps it will be a South African firm that wishes to purchase a mining operation in Angola, but to make the purchase it must convert South African rand to Angolan kwanza. Perhaps it will be an American tourist visiting China, who wishes to convert U.S. dollars to Chinese yuan to pay the hotel bill.

Exchange rates can sometimes change very swiftly. For example, in the United Kingdom the pound was worth $2 in U.S. currency in spring 2008, but was worth only $1.40 in U.S. currency six months later. For firms engaged in international buying, selling, lending, and borrowing, these swings in exchange rates can have an enormous effect on profits.

This chapter discusses the international dimension of money, which involves conversions from one currency to another at an exchange rate. An exchange rate is nothing more than a price—that is, the price of one currency in terms of another currency—and so they can be analyzed with the tools of supply and demand. The first module of this chapter begins with an overview of foreign exchange markets: their size, their main participants, and the vocabulary for discussing movements of exchange rates. The following module uses demand and supply graphs to analyze some of the main factors that cause shifts in exchange rates. A final module then brings the central bank and monetary policy back into the picture. Each country must decide whether to allow its exchange rate to be determined in the market, or have the central bank intervene in the exchange rate market. All the choices for exchange rate policy involve distinctive tradeoffs and risks.

15.1 | How the Foreign Exchange Market Works

By the end of this section, you will be able to:
- Define "foreign exchange market"
- Describe different types of investments like foreign direct investments (FDI), portfolio investments, and hedging
- Explain how the appreciating or depreciating of currency affects exchange rates
- Identify who benefits from a stronger currency and benefits from a weaker currency

Most countries have different currencies, but not all. Sometimes small economies use the currency of an economically larger neighbor. For example, Ecuador, El Salvador, and Panama have decided to **dollarize**—that is, to use the U.S. dollar as their currency. Sometimes nations share a common currency. A large-scale example of a common currency is the decision by 17 European nations—including some very large economies such as France, Germany, and Italy—to replace their former currencies with the euro. With these exceptions duly noted, most of the international economy takes place in a situation of multiple national currencies in which both people and firms need to convert from one currency to another when selling, buying, hiring, borrowing, traveling, or investing across national borders. The market in which people or firms use one currency to purchase another currency is called the **foreign exchange market**.

You have encountered the basic concept of exchange rates in earlier chapters. In **The International Trade and Capital Flows (http://cnx.org/content/m57383/latest/)** , for example, we discussed how exchange rates are used to compare GDP statistics from countries where GDP is measured in different currencies. These earlier examples, however, took the actual exchange rate as given, as if it were a fact of nature. In reality, the exchange rate is a price—the price of one currency expressed in terms of units of another currency. The key framework for analyzing prices, whether in this course, any other economics course, in public policy, or business examples, is the operation of supply and demand in markets.

Link It Up ⌾

Visit this website (http://openstaxcollege.org/l/exratecalc) for an exchange rate calculator.

The Extraordinary Size of the Foreign Exchange Markets

The quantities traded in foreign exchange markets are breathtaking. A survey done in April, 2013 by the Bank of International Settlements, an international organization for banks and the financial industry, found that $5.3 trillion *per day* was traded on foreign exchange markets, which makes the foreign exchange market the largest market in the world economy. In contrast, 2013 U.S. real GDP was $15.8 trillion *per year*.

Table 15.1 shows the currencies most commonly traded on foreign exchange markets. The foreign exchange market is dominated by the U.S. dollar, the currencies used by nations in Western Europe (the euro, the British pound, and the Australian dollar), and the Japanese yen.

Currency	% Daily Share
U.S. dollar	87.0%
Euro	33.4%
Japanese yen	23.0%
British pound	11.8%
Australian dollar	8.6%
Swiss franc	5.2%
Canadian dollar	4.6%
Mexican peso	2.5%
Chinese yuan	2.2%

Table 15.1 Currencies Traded Most on Foreign Exchange Markets as of April, 2013 (Source: http://www.bis.org/publ/rpfx13fx.pdf)

Demanders and Suppliers of Currency in Foreign Exchange Markets

In foreign exchange markets, demand and supply become closely interrelated, because a person or firm who demands one currency must at the same time supply another currency—and vice versa. To get a sense of this, it is useful to consider four groups of people or firms who participate in the market: (1) firms that are involved in international trade of goods and services; (2) tourists visiting other countries; (3) international investors buying ownership (or part-ownership) of a foreign firm; (4) international investors making financial investments that do not involve ownership. Let's consider these categories in turn.

Firms that buy and sell on international markets find that their costs for workers, suppliers, and investors are measured in the currency of the nation where their production occurs, but their revenues from sales are measured in the currency of the different nation where their sales happened. So, a Chinese firm exporting abroad will earn some other currency—say, U.S. dollars—but will need Chinese yuan to pay the workers, suppliers, and investors who are based in China. In the foreign exchange markets, this firm will be a supplier of U.S. dollars and a demander of Chinese yuan.

International tourists will supply their home currency to receive the currency of the country they are visiting. For example, an American tourist who is visiting China will supply U.S. dollars into the foreign exchange market and demand Chinese yuan.

Financial investments that cross international boundaries, and require exchanging currency, are often divided into two categories. **Foreign direct investment (FDI)** refers to purchasing a firm (at least ten percent) in another country or starting up a new enterprise in a foreign country For example, in 2008 the Belgian beer-brewing company InBev bought the U.S. beer-maker Anheuser-Busch for $52 billion. To make this purchase of a U.S. firm, InBev would have to supply euros (the currency of Belgium) to the foreign exchange market and demand U.S. dollars.

The other kind of international financial investment, **portfolio investment**, involves a purely financial investment that does not entail any management responsibility. An example would be a U.S. financial investor who purchased bonds issued by the government of the United Kingdom, or deposited money in a British bank. To make such investments, the American investor would supply U.S. dollars in the foreign exchange market and demand British pounds.

Portfolio investment is often linked to expectations about how exchange rates will shift. Look at a U.S. financial investor who is considering purchasing bonds issued in the United Kingdom. For simplicity, ignore any interest paid by the bond (which will be small in the short run anyway) and focus on exchange rates. Say that a British pound is currently worth $1.50 in U.S. currency. However, the investor believes that in a month, the British pound will be worth $1.60 in U.S. currency. Thus, as Figure 15.2 (a) shows, this investor would change $24,000 for 16,000 British pounds. In a month, if the pound is indeed worth $1.60, then the portfolio investor can trade back to U.S. dollars at the new exchange rate, and have $25,600—a nice profit. A portfolio investor who believes that the foreign exchange rate for the pound will work in the opposite direction can also invest accordingly. Say that an investor expects that the pound, now worth $1.50 in U.S. currency, will decline to $1.40. Then, as shown in Figure 15.2 (b), that investor could start off with £20,000 in British currency (borrowing the money if necessary), convert it to $30,000 in U.S. currency, wait a month, and then convert back to approximately £21,429 in British currency—again making a nice profit. Of course, this kind of investing comes without guarantees, and an investor will suffer losses if the exchange rates do not move as predicted.

(a) An international investor who expects that, in the future, a British pound(£) will buy $1.60 in U.S. currency instead of its current exchange rate of $1.50 may hope for the following chain of events to occur:

Take $24,000 in U.S. currency convert it to £16,000 in British currency. → Exchange rate for pound(£) changes from $1.50 to $1.60 → Now convert £16,000 back to $25,000—and earn a profit of $1,000.

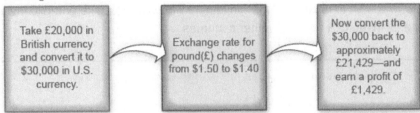

(b) An international investor who expects that, in the future, a British pound(£) will buy only $1.40 in U.S. currency instead of its current exchange rate of $1.50 may hope for the following chain of events to occur:

Take £20,000 in British currency and convert it to $30,000 in U.S. currency. → Exchange rate for pound(£) changes from $1.50 to $1.40 → Now convert the $30,000 back to approximately £21,429—and earn a profit of £1,429.

Figure 15.2 A Portfolio Investor Trying to Benefit from Exchange Rate Movements Expectations of the future value of a currency can drive demand and supply of that currency in foreign exchange markets.

Many portfolio investment decisions are not as simple as betting that the value of the currency will change in one direction or the other. Instead, they involve firms trying to protect themselves from movements in exchange rates. Imagine you are running a U.S. firm that is exporting to France. You have signed a contract to deliver certain products and will receive 1 million euros a year from now. But you do not know how much this contract will be worth in U.S. dollars, because the dollar/euro exchange rate can fluctuate in the next year. Let's say you want to know for sure what the contract will be worth, and not take a risk that the euro will be worth less in U.S. dollars than it currently is. You can **hedge**, which means using a financial transaction to protect yourself against a risk from one of your investments (in this case, currency risk from the contract). Specifically, you can sign a financial contract and pay a fee that guarantees you a certain exchange rate one year from now—regardless of what the market exchange rate is at that time. Now, it is possible that the euro will be worth more in dollars a year from now, so your hedging contract will be unnecessary, and you will have paid a fee for nothing. But if the value of the euro in dollars declines, then you are protected by the hedge. Financial contracts like hedging, where parties wish to be protected against exchange rate movements, also commonly lead to a series of portfolio investments by the firm that is receiving a fee to provide the hedge.

Both foreign direct investment and portfolio investment involve an investor who supplies domestic currency and demands a foreign currency. With portfolio investment less than ten percent of a company is purchased. As such, portfolio investment is often made with a short term focus. With foreign direct investment more than ten percent of a company is purchased and the investor typically assumes some managerial responsibility; thus foreign direct investment tends to have a more long-run focus. As a practical matter, portfolio investments can be withdrawn from a country much more quickly than foreign direct investments. A U.S. portfolio investor who wants to buy or sell bonds issued by the government of the United Kingdom can do so with a phone call or a few clicks of a computer key. However, a U.S. firm that wants to buy or sell a company, such as one that manufactures automobile parts in the United Kingdom, will find that planning and carrying out the transaction takes a few weeks, even months. Table 15.2 summarizes the main categories of demanders and suppliers of currency.

Demand for the U.S. Dollar Comes from...	Supply of the U.S. Dollar Comes from...
A U.S. exporting firm that earned foreign currency and is trying to pay U.S.-based expenses	A foreign firm that has sold imported goods in the United States, earned U.S. dollars, and is trying to pay expenses incurred in its home country
Foreign tourists visiting the United States	U.S. tourists leaving to visit other countries
Foreign investors who wish to make direct investments in the U.S. economy	U.S. investors who want to make foreign direct investments in other countries
Foreign investors who wish to make portfolio investments in the U.S. economy	U.S. investors who want to make portfolio investments in other countries

Table 15.2 The Demand and Supply Line-ups in Foreign Exchange Markets

Participants in the Exchange Rate Market

The foreign exchange market does not involve the ultimate suppliers and demanders of foreign exchange literally seeking each other out. If Martina decides to leave her home in Venezuela and take a trip in the United States, she does not need to find a U.S. citizen who is planning to take a vacation in Venezuela and arrange a person-to-person currency trade. Instead, the foreign exchange market works through financial institutions, and it operates on several levels.

Most people and firms who are exchanging a substantial quantity of currency go to a bank, and most banks provide foreign exchange as a service to customers. These banks (and a few other firms), known as dealers, then trade the foreign exchange. This is called the interbank market.

In the world economy, roughly 2,000 firms are foreign exchange dealers. The U.S. economy has less than 100 foreign exchange dealers, but the largest 12 or so dealers carry out more than half the total transactions. The foreign exchange market has no central location, but the major dealers keep a close watch on each other at all times.

The foreign exchange market is huge not because of the demands of tourists, firms, or even foreign direct investment, but instead because of portfolio investment and the actions of interlocking foreign exchange dealers. International tourism is a very large industry, involving about $1 trillion per year. Global exports are about 23% of global GDP; which is about $18 trillion per year. Foreign direct investment totaled about $1.5 trillion in the end of 2013. These quantities are dwarfed, however, by the $5.3 trillion *per day* being traded in foreign exchange markets. Most transactions in the foreign exchange market are for portfolio investment—relatively short-term movements of financial capital between currencies—and because of the actions of the large foreign exchange dealers as they constantly buy and sell with each other.

Strengthening and Weakening Currency

When the prices of most goods and services change, the price is said to "rise" or "fall." For exchange rates, the terminology is different. When the exchange rate for a currency rises, so that the currency exchanges for more of other currencies, it is referred to as **appreciating** or "strengthening." When the exchange rate for a currency falls, so that a currency trades for less of other currencies, it is referred to as **depreciating** or "weakening."

To illustrate the use of these terms, consider the exchange rate between the U.S. dollar and the Canadian dollar since 1980, shown in **Figure 15.3** (a). The vertical axis in **Figure 15.3** (a) shows the price of $1 in U.S. currency, measured in terms of Canadian currency. Clearly, exchange rates can move up and down substantially. A U.S. dollar traded for $1.17 Canadian in 1980. The U.S. dollar appreciated or strengthened to $1.39 Canadian in 1986, depreciated or weakened to $1.15 Canadian in 1991, and then appreciated or strengthened to $1.60 Canadian by early in 2002, fell to roughly $1.20 Canadian in 2009, and then had a sharp spike up and decline in 2009 and 2010. The units in which exchange rates are measured can be confusing, because the exchange rate of the U.S. dollar is being measured using a different currency—the Canadian dollar. But exchange rates always measure the price of one unit of currency by using a different currency.

(a) U.S. dollar exchange rate in Canadian dollars

(b) Canadian dollar exchange rate in U.S. dollars

Figure 15.3 Strengthen or Appreciate vs. Weaken or Depreciate Exchange rates tend to fluctuate substantially, even between bordering companies such as the United States and Canada. By looking closely at the time values (the years vary slightly on these graphs), it is clear that the values in part (a) are a mirror image of part (b), which demonstrates that the depreciation of one currency correlates to the appreciation of the other and vice versa. This means that when comparing the exchange rates between two countries (in this case, the United States and Canada), the depreciation (or weakening) of one country (the U.S. dollar for this example) indicates the appreciation (or strengthening) of the other currency (which in this example is the Canadian dollar). (Source: Federal Reserve Economic Data (FRED) (a) https://research.stlouisfed.org/fred2/series/EXCAUS ; (b) https://research.stlouisfed.org/fred2/series/CCUSSP01CAQ650N)

In looking at the exchange rate between two currencies, the appreciation or strengthening of one currency must mean the depreciation or weakening of the other. Figure 15.3 (b) shows the exchange rate for the Canadian dollar, measured in terms of U.S. dollars. The exchange rate of the U.S. dollar measured in Canadian dollars, shown in Figure 15.3 (a), is a perfect mirror image with the exchange rate of the Canadian dollar measured in U.S. dollars, shown in Figure 15.3 (b). A fall in the Canada $/U.S. $ ratio means a rise in the U.S. $/Canada $ ratio, and vice versa.

With the price of a typical good or service, it is clear that higher prices benefit sellers and hurt buyers, while lower prices benefit buyers and hurt sellers. In the case of exchange rates, where the buyers and sellers are not always intuitively obvious, it is useful to trace through how different participants in the market will be affected by a stronger or weaker currency. Consider, for example, the impact of a stronger U.S. dollar on six different groups of economic actors, as shown in Figure 15.4: (1) U.S. exporters selling abroad; (2) foreign exporters (that is, firms selling imports in the U.S. economy); (3) U.S. tourists abroad; (4) foreign tourists visiting the United States; (5) U.S. investors (either foreign direct investment or portfolio investment) considering opportunities in other countries; (6) and foreign investors considering opportunities in the U.S. economy.

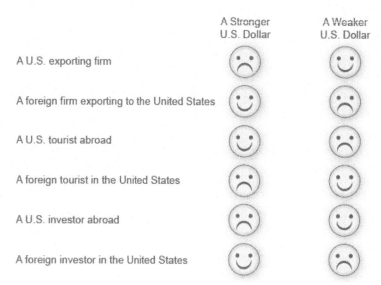

Figure 15.4 How Do Exchange Rate Movements Affect Each Group? Exchange rate movements affect exporters, tourists, and international investors in different ways.

For a U.S. firm selling abroad, a stronger U.S. dollar is a curse. A strong U.S. dollar means that foreign currencies are correspondingly weak. When this exporting firm earns foreign currencies through its export sales, and then converts them back to U.S. dollars to pay workers, suppliers, and investors, the stronger dollar means that the foreign currency buys fewer U.S. dollars than if the currency had not strengthened, and that the firm's profits (as measured in dollars) fall. As a result, the firm may choose to reduce its exports, or it may raise its selling price, which will also tend to reduce its exports. In this way, a stronger currency reduces a country's exports.

Conversely, for a foreign firm selling in the U.S. economy, a stronger dollar is a blessing. Each dollar earned through export sales, when traded back into the home currency of the exporting firm, will now buy more of the home currency than expected before the dollar had strengthened. As a result, the stronger dollar means that the importing firm will earn higher profits than expected. The firm will seek to expand its sales in the U.S. economy, or it may reduce prices, which will also lead to expanded sales. In this way, a stronger U.S. dollar means that consumers will purchase more from foreign producers, expanding the country's level of imports.

For a U.S. tourist abroad, who is exchanging U.S. dollars for foreign currency as necessary, a stronger U.S. dollar is a benefit. The tourist receives more foreign currency for each U.S. dollar, and consequently the cost of the trip in U.S. dollars is lower. When a country's currency is strong, it is a good time for citizens of that country to tour abroad. Imagine a U.S. tourist who has saved up $5,000 for a trip to South Africa. In January 2008, $1 bought 7 South African rand, so the tourist had 35,000 rand to spend. In January 2009, $1 bought 10 rand, so the tourist had 50,000 rand to spend. By January 2010, $1 bought only 7.5 rand. Clearly, 2009 was the year for U.S. tourists to visit South Africa. For foreign visitors to the United States, the opposite pattern holds true. A relatively stronger U.S. dollar means that their own currencies are relatively weaker, so that as they shift from their own currency to U.S. dollars, they have fewer U.S. dollars than previously. When a country's currency is strong, it is not an especially good time for foreign tourists to visit.

A stronger dollar injures the prospects of a U.S. financial investor who has already invested money in another country. A U.S. financial investor abroad must first convert U.S. dollars to a foreign currency, invest in a foreign country, and then later convert that foreign currency back to U.S. dollars. If in the meantime the U.S. dollar becomes stronger and the foreign currency becomes weaker, then when the investor converts back to U.S. dollars, the rate of return on that investment will be less than originally expected at the time it was made.

However, a stronger U.S. dollar boosts the returns of a foreign investor putting money into a U.S. investment. That foreign investor converts from the home currency to U.S. dollars and seeks a U.S. investment, while later planning to switch back to the home currency. If, in the meantime, the dollar grows stronger, then when the time comes to convert from U.S. dollars back to the foreign currency, the investor will receive more foreign currency than expected at the time the original investment was made.

The preceding paragraphs all focus on the case where the U.S. dollar becomes stronger. The corresponding happy or unhappy economic reactions are illustrated in the first column of Figure 15.4. The following Work It Out feature centers the analysis on the opposite: a weaker dollar.

Work It Out ─○─○─○

Effects of a Weaker Dollar

Let's work through the effects of a weaker dollar on a U.S. exporter, a foreign exporter into the United States, a U.S. tourist going abroad, a foreign tourist coming to the United States, a U.S. investor abroad, and a foreign investor in the United States.

Step 1. Note that the demand for U.S. exports is a function of the price of those exports, which depends on the dollar price of those goods and the exchange rate of the dollar in terms of foreign currency. For example, a Ford pickup truck costs $25,000 in the United States. When it is sold in the United Kingdom, the price is $25,000 / $1.50 per British pound, or £16,667. The dollar affects the price faced by foreigners who may purchase U.S. exports.

Step 2. Consider that, if the dollar weakens, the pound rises in value. If the pound rises to $2.00 per pound, then the price of a Ford pickup is now $25,000 / $2.00 = £12,500. A weaker dollar means the foreign currency buys more dollars, which means that U.S. exports appear less expensive.

Step 3. Summarize that a weaker U.S. dollar leads to an increase in U.S. exports. For a foreign exporter, the outcome is just the opposite.

Step 4. Suppose a brewery in England is interested in selling its Bass Ale to a grocery store in the United States. If the price of a six pack of Bass Ale is £6.00 and the exchange rate is $1.50 per British pound, the price for the grocery store is 6.00 × $1.50 = $9.00 per six pack. If the dollar weakens to $2.00 per pound, the price of Bass Ale is now 6.00 × $2.00 = $12.

Step 5. Summarize that, from the perspective of U.S. purchasers, a weaker dollar means that foreign currency is more expensive, which means that foreign goods are more expensive also. This leads to a decrease in U.S. imports, which is bad for the foreign exporter.

Step 6. Consider U.S. tourists going abroad. They face the same situation as a U.S. importer—they are purchasing a foreign trip. A weaker dollar means that their trip will cost more, since a given expenditure of foreign currency (e.g., hotel bill) will take more dollars. The result is that the tourist may not stay as long abroad, and some may choose not to travel at all.

Step 7. Consider that, for the foreign tourist to the United States, a weaker dollar is a boon. It means their currency goes further, so the cost of a trip to the United States will be less. Foreigners may choose to take longer trips to the United States, and more foreign tourists may decide to take U.S. trips.

Step 8. Note that a U.S. investor abroad faces the same situation as a U.S. importer—they are purchasing a foreign asset. A U.S. investor will see a weaker dollar as an increase in the "price" of investment, since the same number of dollars will buy less foreign currency and thus less foreign assets. This should decrease the amount of U.S. investment abroad.

Step 9. Note also that foreign investors in the Unites States will have the opposite experience. Since foreign currency buys more dollars, they will likely invest in more U.S. assets.

At this point, you should have a good sense of the major players in the foreign exchange market: firms involved in international trade, tourists, international financial investors, banks, and foreign exchange dealers. The next module shows how the tools of demand and supply can be used in foreign exchange markets to explain the underlying causes of stronger and weaker currencies ("stronger" and "weaker" addressed more in the following Clear It Up feature).

Why is a stronger currency not necessarily better?

One common misunderstanding about exchange rates is that a "stronger" or "appreciating" currency must be better than a "weaker" or "depreciating" currency. After all, is it not obvious that "strong" is better than "weak"? But do not let the terminology confuse you. When a currency becomes stronger, so that it purchases more of other currencies, it benefits some in the economy and injures others. Stronger currency is not necessarily better, it is just different.

15.2 | Demand and Supply Shifts in Foreign Exchange Markets

By the end of this section, you will be able to:
- Explain supply and demand for exchange rates
- Define arbitrage
- Explain purchasing power parity's importance when comparing countries.

The foreign exchange market involves firms, households, and investors who demand and supply currencies coming together through their banks and the key foreign exchange dealers. **Figure 15.5** (a) offers an example for the exchange rate between the U.S. dollar and the Mexican peso. The vertical axis shows the exchange rate for U.S. dollars, which in this case is measured in pesos. The horizontal axis shows the quantity of U.S. dollars being traded in the foreign exchange market each day. The demand curve (D) for U.S. dollars intersects with the supply curve (S) of U.S. dollars at the equilibrium point (E), which is an exchange rate of 10 pesos per dollar and a total volume of $8.5 billion.

(a) The U.S. dollar exchange rate   (b) The Mexican peso exchange rate

Figure 15.5 Demand and Supply for the U.S. Dollar and Mexican Peso Exchange Rate (a) The quantity measured on the horizontal axis is in U.S. dollars, and the exchange rate on the vertical axis is the price of U.S. dollars measured in Mexican pesos. (b) The quantity measured on the horizontal axis is in Mexican pesos, while the price on the vertical axis is the price of pesos measured in U.S. dollars. In both graphs, the equilibrium exchange rate occurs at point E, at the intersection of the demand curve (D) and the supply curve (S).

Figure 15.5 (b) presents the same demand and supply information from the perspective of the Mexican peso. The vertical axis shows the exchange rate for Mexican pesos, which is measured in U.S. dollars. The horizontal axis shows the quantity of Mexican pesos traded in the foreign exchange market. The demand curve (D) for Mexican pesos intersects with the supply curve (S) of Mexican pesos at the equilibrium point (E), which is an exchange rate of 10 cents in U.S. currency for each Mexican peso and a total volume of 85 billion pesos. Note that the two exchange rates are inverses: 10 pesos per dollar is the same as 10 cents per peso (or $0.10 per peso). In the actual foreign exchange market, almost all of the trading for Mexican pesos is done for U.S. dollars. What factors would cause the demand or supply to shift, thus leading to a change in the equilibrium exchange rate? The answer to this question is discussed in the following section.

Expectations about Future Exchange Rates

One reason to demand a currency on the foreign exchange market is the belief that the value of the currency is about to increase. One reason to supply a currency—that is, sell it on the foreign exchange market—is the expectation that the value of the currency is about to decline. For example, imagine that a leading business newspaper, like the *Wall Street Journal* or the *Financial Times*, runs an article predicting that the Mexican peso will appreciate in value. The likely effects of such an article are illustrated in Figure 15.6. Demand for the Mexican peso shifts to the right, from D_0 to D_1, as investors become eager to purchase pesos. Conversely, the supply of pesos shifts to the left, from S_0 to S_1, because investors will be less willing to give them up. The result is that the equilibrium exchange rate rises from 10 cents/peso to 12 cents/peso and the equilibrium exchange rate rises from 85 billion to 90 billion pesos as the equilibrium moves from E_0 to E_1.

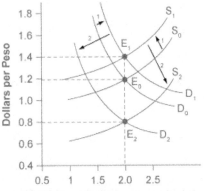

Figure 15.6 Exchange Rate Market for Mexican Peso Reacts to Expectations about Future Exchange Rates
An announcement that the peso exchange rate is likely to strengthen in the future will lead to greater demand for the peso in the present from investors who wish to benefit from the appreciation. Similarly, it will make investors less likely to supply pesos to the foreign exchange market. Both the shift of demand to the right and the shift of supply to the left cause an immediate appreciation in the exchange rate.

Figure 15.6 also illustrates some peculiar traits of supply and demand diagrams in the foreign exchange market. In contrast to all the other cases of supply and demand you have considered, in the foreign exchange market, supply and demand typically both move at the same time. Groups of participants in the foreign exchange market like firms and investors include some who are buyers and some who are sellers. An expectation of a future shift in the exchange rate affects both buyers and sellers—that is, it affects both demand and supply for a currency.

The shifts in demand and supply curves both cause the exchange rate to shift in the same direction; in this example, they both make the peso exchange rate stronger. However, the shifts in demand and supply work in opposing directions on the quantity traded. In this example, the rising demand for pesos is causing the quantity to rise while the falling supply of pesos is causing quantity to fall. In this specific example, the result is a higher quantity. But in other cases, the result could be that quantity remains unchanged or declines.

This example also helps to explain why exchange rates often move quite substantially in a short period of a few weeks or months. When investors expect a country's currency to strengthen in the future, they buy the currency and cause it to appreciate immediately. The appreciation of the currency can lead other investors to believe that future appreciation is likely—and thus lead to even further appreciation. Similarly, a fear that a currency *might* weaken quickly leads to an *actual* weakening of the currency, which often reinforces the belief that the currency is going to weaken further.

Thus, beliefs about the future path of exchange rates can be self-reinforcing, at least for a time, and a large share of the trading in foreign exchange markets involves dealers trying to outguess each other on what direction exchange rates will move next.

Differences across Countries in Rates of Return

The motivation for investment, whether domestic or foreign, is to earn a return. If rates of return in a country look relatively high, then that country will tend to attract funds from abroad. Conversely, if rates of return in a country look relatively low, then funds will tend to flee to other economies. Changes in the expected rate of return will shift demand and supply for a currency. For example, imagine that interest rates rise in the United States as compared with Mexico. Thus, financial investments in the United States promise a higher return than they previously did. As a result, more investors will demand U.S. dollars so that they can buy interest-bearing assets and fewer investors will be willing to supply U.S. dollars to foreign exchange markets. Demand for the U.S. dollar will shift to the right, from D_0 to D_1, and supply will shift to the left, from S_0 to S_1, as shown in **Figure 15.7**. The new equilibrium (E_1), will occur at an exchange rate of nine pesos/dollar and the same quantity of $8.5 billion. Thus, a higher interest rate or rate of return relative to other countries leads a nation's currency to appreciate or strengthen, and a lower interest rate relative to other countries leads a nation's currency to depreciate or weaken. Since a nation's central bank can use monetary policy to affect its interest rates, a central bank can also cause changes in exchange rates—a connection that will be discussed in more detail later in this chapter.

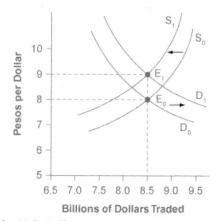

Figure 15.7 Exchange Rate Market for U.S. Dollars Reacts to Higher Interest Rates   A higher rate of return for U.S. dollars makes holding dollars more attractive. Thus, the demand for dollars in the foreign exchange market shifts to the right, from D_0 to D_1, while the supply of dollars shifts to the left, from S_0 to S_1. The new equilibrium (E_1) has a stronger exchange rate than the original equilibrium (E_0), but in this example, the equilibrium quantity traded does not change.

Relative Inflation

If a country experiences a relatively high inflation rate compared with other economies, then the buying power of its currency is eroding, which will tend to discourage anyone from wanting to acquire or to hold the currency. **Figure 15.8** shows an example based on an actual episode concerning the Mexican peso. In 1986–87, Mexico experienced an inflation rate of over 200%. Not surprisingly, as inflation dramatically decreased the purchasing power of the peso in Mexico, the exchange rate value of the peso declined as well. As shown in **Figure 15.8**, demand for the peso on foreign exchange markets decreased from D_0 to D_1, while supply of the peso increased from S_0 to S_1. The equilibrium exchange rate fell from $2.50 per peso at the original equilibrium (E_0) to $0.50 per peso at the new equilibrium (E_1). In this example, the quantity of pesos traded on foreign exchange markets remained the same, even as the exchange rate shifted.

Figure 15.8 Exchange Rate Markets React to Higher Inflation If a currency is experiencing relatively high inflation, then its buying power is decreasing and international investors will be less eager to hold it. Thus, a rise in inflation in the Mexican peso would lead demand to shift from D_0 to D_1, and supply to increase from S_0 to S_1. Both movements in demand and supply would cause the currency to depreciate. The effect on the quantity traded is drawn here as a decrease, but in truth it could be an increase or no change, depending on the actual movements of demand and supply.

Link It Up

Visit this website (http://openstaxcollege.org/l/bigmac) to learn about the Big Mac index.

Purchasing Power Parity

Over the long term, exchange rates must bear some relationship to the buying power of the currency in terms of goods that are internationally traded. If at a certain exchange rate it was much cheaper to buy internationally traded goods—such as oil, steel, computers, and cars—in one country than in another country, businesses would start buying in the cheap country, selling in other countries, and pocketing the profits.

For example, if a U.S. dollar is worth $1.60 in Canadian currency, then a car that sells for $20,000 in the United States should sell for $32,000 in Canada. If the price of cars in Canada was much lower than $32,000, then at least some U.S. car-buyers would convert their U.S. dollars to Canadian dollars and buy their cars in Canada. If the price of cars was much higher than $32,000 in this example, then at least some Canadian buyers would convert their Canadian dollars to U.S. dollars and go to the United States to purchase their cars. This is known as **arbitrage**, the process of buying and selling goods or currencies across international borders at a profit. It may occur slowly, but over time, it will force prices and exchange rates to align so that the price of internationally traded goods is similar in all countries.

The exchange rate that equalizes the prices of internationally traded goods across countries is called the **purchasing power parity (PPP)** exchange rate. A group of economists at the International Comparison Program, run by the

World Bank, have calculated the PPP exchange rate for all countries, based on detailed studies of the prices and quantities of internationally tradable goods.

The purchasing power parity exchange rate has two functions. First, PPP exchange rates are often used for international comparison of GDP and other economic statistics. Imagine that you are preparing a table showing the size of GDP in many countries in several recent years, and for ease of comparison, you are converting all the values into U.S. dollars. When you insert the value for Japan, you need to use a yen/dollar exchange rate. But should you use the market exchange rate or the PPP exchange rate? Market exchange rates bounce around. In summer 2008, the exchange rate was 108 yen/dollar, but in late 2009 the U.S. dollar exchange rate versus the yen was 90 yen/dollar. For simplicity, say that Japan's GDP was ¥500 trillion in both 2008 and 2009. If you use the market exchange rates, then Japan's GDP will be $4.6 trillion in 2008 (that is, ¥500 trillion /(¥108/dollar)) and $5.5 trillion in 2009 (that is, ¥500 trillion /(¥90/dollar)).

Of course, it is not true that Japan's economy increased enormously in 2009—in fact, Japan had a recession like much of the rest of the world. The misleading appearance of a booming Japanese economy occurs only because we used the market exchange rate, which often has short-run rises and falls. However, PPP exchange rates stay fairly constant and change only modestly, if at all, from year to year.

The second function of PPP is that exchanges rates will often get closer and closer to it as time passes. It is true that in the short run and medium run, as exchange rates adjust to relative inflation rates, rates of return, and to expectations about how interest rates and inflation will shift, the exchange rates will often move away from the PPP exchange rate for a time. But, knowing the PPP will allow you to track and predict exchange rate relationships.

15.3 | Macroeconomic Effects of Exchange Rates

By the end of this section you will be able to:
- Explain how exchange rate shifting influences aggregate demand and supply
- Explain how loans and banks can also be influenced by shifting exchange rates

A central bank will be concerned about the exchange rate for multiple reasons: (1) Movements in the exchange rate will affect the quantity of aggregate demand in an economy; (2) frequent substantial fluctuations in the exchange rate can disrupt international trade and cause problems in a nation's banking system–this may contribute to an unsustainable balance of trade and large inflows of international financial capital, which can set the economy up for a deep recession if international investors decide to move their money to another country. Let's discuss these scenarios in turn.

Exchange Rates, Aggregate Demand, and Aggregate Supply

Foreign trade in goods and services typically involves incurring the costs of production in one currency while receiving revenues from sales in another currency. As a result, movements in exchange rates can have a powerful effect on incentives to export and import, and thus on aggregate demand in the economy as a whole.

For example, in 1999, when the euro first became a currency, its value measured in U.S. currency was $1.06/euro. By the end of 2013, the euro had risen (and the U.S. dollar had correspondingly weakened) to $1.37/euro. Consider the situation of a French firm that each year incurs €10 million in costs, and sells its products in the United States for $10 million. In 1999, when this firm converted $10 million back to euros at the exchange rate of $1.06/euro (that is, $10 million × [€1/$1.06]), it received €9.4 million, and suffered a loss. In 2013, when this same firm converted $10 million back to euros at the exchange rate of $1.37/euro (that is, $10 million × [€1 euro/$1.37]), it received approximately €7.3 million and an even larger loss. This example shows how a stronger euro discourages exports by the French firm, because it makes the costs of production in the domestic currency higher relative to the sales revenues earned in another country. From the point of view of the U.S. economy, the example also shows how a weaker U.S. dollar encourages exports.

Since an increase in exports results in more dollars flowing into the economy, and an increase in imports means more dollars are flowing out, it is easy to conclude that exports are "good" for the economy and imports are "bad," but this overlooks the role of exchange rates. If an American consumer buys a Japanese car for $20,000 instead of an American car for $30,000, it may be tempting to argue that the American economy has lost out. However, the Japanese company will have to convert those dollars to yen to pay its workers and operate its factories. Whoever buys those dollars will have to use them to purchase American goods and services, so the money comes right back into the American economy. At the same time, the consumer saves money by buying a less expensive import, and can use the extra money for other purposes.

Fluctuations in Exchange Rates

Exchange rates can fluctuate a great deal in the short run. As yet one more example, the Indian rupee moved from 39 rupees/dollar in February 2008 to 51 rupees/dollar in March 2009, a decline of more than one-fourth in the value of the rupee on foreign exchange markets. Figure 15.9 earlier showed that even two economically developed neighboring economies like the United States and Canada can see significant movements in exchange rates over a few years. For firms that depend on export sales, or firms that rely on imported inputs to production, or even purely domestic firms that compete with firms tied into international trade—which in many countries adds up to half or more of a nation's GDP—sharp movements in exchange rates can lead to dramatic changes in profits and losses. So, a central bank may desire to keep exchange rates from moving too much as part of providing a stable business climate, where firms can focus on productivity and innovation, not on reacting to exchange rate fluctuations.

One of the most economically destructive effects of exchange rate fluctuations can happen through the banking system. Most international loans are measured in a few large currencies, like U.S. dollars, European euros, and Japanese yen. In countries that do not use these currencies, banks often borrow funds in the currencies of other countries, like U.S. dollars, but then lend in their own domestic currency. The left-hand chain of events in Figure 15.9 shows how this pattern of international borrowing can work. A bank in Thailand borrows one million in U.S. dollars. Then the bank converts the dollars to its domestic currency—in the case of Thailand, the currency is the baht—at a rate of 40 baht/dollar. The bank then lends the baht to a firm in Thailand. The business repays the loan in baht, and the bank converts it back to U.S. dollars to pay off its original U.S. dollar loan.

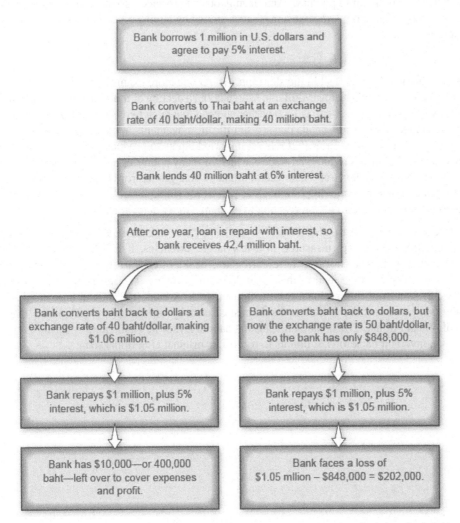

Figure 15.9 International Borrowing The scenario of international borrowing that ends on the left is a success story, but the scenario that ends on the right shows what happens when the exchange rate weakens.

This process of borrowing in a foreign currency and lending in a domestic currency can work just fine, as long as the exchange rate does not shift. In the scenario outlined, if the dollar strengthens and the baht weakens, a problem arises. The right-hand chain of events in **Figure 15.9** illustrates what happens when the baht unexpectedly weakens from 40 baht/dollar to 50 baht/dollar. The Thai firm still repays the loan in full to the bank. But because of the shift in the exchange rate, the bank cannot repay its loan in U.S. dollars. (Of course, if the exchange rate had changed in the other direction, making the Thai currency stronger, the bank could have realized an unexpectedly large profit.)

In 1997–1998, countries across eastern Asia, like Thailand, Korea, Malaysia, and Indonesia, experienced a sharp depreciation of their currencies, in some cases 50% or more. These countries had been experiencing substantial inflows of foreign investment capital, with bank lending increasing by 20% to 30% per year through the mid-1990s. When their exchange rates depreciated, the banking systems in these countries were bankrupt. Argentina experienced a similar chain of events in 2002. When the Argentine peso depreciated, Argentina's banks found themselves unable to pay back what they had borrowed in U.S. dollars.

Banks play a vital role in any economy in facilitating transactions and in making loans to firms and consumers. When most of a country's largest banks become bankrupt simultaneously, a sharp decline in aggregate demand and a deep recession results. Since the main responsibilities of a central bank are to control the money supply and to ensure that the banking system is stable, a central bank must be concerned about whether large and unexpected exchange rate depreciation will drive most of the country's existing banks into bankruptcy. For more on this concern, return to the chapter on **The International Trade and Capital Flows**.

Summing Up Public Policy and Exchange Rates

Every nation would prefer a stable exchange rate to facilitate international trade and reduce the degree of risk and uncertainty in the economy. However, a nation may sometimes want a weaker exchange rate to stimulate aggregate demand and reduce a recession, or a stronger exchange rate to fight inflation. The country must also be concerned that rapid movements from a weak to a strong exchange rate may cripple its export industries, while rapid movements from a strong to a weak exchange rate can cripple its banking sector. In short, every choice of an exchange rate—whether it should be stronger or weaker, or fixed or changing—represents potential tradeoffs.

15.4 | Exchange Rate Policies

By the end of this section, you will be able to:
- Differentiate among a floating exchange rate, a soft peg, a hard peg, and a merged currency
- Identify the tradeoffs that come with a floating exchange rate, a soft peg, a hard peg, and a merged currency

Exchange rate policies come in a range of different forms listed in Figure 15.10: let the foreign exchange market determine the exchange rate; let the market set the value of the exchange rate most of the time, but have the central bank sometimes intervene to prevent fluctuations that seem too large; have the central bank guarantee a specific exchange rate; or share a currency with other countries. Let's discuss each type of exchange rate policy and its tradeoffs.

Figure 15.10 A Spectrum of Exchange Rate Policies A nation may adopt one of a variety of exchange rate regimes, from floating rates in which the foreign exchange market determines the rates to pegged rates where governments intervene to manage the value of the exchange rate, to a common currency where the nation adopts the currency of another country or group of countries.

Floating Exchange Rates

A policy which allows the foreign exchange market to set exchange rates is referred to as a **floating exchange rate**. The U.S. dollar is a floating exchange rate, as are the currencies of about 40% of the countries in the world economy. The major concern with this policy is that exchange rates can move a great deal in a short time.

Consider the U.S. exchange rate expressed in terms of another fairly stable currency, the Japanese yen, as shown in Figure 15.11. On January 1, 2002, the exchange rate was 133 yen/dollar. On January 1, 2005, it was 103 yen/dollar. On June 1, 2007, it was 122 yen/dollar, on January 1, 2012, it was 77 yen per dollar, and on March 1, 2015, it was 120 yen per dollar. As investor sentiment swings back and forth, driving exchange rates up and down, exporters, importers, and banks involved in international lending are all affected. At worst, large movements in exchange rates can drive companies into bankruptcy or trigger a nationwide banking collapse. But even in the moderate case of the yen/dollar exchange rate, these movements of roughly 30 percent back and forth impose stress on both economies as firms must alter their export and import plans to take the new exchange rates into account. Especially in smaller countries where international trade is a relatively large share of GDP, exchange rate movements can rattle their economies.

Figure 15.11 U.S. Dollar Exchange Rate in Japanese Yen Even seemingly stable exchange rates such as the Japanese Yen to the U.S. Dollar can vary when closely looked at over time. This figure shows a relatively stable rate between 2011 and 2013. In 2013, there was a drastic depreciation of the Yen (relative to the U.S. Dollar) by about 14% and again at the end of the year in 2014 also by about 14%. (Source: Federal Reserve Economic Data (FRED) https://research.stlouisfed.org/fred2/series/DEXJPUS)

However, movements of floating exchange rates have advantages, too. After all, prices of goods and services rise and fall throughout a market economy, as demand and supply shift. If an economy experiences strong inflows or outflows of international financial capital, or has relatively high inflation, or if it experiences strong productivity growth so that purchasing power changes relative to other economies, then it makes economic sense for the exchange rate to shift as well.

Floating exchange rate advocates often argue that if government policies were more predictable and stable, then inflation rates and interest rates would be more predictable and stable. Exchange rates would bounce around less, too. The economist Milton Friedman (1912–2006), for example, wrote a defense of floating exchange rates in 1962 in his book *Capitalism and Freedom*:

> Being in favor of floating exchange rates does not mean being in favor of unstable exchange rates. When we support a free price system [for goods and services] at home, this does not imply that we favor a system in which prices fluctuate wildly up and down. What we want is a system in which prices are free to fluctuate but in which the forces determining them are sufficiently stable so that in fact prices move within moderate ranges. This is equally true in a system of floating exchange rates. The ultimate objective is a world in which exchange rates, while free to vary, are, in fact, highly stable because basic economic policies and conditions are stable.

Advocates of floating exchange rates admit that, yes, exchange rates may sometimes fluctuate. They point out, however, that if a central bank focuses on preventing either high inflation or deep recession, with low and reasonably steady interest rates, then exchange rates will have less reason to vary.

Using Soft Pegs and Hard Pegs

When a government intervenes in the foreign exchange market so that the exchange rate of its currency is different from what the market would have produced, it is said to have established a "peg" for its currency. A **soft peg** is the name for an exchange rate policy where the government usually allows the exchange rate to be set by the market, but in some cases, especially if the exchange rate seems to be moving rapidly in one direction, the central bank will intervene in the market. With a **hard peg** exchange rate policy, the central bank sets a fixed and unchanging value for the exchange rate. A central bank can implement soft peg and hard peg policies.

Suppose the market exchange rate for the Brazilian currency, the real, would be 35 cents/real with a daily quantity of 15 billion real traded in the market, as shown at the equilibrium E_0 in **Figure 15.12** (a) and **Figure 15.12** (b). However, the government of Brazil decides that the exchange rate should be 30 cents/real, as shown in **Figure 15.12** (a). Perhaps Brazil sets this lower exchange rate to benefit its export industries. Perhaps it is an attempt to stimulate aggregate demand by stimulating exports. Perhaps Brazil believes that the current market exchange rate is higher than the long-term purchasing power parity value of the real, so it is minimizing fluctuations in the real by keeping it at this lower rate. Perhaps the target exchange rate was set sometime in the past, and is now being maintained for the sake of stability. Whatever the reason, if Brazil's central bank wishes to keep the exchange rate below the market level, it must face the reality that at this weaker exchange rate of 30 cents/real, the quantity demanded of its currency at 17 billion reals is greater than the quantity supplied of 13 billion reals in the foreign exchange market.

Figure 15.12 Pegging an Exchange Rate (a) If an exchange rate is pegged below what would otherwise be the equilibrium, then the quantity demanded of the currency will exceed the quantity supplied. (b) If an exchange rate is pegged above what would otherwise be the equilibrium, then the quantity supplied of the currency exceeds the quantity demanded.

The Brazilian central bank could weaken its exchange rate in two ways. One approach is to use an expansionary monetary policy that leads to lower interest rates. In foreign exchange markets, the lower interest rates will reduce demand and increase supply of the real and lead to depreciation. This technique is not often used because lowering interest rates to weaken the currency may be in conflict with the country's monetary policy goals. Alternatively, Brazil's central bank could trade directly in the foreign exchange market. The central bank can expand the money supply by creating reals, use the reals to purchase foreign currencies, and avoid selling any of its own currency. In this way, it can fill the gap between quantity demanded and quantity supplied of its currency.

Figure 15.12 (b) shows the opposite situation. Here, the Brazilian government desires a stronger exchange rate of 40 cents/real than the market rate of 35 cents/real. Perhaps Brazil desires the stronger currency to reduce aggregate demand and to fight inflation, or perhaps Brazil believes that that current market exchange rate is temporarily lower than the long-term rate. Whatever the reason, at the higher desired exchange rate, the quantity supplied of 16 billion reals exceeds the quantity demanded of 14 billion reals.

Brazil's central bank can use a contractionary monetary policy to raise interest rates, which will increase demand and reduce supply of the currency on foreign exchange markets, and lead to an appreciation. Alternatively, Brazil's central bank can trade directly in the foreign exchange market. In this case, with an excess supply of its own currency in foreign exchange markets, the central bank must use reserves of foreign currency, like U.S. dollars, to demand its own currency and thus cause an appreciation of its exchange rate.

Both a soft peg and a hard peg policy require that the central bank intervene in the foreign exchange market. However, a hard peg policy attempts to preserve a fixed exchange rate at all times. A soft peg policy typically allows the exchange rate to move up and down by relatively small amounts in the short run of several months or a year, and to move by larger amounts over time, but seeks to avoid extreme short-term fluctuations.

Tradeoffs of Soft Pegs and Hard Pegs

When a country decides to alter the market exchange rate, it faces a number of tradeoffs. If it uses monetary policy to alter the exchange rate, it then cannot at the same time use monetary policy to address issues of inflation or recession. If it uses direct purchases and sales of foreign currencies in exchange rates, then it must face the issue of how it will handle its reserves of foreign currency. Finally, a pegged exchange rate can even create additional movements of the exchange rate; for example, even the possibility of government intervention in exchange rate markets will lead to rumors about whether and when the government will intervene, and dealers in the foreign exchange market will react to those rumors. Let's consider these issues in turn.

One concern with pegged exchange rate policies is that they imply a country's monetary policy is no longer focused on controlling inflation or shortening recessions, but now must also take the exchange rate into account. For example, when a country pegs its exchange rate, it will sometimes face economic situations where it would like to have an expansionary monetary policy to fight recession—but it cannot do so because that policy would depreciate its exchange rate and break its hard peg. With a soft peg exchange rate policy, the central bank can sometimes ignore the exchange rate and focus on domestic inflation or recession—but in other cases the central bank may ignore inflation or recession and instead focus on its soft peg exchange rate. With a hard peg policy, domestic monetary policy is effectively no longer determined by domestic inflation or unemployment, but only by what monetary policy is needed to keep the exchange rate at the hard peg.

Another issue arises when a central bank intervenes directly in the exchange rate market. If a central bank ends up in a situation where it is perpetually creating and selling its own currency on foreign exchange markets, it will be buying the currency of other countries, like U.S. dollars or euros, to hold as reserves. Holding large reserves of other currencies has an opportunity cost, and central banks will not wish to boost such reserves without limit.

In addition, a central bank that causes a large increase in the supply of money is also risking an inflationary surge in aggregate demand. Conversely, when a central bank wishes to buy its own currency, it can do so by using its reserves of international currency like the U.S. dollar or the euro. But if the central bank runs out of such reserves, it can no longer use this method to strengthen its currency. Thus, buying foreign currencies in exchange rate markets can be expensive and inflationary, while selling foreign currencies can work only until a central bank runs out of reserves.

Yet another issue is that when a government pegs its exchange rate, it may unintentionally create another reason for additional fluctuation. With a soft peg policy, foreign exchange dealers and international investors react to every rumor about how or when the central bank is likely to intervene to influence the exchange rate, and as they react to rumors the exchange rate will shift up and down. Thus, even though the goal of a soft peg policy is to reduce short-term fluctuations of the exchange rate, the existence of the policy—when anticipated in the foreign exchange market—may sometimes increase short-term fluctuations as international investors try to anticipate how and when the central bank will act. The following Clear It Up feature discusses the effects of **international capital flows**—capital that flows across national boundaries as either portfolio investment or direct investment.

How do Tobin taxes control the flow of capital?

Some countries like Chile and Malaysia have sought to reduce movements in exchange rates by limiting inflows and outflows of international financial capital. This policy can be enacted either through targeted taxes or by regulations.

Taxes on international capital flows are sometimes known as **Tobin taxes**, named after James Tobin, the 1981 Nobel laureate in economics who proposed such a tax in a 1972 lecture. For example, a government might tax all foreign exchange transactions, or attempt to tax short-term portfolio investment while exempting long-term foreign direct investment. Countries can also use regulation to forbid certain kinds of foreign investment in the first place or to make it difficult for international financial investors to withdraw their funds from a country.

The goal of such policies is to reduce international capital flows, especially short-term portfolio flows, in the hope that doing so will reduce the chance of large movements in exchange rates that can bring macroeconomic disaster.

But proposals to limit international financial flows have severe practical difficulties. Taxes are imposed by national governments, not international ones. If one government imposes a Tobin tax on exchange rate transactions carried out within its territory, the exchange rate market might easily be operated by a firm based someplace like the Grand Caymans, an island nation in the Caribbean well-known for allowing some financial wheeling and dealing. In an interconnected global economy, if goods and services are allowed to flow across national borders, then payments need to flow across borders, too. It is very difficult—in fact close to impossible—for a nation to allow only the flows of payments that relate to goods and services, while clamping down or taxing other flows of financial capital. If a nation participates in international trade, it must also participate in international capital movements.

Finally, countries all over the world, especially low-income countries, are crying out for foreign investment to help develop their economies. Policies that discourage international financial investment may prevent some possible harm, but they rule out potentially substantial economic benefits as well.

A hard peg exchange rate policy will not allow short-term fluctuations in the exchange rate. If the government first announces a hard peg and then later changes its mind—perhaps the government becomes unwilling to keep interest rates high or to hold high levels of foreign exchange reserves—then the result of abandoning a hard peg could be a dramatic shift in the exchange rate.

In the mid-2000s, about one-third of the countries in the world used a soft peg approach and about one-quarter used a hard peg approach. The general trend in the 1990s was to shift away from a soft peg approach in favor of either floating rates or a hard peg. The concern is that a successful soft peg policy may, for a time, lead to very little variation in exchange rates, so that firms and banks in the economy begin to act as if a hard peg exists. When the exchange rate does move, the effects are especially painful because firms and banks have not planned and hedged against a possible change. Thus, the argument went, it is better either to be clear that the exchange rate is always flexible, or that it is fixed, but choosing an in-between soft peg option may end up being worst of all.

A Merged Currency

A final approach to exchange rate policy is for a nation to choose a common currency shared with one or more nations is also called a **merged currency**. A merged currency approach eliminates foreign exchange risk altogether. Just as no one worries about exchange rate movements when buying and selling between New York and California, Europeans know that the value of the euro will be the same in Germany and France and other European nations that have adopted the euro.

However, a merged currency also poses problems. Like a hard peg, a merged currency means that a nation has given up altogether on domestic monetary policy, and instead has put its interest rate policies in other hands. When Ecuador uses the U.S. dollar as its currency, it has no voice in whether the Federal Reserve raises or lowers interest rates. The European Central Bank that determines monetary policy for the euro has representatives from all the euro nations. However, from the standpoint of, say, Portugal, there will be times when the decisions of the European Central Bank about monetary policy do not match the decisions that would have been made by a Portuguese central bank.

The lines between these four different exchange rate policies can blend into each other. For example, a soft peg exchange rate policy in which the government almost never acts to intervene in the exchange rate market will look a great deal like a floating exchange rate. Conversely, a soft peg policy in which the government intervenes often to keep the exchange rate near a specific level will look a lot like a hard peg. A decision to merge currencies with another country is, in effect, a decision to have a permanently fixed exchange rate with those countries, which is like a very hard exchange rate peg. The range of exchange rates policy choices, with their advantages and disadvantages, are summarized in Table 15.3.

Situation	Floating Exchange Rates	Soft Peg	Hard Peg	Merged Currency
Large short-run fluctuations in exchange rates?	Often a lot in the short term	Maybe less in the short run, but still large changes over time	None, unless a change in the fixed rate	None

Table 15.3 Tradeoffs of Exchange Rate Policies

Situation	Floating Exchange Rates	Soft Peg	Hard Peg	Merged Currency
Large long-term fluctuations in exchange rates?	Can often happen	Can often happen	Cannot happen unless hard peg changes, in which case substantial volatility can occur	Cannot happen
Power of central bank to conduct countercyclical monetary policy?	Flexible exchange rates make monetary policy stronger	Some power, although conflicts may arise between exchange rate policy and countercyclical policy	Very little; central bank must keep exchange rate fixed	None; nation does not have its own currency
Costs of holding foreign exchange reserves?	Do not need to hold reserves	Hold moderate reserves that rise and fall over time	Hold large reserves	No need to hold reserves
Risk of being stuck with an exchange rate that causes a large trade imbalance and very high inflows or outflows of financial capital?	Adjusts often	Adjusts over the medium term, if not the short term	May become stuck over time either far above or below the market level	Cannot adjust

Table 15.3 Tradeoffs of Exchange Rate Policies

Global macroeconomics would be easier if the whole world had one currency and one central bank. The exchange rates between different currencies complicate the picture. If exchange rates are set solely by financial markets, they fluctuate substantially as short-term portfolio investors try to anticipate tomorrow's news. If the government attempts to intervene in exchange rate markets through soft pegs or hard pegs, it gives up at least some of the power to use monetary policy to focus on domestic inflations and recessions, and it risks causing even greater fluctuations in foreign exchange markets.

There is no consensus among economists about which exchange rate policies are best: floating, soft peg, hard peg, or merged currencies. The choice depends both on how well a nation's central bank can implement a specific exchange rate policy and on how well a nation's firms and banks can adapt to different exchange rate policies. A national economy that does a fairly good job at achieving the four main economic goals of growth, low inflation, low unemployment, and a sustainable balance of trade will probably do just fine most of the time with any exchange rate policy; conversely, no exchange rate policy is likely to save an economy that consistently fails at achieving these goals. On the other hand, a merged currency applied across wide geographic and cultural areas carries with it its own set of problems, such as the ability for countries to conduct their own independent monetary policies.

Bring it Home

Is a Stronger Dollar Good for the U.S. Economy?

The foreign exchange value of the dollar is a price and whether a higher price is good or bad depends on where you are standing: sellers benefit from higher prices and buyers are harmed. A stronger dollar is good for U.S. imports (and people working for U.S. importers) and U.S. investment abroad. It is also good for U.S. tourists going to other countries, since their dollar goes further. But a stronger dollar is bad for U.S. exports (and people working in U.S. export industries); it is bad for foreign investment in the United States (leading, for example, to higher U.S. interest rates); and it is bad for foreign tourists (as well as U.S hotels, restaurants, and others in the tourist industry). In short, whether the U.S. dollar is good or bad is a more complex question than you may have thought. The economic answer is "it depends."

KEY TERMS

appreciating when a currency is worth more in terms of other currencies; also called "strengthening"

arbitrage the process of buying a good and selling goods across borders to take advantage of international price differences

depreciating when a currency is worth less in terms of other currencies; also called "weakening"

dollarize a country that is not the United States uses the U.S. dollar as its currency

floating exchange rate a country lets the value of its currency be determined in the exchange rate market

foreign direct investment (FDI) purchasing more than ten percent of a firm or starting a new enterprise in another country

foreign exchange market the market in which people use one currency to buy another currency

hard peg an exchange rate policy in which the central bank sets a fixed and unchanging value for the exchange rate

hedge using a financial transaction as protection against risk

international capital flows flow of financial capital across national boundaries either as portfolio investment or direct investment

merged currency when a nation chooses to use the currency of another nation

portfolio investment an investment in another country that is purely financial and does not involve any management responsibility

purchasing power parity (PPP) the exchange rate that equalizes the prices of internationally traded goods across countries

soft peg an exchange rate policy in which the government usually allows the exchange rate to be set by the market, but in some cases, especially if the exchange rate seems to be moving rapidly in one direction, the central bank will intervene

Tobin taxes see international capital flows

KEY CONCEPTS AND SUMMARY

15.1 How the Foreign Exchange Market Works

In the foreign exchange market, people and firms exchange one currency to purchase another currency. The demand for dollars comes from those U.S. export firms seeking to convert their earnings in foreign currency back into U.S. dollars; foreign tourists converting their earnings in a foreign currency back into U.S. dollars; and foreign investors seeking to make financial investments in the U.S. economy. On the supply side of the foreign exchange market for the trading of U.S. dollars are foreign firms that have sold imports in the U.S. economy and are seeking to convert their earnings back to their home currency; U.S. tourists abroad; and U.S. investors seeking to make financial investments in foreign economies. When currency A can buy more of currency B, then currency A has strengthened or appreciated relative to B. When currency A can buy less of currency B, then currency A has weakened or depreciated relative to B. If currency A strengthens or appreciates relative to currency B, then currency B must necessarily weaken or depreciate with regard to currency A. A stronger currency benefits those who are buying with that currency and injures those who are selling. A weaker currency injures those, like importers, who are buying with that currency and benefits those who are selling with it, like exporters.

15.2 Demand and Supply Shifts in Foreign Exchange Markets

In the extreme short run, ranging from a few minutes to a few weeks, exchange rates are influenced by speculators who are trying to invest in currencies that will grow stronger, and to sell currencies that will grow weaker. Such speculation can create a self-fulfilling prophecy, at least for a time, where an expected appreciation leads to a stronger currency and vice versa. In the relatively short run, exchange rate markets are influenced by differences in rates of return. Countries with relatively high real rates of return (for example, high interest rates) will tend to experience stronger currencies as they attract money from abroad, while countries with relatively low rates of return will tend to experience weaker exchange rates as investors convert to other currencies.

In the medium run of a few months or a few years, exchange rate markets are influenced by inflation rates. Countries with relatively high inflation will tend to experience less demand for their currency than countries with lower inflation, and thus currency depreciation. Over long periods of many years, exchange rates tend to adjust toward the purchasing power parity (PPP) rate, which is the exchange rate such that the prices of internationally tradable goods in different countries, when converted at the PPP exchange rate to a common currency, are similar in all economies.

15.3 Macroeconomic Effects of Exchange Rates

A central bank will be concerned about the exchange rate for several reasons. Exchange rates will affect imports and exports, and thus affect aggregate demand in the economy. Fluctuations in exchange rates may cause difficulties for many firms, but especially banks. The exchange rate may accompany unsustainable flows of international financial capital.

15.4 Exchange Rate Policies

In a floating exchange rate policy, a country's exchange rate is determined in the foreign exchange market. In a soft peg exchange rate policy, a country's exchange rate is usually determined in the foreign exchange market, but the government sometimes intervenes to strengthen or weaken the exchange rate. In a hard peg exchange rate policy, the government chooses an exchange rate. A central bank can intervene in exchange markets in two ways. It can raise or lower interest rates to make the currency stronger or weaker. Or it can directly purchase or sell its currency in foreign exchange markets. All exchange rates policies face tradeoffs. A hard peg exchange rate policy will reduce exchange rate fluctuations, but means that a country must focus its monetary policy on the exchange rate, not on fighting recession or controlling inflation. When a nation merges its currency with another nation, it gives up on nationally oriented monetary policy altogether.

A soft peg exchange rate may create additional volatility as exchange rate markets try to anticipate when and how the government will intervene. A flexible exchange rate policy allows monetary policy to focus on inflation and unemployment, and allows the exchange rate to change with inflation and rates of return, but also raises a risk that exchange rates may sometimes make large and abrupt movements. The spectrum of exchange rate policies includes: (a) a floating exchange rate, (b) a pegged exchange rate, soft or hard, and (c) a merged currency. Monetary policy can focus on a variety of goals: (a) inflation; (b) inflation or unemployment, depending on which is the most dangerous obstacle; and (c) a long-term rule based policy designed to keep the money supply stable and predictable.

SELF-CHECK QUESTIONS

1. How will a stronger euro affect the following economic agents?
   a. A British exporter to Germany.
   b. A Dutch tourist visiting Chile.
   c. A Greek bank investing in a Canadian government bond.
   d. A French exporter to Germany.

2. Suppose that political unrest in Egypt leads financial markets to anticipate a depreciation in the Egyptian pound. How will that affect the demand for pounds, supply of pounds, and exchange rate for pounds compared to, say, U.S. dollars?

3. Suppose U.S. interest rates decline compared to the rest of the world. What would be the likely impact on the demand for dollars, supply of dollars, and exchange rate for dollars compared to, say, euros?

4. Suppose Argentina gets inflation under control and the Argentine inflation rate decreases substantially. What would likely happen to the demand for Argentine pesos, the supply of Argentine pesos, and the peso/U.S. dollar exchange rate?

5. This chapter has explained that "one of the most economically destructive effects of exchange rate fluctuations can happen through the banking system," if banks borrow from abroad to lend domestically. Why is this less likely to be a problem for the U.S. banking system?

6. A booming economy can attract financial capital inflows, which promote further growth. But capital can just as easily flow out of the country, leading to economic recession. Is a country whose economy is booming because it decided to stimulate consumer spending more or less likely to experience capital flight than an economy whose boom is caused by economic investment expenditure?

7. How would a contractionary monetary policy affect the exchange rate, net exports, aggregate demand, and aggregate supply?

8. A central bank can allow its currency to fall indefinitely, but it cannot allow its currency to rise indefinitely. Why not?

9. Is a country for which imports and exports make up a large fraction of the GDP more likely to adopt a flexible exchange rate or a fixed (hard peg) exchange rate?

REVIEW QUESTIONS

10. What is the foreign exchange market?

11. Describe some buyers and some sellers in the market for U.S. dollars.

12. What is the difference between foreign direct investment and portfolio investment?

13. What does it mean to hedge a financial transaction?

14. What does it mean to say that a currency appreciates? Depreciates? Becomes stronger? Becomes weaker?

15. Does an expectation of a stronger exchange rate in the future affect the exchange rate in the present? If so, how?

16. Does a higher rate of return in a nation's economy, all other things being equal, affect the exchange rate of its currency? If so, how?

17. Does a higher inflation rate in an economy, other things being equal, affect the exchange rate of its currency? If so, how?

18. What is the purchasing power parity exchange rate?

19. What are some of the reasons a central bank is likely to care, at least to some extent, about the exchange rate?

20. How can an unexpected fall in exchange rates injure the financial health of a nation's banks?

21. What is the difference between a floating exchange rate, a soft peg, a hard peg, and dollarization?

22. List some advantages and disadvantages of the different exchange rate policies.

CRITICAL THINKING QUESTIONS

23. Why would a nation "dollarize"—that is, adopt another country's currency instead of having its own?

24. Can you think of any major disadvantages to dollarization? How would a central bank work in a country that has dollarized?

25. If a country's currency is expected to appreciate in value, what would you think will be the impact of expected exchange rates on yields (e.g., the interest rate paid on government bonds) in that country? *Hint*: Think about how expected exchange rate changes and interest rates affect demand and supply for a currency.

26. Do you think that a country experiencing hyperinflation is more or less likely to have an exchange rate equal to its purchasing power parity value when compared to a country with a low inflation rate?

27. Suppose a country has an overall balance of trade so that exports of goods and services equal imports of goods and services. Does that imply that the country has balanced trade with *each* of its trading partners?

28. We learned that monetary policy is amplified by changes in exchange rates and the corresponding changes in the balance of trade. From the perspective of a nation's central bank, is this a good thing or a bad thing?

29. If a developing country needs foreign capital inflows, management expertise, and technology, how can it encourage foreign investors while at the same time protect itself against capital flight and banking system collapse, as happened during the Asian financial crisis?

30. Many developing countries, like Mexico, have moderate to high rates of inflation. At the same time, international trade plays an important role in their economies. What type of exchange rate regime would be best for such a country's currency *vis à vis* the U.S. dollar?

31. What would make a country decide to change from a common currency, like the euro, back to its own currency?

PROBLEMS

32. A British pound cost $1.56 in U.S. dollars in 1996, but $1.66 in U.S. dollars in 1998. Was the pound weaker or stronger against the dollar? Did the dollar appreciate or depreciate versus the pound?

33. In Exercise 15.32 calculate the cost of a U.S. dollar in terms of British pounds in 1996 and 1998.

16 | Government Budgets and Fiscal Policy

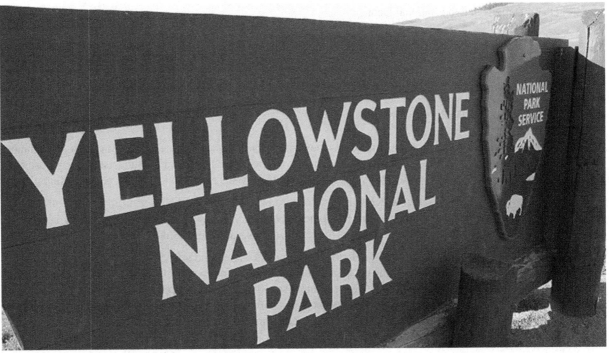

Figure 16.1 Shut Downs and Parks Yellowstone National Park is one of the many national parks forced to close down during the government shut down in October 2013. (Credit: modification of work by "daveynin"/flickr Creative Commons)

Bring it Home

No Yellowstone Park?

So you had trekked all the way to see Yellowstone National Park in the beautiful month of October 2013, only to find it… closed. Closed! Why?

For two weeks in October 2013, the U.S. federal government shut down. Many federal services, like the national parks, closed and 800,000 federal employees were furloughed. Tourists were shocked and so was the rest of the world: Congress and the President could not agree on a budget. Inside the Capitol, Republicans and Democrats argued about spending priorities and whether to increase the national debt limit. Each year's budget, which is over $3 trillion of spending, must be approved by Congress and signed by the President. Two thirds of the budget is entitlements and other mandatory spending which occur without congressional or presidential action once the programs are set up. Tied to the budget debate was the issue of increasing the debt ceiling—how high the national debt of the U.S. government can be. The House of Representatives refused to sign on to the bills to fund the government unless they included provisions to stop or change the Affordable Health Care Act (more colloquially known as Obamacare). As the days ticked by, the United States came very close to defaulting on its debt.

Why does the federal budget create such intense debates? What would happen if the United States actually defaulted on its debt? In this chapter, we will examine the federal budget, taxation, and fiscal policy. We will also look at the annual federal budget deficits and the national debt.

Introduction to Government Budgets and Fiscal Policy

In this chapter, you will learn about:

- Government Spending

- Taxation

- Federal Deficits and the National Debt

- Using Fiscal Policy to Fight Recessions, Unemployment, and Inflation

- Automatic Stabilizers

- Practical Problems with Discretionary Fiscal Policy

- The Question of a Balanced Budget

All levels of government—federal, state, and local—have budgets that show how much revenue the government expects to receive in taxes and other income and how the government plans to spend it. Budgets, however, can shift dramatically within a few years, as policy decisions and unexpected events shake up earlier tax and spending plans.

In this chapter, we revisit fiscal policy, which was first covered in **Welcome to Economics!** Fiscal policy is one of two policy tools for fine tuning the economy (the other is monetary policy). While monetary policy is made by policymakers at the Federal Reserve, fiscal policy is made by Congress and the President.

The discussion of fiscal policy focuses on how federal government taxing and spending affects aggregate demand. All government spending and taxes affect the economy, but fiscal policy focuses strictly on the policies of the federal government. We begin with an overview of U.S. government spending and taxes. We then discuss fiscal policy from a short-run perspective; that is, how government uses tax and spending policies to address recession, unemployment, and inflation; how periods of recession and growth affect government budgets; and the merits of balanced budget proposals.

16.1 | Government Spending

By the end of this section, you will be able to:
- Identify U.S. budget deficit and surplus trends over the past five decades
- Explain the differences between the U.S. federal budget, and state and local budgets

Government spending covers a range of services provided by the federal, state, and local governments. When the federal government spends more money than it receives in taxes in a given year, it runs a **budget deficit**. Conversely, when the government receives more money in taxes than it spends in a year, it runs a **budget surplus**. If government spending and taxes are equal, it is said to have a **balanced budget**. For example, in 2009, the U.S. government experienced its largest budget deficit ever, as the federal government spent $1.4 trillion more than it collected in taxes. This deficit was about 10% of the size of the U.S. GDP in 2009, making it by far the largest budget deficit relative to GDP since the mammoth borrowing used to finance World War II.

This section presents an overview of government spending in the United States.

Total U.S. Government Spending

Federal spending in nominal dollars (that is, dollars not adjusted for inflation) has grown by a multiple of more than 38 over the last four decades, from $93.4 billion in 1960 to $3.9 trillion in 2014. Comparing spending over time in nominal dollars is misleading because it does not take into account inflation or growth in population and the real economy. A more useful method of comparison is to examine government spending as a percent of GDP over time.

The top line in **Figure 16.2** shows the level of federal spending since 1960, expressed as a share of GDP. Despite a widespread sense among many Americans that the federal government has been growing steadily larger, the graph shows that federal spending has hovered in a range from 18% to 22% of GDP most of the time since 1960. The other lines in **Figure 16.2** show the major federal spending categories: national defense, Social Security, health programs, and interest payments. From the graph, we see that national defense spending as a share of GDP has generally declined since the 1960s, although there were some upward bumps in the 1980s buildup under President Ronald Reagan and in the aftermath of the terrorist attacks on September 11, 2001. In contrast, Social Security and healthcare have grown steadily as a percent of GDP. Healthcare expenditures include both payments for senior citizens (Medicare), and payments for low-income Americans (Medicaid). Medicaid is also partially funded by state governments. Interest payments are the final main category of government spending shown in the figure.

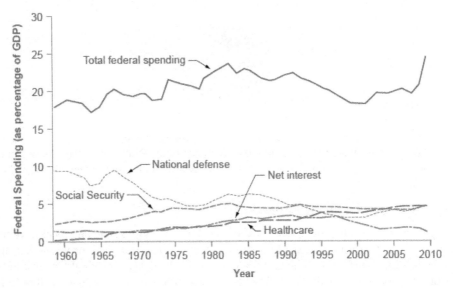

Figure 16.2 Federal Spending, 1960–2014 Since 1960, total federal spending has ranged from about 18% to 22% of GDP, although it climbed above that level in 2009, but quickly dropped back down to that level by 2013. The share spent on national defense has generally declined, while the share spent on Social Security and on healthcare expenses (mainly Medicare and Medicaid) has increased. (Source: *Economic Report of the President*, Tables B-2 and B-22, http://www.gpo.gov/fdsys/pkg/ERP-2014/content-detail.html)

Each year, the government borrows funds from U.S. citizens and foreigners to cover its budget deficits. It does this by selling securities (Treasury bonds, notes, and bills)—in essence borrowing from the public and promising to repay with interest in the future. From 1961 to 1997, the U.S. government has run budget deficits, and thus borrowed funds, in almost every year. It had budget surpluses from 1998 to 2001, and then returned to deficits.

The interest payments on past federal government borrowing were typically 1–2% of GDP in the 1960s and 1970s but then climbed above 3% of GDP in the 1980s and stayed there until the late 1990s. The government was able to repay some of its past borrowing by running surpluses from 1998 to 2001 and, with help from low interest rates, the interest payments on past federal government borrowing had fallen back to 1.4% of GDP by 2012.

We investigate the patterns of government borrowing and debt in more detail later in this chapter, but first we need to clarify the difference between the deficit and the debt. *The deficit is not the debt.* The difference between the deficit and the debt lies in the time frame. The government deficit (or surplus) refers to what happens with the federal government budget each year. The government debt is accumulated over time; it is the sum of all past deficits and surpluses. If you borrow $10,000 per year for each of the four years of college, you might say that your annual deficit was $10,000, but your accumulated debt over the four years is $40,000.

These four categories—national defense, Social Security, healthcare, and interest payments—account for roughly 73% of all federal spending, as **Figure 16.3** shows. The remaining 27% wedge of the pie chart covers all other categories of federal government spending: international affairs; science and technology; natural resources and the environment; transportation; housing; education; income support for the poor; community and regional development; law enforcement and the judicial system; and the administrative costs of running the government.

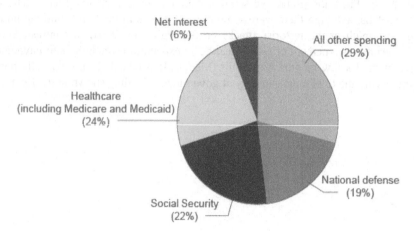

Figure 16.3 Slices of Federal Spending, 2014 About 73% of government spending goes to four major areas: national defense, Social Security, healthcare, and interest payments on past borrowing. This leaves about 29% of federal spending for all other functions of the U.S. government. (Source: https://www.whitehouse.gov/omb/budget/Historicals/)

State and Local Government Spending

Although federal government spending often gets most of the media attention, state and local government spending is also substantial—at about $3.1 trillion in 2014. **Figure 16.4** shows that state and local government spending has increased during the last four decades from around 8% to around 14% today. The single biggest item is education, which accounts for about one-third of the total. The rest covers programs like highways, libraries, hospitals and healthcare, parks, and police and fire protection. Unlike the federal government, all states (except Vermont) have balanced budget laws, which means any gaps between revenues and spending must be closed by higher taxes, lower spending, drawing down their previous savings, or some combination of all of these.

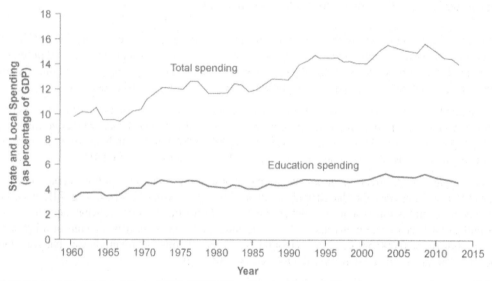

Figure 16.4 State and Local Spending, 1960–2013 Spending by state and local government increased from about 10% of GDP in the early 1960s to 14–16% by the mid-1970s. It has remained at roughly that level since. The single biggest spending item is education, including both K–12 spending and support for public colleges and universities, which has been about 4–5% of GDP in recent decades. Source: (Source: Bureau of Economic Analysis.)

U.S. presidential candidates often run for office pledging to improve the public schools or to get tough on crime. However, in the U.S. system of government, these tasks are primarily the responsibilities of state and local governments. Indeed, in fiscal year 2014 state and local governments spent about $840 billion per year on education (including K–12 and college and university education), compared to only $100 billion by the federal government, according to usgovernmentspending.com. In other words, about 90 cents of every dollar spent on education happens at the state and local level. A politician who really wants hands-on responsibility for reforming education or reducing crime might do better to run for mayor of a large city or for state governor rather than for president of the United States.

16.2 | Taxation

By the end of this section, you will be able to:
- Differentiate among a regressive tax, a proportional tax, and a progressive tax
- Identify the major sources of revenue for the U.S. federal budget

There are two main categories of taxes: those collected by the federal government and those collected by state and local governments. What percentage is collected and what that revenue is used for varies greatly. The following sections will briefly explain the taxation system in the United States.

Federal Taxes

Just as many Americans erroneously think that federal spending has grown considerably, many also believe that taxes have increased substantially. The top line of **Figure 16.5** shows total federal taxes as a share of GDP since 1960. Although the line rises and falls, it typically remains within the range of 17% to 20% of GDP, except for 2009, when taxes fell substantially below this level, due to recession.

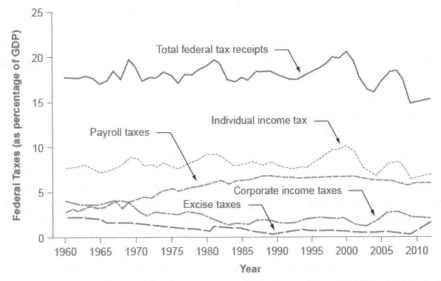

Figure 16.5 Federal Taxes, 1960–2014 Federal tax revenues have been about 17–20% of GDP during most periods in recent decades. The primary sources of federal taxes are individual income taxes and the payroll taxes that finance Social Security and Medicare. Corporate income taxes and social insurance taxes provide smaller shares of revenue. (Source: *Economic Report of the President, 2015.* Table B-21, https://www.whitehouse.gov/administration/eop/cea/economic-report-of-the-President/2015)

Figure 16.5 also shows the patterns of taxation for the main categories of taxes levied by the federal government: individual income taxes, corporate income taxes, and social insurance and retirement receipts. When most people think of taxes levied by the federal government, the first tax that comes to mind is the **individual income tax** that is due every year on April 15 (or the first business day after). The personal income tax is the largest single source of federal government revenue, but it still represents less than half of federal tax revenue.

The second largest source of federal revenue is the **payroll tax** (captured in social insurance and retirement receipts), which provides funds for Social Security and Medicare. Payroll taxes have increased steadily over time. Together, the personal income tax and the payroll tax accounted for about 80% of federal tax revenues in 2014. Although personal income tax revenues account for more total revenue than the payroll tax, nearly three-quarters of households pay more in payroll taxes than in income taxes.

The income tax is a **progressive tax**, which means that the tax rates increase as a household's income increases. Taxes also vary with marital status, family size, and other factors. The **marginal tax rates** (the tax that must be paid on all yearly income) for a single taxpayer range from 10% to 35%, depending on income, as the following Clear It Up feature explains.

How does the marginal rate work?

Suppose that a single taxpayer's income is $35,000 per year. Also suppose that income from $0 to $9,075 is taxed at 10%, income from $9,075 to $36,900 is taxed at 15%, and, finally, income from $36,900 and beyond is taxed at 25%. Since this person earns $35,000, their marginal tax rate is 15%.

The key fact here is that the federal income tax is designed so that tax rates increase as income increases, up to a certain level. The payroll taxes that support Social Security and Medicare are designed in a different way. First, the payroll taxes for Social Security are imposed at a rate of 12.4% up to a certain wage limit, set at $118,500 in 2015. Medicare, on the other hand, pays for elderly healthcare, and is fixed at 2.9%, with no upper ceiling.

In both cases, the employer and the employee split the payroll taxes. An employee only sees 6.2% deducted from his paycheck for Social Security, and 1.45% from Medicare. However, as economists are quick to point out, the employer's half of the taxes are probably passed along to the employees in the form of lower wages, so in reality, the worker pays all of the payroll taxes.

The Medicare payroll tax is also called a **proportional tax**; that is, a flat percentage of all wages earned. The Social Security payroll tax is proportional up to the wage limit, but above that level it becomes a **regressive tax**, meaning that people with higher incomes pay a smaller share of their income in tax.

The third-largest source of federal tax revenue, as shown in **Figure 16.5** is the **corporate income tax**. The common name for corporate income is "profits." Over time, corporate income tax receipts have declined as a share of GDP, from about 4% in the 1960s to an average of 1% to 2% of GDP in the first decade of the 2000s.

The federal government has a few other, smaller sources of revenue. It imposes an **excise tax**—that is, a tax on a particular good—on gasoline, tobacco, and alcohol. As a share of GDP, the amount collected by these taxes has stayed nearly constant over time, from about 2% of GDP in the 1960s to roughly 3% by 2014, according to the nonpartisan Congressional Budget Office. The government also imposes an **estate and gift tax** on people who pass large amounts of assets to the next generation—either after death or during life in the form of gifts. These estate and gift taxes collected about 0.2% of GDP in the first decade of the 2000s. By a quirk of legislation, the estate and gift tax was repealed in 2010, but reinstated in 2011. Other federal taxes, which are also relatively small in magnitude, include tariffs collected on imported goods and charges for inspections of goods entering the country.

State and Local Taxes

At the state and local level, taxes have been rising as a share of GDP over the last few decades to match the gradual rise in spending, as **Figure 16.6** illustrates. The main revenue sources for state and local governments are sales taxes, property taxes, and revenue passed along from the federal government, but many state and local governments also levy personal and corporate income taxes, as well as impose a wide variety of fees and charges. The specific sources of tax revenue vary widely across state and local governments. Some states rely more on property taxes, some on sales taxes, some on income taxes, and some more on revenues from the federal government.

Figure 16.6 State and Local Tax Revenue as a Share of GDP, 1960–2014 State and local tax revenues have increased to match the rise in state and local spending. (Source: *Economic Report of the President, 2015.* Table B-21, https://www.whitehouse.gov/administration/eop/cea/economic-report-of-the-President/2015)

16.3 | Federal Deficits and the National Debt

By the end of this section, you will be able to:
- Explain the U.S. federal budget in terms of annual debt and accumulated debt
- Understand how economic growth or decline can influence a budget surplus or budget deficit

Having discussed the revenue (taxes) and expense (spending) side of the budget, we now turn to the annual budget deficit or surplus, which is the difference between the tax revenue collected and spending over a fiscal year, which starts October 1 and ends September 30 of the next year.

Figure 16.7 shows the pattern of annual federal budget deficits and surpluses, back to 1930, as a share of GDP. When the line is above the horizontal axis, the budget is in surplus; when the line is below the horizontal axis, a budget deficit occurred. Clearly, the biggest deficits as a share of GDP during this time were incurred to finance World War II. Deficits were also large during the 1930s, the 1980s, the early 1990s, and most recently during the recession of 2008–2009.

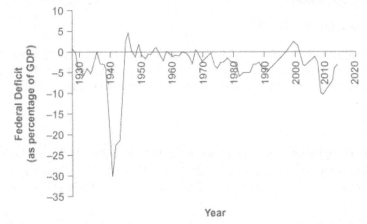

Figure 16.7 Pattern of Federal Budget Deficits and Surpluses, 1929–2014 The federal government has run budget deficits for decades. The budget was briefly in surplus in the late 1990s, before heading into deficit again in the first decade of the 2000s—and especially deep deficits in the recession of 2008–2009. (Source: Federal Reserve Bank of St. Louis (FRED). http://research.stlouisfed.org/fred2/series/FYFSGDA188S)

Debt/GDP Ratio

Another useful way to view the budget deficit is through the prism of accumulated debt rather than annual deficits. The **national debt** refers to the total amount that the government has borrowed over time; in contrast, the budget deficit refers to how much has been borrowed in one particular year. Figure 16.8 shows the ratio of debt/GDP since 1940. Until the 1970s, the debt/GDP ratio revealed a fairly clear pattern of federal borrowing. The government ran up large deficits and raised the debt/GDP ratio in World War II, but from the 1950s to the 1970s the government ran either surpluses or relatively small deficits, and so the debt/GDP ratio drifted down. Large deficits in the 1980s and early 1990s caused the ratio to rise sharply. When budget surpluses arrived from 1998 to 2001, the debt/GDP ratio declined substantially. The budget deficits starting in 2002 then tugged the debt/GDP ratio higher—with a big jump when the recession took hold in 2008–2009.

Figure 16.8 Federal Debt as a Percentage of GDP, 1942–2014 Federal debt is the sum of annual budget deficits and surpluses. Annual deficits do not always mean that the debt/GDP ratio is rising. During the 1960s and 1970s, the government often ran small deficits, but since the debt was growing more slowly than the economy, the debt/GDP ratio was declining over this time. In the 2008–2009 recession, the debt/GDP ratio rose sharply. (Source: *Economic Report of the President, Table B-20*, http://www.gpo.gov/fdsys/pkg/ERP-2015/content-detail.html)

The next Clear it Up feature discusses how the government handles the national debt.

Clear It Up

What is the national debt?

One year's federal budget deficit causes the federal government to sell Treasury bonds to make up the difference between spending programs and tax revenues. The dollar value of all the outstanding Treasury bonds on which the federal government owes money is equal to the national debt.

The Path from Deficits to Surpluses to Deficits

Why did the budget deficits suddenly turn to surpluses from 1998 to 2001? And why did the surpluses return to deficits in 2002? Why did the deficit become so large after 2007? Figure 16.9 suggests some answers. The graph combines the earlier information on total federal spending and taxes in a single graph, but focuses on the federal budget since 1990.

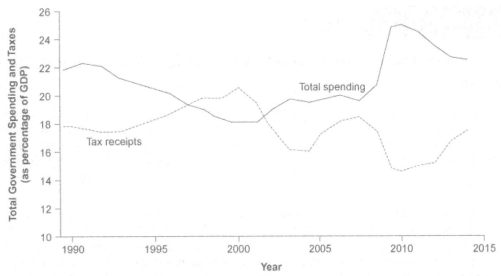

Figure 16.9 Total Government Spending and Taxes as a Share of GDP, 1990–2014 When government spending exceeds taxes, the gap is the budget deficit. When taxes exceed spending, the gap is a budget surplus. The recessionary period starting in late 2007 saw higher spending and lower taxes, combining to create a large deficit in 2009. (Source: *Economic Report of the President, Tables B-21 and B-1,*"http://www.gpo.gov/fdsys/pkg/ERP-2015/content-detail.html)

Government spending as a share of GDP declined steadily through the 1990s. The biggest single reason was that defense spending declined from 5.2% of GDP in 1990 to 3.0% in 2000, but interest payments by the federal government also fell by about 1.0% of GDP. However, federal tax collections increased substantially in the later 1990s, jumping from 18.1% of GDP in 1994 to 20.8% in 2000. Powerful economic growth in the late 1990s fueled the boom in taxes. Personal income taxes rise as income goes up; payroll taxes rise as jobs and payrolls go up; corporate income taxes rise as profits go up. At the same time, government spending on transfer payments such as unemployment benefits, foods stamps, and welfare declined with more people working.

This sharp increase in tax revenues and decrease in expenditures on transfer payments was largely unexpected even by experienced budget analysts, and so budget surpluses came as a surprise. But in the early 2000s, many of these factors started running in reverse. Tax revenues sagged, due largely to the recession that started in March 2001, which reduced revenues. A series of tax cuts was enacted by Congress and signed into law by President George W. Bush, starting in 2001. In addition, government spending swelled due to increases in defense, healthcare, education, Social Security, and support programs for those who were hurt by the recession and the slow growth that followed. Deficits returned. When the severe recession hit in late 2007, spending climbed and tax collections fell to historically unusual levels, resulting in enormous deficits.

Longer-term forecasts of the U.S. budget, a decade or more into the future, predict enormous deficits. The higher deficits run during the recession of 2008–2009 have repercussions, and the demographics will be challenging. The primary reason is the "baby boom"—the exceptionally high birthrates that began in 1946, right after World War II, and lasted for about two decades. Starting in 2010, the front edge of the baby boom generation began to reach age 65, and in the next two decades, the proportion of Americans over the age of 65 will increase substantially. The current level of the payroll taxes that support Social Security and Medicare will fall well short of the projected expenses of these programs, as the following Clear It Up feature shows; thus, the forecast is for large budget deficits. A decision to collect more revenue to support these programs or to decrease benefit levels would alter this long-term forecast.

What is the long-term budget outlook for Social Security and Medicare?

In 1946, just one American in 13 was over age 65. By 2000, it was one in eight. By 2030, one American in five will be over age 65. Two enormous U.S. federal programs focus on the elderly—Social Security and Medicare. The growing numbers of elderly Americans will increase spending on these programs, as well as on Medicaid. The current payroll tax levied on workers, which supports all of Social Security and the hospitalization insurance part of Medicare, will not be enough to cover the expected costs. So, what are the options?

Long-term projections from the Congressional Budget Office in 2009 are that Medicare and Social Security spending combined will rise from 8.3% of GDP in 2009 to about 13% by 2035 and about 20% in 2080. If this rise in spending occurs, without any corresponding rise in tax collections, then some mix of changes must occur: (1) taxes will need to be increased dramatically; (2) other spending will need to be cut dramatically; (3) the retirement age and/or age receiving Medicare benefits will need to increase, or (4) the federal government will need to run extremely large budget deficits.

Some proposals suggest removing the cap on wages subject to the payroll tax, so that those with very high incomes would have to pay the tax on the entire amount of their wages. Other proposals suggest moving Social Security and Medicare from systems in which workers pay for retirees toward programs that set up accounts where workers save funds over their lifetimes and then draw out after retirement to pay for healthcare.

The United States is not alone in this problem. Indeed, providing the promised level of retirement and health benefits to a growing proportion of elderly with a falling proportion of workers is an even more severe problem in many European nations and in Japan. How to pay promised levels of benefits to the elderly will be a difficult public policy decision.

In the next module we shift to the use of fiscal policy to counteract business cycle fluctuations. In addition, we will explore proposals requiring a balanced budget—that is, for government spending and taxes to be equal each year. The Impacts of Government Borrowing will also cover how fiscal policy and government borrowing will affect national saving—and thus affect economic growth and trade imbalances.

16.4 | Using Fiscal Policy to Fight Recession, Unemployment, and Inflation

By the end of this section, you will be able to:
- Explain how expansionary fiscal policy can shift aggregate demand and influence the economy
- Explain how contractionary fiscal policy can shift aggregate demand and influence the economy

We need to emphasize that fiscal policy is the use of government spending and tax policy to alter the economy. Fiscal policy does not include all spending (such as the increase in spending that accompanies a war).

Graphically, we see that fiscal policy, whether through change in spending or taxes, shifts the aggregate demand outward in the case of **expansionary fiscal policy** and inward in the case of **contractionary fiscal policy**. Figure 16.10 illustrates the process by using an aggregate demand/aggregate supply diagram in a growing economy. The original equilibrium occurs at E_0, the intersection of aggregate demand curve AD_0 and aggregate supply curve $SRAS_0$, at an output level of 200 and a price level of 90.

One year later, aggregate supply has shifted to the right to $SRAS_1$ in the process of long-term economic growth, and aggregate demand has also shifted to the right to AD_1, keeping the economy operating at the new level of potential GDP. The new equilibrium (E_1) is an output level of 206 and a price level of 92. One more year later, aggregate supply has again shifted to the right, now to SRAS$_2$, and aggregate demand shifts right as well to AD$_2$. Now the equilibrium is E$_2$, with an output level of 212 and a price level of 94. In short, the figure shows an economy that is growing steadily year to year, producing at its potential GDP each year, with only small inflationary increases in the price level.

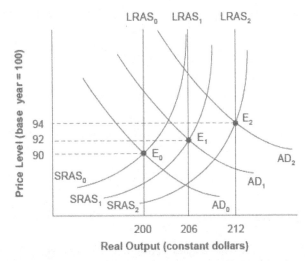

Figure 16.10 A Healthy, Growing Economy In this well-functioning economy, each year aggregate supply and aggregate demand shift to the right so that the economy proceeds from equilibrium E$_0$ to E$_1$ to E$_2$. Each year, the economy produces at potential GDP with only a small inflationary increase in the price level. But if aggregate demand does not smoothly shift to the right and match increases in aggregate supply, growth with deflation can develop.

Aggregate demand and aggregate supply do not always move neatly together. Aggregate demand may fail to increase along with aggregate supply, or aggregate demand may even shift left, for a number of possible reasons: households become hesitant about consuming; firms decide against investing as much; or perhaps the demand from other countries for exports diminishes. For example, investment by private firms in physical capital in the U.S. economy boomed during the late 1990s, rising from 14.1% of GDP in 1993 to 17.2% in 2000, before falling back to 15.2% by 2002. Conversely, if shifts in aggregate demand run ahead of increases in aggregate supply, inflationary increases in the price level will result. Business cycles of recession and recovery are the consequence of shifts in aggregate supply and aggregate demand.

Monetary Policy and Bank Regulation shows us that a central bank can use its powers over the banking system to engage in countercyclical—or "against the business cycle"—actions. If recession threatens, the central bank uses an expansionary monetary policy to increase the supply of money, increase the quantity of loans, reduce interest rates, and shift aggregate demand to the right. If inflation threatens, the central bank uses contractionary monetary policy to reduce the supply of money, reduce the quantity of loans, raise interest rates, and shift aggregate demand to the left. Fiscal policy is another macroeconomic policy tool for adjusting aggregate demand by using either government spending or taxation policy.

Expansionary Fiscal Policy

Expansionary fiscal policy increases the level of aggregate demand, through either increases in government spending or reductions in taxes. Expansionary policy can do this by (1) increasing consumption by raising disposable income through cuts in personal income taxes or payroll taxes; (2) increasing investments by raising after-tax profits through cuts in business taxes; and (3) increasing government purchases through increased spending by the federal government on final goods and services and raising federal grants to state and local governments to increase their expenditures on final goods and services. Contractionary fiscal policy does the reverse: it decreases the level of aggregate demand by decreasing consumption, decreasing investments, and decreasing government spending, either through cuts in government spending or increases in taxes. The aggregate demand/aggregate supply model is useful in judging whether expansionary or contractionary fiscal policy is appropriate.

Consider first the situation in **Figure 16.11**, which is similar to the U.S. economy during the recession in 2008–2009. The intersection of aggregate demand (AD$_0$) and aggregate supply (SRAS$_0$) is occurring below the level of potential GDP as indicated by the LRAS curve. At the equilibrium (E$_0$), a recession occurs and unemployment rises. In this case, expansionary fiscal policy using tax cuts or increases in government spending can shift aggregate demand to AD_1, closer to the full-employment level of output. In addition, the price level would rise back to the level P_1 associated with potential GDP.

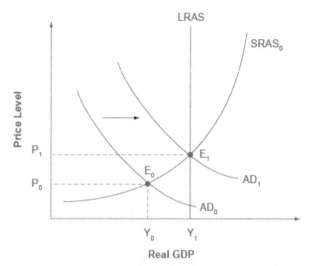

Figure 16.11 Expansionary Fiscal Policy The original equilibrium (E_0) represents a recession, occurring at a quantity of output (Y_0) below potential GDP. However, a shift of aggregate demand from AD_0 to AD_1, enacted through an expansionary fiscal policy, can move the economy to a new equilibrium output of E_1 at the level of potential GDP which is shown by the LRAS curve. Since the economy was originally producing below potential GDP, any inflationary increase in the price level from P_0 to P_1 that results should be relatively small.

Should the government use tax cuts or spending increases, or a mix of the two, to carry out expansionary fiscal policy? After the Great Recession of 2008–2009 (which started, actually, in very late 2007), U.S. government spending rose from 19.6% of GDP in 2007 to 24.6% in 2009, while tax revenues declined from 18.5% of GDP in 2007 to 14.8% in 2009. The choice between whether to use tax or spending tools often has a political tinge. As a general statement, conservatives and Republicans prefer to see expansionary fiscal policy carried out by tax cuts, while liberals and Democrats prefer that expansionary fiscal policy be implemented through spending increases. The Obama administration and Congress passed an $830 billion expansionary policy in early 2009 involving both tax cuts and increases in government spending, according to the Congressional Budget Office. However, state and local governments, whose budgets were also hard hit by the recession, began cutting their spending—a policy that offset federal expansionary policy.

The conflict over which policy tool to use can be frustrating to those who want to categorize economics as "liberal" or "conservative," or who want to use economic models to argue against their political opponents. But the AD–AS model can be used both by advocates of smaller government, who seek to reduce taxes and government spending, and by advocates of bigger government, who seek to raise taxes and government spending. Economic studies of specific taxing and spending programs can help to inform decisions about whether taxes or spending should be changed, and in what ways. Ultimately, decisions about whether to use tax or spending mechanisms to implement macroeconomic policy is, in part, a political decision rather than a purely economic one.

Contractionary Fiscal Policy

Fiscal policy can also contribute to pushing aggregate demand beyond potential GDP in a way that leads to inflation. As shown in **Figure 16.12**, a very large budget deficit pushes up aggregate demand, so that the intersection of aggregate demand (AD_0) and aggregate supply ($SRAS_0$) occurs at equilibrium E_0, which is an output level above potential GDP. This is sometimes known as an "overheating economy" where demand is so high that there is upward pressure on wages and prices, causing inflation. In this situation, contractionary fiscal policy involving federal spending cuts or tax increases can help to reduce the upward pressure on the price level by shifting aggregate demand to the left, to AD_1, and causing the new equilibrium E_1 to be at potential GDP, where aggregate demand intersects the LRAS curve.

Figure 16.12 A Contractionary Fiscal Policy The economy starts at the equilibrium quantity of output Y_0, which is above potential GDP. The extremely high level of aggregate demand will generate inflationary increases in the price level. A contractionary fiscal policy can shift aggregate demand down from AD_0 to AD_1, leading to a new equilibrium output E_1, which occurs at potential GDP, where AD1 intersects the LRAS curve.

Again, the AD–AS model does not dictate how this contractionary fiscal policy is to be carried out. Some may prefer spending cuts; others may prefer tax increases; still others may say that it depends on the specific situation. The model only argues that, in this situation, aggregate demand needs to be reduced.

16.5 | Automatic Stabilizers

By the end of this section, you will be able to:
- Describe how discretionary fiscal policy can be used by the federal government to stabilize the economy.
- Identify examples of automatic stabilizers.
- Understand how a standardized employment budget can be used to identify automatic stabilizers.

The millions of unemployed in 2008–2009 could collect unemployment insurance benefits to replace some of their salaries. Federal fiscal policies include **discretionary fiscal policy**, when the government passes a new law that explicitly changes tax or spending levels. The stimulus package of 2009 is an example. Changes in tax and spending levels can also occur automatically, due to **automatic stabilizers**, such as unemployment insurance and food stamps, which are programs that are already laws that stimulate aggregate demand in a recession and hold down aggregate demand in a potentially inflationary boom.

Counterbalancing Recession and Boom

Consider first the situation where aggregate demand has risen sharply, causing the equilibrium to occur at a level of output above potential GDP. This situation will increase inflationary pressure in the economy. The policy prescription in this setting would be a dose of contractionary fiscal policy, implemented through some combination of higher taxes and lower spending. To some extent, *both* changes happen automatically. On the tax side, a rise in aggregate demand means that workers and firms throughout the economy earn more. Because taxes are based on personal income and corporate profits, a rise in aggregate demand automatically increases tax payments. On the spending side, stronger aggregate demand typically means lower unemployment and fewer layoffs, and so there is less need for government spending on unemployment benefits, welfare, Medicaid, and other programs in the social safety net.

The process works in reverse, too. If aggregate demand were to fall sharply so that a recession occurs, then the prescription would be for expansionary fiscal policy—some mix of tax cuts and spending increases. The lower level of aggregate demand and higher unemployment will tend to pull down personal incomes and corporate profits, an effect that will reduce the amount of taxes owed automatically. Higher unemployment and a weaker economy should lead to increased government spending on unemployment benefits, welfare, and other similar domestic programs. In 2009, the stimulus package included an extension in the time allowed to collect unemployment insurance. In addition, the automatic stabilizers react to a weakening of aggregate demand with expansionary fiscal policy and react to a strengthening of aggregate demand with contractionary fiscal policy, just as the AD/AS analysis suggests.

The very large budget deficit of 2009 was produced by a combination of automatic stabilizers and discretionary fiscal policy. The Great Recession, starting in late 2007, meant less tax-generating economic activity, which triggered the automatic stabilizers that reduce taxes. Most economists, even those who are concerned about a possible pattern of persistently large budget deficits, are much less concerned or even quite supportive of larger budget deficits in the short run of a few years during and immediately after a severe recession.

A glance back at economic history provides a second illustration of the power of automatic stabilizers. Remember that the length of economic upswings between recessions has become longer in the U.S. economy in recent decades (as discussed in **Unemployment**). The three longest economic booms of the twentieth century happened in the 1960s, the 1980s, and the 1991–2001 time period. One reason why the economy has tipped into recession less frequently in recent decades is that the size of government spending and taxes has increased in the second half of the twentieth century. Thus, the automatic stabilizing effects from spending and taxes are now larger than they were in the first half of the twentieth century. Around 1900, for example, federal spending was only about 2% of GDP. In 1929, just before the Great Depression hit, government spending was still just 4% of GDP. In those earlier times, the smaller size of government made automatic stabilizers far less powerful than in the last few decades, when government spending often hovers at 20% of GDP or more.

The Standardized Employment Deficit or Surplus

Each year, the nonpartisan Congressional Budget Office (CBO) calculates the **standardized employment budget**—that is, what the budget deficit or surplus would be if the economy were producing at potential GDP, where people who look for work were finding jobs in a reasonable period of time and businesses were making normal profits, with the result that both workers and businesses would be earning more and paying more taxes. In effect, the standardized employment deficit eliminates the impact of the automatic stabilizers. **Figure 16.13** compares the actual budget deficits of recent decades with the CBO's standardized deficit.

Link It Up @@@

Visit this website (http://openstaxcollege.org/l/CBO) to learn more from the Congressional Budget Office.

Figure 16.13 Comparison of Actual Budget Deficits with the Standardized Employment Deficit When the economy is in recession, the standardized employment budget deficit is less than the actual budget deficit because the economy is below potential GDP, and the automatic stabilizers are reducing taxes and increasing spending. When the economy is performing extremely well, the standardized employment deficit (or surplus) is higher than the actual budget deficit (or surplus) because the economy is producing about potential GDP, so the automatic stabilizers are increasing taxes and reducing the need for government spending. (Sources: *Actual and Cyclically Adjusted Budget Surpluses/Deficits,* http://www.cbo.gov/publication/43977; and *Economic Report of the President, Table B-1,* http://www.gpo.gov/fdsys/pkg/ERP-2013/content-detail.html)

Notice that in recession years, like the early 1990s, 2001, or 2009, the standardized employment deficit is smaller than the actual deficit. During recessions, the automatic stabilizers tend to increase the budget deficit, so if the economy was instead at full employment, the deficit would be reduced. However, in the late 1990s the standardized employment budget surplus was lower than the actual budget surplus. The gap between the standardized budget deficit or surplus and the actual budget deficit or surplus shows the impact of the automatic stabilizers. More generally, the standardized budget figures allow you to see what the budget deficit would look like with the economy held constant—at its potential GDP level of output.

Automatic stabilizers occur quickly. Lower wages means that a lower amount of taxes is withheld from paychecks right away. Higher unemployment or poverty means that government spending in those areas rises as quickly as people apply for benefits. However, while the automatic stabilizers offset part of the shifts in aggregate demand, they do not offset all or even most of it. Historically, automatic stabilizers on the tax and spending side offset about 10% of any initial movement in the level of output. This offset may not seem enormous, but it is still useful. Automatic stabilizers, like shock absorbers in a car, can be useful if they reduce the impact of the worst bumps, even if they do not eliminate the bumps altogether.

16.6 | Practical Problems with Discretionary Fiscal Policy

By the end of this section, you will be able to:
- Understand how fiscal policy and monetary policy are interconnected
- Explain the three lag times that often occur when solving economic problems.
- Identify the legal and political challenges of responding to an economic problem.

In the early 1960s, many leading economists believed that the problem of the business cycle, and the swings between cyclical unemployment and inflation, were a thing of the past. On the cover of its December 31, 1965, issue, *Time* magazine, then the premier news magazine in the United States, ran a picture of John Maynard Keynes, and the story inside identified Keynesian theories as "the prime influence on the world's economies." The article reported that policymakers have "used Keynesian principles not only to avoid the violent [business] cycles of prewar days but to produce phenomenal economic growth and to achieve remarkably stable prices."

This happy consensus, however, did not last. The U.S. economy suffered one recession from December 1969 to November 1970, a deeper recession from November 1973 to March 1975, and then double-dip recessions from

January to June 1980 and from July 1981 to November 1982. At various times, inflation and unemployment both soared. Clearly, the problems of macroeconomic policy had not been completely solved. As economists began to consider what had gone wrong, they identified a number of issues that make discretionary fiscal policy more difficult than it had seemed in the rosy optimism of the mid-1960s.

Fiscal Policy and Interest Rates

Because fiscal policy affects the quantity that the government borrows in financial capital markets, it not only affects aggregate demand—it can also affect interest rates. In **Figure 16.14**, the original equilibrium (E_0) in the financial capital market occurs at a quantity of $800 billion and an interest rate of 6%. However, an increase in government budget deficits shifts the demand for financial capital from D_0 to D_1. The new equilibrium (E_1) occurs at a quantity of $900 billion and an interest rate of 7%.

A consensus estimate based on a number of studies is that an increase in budget deficits (or a fall in budget surplus) by 1% of GDP will cause an increase of 0.5–1.0% in the long-term interest rate.

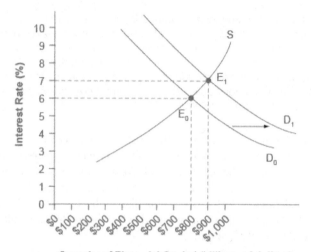

Figure 16.14 Fiscal Policy and Interest Rates   When a government borrows money in the financial capital market, it causes a shift in the demand for financial capital from D_0 to D_1. As the equilibrium moves from E_0 to E_1, the equilibrium interest rate rises from 6% to 7% in this example. In this way, an expansionary fiscal policy intended to shift aggregate demand to the right can also lead to a higher interest rate, which has the effect of shifting aggregate demand back to the left.

A problem arises here. An expansionary fiscal policy, with tax cuts or spending increases, is intended to increase aggregate demand. If an expansionary fiscal policy also causes higher interest rates, then firms and households are discouraged from borrowing and spending (as occurs with tight monetary policy), thus reducing aggregate demand. Even if the direct effect of expansionary fiscal policy on increasing demand is not totally offset by lower aggregate demand from higher interest rates, fiscal policy can end up being less powerful than was originally expected. This is referred to as **crowding out**, where government borrowing and spending results in higher interest rates, which reduces business investment and household consumption.

The broader lesson is that fiscal and monetary policy must be coordinated. If expansionary fiscal policy is to work well, then the central bank can also reduce or keep short-term interest rates low. Conversely, monetary policy can also help to ensure that contractionary fiscal policy does not lead to a recession.

Long and Variable Time Lags

Monetary policy can be changed several times each year, but fiscal policy is much slower to be enacted. Imagine that the economy starts to slow down. It often takes some months before the economic statistics signal clearly that a downturn has started, and a few months more to confirm that it is truly a recession and not just a one- or two-month blip. The time it takes to determine that a recession has occurred is often called the **recognition lag**. After this lag, policymakers become aware of the problem and propose fiscal policy bills. The bills go into various congressional committees for hearings, negotiations, votes, and then, if passed, eventually for the president's signature. Many fiscal policy bills about spending or taxes propose changes that would start in the next budget year or would be phased in gradually over time. The time to get a bill passed is often referred to as the **legislative lag**. Finally, once the bill is passed it takes some time for the funds to be dispersed to the appropriate agencies to implement the programs. The time to get the projects started is often called the **implementation lag**.

Moreover, the exact level of fiscal policy to be implemented is never completely clear. Should the budget deficit be increased by 0.5% of GDP? By 1% of GDP? By 2% of GDP? In an AD/AS diagram, it is straightforward to sketch an aggregate demand curve shifting to the potential GDP level of output. In the real world, the actual level of potential output is known only roughly, not precisely, and exactly how a spending cut or tax increase will affect aggregate demand is always somewhat controversial. Also unknown is the state of the economy at any point in time. During the early days of the Obama administration, for example, no one knew how deep in the hole the economy really was. During the financial crisis of 2008-09, the rapid collapse of the banking system and automotive sector made it difficult to assess how quickly the economy was collapsing.

Thus, it can take many months or even more than a year to begin an expansionary fiscal policy after a recession has started—and even then, uncertainty will remain over exactly how much to expand or contract taxes and spending. When politicians attempt to use countercyclical fiscal policy to fight recession or inflation, they run the risk of responding to the macroeconomic situation of two or three years ago, in a way that may be exactly wrong for the economy at that time. George P. Schultz, a professor of economics, former Secretary of the Treasury, and Director of the Office of Management and Budget, once wrote: "While the economist is accustomed to the concept of lags, the politician likes instant results. The tension comes because, as I have seen on many occasions, the economist's lag is the politician's nightmare."

Temporary and Permanent Fiscal Policy

A temporary tax cut or spending increase will explicitly last only for a year or two, and then revert back to its original level. A permanent tax cut or spending increase is expected to stay in place for the foreseeable future. The effect of temporary and permanent fiscal policies on aggregate demand can be very different. Consider how you would react if the government announced a tax cut that would last one year and then be repealed, in comparison with how you would react if the government announced a permanent tax cut. Most people and firms will react more strongly to a permanent policy change than a temporary one.

This fact creates an unavoidable difficulty for countercyclical fiscal policy. The appropriate policy may be to have an expansionary fiscal policy with large budget deficits during a recession, and then a contractionary fiscal policy with budget surpluses when the economy is growing well. But if both policies are explicitly temporary ones, they will have a less powerful effect than a permanent policy.

Structural Economic Change Takes Time

When an economy recovers from a recession, it does not usually revert back to its exact earlier shape. Instead, the internal structure of the economy evolves and changes and this process can take time. For example, much of the economic growth of the mid-2000s was in the sectors of construction (especially of housing) and finance. However, when housing prices started falling in 2007 and the resulting financial crunch led into recession (as discussed in Monetary Policy and Bank Regulation), both sectors contracted. The manufacturing sector of the U.S. economy has been losing jobs in recent years as well, under pressure from technological change and foreign competition. Many of the people thrown out of work from these sectors in the Great Recession of 2008–2009 will never return to the same jobs in the same sectors of the economy; instead, the economy will need to grow in new and different directions, as the following Clear It Up feature shows. Fiscal policy can increase overall demand, but the process of structural economic change—the expansion of a new set of industries and the movement of workers to those industries—inevitably takes time.

Clear It Up

Why do jobs vanish?

People can lose jobs for a variety of reasons: because of a recession, but also because of longer-run changes in the economy, such as new technology. Productivity improvements in auto manufacturing, for example, can reduce the number of workers needed, and eliminate these jobs in the long run. The Internet has created jobs but also caused the loss of jobs as well, from travel agents to book store clerks. Many of these jobs may never come back. Short-run fiscal policy to reduce unemployment can create jobs, but it cannot replace jobs that will never return.

The Limitations of Fiscal Policy

Fiscal policy can help an economy that is producing below its potential GDP to expand aggregate demand so that it produces closer to potential GDP, thus lowering unemployment. But fiscal policy cannot help an economy produce at an output level above potential GDP without causing inflation At this point, unemployment becomes so low that workers become scarce and wages rise rapidly.

Link It Up

Visit this website (http://openstaxcollege.org/l/fiscalpolicy) to read about how the recovery is being affected by fiscal policies.

Political Realties and Discretionary Fiscal Policy

A final problem for discretionary fiscal policy arises out of the difficulties of explaining to politicians how countercyclical fiscal policy that runs against the tide of the business cycle should work. Politicians often have a gut-level belief that when the economy and tax revenues slow down, it is time to hunker down, pinch pennies, and trim expenses. Countercyclical policy, however, says that when the economy has slowed down, it is time for the government to go on a spree, raising spending, and cutting taxes. This offsets the drop in the economy in the other sectors. Conversely, when economic times are good and tax revenues are rolling in, politicians often feel that it is time for tax cuts and new spending. But countercyclical policy says that this economic boom should be an appropriate time for keeping taxes high and restraining spending.

Politicians tend to prefer expansionary fiscal policy over contractionary policy. There is rarely a shortage of proposals for tax cuts and spending increases, especially during recessions. However, politicians are less willing to hear the message that in good economic times, they should propose tax increases and spending limits. In the economic upswing of the late 1990s and early 2000s, for example, the U.S. GDP grew rapidly. Estimates from respected government economic forecasters like the nonpartisan Congressional Budget Office and the Office of Management and Budget stated that the GDP was above potential GDP, and that unemployment rates were unsustainably low. However, no mainstream politician took the lead in saying that the booming economic times might be an appropriate time for spending cuts or tax increases.

Discretionary Fiscal Policy: Summing Up

Expansionary fiscal policy can help to end recessions and contractionary fiscal policy can help to reduce inflation. Given the uncertainties over interest rate effects, time lags, temporary and permanent policies, and unpredictable political behavior, many economists and knowledgeable policymakers had concluded by the mid-1990s that discretionary fiscal policy was a blunt instrument, more like a club than a scalpel. It might still make sense to use it in extreme economic situations, like an especially deep or long recession. For less extreme situations, it was often preferable to let fiscal policy work through the automatic stabilizers and focus on monetary policy to steer short-term countercyclical efforts.

16.7 | The Question of a Balanced Budget

By the end of this section, you will be able to:

- Understand the arguments for and against requiring the U.S. federal budget to be balanced
- Consider the long-run and short-run effects of a federal budget deficit

For many decades, going back to the 1930s, proposals have been put forward to require that the U.S. government balance its budget every year. In 1995, a proposed constitutional amendment that would require a balanced budget passed the U.S. House of Representatives by a wide margin, and failed in the U.S. Senate by only a single vote. (For the balanced budget to have become an amendment to the Constitution would have required a two-thirds vote by Congress and passage by three-quarters of the state legislatures.)

Most economists view the proposals for a perpetually balanced budget with bemusement. After all, in the short term, economists would expect the budget deficits and surpluses to fluctuate up and down with the economy and the automatic stabilizers. Economic recessions should automatically lead to larger budget deficits or smaller budget surpluses, while economic booms lead to smaller deficits or larger surpluses. A requirement that the budget be balanced each and every year would prevent these automatic stabilizers from working and would worsen the severity of economic fluctuations.

Some supporters of the balanced budget amendment like to argue that, since households must balance their own budgets, the government should too. But this analogy between household and government behavior is severely flawed. Most households do not balance their budgets every year. Some years households borrow to buy houses or cars or to pay for medical expenses or college tuition. Other years they repay loans and save funds in retirement accounts. After retirement, they withdraw and spend those savings. Also, the government is not a household for many reasons, one of which is that the government has macroeconomic responsibilities. The argument of Keynesian macroeconomic policy is that the government needs to lean against the wind, spending when times are hard and saving when times are good, for the sake of the overall economy.

There is also no particular reason to expect a government budget to be balanced in the medium term of a few years. For example, a government may decide that by running large budget deficits, it can make crucial long-term investments in human capital and physical infrastructure that will build the long-term productivity of a country. These decisions may work out well or poorly, but they are not always irrational. Such policies of ongoing government budget deficits may persist for decades. As the U.S. experience from the end of World War II up to about 1980 shows, it is perfectly possible to run budget deficits almost every year for decades, but as long as the percentage increases in debt are smaller than the percentage growth of GDP, the debt/GDP ratio will decline at the same time.

Nothing in this argument should be taken as a claim that budget deficits are always a wise policy. In the short run, a government that runs a very large budget deficit can shift aggregate demand to the right and trigger severe inflation. Additionally, governments may borrow for foolish or impractical reasons. The Macroeconomics Impacts of Government Borrowing will discuss how large budget deficits, by reducing national saving, can in certain cases reduce economic growth and even contribute to international financial crises. A requirement that the budget be balanced in each calendar year, however, is a misguided overreaction to the fear that in some cases, budget deficits can become too large.

Bring it Home

No Yellowstone Park?

The federal budget shutdown of 2013 illustrated the many sides to fiscal policy and the federal budget. In 2013, Republicans and Democrats could not agree on which spending policies to fund and how large the government debt should be. Due to the severity of the recession in 2008–2009, the fiscal stimulus, and previous policies, the federal budget deficit and debt was historically high. One way to try to cut federal spending and borrowing was to refuse to raise the legal federal debt limit, or tie on conditions to appropriation bills to stop the Affordable Health Care Act. This disagreement led to a two-week shutdown of the federal government and got close to the deadline where the federal government would default on its Treasury bonds. Finally, however, a compromise emerged and default was avoided. This shows clearly how closely fiscal policies are tied to politics.

KEY TERMS

automatic stabilizers tax and spending rules that have the effect of slowing down the rate of decrease in aggregate demand when the economy slows down and restraining aggregate demand when the economy speeds up, without any additional change in legislation

balanced budget when government spending and taxes are equal

budget deficit when the federal government spends more money than it receives in taxes in a given year

budget surplus when the government receives more money in taxes than it spends in a year

contractionary fiscal policy fiscal policy that decreases the level of aggregate demand, either through cuts in government spending or increases in taxes

corporate income tax a tax imposed on corporate profits

crowding out federal spending and borrowing causes interest rates to rise and business investment to fall

discretionary fiscal policy the government passes a new law that explicitly changes overall tax or spending levels with the intent of influencing the level or overall economic activity

estate and gift tax a tax on people who pass assets to the next generation—either after death or during life in the form of gifts

excise tax a tax on a specific good—on gasoline, tobacco, and alcohol

expansionary fiscal policy fiscal policy that increases the level of aggregate demand, either through increases in government spending or cuts in taxes

implementation lag the time it takes for the funds relating to fiscal policy to be dispersed to the appropriate agencies to implement the programs

individual income tax a tax based on the income, of all forms, received by individuals

legislative lag the time it takes to get a fiscal policy bill passed

marginal tax rates or the tax that must be paid on all yearly income

national debt the total accumulated amount the government has borrowed, over time, and not yet paid back

payroll tax a tax based on the pay received from employers; the taxes provide funds for Social Security and Medicare

progressive tax a tax that collects a greater share of income from those with high incomes than from those with lower incomes

proportional tax a tax that is a flat percentage of income earned, regardless of level of income

recognition lag the time it takes to determine that a recession has occurred

regressive tax a tax in which people with higher incomes pay a smaller share of their income in tax

standardized employment budget the budget deficit or surplus in any given year adjusted for what it would have been if the economy were producing at potential GDP

KEY CONCEPTS AND SUMMARY

16.1 Government Spending

Fiscal policy is the set of policies that relate to federal government spending, taxation, and borrowing. In recent decades, the level of federal government spending and taxes, expressed as a share of GDP, has not changed much, typically fluctuating between about 18% to 22% of GDP. However, the level of state spending and taxes, as a share of GDP, has risen from about 12–13% to about 20% of GDP over the last four decades. The four main areas of federal spending are national defense, Social Security, healthcare, and interest payments, which together account for about 70% of all federal spending. When a government spends more than it collects in taxes, it is said to have a budget deficit. When a government collects more in taxes than it spends, it is said to have a budget surplus. If government spending and taxes are equal, it is said to have a balanced budget. The sum of all past deficits and surpluses make up the government debt.

16.2 Taxation

The two main federal taxes are individual income taxes and payroll taxes that provide funds for Social Security and Medicare; these taxes together account for more than 80% of federal revenues. Other federal taxes include the corporate income tax, excise taxes on alcohol, gasoline and tobacco, and the estate and gift tax. A progressive tax is one, like the federal income tax, where those with higher incomes pay a higher share of taxes out of their income than those with lower incomes. A proportional tax is one, like the payroll tax for Medicare, where everyone pays the same share of taxes regardless of income level. A regressive tax is one, like the payroll tax (above a certain threshold) that supports Social Security, where those with high income pay a lower share of income in taxes than those with lower incomes.

16.3 Federal Deficits and the National Debt

For most of the twentieth century, the U.S. government took on debt during wartime and then paid down that debt slowly in peacetime. However, it took on quite substantial debts in peacetime in the 1980s and early 1990s, before a brief period of budget surpluses from 1998 to 2001, followed by a return to annual budget deficits since 2002, with very large deficits in the recession of 2008 and 2009. A budget deficit or budget surplus is measured annually. Total government debt or national debt is the sum of budget deficits and budget surpluses over time.

16.4 Using Fiscal Policy to Fight Recession, Unemployment, and Inflation

Expansionary fiscal policy increases the level of aggregate demand, either through increases in government spending or through reductions in taxes. Expansionary fiscal policy is most appropriate when an economy is in recession and producing below its potential GDP. Contractionary fiscal policy decreases the level of aggregate demand, either through cuts in government spending or increases in taxes. Contractionary fiscal policy is most appropriate when an economy is producing above its potential GDP.

16.5 Automatic Stabilizers

Fiscal policy is conducted both through discretionary fiscal policy, which occurs when the government enacts taxation or spending changes in response to economic events, or through automatic stabilizers, which are taxing and spending mechanisms that, by their design, shift in response to economic events without any further legislation. The standardized employment budget is the calculation of what the budget deficit or budget surplus would have been in a given year if the economy had been producing at its potential GDP in that year. Many economists and politicians criticize the use of fiscal policy for a variety of reasons, including concerns over time lags, the impact on interest rates, and the inherently political nature of fiscal policy. We cover the critique of fiscal policy in the next module.

16.6 Practical Problems with Discretionary Fiscal Policy

Because fiscal policy affects the quantity of money that the government borrows in financial capital markets, it not only affects aggregate demand—it can also affect interest rates. If an expansionary fiscal policy also causes higher interest rates, then firms and households are discouraged from borrowing and spending, reducing aggregate demand in a situation called crowding out. Given the uncertainties over interest rate effects, time lags (implementation lag, legislative lag, and recognition lag), temporary and permanent policies, and unpredictable political behavior, many economists and knowledgeable policymakers have concluded that discretionary fiscal policy is a blunt instrument and better used only in extreme situations.

16.7 The Question of a Balanced Budget

Balanced budget amendments are a popular political idea, but the economic merits behind such proposals are questionable. Most economists accept that fiscal policy needs to be flexible enough to accommodate unforeseen expenditures, such as wars or recessions. While persistent, large budget deficits can indeed be a problem, a balanced budget amendment prevents even small, temporary deficits that might, in some cases, be necessary.

SELF-CHECK QUESTIONS

1. When governments run budget deficits, how do they make up the differences between tax revenue and spending?

2. When governments run budget surpluses, what is done with the extra funds?

3. Is it possible for a nation to run budget deficits and still have its debt/GDP ratio fall? Explain your answer. Is it possible for a nation to run budget surpluses and still have its debt/GDP ratio rise? Explain your answer.

4. Suppose that gifts were taxed at a rate of 10% for amounts up to $100,000 and 20% for anything over that amount. Would this tax be regressive or progressive?

5. If an individual owns a corporation for which he is the only employee, which different types of federal tax will he have to pay?

6. What taxes would an individual pay if he were self-employed and the business is not incorporated?

7. The social security tax is 6.2% on employees' income earned below $113,000. Is this tax progressive, regressive or proportional?

8. Debt has a certain self-reinforcing quality to it. There is one category of government spending that automatically increases along with the federal debt. What is it?

9. True or False:
    a. Federal spending has grown substantially in recent decades.
    b. By world standards, the U.S. government controls a relatively large share of the U.S. economy.
    c. A majority of the federal government's revenue is collected through personal income taxes.
    d. Education spending is slightly larger at the federal level than at the state and local level.
    e. State and local government spending has not risen much in recent decades.
    f. Defense spending is higher now than ever.
    g. The share of the economy going to federal taxes has increased substantially over time.
    h. Foreign aid is a large portion, although less than half, of federal spending.
    i. Federal deficits have been very large for the last two decades.
    j. The accumulated federal debt as a share of GDP is near an all-time high.

10. What is the main reason for employing contractionary fiscal policy in a time of strong economic growth?

11. What is the main reason for employing expansionary fiscal policy during a recession?

12. In a recession, does the actual budget surplus or deficit fall above or below the standardized employment budget?

13. What is the main advantage of automatic stabilizers over discretionary fiscal policy?

14. Explain how automatic stabilizers work, both on the taxation side and on the spending side, first in a situation where the economy is producing less than potential GDP and then in a situation where the economy is producing more than potential GDP.

15. What would happen if expansionary fiscal policy was implemented in a recession but, due to lag, did not actually take effect until after the economy was back to potential GDP?

16. What would happen if contractionary fiscal policy were implemented during an economic boom but, due to lag, it did not take effect until the economy slipped into recession?

17. Do you think the typical time lag for fiscal policy is likely to be longer or shorter than the time lag for monetary policy? Explain your answer?

18. How would a balanced budget amendment affect a decision by Congress to grant a tax cut during a recession?

19. How would a balanced budget amendment change the effect of automatic stabilizer programs?

REVIEW QUESTIONS

20. Give some examples of changes in federal spending and taxes by the government that would be fiscal policy and some that would not.

21. Have the spending and taxes of the U.S. federal government generally had an upward or a downward trend in the last few decades?

22. What are the main categories of U.S. federal government spending?

23. What is the difference between a budget deficit, a balanced budget, and a budget surplus?

24. Have spending and taxes by state and local governments in the United States had a generally upward or downward trend in the last few decades?

25. What are the main categories of U.S. federal government taxes?

26. What is the difference between a progressive tax, a proportional tax, and a regressive tax?

27. What has been the general pattern of U.S. budget deficits in recent decades?

28. What is the difference between a budget deficit and the national debt?

29. What is the difference between expansionary fiscal policy and contractionary fiscal policy?

30. Under what general macroeconomic circumstances might a government use expansionary fiscal policy? When might it use contractionary fiscal policy?

31. What is the difference between discretionary fiscal policy and automatic stabilizers?

32. Why do automatic stabilizers function "automatically?"

33. What is the standardized employment budget?

34. What are some practical weaknesses of discretionary fiscal policy?

35. What are some of the arguments for and against a requirement that the federal government budget be balanced every year?

CRITICAL THINKING QUESTIONS

36. Why is government spending typically measured as a percentage of GDP rather than in nominal dollars?

37. Why are expenditures such as crime prevention and education typically done at the state and local level rather than at the federal level?

38. Why is spending by the U.S. government on scientific research at NASA fiscal policy while spending by the University of Illinois is not fiscal policy? Why is a cut in the payroll tax fiscal policy whereas a cut in a state income tax is not fiscal policy?

39. Excise taxes on tobacco and alcohol and state sales taxes are often criticized for being regressive. Although

everyone pays the same rate regardless of income, why might this be so?

40. What is the benefit of having state and local taxes on income instead of collecting all such taxes at the federal level?

41. In a booming economy, is the federal government more likely to run surpluses or deficits? What are the various factors at play?

42. Economist Arthur Laffer famously pointed out that, in some cases, income tax revenue can actually go up when tax rates go down. Why might this be the case?

43. Is it possible for a nation to run budget deficits and still have its debt/GDP ratio fall? Explain your answer. Is it possible for a nation to run budget surpluses and still have its debt/GDP ratio rise? Explain your answer.

44. How will cuts in state budget spending affect federal expansionary policy?

45. Is expansionary fiscal policy more attractive to politicians who believe in larger government or to politicians who believe in smaller government? Explain your answer.

46. Is Medicaid (federal government aid to low-income families and individuals) an automatic stabilizer?

47. What is a potential problem with a temporary tax increase designed to increase aggregate demand if people know that it is temporary?

48. If the government gives a $300 tax cut to everyone in the country, explain the mechanism by which this will cause interest rates to rise.

49. Do you agree or disagree with this statement: "It is in the best interest of our economy for Congress and the President to run a balanced budget each year." Explain your answer.

50. During the Great Recession of 2008–2009, what actions would have been required of Congress and the President had a balanced budget amendment to the Constitution been ratified? What impact would that have had on the unemployment rate?

PROBLEMS

51. A government starts off with a total debt of $3.5 billion. In year one, the government runs a deficit of $400 million. In year two, the government runs a deficit of $1 billion. In year three, the government runs a surplus of $200 million. What is the total debt of the government at the end of year three?

52. If a government runs a budget deficit of $10 billion dollars each year for ten years, then a surplus of $1 billion for five years, and then a balanced budget for another ten years, what is the government debt?

53. Specify whether expansionary or contractionary fiscal policy would seem to be most appropriate in response to each of the situations below and sketch a diagram using aggregate demand and aggregate supply curves to illustrate your answer:
   a. A recession.
   b. A stock market collapse that hurts consumer and business confidence.
   c. Extremely rapid growth of exports.
   d. Rising inflation.
   e. A rise in the natural rate of unemployment.
   f. A rise in oil prices.

17 | The Impacts of Government Borrowing

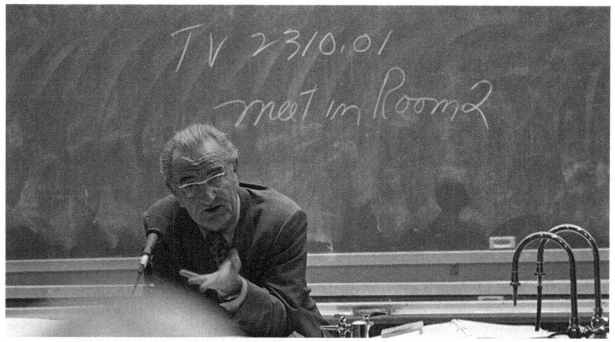

Figure 17.1 President Lyndon B. Johnson President Lyndon Johnson played a pivotal role in financing higher education. (Credit: modification of image by LBJ Museum & Library)

Bring it Home

Financing Higher Education

On November 8, 1965, President Lyndon B. Johnson signed The Higher Education Act of 1965 into law. With a stroke of the pen, he implemented what we know as the financial aid, work study, and student loan programs to help Americans pay for a college education. In his remarks, the President said:

> Here the seeds were planted from which grew my firm conviction that for the individual, education is the path to achievement and fulfillment; for the Nation, it is a path to a society that is not only free but civilized; and for the world, it is the path to peace—for it is education that places reason over force.

This Act, he said, "is responsible for funding higher education for millions of Americans. It is the embodiment of the United States' investment in 'human capital'." Since the Act was first signed into law, it has been renewed several times.

The purpose of The Higher Education Act of 1965 was to build the country's human capital by creating educational opportunity for millions of Americans. The three criteria used to judge eligibility are income, full-time or part-time attendance, and the cost of the institution. According to the 2011–2012 National Postsecondary Student Aid Study (NPSAS:12), in the 2011–2012 school year, over 70% of all full-time college students received some form of federal financial aid; 47% received grants; and another 55% received federal government student loans. The budget to support financial aid has increased not only because of increased enrollment, but also because of increased tuition and fees for higher education. These increases are currently being questioned. The President and Congress are charged with balancing fiscal responsibility and important government-financed expenditures like investing in human capital.

Introduction to the Impacts of Government Borrowing

In this chapter, you will learn about:

- How Government Borrowing Affects Investment and the Trade Balance
- Fiscal Policy, Investment, and Economic Growth
- How Government Borrowing Affects Private Saving
- Fiscal Policy and the Trade Balance

Governments have many competing demands for financial support. Any spending should be tempered by fiscal responsibility and by looking carefully at the spending's impact. When a government spends more than it collects in taxes, it runs a budget deficit. It then needs to borrow. When government borrowing becomes especially large and sustained, it can substantially reduce the financial capital available to private sector firms, as well as lead to trade imbalances and even financial crises.

The **Government Budgets and Fiscal Policy** chapter introduced the concepts of deficits and debt, as well as how a government could use fiscal policy to address recession or inflation. This chapter begins by building on the national savings and investment identity, first introduced in **The International Trade and Capital Flows** chapter, to show how government borrowing affects firms' physical capital investment levels and trade balances. A prolonged period of budget deficits may lead to lower economic growth, in part because the funds borrowed by the government to fund its budget deficits are typically no longer available for private investment. Moreover, a sustained pattern of large budget deficits can lead to disruptive economic patterns of high inflation, substantial inflows of financial capital from abroad, plummeting exchange rates, and heavy strains on a country's banking and financial system.

17.1 | How Government Borrowing Affects Investment and the Trade Balance

By the end of this section, you will be able to:
- Explain the national saving and investment identity in terms of demand and supply
- Evaluate the role of budget surpluses and trade surpluses in national saving and investment identity

When governments are borrowers in financial markets, there are three possible sources for the funds from a macroeconomic point of view: (1) households might save more; (2) private firms might borrow less; and (3) the additional funds for government borrowing might come from outside the country, from foreign financial investors. Let's begin with a review of why one of these three options must occur, and then explore how interest rates and exchange rates adjust to these connections.

The National Saving and Investment Identity

The national saving and investment identity, first introduced in **The International Trade and Capital Flows** chapter, provides a framework for showing the relationships between the sources of demand and supply in financial capital markets. The identity begins with a statement that must always hold true: the quantity of financial capital supplied in the market must equal the quantity of financial capital demanded.

The U.S. economy has two main sources for financial capital: private savings from inside the U.S. economy and public savings.

$$\text{Total savings} = \text{Private savings (S)} + \text{Public savings (T} - \text{G)}$$

These include the inflow of foreign financial capital from abroad. The inflow of savings from abroad is, by definition, equal to the trade deficit, as explained in The International Trade and Capital Flows chapter. So this inflow of foreign investment capital can be written as imports (M) minus exports (X). There are also two main sources of demand for financial capital: private sector investment (I) and government borrowing. Government borrowing in any given year is equal to the budget deficit, and can be written as the difference between government spending (G) and net taxes (T). Let's call this equation 1.

$$\text{Quantity supplied of financial capital} = \text{Quantity demanded of financial capital}$$
$$\text{Private savings} + \text{Inflow of foreign savings} = \text{Private investment} + \text{Government budget deficit}$$
$$S + (M - X) = I + (G - T)$$

Governments often spend more than they receive in taxes and, therefore, public savings (T – G) is negative. This causes a need to borrow money in the amount of (G – T) instead of adding to the nation's savings. If this is the case, governments can be viewed as demanders of financial capital instead of suppliers. So, in algebraic terms, the national savings and investment identity can be rewritten like this:

$$\text{Private investment} = \text{Private savings} + \text{Public savings} + \text{Trade deficit}$$
$$I = S + (T - G) + (M - X)$$

Let's call this equation 2. A change in any part of the national saving and investment identity must be accompanied by offsetting changes in at least one other part of the equation because the equality of quantity supplied and quantity demanded is always assumed to hold. If the government budget deficit changes, then either private saving or investment or the trade balance—or some combination of the three—must change as well. Figure 17.2 shows the possible effects.

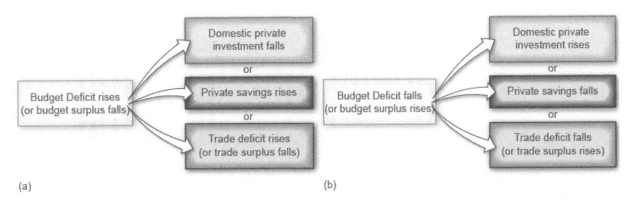

Figure 17.2 Effects of Change in Budget Surplus or Deficit on Investment, Savings, and The Trade Balance Chart (a) shows the potential results when the budget deficit rises (or budget surplus falls). Chart (b) shows the potential results when the budget deficit falls (or budget surplus rises).

What about Budget Surpluses and Trade Surpluses?

The national saving and investment identity must always hold true because, by definition, the quantity supplied and quantity demanded in the financial capital market must always be equal. However, the formula will look somewhat different if the government budget is in deficit rather than surplus or if the balance of trade is in surplus rather than deficit. For example, in 1999 and 2000, the U.S. government had budget surpluses, although the economy was still experiencing trade deficits. When the government was running budget surpluses, it was acting as a saver rather than a borrower, and supplying rather than demanding financial capital. As a result, the national saving and investment identity during this time would be more properly written:

$$\text{Quantity supplied of financial capital} = \text{Quantity demanded of financial capital}$$
$$\text{Private savings} + \text{Trade deficit} + \text{Government surplus} = \text{Private investment}$$
$$S + (M - X) + (T - G) = I$$

Let's call this equation 3. Notice that this expression is mathematically the same as equation 2 except the savings and investment sides of the identity have simply flipped sides.

During the 1960s, the U.S. government was often running a budget deficit, but the economy was typically running trade surpluses. Since a trade surplus means that an economy is experiencing a net outflow of financial capital, the national saving and investment identity would be written:

Quantity supplied of financial capital = Quantity demanded of financial capital

Private savings = Private investment + Outflow of foreign savings + Government budget deficit

$$S = I + (X - M) + (G - T)$$

Instead of the balance of trade representing part of the supply of financial capital, which occurs with a trade deficit, a trade surplus represents an outflow of financial capital leaving the domestic economy and being invested elsewhere in the world.

Quantity supplied of financial capital = Quantity demanded of financial capital demand

Private savings = Private investment + Government budget deficit + Trade surplus

$$S = I + (G - T) + (X - M)$$

The point to this parade of equations is that the national saving and investment identity is assumed to always hold. So when you write these relationships, it is important to engage your brain and think about what is on the supply side and what is on the demand side of the financial capital market before you put pencil to paper.

As can be seen in **Figure 17.3**, the Office of Management and Budget shows that the United States has consistently run budget deficits since 1977, with the exception of 1999 and 2000. What is alarming is the dramatic increase in budget deficits that has occurred since 2008, which in part reflects declining tax revenues and increased safety net expenditures due to the Great Recession. (Recall that T is net taxes. When the government must transfer funds back to individuals for safety net expenditures like Social Security and unemployment benefits, budget deficits rise.) These deficits have implications for the future health of the U.S. economy.

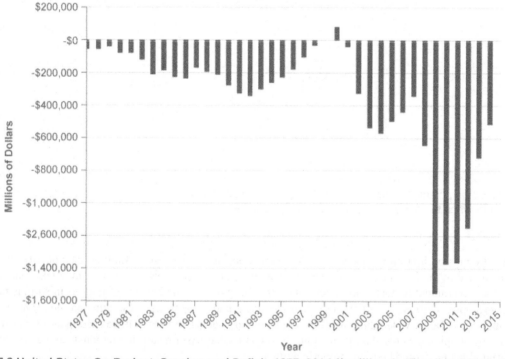

Figure 17.3 United States On-Budget, Surplus, and Deficit, 1977–2014 ($ millions)   The United States has run a budget deficit for over 30 years, with the exception of 1999 and 2000. Military expenditures, entitlement programs, and the decrease in tax revenue coupled with increased safety net support during the Great Recession are major contributors to the dramatic increases in the deficit after 2008. (Source: Table 1.1, "Summary of Receipts, Outlays, and Surpluses or Deficits," https://www.whitehouse.gov/omb/budget/Historicals)

A rising budget deficit may result in a fall in domestic investment, a rise in private savings, or a rise in the trade deficit. The following modules discuss each of these possible effects in more detail.

17.2 | Fiscal Policy, Investment, and Economic Growth

By the end of this section, you will be able to:
- Explain crowding out and its effect on physical capital investment
- Explain the relationship between budget deficits and interest rates
- Identify why economic growth is tied to investments in physical capital, human capital, and technology

The underpinnings of economic growth are investments in physical capital, human capital, and technology, all set in an economic environment where firms and individuals can react to the incentives provided by well-functioning markets and flexible prices. Government borrowing can reduce the financial capital available for private firms to invest in physical capital. But government spending can also encourage certain elements of long-term growth, such as spending on roads or water systems, on education, or on research and development that creates new technology.

Crowding Out Physical Capital Investment

A larger budget deficit will increase demand for financial capital. If private saving and the trade balance remain the same, then less financial capital will be available for private investment in physical capital. When government borrowing soaks up available financial capital and leaves less for private investment in physical capital, the result is known as crowding out.

To understand the potential impact of crowding out, consider the situation of the U.S. economy before the exceptional circumstances of the recession that started in late 2007. In 2005, for example, the budget deficit was roughly 4% of GDP. Private investment by firms in the U.S. economy has hovered in the range of 14% to 18% of GDP in recent decades. However, in any given year, roughly half of U.S. investment in physical capital just replaces machinery and equipment that has worn out or become technologically obsolete. Only about half represents an increase in the total quantity of physical capital in the economy. So investment in new physical capital in any year is about 7% to 9% of GDP. In this situation, even U.S. budget deficits in the range of 4% of GDP can potentially crowd out a substantial share of new investment spending. Conversely, a smaller budget deficit (or an increased budget surplus) increases the pool of financial capital available for private investment.

Link It Up

Visit this website (http://openstaxcollege.org/l/debtclock) to view the "U.S. Debt Clock."

The patterns of U.S. budget deficits and private investment since 1980 are shown in **Figure 17.4**. If greater government deficits lead to less private investment in physical capital, and reduced government deficits or budget surpluses lead to more investment in physical capital, these two lines should move up and down at the same time. This pattern occurred in the late 1990s and early 2000s. The U.S. federal budget went from a deficit of 2.2% of GDP in 1995 to a budget surplus of 2.4% of GDP in 2000—a swing of 4.6% of GDP. From 1995 to 2000, private investment in physical capital rose from 15% to 18% of GDP—a rise of 3% of GDP. Then, when the U.S. government again started running budget deficits in the early 2000s, less financial capital became available for private investment, and the rate of private investment fell back to about 15% of GDP by 2003.

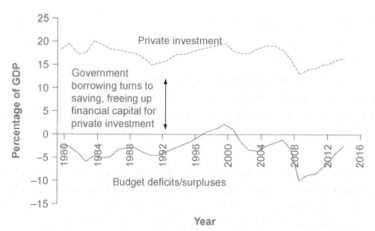

Figure 17.4 U.S. Budget Deficits/Surpluses and Private Investment The connection between private savings and flows of international capital plays a role in budget deficits and surpluses. Consequently, government borrowing and private investment sometimes rise and fall together. For example, the 1990s show a pattern in which reduced government borrowing helped to reduce crowding out so that more funds were available for private investment.

This argument does not claim that a government's budget deficits will exactly shadow its national rate of private investment; after all, private saving and inflows of foreign financial investment must also be taken into account. In the mid-1980s, for example, government budget deficits increased substantially without a corresponding drop off in private investment. In 2009, nonresidential private fixed investment dropped by $300 billion from its previous level of $1,941 billion in 2008, primarily because, during a recession, firms lack both the funds and the incentive to invest. Investment growth between 2009 and 2014 averaged approximately 5.9% to $2,210.5 billion—only slightly above its 2008 level, according to the Bureau of Economic Analysis. During that same period, interest rates dropped from 3.94% to less than a quarter percent as the Federal Reserve took dramatic action to prevent a depression by increasing the money supply through lowering short-term interest rates. The "crowding out" of private investment due to government borrowing to finance expenditures appears to have been suspended during the Great Recession. However, as the economy improves and interest rates rise, borrowing by the government may potentially create pressure on interest rates.

The Interest Rate Connection

Assume that government borrowing of substantial amounts will have an effect on the quantity of private investment. How will this affect interest rates in financial markets? In **Figure 17.5**, the original equilibrium (E_0) where the demand curve (D_0) for financial capital intersects with the supply curve (S_0) occurs at an interest rate of 5% and an equilibrium quantity equal to 20% of GDP. However, as the government budget deficit increases, the demand curve for financial capital shifts from D_0 to D_1. The new equilibrium (E_1) occurs at an interest rate of 6% and an equilibrium quantity of 21% of GDP.

Figure 17.5 Budget Deficits and Interest Rates   In the financial market, an increase in government borrowing can shift the demand curve for financial capital to the right from D_0 to D_1. As the equilibrium interest rate shifts from E_0 to E_1, the interest rate rises from 5% to 6% in this example. The higher interest rate is one economic mechanism by which government borrowing can crowd out private investment.

A survey of economic studies on the connection between government borrowing and interest rates in the U.S. economy suggests that an increase of 1% in the budget deficit will lead to a rise in interest rates of between 0.5 and 1.0%, other factors held equal. In turn, a higher interest rate tends to discourage firms from making physical capital investments. One reason government budget deficits crowd out private investment, therefore, is the increase in interest rates. There are, however, economic studies that show a limited connection between the two (at least in the United States), but as the budget deficit grows, the dangers of rising interest rates become more real.

At this point, you may wonder about the Federal Reserve. After all, can the Federal Reserve not use expansionary monetary policy to reduce interest rates, or in this case, to prevent interest rates from rising? This useful question emphasizes the importance of considering how fiscal and monetary policies work in relation to each other. Imagine a central bank faced with a government that is running large budget deficits, causing a rise in interest rates and crowding out private investment. If the budget deficits are increasing aggregate demand when the economy is already producing near potential GDP, threatening an inflationary increase in price levels, the central bank may react with a contractionary monetary policy. In this situation, the higher interest rates from the government borrowing would be made even higher by contractionary monetary policy, and the government borrowing might crowd out a great deal of private investment.

On the other hand, if the budget deficits are increasing aggregate demand when the economy is producing substantially less than potential GDP, an inflationary increase in the price level is not much of a danger and the central bank might react with expansionary monetary policy. In this situation, higher interest rates from government borrowing would be largely offset by lower interest rates from expansionary monetary policy, and there would be little crowding out of private investment.

However, even a central bank cannot erase the overall message of the national savings and investment identity. If government borrowing rises, then private investment must fall, or private saving must rise, or the trade deficit must fall. By reacting with contractionary or expansionary monetary policy, the central bank can only help to determine which of these outcomes is likely.

Public Investment in Physical Capital

Government can invest in physical capital directly: roads and bridges; water supply and sewers; seaports and airports; schools and hospitals; plants that generate electricity, like hydroelectric dams or windmills; telecommunications facilities; and weapons used by the military. In 2014, the U.S. federal government budget for Fiscal Year 2014 shows that the United States spent about $92 billion on transportation, including highways, mass transit, and airports. Table 17.1 shows the total outlay for 2014 for major public physical capital investment by the federal government in the United States. Physical capital related to the military or to residences where people live is omitted from this table, because the focus here is on public investments that have a direct effect on raising output in the private sector.

Type of Public Physical Capital	Federal Outlays 2014 ($ millions)
Transportation	$91,915
Community and regional development	$20,670
Natural resources and the environment	$36,171
Education, training, employment, and social services	$90,615
Other	$37,282
Total	$276,653

Table 17.1 Grants for Major Physical Capital Investment, 2014

Public physical capital investment of this sort can increase the output and productivity of the economy. An economy with reliable roads and electricity will be able to produce more. But it is hard to quantify how much government investment in physical capital will benefit the economy, because government responds to political as well as economic incentives. When a firm makes an investment in physical capital, it is subject to the discipline of the market: If it does not receive a positive return on investment, the firm may lose money or even go out of business.

In some cases, lawmakers make investments in physical capital as a way of spending money in the districts of key politicians. The result may be unnecessary roads or office buildings. Even if a project is useful and necessary, it might be done in a way that is excessively costly, because local contractors who make campaign contributions to politicians appreciate the extra business. On the other hand, governments sometimes do not make the investments they should because a decision to spend on infrastructure does not need to just make economic sense; it must be politically popular as well. Managing public investment so that it is done in a cost-effective way can be difficult.

If a government decides to finance an investment in public physical capital with higher taxes or lower government spending in other areas, it need not worry that it is directly crowding out private investment. Indirectly however, higher household taxes could cut down on the level of private savings available and have a similar effect. If a government decides to finance an investment in public physical capital by borrowing, it may end up increasing the quantity of public physical capital at the cost of crowding out investment in private physical capital, which is more beneficial to the economy would be dependent on the project being considered.

Public Investment in Human Capital

In most countries, the government plays a large role in society's investment in human capital through the education system. A highly educated and skilled workforce contributes to a higher rate of economic growth. For the low-income nations of the world, additional investment in human capital seems likely to increase productivity and growth. For the United States, tough questions have been raised about how much increases in government spending on education will improve the actual level of education.

Among economists, discussions of education reform often begin with some uncomfortable facts. As shown in **Figure 17.6**, spending per student for kindergarten through grade 12 (K–12) increased substantially in real dollars through 2010. The U.S. Census Bureau reports that current spending per pupil for elementary and secondary education rose from $5,001 in 1998 to $10,608 in 2012. However, as measured by standardized tests like the SAT, the level of student academic achievement has barely budged in recent decades. Indeed, on international tests, U.S. students lag behind students from many other countries. (Of course, test scores are an imperfect measure of education for a variety of reasons. It would be difficult, however, to argue that there are not real problems in the U.S. education system and that the tests are just inaccurate.)

Figure 17.6 Total Spending for Elementary, Secondary, and Vocational Education (1998–2014) in the United States   The graph shows that government spending on education was continually increasing up until 2006 where it leveled off until 2008 when it increased dramatically. Since 2010, spending has steadily decreased. (Source: Office of Management and Budget)

The fact that increased financial resources have not brought greater measurable gains in student performance has led some education experts to question whether the problems may be due to structure, not just to the resources spent.

Other government programs seek to increase human capital either before or after the K–12 education system. Programs for early childhood education, like the federal **Head Start program**, are directed at families where the parents may have limited educational and financial resources. Government also offers substantial support for universities and colleges. For example, in the United States about 60% of students take at least a few college or university classes beyond the high school level. In Germany and Japan, about half of all students take classes beyond the comparable high school level. In the countries of Latin America, only about one student in four takes classes beyond the high school level, and in the nations of sub-Saharan Africa, only about one student in 20.

Not all spending on educational human capital needs to happen through the government: many college students in the United States pay a substantial share of the cost of their education. If low-income countries of the world are going to experience a widespread increase in their education levels for grade-school children, government spending seems likely to play a substantial role. For the U.S. economy, and for other high-income countries, the primary focus at this time is more on how to get a bigger return from existing spending on education and how to improve the performance of the average high school graduate, rather than dramatic increases in education spending.

How Fiscal Policy Can Improve Technology

Research and development (R&D) efforts are the lifeblood of new technology. According to the National Science Foundation, federal outlays for research, development, and physical plant improvements to various governmental agencies have remained at an average of 8.8% of GDP. About one-fifth of U.S. R&D spending goes to defense and space-oriented research. Although defense-oriented R&D spending may sometimes produce consumer-oriented spinoffs, R&D that is aimed at producing new weapons is less likely to benefit the civilian economy than direct civilian R&D spending.

Fiscal policy can encourage R&D using either direct spending or tax policy. Government could spend more on the R&D that is carried out in government laboratories, as well as expanding federal R&D grants to universities and colleges, nonprofit organizations, and the private sector. By 2014, the federal share of R&D outlays totaled $135.5 billion, or about 4% of the federal government's total budget outlays, according to data from the National Science Foundation. Fiscal policy can also support R&D through tax incentives, which allow firms to reduce their tax bill as they increase spending on research and development.

Summary of Fiscal Policy, Investment, and Economic Growth

Investment in physical capital, human capital, and new technology is essential for long-term economic growth, as summarized in Table 17.2. In a market-oriented economy, private firms will undertake most of the investment in physical capital, and fiscal policy should seek to avoid a long series of outsized budget deficits that might crowd out such investment. The effects of many growth-oriented policies will be seen very gradually over time, as students are better educated, physical capital investments are made, and new technologies are invented and implemented.

	Physical Capital	**Human Capital**	**New Technology**
Private Sector	New investment in property and equipment	On-the-job training	Research and development
Public Sector	Public infrastructure	Public education Job training	Research and development encouraged through private sector incentives and direct spending.

Table 17.2 Investment Role of Public and Private Sector in a Market Economy

17.3 | How Government Borrowing Affects Private Saving

By the end of this section, you will be able to:

- Apply Ricardian equivalence to evaluate how government borrowing affects private saving
- Interpret a graphic representation of Ricardian equivalence

A change in government budgets may impact private saving. Imagine that people watch government budgets and adjust their savings accordingly. For example, whenever the government runs a budget deficit, people might reason: "Well, a higher budget deficit means that I'm just going to owe more taxes in the future to pay off all that government borrowing, so I'll start saving now." If the government runs budget surpluses, people might reason: "With these budget surpluses (or lower budget deficits), interest rates are falling, so that saving is less attractive. Moreover, with a budget surplus the country will be able to afford a tax cut sometime in the future. I won't bother saving as much now."

The theory that rational private households might shift their saving to offset government saving or borrowing is known as **Ricardian equivalence** because the idea has intellectual roots in the writings of the early nineteenth-century economist David Ricardo (1772–1823). If Ricardian equivalence holds completely true, then in the national saving and investment identity, any change in budget deficits or budget surpluses would be completely offset by a corresponding change in private saving. As a result, changes in government borrowing would have no effect at all on either physical capital investment or trade balances.

In practice, the private sector only sometimes and partially adjusts its savings behavior to offset government budget deficits and surpluses. **Figure 17.7** shows the patterns of U.S. government budget deficits and surpluses and the rate of private saving—which includes saving by both households and firms—since 1980. The connection between the two is not at all obvious. In the mid-1980s, for example, government budget deficits were quite large, but there is no corresponding surge of private saving. However, when budget deficits turn to surpluses in the late 1990s, there is a simultaneous decline in private saving. When budget deficits get very large in 2008 and 2009, on the other hand, there is some sign of a rise in saving. A variety of statistical studies based on the U.S. experience suggests that when government borrowing increases by $1, private saving rises by about 30 cents. A World Bank study done in the late 1990s, looking at government budgets and private saving behavior in countries around the world, found a similar result.

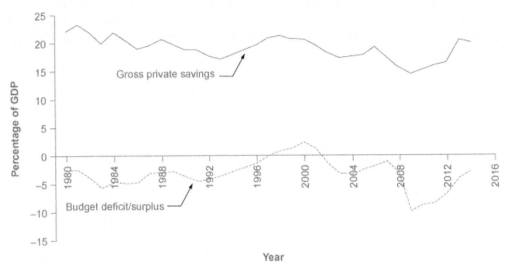

Figure 17.7 U.S. Budget Deficits and Private Savings The theory of Ricardian equivalence suggests that any increase in government borrowing will be offset by additional private saving, while any decrease in government borrowing will be offset by reduced private saving. Sometimes this theory holds true, and sometimes it does not hold true at all. (Source: Bureau of Economic Analysis and Federal Reserve Economic Data)

So private saving does increase to some extent when governments run large budget deficits, and private saving falls when governments reduce deficits or run large budget surpluses. However, the offsetting effects of private saving compared to government borrowing are much less than one-to-one. In addition, this effect can vary a great deal from country to country, from time to time, and over the short run and the long run.

If the funding for a larger budget deficit comes from international financial investors, then a budget deficit may be accompanied by a trade deficit. In some countries, this pattern of a **twin deficits** has set the stage for international financial investors first to send their funds to a country and cause an appreciation of its exchange rate and then to pull their funds out and cause a depreciation of the exchange rate and a financial crisis as well. It depends on whether funding comes from international financial investors.

17.4 | Fiscal Policy and the Trade Balance

By the end of this section, you will be able to:
- Discuss twin deficits as they related to budget and trade deficit
- Explain the relationship between budget deficits and exchange rates
- Explain the relationship between budget deficits and inflation
- Identify causes of recessions

Government budget balances can affect the trade balance. As The Keynesian Perspective chapter discusses, a net inflow of foreign financial investment always accompanies a trade deficit, while a net outflow of financial investment always accompanies a trade surplus. One way to understand the connection from budget deficits to trade deficits is that when government creates a budget deficit with some combination of tax cuts or spending increases, it will increase aggregate demand in the economy, and some of that increase in aggregate demand will result in a higher level of imports. A higher level of imports, with exports remaining fixed, will cause a larger trade deficit. That means foreigners' holdings of dollars increase as Americans purchase more imported goods. Foreigners use those dollars to invest in the United States, which leads to an inflow of foreign investment. One possible source of funding our budget deficit is foreigners buying Treasury securities that are sold by the U.S. government. So a budget deficit is often accompanied by a trade deficit.

Twin Deficits?

In the mid-1980s, it was common to hear economists and even newspaper articles refer to the twin deficits, as the budget deficit and trade deficit both grew substantially. **Figure 17.8** shows the pattern. The federal budget deficit went from 2.6% of GDP in 1981 to 5.1% of GDP in 1985—a drop of 2.5% of GDP. Over that time, the trade deficit moved from 0.5% in 1981 to 2.9% in 1985—a drop of 2.4% of GDP. In the mid-1980s, the considerable increase in government borrowing was matched by an inflow of foreign investment capital, so the government budget deficit and the trade deficit moved together.

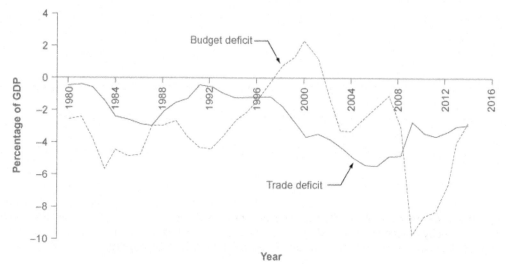

Figure 17.8 U.S. Budget Deficits and Trade Deficits   In the 1980s, the budget deficit and the trade deficit declined at the same time. However, since then, the deficits have stopped being twins. The trade deficit grew smaller in the early 1990s as the budget deficit increased, and then the trade deficit grew larger in the late 1990s as the budget deficit turned into a surplus. In the first half of the 2000s, both budget and trade deficits increased. But in 2009, the trade deficit declined as the budget deficit increased.

Of course, no one should expect the budget deficit and trade deficit to move in lockstep, because the other parts of the national saving and investment identity—investment and private savings—will often change as well. In the late 1990s, for example, the government budget balance turned from deficit to surplus, but the trade deficit remained large and growing. During this time, the inflow of foreign financial investment was supporting a surge of physical capital investment by U.S. firms. In the first half of the 2000s, the budget and trade deficits again increased together, but in 2009, the budget deficit increased while the trade deficit declined. The budget deficit and the trade deficits are related to each other, but they are more like cousins than twins.

Budget Deficits and Exchange Rates

Exchange rates can also help to explain why budget deficits are linked to trade deficits. **Figure 17.9** shows a situation using the exchange rate for the U.S. dollar, measured in euros. At the original equilibrium (E_0), where the demand for U.S. dollars (D_0) intersects with the supply of U.S. dollars (S_0) on the foreign exchange market, the exchange rate is 0.9 euros per U.S. dollar and the equilibrium quantity traded in the market is $100 billion per day (which was roughly the quantity of dollar–euro trading in exchange rate markets in the mid-2000s). Then the U.S. budget deficit rises and foreign financial investment provides the source of funds for that budget deficit.

International financial investors, as a group, will demand more U.S. dollars on foreign exchange markets to purchase the U.S. government bonds, and they will supply fewer of the U.S. dollars that they already hold in these markets. Demand for U.S. dollars on the foreign exchange market shifts from D_0 to D_1 and the supply of U.S. dollars falls from S_0 to S_1. At the new equilibrium (E_1), the exchange rate has appreciated to 1.05 euros per dollar while, in this example, the quantity of dollars traded remains the same.

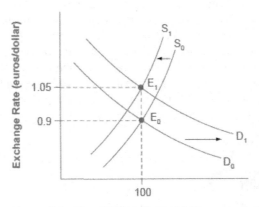

Figure 17.9 Budget Deficits and Exchange Rates Imagine that the U.S. government increases its borrowing and the funds come from European financial investors. To purchase U.S. government bonds, those European investors will need to demand more U.S. dollars on foreign exchange markets, causing the demand for U.S. dollars to shift to the right from D_0 to D_1. European financial investors as a group will also be less likely to supply U.S. dollars to the foreign exchange markets, causing the supply of U.S. dollars to shift from S_0 to S_1. The equilibrium exchange rate strengthens from 0.9 euro/ dollar at E_0 to 1.05 euros/dollar at E_1.

A stronger exchange rate, of course, makes it more difficult for exporters to sell their goods abroad while making imports cheaper, so a trade deficit (or a reduced trade surplus) results. Thus, a budget deficit can easily result in an inflow of foreign financial capital, a stronger exchange rate, and a trade deficit.

You can also imagine this appreciation of the exchange rate as being driven by interest rates. As explained earlier in **Budget Deficits and Interest Rates in Fiscal Policy, Investment, and Economic Growth**, a budget deficit increases demand in markets for domestic financial capital, raising the domestic interest rate. A higher interest rate will attract an inflow of foreign financial capital, and appreciate the exchange rate in response to the increase in demand for U.S. dollars by foreign investors and a decrease in supply of U. S. dollars. Because of higher interest rates in the United States, Americans find U.S. bonds more attractive than foreign bonds. When Americans are buying fewer foreign bonds, they are supplying fewer U.S. dollars. The depreciation of the U.S. dollar leads to a larger trade deficit (or reduced surplus). The connections between inflows of foreign investment capital, interest rates, and exchange rates are all just different ways of drawing the same economic connections: a larger budget deficit can result in a larger trade deficit, although the connection should not be expected to be one-to-one.

From Budget Deficits to International Economic Crisis

The economic story of how an outflow of international financial capital can cause a deep recession is laid out, step-by-step, in the **Exchange Rates and International Capital Flows** chapter. When international financial investors decide to withdraw their funds from a country like Turkey, they increase the supply of the Turkish lira and reduce the demand for lira, depreciating the lira exchange rate. When firms and the government in a country like Turkey borrow money in international financial markets, they typically do so in stages. First, banks in Turkey borrow in a widely used currency like U.S. dollars or euros, then convert those U.S. dollars to lira, and then lend the money to borrowers in Turkey. If the value of the lira exchange rate depreciates, then Turkey's banks will find it impossible to repay the international loans that are in U.S. dollars or euros.

The combination of less foreign investment capital and banks that are bankrupt can sharply reduce aggregate demand, which causes a deep recession. Many countries around the world have experienced this kind of recession in recent years: along with Turkey in 2002, this general pattern was followed by Mexico in 1995, Thailand and countries across East Asia in 1997–1998, Russia in 1998, and Argentina in 2002. In many of these countries, large government budget deficits played a role in setting the stage for the financial crisis. A moderate increase in a budget deficit that leads to a moderate increase in a trade deficit and a moderate appreciation of the exchange rate is not necessarily a cause for concern. But beyond some point that is hard to define in advance, a series of large budget deficits can become a cause for concern among international investors.

One reason for concern is that extremely large budget deficits mean that aggregate demand may shift so far to the right as to cause high inflation. The example of Turkey is a situation where very large budget deficits brought inflation rates well into double digits. In addition, very large budget deficits at some point begin to raise a fear that the borrowing will not be repaid. In the last 175 years, the government of Turkey has been unable to pay its debts and defaulted on its loans six times. Brazil's government has been unable to pay its debts and defaulted on its loans seven times; Venezuela, nine times; and Argentina, five times. The risk of high inflation or a default on repaying international loans will worry international investors, since both factors imply that the rate of return on their investments in that country may end up lower than expected. If international investors start withdrawing the funds from a country rapidly, the scenario of less investment, a depreciated exchange rate, widespread bank failure, and deep recession can occur. The following Clear It Up feature explains other impacts of large deficits.

What are the risks of chronic large deficits in the United States?

If a government runs large budget deficits for a sustained period of time, what can go wrong? According to a recent report by the Brookings Institution, a key risk of a large budget deficit is that government debt may grow too high compared to the country's GDP growth. As debt grows, the national savings rate will decline, leaving less available in financial capital for private investment. The impact of chronically large budget deficits is as follows:

- As the population ages, there will be an increasing demand for government services that may cause higher government deficits. Government borrowing and its interest payments will pull resources away from domestic investment in human capital and physical capital that is essential to economic growth.

- Interest rates may start to rise so that the cost of financing government debt will rise as well, creating pressure on the government to reduce its budget deficits through spending cuts and tax increases. These steps will be politically painful, and they will also have a contractionary effect on aggregate demand in the economy.

- Rising percentage of debt to GDP will create uncertainty in the financial and global markets that might cause a country to resort to inflationary tactics to reduce the real value of the debt outstanding. This will decrease real wealth and damage confidence in the country's ability to manage its spending. After all, if the government has borrowed at a fixed interest rate of, say, 5%, and it lets inflation rise above that 5%, then it will effectively be able to repay its debt at a negative real interest rate.

The conventional reasoning suggests that the relationship between sustained deficits that lead to high levels of government debt and long-term growth is negative. How significant this relationship is, how big an issue it is compared to other macroeconomic issues, and the direction of causality, is less clear.

What remains important to acknowledge is that the relationship between debt and growth is negative and that for some countries, the relationship may be stronger than in others. It is also important to acknowledge the direction of causality: does high debt cause slow growth, slow growth cause high debt, or are both high debt and slow growth the result of third factors? In our analysis, we have argued simply that high debt causes slow growth. There may be more to this debate than we have space to discuss here.

Using Fiscal Policy to Address Trade Imbalances

If a nation is experiencing the inflow of foreign investment capital associated with a trade deficit because foreign investors are making long-term direct investments in firms, there may be no substantial reason for concern. After all, many low-income nations around the world would welcome direct investment by multinational firms that ties them more closely into the global networks of production and distribution of goods and services. In this case, the inflows of foreign investment capital and the trade deficit are attracted by the opportunities for a good rate of return on private sector investment in an economy.

However, governments should beware of a sustained pattern of high budget deficits and high trade deficits. The danger arises in particular when the inflow of foreign investment capital is not funding long-term physical capital investment by firms, but instead is short-term portfolio investment in government bonds. When inflows of foreign financial investment reach high levels, foreign financial investors will be on the alert for any reason to fear that the country's exchange rate may decline or the government may be unable to repay what it has borrowed on time. Just as a few falling rocks can trigger an avalanche; a relatively small piece of bad news about an economy can trigger an enormous outflow of short-term financial capital.

Reducing a nation's budget deficit will not always be a successful method of reducing its trade deficit, because other elements of the national saving and investment identity, like private saving or investment, may change instead. In those cases when the budget deficit is the main cause of the trade deficit, governments should take steps to reduce their budget deficits, lest they make their economy vulnerable to a rapid outflow of international financial capital that could bring a deep recession.

Bring it Home

Financing Higher Education

Over the period between 1982 and 2012, the increases in the cost of a college education had far outpaced that of the income of the typical American family. According to the research done by the President Obama's staff, the cost of education at a four-year public college increased by 257% compared to an increase in family incomes of only 16% over the prior 30 years. The ongoing debate over a balanced budget and proposed cutbacks accentuated the need to increase investment in human capital to grow the economy versus deepening the already significant debt levels of the U.S. government. In the summer of 2013, President Obama presented a plan to make college more affordable that included increasing Pell Grant awards and the number of recipients, caps on interest rates for student loans, and providing education tax credits. In addition, the plan includes an accountability method for institutions of higher education that focuses on completion rates and creates a College Scorecard. Whether or not all these initiatives come to fruition remains to be seen, but they are indicative of creative approaches that government can take to meet its obligation from both a public and fiscal policy perspective.

KEY TERMS

Head Start program a program for early childhood education directed at families with limited educational and financial resources.

Ricardian equivalence the theory that rational private households might shift their saving to offset government saving or borrowing

twin deficits deficits that occur when a country is running both a trade and a budget deficit

KEY CONCEPTS AND SUMMARY

17.1 How Government Borrowing Affects Investment and the Trade Balance
A change in any part of the national saving and investment identity suggests that if the government budget deficit changes, then either private savings, private investment in physical capital, or the trade balance—or some combination of the three—must change as well.

17.2 Fiscal Policy, Investment, and Economic Growth
Economic growth comes from a combination of investment in physical capital, human capital, and technology. Government borrowing can crowd out private sector investment in physical capital, but fiscal policy can also increase investment in publicly owned physical capital, human capital (education), and research and development. Possible methods for improving education and society's investment in human capital include spending more money on teachers and other educational resources, and reorganizing the education system to provide greater incentives for success. Methods for increasing research and development spending to generate new technology include direct government spending on R&D and tax incentives for businesses to conduct additional R&D.

17.3 How Government Borrowing Affects Private Saving
The theory of Ricardian equivalence holds that changes in government borrowing or saving will be offset by changes in private saving. Thus, higher budget deficits will be offset by greater private saving, while larger budget surpluses will be offset by greater private borrowing. If the theory holds true, then changes in government borrowing or saving would have no effect on private investment in physical capital or on the trade balance. However, empirical evidence suggests that the theory holds true only partially.

17.4 Fiscal Policy and the Trade Balance
The government need not balance its budget every year. However, a sustained pattern of large budget deficits over time risks causing several negative macroeconomic outcomes: a shift to the right in aggregate demand that causes an inflationary increase in the price level; crowding out private investment in physical capital in a way that slows down economic growth; and creating a dependence on inflows of international portfolio investment which can sometimes turn into outflows of foreign financial investment that can be injurious to a macroeconomy.

SELF-CHECK QUESTIONS

1. In a country, private savings equals 600, the government budget surplus equals 200, and the trade surplus equals 100. What is the level of private investment in this economy?

2. Assume an economy has a budget surplus of 1,000, private savings of 4,000, and investment of 5,000.
   a. Write out a national saving and investment identity for this economy.
   b. What will be the balance of trade in this economy?
   c. If the budget surplus changes to a budget deficit of 1000, with private saving and investment unchanged, what is the new balance of trade in this economy?

3. Why have many education experts recently placed an emphasis on altering the incentives faced by U.S. schools rather than on increasing their budgets? Without endorsing any of these proposals as especially good or bad, list some of the ways in which incentives for schools might be altered.

4. What are some steps the government can take to encourage research and development?

5. Imagine an economy in which Ricardian equivalence holds. This economy has a budget deficit of 50, a trade deficit of 20, private savings of 130, and investment of 100. If the budget deficit rises to 70, how are the other terms in the national saving and investment identity affected?

6. In the late 1990s, the U.S. government moved from a budget deficit to a budget surplus and the trade deficit in the U.S. economy grew substantially. Using the national saving and investment identity, what can you say about the direction in which saving and/or investment must have changed in this economy?

REVIEW QUESTIONS

7. Based on the national saving and investment identity, what are the three ways the macroeconomy might react to greater government budget deficits?

8. How would you expect larger budget deficits to affect private sector investment in physical capital? Why?

9. What are some of the ways fiscal policy might encourage economic growth?

10. What are some fiscal policies for improving a society's human capital?

11. What are some fiscal policies for improving the technologies that the economy will have to draw upon in the future?

12. Explain how cuts in funding for programs such as Head Start might affect the development of human capital in the United States.

13. What is the theory of Ricardian equivalence?

14. What does the concept of rationality have to do with Ricardian equivalence?

15. Under what conditions will a larger budget deficit cause a trade deficit?

CRITICAL THINKING QUESTIONS

16. Assume there is no discretionary increase in government spending. Explain how an improving economy will affect the budget balance and, in turn, investment and the trade balance.

17. Explain how decreased domestic investments that occur due to a budget deficit will affect future economic growth.

18. The U.S. government has shut down a number of times in recent history. Explain how a government shutdown will affect the variables in the national investment and savings identity. Could the shutdown affect the government budget deficit?

19. Explain why the government might prefer to provide incentives to private firms to do investment or research and development, rather than simply doing the spending itself?

20. Under what condition would crowding out not inhibit long-run economic growth? Under what condition would crowding out impede long-run economic growth?

21. What must take place for the government to run deficits without any crowding out?

22. Explain whether or not you agree with the premise of the Ricardian equivalence theory that rational people might reason: "Well, a higher budget deficit (surplus) means that I'm just going to owe more (less) taxes in the future to pay off all that government borrowing, so I'll start saving (spending) now." Why or why not?

23. Explain how a shift from a government budget deficit to a budget surplus might affect the exchange rate.

24. Describe how a plan for reducing the government deficit might affect a college student, a young professional, and a middle-income family.

PROBLEMS

25. During the most recent recession, some economists argued that the change in the interest rates that comes about due to deficit spending implied in the demand and supply of financial capital graph would not occur. A simple reason was that the government was stepping in to invest when private firms were not. Using a graph, explain how the deficit demand is offset by the use by government in investment.

26. Illustrate the concept of Ricardian equivalence using the demand and supply of financial capital graph.

27. Sketch a diagram of how a budget deficit causes a trade deficit. (*Hint*: Begin with what will happen to the exchange rate when foreigners demand more U.S. government debt.)

28. Sketch a diagram of how sustained budget deficits cause low economic growth.

29. Assume that you are employed by the government of Tanzania in 1964, a new nation recently independent from Britain. The Tanzanian parliament has decided that it will spend 10 million shillings on schools, roads, and healthcare for the year. You estimate that the net taxes for the year are eight million shillings. The difference will be financed by selling 10-year government bonds at 12% interest per year. The interest on outstanding bonds must be added to government expenditure each year. Assume that additional taxes are added to finance this increase in government expenditure so the gap between government spending is always two million. If the school, road, and healthcare budget are unchanged, compute the value of the accumulated debt in 10 years.

18 | Macroeconomic Policy Around the World

Figure 18.1 Looking for Work Job fairs and job centers are often available to help match people to jobs. This fair took place in the U.S. (Hawaii), a high-income country with policies to keep unemployment levels in check. Unemployment is an issue that has different causes in different countries, and is especially severe in the low- and middle-income economies around the world. (Credit: modification of work by Daniel Ramirez/Flickr Creative Commons)

Bring it Home

Youth Unemployment: Three Cases

Chad Harding, a young man from Cape Town, South Africa, completed school having done well on his exams. He had high hopes for the future. Like many young South Africans, however, he had difficulty finding a job. "I was just stuck at home waiting, waiting for something to come up," he said in a BBC interview in 2012. In South Africa 54.6% of young females and 47.2% of males are unemployed. In fact, the problem is not limited to South Africa. Seventy-three million of the world's youth aged 15 to 24 are currently unemployed, according to the International Labour Organization.

According to the *Wall Street Journal,* in India, 60% of the labor force is self-employed, largely because of labor market regulation. A recent World Development Report by The World Bank says that India's unemployed youth accounted for 9.9% of the youth work force in 2010. In Spain (a far richer country) in the same year, the female/male youth unemployment rate was 39.8% and 43.2% respectively.

Youth unemployment is a significant issue in many parts of the world. However, despite the apparent similarities in rates between South Africa, Spain, and India, macroeconomic policy solutions to decrease youth unemployment in these three countries are different. This chapter will look at macroeconomic policies around the world, specifically those related to reducing unemployment, promoting economic growth, and stable inflation and exchange rates. Then we will look again at the three cases of South Africa, Spain, and India.

Introduction to Macroeconomic Policy around the World

In this chapter, you will learn about:

- The Diversity of Countries and Economies across the World

- Improving Countries' Standards of Living

- Causes of Unemployment around the World

- Causes of Inflation in Various Countries and Regions

- Balance of Trade Concerns

There are extraordinary differences in the composition and performance of economies across the world. What explains these differences? Are countries motivated by similar goals when it comes to macroeconomic policy? Can we apply the same macroeconomic framework developed in this text to understand the performance of these countries? Let's take each of these questions in turn.

Explaining differences: Recall from **Unemployment** that we explained the difference in composition and performance of economies by appealing to an aggregate production function. We argued that the diversity of average incomes across the world was explained by differences in productivity, which in turn were affected by inputs such as capital deepening, human capital, and "technology." Every economy has its own distinctive economic characteristics, institutions, history, and political realities, which imply that access to these "ingredients" will vary by country and so will economic performance.

For example, South Korea invested heavily in education and technology to increase agricultural productivity in the early 1950s. Some of this investment came from its historical relationship with the United States. As a result of these and many other institutions, its economy has managed to converge to the levels of income in leading economies like Japan and the United States.

Similar goals and frameworks: Many economies that have performed well in terms of per capita income have—for better or worse—been motivated by a similar goal: to maintain the quality of life of their citizens. Quality of life is a broad term, but as you can imagine it includes but is not limited to such things as low level of unemployment, price stability (low levels of inflation), and the ability to trade. These seem to be universal macroeconomic goals as discussed in **The Macroeconomic Perspective**. No country would argue against them. To study macroeconomic policy around the world, we begin by comparing standards of living. In keeping with these goals, we also look at indicators such as unemployment, inflation, and the balance of trade policies across countries. Remember that every country has had a diverse set of experiences; therefore although our goals may be similar, each country may well require macroeconomic policies tailored to its circumstances.

Link It Up 🔗

For more reading on the topic of youth unemployment, visit this website (http://openstaxcollege.org/l/genjobless) to read "Generation Jobless" in the *Economist*.

18.1 | The Diversity of Countries and Economies across the World

By the end of this section, you will be able to:
- Analyze GDP per capita as a measure of the diversity of international standards of living
- Identify what classifies a country as low-income, middle-income, or high-income
- Explain how standards of living are influenced by geography, demographics, industry structure, and economic institutions

The national economies that make up the global economy are remarkably diverse. Let us use one key indicator of the standard of living, GDP per capita, to quantify this diversity. You will quickly see that quantifying this diversity is fraught with challenges and limitations. As explained in **The Macroeconomic Perspective**, we must consider using purchasing power parity or "international dollars" to convert average incomes into comparable units. Purchasing power parity, as formally defined in **Exchange Rates and International Capital Flows**, takes into account the fact that prices of the same good are different across countries.

The Macroeconomic Perspective explained how to measure GDP, the challenges of using GDP to compare standards of living, and the difficulty of confusing economic size with distribution. In China's case, for example, China ranks as the second largest global economy, second to only the United States, with Japan being third. But, when we take China's GDP of $9.2 trillion and divide it by its population of 1.4 billion, then the per capita GDP is only $6,900, which is significantly lower than that of Japan, at $38,500, and that of the United States, at $52,800. Measurement issues aside, it's worth repeating that the goal, then, is to not only increase GDP, but to strive toward increased GDP per capita to increase overall standards of living for individuals. As we have learned from **Economic Growth**, this can be achieved at the national level by designing policies that increase worker productivity, deepen capital, and advance technology.

GDP per capita also allows us to rank countries into high-, middle-, or low-income groups. Low-income countries are those with $1,025 per capita GDP per year; middle-income countries have a per capita GDP between $1,025 and $12,475; while high-income countries have over $12,475 per year per capita income. As seen in **Table 18.1** and **Figure 18.2**, high-income countries earn 68% of world income, but represent just 12% of the global population. Low-income countries earn 1% of total world income, but represent 18.5% of global population.

Ranking based on GDP/capita	GDP (in billions)	% of Global GDP	Population	% of Global Population
Low income ($1,025 or less)	$612.7	0.8%	848,700,000	11.8%
Middle income ($1,025 - $12,475)	$23,930	31.7%	4,970,000,000	69.4%

Table 18.1 World Income versus Global Population (Source:http://databank.worldbank.org/data/views/reports/tableview.aspx?isshared=true&ispopular=series&pid=20)

Ranking based on GDP/capita	GDP (in billions)	% of Global GDP	Population	% of Global Population
High income (more than $12,475)	$51,090,000,000	67.5%	1,306,000,000	18.8%
World Total income	*$75,592,941*		*7,162,119,434*	

Table 18.1 World Income versus Global Population   (Source:http://databank.worldbank.org/data/views/reports/tableview.aspx?isshared=true&ispopular=series&pid=20)

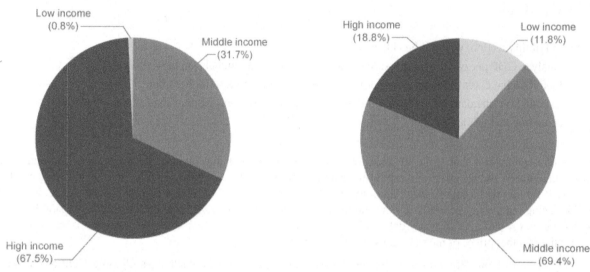

(a) Percentage of global GDP by country income   (b) Percentage of population by country income

Figure 18.2 Percent of Global GDP and Percent of Population The pie charts show the GDP (from 2011) for countries categorized into low, middle, or high income. Low-income are those earning less than $1,025 (less than 1% of global income). They represent 18.5% of the world population. Middle-income countries are those with per capita income of $1,025–$12,475 (31.1% of global income). They represent 69.5% of world population. High-income countries have 68.3% of global income and 12% of the world's population. (Source: http://databank.worldbank.org/data/views/reports/tableview.aspx?isshared=true&ispopular=series&pid=20)

An overview of the regional averages of GDP per person for developing countries, measured in comparable international dollars as well as population in 2008 (**Figure 18.3**), shows that the differences across these regions are stark. As **Table 18.2** shows, nominal GDP per capita in 2012 for the 581.4 million people living in Latin America and the Caribbean region was $9,190, which far exceeds that of South Asia and sub-Saharan Africa. In turn, people in the high-income nations of the world, such as those who live in the European Union nations or North America, have a per capita GDP three to four times that of the people of Latin America. To put things in perspective, North America and the European Union have slightly more than 9% of the world's population, but they produce and consume close to 70% of the world's GDP.

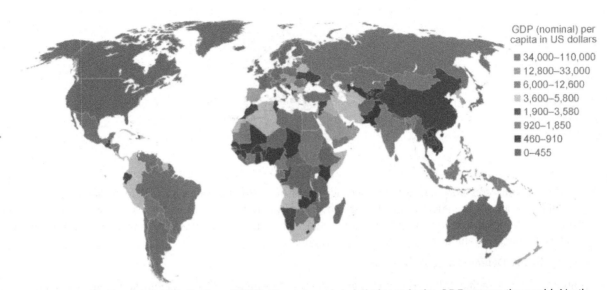

Figure 18.3 GDP Per Capita in U.S. Dollars (2008) There is a clear imbalance in the GDP across the world. North America, Australia, and Western Europe have the highest GDPs while large areas of the world have dramatically lower GDPs. (Credit: modification of work by Bsrboy/Wikimedia Commons)

	Population (in millions)	**GDP Per Capita**
East Asia and Pacific	2,006	$5,536
South Asia	1,671	$1,482
Sub-Saharan Africa	936.1	$1,657
Latin America and Caribbean	588	$9,536
Middle East and North Africa	345.4	$3,456
Europe and Central Asia	272.2	$7,118

Table 18.2 Regional Comparisons of Nominal GDP per Capita and Population in 2013 (Source: http://databank.worldbank.org/data/home.aspx)

Such comparisons between regions are admittedly rough. After all, per capita GDP cannot fully capture the quality of life. Many other factors have a large impact on the standard of living, like health, education, human rights, crime and personal safety, and environmental quality. These measures also reveal very wide differences in the standard of living across the regions of the world. Much of this is correlated with per capita income, but there are exceptions. For example, life expectancy at birth in many low-income regions approximates those who are more affluent. The data also illustrate that nobody can claim to have perfect standards of living. For instance, despite very high income levels, there is still undernourishment in Europe and North America.

Link It Up ⚭

Economists know that there are many factors that contribute to your standard of living. People in high-income countries may have very little time due to heavy workloads and may feel disconnected from their community. Lower-income countries may be more community centered, but have little in the way of material wealth. It is hard to measure these characteristics of standard of living. The Organization for Economic Co-Operation and Development has developed the "OECD Better Life Index." Visit this website (http://openstaxcollege.org/l/standofliving) to see how countries measure up to your expected standard of living.

The differences in economic statistics and other measures of well-being, substantial though they are, do not fully capture the reasons for the enormous differences between countries. Aside from the neoclassical determinants of growth, four additional determinants are significant in a wide range of statistical studies and are worth mentioning: geography, demography, industrial structure, and institutions.

Geographic and Demographic Differences

Countries have geographic differences: some have extensive coastlines, some are landlocked. Some have large rivers that have been a path of commerce for centuries, or mountains that have been a barrier to trade. Some have deserts, some have rain forests. These differences create different positive and negative opportunities for commerce, health, and the environment.

Countries also have considerable differences in the age distribution of the population. Many high-income nations are approaching a situation by 2020 or so in which the elderly will form a much larger share of the population. Most low-income countries still have a higher proportion of youth and young adults, but by about 2050, the elderly populations in these low-income countries are expected to boom as well. These demographic changes will have considerable impact on the standard of living of the young and the old.

Differences in Industry Structure and Economic Institutions

Countries have differences in industry structure. In the high-income economies of the world, only about 2% of GDP comes from agriculture; the average for the rest of the world is 12%. Countries have strong differences in degree of urbanization.

Countries also have strong differences in economic institutions: some nations have economies that are extremely market-oriented, while other nations have command economies. Some nations are open to international trade, while others use tariffs and import quotas to limit the impact of trade. Some nations are torn by long-standing armed conflicts; other nations are largely at peace. There are differences in political, religious, and social institutions as well.

No nation intentionally aims for a low standard of living, high rates of unemployment and inflation, or an unsustainable trade imbalance. However, nations will differ in their priorities and in the situations in which they find themselves, and so their policy choices can reasonably vary, too. The next modules will discuss how nations around the world, from high income to low income, approach the four macroeconomic goals of economic growth, low unemployment, low inflation, and a sustainable balance of trade.

18.2 | Improving Countries' Standards of Living

By the end of this section, you will be able to:
- Analyze the growth policies of low-income countries seeking to improve standards of living
- Analyze the growth policies of middle-income countries, particularly the East Asian Tigers with their focus on technology and market-oriented incentives
- Analyze the struggles facing economically-challenged countries wishing to enact growth policies
- Evaluate the success of sending aid to low-income countries

Jobs are created in economies that grow. Where does economic growth come from? According to most economists who believe in the **growth consensus**, economic growth (as discussed in Economic Growth) is built on a foundation of productivity improvements. In turn, productivity increases are the result of greater human and physical capital and technology, all interacting in a market-driven economy. In the pursuit of economic growth, however, some countries and regions start from different levels, as illustrated by the differences in per capita GDP presented earlier in Table 18.2.

Growth Policies for the High-Income Countries

For the high-income countries, the challenge of economic growth is to push continually for a more educated workforce that can create, invest in, and apply new technologies. In effect, the goal of their growth-oriented public policy is to shift their aggregate supply curves to the right (refer to The Aggregate Demand/Aggregate Supply Model). The main public policies targeted at achieving this goal are fiscal policies focused on investment, including investment in human capital, in technology, and in physical plant and equipment. These countries also recognize that economic growth works best in a stable and market-oriented economic climate. For this reason, they use monetary policy to keep inflation low and stable, and to minimize the risk of exchange rate fluctuations, while also encouraging domestic and international competition.

However, early in the second decade of the 2000s, many high-income countries found themselves more focused on the short term than on the long term. The United States, Western Europe, and Japan all experienced a combination of financial crisis and deep recession, and the after-effects of the recession—like high unemployment rates—seemed likely to linger for several years. Most of these governments took aggressive, and in some cases controversial, steps to jump-start their economies by running very large budget deficits as part of expansionary fiscal policy. These countries must adopt a course that combines lower government spending and higher taxes.

Similarly, many central banks ran highly expansionary monetary policies, with both near-zero interest rates and unconventional loans and investments. For example, in 2012, Shinzo Abe (see Figure 18.4), then newly-elected Prime Minister of Japan, unveiled a plan to get his country out of its two-decade-long slump in economic growth. It included both fiscal stimulus and an increase in the money supply. The plan was quite successful in the short run. However, according to the *Economist*, with public debt "expected to approach 240% of GDP," (as of 2012 it was 226% of GDP) printing money and public-works spending were only short-term solutions.

Figure 18.4 Japan's Prime Minister, Shinzo Abe Japan's Prime Minister used fiscal and monetary policies to stimulate his country's economy, which has worked in only the short run. (Credit: modification of work by Chatham House/Flickr Creative Commons)

As other chapters discuss, macroeconomics needs to have both a short-run and a long-run focus. The challenge for many of the developed countries in the next few years will be to exit from the short-term policies that were used to correct the 2008–2009 recession. Since the return to growth has been sluggish, it has been politically challenging for these governments to refocus their efforts on new technology, education, and physical capital investment.

Growth Policies for the Middle-Income Economies

The world's great economic success stories in the last few decades began in the 1970s with that group of nations sometimes known as the **East Asian Tigers**: South Korea, Thailand, Malaysia, Indonesia, and Singapore. The list sometimes includes Hong Kong and Taiwan, although these are often treated under international law as part of China, rather than as separate countries. The economic growth of the Tigers has been phenomenal, typically averaging 5.5% real per capita growth for several decades. In the 1980s, other countries began to show signs of convergence. China began growing rapidly, often at annual rates of 8% to 10% per year. India began growing rapidly, first at rates of about 5% per year in the 1990s, but then higher still in the first decade of the 2000s.

The underlying causes of these rapid growth rates are known:

- China and the East Asian Tigers, in particular, have been among the highest savers in the world, often saving one-third or more of GDP as compared to the roughly one-fifth of GDP, which would be a more typical saving rate in Latin America and Africa. These higher savings were harnessed for domestic investment to build physical capital.

- These countries had policies that supported heavy investments in human capital, first building up primary-level education and then expanding secondary-level education. Many focused on encouraging math and science education, which is useful in engineering and business.

- Governments made a concerted effort to seek out applicable technology, by sending students and government commissions abroad to look at the most efficient industrial operations elsewhere. They also created policies to support innovative companies that wished to build production facilities to take advantage of the abundant and inexpensive human capital.

- China and India in particular also allowed far greater freedom for market forces, both within their own domestic economies and also in encouraging their firms to participate in world markets.

This combination of technology, human capital, and physical capital, combined with the incentives of a market-oriented economic context, proved an extremely powerful stimulant to growth. Challenges faced by these middle-income countries are a legacy of government economic controls that for political reasons can be dismantled only slowly over time. In many of them, the banking and financial sector is heavily regulated. Governments have also sometimes selected certain industries to receive low-interest loans or government subsidies. These economies have found that an increased dose of market-oriented incentives for firms and workers has been a critical ingredient in the recipe for faster growth. To learn more about measuring economic growth, read the following Clear It Up feature.

What is the rule of 72?

It is worth pausing a moment to marvel at the growth rates of the East Asian Tigers. If per capita GDP grows at, say, 6% per year, then you can apply the formula for compound growth rates—that is $(1 + 0.06)^{30}$—meaning a nation's level of per capita GDP will rise by a multiple of almost six over 30 years. Another strategy is to apply the rule of 72. The rule of 72 is an approximation to figure out doubling time. The rule number, 72, is divided by the annual growth rate to obtain the approximate number of years it will take for income to double. So if we have a 6% growth rate, it will take 72/6, or 12 years, for incomes to double. Using this rule here suggests that a Tiger that grows at 6% will double its GDP every 12 years. In contrast, a technological leader, chugging along with per capita growth rates of about 2% per year, would double its income in 36 years.

Growth Policies for Economically-Challenged Countries

Many economically-challenged or low-income countries are geographically located in Sub-Saharan Africa. Other pockets of low income are found in the former Soviet Bloc, and in parts of Central America and the Caribbean.

There are macroeconomic policies and prescriptions that might alleviate the extreme poverty and low standard of living. However, many of these countries lack the economic and legal stability, along with market-oriented institutions, needed to provide a fertile climate for domestic economic growth and to attract foreign investment. Thus, macroeconomic policies for low income economies are vastly different from those of the high income economies. The World Bank has made it a priority to combat poverty and raise overall income levels through 2030. One of the key obstacles to achieving this is the political instability that seems to be a common feature of low-income countries.

Figure 18.5 shows the ten lowest income countries as ranked by The World Bank in 2013. These countries share some common traits, the most significant of which is the recent failures of their governments to provide a legal framework for economic growth. Ethiopia and Eritrea recently ended a long-standing war in 2000. Civil and ethnic wars have plagued countries such as Burundi and Liberia. Command economies, corruption, as well as political factionalism and infighting are commonly adopted elements in these low-income countries. The Democratic Republic of the Congo (often referred to as "Congo") is a resource-wealthy country that has not been able to increase its subsistence standard of living due to the political environment.

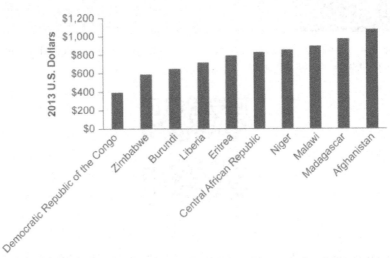

Figure 18.5 The Ten Lowest Income Countries This bar chart that shows ten low-income countries, which include, from lowest income to highest: Democratic Republic of the Congo, Zimbabwe, Burundi, Liberia, Eritrea, Central African Republic, Niger, Madagascar, and Afghanistan. (Source: http://databank.worldbank.org/data/views/reports/map.aspx#)

Low-income countries are at a disadvantage because any incomes received are spent immediately on necessities such as food. People in these countries live on less than $1,035 per year, which is less than $100 per month. Lack of saving means a lack of capital accumulation and a lack of loanable funds for investment in physical and human capital. Recent research by two MIT economists, Abhijit Bannerjee and Esther Duflo, has confirmed that the households in these economies are trapped in low incomes because they cannot muster enough investment to push themselves out of poverty.

For example, the average citizen of Burundi, the lowest-income country, subsists on $150 per year (adjusted to 2005 dollars). According to data collected by the Central Intelligence Agency in its CIA Factbook, as of 2013, 90% of Burundi's population is agrarian, with coffee and tea as the main income producing crop. Only one in two children attends school and, as shown in **Figure 18.6**, many are not in schools comparable to what is found in developed countries. The CIA Factbook also estimates that 15% of Burundi's population suffers from HIV/AIDS. Political instability has made it difficult for Burundi to make significant headway toward growth, as verified by the electrification of only 2% of households and 42% of its national income coming from foreign aid.

Figure 18.6 Lack of Funds for Investing in Human Capital In low-income countries, all income is often spent on necessities for living and cannot be accumulated or invested in physical or human capital. The students in this photograph learn in an outside "classroom" void of not only technology, but even chairs and desks. (Credit: Rafaela Printes/Flickr Creative Commons)

Link It Up

The World Factbook website (http://openstaxcollege.org/l/worldfactbook) is loaded with maps, flags, and other information about countries across the globe.

Other low-income countries share similar stories. These countries have found it difficult to generate investments for themselves or to find foreign investors willing to put up the money for more than the basic needs. Foreign aid and external investment comprise significant portions of the income in these economies, but are not sufficient to allow for the capital accumulation necessary to invest in physical and human capital. But is foreign aid always a contributor to economic growth? It can be a controversial issue, as the next Clear it Up feature points out.

Clear It Up

Does foreign aid to low-income countries work?

According to the Organization of Economic Cooperation and Development (OECD), about $134 billion per year in foreign aid flows from the high-income countries of the world to the low-income ones. Relative to the size of their populations or economies, this is not a large amount for either donors or recipients. For low-income countries, aid averages about 1.3 percent of their GDP. But even this relatively small amount has been highly controversial.

Supporters of additional foreign aid point to the extraordinary human suffering in the low-and middle-income countries of the world. They see opportunities all across Africa, Asia, and Latin America to set up health clinics and schools. They want to help with the task of building economic infrastructure: clean water, plumbing, electricity, and roads. Supporters of this aid include formal state-sponsored institutions like the United Kingdom's Department for International Development (DFID) or independent non-governmental organizations (NGOs) like CARE International that also receive donor government funds. For example, because of an outbreak of meningitis in Ethiopia in 2010, DFID channeled significant funds to the Ethiopian Ministry of Health to train rural health care workers and also for vaccines. These monies helped the Ministry offset shortfalls in their budget.

Opponents of increased aid do not quarrel with the goal of reducing human suffering, but they suggest that foreign aid has often proved a poor tool for advancing that goal. For example, according to an article in the *Attaché Journal of International Affairs*, the Canadian foreign aid organization (CIDA) provided $100 million to Tanzania to grow wheat. The project did produce wheat, but nomadic pastoralists and other villagers who had lived on the land were driven off 100,000 acres of land to make way for the project. The damage in terms of human rights and lost livelihoods was significant. Villagers were beaten and killed because some refused to leave the land. At times, the unintended collateral damage from foreign aid can be significant.

William Easterly, professor of economics at New York University and author of *The White Man's Burden*, argues that aid is often given for political reasons and ends up doing more harm than good. If the government of a country creates a reasonably stable and market-oriented macroeconomic climate, then foreign investors will be likely to provide funds for many profitable activities. For example, according to *The New York Times*, Facebook is partnering with multiple organizations in a project called Internet.org to provide access in remote and low-income areas of the world, and Google began its own initiative called Project Loon. Facebook's first forays into providing Internet access via mobile phones began in stable, market-oriented countries like India, Brazil, Indonesia, Turkey, and the Philippines.

Policymakers are now wiser about the limitations of foreign aid than they were a few decades ago. In targeted and specific cases, especially if foreign aid is channeled to long-term investment projects, foreign aid can have a modest role to play in reducing the extreme levels of deprivation experienced by hundreds of millions of people around the world.

Link It Up

Watch this video (http://openstaxcollege.org/l/foodafrica) on the complexities of providing economic aid in Africa.

18.3 | Causes of Unemployment around the World

By the end of this section, you will be able to:
- Explain the nature and causes of unemployment
- Analyze the natural rate of unemployment and the factors that affect it
- Identify how undeveloped labor markets can result in the same hardships as unemployment

The causes of unemployment in high-income countries of the world can be categorized in two ways: either cyclical unemployment caused by the economy being in a recession, or the natural rate of unemployment caused by factors in labor markets, such as government regulations regarding hiring and starting businesses.

Unemployment from a Recession

For unemployment caused by a recession, the Keynesian economic model points out that both monetary and fiscal policy tools are available. The monetary policy prescription for dealing with recession is straightforward: run an expansionary monetary policy to increase the quantity of money and loans, drive down interest rates, and increase aggregate demand. In a recession, there is usually relatively little danger of inflation taking off, and so even a central bank, with fighting inflation as its top priority, can usually justify some reduction in interest rates.

With regard to fiscal policy, the automatic stabilizers discussed in Government Budget and Fiscal Policy should be allowed to work, even if this means larger budget deficits in times of recession. There is less agreement over whether, in addition to automatic stabilizers, governments in a recession should try to adopt discretionary fiscal policy of additional tax cuts or spending increases. In the case of the Great Recession, the case for this kind of extra-aggressive expansionary fiscal policy is stronger, but for a smaller recession, given the time lags of implementing fiscal policy, discretionary fiscal policy should be used with caution.

However, the aftermath of the Recession emphasizes that expansionary fiscal and monetary policies do not turn off a recession like flipping a switch turns off a lamp. Even after a recession is officially over, and positive growth has returned, it can take some months—or even a couple of years—before private-sector firms believe the economic climate is healthy enough that they can expand their workforce.

The Natural Rate of Unemployment

Unemployment rates in the nations of Europe have typically been higher than in the United States. In 2006, before the start of the Great Recession, the U.S. unemployment rate was 4.6%, compared with 9% in France, 10.4% in Germany, and 7.1% in Sweden. The pattern of generally higher unemployment rates in Europe, which dates back to the 1970s, is typically attributed to the fact that European economies have a higher natural rate of unemployment because they have a greater number of rules and restrictions that discourage firms from hiring and unemployed workers from taking jobs.

Addressing the natural rate of unemployment is straightforward in theory but difficult in practice. Government can play a useful role in providing unemployment and welfare payments, passing rules about where and when businesses can operate, assuring that the workplace is safe, and so on. But these well-intentioned laws can, in some cases, become so intrusive that businesses decide to place limits on their hiring.

For example, a law that imposes large costs on a business that tries to fire or lay off workers will mean that businesses try to avoid hiring in the first place, as is the case in France. According to *Business Week*, "France has 2.4 times as many companies with 49 employees as with 50 ... according to the French labor code, once a company has at least 50 employees inside France, management must create three worker councils, introduce profit sharing, and submit restructuring plans to the councils if the company decides to fire workers for economic reasons." This labor law essentially limits employment (or raises the natural rate of unemployment).

Undeveloped Labor Markets

Low-income and middle-income countries face employment issues that go beyond unemployment as it is understood in the high-income economies. A substantial number of workers in these economies provide many of their own needs by farming, fishing, or hunting. They barter and trade with others and may take a succession of short-term or one-day jobs, sometimes being paid with food or shelter, sometimes with money. They are not "unemployed" in the sense that the term is used in the United States and Europe, but neither are they employed in a regular wage-paying job.

The starting point of economic activity, as discussed in **Welcome to Economics!**, is the division of labor, in which workers specialize in certain tasks and trade the fruits of their labor with others. Workers who are not connected to a labor market are often unable to specialize very much. Because these workers are not "officially" employed, they are often not eligible for social benefits like unemployment insurance or old-age payments—if such payments are even available in their country. Helping these workers to become more connected to the labor market and the economy is an important policy goal. Indeed, recent research by development economists suggests that one of the key factors in raising people in low-income countries out of the worst kind of poverty is whether they can make a connection to a somewhat regular wage-paying job.

18.4 | Causes of Inflation in Various Countries and Regions

By the end of this section, you will be able to:
- Identify the causes and effects of inflation in various economic markets
- Explain the significance of a converging economy

Policymakers of the high-income economies appear to have learned some lessons about fighting inflation. First, whatever happens with aggregate supply and aggregate demand in the short run, monetary policy can be used to prevent inflation from becoming entrenched in the economy in the medium and long term. Second, there is no long-run gain to letting inflation become established. In fact, allowing inflation to become lasting and persistent poses undesirable risks and tradeoffs. When inflation is high, businesses and individuals need to spend time and effort worrying about protecting themselves against inflation, rather than seeking out better ways to serve customers. In short, the high-income economies appear to have both a political consensus to hold inflation low and the economic tools to do so.

In a number of middle- and low-income economies around the world, inflation is far from a solved problem. In the early 2000s, Turkey experienced inflation of more than 50% per year for several years. Belarus had inflation of about 100% per year from 2000 to 2001. From 2008 to 2010, Venezuela and Myanmar had inflation rates of 20% to 30%

per year. Indonesia, Iran, Nigeria, the Russian Federation, and Ukraine all had double-digit inflation for most of the years from 2000 to 2010. Zimbabwe had hyperinflation, with inflation rates that went from more than 100% per year in the mid-2000s to a rate of several million percent in 2008.

In these countries, the problem of very high inflation generally arises from huge budget deficits, which are financed by the government printing its domestic currency. This is a case of "too much money chasing too few goods." In the case of Zimbabwe, the government covered its widening deficits by printing ever higher currency notes, including a $100 trillion bill. By late 2008, the money was nearly worthless, which led Zimbabwe to adopt the U.S. dollar, immediately halting their hyperinflation. In some countries, the central bank makes loans to politically favored firms, essentially printing money to do so, and this too leads to higher inflation.

A number of countries have managed to sustain solid levels of economic growth for sustained periods of time with levels of inflation that would sound high by recent U.S. standards, like 10% to 30% per year. In such economies, most contracts, wage levels, and interest rates are indexed to inflation. Indexing wage contracts and interest rates means that they will increase when inflation increases to retain purchasing power. When wages do not rise as price levels rise, this leads to a decline in the real wage rate and a decrease in the standard of living. Likewise, interest rates that are not indexed mean that the lenders of money will be paid back in devalued currency and will also lose purchasing power on monies that were lent. It is clearly possible—and perhaps sometimes necessary—for a **converging economy** (the economy of a country that demonstrates the ability to catch up to the technology leaders) to live with a degree of uncertainty over inflation that would be politically unacceptable in the high-income economies.

18.5 | Balance of Trade Concerns

By the end of this section, you will be able to:
- Explain the meaning of trade balance and its implications for the foreign exchange market
- Analyze concerns over international trade in goods and services and international flows of capital
- Identify and evaluate market-oriented economic reforms

In the 1950s and 1960s, and even into the 1970s, openness to global flows of goods, services, and financial capital was often viewed in a negative light by low- and middle-income countries. These countries feared that foreign trade would mean both economic losses as their economy was "exploited" by high-income trading partners and a loss of domestic political control to powerful business interests and multinational corporations.

These negative feelings about international trade have evolved. After all, the great economic success stories of recent years like Japan, the East Asian Tiger economies, China, and India, all took advantage of opportunities to sell in global markets. The economies of Europe thrive with high levels of trade. In the North American Free Trade Agreement (NAFTA), the United States, Canada, and Mexico pledged themselves to reduce trade barriers. Many countries have clearly learned that reducing barriers to trade is at least potentially beneficial to the economy. Indeed, many smaller economies of the world have learned an even tougher lesson: if they do not participate actively in world trade, they are unlikely to join the success stories among the converging economies. There are no examples in world history of small economies that remained apart from the global economy but still attained a high standard of living.

Although almost every country now claims that its goal is to participate in global trade, the possible negative consequences have remained highly controversial. It is useful to divide up these possible negative consequences into issues involving trade of goods and services and issues involving flows of international capital. These issues are related, but not the same. An economy may have a high level of trade in goods and services relative to GDP, but if exports and imports are balanced, the net flow of foreign investment in and out of the economy will be zero. Conversely, an economy may have only a moderate level of trade relative to GDP, but find that it has a substantial current account trade imbalance. Thus, it is useful to consider the concerns over international trade of goods and services and international flows of financial capital separately.

Concerns over International Trade in Goods and Services

There is a long list of worries about foreign trade in goods and services: fear of job loss, environmental dangers, unfair labor practices, and many other concerns. These arguments are discussed at some length in The International Trade and Capital Flows.

Of all of the arguments for limitations on trade, perhaps the most controversial one among economists is the infant industry argument; that is, subsidizing or protecting new industries for a time until they become established. (**Globalization and Protectionism (http://cnx.org/content/m57388/latest/)** explains this concept in more detail.) Such policies have been used with some success at certain points in time, but in the world as a whole, support for key industries is far more often directed at long-established industries with substantial political power that are suffering losses and laying off workers, rather than potentially vibrant new industries that have yet to be established. If government is going to favor certain industries, it needs to do so in a way that is temporary and that orients them toward a future of market competition, rather than a future of unending government subsidies and trade protection.

Concerns over International Flows of Capital

Recall from **The Macroeconomic Perspective** that a trade deficit exists when a nation's imports exceed its exports. In order for a trade deficit to take place, foreign countries must provide loans or investments, which they are willing to do because they expect they will be repaid eventually (that the deficit will become a surplus). A trade surplus, you may remember, exists when a nation's exports exceed its imports. So, in order for a trade deficit to switch to a trade surplus, a nation's exports must rise and its imports must fall. Sometimes this happens when the currency decreases in value. For example, if the U.S. had a trade deficit and the dollar depreciated, imports would become more expensive. This would, in turn, benefit the foreign countries who provided the loans or investments.

The expected pattern of trade imbalances in the world economy has been that high-income economies will run trade surpluses, which means they will experience a net outflow of capital to foreign destinations or export more than they import, while low- and middle-income economies will run trade deficits, which means that they will experience a net inflow of foreign capital.

This pattern of international investing can benefit all sides. Investors in the high-income countries benefit because they can receive high returns on their investments, and also because they can diversify their investments so that they are at less risk of a downturn in their own domestic economy. The low-income economies that receive an inflow of capital presumably have potential for rapid catch-up economic growth, and they can use the inflow of international financial capital to help spur their physical capital investment. In addition, inflows of financial capital often come with management abilities, technological expertise, and training.

However, for the last couple of decades, this cheerful scenario has faced two "dark clouds." The first cloud is the very large trade or current account deficits in the U.S. economy. (See **The International Trade and Capital Flows.**) Instead of offering net financial investment abroad, the U.S. economy is soaking up savings from all over the world. These substantial U.S. trade deficits may not be sustainable according to Sebastian Edwards writing for the National Bureau of Economic Research. While trade deficits on their own are not bad, the question is whether they will be reduced gradually or hastily. In the gradual scenario, U.S. exports could grow more rapidly than imports over a period of years, aided by a depreciation of the U.S. dollar. An unintended consequence of the slow growth since the Great Recession has been a decline in the size of the U.S. current account deficit from 6% pre-recession to 3% most recently.

The other option is that the U.S. trade deficit could be reduced in a rush. Here is one scenario: if foreign investors became less willing to hold U.S. dollar assets, the dollar exchange rate could weaken. As speculators see this process happening, they might rush to unload their dollar assets, which would drive the dollar down still further.

A lower U.S. dollar would stimulate aggregate demand by making exports cheaper and imports more expensive. It would mean higher prices for imported inputs throughout the economy, shifting the short-term aggregate supply curve to the left. The result could be a burst of inflation and, if the Federal Reserve were to run a tight monetary policy to reduce the inflation, it could also lead to recession. People sometimes talk as if the U.S. economy, with its great size, is invulnerable to this sort of pressure from international markets. While it is tough to rock, it is not impossible for the $17 trillion U.S. economy to face these international pressures.

The second "dark cloud" is how the smaller economies of the world should deal with the possibility of sudden inflows and outflows of foreign financial capital. Perhaps the most vivid recent example of the potentially destructive forces of international capital movements occurred in the economies of the East Asian Tigers in 1997–1998. Thanks to their excellent growth performance over the previous few decades, these economies had attracted considerable interest from foreign investors. In the mid-1990s, however, foreign investment into these countries surged even further. Much of this money was funneled through banks that borrowed in U.S. dollars and loaned in their national currencies. Bank lending surged at rates of 20% per year or more. This inflow of foreign capital meant that investment in these economies exceeded the level of domestic savings, so that current account deficits in these countries jumped into the range of 5–10% of GDP.

The surge in bank lending meant that many banks in these East Asian countries did not do an especially good job of screening out safe and unsafe borrowers. Many of the loans—as high as 10% to 15% of all loans in some of these countries—started to turn bad. Fearing losses, foreign investors started pulling their money out. As the foreign money left, the exchange rates of these countries crashed, often falling by 50% or more in a few months. The banks were stuck with a mismatch: even if the rest of their domestic loans were repaid, they could never pay back the U.S. dollars that they owed. The banking sector as a whole went bankrupt. The lack of credit and lending in the economy collapsed aggregate demand, bringing on a deep recession.

If the flow and ebb of international capital markets can flip even the economies of the East Asian Tigers, with their stellar growth records, into a recession, then it is no wonder that other middle- and low-income countries around the world are concerned. Moreover, similar episodes of an inflow and then an outflow of foreign financial capital have rocked a number of economies around the world: for example, in the last few years, economies like Ireland, Iceland, and Greece have all experienced severe shocks when foreign lenders decided to stop extending funds. Especially in Greece, this caused the government to enact austerity measures which led to protests throughout the country (**Figure 18.7**).

Figure 18.7 Protests in Greece The economic conditions in Greece have deteriorated from the Great Recession such that the government had to enact austerity measures, (strict rules) cutting wages and increasing taxes on its population. Massive protests are but one byproduct. (Credit: modification of work by Apostolos/Flickr Creative Commons)

Many nations are taking steps to reduce the risk that their economy will be injured if foreign financial capital takes flight, including having their central banks hold large reserves of foreign exchange and stepping up their regulation of domestic banks to avoid a wave of imprudent lending. The most controversial steps in this area involve whether countries should try to take steps to control or reduce the flows of foreign capital. If a country could discourage some of the inflow of speculative short-term capital, and instead only encourage investment capital that was committed for the medium term and the long term, then it could be at least somewhat less susceptible to swings in the sentiments of global investors.

If economies participate in the global trade of goods and services, they will also need to participate in international flows of financial payments and investments. These linkages can offer great benefits to an economy. However, any nation that is experiencing a substantial and sustained pattern of trade deficits, along with the corresponding net inflow of international financial capital, has some reason for concern. During the Asian Financial Crisis in the late 1990s, countries that grew dramatically in the years leading up to the crisis as international capital flowed in, saw their economies collapse when the capital very quickly flowed out.

Market-Oriented Economic Reforms

The standard of living has increased dramatically for billions of people around the world in the last half century. Such increases have occurred not only in the technological leaders like the United States, Canada, the nations of Europe, and Japan, but also in the East Asian Tigers and in many nations of Latin America and Eastern Europe. The challenge for most of these countries is to maintain these growth rates. The economically-challenged regions of the world have stagnated and become stuck in poverty traps. These countries need to focus on the basics: health and education, or human capital development. As **Figure 18.8** illustrates, modern technology allows for the investment in education and human capital development in ways that would have not been possible just a few short years ago.

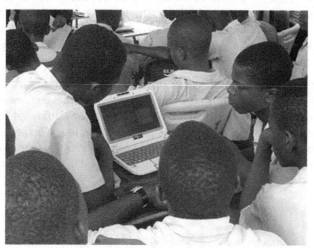

Figure 18.8 Solar-powered Technology Modern technologies, such as solar-power and Wi-Fi, enable education to be delivered to students even in remote parts of a country without electricity. These students in Ghana are sharing a laptop provided by a van with solar-power. (Credit: EIFL/Flickr Creative Commons)

Other than the issue of economic growth, the other three main goals of macroeconomic policy—that is, low unemployment, low inflation, and a sustainable balance of trade—all involve situations in which, for some reason, the economy fails to coordinate the forces of supply and demand. In the case of cyclical unemployment, for example, the intersection of aggregate supply and aggregate demand occurs at a level of output below potential GDP. In the case of the natural rate of unemployment, government regulations create a situation where otherwise-willing employers become unwilling to hire otherwise-willing workers. Inflation is a situation in which aggregate demand outstrips aggregate supply, at least for a time, so that too much buying power is chasing too few goods. A trade imbalance is a situation where, because of a net inflow or outflow of foreign capital, domestic savings are not aligned with domestic investment. Each of these situations can create a range of easier or harder policy choices.

Bring it Home

Youth Unemployment: Three Cases

Spain and South Africa had the same high youth unemployment in 2011, but the reasons for this unemployment are different. Spain's youth unemployment surged due to the Great Recession of 2008–2009 and heavy indebtedness on the part of its citizens and its government. Spain's current account balance is negative, which means it is borrowing heavily. To cure cyclical unemployment during a recession, the Keynesian model suggests increases in government spending—fiscal expansion or monetary expansion. Neither option is open to Spain. It currently can borrow at only high interest rates, which will be a real problem in terms of debt service. In addition, the rest of the European Union (EU) has dragged its feet when it comes to debt forgiveness. Monetary expansion is not possible because Spain uses the euro and cannot devalue its currency unless it convinces all of the EU to do so. So what can be done? The *Economist*, summarizing some of the ideas of economists and policymakers, suggests that Spain's only realistic (although painful) option is to reduce government-mandated wages, which would allow it to reduce government spending. As a result, the government would be able to lower tax rates on the working population. With a lower wage or lower tax environment, firms will hire more workers. This will lower unemployment and stimulate the economy. Spain can also encourage greater foreign investment and try to promote policies that encourage domestic savings.

South Africa has more of a natural rate of unemployment problem. It is an interesting case because its youth unemployment is mostly due to the fact that its young are not ready to work. This is commonly referred to as an employability problem. According to interviews of South African firms as reported in the *Economist*, the young are academically smart but lack practical skills for the workplace. Despite a big push to increase investment in human capital, the results have not yet borne fruit. Recently the government unveiled a plan to pay unemployed youth while they were "trained-up" or apprenticed in South African firms. The government has room to increase fiscal expenditure, encourage domestic savings, and continue to fund investment in education, vocational training, and apprentice programs. South Africa can also improve the climate for foreign investment from technology leaders, which would encourage economic growth.

India has a smaller youth employment problem in terms of percentages. However, bear in mind that since this is a populous country, it turns out to be a significant problem in raw numbers. According to Kaushik Basu, writing for the BBC, "there are 45 national laws governing the hiring and firing decisions of firms and close to four times that amount at the state level". These laws make it difficult for companies to fire workers. To stay nimble and responsive to markets, Indian companies respond to these laws by hiring fewer workers. The Indian government can do much to solve this problem by adjusting its labor laws. Essentially, the government has to remove itself from firms' hiring and firing decisions, so that growing Indian firms can freely employ more workers. Indian workers, like those in South Africa, do not have workforce skills. Again, the government can increase its spending on education, vocational training, and workforce readiness programs.

Finally, India has a significant current account deficit. This deficit is mainly a result of short- and long-term capital flows. To solve this deficit, India has experimented by lifting the limitation on domestic savers from investing abroad. This is a step in the right direction that may dampen the growth in the current account deficit. A final policy possibility is to improve domestic capital markets so many self-employed Indians can get access to capital to realize their business ideas. If more Indians can get access to capital to start businesses, employment might increase.

KEY TERMS

converging economy economy of a country that has demonstrated the ability to catch up to the technology leaders by investing in both physical and human capital

East Asian Tigers the economies of Taiwan, Singapore, Hong Kong, and South Korea, which maintained high growth rates and rapid export-led industrialization between the early 1960s and 1990 allowing them to converge with the technological leaders in high-income countries

growth consensus a series of studies that show, statistically, that 70% of the differences in income per person across the world is explained by differences in physical capital (savings/investment)

high-income country nation with a per capita income of $12,475 or more; typically has high levels of human and physical capital

low-income country a nation that has a per capita income of less than $1,025; a third of the world's population

middle-income country a nation with per capita income between $1,025 and $12, 475 and that has shown some ability, even if not always sustained, to catch up to the technology leaders in high-income countries

KEY CONCEPTS AND SUMMARY

18.1 The Diversity of Countries and Economies across the World

Macroeconomic policy goals for most countries strive toward low levels of unemployment and inflation, as well as stable trade balances. Countries are analyzed based on their GDP per person and ranked as low-, middle-, and high-income countries. Low-income are those earning less than $1,025 (less than 1%) of global income. They currently have 18.5% of the world population. Middle-income countries are those with per capital income of $1,025–$12,475 (31.1% of global income). They have 69.5% of world population. High-income countries are those with per capita income greater than $12,475 (68.3% of global income). They have 12% of the world's population. Regional comparisons tend to be inaccurate because even countries within those regions tend to differ from each other.

18.2 Improving Countries' Standards of Living

The fundamentals of growth are the same in every country: improvements in human capital, physical capital, and technology interacting in a market-oriented economy. Countries that are high-income tend to focus on developing and using new technology. Countries that are middle-income focus on increasing human capital and becoming more connected to technology and global markets. They have charted unconventional paths by relying more on state-led support rather than relying solely on markets. Low-income, economically-challenged countries have many health and human development needs, but they are also challenged by the lack of investment and foreign aid to develop infrastructure like roads. There are some bright spots when it comes to financial development and mobile communications, which suggest that low-income countries can become technology leaders in their own right, but it is too early to claim victory. These countries must do more to connect to the rest of the global economy and find the technologies that work best for them.

18.3 Causes of Unemployment around the World

Cyclical unemployment can be addressed by expansionary fiscal and monetary policy. The natural rate of unemployment can be harder to deal with, because it involves thinking carefully about the tradeoffs involved in laws that affect employment and hiring. Unemployment is understood differently in high-income countries compared to low- and middle-income countries. People in these countries are not "unemployed" in the sense that term is used in the United States and Europe, but neither are they employed in a regular wage-paying job. While some may have regular wage-paying jobs, others are part of a barter economy.

18.4 Causes of Inflation in Various Countries and Regions

Most high-income economies have learned that their central banks can control inflation in the medium and the long term. In addition, they have learned that inflation has no long-term benefits but potentially substantial long-term costs if it distracts businesses from focusing on real productivity gains. However, smaller economies around the world may face more volatile inflation because their smaller economies can be unsettled by international movements of capital and goods.

18.5 Balance of Trade Concerns

There are many legitimate concerns over possible negative consequences of free trade. Perhaps the single strongest response to these concerns is that there are good ways to address them without restricting trade and thus losing its benefits. There are two major issues involving trade imbalances. One is what will happen with the large U.S. trade deficits, and whether they will come down gradually or with a rush. The other is whether smaller countries around the world should take some steps to limit flows of international capital, in the hope that they will not be quite so susceptible to economic whiplash from international financial capital flowing in and out of their economies.

SELF-CHECK QUESTIONS

1. Using the data provided in Table 18.3, rank the seven regions of the world according to GDP and then according to GDP per capita.

	Population (in millions)	GDP Per Capita	GDP = Population × Per Capita GDP (in millions)
East Asia and Pacific	2,006	$5,536	$10,450,032
South Asia	1,671	$1,482	$2,288,812
Sub-Saharan Africa	936.1	$1,657	$1,287,650
Latin America and Caribbean	588	$9,536	$5,339,390
Middle East and North Africa	345.4	$3,456	$1,541,900
Europe and Central Asia	272.2	$7,118	$1,862,384

Table 18.3 GDP and Population of Seven Regions of the World

2. What are the drawbacks to analyzing the global economy on a regional basis?

3. Create a table that identifies the macroeconomic policies for a high-income country, a middle-income country, and a low-income country.

4. Use the data in the text to contrast the policy prescriptions of the high-income, middle-income, and low-income countries.

5. What are the different policy tools for dealing with cyclical unemployment?

6. Explain how the natural rate of unemployment may be higher in low-income countries.

7. How does indexing wage contracts to inflation help workers?

8. Use the AD/AS model to show how increases in government spending can lead to more inflation.

9. Show, using the AD/AS model, how monetary policy can be used to decrease the price level.

10. What do international flows of capital have to do with trade imbalances?

11. Use the demand-and-supply of foreign currency graph to determine what would happen to a small, open economy that experienced capital outflows.

REVIEW QUESTIONS

12. What is the primary way in which economists measure standards of living?

13. What are some of the other ways of comparing the standard of living in countries around the world?

14. What are the four other factors that determine the economic standard of living around the world?

15. What other factors, aside from labor productivity, capital investment, and technology, impact the economic growth of a country? How?

16. What strategies were employed by the East Asian Tigers to stimulate economic growth?

17. What are the two types of unemployment problems?

18. In low-income countries, does it make sense to argue that most of the people without long-term jobs are unemployed?

19. Is inflation likely to be a severe problem for at least some high-income economies in the near future?

20. Is inflation likely to be a problem for at least some low- and middle-income economies in the near future?

21. What are the major issues with regard to trade imbalances for the U.S. economy?

22. What are the major issues with regard to trade imbalances for low- and middle-income countries?

CRITICAL THINKING QUESTIONS

23. Demography can have important economic effects. The United States has an aging population. Explain one economic benefit and one economic cost of an aging population as well as of a population that is very young.

24. Explain why is it difficult to set aside funds for investment when you are in poverty.

25. Why do you think it is difficult for high-income countries to achieve high growth rates?

26. Is it possible to protect workers from being fired without distorting the labor market?

27. Explain what will happen in a nation that tries to solve a structural unemployment problem using

expansionary monetary and fiscal policy. Draw one AD/AS diagram, based on the Keynesian model, for what the nation hopes will happen. Then draw a second AD/AS diagram, based on the neoclassical model, for what is more likely to happen.

28. Why are inflationary dangers lower in the high-income economies than in low-income and middle-income economies?

29. Explain why converging economies may present a strong argument for limiting flows of capital but not for limiting trade.

PROBLEMS

30. Retrieve the following data from The World Bank database (http://databank.worldbank.org/data/home.aspx) for India, Spain, and South Africa for the most recent year available:
- GDP in constant international dollars or PPP
- Population
- GDP per person in constant international dollars

- Mortality rate, infant (per 1,000 live births)
- Health expenditure per capita (current U.S. dollars)
- Life expectancy at birth, total (years)

31. Prepare a chart that compares India, Spain, and South Africa based on the data you find. Describe the key differences between the countries. Rank these as high-, medium-, and low-income countries, explain what is surprising or expected about this data.

32. Use the Rule of 72 to estimate how long it will take for India, Spain, and South Africa to double their standards of living.

33. Using the research skills you have acquired, retrieve the following data from The World Bank database (http://databank.worldbank.org/data/home.aspx) for India, Spain, and South Africa for 2008–2013, if available:
- Telephone lines
- Mobile cellular subscriptions
- Secure Internet servers (per one million people)
- Electricity production (kWh)

Prepare a chart that compares these three countries. Describe the key differences between the countries.

34. Retrieve the unemployment data from The World Bank database (http://databank.worldbank.org/data/home.aspx) for India, Spain, and South Africa for 2008–2012. Prepare a chart that compares India, Spain, and South Africa based on the data. Describe the key differences between the countries. Rank these countries as high-, medium-, and low-income countries. Explain what is surprising or expected about this data. How were these countries impacted by the Great Recession?

35. Retrieve inflation data from The World Bank data base (http://databank.worldbank.org/data/home.aspx) for India, Spain, and South Africa for 2008–2013. Prepare a chart that compares India, Spain, and South Africa based on the data. Describe the key differences between the countries. Rank these countries as high-, medium-, and low-income. Explain what is surprising or expected about the data.

Appendix A

(This appendix should be consulted after first reading Welcome to Eonomics!) Economics is not math. There is no important concept in this course that cannot be explained without mathematics. That said, math is a tool that can be used to illustrate economic concepts. Remember the saying a picture is worth a thousand words? Instead of a picture, think of a graph. It is the same thing. Economists use models as the primary tool to derive insights about economic issues and problems. Math is one way of working with (or manipulating) economic models.

There are other ways of representing models, such as text or narrative. But why would you use your fist to bang a nail, if you had a hammer? Math has certain advantages over text. It disciplines your thinking by making you specify exactly what you mean. You can get away with fuzzy thinking in your head, but you cannot when you reduce a model to algebraic equations. At the same time, math also has disadvantages. Mathematical models are necessarily based on simplifying assumptions, so they are not likely to be perfectly realistic. Mathematical models also lack the nuances which can be found in narrative models. The point is that math is one tool, but it is not the only tool or even always the best tool economists can use. So what math will you need for this book? The answer is: little more than high school algebra and graphs. You will need to know:

- What a function is
- How to interpret the equation of a line (i.e., slope and intercept)
- How to manipulate a line (i.e., changing the slope or the intercept)
- How to compute and interpret a growth rate (i.e., percentage change)
- How to read and manipulate a graph

In this text, we will use the easiest math possible, and we will introduce it in this appendix. So if you find some math in the book that you cannot follow, come back to this appendix to review. Like most things, math has diminishing returns. A little math ability goes a long way; the more advanced math you bring in, the less additional knowledge that will get you. That said, if you are going to major in economics, you should consider learning a little calculus. It will be worth your while in terms of helping you learn advanced economics more quickly.

Algebraic Models

Often economic models (or parts of models) are expressed in terms of mathematical functions. What is a function? A function describes a relationship. Sometimes the relationship is a definition. For example (using words), your professor is Adam Smith. This could be expressed as Professor = Adam Smith. Or Friends = Bob + Shawn + Margaret.

Often in economics, functions describe cause and effect. The variable on the left-hand side is what is being explained ("the effect"). On the right-hand side is what is doing the explaining ("the causes"). For example, suppose your GPA was determined as follows:

$$GPA = 0.25 \times combined\_SAT + 0.25 \times class\_attendance + 0.50 \times hours\_spent\_studying$$

This equation states that your GPA depends on three things: your combined SAT score, your class attendance, and the number of hours you spend studying. It also says that study time is twice as important (0.50) as either combined_SAT score (0.25) or class_attendance (0.25). If this relationship is true, how could you raise your GPA? By not skipping class and studying more. Note that you cannot do anything about your SAT score, since if you are in college, you have (presumably) already taken the SATs.

Of course, economic models express relationships using economic variables, like Budget = money_spent_on_econ_books + money_spent_on_music, assuming that the only things you buy are economics books and music.

Most of the relationships we use in this course are expressed as linear equations of the form:

$$y = b + mx$$

Expressing Equations Graphically

Graphs are useful for two purposes. The first is to express equations visually, and the second is to display statistics or data. This section will discuss expressing equations visually.

To a mathematician or an economist, a variable is the name given to a quantity that may assume a range of values. In the equation of a line presented above, x and y are the variables, with x on the horizontal axis and y on the vertical axis, and b and m representing factors that determine the shape of the line. To see how this equation works, consider a numerical example:

$$y = 9 + 3x$$

In this equation for a specific line, the b term has been set equal to 9 and the m term has been set equal to 3. Table A1 shows the values of x and y for this given equation. Figure A1 shows this equation, and these values, in a graph. To construct the table, just plug in a series of different values for x, and then calculate what value of y results. In the figure, these points are plotted and a line is drawn through them.

x	y
0	9
1	12
2	15
3	18
4	21
5	24
6	27

Table A1 Values for the Slope Intercept Equation

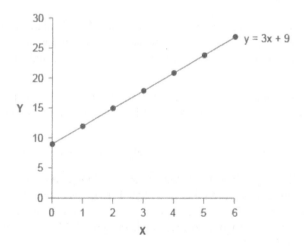

Figure A1 Slope and the Algebra of Straight Lines   This line graph has *x* on the horizontal axis and y on the vertical axis. The y-intercept—that is, the point where the line intersects the y-axis—is 9. The slope of the line is 3; that is, there is a rise of 3 on the vertical axis for every increase of 1 on the horizontal axis. The slope is the same all along a straight line.

This example illustrates how the b and m terms in an equation for a straight line determine the shape of the line. The b term is called the y-intercept. The reason for this name is that, if x = 0, then the b term will reveal where the line intercepts, or crosses, the y-axis. In this example, the line hits the vertical axis at 9. The m term in the equation for the line is the slope. Remember that slope is defined as rise over run; more specifically, the slope of a line from one point to another is the change in the vertical axis divided by the change in the horizontal axis. In this example, each time the x term increases by one (the run), the y term rises by three. Thus, the slope of this line is three. Specifying a y-intercept and a slope—that is, specifying b and m in the equation for a line—will identify a specific line. Although it is rare for real-world data points to arrange themselves as an exact straight line, it often turns out that a straight line can offer a reasonable approximation of actual data.

Interpreting the Slope

The concept of slope is very useful in economics, because it measures the relationship between two variables. A positive slope means that two variables are positively related; that is, when x increases, so does y, or when x decreases, y decreases also. Graphically, a positive slope means that as a line on the line graph moves from left to right, the line rises. The length-weight relationship, shown in **Figure A3** later in this Appendix, has a positive slope. We will learn in other chapters that price and quantity supplied have a positive relationship; that is, firms will supply more when the price is higher.

A negative slope means that two variables are negatively related; that is, when x increases, y decreases, or when x decreases, y increases. Graphically, a negative slope means that, as the line on the line graph moves from left to right, the line falls. The altitude-air density relationship, shown in **Figure A4** later in this appendix, has a negative slope. We will learn that price and quantity demanded have a negative relationship; that is, consumers will purchase less when the price is higher.

A slope of zero means that there is no relationship between x and y. Graphically, the line is flat; that is, zero rise over the run. **Figure A5** of the unemployment rate, shown later in this appendix, illustrates a common pattern of many line graphs: some segments where the slope is positive, other segments where the slope is negative, and still other segments where the slope is close to zero.

The slope of a straight line between two points can be calculated in numerical terms. To calculate slope, begin by designating one point as the "starting point" and the other point as the "end point" and then calculating the rise over run between these two points. As an example, consider the slope of the air density graph between the points representing an altitude of 4,000 meters and an altitude of 6,000 meters:

Rise: Change in variable on vertical axis (end point minus original point)

$$= 0.100 - 0.307$$
$$= -0.207$$

Run: Change in variable on horizontal axis (end point minus original point)

$$= 6,000 - 4,000$$
$$= 2,000$$

Thus, the slope of a straight line between these two points would be that from the altitude of 4,000 meters up to 6,000 meters, the density of the air decreases by approximately 0.1 kilograms/cubic meter for each of the next 1,000 meters

Suppose the slope of a line were to increase. Graphically, that means it would get steeper. Suppose the slope of a line were to decrease. Then it would get flatter. These conditions are true whether or not the slope was positive or negative to begin with. A higher positive slope means a steeper upward tilt to the line, while a smaller positive slope means a flatter upward tilt to the line. A negative slope that is larger in absolute value (that is, more negative) means a steeper downward tilt to the line. A slope of zero is a horizontal flat line. A vertical line has an infinite slope.

Suppose a line has a larger intercept. Graphically, that means it would shift out (or up) from the old origin, parallel to the old line. If a line has a smaller intercept, it would shift in (or down), parallel to the old line.

Solving Models with Algebra

Economists often use models to answer a specific question, like: What will the unemployment rate be if the economy grows at 3% per year? Answering specific questions requires solving the "system" of equations that represent the model.

Suppose the demand for personal pizzas is given by the following equation:

$$Qd = 16 - 2P$$

where Qd is the amount of personal pizzas consumers want to buy (i.e., quantity demanded), and P is the price of pizzas. Suppose the supply of personal pizzas is:

$$Qs = 2 + 5P$$

where Qs is the amount of pizza producers will supply (i.e., quantity supplied).

Finally, suppose that the personal pizza market operates where supply equals demand, or

$$Qd = Qs$$

We now have a system of three equations and three unknowns (Qd, Qs, and P), which we can solve with algebra:

Since Qd = Qs, we can set the demand and supply equation equal to each other:

$$\begin{aligned} Qd &= Qs \\ 16 - 2P &= 2 + 5P \end{aligned}$$

Subtracting 2 from both sides and adding 2P to both sides yields:

$$\begin{aligned} 16 - 2P - 2 &= 2 + 5P - 2 \\ 14 - 2P &= 5P \\ 14 - 2P + 2P &= 5P + 2P \\ 14 &= 7P \\ \frac{14}{7} &= \frac{7P}{7} \\ 2 &= P \end{aligned}$$

In other words, the price of each personal pizza will be $2. How much will consumers buy?

Taking the price of $2, and plugging it into the demand equation, we get:

$$\begin{aligned} Qd &= 16 - 2P \\ &= 16 - 2(2) \\ &= 16 - 4 \\ &= 12 \end{aligned}$$

So if the price is $2 each, consumers will purchase 12. How much will producers supply? Taking the price of $2, and plugging it into the supply equation, we get:

$$\begin{aligned} Qs &= 2 + 5P \\ &= 2 + 5(2) \\ &= 2 + 10 \\ &= 12 \end{aligned}$$

So if the price is $2 each, producers will supply 12 personal pizzas. This means we did our math correctly, since Qd = Qs.

Solving Models with Graphs

If algebra is not your forte, you can get the same answer by using graphs. Take the equations for Qd and Qs and graph them on the same set of axes as shown in **Figure A2**. Since P is on the vertical axis, it is easiest if you solve each equation for P. The demand curve is then P = 8 − 0.5Qs and the demand curve is P = −0.4 + 0.2Qd. Note that the vertical intercepts are 8 and −0.4, and the slopes are −0.5 for demand and 0.2 for supply. If you draw the graphs carefully, you will see that where they cross (Qs = Qd), the price is $2 and the quantity is 12, just like the algebra predicted.

Figure A2 Supply and Demand Graph The equations for Qd and Qs are displayed graphically by the sloped lines.

We will use graphs more frequently in this book than algebra, but now you know the math behind the graphs.

Growth Rates

Growth rates are frequently encountered in real world economics. A growth rate is simply the percentage change in some quantity. It could be your income. It could be a business's sales. It could be a nation's GDP. The formula for computing a growth rate is straightforward:

$$\text{Percentage change} = \frac{\text{Change in quantity}}{\text{Quantity}}$$

Suppose your job pays $10 per hour. Your boss, however, is so impressed with your work that he gives you a $2 per hour raise. The percentage change (or growth rate) in your pay is $2/$10 = 0.20 or 20%.

To compute the growth rate for data over an extended period of time, for example, the average annual growth in GDP over a decade or more, the denominator is commonly defined a little differently. In the previous example, we defined the quantity as the initial quantity—or the quantity when we started. This is fine for a one-time calculation, but when we compute the growth over and over, it makes more sense to define the quantity as the average quantity over the period in question, which is defined as the quantity halfway between the initial quantity and the next quantity. This is harder to explain in words than to show with an example. Suppose a nation's GDP was $1 trillion in 2005 and $1.03 trillion in 2006. The growth rate between 2005 and 2006 would be the change in GDP ($1.03 trillion – $1.00 trillion) divided by the average GDP between 2005 and 2006 ($1.03 trillion + $1.00 trillion)/2. In other words:

$$= \frac{\$1.03 \text{ trillion} - \$1.00 \text{ trillion}}{(\$1.03 \text{ trillion} + \$1.00 \text{ trillion}) / 2}$$
$$= \frac{0.03}{1.015}$$
$$= 0.0296$$
$$= 2.96\% \text{ growth}$$

Note that if we used the first method, the calculation would be ($1.03 trillion – $1.00 trillion) / $1.00 trillion = 3% growth, which is approximately the same as the second, more complicated method. If you need a rough approximation, use the first method. If you need accuracy, use the second method.

A few things to remember: A positive growth rate means the quantity is growing. A smaller growth rate means the quantity is growing more slowly. A larger growth rate means the quantity is growing more quickly. A negative growth rate means the quantity is decreasing.

The same change over times yields a smaller growth rate. If you got a $2 raise each year, in the first year the growth rate would be $2/$10 = 20%, as shown above. But in the second year, the growth rate would be $2/$12 = 0.167 or 16.7% growth. In the third year, the same $2 raise would correspond to a $2/$14 = 14.2%. The moral of the story is this: To keep the growth rate the same, the change must increase each period.

Displaying Data Graphically and Interpreting the Graph

Graphs are also used to display data or evidence. Graphs are a method of presenting numerical patterns. They condense detailed numerical information into a visual form in which relationships and numerical patterns can be seen more easily. For example, which countries have larger or smaller populations? A careful reader could examine a long list of numbers representing the populations of many countries, but with over 200 nations in the world, searching through such a list would take concentration and time. Putting these same numbers on a graph can quickly reveal population patterns. Economists use graphs both for a compact and readable presentation of groups of numbers and for building an intuitive grasp of relationships and connections.

Three types of graphs are used in this book: line graphs, pie graphs, and bar graphs. Each is discussed below. We also provide warnings about how graphs can be manipulated to alter viewers' perceptions of the relationships in the data.

Line Graphs

The graphs we have discussed so far are called line graphs, because they show a relationship between two variables: one measured on the horizontal axis and the other measured on the vertical axis.

Sometimes it is useful to show more than one set of data on the same axes. The data in **Table A2** is displayed in **Figure A3** which shows the relationship between two variables: length and median weight for American baby boys and girls during the first three years of life. (The median means that half of all babies weigh more than this and half weigh less.) The line graph measures length in inches on the horizontal axis and weight in pounds on the vertical axis. For example, point A on the figure shows that a boy who is 28 inches long will have a median weight of about 19 pounds. One line on the graph shows the length-weight relationship for boys and the other line shows the relationship for girls. This kind of graph is widely used by healthcare providers to check whether a child's physical development is roughly on track.

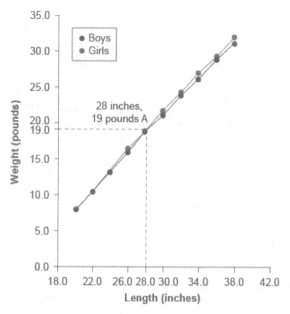

Figure A3 The Length-Weight Relationship for American Boys and Girls   The line graph shows the relationship between height and weight for boys and girls from birth to 3 years. Point A, for example, shows that a boy of 28 inches in height (measured on the horizontal axis) is typically 19 pounds in weight (measured on the vertical axis). These data apply only to children in the first three years of life.

Boys from Birth to 36 Months		Girls from Birth to 36 Months	
Length (inches)	Weight (pounds)	Length (inches)	Weight (pounds)

Table A2 Length to Weight Relationship for American Boys and Girls

Boys from Birth to 36 Months		Girls from Birth to 36 Months	
20.0	8.0	20.0	7.9
22.0	10.5	22.0	10.5
24.0	13.5	24.0	13.2
26.0	16.4	26.0	16.0
28.0	19.0	28.0	18.8
30.0	21.8	30.0	21.2
32.0	24.3	32.0	24.0
34.0	27.0	34.0	26.2
36.0	29.3	36.0	28.9
38.0	32.0	38.0	31.3

Table A2 Length to Weight Relationship for American Boys and Girls

Not all relationships in economics are linear. Sometimes they are curves. Figure A4 presents another example of a line graph, representing the data from Table A3. In this case, the line graph shows how thin the air becomes when you climb a mountain. The horizontal axis of the figure shows altitude, measured in meters above sea level. The vertical axis measures the density of the air at each altitude. Air density is measured by the weight of the air in a cubic meter of space (that is, a box measuring one meter in height, width, and depth). As the graph shows, air pressure is heaviest at ground level and becomes lighter as you climb. Figure A4 shows that a cubic meter of air at an altitude of 500 meters weighs approximately one kilogram (about 2.2 pounds). However, as the altitude increases, air density decreases. A cubic meter of air at the top of Mount Everest, at about 8,828 meters, would weigh only 0.023 kilograms. The thin air at high altitudes explains why many mountain climbers need to use oxygen tanks as they reach the top of a mountain.

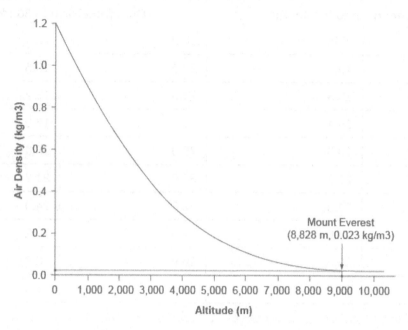

Figure A4 Altitude-Air Density Relationship This line graph shows the relationship between altitude, measured in meters above sea level, and air density, measured in kilograms of air per cubic meter. As altitude rises, air density declines. The point at the top of Mount Everest has an altitude of approximately 8,828 meters above sea level (the horizontal axis) and air density of 0.023 kilograms per cubic meter (the vertical axis).

Altitude (meters)	Air Density (kg/cubic meters)
0	1.200
500	1.093
1,000	0.831
1,500	0.678
2,000	0.569
2,500	0.484
3,000	0.415
3,500	0.357
4,000	0.307
4,500	0.231
5,000	0.182
5,500	0.142
6,000	0.100
6,500	0.085
7,000	0.066

Table A3 Altitude to Air Density Relationship

Altitude (meters)	Air Density (kg/cubic meters)
7,500	0.051
8,000	0.041
8,500	0.025
9,000	0.022
9,500	0.019
10,000	0.014

Table A3 Altitude to Air Density Relationship

The length-weight relationship and the altitude-air density relationships in these two figures represent averages. If you were to collect actual data on air pressure at different altitudes, the same altitude in different geographic locations will have slightly different air density, depending on factors like how far you are from the equator, local weather conditions, and the humidity in the air. Similarly, in measuring the height and weight of children for the previous line graph, children of a particular height would have a range of different weights, some above average and some below. In the real world, this sort of variation in data is common. The task of a researcher is to organize that data in a way that helps to understand typical patterns. The study of statistics, especially when combined with computer statistics and spreadsheet programs, is a great help in organizing this kind of data, plotting line graphs, and looking for typical underlying relationships. For most economics and social science majors, a statistics course will be required at some point.

One common line graph is called a time series, in which the horizontal axis shows time and the vertical axis displays another variable. Thus, a time series graph shows how a variable changes over time. Figure A5 shows the unemployment rate in the United States since 1975, where unemployment is defined as the percentage of adults who want jobs and are looking for a job, but cannot find one. The points for the unemployment rate in each year are plotted on the graph, and a line then connects the points, showing how the unemployment rate has moved up and down since 1975. The line graph makes it easy to see, for example, that the highest unemployment rate during this time period was slightly less than 10% in the early 1980s and 2010, while the unemployment rate declined from the early 1990s to the end of the 1990s, before rising and then falling back in the early 2000s, and then rising sharply during the recession from 2008–2009.

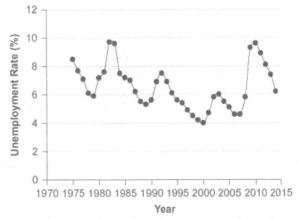

Figure A5 U.S. Unemployment Rate, 1975–2014 This graph provides a quick visual summary of unemployment data. With a graph like this, it is easy to spot the times of high unemployment and of low unemployment.

Pie Graphs

A pie graph (sometimes called a pie chart) is used to show how an overall total is divided into parts. A circle represents a group as a whole. The slices of this circular "pie" show the relative sizes of subgroups.

Figure A6 shows how the U.S. population was divided among children, working age adults, and the elderly in 1970, 2000, and what is projected for 2030. The information is first conveyed with numbers in **Table A4**, and then in three pie charts. The first column of **Table A4** shows the total U.S. population for each of the three years. Columns 2–4 categorize the total in terms of age groups—from birth to 18 years, from 19 to 64 years, and 65 years and above. In columns 2–4, the first number shows the actual number of people in each age category, while the number in parentheses shows the percentage of the total population comprised by that age group.

Year	Total Population	19 and Under	20–64 years	Over 65
1970	205.0 million	77.2 (37.6%)	107.7 (52.5%)	20.1 (9.8%)
2000	275.4 million	78.4 (28.5%)	162.2 (58.9%)	34.8 (12.6%)
2030	351.1 million	92.6 (26.4%)	188.2 (53.6%)	70.3 (20.0%)

Table A4 U.S. Age Distribution, 1970, 2000, and 2030 (projected)

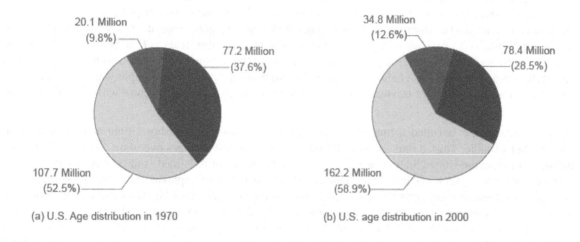

(a) U.S. Age distribution in 1970

(b) U.S. age distribution in 2000

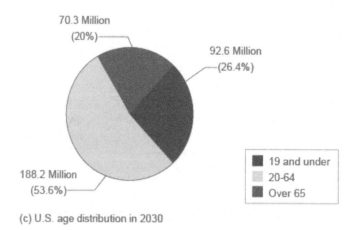

(c) U.S. age distribution in 2030

Figure A6 Pie Graphs of the U.S. Age Distribution (numbers in millions) The three pie graphs illustrate the division of total population into three age groups for the three different years.

In a pie graph, each slice of the pie represents a share of the total, or a percentage. For example, 50% would be half of the pie and 20% would be one-fifth of the pie. The three pie graphs in **Figure A6** show that the share of the U.S. population 65 and over is growing. The pie graphs allow you to get a feel for the relative size of the different age groups from 1970 to 2000 to 2030, without requiring you to slog through the specific numbers and percentages in the table. Some common examples of how pie graphs are used include dividing the population into groups by age, income level, ethnicity, religion, occupation; dividing different firms into categories by size, industry, number of employees; and dividing up government spending or taxes into its main categories.

Bar Graphs

A bar graph uses the height of different bars to compare quantities. Table A5 lists the 12 most populous countries in the world. Figure A7 provides this same data in a bar graph. The height of the bars corresponds to the population of each country. Although you may know that China and India are the most populous countries in the world, seeing how the bars on the graph tower over the other countries helps illustrate the magnitude of the difference between the sizes of national populations.

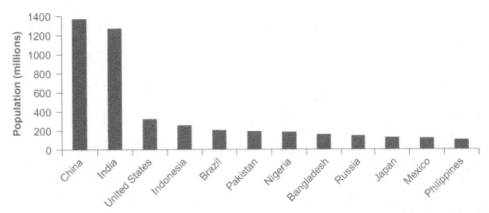

Figure A7 Leading Countries of the World by Population, 2015 (in millions)   The graph shows the 12 countries of the world with the largest populations. The height of the bars in the bar graph shows the size of the population for each country.

Country	Population
China	1,369
India	1,270
United States	321
Indonesia	255
Brazil	204
Pakistan	190
Nigeria	184
Bangladesh	158
Russia	146
Japan	127
Mexico	121
Philippines	101

Table A5 Leading 12 Countries of the World by Population

Bar graphs can be subdivided in a way that reveals information similar to that we can get from pie charts. **Figure A8** offers three bar graphs based on the information from **Figure A6** about the U.S. age distribution in 1970, 2000, and 2030. **Figure A8** (a) shows three bars for each year, representing the total number of persons in each age bracket for each year. **Figure A8** (b) shows just one bar for each year, but the different age groups are now shaded inside the bar. In **Figure A8** (c), still based on the same data, the vertical axis measures percentages rather than the number of persons. In this case, all three bar graphs are the same height, representing 100% of the population, with each bar divided according to the percentage of population in each age group. It is sometimes easier for a reader to run his or her eyes across several bar graphs, comparing the shaded areas, rather than trying to compare several pie graphs.

(a) Bars for separate age groups

(b) Bars show total population divided into age groups

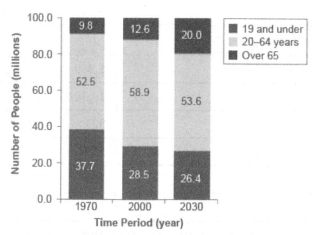

(c) Bars show total population divided into percentages

Figure A8 U.S. Population with Bar Graphs   Population data can be represented in different ways. (a) Shows three bars for each year, representing the total number of persons in each age bracket for each year. (b) Shows just one bar for each year, but the different age groups are now shaded inside the bar. (c) Sets the vertical axis as a measure of percentages rather than the number of persons. All three bar graphs are the same height and each bar is divided according to the percentage of population in each age group.

Figure A7 and **Figure A8** show how the bars can represent countries or years, and how the vertical axis can represent a numerical or a percentage value. Bar graphs can also compare size, quantity, rates, distances, and other quantitative categories.

Comparing Line Graphs with Pie Charts and Bar Graphs

Now that you are familiar with pie graphs, bar graphs, and line graphs, how do you know which graph to use for your data? Pie graphs are often better than line graphs at showing how an overall group is divided. However, if a pie graph has too many slices, it can become difficult to interpret.

Bar graphs are especially useful when comparing quantities. For example, if you are studying the populations of different countries, as in **Figure A7**, bar graphs can show the relationships between the population sizes of multiple countries. Not only can it show these relationships, but it can also show breakdowns of different groups within the population.

A line graph is often the most effective format for illustrating a relationship between two variables that are both changing. For example, time series graphs can show patterns as time changes, like the unemployment rate over time. Line graphs are widely used in economics to present continuous data about prices, wages, quantities bought and sold, the size of the economy.

How Graphs Can Be Misleading

Graphs not only reveal patterns; they can also alter how patterns are perceived. To see some of the ways this can be done, consider the line graphs of **Figure A9**, **Figure A10**, and **Figure A11**. These graphs all illustrate the unemployment rate—but from different perspectives.

(a) Unemployment rate, wide and short

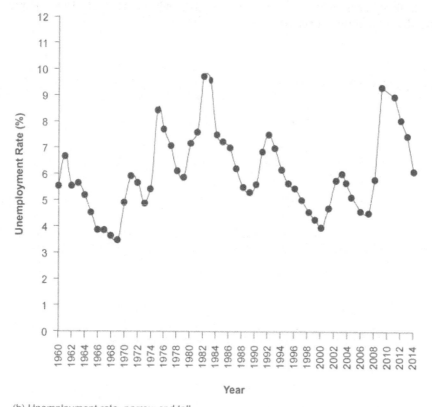

(b) Unemployment rate, narrow and tall

Figure A9

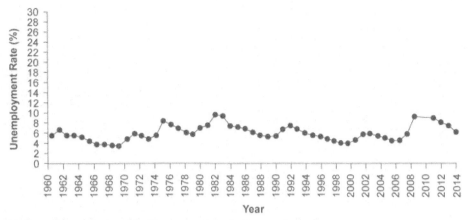

(c) Unemployment rate, with wider range of numbers on vertical axis

(d) Unemployment rate, with smaller range of numbers on vertical axis

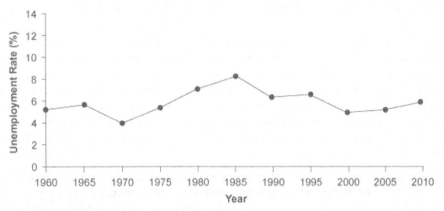

(e) Unemployment rate, five-year averages

Figure A10 Presenting Unemployment Rates in Different Ways, All of Them Accurate Simply changing the width and height of the area in which data is displayed can alter the perception of the data.

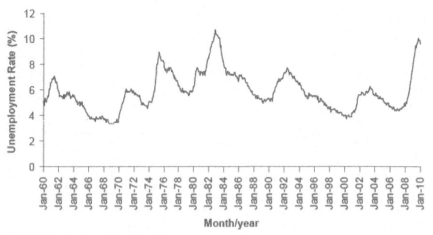

(f) Unemployment rate, monthly data

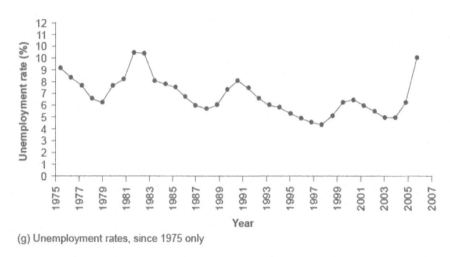

(g) Unemployment rates, since 1975 only

Figure A11 Presenting Unemployment Rates in Different Ways, All of Them Accurate   Simply changing the width and height of the area in which data is displayed can alter the perception of the data.

Suppose you wanted a graph which gives the impression that the rise in unemployment in 2009 was not all that large, or all that extraordinary by historical standards. You might choose to present your data as in **Figure A9** (a). **Figure A9** (a) includes much of the same data presented earlier in **Figure A5**, but stretches the horizontal axis out longer relative to the vertical axis. By spreading the graph wide and flat, the visual appearance is that the rise in unemployment is not so large, and is similar to some past rises in unemployment. Now imagine you wanted to emphasize how unemployment spiked substantially higher in 2009. In this case, using the same data, you can stretch the vertical axis out relative to the horizontal axis, as in **Figure A9** (b), which makes all rises and falls in unemployment appear larger.

A similar effect can be accomplished without changing the length of the axes, but by changing the scale on the vertical axis. In **Figure A10** (c), the scale on the vertical axis runs from 0% to 30%, while in **Figure A10** (d), the vertical axis runs from 3% to 10%. Compared to **Figure A5**, where the vertical scale runs from 0% to 12%, **Figure A10** (c) makes the fluctuation in unemployment look smaller, while **Figure A10** (d) makes it look larger.

Another way to alter the perception of the graph is to reduce the amount of variation by changing the number of points plotted on the graph. **Figure A10** (e) shows the unemployment rate according to five-year averages. By averaging out some of the year- to-year changes, the line appears smoother and with fewer highs and lows. In reality, the unemployment rate is reported monthly, and **Figure A11** (f) shows the monthly figures since 1960, which fluctuate more than the five-year average. **Figure A11** (f) is also a vivid illustration of how graphs can compress lots of data. The graph includes monthly data since 1960, which over almost 50 years, works out to nearly 600 data points.

Reading that list of 600 data points in numerical form would be hypnotic. You can, however, get a good intuitive sense of these 600 data points very quickly from the graph.

A final trick in manipulating the perception of graphical information is that, by choosing the starting and ending points carefully, you can influence the perception of whether the variable is rising or falling. The original data show a general pattern with unemployment low in the 1960s, but spiking up in the mid-1970s, early 1980s, early 1990s, early 2000s, and late 2000s. Figure A11 (g), however, shows a graph that goes back only to 1975, which gives an impression that unemployment was more-or-less gradually falling over time until the 2009 recession pushed it back up to its "original" level—which is a plausible interpretation if one starts at the high point around 1975.

These kinds of tricks—or shall we just call them "presentation choices"— are not limited to line graphs. In a pie chart with many small slices and one large slice, someone must decided what categories should be used to produce these slices in the first place, thus making some slices appear bigger than others. If you are making a bar graph, you can make the vertical axis either taller or shorter, which will tend to make variations in the height of the bars appear more or less.

Being able to read graphs is an essential skill, both in economics and in life. A graph is just one perspective or point of view, shaped by choices such as those discussed in this section. Do not always believe the first quick impression from a graph. View with caution.

Key Concepts and Summary

Math is a tool for understanding economics and economic relationships can be expressed mathematically using algebra or graphs. The algebraic equation for a line is $y = b + mx$, where x is the variable on the horizontal axis and y is the variable on the vertical axis, the b term is the y-intercept and the m term is the slope. The slope of a line is the same at any point on the line and it indicates the relationship (positive, negative, or zero) between two economic variables.

Economic models can be solved algebraically or graphically. Graphs allow you to illustrate data visually. They can illustrate patterns, comparisons, trends, and apportionment by condensing the numerical data and providing an intuitive sense of relationships in the data. A line graph shows the relationship between two variables: one is shown on the horizontal axis and one on the vertical axis. A pie graph shows how something is allotted, such as a sum of money or a group of people. The size of each slice of the pie is drawn to represent the corresponding percentage of the whole. A bar graph uses the height of bars to show a relationship, where each bar represents a certain entity, like a country or a group of people. The bars on a bar graph can also be divided into segments to show subgroups.

Any graph is a single visual perspective on a subject. The impression it leaves will be based on many choices, such as what data or time frame is included, how data or groups are divided up, the relative size of vertical and horizontal axes, whether the scale used on a vertical starts at zero. Thus, any graph should be regarded somewhat skeptically, remembering that the underlying relationship can be open to different interpretations.

Review Questions

Exercise A1

Name three kinds of graphs and briefly state when is most appropriate to use each type of graph.

Exercise A2

What is slope on a line graph?

Exercise A3

What do the slices of a pie chart represent?

Exercise A4

Why is a bar chart the best way to illustrate comparisons?

Exercise A5

How does the appearance of positive slope differ from negative slope and from zero slope?

Appendix B

Economists use a vocabulary of maximizing utility to describe people's preferences. In **Consumer Choices**
(http://cnx.org/content/m57229/latest/) , the level of utility that a person receives is described in numerical
terms. This appendix presents an alternative approach to describing personal preferences, called indifference curves,
which avoids any need for using numbers to measure utility. By setting aside the assumption of putting a numerical
valuation on utility—an assumption that many students and economists find uncomfortably unrealistic—the
indifference curve framework helps to clarify the logic of the underlying model.

What Is an Indifference Curve?

People cannot really put a numerical value on their level of satisfaction. However, they can, and do, identify what
choices would give them more, or less, or the same amount of satisfaction. An indifference curve shows combinations
of goods that provide an equal level of utility or satisfaction. For example, **Figure B1** presents three indifference
curves that represent Lilly's preferences for the tradeoffs that she faces in her two main relaxation activities: eating
doughnuts and reading paperback books. Each indifference curve (Ul, Um, and Uh) represents one level of utility.
First we will explore the meaning of one particular indifference curve and then we will look at the indifference curves
as a group.

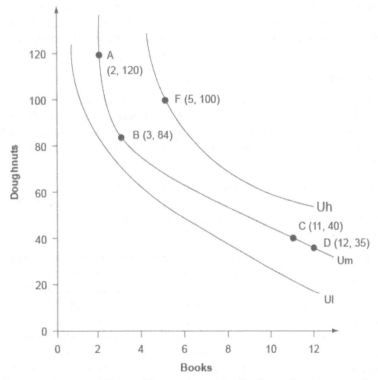

Figure B1 Lilly's Indifference Curves Lilly would receive equal utility from all points on a given indifference curve.
Any points on the highest indifference curve Uh, like F, provide greater utility than any points like A, B, C, and D on
the middle indifference curve Um. Similarly, any points on the middle indifference curve Um provide greater utility
than any points on the lowest indifference curve Ul.

The Shape of an Indifference Curve

The indifference curve Um has four points labeled on it: A, B, C, and D. Since an indifference curve represents a set
of choices that have the same level of utility, Lilly must receive an equal amount of utility, judged according to her
personal preferences, from two books and 120 doughnuts (point A), from three books and 84 doughnuts (point B)
from 11 books and 40 doughnuts (point C) or from 12 books and 35 doughnuts (point D). She would also receive the
same utility from any of the unlabeled intermediate points along this indifference curve.

Indifference curves have a roughly similar shape in two ways: 1) they are downward sloping from left to right; 2) they are convex with respect to the origin. In other words, they are steeper on the left and flatter on the right. The downward slope of the indifference curve means that Lilly must trade off less of one good to get more of the other, while holding utility constant. For example, points A and B sit on the same indifference curve Um, which means that they provide Lilly with the same level of utility. Thus, the marginal utility that Lilly would gain from, say, increasing her consumption of books from two to three must be equal to the marginal utility that she would lose if her consumption of doughnuts was cut from 120 to 84—so that her overall utility remains unchanged between points A and B. Indeed, the slope along an indifference curve is referred to as the marginal rate of substitution, which is the rate at which a person is willing to trade one good for another so that utility will remain the same.

Indifference curves like Um are steeper on the left and flatter on the right. The reason behind this shape involves diminishing marginal utility—the notion that as a person consumes more of a good, the marginal utility from each additional unit becomes lower. Compare two different choices between points that all provide Lilly an equal amount of utility along the indifference curve Um: the choice between A and B, and between C and D. In both choices, Lilly consumes one more book, but between A and B her consumption of doughnuts falls by 36 (from 120 to 84) and between C and D it falls by only five (from 40 to 35). The reason for this difference is that points A and C are different starting points, and thus have different implications for marginal utility. At point A, Lilly has few books and many doughnuts. Thus, her marginal utility from an extra book will be relatively high while the marginal utility of additional doughnuts is relatively low—so on the margin, it will take a relatively large number of doughnuts to offset the utility from the marginal book. At point C, however, Lilly has many books and few doughnuts. From this starting point, her marginal utility gained from extra books will be relatively low, while the marginal utility lost from additional doughnuts would be relatively high—so on the margin, it will take a relatively smaller number of doughnuts to offset the change of one marginal book. In short, the slope of the indifference curve changes because the marginal rate of substitution—that is, the quantity of one good that would be traded for the other good to keep utility constant—also changes, as a result of diminishing marginal utility of both goods.

The Field of Indifference Curves

Each indifference curve represents the choices that provide a single level of utility. Every level of utility will have its own indifference curve. Thus, Lilly's preferences will include an infinite number of indifference curves lying nestled together on the diagram—even though only three of the indifference curves, representing three levels of utility, appear on **Figure B1**. In other words, an infinite number of indifference curves are not drawn on this diagram—but you should remember that they exist.

Higher indifference curves represent a greater level of utility than lower ones. In **Figure B1**, indifference curve Ul can be thought of as a "low" level of utility, while Um is a "medium" level of utility and Uh is a "high" level of utility. All of the choices on indifference curve Uh are preferred to all of the choices on indifference curve Um, which in turn are preferred to all of the choices on Ul.

To understand why higher indifference curves are preferred to lower ones, compare point B on indifference curve Um to point F on indifference curve Uh. Point F has greater consumption of both books (five to three) and doughnuts (100 to 84), so point F is clearly preferable to point B. Given the definition of an indifference curve—that all the points on the curve have the same level of utility—if point F on indifference curve Uh is preferred to point B on indifference curve Um, then it must be true that all points on indifference curve Uh have a higher level of utility than all points on Um. More generally, for any point on a lower indifference curve, like Ul, you can identify a point on a higher indifference curve like Um or Uh that has a higher consumption of both goods. Since one point on the higher indifference curve is preferred to one point on the lower curve, and since all the points on a given indifference curve have the same level of utility, it must be true that all points on higher indifference curves have greater utility than all points on lower indifference curves.

These arguments about the shapes of indifference curves and about higher or lower levels of utility do not require any numerical estimates of utility, either by the individual or by anyone else. They are only based on the assumptions that when people have less of one good they need more of another good to make up for it, if they are keeping the same level of utility, and that as people have more of a good, the marginal utility they receive from additional units of that good will diminish. Given these gentle assumptions, a field of indifference curves can be mapped out to describe the preferences of any individual.

The Individuality of Indifference Curves

Each person determines their own preferences and utility. Thus, while indifference curves have the same general shape—they slope down, and the slope is steeper on the left and flatter on the right—the specific shape of indifference curves can be different for every person. **Figure B1**, for example, applies only to Lilly's preferences. Indifference curves for other people would probably travel through different points.

Utility-Maximizing with Indifference Curves

People seek the highest level of utility, which means that they wish to be on the highest possible indifference curve. However, people are limited by their budget constraints, which show what tradeoffs are actually possible.

Maximizing Utility at the Highest Indifference Curve

Return to the situation of Lilly's choice between paperback books and doughnuts. Say that books cost $6, doughnuts are 50 cents each, and that Lilly has $60 to spend. This information provides the basis for the budget line shown in **Figure B2**. Along with the budget line are shown the three indifference curves from **Figure B1**. What is Lilly's utility-maximizing choice? Several possibilities are identified in the diagram.

Figure B2 Indifference Curves and a Budget Constraint   Lilly's preferences are shown by the indifference curves. Lilly's budget constraint, given the prices of books and doughnuts and her income, is shown by the straight line. Lilly's optimal choice will be point B, where the budget line is tangent to the indifference curve Um. Lilly would have more utility at a point like F on the higher indifference curve Uh, but the budget line does not touch the higher indifference curve Uh at any point, so she cannot afford this choice. A choice like G is affordable to Lilly, but it lies on indifference curve Ul and thus provides less utility than choice B, which is on indifference curve Um.

The choice of F with five books and 100 doughnuts is highly desirable, since it is on the highest indifference curve Uh of those shown in the diagram. However, it is not affordable given Lilly's budget constraint. The choice of H with three books and 70 doughnuts on indifference curve Ul is a wasteful choice, since it is inside Lilly's budget set, and as a utility-maximizer, Lilly will always prefer a choice on the budget constraint itself. Choices B and G are both on the opportunity set. However, choice G of six books and 48 doughnuts is on lower indifference curve Ul than choice B of three books and 84 doughnuts, which is on the indifference curve Um. If Lilly were to start at choice G, and then thought about whether the marginal utility she was deriving from doughnuts and books, she would decide that some additional doughnuts and fewer books would make her happier—which would cause her to move toward her preferred choice B. Given the combination of Lilly's personal preferences, as identified by her indifference curves, and Lilly's opportunity set, which is determined by prices and income, B will be her utility-maximizing choice.

The highest achievable indifference curve touches the opportunity set at a single point of tangency. Since an infinite number of indifference curves exist, even if only a few of them are drawn on any given diagram, there will always exist one indifference curve that touches the budget line at a single point of tangency. All higher indifference curves, like Uh, will be completely above the budget line and, although the choices on that indifference curve would provide higher utility, they are not affordable given the budget set. All lower indifference curves, like Ul, will cross the budget line in two separate places. When one indifference curve crosses the budget line in two places, however, there will be another, higher, attainable indifference curve sitting above it that touches the budget line at only one point of tangency.

Changes in Income

A rise in income causes the budget constraint to shift to the right. In graphical terms, the new budget constraint will now be tangent to a higher indifference curve, representing a higher level of utility. A reduction in income will cause the budget constraint to shift to the left, which will cause it to be tangent to a lower indifference curve, representing a reduced level of utility. If income rises by, for example, 50%, exactly how much will a person alter consumption of books and doughnuts? Will consumption of both goods rise by 50%? Or will the quantity of one good rise substantially, while the quantity of the other good rises only a little, or even declines?

Since personal preferences and the shape of indifference curves are different for each individual, the response to changes in income will be different, too. For example, consider the preferences of Manuel and Natasha in **Figure B3** (a) and **Figure B3** (b). They each start with an identical income of $40, which they spend on yogurts that cost $1 and rental movies that cost $4. Thus, they face identical budget constraints. However, based on Manuel's preferences, as revealed by his indifference curves, his utility-maximizing choice on the original budget set occurs where his opportunity set is tangent to the highest possible indifference curve at W, with three movies and 28 yogurts, while Natasha's utility-maximizing choice on the original budget set at Y will be seven movies and 12 yogurts.

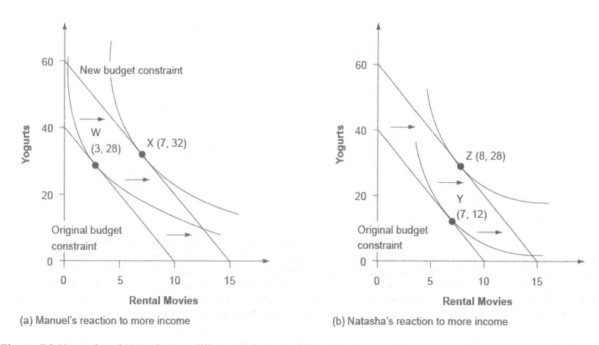

(a) Manuel's reaction to more income   (b) Natasha's reaction to more income

Figure B3 Manuel and Natasha's Indifference Curves Manuel and Natasha originally face the same budget constraints; that is, same prices and same income. However, the indifference curves that illustrate their preferences are not the same. (a) Manuel's original choice at W involves more yogurt and more movies, and he reacts to the higher income by mainly increasing consumption of movies at X. (b) Conversely, Natasha's original choice (Y) involves relatively more movies, but she reacts to the higher income by choosing relatively more yogurts. Even when budget constraints are the same, personal preferences lead to different original choices and to different reactions in response to a change in income.

Now, say that income rises to $60 for both Manuel and Natasha, so their budget constraints shift to the right. As shown in **Figure B3** (a), Manuel's new utility maximizing choice at X will be seven movies and 32 yogurts—that is, Manuel will choose to spend most of the extra income on movies. Natasha's new utility maximizing choice at Z will be eight movies and 28 yogurts—that is, she will choose to spend most of the extra income on yogurt. In this way, the indifference curve approach allows for a range of possible responses. However, if both goods are normal goods, then the typical response to a higher level of income will be to purchase more of them—although exactly how much more is a matter of personal preference. If one of the goods is an inferior good, the response to a higher level of income will be to purchase less of it.

Responses to Price Changes: Substitution and Income Effects

A higher price for a good will cause the budget constraint to shift to the left, so that it is tangent to a lower indifference curve representing a reduced level of utility. Conversely, a lower price for a good will cause the opportunity set to shift to the right, so that it is tangent to a higher indifference curve representing an increased level of utility. Exactly how much a change in price will lead to the quantity demanded of each good will depend on personal preferences.

Anyone who faces a change in price will experience two interlinked motivations: a substitution effect and an income effect. The substitution effect is that when a good becomes more expensive, people seek out substitutes. If oranges become more expensive, fruit-lovers scale back on oranges and eat more apples, grapefruit, or raisins. Conversely, when a good becomes cheaper, people substitute toward consuming more. If oranges get cheaper, people fire up their juicing machines and ease off on other fruits and foods. The income effect refers to how a change in the price of a good alters the effective buying power of one's income. If the price of a good that you have been buying falls, then in effect your buying power has risen—you are able to purchase more goods. Conversely, if the price of a good that you have been buying rises, then the buying power of a given amount of income is diminished. (One common source of confusion is that the "income effect" does not refer to a change in actual income. Instead, it refers to the situation in which the price of a good changes, and thus the quantities of goods that can be purchased with a fixed amount of income change. It might be more accurate to call the "income effect" a "buying power effect," but the "income effect" terminology has been used for decades, and it is not going to change during this economics course.) Whenever a price changes, consumers feel the pull of both substitution and income effects at the same time.

Using indifference curves, you can illustrate the substitution and income effects on a graph. In **Figure B4**, Ogden faces a choice between two goods: haircuts or personal pizzas. Haircuts cost $20, personal pizzas cost $6, and he has $120 to spend.

Figure B4 Substitution and Income Effects   The original choice is A, the point of tangency between the original budget constraint and indifference curve. The new choice is B, the point of tangency between the new budget constraint and the lower indifference curve. Point C is the tangency between the dashed line, where the slope shows the new higher price of haircuts, and the original indifference curve. The substitution effect is the shift from A to C, which means getting fewer haircuts and more pizza. The income effect is the shift from C to B; that is, the reduction in buying power that causes a shift from the higher indifference curve to the lower indifference curve, with relative prices remaining unchanged. The income effect results in less consumed of both goods. Both substitution and income effects cause fewer haircuts to be consumed. For pizza, in this case, the substitution effect and income effect cancel out, leading to the same amount of pizza consumed.

The price of haircuts rises to $30. Ogden starts at choice A on the higher opportunity set and the higher indifference curve. After the price of pizza increases, he chooses B on the lower opportunity set and the lower indifference curve. Point B with two haircuts and 10 personal pizzas is immediately below point A with three haircuts and 10 personal pizzas, showing that Ogden reacted to a higher price of haircuts by cutting back only on haircuts, while leaving his consumption of pizza unchanged.

The dashed line in the diagram, and point C, are used to separate the substitution effect and the income effect. To understand their function, start by thinking about the substitution effect with this question: How would Ogden change his consumption if the relative prices of the two goods changed, but this change in relative prices did not affect his utility? The slope of the budget constraint is determined by the relative price of the two goods; thus, the slope of the original budget line is determined by the original relative prices, while the slope of the new budget line is determined by the new relative prices. With this thought in mind, the dashed line is a graphical tool inserted in a specific way: It is inserted so that it is parallel with the new budget constraint, so it reflects the new relative prices, but it is tangent to the original indifference curve, so it reflects the original level of utility or buying power.

Thus, the movement from the original choice (A) to point C is a substitution effect; it shows the choice that Ogden would make if relative prices shifted (as shown by the different slope between the original budget set and the dashed line) but if buying power did not shift (as shown by being tangent to the original indifference curve). The substitution effect will encourage people to shift away from the good which has become relatively more expensive—in Ogden's case, the haircuts on the vertical axis—and toward the good which has become relatively less expensive—in this case, the pizza on the vertical axis. The two arrows labeled with "s" for "substitution effect," one on each axis, show the direction of this movement.

The income effect is the movement from point C to B, which shows how Ogden reacts to a reduction in his buying power from the higher indifference curve to the lower indifference curve, but holding constant the relative prices (because the dashed line has the same slope as the new budget constraint). In this case, where the price of one good increases, buying power is reduced, so the income effect means that consumption of both goods should fall (if they are both normal goods, which it is reasonable to assume unless there is reason to believe otherwise). The two arrows labeled with "i" for "income effect," one on each axis, show the direction of this income effect movement.

Now, put the substitution and income effects together. When the price of pizza increased, Ogden consumed less of it, for two reasons shown in the exhibit: the substitution effect of the higher price led him to consume less and the income effect of the higher price also led him to consume less. However, when the price of pizza increased, Ogden consumed the same quantity of haircuts. The substitution effect of a higher price for pizza meant that haircuts became relatively less expensive (compared to pizza), and this factor, taken alone, would have encouraged Ogden to consume more haircuts. However, the income effect of a higher price for pizza meant that he wished to consume less of both goods, and this factor, taken alone, would have encouraged Ogden to consume fewer haircuts. As shown in **Figure B4**, in this particular example the substitution effect and income effect on Ogden's consumption of haircuts are offsetting—so he ends up consuming the same quantity of haircuts after the price increase for pizza as before.

The size of these income and substitution effects will differ from person to person, depending on individual preferences. For example, if Ogden's substitution effect away from pizza and toward haircuts is especially strong, and outweighs the income effect, then a higher price for pizza might lead to increased consumption of haircuts. This case would be drawn on the graph so that the point of tangency between the new budget constraint and the relevant indifference curve occurred below point B and to the right. Conversely, if the substitution effect away from pizza and toward haircuts is not as strong, and the income effect on is relatively stronger, then Ogden will be more likely to react to the higher price of pizza by consuming less of both goods. In this case, his optimal choice after the price change will be above and to the left of choice B on the new budget constraint.

Although the substitution and income effects are often discussed as a sequence of events, it should be remembered that they are twin components of a single cause—a change in price. Although you can analyze them separately, the two effects are always proceeding hand in hand, happening at the same time.

Indifference Curves with Labor-Leisure and Intertemporal Choices

The concept of an indifference curve applies to tradeoffs in any household choice, including the labor-leisure choice or the intertemporal choice between present and future consumption. In the labor-leisure choice, each indifference curve shows the combinations of leisure and income that provide a certain level of utility. In an intertemporal choice, each indifference curve shows the combinations of present and future consumption that provide a certain level of utility. The general shapes of the indifference curves—downward sloping, steeper on the left and flatter on the right—also remain the same.

A Labor-Leisure Example

Petunia is working at a job that pays $12 per hour but she gets a raise to $20 per hour. After family responsibilities and sleep, she has 80 hours per week available for work or leisure. As shown in **Figure B5**, the highest level of utility for Petunia, on her original budget constraint, is at choice A, where it is tangent to the lower indifference curve (Ul). Point A has 30 hours of leisure and thus 50 hours per week of work, with income of $600 per week (that is, 50 hours of work at $12 per hour). Petunia then gets a raise to $20 per hour, which shifts her budget constraint to the right. Her new utility-maximizing choice occurs where the new budget constraint is tangent to the higher indifference curve Uh. At B, Petunia has 40 hours of leisure per week and works 40 hours, with income of $800 per week (that is, 40 hours of work at $20 per hour).

Figure B5 Effects of a Change in Petunia's Wage Petunia starts at choice A, the tangency between her original budget constraint and the lower indifference curve Ul. The wage increase shifts her budget constraint to the right, so that she can now choose B on indifference curve Uh. The substitution effect is the movement from A to C. In this case, the substitution effect would lead Petunia to choose less leisure, which is relatively more expensive, and more income, which is relatively cheaper to earn. The income effect is the movement from C to B. The income effect in this example leads to greater consumption of both goods. Overall, in this example, income rises because of both substitution and income effects. However, leisure declines because of the substitution effect but increases because of the income effect—leading, in Petunia's case, to an overall increase in the quantity of leisure consumed.

Substitution and income effects provide a vocabulary for discussing how Petunia reacts to a higher hourly wage. The dashed line serves as the tool for separating the two effects on the graph.

The substitution effect tells how Petunia would have changed her hours of work if her wage had risen, so that income was relatively cheaper to earn and leisure was relatively more expensive, but if she had remained at the same level of utility. The slope of the budget constraint in a labor-leisure diagram is determined by the wage rate. Thus, the dashed line is carefully inserted with the slope of the new opportunity set, reflecting the labor-leisure tradeoff of the new wage rate, but tangent to the original indifference curve, showing the same level of utility or "buying power." The shift from original choice A to point C, which is the point of tangency between the original indifference curve and the dashed line, shows that because of the higher wage, Petunia will want to consume less leisure and more income. The "s" arrows on the horizontal and vertical axes of **Figure B5** show the substitution effect on leisure and on income.

The income effect is that the higher wage, by shifting the labor-leisure budget constraint to the right, makes it possible for Petunia to reach a higher level of utility. The income effect is the movement from point C to point B; that is, it shows how Petunia's behavior would change in response to a higher level of utility or "buying power," with the wage rate remaining the same (as shown by the dashed line being parallel to the new budget constraint). The income effect, encouraging Petunia to consume both more leisure and more income, is drawn with arrows on the horizontal and vertical axis of **Figure B5**.

Putting these effects together, Petunia responds to the higher wage by moving from choice A to choice B. This movement involves choosing more income, both because the substitution effect of higher wages has made income relatively cheaper or easier to earn, and because the income effect of higher wages has made it possible to have more income and more leisure. Her movement from A to B also involves choosing more leisure because, according to Petunia's preferences, the income effect that encourages choosing more leisure is stronger than the substitution effect that encourages choosing less leisure.

Figure B5 represents only Petunia's preferences. Other people might make other choices. For example, a person whose substitution and income effects on leisure exactly counterbalanced each other might react to a higher wage with a choice like D, exactly above the original choice A, which means taking all of the benefit of the higher wages in the form of income while working the same number of hours. Yet another person, whose substitution effect on leisure outweighed the income effect, might react to a higher wage by making a choice like F, where the response to higher wages is to work more hours and earn much more income. To represent these different preferences, you could easily draw the indifference curve Uh to be tangent to the new budget constraint at D or F, rather than at B.

An Intertemporal Choice Example

Quentin has saved up $10,000. He is thinking about spending some or all of it on a vacation in the present, and then will save the rest for another big vacation five years from now. Over those five years, he expects to earn a total 80% rate of return. **Figure B6** shows Quentin's budget constraint and his indifference curves between present consumption and future consumption. The highest level of utility that Quentin can achieve at his original intertemporal budget constraint occurs at point A, where he is consuming $6,000, saving $4,000 for the future, and expecting with the accumulated interest to have $7,200 for future consumption (that is, $4,000 in current financial savings plus the 80% rate of return).

However, Quentin has just realized that his expected rate of return was unrealistically high. A more realistic expectation is that over five years he can earn a total return of 30%. In effect, his intertemporal budget constraint has pivoted to the left, so that his original utility-maximizing choice is no longer available. Will Quentin react to the lower rate of return by saving more, or less, or the same amount? Again, the language of substitution and income effects provides a framework for thinking about the motivations behind various choices. The dashed line, which is a graphical tool to separate the substitution and income effect, is carefully inserted with the same slope as the new opportunity set, so that it reflects the changed rate of return, but it is tangent to the original indifference curve, so that it shows no change in utility or "buying power."

The substitution effect tells how Quentin would have altered his consumption because the lower rate of return makes future consumption relatively more expensive and present consumption relatively cheaper. The movement from the original choice A to point C shows how Quentin substitutes toward more present consumption and less future consumption in response to the lower interest rate, with no change in utility. The substitution arrows on the horizontal and vertical axes of **Figure B6** show the direction of the substitution effect motivation. The substitution effect suggests that, because of the lower interest rate, Quentin should consume more in the present and less in the future.

Quentin also has an income effect motivation. The lower rate of return shifts the budget constraint to the left, which means that Quentin's utility or "buying power" is reduced. The income effect (assuming normal goods) encourages less of both present and future consumption. The impact of the income effect on reducing present and future consumption in this example is shown with "i" arrows on the horizontal and vertical axis of **Figure B6**.

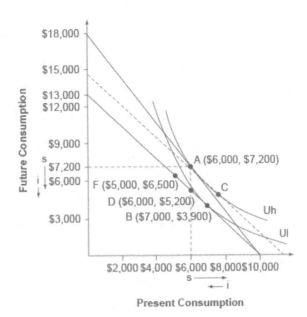

Figure B6 Indifference Curve and an Intertemporal Budget Constraint The original choice is A, at the tangency between the original budget constraint and the original indifference curve Uh. The dashed line is drawn parallel to the new budget set, so that its slope reflects the lower rate of return, but is tangent to the original indifference curve. The movement from A to C is the substitution effect: in this case, future consumption has become relatively more expensive, and present consumption has become relatively cheaper. The income effect is the shift from C to B; that is, the reduction in utility or "buying power" that causes a move to a lower indifference curve Ul, but with the relative price the same. It means less present and less future consumption. In the move from A to B, the substitution effect on present consumption is greater than the income effect, so the overall result is more present consumption. Notice that the lower indifference curve could have been drawn tangent to the lower budget constraint point D or point F, depending on personal preferences.

Taking both effects together, the substitution effect is encouraging Quentin toward more present and less future consumption, because present consumption is relatively cheaper, while the income effect is encouraging him to less present and less future consumption, because the lower interest rate is pushing him to a lower level of utility. For Quentin's personal preferences, the substitution effect is stronger so that, overall, he reacts to the lower rate of return with more present consumption and less savings at choice B. However, other people might have different preferences. They might react to a lower rate of return by choosing the same level of present consumption and savings at choice D, or by choosing less present consumption and more savings at a point like F. For these other sets of preferences, the income effect of a lower rate of return on present consumption would be relatively stronger, while the substitution effect would be relatively weaker.

Sketching Substitution and Income Effects

Indifference curves provide an analytical tool for looking at all the choices that provide a single level of utility. They eliminate any need for placing numerical values on utility and help to illuminate the process of making utility-maximizing decisions. They also provide the basis for a more detailed investigation of the complementary motivations that arise in response to a change in a price, wage or rate of return—namely, the substitution and income effects.

If you are finding it a little tricky to sketch diagrams that show substitution and income effects so that the points of tangency all come out correctly, it may be useful to follow this procedure.

Step 1. Begin with a budget constraint showing the choice between two goods, which this example will call "candy" and "movies." Choose a point A which will be the optimal choice, where the indifference curve will be tangent—but it is often easier not to draw in the indifference curve just yet. See **Figure B7**.

Figure B7

Step 2. Now the price of movies changes: let's say that it rises. That shifts the budget set inward. You know that the higher price will push the decision-maker down to a lower level of utility, represented by a lower indifference curve. But at this stage, draw only the new budget set. See Figure B8.

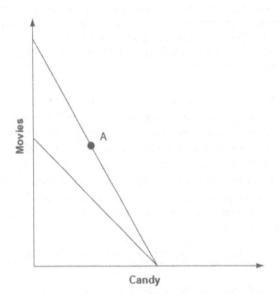

Figure B8

Step 3. The key tool in distinguishing between substitution and income effects is to insert a dashed line, parallel to the new budget line. This line is a graphical tool that allows you to distinguish between the two changes: (1) the effect on consumption of the two goods of the shift in prices—with the level of utility remaining unchanged—which is the substitution effect; and (2) the effect on consumption of the two goods of shifting from one indifference curve to the other—with relative prices staying unchanged—which is the income effect. The dashed line is inserted in this step. The trick is to have the dashed line travel close to the original choice A, but not directly through point A. See Figure B9.

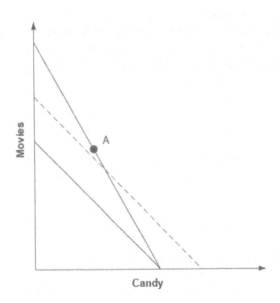

Figure B9

Step 4. Now, draw the original indifference curve, so that it is tangent to both point A on the original budget line and to a point C on the dashed line. Many students find it easiest to first select the tangency point C where the original indifference curve touches the dashed line, and then to draw the original indifference curve through A and C. The substitution effect is illustrated by the movement along the original indifference curve as prices change but the level of utility holds constant, from A to C. As expected, the substitution effect leads to less consumed of the good that is relatively more expensive, as shown by the "s" (substitution) arrow on the vertical axis, and more consumed of the good that is relatively less expensive, as shown by the "s" arrow on the horizontal axis. See **Figure B10**.

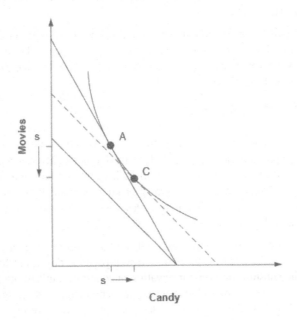

Figure B10

Step 5. With the substitution effect in place, now choose utility-maximizing point B on the new opportunity set. When you choose point B, think about whether you wish the substitution or the income effect to have a larger impact on the good (in this case, candy) on the horizontal axis. If you choose point B to be directly in a vertical line with point A (as is illustrated here), then the income effect will be exactly offsetting the substitution effect on the horizontal axis. If you insert point B so that it lies a little to right of the original point A, then the substitution effect will exceed the income effect. If you insert point B so that it lies a little to the left of point A, then the income effect will exceed the substitution effect. The income effect is the movement from C to B, showing how choices shifted as a result of the decline in buying power and the movement between two levels of utility, with relative prices remaining the same. With normal goods, the negative income effect means less consumed of each good, as shown by the direction of the "i" (income effect) arrows on the vertical and horizontal axes. See Figure B11.

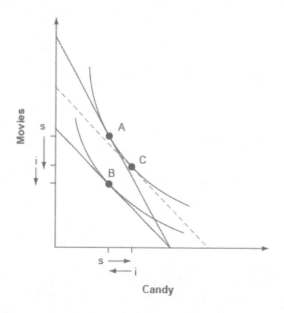

Figure B11

In sketching substitution and income effect diagrams, you may wish to practice some of the following variations: (1) Price falls instead of a rising; (2) The price change affects the good on either the vertical or the horizontal axis; (3) Sketch these diagrams so that the substitution effect exceeds the income effect; the income effect exceeds the substitution effect; and the two effects are equal.

One final note: The helpful dashed line can be drawn tangent to the new indifference curve, and parallel to the original budget line, rather than tangent to the original indifference curve and parallel to the new budget line. Some students find this approach more intuitively clear. The answers you get about the direction and relative sizes of the substitution and income effects, however, should be the same.

Key Concepts and Summary

An indifference curve is drawn on a budget constraint diagram that shows the tradeoffs between two goods. All points along a single indifference curve provide the same level of utility. Higher indifference curves represent higher levels of utility. Indifference curves slope downward because, if utility is to remain the same at all points along the curve, a reduction in the quantity of the good on the vertical axis must be counterbalanced by an increase in the quantity of the good on the horizontal axis (or vice versa). Indifference curves are steeper on the far left and flatter on the far right, because of diminishing marginal utility.

The utility-maximizing choice along a budget constraint will be the point of tangency where the budget constraint touches an indifference curve at a single point. A change in the price of any good has two effects: a substitution effect and an income effect. The substitution effect motivation encourages a utility-maximizer to buy less of what is relatively more expensive and more of what is relatively cheaper. The income effect motivation encourages a utility-maximizer to buy more of both goods if utility rises or less of both goods if utility falls (if they are both normal goods).

In a labor-leisure choice, every wage change has a substitution and an income effect. The substitution effect of a wage increase is to choose more income, since it is cheaper to earn, and less leisure, since its opportunity cost has increased. The income effect of a wage increase is to choose more of leisure and income, since they are both normal goods. The substitution and income effects of a wage decrease would reverse these directions.

In an intertemporal consumption choice, every interest rate change has a substitution and an income effect. The substitution effect of an interest rate increase is to choose more future consumption, since it is now cheaper to earn future consumption and less present consumption (more savings), since the opportunity cost of present consumption in terms of what is being given up in the future has increased. The income effect of an interest rate increase is to choose more of both present and future consumption, since they are both normal goods. The substitution and income effects of an interest rate decrease would reverse these directions.

Review Questions

Exercise B1

What point is preferred along an indifference curve?

Exercise B2

Why do indifference curves slope down?

Exercise B3

Why are indifference curves steep on the left and flatter on the right?

Exercise B4

How many indifference curves does a person have?

Exercise B5

How can you tell which indifference curves represent higher or lower levels of utility?

Exercise B6

What is a substitution effect?

Exercise B7

What is an income effect?

Exercise B8

Does the "income effect" involve a change in income? Explain.

Exercise B9

Does a change in price have both an income effect and a substitution effect? Does a change in income have both an income effect and a substitution effect?

Exercise B10

Would you expect, in some cases, to see only an income effect or only a substitution effect? Explain.

Exercise B11

Which is larger, the income effect or the substitution effect?

Appendix C

As explained in **Financial Markets (http://cnx.org/content/m57283/latest/)** , the prices of stocks and bonds depend on future events. The price of a bond depends on the future payments that the bond is expected to make, including both payments of interest and the repayment of the face value of the bond. The price of a stock depends on the expected future profits earned by the firm. The concept of a present discounted value (PDV), which is defined as the amount you should be willing to pay in the present for a stream of expected future payments, can be used to calculate appropriate prices for stocks and bonds. To place a present discounted value on a future payment, think about what amount of money you would need to have in the present to equal a certain amount in the future. This calculation will require an interest rate. For example, if the interest rate is 10%, then a payment of $110 a year from now will have a present discounted value of $100—that is, you could take $100 in the present and have $110 in the future. We will first shows how to apply the idea of present discounted value to a stock and then we will show how to apply it to a bond.

Applying Present Discounted Value to a Stock

Consider the case of Babble, Inc., a company that offers speaking lessons. For the sake of simplicity, say that the founder of Babble is 63 years old and plans to retire in two years, at which point the company will be disbanded. The company is selling 200 shares of stock and profits are expected to be $15 million right away, in the present, $20 million one year from now, and $25 million two years from now. All profits will be paid out as dividends to shareholders as they occur. Given this information, what will an investor pay for a share of stock in this company?

A financial investor, thinking about what future payments are worth in the present, will need to choose an interest rate. This interest rate will reflect the rate of return on other available financial investment opportunities, which is the opportunity cost of investing financial capital, and also a risk premium (that is, using a higher interest rate than the rates available elsewhere if this investment appears especially risky). In this example, say that the financial investor decides that appropriate interest rate to value these future payments is 15%.

Table C1 shows how to calculate the present discounted value of the future profits. For each time period, when a benefit is going to be received, apply the formula:

$$\text{Present discounted value} = \frac{\text{Future value received years in the future}}{(1 + \text{Interest rate})^{\text{numbers of years t}}}$$

Payments from Firm	Present Value
$15 million in present	$15 million
$20 million in one year	$20 million$/(1 + 0.15)^1$ = $17.4 million
$25 million in two years	$25 million$/(1 + 0.15)^2$ = $18.9 million
Total	*$51.3 million*

Table C1 Calculating Present Discounted Value of a Stock

Next, add up all the present values for the different time periods to get a final answer. The present value calculations ask what the amount in the future is worth in the present, given the 15% interest rate. Notice that a different PDV calculation needs to be done separately for amounts received at different times. Then, divide the PDV of total profits by the number of shares, 200 in this case: 51.3 million/200 = 0.2565 million. The price per share should be about $256,500 per share.

Of course, in the real world expected profits are a best guess, not a hard piece of data. Deciding which interest rate to apply for discounting to the present can be tricky. One needs to take into account both potential capital gains from the future sale of the stock and also dividends that might be paid. Differences of opinion on these issues are exactly why some financial investors want to buy a stock that other people want to sell: they are more optimistic about its future prospects. Conceptually, however, it all comes down to what you are willing to pay in the present for a stream of benefits to be received in the future.

Applying Present Discounted Value to a Bond

A similar calculation works in the case of bonds. Financial Markets (http://cnx.org/content/m57283/latest/) explains that if the interest rate falls after a bond is issued, so that the investor has locked in a higher rate, then that bond will sell for more than its face value. Conversely, if the interest rate rises after a bond is issued, then the investor is locked into a lower rate, and the bond will sell for less than its face value. The present value calculation sharpens this intuition.

Think about a simple two-year bond. It was issued for $3,000 at an interest rate of 8%. Thus, after the first year, the bond pays interest of 240 (which is 3,000 × 8%). At the end of the second year, the bond pays $240 in interest, plus the $3,000 in principle. Calculate how much this bond is worth in the present if the discount rate is 8%. Then, recalculate if interest rates rise and the applicable discount rate is 11%. To carry out these calculations, look at the stream of payments being received from the bond in the future and figure out what they are worth in present discounted value terms. The calculations applying the present value formula are shown in Table C2.

Stream of Payments (for the 8% interest rate)	Present Value (for the 8% interest rate)	Stream of Payments (for the 11% interest rate)	Present Value (for the 11% interest rate)
$240 payment after one year	$240/(1 + 0.08)^1 = $222.20	$240 payment after one year	$240/(1 + 0.11)^1 = $216.20
$3,240 payment after second year	$3,240/(1 + 0.08)^2 = $2,777.80	$3,240 payment after second year	$3,240/(1 + 0.11)^2 = $2,629.60
Total	*$3,000*	*Total*	*$2,845.80*

Table C2 Computing the Present Discounted Value of a Bond

The first calculation shows that the present value of a $3,000 bond, issued at 8%, is just $3,000. After all, that is how much money the borrower is receiving. The calculation confirms that the present value is the same for the lender. The bond is moving money around in time, from those willing to save in the present to those who want to borrow in the present, but the present value of what is received by the borrower is identical to the present value of what will be repaid to the lender.

The second calculation shows what happens if the interest rate rises from 8% to 11%. The actual dollar payments in the first column, as determined by the 8% interest rate, do not change. However, the present value of those payments, now discounted at a higher interest rate, is lower. Even though the future dollar payments that the bond is receiving have not changed, a person who tries to sell the bond will find that the investment's value has fallen.

Again, real-world calculations are often more complex, in part because, not only the interest rate prevailing in the market, but also the riskiness of whether the borrower will repay the loan, will change. In any case, the price of a bond is always the present value of a stream of future expected payments.

Other Applications

Present discounted value is a widely used analytical tool outside the world of finance. Every time a business thinks about making a physical capital investment, it must compare a set of present costs of making that investment to the present discounted value of future benefits. When government thinks about a proposal to, for example, add safety features to a highway, it must compare costs incurred in the present to benefits received in the future. Some academic disputes over environmental policies, like how much to reduce carbon dioxide emissions because of the risk that they will lead to a warming of global temperatures several decades in the future, turn on how one compares present costs of pollution control with long-run future benefits. Someone who wins the lottery and is scheduled to receive a string of payments over 30 years might be interested in knowing what the present discounted value is of those payments.

Whenever a string of costs and benefits stretches from the present into different times in the future, present discounted value becomes an indispensable tool of analysis.

ANSWER KEY

Chapter 1

1. Scarcity means human wants for goods and services exceed the available supply. Supply is limited because resources are limited. Demand, however, is virtually unlimited. Whatever the supply, it seems human nature to want more.

2. 100 people / 10 people per ham = a maximum of 10 hams per month if all residents produce ham. Since consumption is limited by production, the maximum number of hams residents could consume per month is 10.

3. She is very productive at her consulting job, but not very productive growing vegetables. Time spent consulting would produce far more income than it what she could save growing her vegetables using the same amount of time. So on purely economic grounds, it makes more sense for her to maximize her income by applying her labor to what she does best (i.e. specialization of labor).

4. The engineer is better at computer science than at painting. Thus, his time is better spent working for pay at his job and paying a painter to paint his house. Of course, this assumes he does not paint his house for fun!

5. There are many physical systems that would work, for example, the study of planets (micro) in the solar system (macro), or solar systems (micro) in the galaxy (macro).

6. Draw a box outside the original circular flow to represent the foreign country. Draw an arrow from the foreign country to firms, to represents imports. Draw an arrow in the reverse direction representing payments for imports. Draw an arrow from firms to the foreign country to represent exports. Draw an arrow in the reverse direction to represent payments for imports.

7. There are many such problems. Consider the AIDS epidemic. Why are so few AIDS patients in Africa and Southeast Asia treated with the same drugs that are effective in the United States and Europe? It is because neither those patients nor the countries in which they live have the resources to purchase the same drugs.

8. Public enterprise means the factors of production (resources and businesses) are owned and operated by the government.

9. The United States is a large country economically speaking, so it has less need to trade internationally than the other countries mentioned. (This is the same reason that France and Italy have lower ratios than Belgium or Sweden.) One additional reason is that each of the other countries is a member of the European Union, where trade between members occurs without barriers to trade, like tariffs and quotas.

Chapter 2

1. The opportunity cost of bus tickets is the number of burgers that must be given up to obtain one more bus ticket. Originally, when the price of bus tickets was 50 cents per trip, this opportunity cost was 0.50/2 = .25 burgers. The reason for this is that at the original prices, one burger ($2) costs the same as four bus tickets ($0.50), so the opportunity cost of a burger is four bus tickets, and the opportunity cost of a bus ticket is .25 (the inverse of the opportunity cost of a burger). With the new, higher price of bus tickets, the opportunity cost rises to $1/$2 or 0.50. You can see this graphically since the slope of the new budget constraint is flatter than the original one. If Alphonso spends all of his budget on burgers, the higher price of bus tickets has no impact so the horizontal intercept of the budget constraint is the same. If he spends all of his budget on bus tickets, he can now afford only half as many, so the vertical intercept is half as much. In short, the budget constraint rotates clockwise around the horizontal intercept, flattening as it goes and the opportunity cost of bus tickets increases.

2. Because of the improvement in technology, the vertical intercept of the PPF would be at a higher level of healthcare. In other words, the PPF would rotate clockwise around the horizontal intercept. This would make the PPF steeper, corresponding to an increase in the opportunity cost of education, since resources devoted to education would now mean forgoing a greater quantity of healthcare.

3. No. Allocative efficiency requires productive efficiency, because it pertains to choices along the production possibilities frontier.

4. Both the budget constraint and the PPF show the constraint that each operates under. Both show a tradeoff between having more of one good but less of the other. Both show the opportunity cost graphically as the slope of the constraint (budget or PPF).

5. When individuals compare cost per unit in the grocery store, or characteristics of one product versus another, they are behaving approximately like the model describes.

6. Since an op-ed makes a case for what should be, it is considered normative.

7. Assuming that the study is not taking an explicit position about whether soft drink consumption is good or bad, but just reporting the science, it would be considered positive.

Chapter 3

1. Since $1.60 per gallon is above the equilibrium price, the quantity demanded would be lower at 550 gallons and the quantity supplied would be higher at 640 gallons. (These results are due to the laws of demand and supply, respectively.) The outcome of lower Qd and higher Qs would be a surplus in the gasoline market of 640 – 550 = 90 gallons.

2. To make it easier to analyze complex problems. *Ceteris paribus* allows you to look at the effect of one factor at a time on what it is you are trying to analyze. When you have analyzed all the factors individually, you add the results together to get the final answer.

3.
    a. An improvement in technology that reduces the cost of production will cause an increase in supply. Alternatively, you can think of this as a reduction in price necessary for firms to supply any quantity. Either way, this can be shown as a rightward (or downward) shift in the supply curve.
    b. An improvement in product quality is treated as an increase in tastes or preferences, meaning consumers demand more paint at any price level, so demand increases or shifts to the right. If this seems counterintuitive, note that demand in the future for the longer-lasting paint will fall, since consumers are essentially shifting demand from the future to the present.
    c. An increase in need causes an increase in demand or a rightward shift in the demand curve.
    d. Factory damage means that firms are unable to supply as much in the present. Technically, this is an increase in the cost of production. Either way you look at it, the supply curve shifts to the left.

4.

a. More fuel-efficient cars means there is less need for gasoline. This causes a leftward shift in the demand for gasoline and thus oil. Since the demand curve is shifting down the supply curve, the equilibrium price and quantity both fall.

b. Cold weather increases the need for heating oil. This causes a rightward shift in the demand for heating oil and thus oil. Since the demand curve is shifting up the supply curve, the equilibrium price and quantity both rise.

c. A discovery of new oil will make oil more abundant. This can be shown as a rightward shift in the supply curve, which will cause a decrease in the equilibrium price along with an increase in the equilibrium quantity. (The supply curve shifts down the demand curve so price and quantity follow the law of demand. If price goes down, then the quantity goes up.)

d. When an economy slows down, it produces less output and demands less input, including energy, which is used in the production of virtually everything. A decrease in demand for energy will be reflected as a decrease in the demand for oil, or a leftward shift in demand for oil. Since the demand curve is shifting down the supply curve, both the equilibrium price and quantity of oil will fall.

e. Disruption of oil pumping will reduce the supply of oil. This leftward shift in the supply curve will show a movement up the demand curve, resulting in an increase in the equilibrium price of oil and a decrease in the equilibrium quantity.

f. Increased insulation will decrease the demand for heating. This leftward shift in the demand for oil causes a movement down the supply curve, resulting in a decrease in the equilibrium price and quantity of oil.

g. Solar energy is a substitute for oil-based energy. So if solar energy becomes cheaper, the demand for oil will decrease as consumers switch from oil to solar. The decrease in demand for oil will be shown as a leftward shift in the demand curve. As the demand curve shifts down the supply curve, both equilibrium price and quantity for oil will fall.

h. A new, popular kind of plastic will increase the demand for oil. The increase in demand will be shown as a rightward shift in demand, raising the equilibrium price and quantity of oil.

5. Step 1. Draw the graph with the initial supply and demand curves. Label the initial equilibrium price and quantity. Step 2. Did the economic event affect supply or demand? Jet fuel is a cost of producing air travel, so an increase in jet fuel price affects supply. Step 3. An increase in the price of jet fuel caused a decrease in the cost of air travel. We show this as a downward or rightward shift in supply. Step 4. A rightward shift in supply causes a movement down the demand curve, lowering the equilibrium price of air travel and increasing the equilibrium quantity.

6. Step 1. Draw the graph with the initial supply and demand curves. Label the initial equilibrium price and quantity. Step 2. Did the economic event affect supply or demand? A tariff is treated like a cost of production, so this affects supply. Step 3. A tariff reduction is equivalent to a decrease in the cost of production, which we can show as a rightward (or downward) shift in supply. Step 4. A rightward shift in supply causes a movement down the demand curve, lowering the equilibrium price and raising the equilibrium quantity.

7. A price ceiling (which is below the equilibrium price) will cause the quantity demanded to rise and the quantity supplied to fall. This is why a price ceiling creates a shortage.

8. A price ceiling is just a legal restriction. Equilibrium is an economic condition. People may or may not obey the price ceiling, so the actual price may be at or above the price ceiling, but the price ceiling does not change the equilibrium price.

9. A price ceiling is a legal maximum price, but a price floor is a legal minimum price and, consequently, it would leave room for the price to rise to its equilibrium level. In other words, a price floor below equilibrium will not be binding and will have no effect.

Chapter 4

1. Changes in the wage rate (the price of labor) cause a movement along the demand curve. A change in anything else that affects demand for labor (e.g., changes in output, changes in the production process that use more or less labor, government regulation) causes a shift in the demand curve.

2. Changes in the wage rate (the price of labor) cause a movement along the supply curve. A change in anything else that affects supply of labor (e.g., changes in how desirable the job is perceived to be, government policy to promote training in the field) causes a shift in the supply curve.

3. Since a living wage is a suggested minimum wage, it acts like a price floor (assuming, of course, that it is followed). If the living wage is binding, it will cause an excess supply of labor at that wage rate.

4. Changes in the interest rate (i.e., the price of financial capital) cause a movement along the demand curve. A change in anything else (non-price variable) that affects demand for financial capital (e.g., changes in confidence about the future, changes in needs for borrowing) would shift the demand curve.

5. Changes in the interest rate (i.e., the price of financial capital) cause a movement along the supply curve. A change in anything else that affects the supply of financial capital (a non-price variable) such as income or future needs would shift the supply curve.

6. If market interest rates stay in their normal range, an interest rate limit of 35% would not be binding. If the equilibrium interest rate rose above 35%, the interest rate would be capped at that rate, and the quantity of loans would be lower than the equilibrium quantity, causing a shortage of loans.

7. b and c will lead to a fall in interest rates. At a lower demand, lenders will not be able to charge as much, and with more available lenders, competition for borrowers will drive rates down.

8. a and c will increase the quantity of loans. More people who want to borrow will result in more loans being given, as will more people who want to lend.

9. A price floor prevents a price from falling below a certain level, but has no effect on prices above that level. It will have its biggest effect in creating excess supply (as measured by the entire area inside the dotted lines on the graph, from D to S) if it is substantially above the equilibrium price. This is illustrated in the following figure.

It will have a lesser effect if it is slightly above the equilibrium price. This is illustrated in the next figure.

It will have no effect if it is set either slightly or substantially below the equilibrium price, since an equilibrium price above a price floor will not be affected by that price floor. The following figure illustrates these situations.

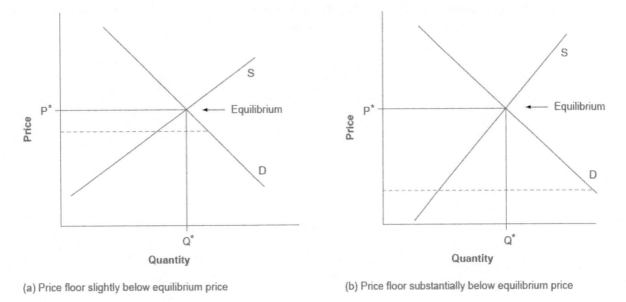

(a) Price floor slightly below equilibrium price

(b) Price floor substantially below equilibrium price

10. A price ceiling prevents a price from rising above a certain level, but has no effect on prices below that level. It will have its biggest effect in creating excess demand if it is substantially below the equilibrium price. The following figure illustrates these situations.

(a) Price ceiling substantially below equilibrium price

(b) Price ceiling slightly below equilibrium price

When the price ceiling is set substantially or slightly above the equilibrium price, it will have no effect on creating excess demand. The following figure illustrates these situations.

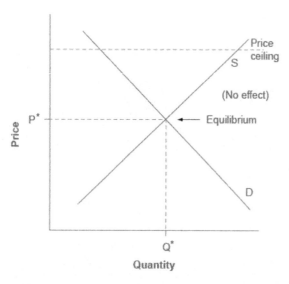

(a) Price ceiling substantially above equilibrium price

(b) Price ceiling slightly above equilibrium price

11. Neither. A shift in demand or supply means that at every price, either a greater or a lower quantity is demanded or supplied. A price floor does not shift a demand curve or a supply curve. However, if the price floor is set above the equilibrium, it will cause the quantity supplied on the supply curve to be greater than the quantity demanded on the demand curve, leading to excess supply.

12. Neither. A shift in demand or supply means that at every price, either a greater or a lower quantity is demanded or supplied. A price ceiling does not shift a demand curve or a supply curve. However, if the price ceiling is set below the equilibrium, it will cause the quantity demanded on the demand curve to be greater than the quantity supplied on the supply curve, leading to excess demand.

Chapter 5

1. GDP is C + I + G + (X − M). GDP = $2,000 billion + $50 billion + $1,000 billion + ($20 billion − $40 billion) = $3,030

2.
    a. Hospital stays are part of GDP.
    b. Changes in life expectancy are not market transactions and not part of GDP.
    c. Child care that is paid for is part of GDP.
    d. If Grandma gets paid and reports this as income, it is part of GDP, otherwise not.
    e. A used car is not produced this year, so it is not part of GDP.
    f. A new car is part of GDP.
    g. Variety does not count in GDP, where the cheese could all be cheddar.
    h. The iron is not counted because it is an intermediate good.

3. From 1980 to 1990, real GDP grew by (8,225.0 − 5,926.5) / (5,926.5) = 39%. Over the same period, prices increased by (72.7 − 48.3) / (48.3/100) = 51%. So about 57% of the growth 51 / (51 + 39) was inflation, and the remainder: 39 / (51 + 39) = 43% was growth in real GDP.

4. Two other major recessions are visible in the figure as slight dips: those of 1973–1975, and 1981–1982. Two other recessions appear in the figure as a flattening of the path of real GDP. These were in 1990–1991 and 2001.

5. 11 recessions in approximately 70 years averages about one recession every six years.

6. The table lists the "Months of Contraction" for each recession. Averaging these figures for the post-WWII recessions gives an average duration of 11 months, or slightly less than a year.

7. The table lists the "Months of Expansion." Averaging these figures for the post-WWII expansions gives an average expansion of 60.5 months, or more than five years.

8. Yes. The answer to both questions depends on whether GDP is growing faster or slower than population. If population grows faster than GDP, GDP increases, while GDP per capita decreases. If GDP falls, but population falls faster, then GDP decreases, while GDP per capita increases.

9. Start with Central African Republic's GDP measured in francs. Divide it by the exchange rate to convert to U.S. dollars, and then divide by population to obtain the per capita figure. That is, 1,107,689 million francs / 284.681 francs per dollar / 4.862 million people = $800.28 GDP per capita.

10.
    a. A dirtier environment would reduce the broad standard of living, but not be counted in GDP, so a rise in GDP would overstate the standard of living.
    b. A lower crime rate would raise the broad standard of living, but not be counted directly in GDP, and so a rise in GDP would understate the standard of living.
    c. A greater variety of goods would raise the broad standard of living, but not be counted directly in GDP, and so a rise in GDP would understate the rise in the standard of living.
    d. A decline in infant mortality would raise the broad standard of living, but not be counted directly in GDP, and so a rise in GDP would understate the rise in the standard of living.

Chapter 6

1. The Industrial Revolution refers to the widespread use of power-driven machinery and the economic and social changes that resulted in the first half of the 1800s. Ingenious machines—the steam engine, the power loom, and the steam locomotive—performed tasks that would have taken vast numbers of workers to do. The Industrial Revolution began in Great Britain, and soon spread to the United States, Germany, and other countries.

2. Property rights are the rights of individuals and firms to own property and use it as they see fit. Contractual rights are based on property rights and they allow individuals to enter into agreements with others regarding the use of their property providing recourse through the legal system in the event of noncompliance. Economic growth occurs when the standard of living increases in an economy, which occurs when output is increasing and incomes are rising. For this to happen, societies must create a legal environment that gives individuals the ability to use their property to their fullest and highest use, including the right to trade or sell that property. Without a legal system that enforces contracts, people would not be likely to enter into contracts for current or future services because of the risk of non-payment. This would make it difficult to transact business and would slow economic growth.

3. Yes. Since productivity is output per unit of input, we can measure productivity using GDP (output) per worker (input).

4. In 20 years the United States will have an income of $10,000 \times (1 + 0.01)^{20} = \$12,201.90$, and South Korea will have an income of $10,000 \times (1 + 0.04)^{20} = \$21,911.23$. South Korea has grown by a multiple of 2.1 and the United States by a multiple of 1.2.

5. Capital deepening and technology are important. What seems to be more important is how they are combined.

6. Government can contribute to economic growth by investing in human capital through the education system, building a strong physical infrastructure for transportation and commerce, increasing investment by lowering capital gains taxes, creating special economic zones that allow for reduced tariffs, and investing in research and development.

7. Public education, low investment taxes, funding for infrastructure projects, special economic zones

8. A good way to think about this is how a runner who has fallen behind in a race feels psychologically and physically as he catches up. Playing catch-up can be more taxing than maintaining one's position at the head of the pack.

9.
   a. No. Capital deepening refers to an increase in the amount of capital per person in an economy. A decrease in investment by firms will actually cause the opposite of capital deepening (since the population will grow over time).
   b. There is no direct connection between and increase in international trade and capital deepening. One could imagine particular scenarios where trade could lead to capital deepening (for example, if international capital inflows which are the counterpart to increasing the trade deficit) lead to an increase in physical capital investment), but in general, no.
   c. Yes. Capital deepening refers to an increase in either physical capital or human capital per person. Continuing education or any time of lifelong learning adds to human capital and thus creates capital deepening.

10. The advantages of backwardness include faster growth rates because of the process of convergence, as well as the ability to adopt new technologies that were developed first in the "leader" countries. While being "backward" is not inherently a good thing, Gerschenkron stressed that there are certain advantages which aid countries trying to "catch up."

11. Capital deepening, by definition, should lead to diminished returns because you're investing more and more but using the same methods of production, leading to the marginal productivity declining. This is shown on a production function as a movement along the curve. Improvements in technology should not lead to diminished returns because you are finding new and more efficient ways of using the same amount of capital. This can be illustrated as a shift upward of the production function curve.

12. Productivity growth from new advances in technology will not slow because the new methods of production will be adopted relatively quickly and easily, at very low marginal cost. Also, countries that are seeing technology growth usually have a vast and powerful set of institutions for training workers and building better machines, which allows the maximum amount of people to benefit from the new technology. These factors have the added effect of making additional technological advances even easier for these countries.

Chapter 7

1. The population is divided into those "in the labor force" and those "not in the labor force." Thus, the number of adults not in the labor force is 237.8 – 153.9 = 83.9 million. Since the labor force is divided into employed persons and unemployed persons, the number of unemployed persons is 153.9 – 139.1 = 14.8 million. Thus, the adult population has the following proportions:

- 139.1/237.8 = 58.5% employed persons
- 14.8/237.8 = 6.2% unemployed persons
- 83.9/237.8 = 35.3% persons out of the labor force

2. The unemployment rate is defined as the number of unemployed persons as a percentage of the labor force or 14.8/153.9 = 9.6%. This is higher than the February 2015 unemployment rate, computed earlier, of 5.5%.

3. Over the long term, the U.S. unemployment rate has remained basically the same level.

4.

a. Nonwhites
b. The young
c. High school graduates

5. Because of the influx of women into the labor market, the supply of labor shifts to the right. Since wages are sticky downward, the increased supply of labor causes an increase in people looking for jobs (Qs), but no change in the number of jobs available (Qe). As a result, unemployment increases by the amount of the increase in the labor supply. This can be seen in the following figure. Over time, as labor demand grows, the unemployment will decline and eventually wages will begin to increase again. But this increase in labor demand goes beyond the scope of this problem.

6. The increase in labor supply was a social demographic trend—it was not caused by the economy falling into a recession. Therefore, the influx of women into the work force increased the natural rate of unemployment.

7. New entrants to the labor force, whether from college or otherwise, are counted as frictionally unemployed until they find a job.

Chapter 8

1. To compute the amount spent on each fruit in each year, you multiply the quantity of each fruit by the price.

- 10 apples × 50 cents each = $5.00 spent on apples in 2001.
- 12 bananas × 20 cents each = $2.40 spent on bananas in 2001.
- 2 bunches of grapes at 65 cents each = $1.30 spent on grapes in 2001.

- 1 pint of raspberries at $2 each = $2.00 spent on raspberries in 2001.

Adding up the amounts gives you the total cost of the fruit basket. The total cost of the fruit basket in 2001 was $5.00 + $2.40 + $1.30 + $2.00 = $10.70. The total costs for all the years are shown in the following table.

2001	2002	2003	2004
$10.70	$13.80	$15.35	$16.31

2. If 2003 is the base year, then the index number has a value of 100 in 2003. To transform the cost of a fruit basket each year, we divide each year's value by $15.35, the value of the base year, and then multiply the result by 100. The price index is shown in the following table.

2001	2002	2003	2004
69.71	84.61	100.00	106.3

Note that the base year has a value of 100; years before the base year have values less than 100; and years after have values more than 100.

3. The inflation rate is calculated as the percentage change in the price index from year to year. For example, the inflation rate between 2001 and 2002 is $(84.61 − 69.71) / 69.71 = 0.2137 = 21.37\%$. The inflation rates for all the years are shown in the last row of the following table, which includes the two previous answers.

Items	Qty	(2001) Price	(2001) Amount Spent	(2002) Price	(2002) Amount Spent	(2003) Price	(2003) Amount Spent	(2004) Price	(2004) Amount Spent
Apples	10	$0.50	$5.00	$0.75	$7.50	$0.85	$8.50	$0.88	$8.80
Bananas	12	$0.20	$2.40	$0.25	$3.00	$0.25	$3.00	$0.29	$3.48
Grapes	2	$0.65	$1.30	$0.70	$1.40	$0.90	$1.80	$0.95	$1.90
Raspberries	1	$2.00	$2.00	$1.90	$1.90	$2.05	$2.05	$2.13	$2.13
Total			$10.70		$13.80		$15.35		$16.31
Price Index			69.71		84.61		100.00		106.3
Inflation Rate					21.37%		18.19%		6.3%

4. Begin by calculating the total cost of buying the basket in each time period, as shown in the following table.

Items	Quantity	(Time 1) Price	(Time 1) Total Cost	(Time 2) Price	(Time 2) Total Cost
Gifts	12	$50	$600	$60	$720
Pizza	24	$15	$360	$16	$384
Blouses	6	$60	$360	$50	$300

Items	Quantity	(Time 1) Price	(Time 1) Total Cost	(Time 2) Price	(Time 2) Total Cost
Trips	2	$400	$800	$420	$840
Total Cost			$2,120		$2,244

The rise in cost of living is calculated as the percentage increase: (2244 – 2120) / 2120 = 0.0585 = 5.85%.

5. Since the CPI measures the prices of the goods and services purchased by the typical urban consumer, it measures the prices of things that people buy with their paycheck. For that reason, the CPI would be the best price index to use for this purpose.

6. The PPI is subject to those biases for essentially the same reasons as the CPI is. The GDP deflator picks up prices of what is actually purchased that year, so there are no biases. That is the advantage of using the GDP deflator over the CPI.

7. The calculator requires you to input three numbers:
- The first year, in this case the year of your birth
- The amount of money you would want to translate in terms of its purchasing power
- The last year—now or the most recent year the calculator will accept

My birth year is 1955. The amount is $1. The year 2012 is currently the latest year the calculator will accept. The simple purchasing power calculator shows that $1 of purchases in 1955 would cost $8.57 in 2012. The website also explains how the true answer is more complicated than that shown by the simple purchasing power calculator.

8. The state government would benefit because it would repay the loan in less valuable dollars than it borrowed. Plus, tax revenues for the state government would increase because of the inflation.

9. Higher inflation reduces real interest rates on fixed rate mortgages. Because ARMs can be adjusted, higher inflation leads to higher interest rates on ARMs.

10. Because the mortgage has an adjustable rate, the rate should fall by 3%, the same as inflation, to keep the real interest rate the same.

Chapter 9

1. The stock and bond values will not show up in the current account. However, the dividends from the stocks and the interest from the bonds show up as an import to income in the current account.

2. It becomes more negative as imports, which are a negative to the current account, are growing faster than exports, which are a positive.

3.
 a. Money flows out of the Mexican economy.
 b. Money flows into the Mexican economy.
 c. Money flows out of the Mexican economy.

4. GDP is a dollar value of all production of goods and services. Exports are produced domestically but shipped abroad. The percent ratio of exports to GDP gives us an idea of how important exports are to the national economy out of all goods and services produced. For example, exports represent only 14% of U.S. GDP, but 50% of Germany's GDP

5. Divide $542 billion by $1,800 billion.

6. Divide –$400 billion by $16,800 billion.

7. The trade balance is the difference between exports and imports. The current account balance includes this number (whether it is a trade balance or a trade surplus), but also includes international flows of money from global investments.

8.
   a. An export sale to Germany involves a financial flow from Germany to the U.S. economy.
   b. The issue here is not U.S. investments in Brazil, but the return paid on those investments, which involves a financial flow from the Brazilian economy to the U.S. economy.
   c. Foreign aid from the United States to Egypt is a financial flow from the United States to Egypt.
   d. Importing oil from the Russian Federation means a flow of financial payments from the U.S. economy to the Russian Federation.
   e. Japanese investors buying U.S. real estate is a financial flow from Japan to the U.S. economy.

9. The top portion tracks the flow of exports and imports and the payments for those. The bottom portion is looking at international financial investments and the outflow and inflow of monies from those investments. These investments can include investments in stocks and bonds or real estate abroad, as well as international borrowing and lending.

10. If more monies are flowing out of the country (for example, to pay for imports) it will make the current account more negative or less positive, and if more monies are flowing into the country, it will make the current account less negative or more positive.

11. Write out the national savings and investment identity for the situation of the economy implied by this question:

$$\text{Supply of capital} \ = \ \text{Demand for capital}$$
$$\text{S} + (\text{M} - \text{X}) + (\text{T} - \text{G}) \ = \ \text{I} \qquad \text{If domestic savings increases and}$$
$$\text{Savings} + (\text{trade deficit}) + (\text{government budget surplus}) \ = \ \text{Investment}$$

nothing else changes, then the trade deficit will fall. In effect, the economy would be relying more on domestic capital and less on foreign capital. If the government starts borrowing instead of saving, then the trade deficit must rise. In effect, the government is no longer providing savings and so, if nothing else is to change, more investment funds must arrive from abroad. If the rate of domestic investment surges, then, *ceteris paribus*, the trade deficit must also rise, to provide the extra capital. The *ceteris paribus*—or "other things being equal"—assumption is important here. In all of these situations, there is no reason to expect in the real world that the original change will affect only, or primarily, the trade deficit. The identity only says that something will adjust—it does not specify what.

12. The government is saving rather than borrowing. The supply of savings, whether private or public, is on the left side of the identity.

13. A trade deficit is determined by a country's level of private and public savings and the amount of domestic investment.

14. The trade deficit must increase. To put it another way, this increase in investment must be financed by an inflow of financial capital from abroad.

15. Incomes fall during a recession, and consumers buy fewer good, including imports.

16. A booming economy will increase the demand for goods in general, so import sales will increase. If our trading partners' economies are doing well, they will buy more of our products and so U.S. exports will increase.

17.
   a. Increased federal spending on Medicare may not increase productivity, so a budget deficit is not justified.
   b. Increased spending on education will increase productivity and foster greater economic growth, so a budget deficit is justified.
   c. Increased spending on the space program may not increase productivity, so a budget deficit is not justified.
   d. Increased spending on airports and air traffic control will increase productivity and foster greater economic growth, so a budget deficit is justified.

18. Foreign investors worried about repayment so they began to pull money out of these countries. The money can be pulled out of stock and bond markets, real estate, and banks.

19. A rapidly growing trade surplus could result from a number of factors, so you would not want to be too quick to assume a specific cause. However, if the choice is between whether the economy is in recession or growing rapidly, the answer would have to be recession. In a recession, demand for all goods, including imports, has declined; however, demand for exports from other countries has not necessarily altered much, so the result is a larger trade surplus.

20. Germany has a higher level of trade than the United States. The United States has a large domestic economy so it has a large volume of internal trade.

21.
    a. A large economy tends to have lower levels of international trade, because it can do more of its trade internally, but this has little impact on its trade imbalance.
    b. An imbalance between domestic physical investment and domestic saving (including government and private saving) will always lead to a trade imbalance, but has little to do with the level of trade.
    c. Many large trading partners nearby geographically increases the level of trade, but has little impact one way or the other on a trade imbalance.
    d. The answer here is not obvious. An especially large budget deficit means a large demand for financial capital which, according to the national saving and investment identity, makes it somewhat more likely that there will be a need for an inflow of foreign capital, which means a trade deficit.
    e. A strong tradition of discouraging trade certainly reduces the level of trade. However, it does not necessarily say much about the balance of trade, since this is determined by both imports and exports, and by national levels of physical investment and savings.

Chapter 10

1. In order to supply goods, suppliers must employ workers, whose incomes increase as a result of their labor. They use this additional income to demand goods of an equivalent value to those they supply.

2. When consumers demand more goods than are available on the market, prices are driven higher and the additional opportunities for profit induce more suppliers to enter the market, producing an equivalent amount to that which is demanded.

3. Higher input prices make output less profitable, decreasing the desired supply. This is shown graphically as a leftward shift in the AS curve.

4. Equilibrium occurs at the level of GDP where AD = AS. Insufficient aggregate demand could explain why the equilibrium occurs at a level of GDP less than potential. A decrease (or leftward shift) in aggregate supply could be another reason.

5. Immigration reform as described should increase the labor supply, shifting SRAS to the right, leading to a higher equilibrium GDP and a lower price level.

6. Given the assumptions made here, the cuts in R&D funding should reduce productivity growth. The model would show this as a leftward shift in the SRAS curve, leading to a lower equilibrium GDP and a higher price level.

7. An increase in the value of the stock market would make individuals feel wealthier and thus more confident about their economic situation. This would likely cause an increase in consumer confidence leading to an increase in consumer spending, shifting the AD curve to the right. The result would be an increase in the equilibrium level of GDP and an increase in the price level.

8. Since imports depend on GDP, if Mexico goes into recession, its GDP declines and so do its imports. This decline in our exports can be shown as a leftward shift in AD, leading to a decrease in our GDP and price level.

9. Tax cuts increase consumer and investment spending, depending on where the tax cuts are targeted. This would shift AD to the right, so if the tax cuts occurred when the economy was in recession (and GDP was less than potential), the tax cuts would increase GDP and "lead the economy out of recession."

10. A negative report on home prices would make consumers feel like the value of their homes, which for most Americans is a major portion of their wealth, has declined. A negative report on consumer confidence would make consumers feel pessimistic about the future. Both of these would likely reduce consumer spending, shifting AD to the left, reducing GDP and the price level. A positive report on the home price index or consumer confidence would do the opposite.

11. A smaller labor force would be reflected in a leftward shift in AS, leading to a lower equilibrium level of GDP and higher price level.

12. Higher EU growth would increase demand for U.S. exports, reducing our trade deficit. The increased demand for exports would show up as a rightward shift in AD, causing GDP to rise (and the price level to rise as well). Higher GDP would require more jobs to fulfill, so U.S. employment would also rise.

13. Expansionary monetary policy shifts AD to the right. A continuing expansionary policy would cause larger and larger shifts (given the parameters of this problem). The result would be an increase in GDP and employment (a decrease in unemployment) and higher prices until potential output was reached. After that point, the expansionary policy would simply cause inflation.

14. Since the SRAS curve is vertical in the neoclassical zone, unless the economy is bordering the intermediate zone, a decrease in AS will cause a decrease in the price level, but no effect on real economic activity (for example, real GDP or employment).

15. Because the SRAS curve is horizontal in the Keynesian zone, a decrease in AD should depress real economic activity but have no effect on prices.

Chapter 11

1.

  a. An increase in home values will increase consumption spending (due to increased wealth). AD will shift to the right and may cause inflation if it goes beyond potential GDP.
  b. Rapid growth by a major trading partner will increase demand for exports. AD will shift to the right and may cause inflation if it goes beyond potential GDP.
  c. Increased profit opportunities will increase business investment. AD will shift to the right and may cause inflation if it goes beyond potential GDP.
  d. Higher interest rates reduce investment spending. AD will shift to the left and may cause recession if it falls below potential GDP.
  e. Demand for cheaper imports increases, reducing demand for domestic products. AD will shift to the left and may be recessionary.

2.

  a. A tax increase on consumer income will cause consumption to fall, pushing the AD curve left, and is a possible solution to inflation.
  b. A surge in military spending is an increase in government spending. This will cause the AD curve to shift to the right. If real GDP is less than potential GDP, then this spending would pull the economy out of a recession. If real GDP is to the right of potential GDP, then the AD curve will shift farther to the right and military spending will be inflationary.
  c. A tax cut focused on business investment will shift AD to the right. If the original macroeconomic equilibrium is below potential GDP, then this policy can help move an economy out of a recession.
  d. Government spending on healthcare will cause the AD curve to shift to the right. If real GDP is less than potential GDP, then this spending would pull the economy out of a recession. If real GDP is to th right of potential GDP, then the AD curve will shift farther to the right and healthcare spending will be inflationary.

3. An inflationary gap is the result of an increase in aggregate demand when the economy is at potential output. Since the AS curve is vertical at potential GDP, any increase in AD will lead to a higher price level (i.e. inflation) but no higher real GDP. This is easy to see if you draw AD_1 to the right of AD_0.

4. A decrease in government spending will shift AD to the left.

5. The following figure shows the aggregate expenditure-output diagram with the recessionary gap.

6. The following figure shows the aggregate expenditure-output diagram with an inflationary gap.

7. First, set up the calculation.
$$AE = 400 + 0.85(Y - T) + 300 + 200 + 500 - 0.1(Y - T)$$
$$AE = Y$$

Then insert Y for AE and 0.25Y for T.
$$Y = 400 + 0.85(Y - 0.25Y) + 300 + 200 + 500 - 0.1(Y - 0.25Y)$$
$$Y = 1400 + 0.6375Y - 0.075Y$$
$$0.4375Y = 1400$$
$$Y = 3200$$

If full employment is 3,500, then one approach is to plug in 3,500 for Y throughout the equation, but to leave G as a separate variable.

$$Y = 400 + 0.85(Y - 0.25Y) + 300 + G + 500 + 0.1(Y - 0.25Y)$$
$$3500 = 400 + 0.85(3500 - 0.25(3500)) + 300 + G + 500 - 0.1(3500 - 0.25(3500))$$
$$G = 3500 - 400 - 2231.25 - 1300 - 500 + 262.5$$
$$G = 331.25$$

A G value of 331.25 is an increase of 131.25 from its original level of 200. Alternatively, the multiplier is that, out of every dollar spent, 0.25 goes to taxes, leaving 0.75, and out of after-tax income, 0.15 goes to savings and 0.1 to imports. Because $(0.75)(0.15) = 0.1125$ and $(0.75)(0.1) = 0.075$, this means that out of every dollar spent: $1 - 0.25 - 0.1125 - 0.075 = 0.5625$. Thus, using the formula, the multiplier is:

$$\frac{1}{1 - 0.5625} = 2.2837$$

To increase equilibrium GDP by 300, it will take a boost of 300/2.2837, which again works out to 131.25.

8. The following table illustrates the completed table. The equilibrium is level is italicized.

National Income	After-Tax Income	Consumption	I + G + X	Minus Imports	Aggregate Expenditures
$8,000	$4,800	$4,340	$5,000	$240	$9,100
$9,000	$5,400	$4,820	$5,000	$270	$9,550
$10,000	*$6,000*	*$5,300*	*$5,000*	*$300*	*$10,000*
$11,000	$6,600	$5,780	$5,000	$330	$10,450
$12,000	$7,200	$6,260	$5,000	$360	$10,900
$13,000	$7,800	$46,740	$5,000	$4,390	$11,350

The alternative way of determining equilibrium is to solve for Y, where Y = national income, using: Y = AE = C + I + G + X − M Y = $500 + 0.8(Y − T) + $2,000 + $1,000 + $2,000 − 0.05(Y − T) Solving for Y, we see that the equilibrium level of output is Y = $10,000.

9. The multiplier refers to how many times a dollar will turnover in the economy. It is based on the Marginal Propensity to Consume (MPC) which tells how much of every dollar received will be spent. If the MPC is 80% then this means that out of every one dollar received by a consumer, $0.80 will be spent. This $0.80 is received by another person. In turn, 80% of the $0.80 received, or $0.64, will be spent, and so on. The impact of the multiplier is diluted when the effect of taxes and expenditure on imports is considered. To derive the multiplier, take the 1/1 − F; where F is equal to percent of savings, taxes, and expenditures on imports.

10. A decrease in energy prices, a positive supply shock, would cause the AS curve to shift out to the right, yielding more real GDP at a lower price level. This would shift the Phillips curve down toward the origin, meaning the economy would experience lower unemployment and a lower rate of inflation.

11. Keynesian economics does not require microeconomic price controls of any sort. It is true that many Keynesian economic prescriptions were for the government to influence the total amount of aggregate demand in the economy, often through government spending and tax cuts.

12. The three problems center on government's ability to estimate potential GDP, decide whether to influence aggregate demand through tax changes or changes in government spending, and the lag time that occurs as Congress and the President attempt to pass legislation.

Chapter 12

1. No, this statement is false. It would be more accurate to say that rational expectations seek to predict the future as accurately as possible, using all of past experience as a guide. Adaptive expectations are largely backward looking; that is, they adapt as experience accumulates, but without attempting to look forward.

2. An unemployment rate of zero percent is presumably well below the rate that is consistent with potential GDP and with the natural rate of unemployment. As a result, this policy would be attempting to push AD out to the right. In the short run, it is possible to have unemployment slightly below the natural rate for a time, at a price of higher inflation, as shown by the movement from E_0 to E_1 along the short-run AS curve. However, over time the extremely low unemployment rates will tend to cause wages to be bid up, and shift the short-run AS curve back to the left. The result would be a higher price level, but an economy still at potential GDP and the natural rate of unemployment, as determined by the long-run AS curve. If the government continues this policy, it will continually be pushing the price level higher and higher, but it will not be able to achieve its goal of zero percent unemployment, because that goal is inconsistent with market forces.

3. The statement is accurate. Rational expectations can be thought of as a version of neoclassical economics because it argues that potential GDP and the rate of unemployment are shaped by market forces as wages and prices adjust. However, it is an "extreme" version because it argues that this adjustment takes place very quickly. Other theories, like adaptive expectations, suggest that adjustment to the neoclassical outcome takes a few years.

4. The short-term Keynesian model is built on the importance of aggregate demand as a cause of business cycles and a degree of wage and price rigidity, and thus does a sound job of explaining many recessions and why cyclical unemployment rises and falls. The neoclassical model emphasizes aggregate supply by focusing on the underlying determinants of output and employment in markets, and thus tends to put more emphasis on economic growth and how labor markets work.

Chapter 13

1. As long as you remain within the walls of the casino, chips fit the definition of money; that is, they serve as a medium of exchange, a unit of account, and a store of value. Chips do not work very well as money once you leave the casino, but many kinds of money do not work well in other areas. For example, it is hard to spend money from Turkey or Brazil at your local supermarket or at the movie theater.

2. Many physical items that a person buys at one time but may sell at another time can serve as an answer to this question. Examples include a house, land, art, rare coins or stamps, and so on.

3. The currency and checks in M1 are easiest to spend. It is harder to spend M2 directly, although if there is an automatic teller machine in the shopping mall, you can turn M2 from your savings account into an M1 of currency quite quickly. If your answer is about "credit cards," then you are really talking about spending M1—although it is M1 from the account of the credit card company, which you will repay later when you credit card bill comes due.

4.
   a. Neither in M1 or M2
   b. That is part of M1, and because M2 includes M1 it is also part of M2
   c. Currency out in the public hands is part of M1 and M2
   d. Checking deposits are in M1 and M2
   e. Money market accounts are in M2

5. A bank's assets include cash held in their vaults, but assets also include monies that the bank holds at the Federal Reserve Bank (called "reserves"), loans that are made to customers, and bonds.

6.
   a. A borrower who has been late on a number of loan payments looks perhaps less likely to repay the loan, or to repay it on time, and so you would want to pay less for that loan.

b. If interest rates generally have risen, then this loan made at a time of relatively lower interest rates looks less attractive, and you would pay less for it.

c. If the borrower is a firm with a record of high profits, then it is likely to be able to repay the loan, and you would be willing to pay more for the loan.

d. If interest rates in the economy have fallen, then the loan is worth more.

Chapter 14

1. Longer terms insulate the Board from political forces. Since the presidency can potentially change every four years, the Federal Reserve's independence prevents drastic swings in monetary policy with every new administration and allows policy decisions to be made only on economic grounds.

2. Banks make their money from issuing loans and charging interest. The more money that is stored in the bank's vault, the less is available for lending and the less money the bank stands to make.

3. The fear and uncertainty created by the suggestion that a bank might fail can lead depositors to withdraw their money. If many depositors do this at the same time, the bank may not be able to meet their demands and will, indeed, fail.

4. The bank has to hold $1,000 in reserves, so when it buys the $500 in bonds, it will have to reduce its loans by $500 to make up the difference. The money supply decreases by the same amount.

5. An increase in reserve requirements would reduce the supply of money, since more money would be held in banks rather than circulating in the economy.

6. Contractionary policy reduces the amount of loanable funds in the economy. As with all goods, greater scarcity leads a greater price, so the interest rate, or the price of borrowing money, rises.

7. An increase in the amount of available loanable funds means that there are more people who want to lend. They, therefore, bid the price of borrowing (the interest rate) down.

8. In times of economic uncertainty, banks may worry that borrowers will lose the ability to repay their loans. They may also fear that a panic is more likely and they will need the excess reserves to meet their obligations.

9. If consumer optimism changes, spending can speed up or slow down. This could also happen in a case where consumers need to buy a large number of items quickly, such as in a situation of national emergency.

Chapter 15

1.

a. The British use the pound sterling, while Germans use the euro, so a British exporter will receive euros from export sales, which will need to be exchanged for pounds. A stronger euro will mean more pounds per euro, so the exporter will be better off. In addition, the lower price for German imports will stimulate demand for British exports. For both these reasons, a stronger euro benefits the British exporter.

b. The Dutch use euros while the Chileans use pesos, so the Dutch tourist needs to turn euros into Chilean pesos. An increase in the euro means that the tourist will get more pesos per euro. As a consequence, the Dutch tourist will have a less expensive vacation than he planned, so the tourist will be better off.

c. The Greek use euros while the Canadians use dollars. An increase in the euro means it will buy more Canadian dollars. As a result, the Greek bank will see a decrease in the cost of the Canadian bonds, so it may purchase more bonds. Either way, the Greek bank benefits.

d. Since both the French and Germans use the euro, an increase in the euro, in terms of other currencies, should have no impact on the French exporter.

2. Expected depreciation in a currency will lead people to divest themselves of the currency. We should expect to see an increase in the supply of pounds and a decrease in demand for pounds. The result should be a decrease in the value of the pound *vis à vis* the dollar.

3. Lower U.S. interest rates make U.S. assets less desirable compared to assets in the European Union. We should expect to see a decrease in demand for dollars and an increase in supply of dollars in foreign currency markets. As a result, we should expect to see the dollar depreciate compared to the euro.

4. A decrease in Argentine inflation relative to other countries should cause an increase in demand for pesos, a decrease in supply of pesos, and an appreciation of the peso in foreign currency markets.

5. The problem occurs when banks borrow foreign currency but lend in domestic currency. Since banks' assets (loans they made) are in domestic currency, while their debts (money they borrowed) are in foreign currency, when the domestic currency declines, their debts grow larger. If the domestic currency falls substantially in value, as happened during the Asian financial crisis, then the banking system could fail. This problem is unlikely to occur for U.S. banks because, even when they borrow from abroad, they tend to borrow dollars. Remember, there are trillions of dollars in circulation in the global economy. Since both assets and debts are in dollars, a change in the value of the dollar does not cause banking system failure the way it can when banks borrow in foreign currency.

6. While capital flight is possible in either case, if a country borrows to invest in real capital it is more likely to be able to generate the income to pay back its debts than a country that borrows to finance consumption. As a result, an investment-stimulated economy is less likely to provoke capital flight and economic recession.

7. A contractionary monetary policy, by driving up domestic interest rates, would cause the currency to appreciate. The higher value of the currency in foreign exchange markets would reduce exports, since from the perspective of foreign buyers, they are now more expensive. The higher value of the currency would similarly stimulate imports, since they would now be cheaper from the perspective of domestic buyers. Lower exports and higher imports cause net exports (EX – IM) to fall, which causes aggregate demand to fall. The result would be a decrease in GDP working through the exchange rate mechanism reinforcing the effect contractionary monetary policy has on domestic investment expenditure. However, cheaper imports would stimulate aggregate supply, bringing GDP back to potential, though at a lower price level.

8. For a currency to fall, a central bank need only supply more of its currency in foreign exchange markets. It can print as much domestic currency as it likes. For a currency to rise, a central bank needs to buy its currency in foreign exchange markets, paying with foreign currency. Since no central bank has an infinite amount of foreign currency reserves, it cannot buy its currency indefinitely.

9. Variations in exchange rates, because they change import and export prices, disturb international trade flows. When trade is a large part of a nation's economic activity, government will find it more advantageous to fix exchange rates to minimize disruptions of trade flows.

Chapter 16

1. The government borrows funds by selling Treasury bonds, notes, and bills.

2. The funds can be used to pay down the national debt or else be refunded to the taxpayers.

3. Yes, a nation can run budget deficits and see its debt/GDP ratio fall. In fact, this is not uncommon. If the deficit is small in a given year, than the addition to debt in the numerator of the debt/GDP ratio will be relatively small, while the growth in GDP is larger, and so the debt/GDP ratio declines. This was the experience of the U.S. economy for the period from the end of World War II to about 1980. It is also theoretically possible, although not likely, for a nation to have a budget surplus and see its debt/GDP ratio rise. Imagine the case of a nation with a small surplus, but in a recession year when the economy shrinks. It is possible that the decline in the nation's debt, in the numerator of the debt/GDP ratio, would be proportionally less than the fall in the size of GDP, so the debt/GDP ratio would rise.

4. Progressive. People who give larger gifts subject to the higher tax rate would typically have larger incomes as well.

5. Corporate income tax on his profits, individual income tax on his salary, and payroll tax taken out of the wages he pays himself.

6. individual income taxes

7. The tax is regressive because wealthy income earners are not taxed at all on income above $113,000. As a percent of total income, the social security tax hits lower income earners harder than wealthier individuals.

8. As debt increases, interest payments also rise, so that the deficit grows even if we keep other government spending constant.

9.
- a. As a share of GDP, this is false. In nominal dollars, it is true.
- b. False.
- c. False.
- d. False. Education spending is much higher at the state level.
- e. False. As a share of GDP, it is up about 50.
- f. As a share of GDP, this is false, and in real dollars, it is also false.
- g. False.
- h. False; it's about 1%.
- i. False. Although budget deficits were large in 2003 and 2004, and continued into the later 2000s, the federal government ran budget surpluses from 1998–2001.
- j. False.

10. To keep prices from rising too much or too rapidly.

11. To increase employment.

12. It falls below because less tax revenue than expected is collected.

13. Automatic stabilizers take effect very quickly, whereas discretionary policy can take a long time to implement.

14. In a recession, because of the decline in economic output, less income is earned, and so less in taxes is automatically collected. Many welfare and unemployment programs are designed so that those who fall into certain categories, like "unemployed" or "low income," are eligible for benefits. During a recession, more people fall into these categories and become eligible for benefits automatically. The combination of reduced taxes and higher spending is just what is needed for an economy in recession producing below potential GDP. With an economic boom, average income levels rise in the economy, so more in taxes is automatically collected. Fewer people meet the criteria for receiving government assistance to the unemployed or the needy, so government spending on unemployment assistance and welfare falls automatically. This combination of higher taxes and lower spending is just what is needed if an economy is producing above its potential GDP.

15. Prices would be pushed up as a result of too much spending.

16. Employment would suffer as a result of too little spending.

17. Monetary policy probably has shorter time lags than fiscal policy. Imagine that the data becomes fairly clear that an economy is in or near a recession. Expansionary monetary policy can be carried out through open market operations, which can be done fairly quickly, since the Federal Reserve's Open Market Committee meets six times a year. Also, monetary policy takes effect through interest rates, which can change fairly quickly. However, fiscal policy is carried out through acts of Congress that need to be signed into law by the president. Negotiating such laws often takes months, and even after the laws are negotiated, it takes more months for spending programs or tax cuts to have an effect on the macroeconomy.

18. The government would have to make up the revenue either by raising taxes in a different area or cutting spending.

19. Programs where the amount of spending is not fixed, but rather determined by macroeconomic conditions, such as food stamps, would lose a great deal of flexibility if spending increases had to be met by corresponding tax increases or spending cuts.

Chapter 17

1. We use the national savings and investment identity to solve this question. In this case, the government has a budget surplus, so the government surplus appears as part of the supply of financial capital. Then:

$$\text{Quantity supplied of financial capital} = \text{Quantity demanded of financial capital}$$
$$S + (T - G) = I + (X - M)$$
$$600 + 200 = I + 100$$
$$I = 700$$

2.

a. Since the government has a budget surplus, the government budget term appears with the supply of capital. The following shows the national savings and investment identity for this economy.

$$\text{Quantity supplied of financial capital} = \text{Quantity demanded of financial capital}$$
$$S + (T - G) = I + (X - M)$$

b. Plugging the given values into the identity shown in part (a), we find that $(X - M) = 0$.

c. Since the government has a budget deficit, the government budget term appears with the demand for capital. You do not know in advance whether the economy has a trade deficit or a trade surplus. But when you see that the quantity demanded of financial capital exceeds the quantity supplied, you know that there must be an additional quantity of financial capital supplied by foreign investors, which means a trade deficit of 2000. This example shows that in this case there is a higher budget deficit, and a higher trade deficit.

$$\text{Quantity supplied of financial capital} = \text{Quantity demanded of financial capital}$$
$$S + (M - X) = I + (G - T)$$
$$4000 + 2000 = 5000 + 1000$$

3. In the last few decades, spending per student has climbed substantially. However, test scores have fallen over this time. This experience has led a number of experts to argue that the problem is not resources—or is not just resources by itself—but is also a problem of how schools are organized and managed and what incentives they have for success. There are a number of proposals to alter the incentives that schools face, but relatively little hard evidence on what proposals work well. Without trying to evaluate whether these proposals are good or bad ideas, you can just list some of them: testing students regularly; rewarding teachers or schools that perform well on such tests; requiring additional teacher training; allowing students to choose between public schools; allowing teachers and parents to start new schools; giving student "vouchers" that they can use to pay tuition at either public or private schools.

4. The government can direct government spending to R&D. It can also create tax incentives for business to invest in R&D.

5. Ricardian equivalence means that private saving changes to offset exactly any changes in the government budget. So, if the deficit increases by 20, private saving increases by 20 as well, and the trade deficit and the budget deficit will not change from their original levels. The original national saving and investment identity is written below. Notice that if any change in the $(G - T)$ term is offset by a change in the S term, then the other terms do not change. So if $(G - T)$ rises by 20, then S must also increase by 20.

$$\text{Quantity supplied of financial capital} = \text{Quantity demanded of financial capital}$$
$$S + (M - X) = I + (G - T)$$
$$130 + 20 = 100 + 50$$

6. In this case, the national saving and investment identity is written in this way:

$$\text{Quantity supplied of financial capital} = \text{Quantity demanded of financial capital}$$
$$(T - G) + (M - X) + S = I$$

The increase in the government budget surplus and the increase in the trade deficit both increased the supply of financial capital. If investment in physical capital remained unchanged, then private savings must go down, and if savings remained unchanged, then investment must go up. In fact, both effects happened; that is, in the late 1990s, in the U.S. economy, savings declined and investment rose.

Chapter 18

1. The answers are shown in the following two tables.

Region	GDP (in millions)
East Asia	$10,450,032
Latin America	$5,339,390
South Asia	$2,288,812
Europe and Central Asia	$1,862,384
Middle East and North Africa	$1,541,900
Sub-Saharan Africa	$1,287,650

Region	GDP Per Capita (in millions)
East Asia	$5,246
Latin America	$1,388
South Asia	$1,415
Europe and Central Asia	$9,190
Middle East and North Africa	$4,535
Sub-Saharan Africa	$6,847

East Asia appears to be the largest economy on GDP basis, but on a per capita basis it drops to third, after Europe and Central Asia and Sub-Saharan Africa.

2. A region can have some of high-income countries and some of the low-income countries. Aggregating per capita real GDP will vary widely across countries within a region, so aggregating data for a region has little meaning. For example, if you were to compare per capital real GDP for the United States, Canada, Haiti, and Honduras, it looks much different than if you looked at the same data for North America as a whole. Thus, regional comparisons are broad-based and may not adequately capture an individual country's economic attributes.

3. The following table provides a summary of possible answers.

High-Income Countries	Middle-Income Countries	Low-Income Countries
• Foster a more educated workforce • Create, invest in, and apply new technologies • Adopt fiscal policies focused on investment, including investment in human capital, in technology, and in physical plant and equipment • Create stable and market-oriented economic climate • Use monetary policy to keep inflation low and stable • Minimize the risk of exchange rate fluctuations, while also encouraging domestic and international competition	• Invest in technology, human capital, and physical capital • Provide incentives of a market-oriented economic context • Work to reduce government economic controls on market activities • Deregulate the banking and financial sector • Reduce protectionist policies	• Eradicate poverty and extreme hunger • Achieve universal primary education • Promote gender equality • Reduce child mortality rates • Improve maternal health • Combat HIV/AIDS, malaria, and other diseases • Ensure environmental sustainability • Develop global partnerships for development

4. Low-income countries must adopt government policies that are market-oriented and that educate the workforce and population. After this is done, low-income countries should focus on eradicating other social ills that inhibit their growth. The economically challenged are stuck in poverty traps. They need to focus more on health and education and create a stable macroeconomic and political environment. This will attract foreign aid and foreign investment. Middle-income countries strive for increases in physical capital and innovation, while higher-income countries must work to maintain their economies through innovation and technology.

5. If there is a recession and unemployment increases, we can call on an expansionary fiscal policy (lower taxes or increased government spending) or an expansionary monetary policy (increase the money supply and lower interest rates). Both policies stimulate output and decrease unemployment.

6. Aside from a high natural rate of unemployment due to government regulations, subsistence households may be counted as not working.

7. Indexing wage contracts means wages rise when prices rise. This means what you can buy with your wages, your standard of living, remains the same. When wages are not indexed, or rise with inflation, your standard of living falls.

8. An increase in government spending shifts the AD curve to the right, raising both income and price levels.

9. A decrease in the money supply will shift the AD curve leftward and reduce income and price levels. Banks will have less money to lend. Interest rates will increase, affecting consumption and investment, which are both key determinants of aggregate demand.

10. Given the high level of activity in international financial markets, it is typically believed that financial flows across borders are the real reason for trade imbalances. For example, the United States had an enormous trade deficit in the late 1990s and early 2000s because it was attracting vast inflows of foreign capital. Smaller countries that have attracted such inflows of international capital worry that if the inflows suddenly turn to outflows, the resulting decline in their currency could collapse their banking system and bring on a deep recession.

11. The demand for the country's currency would decrease, lowering the exchange rate.

REFERENCES

Welcome to Economics!

Bureau of Labor Statistics, U.S. Department of Labor. 2015. "The Employment Situation—February 2015." Accessed March 27, 2015. http://www.bls.gov/news.release/pdf/empsit.pdf.

Williamson, Lisa. "US Labor Market in 2012." *Bureau of Labor Statistics*. Accessed December 1, 2013. http://www.bls.gov/opub/mlr/2013/03/art1full.pdf.

The Heritage Foundation. 2015. "2015 Index of Economic Freedom." Accessed March 11, 2015. http://www.heritage.org/index/ranking.

Garling, Caleb. "S.F. plane crash: Reporting, emotions on social media," *The San Francisco Chronicle*. July 7, 2013. http://www.sfgate.com/news/article/S-F-plane-crash-Reporting-emotions-on-social-4651639.php.

Irvine, Jessica. "Social Networking Sites are Factories of Modern Ideas." *The Sydney Morning Herald*. November 25, 2011.http://www.smh.com.au/federal-politics/society-and-culture/social-networking-sites-are-factories-of-modern-ideas-20111124-1nwy3.html#ixzz2YZhPYeME.

Pew Research Center. 2015. "Social Networking Fact Sheet." Accessed March 11, 2015. http://www.pewinternet.org/fact-sheets/social-networking-fact-sheet/.

The World Bank Group. 2015. "World Data Bank." Accessed March 30, 2014. http://databank.worldbank.org/data/.

Choice in a World of Scarcity

Bureau of Labor Statistics, U.S. Department of Labor. 2015. "Median Weekly Earnings by Educational Attainment in 2014." Accessed March 27, 2015. http://www.bls.gov/opub/ted/2015/median-weekly-earnings-by-education-gender-race-and-ethnicity-in-2014.htm.

Robbins, Lionel. *An Essay on the Nature and Significance of Economic Science*. London: Macmillan. 1932.

United States Department of Transportation. "Total Passengers on U.S Airlines and Foreign Airlines U.S. Flights Increased 1.3% in 2012 from 2011." Accessed October 2013. http://www.rita.dot.gov/bts/press_releases/bts016_13

Smith, Adam. "Of Restraints upon the Importation from Foreign Countries." In *The Wealth of Nations*. London: Methuen & Co., 1904, first pub 1776), I.V. 2.9.

Smith, Adam. "Of the Propriety of Action." In *The Theory of Moral Sentiments*. London: A. Millar, 1759, 1.

Demand and Supply

Costanza, Robert, and Lisa Wainger. "No Accounting For Nature: How Conventional Economics Distorts the Value of Things." *The Washington Post*. September 2, 1990.

European Commission: Agriculture and Rural Development. 2013. "Overview of the CAP Reform: 2014-2024." Accessed April 13, 205. http://ec.europa.eu/agriculture/cap-post-2013/.

Radford, R. A. "The Economic Organisation of a P.O.W. Camp." *Economica*. no. 48 (1945): 189-201. http://www.jstor.org/stable/2550133.

Landsburg, Steven E. *The Armchair Economist: Economics and Everyday Life*. New York: The Free Press. 2012. specifically Section IV: How Markets Work.

National Chicken Council. 2015. "Per Capita Consumption of Poultry and Livestock, 1965 to Estimated 2015, in Pounds." Accessed April 13, 2015. http://www.nationalchickencouncil.org/about-the-industry/statistics/per-capita-consumption-of-poultry-and-livestock-1965-to-estimated-2012-in-pounds/.

Wessel, David. "Saudi Arabia Fears $40-a-Barrel Oil, Too." *The Wall Street Journal*. May 27, 2004, p. 42. http://online.wsj.com/news/articles/SB108561000087822300.

Pew Research Center. "Pew Research: Center for the People & the Press." http://www.people-press.org/.

Labor and Financial Markets

American Community Survey. 2012. "School Enrollment and Work Status: 2011." Accessed April 13, 2015. http://www.census.gov/prod/2013pubs/acsbr11-14.pdf.

National Center for Educational Statistics. "Digest of Education Statistics." (2008 and 2010). Accessed December 11, 2013. nces.ed.gov.

CreditCards.com. 2013. http://www.creditcards.com/credit-card-news/credit-card-industry-facts-personal-debt-statistics-1276.php.

The Macroeconomic Perspective

U.S. Department of Commerce: Bureau of Economic Analysis. "National data: National Income and Product Accounts Tables." http://bea.gov/iTable/iTable.cfm?ReqID=9&step=1.

U.S. Department of Commerce: United States Census Bureau. "Census of Governments: 2012 Census of Governments." http://www.census.gov/govs/cog/.

United States Department of Transportation. "About DOT." Last modified March 2, 2012. http://www.dot.gov/about.

U.S. Department of Energy. "Energy.gov." http://energy.gov/.

U.S. Department of Health & Human Services. "Agency for Healthcare Research and Quality." http://www.ahrq.gov/.

United States Department of Agriculture. "USDA." http://www.usda.gov/wps/portal/usda/usdahome.

Schneider, Friedrich. Department of Economics. "Size and Development of the Shadow Economy of 31 European and 5 other OECD Countries from 2003 to 2013: A Further Decline." *Johannes Kepler University*. Last modified April 5, 2013. http://www.econ.jku.at/members/Schneider/files/publications/2013/ShadEcEurope31_Jan2013.pdf.

The National Bureau of Economic Research. "Information on Recessions and Recoveries, the NBER Business Cycle Dating Committee, and related topics." http://www.nber.org/cycles/main.html.

Economic Growth

Bolt, Jutta, and Jan Luiten van Zanden. "The Maddison Project: The First Update of the Maddison Project Re-Estimating Growth Before 1820 (Maddison-Project Working Paper WP-4)." *University of Groningen: Groningen Growth and Development Centre*. Last modified January 2013. http://www.ggdc.net/maddison/publications/pdf/wp4.pdf.

Central Intelligence Agency. "The World Factbook: Country Comparison GDP (Purchasing Power Parity)." https://www.cia.gov/library/publications/the-world-factbook/rankorder/2001rank.html.

DeLong, Brad. "Lighting the Rocket of Growth and Lightening the Toil of Work: Another Outtake from My 'Slouching Towards Utopia' MS...." *This is Brad DeLong's Grasping Reality* (blog). September 3, 2013. http://delong.typepad.com/sdj/2013/09/lighting-the-rocket-of-growth-and-lightening-the-toil-of-work-another-outtake-from-my-slouching-towards-utopia-ms.html.

Easterlin, Richard A. "The Worldwide Standard of Living since 1800." *The Journal of Economic Perspectives*. no. 1 (2000): 7–26. http://pubs.aeaweb.org/doi/pdfplus/10.1257/jep.14.1.7.

Maddison, Angus. *Contours of the World Economy 1-2030 AD: Essays in Macro-Economic History*. Oxford: Oxford University Press, 2007.

British Library. "Treasures in Full: Magna Carta." http://www.bl.uk/treasures/magnacarta/.

Rothbard, Murray N. Ludwig von Mises Institute. "Property Rights and the Theory of Contracts." *The Ethics of Liberty*. Last modified June 22, 2007. http://mises.org/daily/2580.

Salois, Matthew J., J. Richard Tiffin, and Kelvin George Balcombe. IDEAS: Research Division of the Federal Reserve Bank of St. Louis. "Impact of Income on Calorie and Nutrient Intakes: A Cross-Country Analysis." Presention at the annual meeting of the Agricultural and Applied Economics Association, Pittsburg, PA, July 24–26, 2011. http://ideas.repec.org/p/ags/aaea11/103647.html.

van Zanden, Jan Luiten. *The Long Road to the Industrial Revolution: The European Economy in a Global Perspective, 1000–1800 (Global Economic History Series)*. Boston: Brill, 2009.

The World Bank. "CPIA Property Rights and Rule-based Governance Rating (1=low to 6=high)." http://data.worldbank.org/indicator/IQ.CPA.PROP.XQ.

Rex A. Hudson, ed. *Brazil: A Country Study.* "Spectacular Growth, 1968–73." Washington: GPO for the Library of Congress, 1997. http://countrystudies.us/brazil/64.htm.

"Women and the World Economy: A Guide to Womenomics." *The Economist,* April 12, 2006. http://www.economist.com/node/6802551.

Farole, Thomas, and Gokhan Akinci, eds. *Special Economic Zones: Progress, Emerging Challenges, and Future Directions.* Washington: The World Bank, 2011. http://publications.worldbank.org/index.php?main_page=product_info&products_id=24138.

Garcia, Abraham, and Pierre Mohnen. United Nations University, Maastricht Economic and Social Research and Training Centre on Innovation and Technology: UNU-MERIT. "Impact of Government Support on R&D and Innovation (Working Paper Series #2010-034)." http://www.merit.unu.edu/publications/wppdf/2010/wp2010-034.pdf.

Heston, Alan, Robert Summers, and Bettina Aten. "Penn World Table Version 7.1." *Center for International Comparisons of Production, Income and Prices at the University of Pennsylvania.* Last modified July 2012. https://pwt.sas.upenn.edu/php_site/pwt71/pwt71_form.php.

United States Department of Labor: Bureau of Labor Statistics. "Women at Work: A Visual Essay." *Monthly Labor Review,* October 2003, 45–50. http://www.bls.gov/opub/mlr/2003/10/ressum3.pdf.

Central Intelligence Agency. "The World Factbook: Country Comparison: GDP–Real Growth Rate." https://www.cia.gov/library/publications/the-world-factbook/rankorder/2003rank.html.

Sen, Amartya. "Hunger in the Contemporary World (Discussion Paper DEDPS/8)." *The Suntory Centre: London School of Economics and Political Science.* Last modified November 1997. http://sticerd.lse.ac.uk/dps/de/dedps8.pdf.

Unemployment

Bureau of Labor Statistics. Labor Force Statistics from the Current Population Survey. *Accessed March 6, 2015* http://data.bls.gov/timeseries/LNS14000000.

Cappelli, P. (20 June 2012). "Why Good People Can't Get Jobs: Chasing After the Purple Squirrel." http://knowledge.wharton.upenn.edu/article.cfm?articleid=3027.

Inflation

Sources for **Table 8.1**:
    http://www.eia.gov/dnav/pet/pet_pri_gnd_a_epmr_pte_dpgal_w.htm
    http://data.bls.gov/cgi-bin/surveymost?ap
    http://www.bls.gov/ro3/apmw.htm
    http://www.autoblog.com/2014/03/12/who-can-afford-the-average-car-price-only-folks-in-washington/
    https://www.census.gov/construction/nrs/pdf/uspricemon.pdf
    http://www.bls.gov/news.release/empsit.t24.htm
    http://variety.com/2015/film/news/movie-ticket-prices-increased-in-2014-1201409670/

US Inflation Calculator. "Historical Inflation Rates: 1914-2013." Accessed March 4, 2015. http://www.usinflationcalculator.com/inflation/historical-inflation-rates/.

Bernhard, Kent. "Pump Prices Jump Across U.S. after Katrina." *NBC News,* September 1, 2005. http://www.nbcnews.com/id/9146363/ns/business-local_business/t/pump-prices-jump-across-us-after-katrina/#.U00kRfk7um4.

Wynne, Mark A. "Core Inflation, A Review of Some Conceptual Issues." *Federal Reserve Bank of St. Louis.* p. 209. Accessed April 14, 2014. http://research.stlouisfed.org/publications/review/08/05/part2/Wynne.pdf

Shiller, Robert. "Why Do People Dislike Inflation?" *NBER Working Paper Series, National Bureau of Economic Research,* p. 52. 1996.

Wines, Michael. "How Bad is Inflation in Zimbabwe?" *The New York Times,* May 2, 2006. http://www.nytimes.com/2006/05/02/world/africa/02zimbabwe.html?pagewanted=all&_r=0.

Hanke, Steve H. "R.I.P. Zimbabwe Dollar." *CATO Institute*. Accessed December 31, 2013. http://www.cato.org/zimbabwe.

Massachusetts Institute of Technology. 2015. "Billion Prices Project." Accessed March 4, 2015. http://bpp.mit.edu/usa/.

The International Trade and Capital Flows

Central Intelligence Agency. "The World Factbook." Last modified October 31, 2013. https://www.cia.gov/library/publications/the-world-factbook/geos/gm.html.

U.S. Department of Commerce. "Bureau of Economic Analysis." Last modified December 1, 2013. http://www.bea.gov/.

U.S. Department of Commerce. "United States Census Bureau." http://www.census.gov/.

Tabuchi, Hiroko. "Japan Reports a $78 Billion Trade Deficit for 2012." *The New York Times*, January 23, 2013. http://www.nytimes.com/2013/01/24/business/global/japan-reports-a-78-billion-trade-deficit-for-2012.html?_r=0.

World Bank. 2014. "Exports of Goods and Services (% of GDP)." Accesed April 13, 2015. http://data.worldbank.org/indicator/NE.EXP.GNFS.ZS/countries.

The Aggregate Demand/Aggregate Supply Model

Keynes, John Maynard. *The General Theory of Employment, Interest and Money*. London: Palgrave Macmillan, 1936.

U.S. Department of Commerce: United States Census Bureau. "New Residential Sales: Historical Data." http://www.census.gov/construction/nrs/historical_data/.

Library of Economics and Liberty. "The Concise Encyclopedia of Economics: Jean-Baptiste Say." http://www.econlib.org/library/Enc/bios/Say.html.

Library of Economics and Liberty. "The Concise Encyclopedia of Economics: John Maynard Keynes." http://www.econlib.org/library/Enc/bios/Keynes.html.

Organization for Economic Cooperation and Development. 2015. "Business Tendency Surveys: Construction." Accessed March 4, 2015. http://stats.oecd.org/mei/default.asp?lang=e&subject=6.

University of Michigan. 2015. "Surveys of Consumers." Accessed March 4, 2015. http://www.sca.isr.umich.edu/tables.html.

The Keynesian Perspective

Mahapatra, Lisa. "US Exports To China Have Grown 294% Over The Past Decade." *International Business Times*. Last modified July 09, 2013. http://www.ibtimes.com/us-exports-china-have-grown-294-over-past-decade-1338693.

The Conference Board, Inc. "Global Economic Outlook 2014, November 2013." http://www.conference-board.org/data/globaloutlook.cfm.

Thomas, G. Scott. "Recession claimed 170,000 small businesses in two years." *The Business Journals*. Last modified July 24, 2012. http://www.bizjournals.com/bizjournals/on-numbers/scott-thomas/2012/07/recession-claimed-170000-small.html.

United States Department of Labor: Bureau of Labor Statistics. "Top Picks." http://data.bls.gov/cgi-bin/surveymost?bls.

Joyner, James. Outside the Beltway. "Public Financing of Private Sports Stadiums." Last modified May 23, 2012. http://www.outsidethebeltway.com/public-financing-of-private-sports-stadiums/.

Siegfried, John J., and Andrew Zimbalist. "The Economics of Sports Facilities and Their Communities." *Journal of Economic Perspectives*. no. 3 (2000): 95-114. http://pubs.aeaweb.org/doi/pdfplus/10.1257/jep.14.3.95.

Harford, Tim. "What Price Supply and Demand?" http://timharford.com/2014/01/what-price-supply-and-demand/?utm_source=dlvr.it&utm_medium=twitter.

National Employment Law Project. "Job Creation and Economic Recovery." http://www.nelp.org/index.php/content/content_issues/category/job_creation_and_economic_recovery/.

Hoover, Kevin. "Phillips Curve." *The Concise Encyclopedia of Economics*. http://www.econlib.org/library/Enc/PhillipsCurve.html.

U.S. Government Printing Office. "Economic Report of the President." http://1.usa.gov/1c3psdL.

Blinder, Alan S., and Mark Zandi. "How the Great Recession Was Brought to an End." Last modified July 27, 2010. http://www.princeton.edu/~blinder/End-of-Great-Recession.pdf.

The Neoclassical Perspective

Lumina Foundation. 2014. "A Stronger Nation Through Higher Education." Accessed March 4, 2015. http://www.luminafoundation.org/publications/A_stronger_nation_through_higher_education-2014.pdf.

The National Bureau of Economic Research. http://www.nber.org/.

U.S. Department of Commerce: United States Census Bureau. "The 2012 Statistical Abstract." http://www.census.gov/compendia/statab/cats/education.html.

U.S. Department of the Treasury. "TARP Programs." Last modified December 12, 2013. http://www.treasury.gov/initiatives/financial-stability/TARP-Programs/Pages/default.aspx.

United States Government. "Recovery.gov: Track the Money." Last modified October 30, 2013. http://www.recovery.gov/Pages/default.aspx.

American Statistical Association. "ASA Headlines." http://www.amstat.org/.

Haubrich, Joseph G., George Pennacchi, and Peter Ritchken. "Working Paper 11-07: Inflation Expectations, Real Rates, and Risk Premia: Evidence from Inflation Swaps." *Federal Reserve Bank of Cleveland*. Last modified March 2011. http://www.clevelandfed.org/research/workpaper/2011/wp1107.pdf.

University of Michigan: Institute for Social Research. "Survey Research Center." http://www.src.isr.umich.edu/.

Carvalho, Carlos, Stefano Eusepi, and Christian Grisse. "Policy Initiatives in the Global Recession: What Did Forecasters Expect?" *Federal Reserve Bank of New York: Current Issues in Economics and Finance*, 18, no. 2 (2012). http://www.newyorkfed.org/research/current_issues/ci18-2.pdf.

Money and Banking

Hogendorn, Jan and Marion Johnson. *The Shell Money of the Slave Trade*. Cambridge University Press, 2003. 6.

Federal Reserve Statistical Release. November 23, 2013. http://www.federalreserve.gov/RELEASES/h6/current/default.htm#t2tg1link.

Credit Union National Association. 2014. "Monthly Credit Union Estimates." Last accessed March 4, 2015. http://www.cuna.org/Research-And-Strategy/Credit-Union-Data-And-Statistics/.

Dallas Federal Reserve. 2013. "Ending `Too Big To Fail': A Proposal for Reform Before It's Too Late". Accessed March 4, 2015. http://www.dallasfed.org/news/speeches/fisher/2013/fs130116.cfm.

Richard W. Fisher. "Ending 'Too Big to Fail': A Proposal for Reform Before It's Too Late (With Reference to Patrick Henry, Complexity and Reality) Remarks before the Committee for the Republic, Washington, D.C. Dallas Federal Reserve. January 16, 2013.

"Commercial Banks in the U.S." Federal Reserve Bank of St. Louis. Accessed November 2013. http://research.stlouisfed.org/fred2/series/USNUM.

Bitcoin. 2013. www.bitcoin.org.

National Public Radio. *Lawmakers and Regulators Take Closer Look at Bitcoin*. November 19, 2013. http://thedianerehmshow.org/shows/2013-11-19/lawmakers-and-regulators-take-closer-look-bitcoin.

Monetary Policy and Bank Regulation

Matthews, Dylan. "Nine amazing facts about Janet Yellen, our next Fed chair." Wonkblog. *The Washington Post*. Posted October 09, 2013. http://www.washingtonpost.com/blogs/wonkblog/wp/2013/10/09/nine-amazing-facts-about-janet-yellen-our-next-fed-chair/.

Appelbaum, Binyamin. "Divining the Regulatory Goals of Fed Rivals." *The New York Times*. Posted August 14, 2013. http://www.nytimes.com/2013/08/14/business/economy/careers-of-2-fed-contenders-reveal-little-on-regulatory-approach.html?pagewanted=3.

U.S. Department of the Treasury. "Office of the Comptroller of the Currency." Accessed November 2013. http://www.occ.gov/.

National Credit Union Administration. "About NCUA." Accessed November 2013. http://www.ncua.gov/about/Pages/default.aspx.

Board of Governors of the Federal Reserve System. "Federal Open Market Committee." Accessed September 3, 2013. http://www.federalreserve.gov/monetarypolicy/fomc.htm.

Board of Governors of the Federal Reserve System. "Reserve Requirements." Accessed November 5, 2013. http://www.federalreserve.gov/monetarypolicy/reservereq.htm.

Cox, Jeff. 2014. "Fed Completes the Taper." Accessed March 31, 2015. http://www.cnbc.com/id/102132961.

Jahan, Sarwat. n.d. "Inflation Targeting: Holding the Line." International Monetary Fund. Accessed March 31, 2015. http://www.imf.org/external/pubs/ft/fandd/basics/target.htm.

Tobin, James. "The Concise Encyclopedia of Economics: Monetary Policy." *Library of Economics and Liberty*. Accessed November 2013. http://www.econlib.org/library/Enc/MonetaryPolicy.html.

Federal Reserve Bank of New York. "The Founding of the Fed." Accessed November 2013. http://www.newyorkfed.org/aboutthefed/history_article.html.

Exchange Rates and International Capital Flows

Friedman, Milton. *Capitalism and Freedom*. Chicago: University of Chicago Press, 1962.

Government Budgets and Fiscal Policy

Kramer, Mattea, et. al. *A People's Guide to the Federal Budget*. National Priorities Project. Northampton: Interlink Books, 2012.

Kurtzleben, Danielle. "10 States With The Largest Budget Shortfalls." *U.S. News & World Report*. Januray 14, 2011. http://www.usnews.com/news/articles/2011/01/14/10-states-with-the-largest-budget-shortfalls.

Miller, Rich, and William Selway. "U.S. Cities and States Start Spending Again." *BloombergBusinessweek*, January 10, 2013. http://www.businessweek.com/articles/2013-01-10/u-dot-s-dot-cities-and-states-start-spending-again.

Weisman, Jonathan. "After Year of Working Around Federal Cuts, Agencies Face Fewer Options." *The New York Times*, October 26, 2013. http://www.nytimes.com/2013/10/27/us/politics/after-year-of-working-around-federal-cuts-agencies-face-fewer-options.html?_r=0.

Chantrill, Christopher. USGovernmentSpending.com. "Government Spending Details: United States Federal State and Local Government Spending, Fiscal Year 2013." http://www.usgovernmentspending.com/year_spending_2013USbn_15bs2n_20.

Burman, Leonard E., and Joel Selmrod. *Taxes in America: What Everyone Needs to Know*. New York: Oxford University Press, 2012.

Hall, Robert E., and Alvin Rabushka. *The Flat Tax (Hoover Classics)*. Stanford: Hoover Institution Press, 2007.

Kliff, Sarah. "How Congress Paid for Obamacare (in Two Charts)." *The Washington Post: WonkBlog* (blog), August 30, 2012. http://www.washingtonpost.com/blogs/wonkblog/wp/2012/08/30/how-congress-paid-for-obamacare-in-two-charts/.

Matthews, Dylan. "America's Taxes are the Most Progressive in the World. Its Government is Among the Least." *The Washington Post: WonkBlog* (blog). April 5, 2013. http://www.washingtonpost.com/blogs/wonkblog/wp/2013/04/05/americas-taxes-are-the-most-progressive-in-the-world-its-government-is-among-the-least/.

Eisner, Robert. *The Great Deficit Scares: The Federal Budget, Trade, and Social Security*. New York: Priority Press Publications, 1997.

Weisman, Jonathan, and Ashley Parker. "Republicans Back Down, Ending Crisis Over Shutdown and Debt Limit." *The New York Times*, October 16, 2013. http://www.nytimes.com/2013/10/17/us/congress-budget-debate.html.

Wessel, David. *Red Ink: Inside the High-Stakes Politics of Federal Budget*. New York: Crown Publishing Group, 2013.

Alesina, Alberto, and Francesco Giavazzi. *Fiscal Policy after the Financial Crisis (National Bureau of Economic Research Conference Report)*. Chicago: University Of Chicago Press, 2013.

Martin, Fernando M. "Fiscal Policy in the Great Recession and Lessons from the Past." Federal Reserve Bank of St. Louis: *Economic Synopses*. no. 1 (2012). http://research.stlouisfed.org/publications/es/12/ES_2012-01-06.pdf.

Bivens, Josh, Andrew Fieldhouse, and Heidi Shierholz. "From Free-fall to Stagnation: Five Years After the Start of the Great Recession, Extraordinary Policy Measures Are Still Needed, But Are Not Forthcoming." *Economic Policy Institute*. Last modified February 14, 2013. http://www.epi.org/publication/bp355-five-years-after-start-of-great-recession/.

Lucking, Brian, and Dan Wilson. Federal Reserve Bank of San Francisco, "FRBSF Economic Letter—U.S. Fiscal Policy: Headwind or Tailwind?" Last modified July 2, 2012. http://www.frbsf.org/economic-research/publications/economic-letter/2012/july/us-fiscal-policy/.

Greenstone, Michael, and Adam Looney. Brookings. "The Role of Fiscal Stimulus in the Ongoing Recovery." Last modified July 6, 2012. http://www.brookings.edu/blogs/jobs/posts/2012/07/06-jobs-greenstone-looney.

Leduc, Sylvain, and Daniel Wilson. Federal Reserve Bank of San Francisco: Working Paper Series. "Are State Governments Roadblocks to Federal Stimulus? Evidence from Highway Grants in the 2009 Recovery Act. (Working Paper 2013-16)." Last modified July 2013. http://www.frbsf.org/economic-research/files/wp2013-16.pdf.

Lucking, Brian, and Daniel Wilson. "FRBSF Economic Letter-Fiscal Headwinds: Is the Other Shoe About to Drop?" *Federal Reserve Bank of San Francisco*. Last modified June 3, 2013. http://www.frbsf.org/economic-research/publications/economic-letter/2013/june/fiscal-headwinds-federal-budget-policy/.

Recovery.gov. "Track the Money." http://www.recovery.gov/Pages/default.aspx.

Bastagli, Francesca, David Coady, and Sanjeev Gupta. International Monetary Fund. "IMF Staff Discussion Note: Income Inequality and Fiscal Policy." Last modified June 28, 2012. http://www.imf.org/external/pubs/ft/sdn/2012/sdn1208.pdf.

The Impacts of Government Borrowing

U.S. Department of Commerce: Bureau of Economic Analysis. "National Data: National Income and Product Accounts Tables." Accessed December 1, 2013. http://www.bea.gov/iTable/iTable.cfm?ReqID=9&step=1#reqid=9&step=3&isuri=1&910=X&911=0&903=146&904=2008&905=2013&906=A.

Board of Governors of the Federal Reserve System, "Selected Interest Rates (Daily) – H.15." Accessed December 10, 2013. http://www.federalreserve.gov/releases/h15/data.htm.

The White House. "Fiscal Year 2013 Historical Tables: Budget of the U.S. Government." Accessed December 12, 2013. http://www.whitehouse.gov/sites/default/files/omb/budget/fy2013/assets/hist.pdf.

The National Science Foundation. Accessed December 19, 2013. http://www.nsf.gov/.

The White House. "This is why it's time to make college more affordable." Last modified August 20, 2013. http://www.whitehouse.gov/share/college-affordability.

Rubin, Robert E., Peter R. Orszag, and Allen Sinai. "Sustained Budget Deficits: Longer-Run U.S. Economic Performance and the Risk of Financial and Fiscal Disarray." Last modified January 4, 2004. http://www.brookings.edu/~/media/research/files/papers/2004/1/05budgetdeficit%20orszag/20040105.pdf.

Macroeconomic Policy Around the World

International Labour Organization. "Global Employment Trends for Youth 2013." http://www.ilo.org/global/research/global-reports/global-employment-trends/youth/2013/lang--en/index.htm

International Monetary Fund. "World Economic and Financial Surveys: World Economic Outlook—Transitions and Tensions." Last modified October 2013. http://www.imf.org/external/pubs/ft/weo/2013/02/pdf/text.pdf.

Nobelprize.org. "The Prize in Economics 1987 - Press Release." *Nobel Media AB 2013*. Last modified October 21, 1987. http://www.nobelprize.org/nobel_prizes/economic-sciences/laureates/1987/press.html.

Redvers, Louise. BBC News Business. "Youth unemployment: The big question and South Africa." Last modified October 31, 2012. http://www.bbc.co.uk/news/business-20125053.

The World Bank. "The Complete World Development Report Online." http://www.wdronline.worldbank.org/.

The World Bank. "World DataBank." http://databank.worldbank.org/data/home.aspx.

Todaro, Michael P., and Stephen C Smith. *Economic Development (11ᵗʰEdition)*. Boston, MA: Addison-Wesley: Pearson, 2011, chap. 1–2.

"Shinzo Abe's Government Looks Likely to Disappoint on Fiscal Consolidation." *The Economist*, May 4, 2013. http://www.economist.com/news/finance-and-economics/21577080-shinzo-abes-government-looks-likely-disappoint-fiscal-consolidation-dont.

Banerjee, Abhijit V., and Esther Duflo. *Poor Economics*. "About the Book: Overview." http://pooreconomics.com/about-book.

CARE International. "About Us." Accessed January 14, 2014. http://www.care-international.org/about-us.aspx.

Central Intelligence Agency. "The World Factbook: Africa, Burundi." Last modified November 12, 2013. https://www.cia.gov/library/publications/the-world-factbook/geos/by.html.

Central Intelligence Agency. "The World Factbook: Africa, Democratic Republic of the Congo." Last modified November 12, 2013. https://www.cia.gov/library/publications/the-world-factbook/geos/cg.html.

Easterly, William. *The White Man's Burden: Why the West's Efforts to Aid the Rest Have Done So Much Ill and So Little Good*. Penguin Group (USA), 2006.

Goel, Vindu. "Facebook Leads an Effort to Lower Barriers to Internet Access," *The New York Times*. Last modified August 20, 2013.

Google. "Project Loon." http://www.google.com/loon/.

GOV.UK. "Department for International Development." https://www.gov.uk/government/organisations/department-for-international-development.

The World Bank. "Millennium Development Goals." http://www.worldbank.org/mdgs/.

Todaro, Michael P., and Stephen C Smith. *Economic Development (11ᵗʰ Edition)*. Boston, MA: Addison-Wesley: Pearson, 2011, chap. 3.

Vercillo, Siera. "The Failures of Canadian Foreign Aid: Tied, Mismanaged and Uncoordinated." *The Attaché Journal of International Affairs*. (2010). http://theattachejia.files.wordpress.com/2013/10/the-attache-2010-issue.pdf.

Viscusi, Gregory, and Mark Deen. "Why France Has So Many 49-Employee Companies." *Business Week*. Last modified May 3, 2012. http://www.businessweek.com/articles/2012-05-03/why-france-has-so-many-49-employee-companies.

Edwards, S. (n.d.). "America's Unsustainable Current Account Deficit." *National Bureau of Economic Research Digest*. http://www.nber.org/digest/mar06/w11541.html. http://www.ustr.gov/trade-agreements/free-trade-agreements/north-american-free-trade-agreement-nafta.

New Country Classifications | Data. (n.d.). Accessed January 14, 2014. http://data.worldbank.org/news/new-country-classifications.

Office of the United States Trade Representative: Executive Office of the President. "North American Free Trade Agreement (NAFTA)."

Why India's Labour Laws are a Problem. (2006, May 18). *BBC*. May 18, 2006. http://news.bbc.co.uk/2/hi/south_asia/4984256.stm.

INDEX

Symbols

401(k), 197

A

A.W. Phillips, 289
Abhijit Bannerjee, 445
Abraham García, 145
Adam Smith, 10, 37, 235
adaptive expectations, 306, 315
adjustable-rate mortgage
(ARM), 200, 203
adverse selection of wage cuts
argument, 167, 177
aggregate demand, 235, 263,
302, 306, 311, 353, 357, 378,
402, 447
aggregate demand (AD), 105,
254
Aggregate demand (AD), 238
aggregate demand (AD) curve,
238, 254
aggregate demand/aggregate
supply (AD/AS), 320
aggregate demand/aggregate
supply model, 236, 254, 301
aggregate production function,
136, 141, 150, 151
aggregate supply, 235, 302, 402
aggregate supply (AS), 105, 254
Aggregate supply (AS), 236
aggregate supply (AS) curve,
237, 254
aggregate supply curve, 311
Alexander Gerschenkron, 147
Allocative efficiency, 34
allocative efficiency, 40
American Recovery and
Reinvestment Act of 2009, 270
appreciating, 370, 388
arbitrage, 377, 388
Asian Financial Crisis, 451
asset, 326, 334
asset-liability time mismatch,
329
assets, 344
asset–liability time mismatch,
334
automatic stabilizers, 405, 413,
447

B

balance of payments, 218
balance of trade, 210, 226, 386
balance of trade (trade
balance), 228
balance sheet, 326, 334
balanced budget, 394, 411, 413
bank capital, 327, 334
Bank capital, 343
Bank regulation, 343
bank run, 344, 361
banking system, 324
bankrupt, 380
bar graph, 469
Barter, 320
barter, 334
base year, 185, 203
basic quantity equation of
money, 356, 361
basket of goods and services,
183, 203
bonds, 201, 327, 347, 491
budget constraint, 26, 40, 480
budget deficit, 394, 413
budget line, 479
budget surplus, 394, 413
Bureau of Economic Analysis
(BEA), 211
Bureau of Labor Statistics, 124
business confidence, 244
business cycle, 119, 126

C

capital deepening, 141, 151
central bank, 340, 354, 361,
378, 384
certificates of deposit (CDs),
323
ceteris paribus, 50, 62, 71, 82
circular flow diagram, 14, 21
coins and currency in
circulation, 323, 334
command economy, 16, 21
commodity money, 321, 334
Commodity-backed currencies,
321
commodity-backed currencies,
334
comparative advantage, 11, 35,
40, 217
complements, 52, 71

compound growth rate, 140, 151
consumer confidence, 245
Consumer Price Index (CPI),
186, 203
consumer surplus, 68
consumption budget constraint,
33
consumption demand, 107
contractionary fiscal policy, 291,
294, 402, 413
contractionary monetary policy,
349, 361, 383, 425
contractual rights, 134, 151
convergence, 145, 151
converging economy, 449, 454
coordination argument, 267, 294
core competency, 11
core inflation index, 189, 203
corporate income tax, 398, 413
cost, 33
cost of living, 187
cost-of-living adjustments
(COLAs), 200, 203
countercyclical, 351, 361
credit card, 324, 334
credit union, 326
crowding out, 408, 413, 423
current account balance, 211,
228
cyclical unemployment, 166,
177, 310
Cyclical unemployment, 248

D

deadweight loss, 69
dealers, 370
debit card, 324, 334
deficit, 421
deflation, 191, 203
Deflation, 356
demand, 45, 71, 105, 235, 366
demand and supply diagram, 68
demand and supply models, 94
demand curve, 45, 50, 71, 375,
424
demand deposit, 334
demand deposits, 323
demand schedule, 45, 71
deposit insurance, 345, 361
depository institution, 334
depository institutions, 325
depreciating, 370, 388

CPSIA information can be obtained
at www.ICGtesting.com
Printed in the USA
LVOW04s0422230118
563656LV00005B/30/P

9 781680 921311